MASTERING STRATEGY

Insights from the World's Greatest Leaders and Thinkers

JEFFREY A. RIGSBY
GUY GRECO

McGraw-Hill

New York   Chicago   San Francisco   Lisbon   London
Madrid   Mexico City   Milan   New Delhi
San Juan   Seoul   Singapore
Sydney   Toronto

Dedications

To my parents, Betty and Glen. Without their guidance and examples of commitment
and perseverance, my achievements would not have been possible.

And to my wife, Pam, and daughters Kristen, Sara, Katie, Julianne,
and Laurel—thank you for your unbelievable support and tolerance
while I've pursued my professional and educational goals.

JR

To my father, Leon, who gave me a sense of humor, and my mother, Mildred, who gave me
a sense of compassion. Thank you both for your unconditional support of my dreams.

GG

Copyright © 2003 by Jeffrey A. Rigsby and Guy Greco. Printed in the United States of America.
Except as permitted under the United States Copyright Act of 1976, no part of this publication
may be reproduced or distributed in any form or by any means, or stored in a database or
retrieval system, without the prior written permission of the publisher.

4 5 6 7 8 9 0   DOC/DOC   0 9 8 7 6

ISBN 0-07-140286-1

McGraw-Hill books are available at special quantity discounts to use as premiums and sales promotions, or for use in corporate training programs. For more information, please write to the
Director of Special Sales, Professional Publishing, McGraw-Hill, 2 Penn Plaza, New York, NY
10121-2298. Or contact your local bookstore.

This publication is designed to provide accurate and authoritative information in regard to the
subject matter covered. It is sold with the understanding that neither the author nor the publisher
is engaged in rendering legal, accounting, or other professional service. If legal advice or other
expert assistance is required, the services of a competent professional person should be sought.
—*From a Declaration of Principles jointly adopted by a Committee of the American Bar Association and a Committee of Publishers.*

Library of Congress Cataloging-in-Publication Data
Rigsby, Jeffrey A.
Mastering strategy : insights from the world's greatest leaders and thinkers / by Jeffrey A. Rigsby
and Guy Greco.
  p.   cm.
Includes bibliographical references and index.
ISBN 0-07-140286-1 (hardcover : alk. paper)
1. Strategic planning.   2. Business planning.   3. Strategic planning—United States.
4. Business planning—United States.   I. Greco, Guy.   II. Title.
HD30.28 .R54 2002
658.4'012—dc21

                                                                                    2002011889

Contents

Preface

All models are wrong, but some are useful.

GEORGE E.P. BOX
PROFESSOR-EMERITUS, UNIVERSITY OF WISCONSIN
WORLD-RENOWN STATISTICIAN

W E THINK THAT Professor Box offers a sound perspective. What we have developed is a very useful model for understanding how the myriad of factors that define organizational life might be arranged and assessed. Over the last several years, we have received very positive responses from users of our model. Part of this appeal may be that the *Organization Dynamic Model*® creates a picture of an organization that makes sense.

A fundamental question for any author is: Who are you writing this book for? Although we hope the book has great appeal and practicality for anyone who wants to understand more about the art of business, we are particularly interested in offering this information to four audiences:

CEOs

If you're like most Chief Executive Officers, you may have come up through the company ranks primarily through one functional discipline. You could have made it to the top position by way of finance, operations, marketing and sales, legal, even the occasional Human Resources route. In any case, you most likely have significant vertical depth related to your functional background, but may rely on your executive team for their expertise in other functional areas. This book provides you with a clear understanding of best practices tied to 41 organizational disciplines. Reading a few chapters related to areas outside your personal background will provide you with more horizontal depth. This is a book intended to provide a balance of knowledge. If nothing else, it will make you think about your company and your personal strengths and weaknesses in leading that company.

Those of You Who Appear Headed for CEO

So here you are. Over the years, your career has continued to move in the right direction. You may have had a few precarious moments, but no fatal mistakes that derailed your trek to the top. Now you're at a point where you are among the select few being seriously considered as a successor to the current CEO. The move from an accomplished division head to being a successful CEO is not guaranteed. It would be natural to wonder if you're ready. Anyone is this position, no matter how confident in nature, might easily wonder if they can handle the personal exposure and scrutiny that comes from running the whole show. Will the business community, local or national, rally behind your expertise or uncover your lesser talents? This book can be your primer. Read it and confirm the things you know and discover the things you don't.

Business Owners and Entrepreneurs

The dot.com era taught us time and again that a good idea is not enough. Companies must understand the business disciplines that are required to bring a good product or service to market. The world counts on visionaries like Fred Smith and Bill Gates. But the reasons these business leaders become known beyond their humble beginnings is that they either understood or quickly learned how to develop a business plan that could attract the necessary investment dollars and then put the right team together to enter the market, grow, and prevail. *Mastering Strategy* will provide a framework to evaluate if you have what it takes to turn a good idea into a great company. Motorola started out in 1928 as a humble battery repair business. In 1837, Mr. Proctor and Mr. Gamble—two brothers-in-law, pooled their money and formed a partnership to sell soap and candles. In 1923, Walt Disney set up his first animation studio in his uncle's garage. If you are passionate about your business (or your concept for a business) we applaud you. We understand the feeling. But this is only the first of a long series of steps required to be successful. Read this book and learn about the other factors adopted and institutionalized by the best-run companies to achieve success.

Students Who Have Set Out to Achieve a Masters in Business Administration

Achieving an MBA is a time- and money-consuming quest. And, although there are many fine business schools who do an outstanding job of providing this education, you may find that each course feels like independent study, leaving you with no clear sense of how they are connected. This book will help you understand how the many classes you will take en route to your MBA fit together in an organizational context. Are we saying that this book provides business information at the same level and scope as a two- to three-year MBA curriculum? Absolutely not. We would run the serious risk of insulting our friends and associates on the MBA faculties at UCLA and Pepperdine to suggest anything close to this. We are suggesting, however, that our model is a "useful" tool for helping you better understand how all the information provided by your professors is connected. Many MBA students at leading universities have told us so.

For the last six years, we have spent 100 percent of our time studying successful companies, poring over the primary and secondary research performed by the thought leaders in business, and developing our own model and opinions around management "best practices."

Why?

We believe the foundation to sustainable business success comes in the form of flawless execution and by leaving little or nothing to chance.

We submit that flawless execution can come through mastering best practices that have the highest impact on your business. We have organized these best practices under three interdependent core drivers, *Organization Strategy*, *Organization Design*, and *Organization Culture*. Together, they form the *Organization Dynamic Model*®. Rather than bore you with the process we've gone through to distill our views into this model, we will seek your trust now and ask that you evaluate our thesis once you finish the book.

Our point is this: Whether you are striving for greatness, fighting to maintain your organization's position of dominance, or slugging it out for your very existence—these three drivers are at the root of your success or failure.

Looking at these three drivers from a different perspective, we are providing a means to evaluate whether:

1. Your company knows where it's going and how it's going to get there.
2. You have created the right infrastructure and systems to support your strategy.
3. You have aligned the right people in the right jobs to make things happen.

We don't know if Michael Dell, Bill Gates, Sam Walton, Herb Kelleher, Hugh McColl, or any of the great visionaries of our time examined their companies through this lens—but we can demonstrate that the essence was there.

The question we ask you is, which "best practices" does *your* organization need to master in order to fulfill your strategic intent?

The central purpose of this book is to provide you and your organization with the vehicle to gain business knowledge in order to strengthen your ability to execute flawlessly, leaving little or nothing to chance.

Introduction:
A Readers' Guide

OUR GOAL IS to provide our readers with an experience that makes the effort to purchase and read our book worth the investment. This brief "readers' guide" will describe our model and highlight three methods in which to maximize the use of our book.

The Model

In the business world, there are many excellent models that provide us with an understanding of the characteristics and dynamics of specific organizational disciplines. A review of business literature produces outstanding models on topics like Competitive Analysis (Porter), Core Competence (Hamel and Prahalad), Leadership (Blanchard), Change Management (Kotter), and many others. An analysis of these models provides a deeper understanding into a particular discipline. After years of research, what appears to be missing is a means to link these models into a cohesive structure.

Our intent was to create a model that would provide a framework for understanding how these and other independent disciplines interrelate within an entire organization. To that end, we submit The *Organization Dynamic Model* ® (ODM) (Figure I-1). The model identifies 41 fundamental organizational disciplines. Each of these disciplines are linked to 1 of 12 *Key Components* which in turn are tied to the 3 *Core Drivers* of organization: *strategy, design,* and *culture.*

Figure I.1 The Organization Dynamic Model® (ODM)

	Organization Strategy	Organization Design		Organization Culture	
Mission, Vision, & Competitive Advantage	• Focused Purpose • Future Perspective • Strategic Advantage	**Basic Structure**	• Structure Criteria • Structure Evolution	**Values & Beliefs**	• Values Integration • Values Credibility
External Assessment	• Customer Profile • Industry & Competitive Analysis • Environmental Assessment	**Core Competence**	• Identifying Core Competence • Leveraging Core Competence	**Leadership**	• Management Modeling • Strategic/Tactical Balance • Empowerment • Developmental Coaching • Building Effective Teams
Internal Assessment	• Finance • Research & Development • Production • Marketing • Sales/Effectiveness • Customer Service	**Information, Systems, & Technology**	• Organization Communication • Targeted Information • Enterprising Systems • Applied Technology	**Human Resource Systems**	• Selective Recruitment • Employee Orientation • Continuous Learning • Performance Management • Reward Systems
Objectives, Initiatives, & Goals	• Vital Direction • Resource Alignment • Organization Accountabilities	**Organization Efficiency**	• Balanced Oversight & Direction • Synthesized Roles & Responsibilities • Managed Outsource/Strategic Alliances	**Organization Character**	• Informal Communication • Organization Feedback • Adaptability to Change

If we use a house analogy, *strategy* is the blueprint of the house: What will the house look like? How will we build it? How big? How small? *Design* is the infrastructure: How will the house be wired? What type of electrical, plumbing, cable, and phone systems are required? How simple or difficult is it to get from room to room? How will it function? *Culture* describes how it feels to live in the house: Is it a formal or informal place? Warm or cold? Open or closed? What is the "personality" of the house?

How to Use This Book

We invite you to use this book as it best suits you, whether you are a CEO, business executive, business owner, or student. It is our sincere hope that the information contained in each chapter will be both instructive and immediately applicable. We have made every effort to keep the information direct and to the point.

Essentially, there are three approaches to using the book:

1. **Read it—from cover to cover.**

   This approach is heartily endorsed by the authors, but not just for the reason you might suspect. Reading the book in sequence provides a linear and comprehensive look at the moving parts of an organization. The chapters follow the sequence outlined in *Organization Dynamic Model®*, starting with Strategy, then Design, and finally Culture. The content in each chapter elaborates on scope of the 3 Core Drivers, the 12 Key Components, and each of the 41 disciplines. If you read the full book, you will reinforce the business skills you already know and learn a good deal about those you don't.

2. **A Reference Guide—Chose the topics that you want to understand better now.**

   Use the ODM® in conjunction with the table of contents to focus on those disciplines that are of most interest to you. You can quickly locate the topic and read about how the best-run companies execute this particular discipline. All of us who have spent significant amounts of time in a corporation or government agency have some degree of depth and knowledge in certain functional areas. Likewise, there are other areas where our knowledge is less broad. Reading particular topics in this book will help to develop your understanding of business disciplines that may be less familiar to you. If you are a Human Resources Director, you can broaden your knowledge of Finance. If you are a CFO, you can learn more about what is takes to manage an effective Training and Development department.

3. **A Shared Learning Tool.**
   Whether you are an executive or student, this book is structured in a manner that highlights key business disciplines. Each chapter and subsection can be reviewed and discussed at staff meetings, within a study group, or as the foundation of a full course of study.

We encourage managers to share the book with their direct reports and peers. *Mastering Strategy* can provide managers and their organizations with the means to create a common and informed business language.

University professors seeking a means to provide their students with a "holistic" view of what it takes to run a company can use this text to highlight the multiple dimensions of an organization.

In all cases, we hope you enjoy the read.

JEFFREY A. RIGSBY, MBA is cofounder, CEO, and president of Virtual CEO, Inc., a strategic consulting and "best practice" research firm. Board members, CEOs, and senior executives engage Mr. Rigsby in the areas of organization strategy, business execution, and board governance. He has been featured in several national publications and is a frequent speaker at corporate and other global business events.

GUY GRECO is cofounder and executive vice president of Virtual CEO, Inc. For more than two decades, Mr. Greco has consulted with global companies on topics including leadership, executive alignment, core values, and organizational character. He is a frequent speaker for Fortune 500 companies as well as the Department of Defense.

Organization Strategy

There is no "perfect" strategic decision. One always has to pay a price. One always has to balance conflicting objectives, conflicting opinions, and conflicting priorities. The best strategic decision is only an approximation—and a risk.

—PETER F. DRUCKER

The task of formulating and effectively executing an organization's strategy in today's dynamic world has become increasingly difficult. The accelerated rate of technological change, increased global competition, and a more sophisticated customer base have combined to challenge managers to rethink their business models, techniques, and tools in favor of faster, more responsive approaches.

Successful strategy formulation is becoming increasingly dependent on how well an organization gathers, manages, and synthesizes vital information into targeted, actionable activities.[1] This information should not only contain hard data from secondary and primary research and analysis, but the soft views and intuitions of those in key positions throughout the organization.[2]

The former chief executive officer of Rockwell International, Don Beal, explains, "We expect every business segment head to be responsible for the strategic direction of the business and the business team to be very knowledgeable about their business in the worldwide marketplace, to know where they are taking the business long term; and how they are going to position the business."[3] Strategic dialogue and debate among key employees and managers is a vital component of a successful strategic planning process.

Michael Porter captured the essence of the assessment process by identifying the key questions that need to be answered in order to advance a company's strategic intent. (See Table 1.)

Involving strategic team members in prioritizing and validating significant issues is critical to empowering employees to respond in ways consistent with the overall objectives of the organization.

For the purposes of this section, we have arranged the discussion of strategy into four chapters:

- Chapter 1. Mission, Vision, and Competitive Advantage—Harley David-son and Wal-Mart—Keeping the Tradition Alive
- Chapter 2. The External Assessment—Inside Looking Out
- Chapter 3. The Internal Assessment—Dell, Microsoft, Nike, and the Four Seasons Hotels and Resorts
- Chapter 4. Execution and Action Plans—The Army Corps of Engineers, Leaving Nothing to Chance

In addition to outlining the best practices required to perform well within each of these disciplines, we explore how known best-practice companies

Table I Process for Formulating a Competitive Strategy[4]

A. What Is the Business Doing Now?	1. Identification What is the implicit or explicit current strategy? 2. Implied Assumptions What assumptions about the company's relative position, strengths and weaknesses, competitors, and industry trends must be made for the current strategy to make sense?
B. What Is Happening in the Environment?	1. Industry Analysis What are the key factors for competitive success, and the important industry opportunities and threats? 2. Competitor Analysis What are the capabilities and limitations of existing and potential competitors, and their probable future moves? 3. Societal Analysis What important governmental, social, and political factors will present opportunities or threats? 4. Strengths and Weaknesses Given an analysis of industry competitors, what are the company's strengths and weaknesses relative to present and future competitors?
C. What Should the Business Be Doing?	1. Test of Assumptions and Strategy How do the assumptions embodied in the current strategy compare with B above? Is the strategy consistent or does it fit with your core competence, your capital, and people and technology resource? Does your design and culture support your strategy? 2. Strategic Alternatives What are the feasible strategic alternatives given the analysis above? (Is the current strategy one of these?) 3. Strategic Choice Which alternative best relates the company's situation to external opportunities and threats?

excel in specific strategic areas. It is one thing to highlight a strategic best practice and suggest that you do it; it's another to illustrate how organizations like Harley-Davidson, Microsoft, Four Seasons Hotels and Resorts, and Dell leverage these best practices to sustain leadership roles within their respective industries.

CHAPTER

1

Mission, Vision, and Competitive Advantage— Harley-Davidson and Wal-Mart—Keeping the Tradition Alive

> *The general who wins the battle makes many calculations in his temple before the battle is fought. The general who loses makes but few calculations beforehand.*
>
> —SUN-TZU

HARLEY-DAVIDSON AND WAL-MART are perfect examples of two American companies rooted in founders' traditions. When you think of either of these companies, is there any question as to what they do, how they do it, or whom they serve? Both companies have a very clear, near and long-term view of where they're going, and they know exactly how they stack up against their competition. And they execute, execute, execute! As we explore the multiple dimensions of "best practices" and the disciplines required to build and sustain a successful business, it will always come back to an enterprise's ability to execute. The best-crafted mission and vision without diligent and relentless execution is nothing more than an exercise in creative writing.

Why develop a mission and vision statement? It's generally accepted that the clearer the view you have of where you are going, the more likely the chances you have of getting there. With a clearly defined mission and vision, you can more easily communicate your critical success factors, motivate and direct your organization, and ultimately, move more rapidly in the pursuit of your competitive advantage.

Focused Purpose—Harley-Davidson: We're Carrying on a Legend

"He who wishes to fulfill his mission in the world must be a man of one idea, that is, of one great overmastering purpose, overshadowing all his aims, and guiding and controlling his entire life."—Julius Bates

When we look at creating and sustaining a focused purpose, few companies provide an example as relevant as Harley-Davidson. HD has established itself not only as a leader in its field, but as an American icon. Let's look at how HD set the stage for its success.

Harley-Davidson Mission Statement:[1]
We fulfill dreams through the experiences of motorcycling—by providing to motorcyclists and the general public an expanding line of motorcycles, branded products and services in selected market segments.

INSPIRING THE DREAM. Every Harley-Davidson enthusiast has a story. For some, it is part of their family tradition, handed down from generation to generation. For others it's a memory of standing on a curb, feeling the rumble of a parade of Harleys and cheering as they passed. One thing is certain: there is no single pattern to the way that Harley-Davidson becomes a part of peoples' lives. But once ignited, the passion takes hold and the dream begins.

EXPERIENCING THE DREAM. The dreams of each of our enthusiasts are unique, and at Harley-Davidson it is our mission to fulfill every one of them in a memorable way. We are skilled at providing our customers with a continuous stream of new ways to experience the Harley-Davidson mystique. While motorcycles are most often the way we fulfill dreams, the Company offers a broad range of ways to be captivated by Harley-Davidson.

SHARING THE DREAM. **At Harley-Davidson we are committed to developing mutually beneficial relationships with our stakeholders. It is not enough to inspire and fulfill the dreams of just our customers, because our employees, suppliers, the government, our investors, and society all have a stake in our future. By enriching the relationships we have with our stakeholders, and making their dreams come true, we ensure the sustained growth of Harley-Davidson for many years to come.**

There is no ambiguity about where Harley-Davidson is going, whom they serve, or how they are different. Their mission is clear. A company's mission is nothing more than effectively mapping a course of action for the near term, understanding the needs of the company's primary stakeholders, and aligning current processes to support the company's competitive positioning.

Harley-Davidson

We could have jumped into this chapter with any number of impressive companies. It would have been very easy to lead with GE, Microsoft, Pfizer, IKEA, or Southwest. The list of strongly focused companies is long. However, to establish a foundation for our book and to celebrate a company's sense of purpose, we couldn't resist featuring Harley-Davidson, which is approaching its 100th anniversary. Though the HD team could cite many challenges on their road to success (ask anyone on the team who went through the AMF/Brunswick period), few companies have demonstrated their clear and unwavering mission.

When we evaluate an organization's alignment with their mission, we analyze their position against four simple attributes:

1. Their mission statement clearly articulates their purpose.
2. Their mission statement is realistic.
3. Their mission serves the best interests of all their primary stakeholders.
4. Their mission statement clearly differentiates their company from their competition.

Review the HD Mission Statement. It's not enough to have a mission; the test is whether the entire stakeholder community scores the company in a similar manner? Clearly, whether you're an HD shareholder, employee, customer, dealer, or supplier, we would argue that each stakeholder would confirm that the HD mission complies with the following elements:

1. Does their Mission Statement clearly articulate their purpose?

   "Stay true to the things that make Harley-Davidson a Harley-Davidson. Keep the heritage alive."[2]

   This is a purpose that rings clear to all Harley-Davidson stakeholders. It could be argued that this purpose is why they are Harley-Davidson stakeholders.

2. Is their Mission Statement realistic?

   Can they achieve their mission? Does it instill a sense of reality, yet challenge the organization to grow and move beyond where they are today? In HD's case, they have been living the Mission for so long, it's managements' responsibility to keep the company statement of purpose relevant to new generations of employees, customers, and other stakeholders.

3. Does their mission serve the best interests of all their primary stakeholders?

   Can employees, customers, suppliers, shareholders, and communities read Harley's Mission Statement and determine what's in it for them? The Harley-Davidson organization understands their "space." They have dealers that are an intimate part of their value proposition. While they continue to seek the best methods to serve their customers, their commitment to the "legend" ensures their maintaining what makes them Harley-Davidson.

4. Does their mission clearly spell out how they're different from their competition?

   "We're carrying on a legend."[3] How many motorcycle companies are carrying on a legend? There is a handful out there. Unfortunately, the challenge that competitors are faced with is the passion, commitment, and history of Harley-Davidson Corporation. The people at HD do believe that they are "carrying on a legend." And with that sense of purpose, they retain their existing customer base and continue to forge and expand a whole new generation of Harley enthusiasts.

Understanding "Mission"

One necessary step in creating a mission is to understand the arena in which you compete. Understanding your industry may sound like a basic exercise, but in so doing, a business builds the foundation that will shape every strategic decision it makes. Industry awareness establishes a general understanding of the environment in which the business competes, the customers it serves, and the industry dynamics that establish the rules of engagement. Some examples of industry categories would include the following:

- United Airlines is in the transportation business.
- Wells Fargo Bank is in the banking or financial service business.
- Pfizer is in the pharmaceutical business.
- Oracle is in the information technology business.
- Wal-Mart is in the retail/general merchandise business.

While these may seem obvious, industry descriptions provide not only the scope of what business you are in, but clearly identify activities in which you do not participate. It separates your direct competitors from your substitutes.

Understanding the nature of your industry can also help determine whether you should diversify your risk from business cycles, or focus on a limited business arena. McDonald's, for example, has concentrated for the most part on the fast food business, while firms such as Allied Signal have minimized their cycle risk by operating businesses in several related and unrelated industries.

A company's mission, simply stated, should reflect: who they are, what they do, to whom they offer product and services, and how they will be offering those products and services in terms of being different and better.

Additionally, an effective mission statement will reflect an organization's core competency and match it with elements of its customers' needs. This statement of strategic intent is effective when it is integrated into the organization to such an extent that it aligns the interests of the employees with those of the organization. Alignment is key. *Alignment*—meaning that all resources within an organization are positioned to fulfill the mission.

King and Cleland recommend that organizations carefully develop a written mission statement for the following reasons:[4] (See Table 1.1 below)

Table 1.1 Reasons to Develop a Mission Statement

1. To ensure unanimity of purpose within the organization.
2. To provide a basis, or standard, for allocating organizational resources.
3. To establish a general tone or organizational climate.
4. To serve as a focal point for individuals to identify with the organization's purpose and direction, and to deter those who cannot from participating further in the organization's activities.
5. To facilitate the translation of objectives into a work structure involving the assignment of tasks to responsible elements within the organization.
6. To specify organizational purposes and the translation of these purposes into objectives in such a way that cost, time, and performance parameters can be assessed and controlled.

Why Mission and Vision?

The mission statement generally deals with a shorter-term outlook, usually one to three years out, while the vision statement paints a broader, longer-term view of the company's desired state. In this section, we work through the purpose and approach to building an effective mission statement. In the next section, we weave in the vision statement and its value to the organization.

Peter Drucker described a mission this way:

> **A business mission is the foundation for priorities, strategies, plans, and work assignments. It is the starting point for the design of managerial jobs and, above all, for the design of managerial structures. Nothing may seem simpler or more obvious than to know what a company's business is . . . Actually, "What is our business?" is almost always a difficult question and the right answer is usually anything but obvious.[5]**

Derek F. Abell's response to the question posed by Drucker, "What is our business?" takes the form of three customer-oriented questions:

- "Who is being satisfied?" (customer groups)
- "What is being satisfied?" (customer needs)
- "How are these needs being satisfied?" (distinctive competencies)[6]

What are the key components that make up an effective mission statement? We have said that a mission statement must articulate an organization's purpose, it should be realistic, serve the stakeholders, and call out their competitive advantage. The following example breaks out nine essential components of a mission statement. (See Table 1.2)[7]

When crafting a mission statement, one should avoid financial or other goal-related language. "Creating profit," for example, is why you're in business; therefore, the mission statement should speak to *how* to create profit.

What to Do

Identify the team that will be responsible for delivering the final product (the mission statement). This can be the management team or a group of participants from throughout the organization recommending to the management team. If you delegate it to a participating team, ensure that the management team is prepared and willing to accept the outcome. There is nothing worse than empowering a team and then diluting or discarding their contribution. A facilitator or consultant is recommended to coordinate the effort.

Craft a Mission Statement that Clearly Articulates Your Purpose

Your mission should simply state your purpose. (Purpose:[8] *noun* 1. object to be attained; thing intended. 2. intention to act; resolution, determination. 3. *reason for existing;* use. ·*noun* 1. aim, ambition, aspiration, design, end, goal, hope, intent, intention, motivation, motive, object, objective, plan, point, target, wish. 2. determination, devotion, drive, firmness, persistence, resolution, resolve, steadfastness, tenacity, will, zeal.)

In other words, your mission statement will communicate to your stakeholders the reason you exist.

Make It Doable

Your mission statement can be ambitious and inspiring. Remember, the mission you produce will be the foundation for business decisions and resource allocations. It will also serve as your employees' beacon. If the mission is too complex, unrealistic, or too vague, your employees may become frustrated or just not adopt the mission as their own. We strongly encourage you to reach out to your workforce for their input. They are most likely closer to your customers and where the action is. Being a part of the mission development process increases the likelihood of internal buy-in and adoption.

Table 1.2 Nine Essential Components of a Mission Statement

Component	Test/Question	Example
1. Customers	Who are our firm's customers?	"We believe our first responsibility is to the doctors, nurses, and patients, to mothers and all others who use our products and services…"—Johnson & Johnson
2. Products and Services	What are the firm's major products or services?	"AMAX's principal products are molybdenum, coals, iron ore, and magnesium."—AMAX
3. Markets	Geographically, where does the firm compete?	"We are dedicated to the total success of Corning Glass Works as a worldwide competitor…"—Corning Glass Works
4. Technology	Is the firm technologically current?	"Control Data is in the business of applying microelectronics and computer technology in two general areas: computer-related hardware and computer-enhancing services."—Control Data
5. Concern for Survival, Growth, and Profitability	Is the firm committed to growth and financial soundness?	"In this respect, the company will conduct its operations prudently and will provide the profits and growth which will assure Hoover's ultimate success." —Hoover Universal
6. Philosophy	What are the basic beliefs, values, aspirations, and ethical priorities of the firm?	"We believe human development to be the worthiest of goals of civilization and independence to be the superior condition for nurturing growth in the capabilities of people."—Sun Company
7. Self-Concept	What is the firm's distinctive competence or major competitive advantage?	"Crown Zellerbach is committed to leapfrogging competition with 1,000 days by unleashing the constructive and creative abilities and energies of each of its employees."—Crown Zellerbach
8. Concern for Public Image	Is the firm responsive to social, community, and environmental concerns?	"…To share the world's obligation for the protection of the environment."—Dow Chemical
9. Concern for Employees	Are employees a valuable asset of the firm?	"To recruit, develop, motivate, reward, and retain personnel of exceptional ability, character, and dedication by providing good working conditions, superior leadership, performance based compensation…and a high degree of employment security." —The Wachovia Corporation

See That Your Mission Serves the Best Interests of All Stakeholders

We often get caught up in focusing on driving shareholder value and often lose sight of the fact that there are other critical stakeholders within the enterprise. Your stakeholders are employees, shareholders, suppliers, regulators (in some cases), and the communities in which you provide your products or services. Create a grid that allows you to highlight what you do for each constituency, and tie that data back into your statement.

Illustrate How You're Different

What makes you the best choice over your competitors? Whether it's cost, innovation, or service, call it out. Your point of differentiation is the driver to sustainability and maximum return. (Please see the section on strategic advantage at the end of this chapter to gain insight and methodology.)

The Future Perspective—
Build Your Vision—Live the Dream

"A strategist's job is to see the company not as it is . . . but as it can become."—John W. Teets, Chairman of Greyhound, Inc.

As we discuss the vision statement, let's stay with Harley. They've built a mission statement that aligns itself to their purpose. What do they do, day in and day out, to create value for their stakeholders? How does their vision statement tie in?

Harley-Davidson's Vision Statement

Harley-Davidson, Inc. is an action oriented, international company—A leader in its commitment to continuously improve the quality of profitable relationships with stakeholders [customers, employees, suppliers, shareholders, governments, and society]. Harley-Davidson believes the key to success is to balance stakeholder interests through the empowerment of all employees to focus on value-added activities. Our vision is our corporate conscience and helps us to eliminate short-term thinking, such as cashing in on demand for our new motorcycles by giving quantity precedence over quality or cutting corners in recreational or commercial vehicles to save a few dollars per unit. It also encourages every employee in our organization to be acutely aware of his or her role in satisfying our stakeholders.

Equally important to our Vision, we live by a Code of Business Conduct that is driven by a value system that promotes honesty, integrity, and personal growth in all our dealings with stakeholders. Our values are the rules by which we operate: Tell the truth; be fair; keep your promises; respect the individual; and encourage intellectual curiosity. In addition, we never lose sight of the issues we feel must be addressed in order for us to be successful in the future: Quality, participation, productivity, and cash flow. As a shareholder, you should expect no less from us.

A *future perspective* or long-term vision involves an intuitive understanding of what the firm wants to become. Like a mission statement, the vision statement serves as a reference point for making strategic decisions, conveying benefits to stakeholders, articulating competitive advantage, and underscoring the driving principles of the organization.

When we evaluate an organization's vision, we zero in on three overriding themes:

1. Does the vision statement clearly describe their future state?
2. Does the vision serve the long-term interest of their primary stakeholders?
3. Does the vision provide a foundation for decision making?

Harley-Davidson's results are consistent with what they stand for and what they promise through the mission and vision statements. Harley's success is no accident. How many times have they said "no" to compelling one-off opportunities? Such discipline requires strong leadership and a forward-thinking culture. John Kotter, in his book, *Leading Change,* outlines what his research uncovered as "effective vision characteristics." (See Table 1.3 below.)[9]

A vision statement is often articulated within a documented mission statement, yet its purpose can be clearly distinguished from a short-term mission. Visionary CEOs will postulate on the future, consider where the trends of technology, society, and economics are going, and match the strengths of their companies to the emerging opportunities within that *future perspective.* The vision statement is used to prepare the company for the future. Resource alignment, including financial requirements for the future, can only be determined with a firm future grasp of the company's ultimate destination.

Table 1.3   Characteristics of an Effective Vision

1. Imaginable	Conveys a picture of what the future will look like
2. Desirable	Appeals to the long-term interest of employees, customers, stockholders, and others who have a stake in the enterprise
3. Feasible	Comprises realistic, attainable goals
4. Focused	Is clear enough to provide guidance in decision making
5. Flexible	Is general enough to allow individual initiative and alternative responses in light of changing conditions
6. Communicable	Is easy to communicate; can be successfully explained within five minutes

The vision should remain flexible enough to take advantage of any new emerging opportunities as well.

What a Vision Is *Not*

Often it's easier to say what something is not than what it is. Burt Nanus[10] in *Visionary Leadership* did an effective job of articulating what a vision is *not:*

- While a vision is about the future, it is not a prophecy (although after the fact it may seem so)...Mahatma Gandhi's vision of an independent India or Henry Ford's vision of a car in every garage—these visions had power not because they were prophecies but because of the way they captured the imagination of others, mobilized resources, and reshaped the reality of their times.
- A vision is not a mission. To state that an organization has a mission is to state its purpose, not its direction.
- A vision is not factual. It doesn't exist and may never be realized as originally imagined. It deals not with reality but with possible and desirable futures. It is full of speculation, assumptions, and value judgments.
- A vision cannot be true or false. In can be evaluated only relative to other possible directions for the organization. That is, it can be seen as better or worse, more or less rational, safer or riskier, more or less appropriate, or even just good enough.
- A vision is not—or at least should not be—static, enunciated once for all time. Rather, vision formulation should be seen as a dynamic

process, an integral part of the ongoing task of visionary leadership. (Writers' comment: caution—dynamic process, yes, but consider the required communication necessary to ensure understanding among all stakeholders.)

- A vision is not a constraint on actions, except for those inconsistent with the vision. Instead, it is designed to unleash and then orient the energies of the organization in a common direction.

For both the mission and vision statements to be truly effective, look for them to instill a sense of urgency, direction, and success throughout the organization. Porsche CEO Peter Schultz relates this illustration of how an effective vision can motivate others and increase their productivity:[11]

Three people were at work on a construction site. All three were doing the same job, but when each was asked what his job was, the answers varied. "Breaking rocks," the first replied, "Earning a living," responded the second. "Helping to build a cathedral," said the third. Few of us can build cathedrals. But to the extent we can see the cathedral in whatever cause we are following, the job seems more worthwhile. Good strategists and a clear mission help us find those cathedrals in what otherwise could be dismal issues and empty causes.

Here's a closing thought on Harley-Davidson. Given everything that we've reviewed, the proof is in the pudding. (See Table 1.4 below.)

HD over the last five years has increased its stock price five fold (and is up almost 200 percent in 2001 alone—not bad during a recession), increased earnings per share over three fold, and has almost doubled total sales from $1.7 billion to over $3 billion.

Table 1.4 Harley-Davidson Financial Performance—1997–2001[12]

Consideration	2001	2000	1999	1998	1997
Stock Price	$55.08	$32.03	$23.69	$13.63	$11.75
Total Sales in Millions	$3.363	$2,906	$2,453	$2,064	$1,763
EPS	$1.447	$1.15	$.863	$.69	$.565

What to Do

As you're developing your mission statement, identify the team that will be responsible for delivering the final product (the vision statement). This can be the management team, or a group of participants from throughout the organization recommending to the management team. If you delegate this to a participating team, ensure that the management team is prepared and willing to accept the outcome. As mentioned earlier, there is nothing worse than empowering a team and then diluting or discarding their contribution.

As part of your prework, it will be necessary to evaluate the trends and shifts you anticipate within your industry. Ask the right questions: How will my customers' needs change? What form will my products or services take? Will today's barriers exist tomorrow; will regulations, socioeconomics, or methods of distribution alter how we do business today; will the competitive landscape as I know it alter in a material way? Consider the impact that these changes might have on your business. Will the rules of engagement of business support or alter your current way of doing business?

Define Your Future State—Paint the Picture

Once you have evaluated the potential changes that you and your industry may face, develop brief scenarios on how your organization might change. Creating tangible images of how you would respond to change begins the visioning process. What role do you want your organization to play in these future markets? What form will your leadership take? When all is said and done, your future state must be one of your choosing. It should reflect and describe how you choose to position yourself beyond where you are today. Dare to be great!

- Be ambitious.
- Be unique.
- Be focused.
- Be a beacon.

Create the Emotional Bond

As you consider various scenarios, you must test these scenarios against the needs and desires of your primary stakeholders. Integrating your values and guiding principles will also contribute to the appeal of your vision. Do not resist setting forth high standards and ideals. How will your customers respond to your evolved look and feel? Will your employees embrace and share your passion for the future? Will they be drawn and motivated by the course you've selected? What impact will this future have on your suppliers and partners? Will they play a material role? How will your shareholders react? Will they ride with you, increase their holdings, or might they run for cover? Will society and the communities you serve get behind you? These questions must be answered. Ideally, your vision will paint a picture that will enrich the relationships of current stakeholders, while expanding and drawing new stakeholders that want to be a part of your future.

Provide Clarity

Providing clarity in your vision statement will ensure that resources and decisions align with your strategic intent. This is probably a good time to introduce the "KISS" model—Keep It Simple, Stupid. People have to "get it." In order to provide a basis for sound and aligned business decisions, enthusiasm and loyalty, along with a resilient sense of purpose, craft your vision in a manner that is easily understood, embraced, and aggressively pursued.

Strategic (Competitive) Advantage— Wal-Mart: Making "Lower Prices Every Day" into Shareholder Gold

"We're all working together; that's the secret. And we'll lower the cost of living for everyone, not just in America, but we'll give the world an opportunity to see what it's like to save and have a better lifestyle, a better life for all. We're proud of what we've accomplished; we've just begun."—Sam Walton (1918–1992)

How are you different, and why does it make you better? Answer those questions, and you are on your way to building better margins and setting the foundation for every business decision that you and your team are ever going to make. In the pages that follow, we explore identifying what a company perceives to be its competitive advantage, and what activities are initiated to support the company's point of differentiation within their industry. We also review how having a fundamental understanding of structure and resource alignment is necessary to fulfill a strategy. True differentiation will come in the form of low cost, innovation, or service, or in some cases, a unique hybrid.

Driving to one's strategic advantage is one of the single greatest challenges that today's CEOs face. We've titled this section "Strategic Advantage" instead of "Competitive Advantage" because we believe that a true "edge" must be well thought out and sustainable. An organization's competitive advantage must be rooted in its strategic thought process and strategic positioning. It must be consistently challenged and refined to respond ahead of the competition.

Wal-Mart—Low-Cost Provider

Wal-Mart has demonstrated a consistent edge in its pursuit for "Lower Prices Every Day." The following synopsis reflects Wal-Mart's strategic thought process and clearly defined course.

Wal-Mart Pricing Philosophy:[13]
Sam Walton always knew he wanted to be in the retailing business. He started his career by running a Ben Franklin franchise store and learned about buying, pricing, and passing good deals on to customers.

He credits a manufacturer's agent from New York, Harry Weiner, with his first real lesson about pricing:

"Harry was selling ladies' panties for $2 a dozen. We'd been buying similar panties from Ben Franklin for $2.50 a dozen and selling them at three pair for $1. Well, at Harry's price of $2, we could put them out at four for $1 and make a great promotion for our store.

"Here's the simple lesson we learned . . . say I bought an item for 80 cents. I found that by pricing it at $1.00, I could sell three times more of it than by pricing it at $1.20. I might make only half the profit per item, but because I was selling three times as many, the overall profit was much greater. Simple enough. But this is really the essence of discounting: by cutting your price, you can boost your sales to a point where you earn far more at the cheaper retail than you would have by selling the item at the higher price. In retailer language, you can lower your markup but earn more because of the increased volume."

Sam's adherence to this pricing philosophy was unshakable, as one of Wal-Mart's first store managers recalls:

"Sam wouldn't let us hedge on a price at all. Say the list price was $1.98, but we had paid only 50 cents. Initially, I would say, 'Well, it's originally $1.98, so why don't we sell it for $1.25?' And, he'd say, 'No. We paid 50 cents for it. Mark it up 30 percent, and that's it. No matter what you pay for it, if we get a great deal, pass it on to the customer.' And of course that's what we did."

And that's what we continue to do—work diligently to find great deals to pass on to our customers. Thanks to the legacy of Sam Walton, Wal-Mart is a store you can count on every day to bring you value for your dollar. And that's why at Wal-Mart, you never have to wait for a sale to get your money's worth!

Here are three of our pricing philosophies we follow at Wal-Mart:

1. **Every Day Low Price (EDLP)**
   Because you work hard for every dollar, you deserve the lowest price we can offer every time you make a purchase. You deserve our Every Day Low Price. It's not a sale; it's a great price you can count on every day to make your dollar go further at Wal-Mart.

2. **Rollback**
   This is our ongoing commitment to pass even more savings on to you by lowering our Every Day Low Prices whenever we can. When our costs get rolled back, it allows us to lower our prices for you. Just look for the Rollback smiley face throughout the store. You'll smile too.

3. **Special Buy**
   When you see items with the Special Buy logo, you'll know you're getting an exceptional value. It may be an item we carry every day that includes an additional amount of the same product or another product for a limited time. Or, it could be an item we carry while supplies last, at a very special price.

Wal-Mart Stores, Inc.[14] provide an excellent example of a company defining its competitive advantage and relentlessly pursuing its fulfillment. Wal-Mart's strategy is clearly described as a "low-cost" provider. As such,

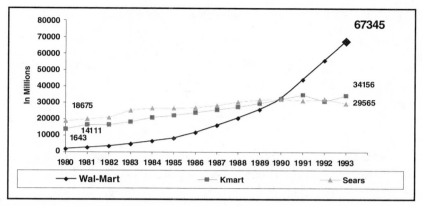

Figure 1.1 Wal-Mart Sales Performance versus Major Competitors, 1980–1993

they developed an organizational push and market outreach that supported their "Every Day Low Price" mantra.

As a low-cost provider, they determined that they must dominate share per market, and in order to do that, they would drive down their costs at every opportunity. They did not sacrifice quality, but did emphasize best price and good selection, and they built their theme by creating a highly motivated organization that viewed themselves as a part of the Wal-Mart family.

Retailer of the Century

From 1980 to 1993, Wal-Mart grew in sales from $1.6 billion to $67 billion. During the same period, Sears, considered the industry leader, went from $18.6 billion to $29.5 billion (Merchandise Group Operations only). (See Figure 1.1 above.) While Sears and K-Mart struggled to define their market positions going forward, Wal-Mart had clearly defined its own market position, had aligned human capabilities and organizational resources, and had met financial and physical requirements to achieve their overall strategic intent.

Wal-Mart Stores, Inc. is the world's largest retailer, with $220 billion in sales in the fiscal year ending Jan. 31, 2002. The company employs more than one million associates worldwide through nearly 3500 facilities in the United States and more than 1000 units in Mexico, Puerto Rico, Canada, Argentina,

Table 1.5 Wal-Mart Financial Performance—1997–2001[15]

Consideration	2001	2000	1999	1998	1997
Stock Price	$57.55	$53.13	$69.13	$40.72	$19.72
Total Sales in Billions	$220	$193	$167	$139	$119
EPS	$1.49	$1.39	$1.19	$.98	$.77

Brazil, China, Korea, Germany, and the United Kingdom. More than 100 million customers per week visit Wal-Mart stores around the world.

Wal-Mart continues to demonstrate consistent growth and shareholder value. (See Table 1.5 for their five-year financial and stock market performance.)

Guided by founder Sam Walton's passion for customer satisfaction and "Every Day Low Prices," Wal-Mart's four retail divisions—Wal-Mart Supercenters, Discount Stores, Neighborhood Markets, and Sam's Club warehouses—offer a wide variety of quality merchandise to consumers around the world.

By the turn of the century, Wal-Mart had been named "Retailer of the Century" by *Discount Store News;* made *Fortune* magazine's lists of the "Most Admired Companies in America" and the "100 Best Companies to Work For;" and was highly ranked on *Financial Times'* "Most Respected in the World" list.

Today, Wal-Mart sales exceed $200 billion, their earnings per share is up over 90 percent since 1997, and their stock value, though slightly impacted by the recent adverse economy, is still up over 250 percent in the last five years. Wal-Mart stock trades on the New York and Pacific Stock Exchanges under the ticker symbol WMT.

When we test an organization's ability to understand and pursue their point of differentiation or competitive advantage, we zero in on three enterprise-wide attributes:

1. Their company focuses on a primary point of differentiation (such as cost, innovation, or service) as a key factor in formulating their strategic plan.
2. Their company's competitive advantage is clearly understood by all its primary stakeholders.
3. Their employees clearly understand how their performance supports their competitive advantage.

Is it clear that Wal-Mart understands and focuses on its primary point of differentiation, and that their point of differentiation is the foundation for their strategic planning and intent? Do you believe that Wal-Mart stakeholders, shareholders, employees, suppliers, management, and the communities they serve fully understand their competitive advantage and its value? And lastly, do you believe that all Wal-Mart associates (employees) understand their role in Wal-Mart's success?

Understand Competitive Advantage

In order for a company to define its strategic intent, it must have a clear understanding of its competitive advantage, or that bundle of skills, knowledge, and special abilities that help the company outperform its competitors. Michael Treacy and Fred Wiersema[16] have defined three areas into which competitive advantages generally fall. (See Table 1.6 below.) Although they are usually mutually exclusive, the advent of cutting-edge technology has led some companies to excel in more than one area. If the organization under review has an expressed competitive advantage that does not clearly fall into one of these three categories, management may want to revisit their understanding of competitive advantage.

These three competitive advantage areas leverage a distinctive segment of customer demand: the elastic demand for lower prices, the inelastic demand for highly innovative products, or the inelastic demand for extraordinary personalized service.

Table 1.6 Competitive Advantage Areas

Low-Cost Provider	Does the company emphasize cost control and containment in producing goods or services at the best cost for the quality delivered?
Product or Innovation Leader	Are the company's products or services innovative and consistently first-to-market?
Service Leader—High "Customer Intimacy"	Does the company's customer service consistently exceed customer expectations and lead the industry for personalized attention?

A company's ability to articulate its competitive advantage thoroughly to its stakeholders will launch the organization towards achieving its strategic intent. Hamel and Prahalad describe strategic intent to include:

- focusing the organization's attention on the essence of winning
- motivating people by communicating the value of the target
- leaving room for individual and team contributions
- sustaining enthusiasm by providing new operational definitions as circumstances change
- using intent consistently to guide resource allocations.[17]

By utilizing organizational capabilities and resources that are valuable and rare, that lack substitutes, and that are difficult to imitate, organizations can enjoy a sustainable competitive advantage.[18] These four characteristics are essential to competitive advantage.

Certainly, resources and capabilities that are common to all competitors could not be leveraged to obtain a competitive advantage. Common valuable resources lead to parity in the marketplace. Possessing scarce resources will give an organization an advantage, but the sustainability is questionable since the resource may have substitutes or be easily imitated. It is only when an organization's capabilities include all four characteristics (value, rarity, lack of substitutes, and difficulty to imitate) that a firm can establish and sustain a competitive advantage.

Strategic intent has been formed effectively when all activities, capabilities, resources, and core competencies are in alignment with the mission, vision, and competitive advantage of a company. It is most influential when personnel believe fervently in their product and industry, and when they are focused entirely on their firm's ability to outdo its competitors.[19] Some would argue that strategic intent provides employees with the only goal worthy of the personal effort and commitment to unseat the best or remain the best, worldwide.[20]

Take the time to challenge your business model. If you're seeking a starting point, review companies that have built their brand on their strategic advantages. Meet with your management team to discuss how a company or a direct competitor is leveraging their advantage to generate better margins, greater market share, or expand into new markets. To get you started, we've listed a handful of well-recognized companies and their specific market advantages. (See Table 1.7 below.)

Table 1.7 Competitive Advantage Examples

Low-Cost Providers	• World Savings
	• Southwest Airlines
	• IKEA
	• Best Buy
	• Costco
Product or Innovation Leaders	• Microsoft
	• Cisco
	• Pfizer
	• Nokia
	• Wells Fargo Bank
Service Leaders—High "Customer Intimacy"	• Four Season's Hotels
	• Nordstrom's
	• Walt Disney Company
	• Lexus
	• Starbuck's Coffee

What to Do

If you haven't done so before, get your team off site. A fresh surrounding with no distractions will serve you well throughout the course of this process. Gather industry data, including competitive analysis, market size, and customer profiles, as well as current and anticipated channel and service requirements. If you have the skill set internally to facilitate such an exercise, great. However, we encourage you to seek the assistance of a professional. The process alone can kill you.

Choose Your Point of Difference—What Makes You Unique?

You have one of three, or, best case, four ways to go. Will you gain advantage through being a low-cost provider, a product innovator, or a superior service provider? Or, if you are particularly skilled, are you a hybrid of two of the three? Make no mistake; confusion at this stage of your decision-making can affect resources in every category. Each of these characteristics possesses its own decision tree, so don't hedge. Evaluate where your strengths are today, and how you shape up against the competition. Your selection will be the foundation for most, if not all, of your decisions going forward. Recruitment, training, technology, physical plant, reward systems, and values will all be guided by how you choose to compete.

Make Sure All Stakeholders Get It!

Ensure that all parties that play a role in your organization's success "get it." Employees, customers, regulators, communities that you serve, and suppliers all need to understand your advantage and how they either can support it or benefit from it. Communicate—Communicate—Communicate! Forms of communication include: internal and external newsletters, investor relations, advertising, town meetings (informal setting to discuss the organization's value proposition), press releases, collateral material, etc.

Get All Employees on Board—It's Not Negotiable!

All employees should have a crystal clear view of how their role in the company supports its competitive advantage. It should be tied to training, internal communications, performance management systems, and reward systems. Misaligned or mismatched employees create a situation that does not heal itself. Ensure that your recruitment, orientation, training, incentive compensation, and succession planning processes and systems are in total synch with your competitive advantage.

Align and Invest in the Right Resources

Identify the physical plant, technology, capital, human resources, and competence required to achieve your strategic intent. Prioritize and fund these resources in a manner that leaves little to chance. Everything cannot be an "A" item. The exercise of prioritization will test your leadership abilities.

Three influences that enable or inhibit your mission, vision, and competitive advantage are the environment in which you compete, the internal capabilities you possess, and a clearly defined plan to fulfill your strategic intent.

The next three chapters are crafted to provide insights and direction in the areas of environmental assessment, assessing your internal capabilities and constraints, and developing an action plan. Management and leadership are all about leaving nothing to chance in pursuit of a sustainable competitive advantage and maximizing shareholder value. The following chapters have been structured to assist you and your organization in understanding how you can leave little or nothing to chance.

The External Assessment—
Inside Looking Out

*When an industry with a reputation for bad
economics meets a manager with a reputation for
excellence, it's usually the industry that leaves with
its reputation intact.*

—ATTRIBUTED TO WARREN BUFFETT

EFFECTIVELY ASSESSING AN external business environment
requires an organization to possess the ability to gather and analyze essential market data. This data includes target customers' profiles, market size, competitive landscape, macro and microeconomic studies, industry opportunities and threats, and key success factors.

Researching this chapter has been paradoxical. The very nature of effective external analysis is extremely private to the "best practice" companies we've attempted to profile. Competitive analysis, certain market research, and defining key success factors for many great companies are part of their intellectual property, and are well guarded. Competitive analysis and market analysis is private and sacred to successful competitive companies. So, with that in mind, we explore what both primary and secondary research teaches us about effective external and business environmental assessment.

We do know that successful strategies and organizational performance is often dictated or at least influenced by the attractiveness of the environment in which the firm competes. This attractiveness is linked to a number of interrelated factors that shape the size and opportunity within a target market. Figure 2.1 (below) illustrates the concept.

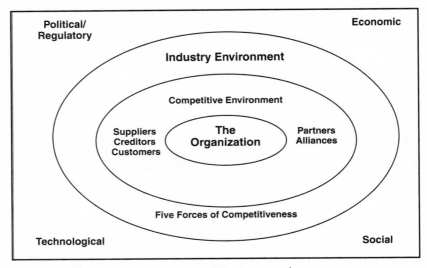

Figure 2.1 An Organization External Environment[1]

It is the combination of these factors that presents opportunities and threats to the organization as it competes in a new global marketplace. Understanding these factors, such as relative benchmarks for performance, the strategic intents of competitors, and customer preferences, is essential to crafting and implementing a viable strategy. Without a frame of reference, strategy would have no durability and no influence.

While working with a certain management team, one of our associates discovered that the team was congratulating themselves for obtaining their goal of 12-percent growth, but later discovered that their industry had grown 20 percent in the same period, leaving them 8 percent behind the average industry growth.

The goal of employing an effective market research and analysis approach is not to develop a comprehensive list of every potentially influential factor, but rather to identify key trends and market opportunities, avoid environmental pitfalls, and gain an ability to expand market presence, operate more efficiently, and enjoy a longer harvest period than key competitors.

The sophistication of computer technology has made data relatively inexpensive to obtain. The following partial list of Web sites contains links to other useful sources of data. (See Table 2.1 below.)

We explore the organizations' internal capabilities and constraints in Chapter 3. In this chapter, we review the manner in which organizations

Table 2.1   Useful Web Sites

American Management Association	www.amanet.org
American Stock Exchange	www.amex.com
Better Business Bureau	www.bbb.org
Census Bureau	www.census.gov
Competitive Intelligence Guide	www.fuld.com
DBC Online	www.dbc.com
Federal Trade Commission	www.ftc.gov
Hoover's Online	www.hoover.com
Investor's Guide	www.investorguide.com
NASDAQ	www.nasdaq.com
New York Stock Exchange	www.nyse.com/public/home.htm
PC Financial Network	www.dljdirect.com
Small Business Administration	www.sba.gov
Strategic Leadership Forum	www.slfnet.org
Strategic Management Society	www.virtual-indiana.com/sms/
Thomas Publishing Co.	www.thomaspublishing.com
U.S. Business Advisor	www.business.gov/business.htm
U.S. Department of Commerce	www.doc.gov
Wall Street Research Net	www.wsm.com

define their market opportunities, define target customers, define competitive positioning, examine economic influences, and ultimately select and develop the key success factors to create a sustainable and expandable competitive advantage.

Industry, Market, and Competitive Analysis

> *"Competitive strategy must grow out of a sophisticated understanding of the rules of competition that determine an industry's attractiveness."—Michael Porter*

Industries and markets change. When Barnes and Noble was evaluating its market and industry in 1995, did it dawn on them that a little upstart called Amazon.com was changing the manner in which customers shop for and purchase books? Did IBM, Compaq, or ACER know in the early 1980s that Michael Dell was looking to carve out the middleman and introduce just-in-time manufacturing to an industry and customer base that those companies had been dominating for years? What was going through the minds of Merrill Lynch or Dean Witter when the likes of E*Trade and AmeriTrade jumped into their space and created an alternative channel for investors to trade and gain quality investment information? Today more than ever, companies must maintain a constant awareness of their industry and their market position. Additionally, they must understand their proprietary position, market share, and the outlook for a growing customer base. The latter items are reviewed later in this chapter.

When working with organizations, especially young or less-experienced management teams, we evaluate whether:

1. They have the necessary resources to put critical industry and competitive data at their disposal.
2. They're assessing the outlook for industry growth, the rising sales of substitute products, and the industry's key market drivers.
3. They're maintaining sufficient data relating to specific direct and indirect competitors—their strengths, weaknesses, and strategic intent.

What are some of the key questions an organization must ask about their industry? Economic characteristics tell us much about an industry. Thompson and Strickland[2] crafted an effective checklist (Table 2.2) to get organizations thinking and to guide them through a thorough evaluation process.

Though information of this nature has never been more readily available, for many organizations it remains a daunting process that more times than not ends up incomplete.

Southwest Airlines[3] is a classic example of a company that thoughtfully considered its industry and market position before opening it doors to commuter passenger traffic over 30 years ago. The company launched their operations in the midst of a rather closed, highly regulatory environment. By positioning itself as a high-frequency, no-frills airline that specialized in short hop flights of less than two hours, often connecting passengers with other long-distance carriers, Southwest obtained a unique market position.

The company quickly became a dominant player in their market, and with the coming of deregulation, followed a brilliantly aligned low-cost strategy by implementing fast turnarounds at their gates, producing more

Table 2.2 What Are the Industry's Dominant Economic Features?

1. How big is the market?

2. What is the scope of competitive rivalry (local, regional, national, international, or global)?

3. What is the market growth rate, and where is the industry in its growth cycle (early development, rapid growth and takeoff, early maturity, maturity, saturated and stagnant, declining)?

4. Number of rivals and their relative sizes—is the industry fragmented with many small companies or concentrated and dominated by a few large companies?

5. The number of buyers and their relative sizes?

6. What is the prevalence of backward and forward integration?

7. What types of distribution channels are used to access buyers?

8. What is the pace of technological change in both production process innovation and new product introductions?

9. Are the products/services of rival firms highly differentiated, weakly differentiated, or essentially identical?

10. Can companies within the industry realize economies of scale in purchasing, manufacturing, transportation, marketing, or advertising?

11. Can certain industry activities be characterized by strong learning and experience effects, such that unit costs decline as cumulative output (and thus the experience of "learning by doing") grows?

12. Can you determine if high rates of capacity utilization are crucial to achieving low-cost production efficiency?

13. What are the resource requirements and the ease of entry and exit?

14. Is the industry profitability above or below par?

on-time flights per day with less aircraft, no meals, no assigned seating or baggage transfer to connecting airlines, or automated ticketing.

These cost-saving measures delivered to their customers the benefits of low cost, frequent service, and on-time flights. It keeps their cost per passenger mile well below that of their next competitor. Competitors who were frustrated in their attempts to emulate Southwest's winning strategy perceived Southwest as the dominant player. Southwest continues to dominate the "low-cost" provider space within the airline industry.

Worth noting, as we have when citing Southwest throughout this book, is the fact that they support their strategic market position by fostering an innovative work environment and only recruiting personnel who reflect the innovative, fun, people-oriented culture that breeds so much success.

Harvard Professor Michael E. Porter, in his book *Competitive Strategy*, introduces the notion of industry environment and the influences that the five forces within the industry have on competition.[4] Porter's model examines the five forces that influence and challenge competition within an industry, and how to strive for a sustainable competitive advantage. (See Figure 2.2.)

Porter submits that by identifying and assessing the key structural features of industries, you can determine the strength of the competitive forces, and hence, potential industry profitability. Utilizing Porter's model, or a variation that accomplishes the same intent will put you in a position to make the following assessments:

1. Identify the main structural features of an industry that influence competitive behavior and profitability, and analyze relationships between industry structure, competition, and the level of profitability.
2. Assess the attractiveness of an industry in terms of the industry's potential for generating above-average or below-average returns.
3. Use evidence on structural trends within industries to forecast changes in industry profitability in the future.

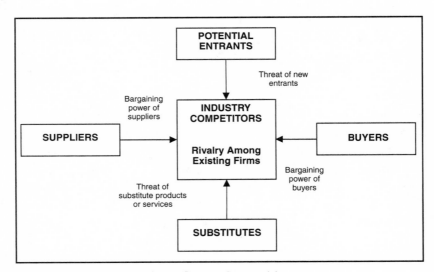

Figure 2.2 Five Forces that Influence Competition

4. Identify the opportunities available to a firm to influence industry structure in order to moderate the intensity of competition and improve industry profitability.
5. Analyze competition and customer requirements in an industry in order to identify key success factors—opportunities for competitive advantage within an industry.

The following table (Table 2.3) is an example of one approach to assessing your competition, and evaluating competitive positioning.

Many organizations conduct this industry and competitive analysis formally once per year. Successful companies continuously monitor changes in the environment, competitive conditions, and emerging trends, and respond to opportunities in a rapid and timely fashion.

The range of support and systems that organizations use to support this process is extremely broad. Large, Fortune 3000 companies have multiple departments, consultants, and sophisticated systems that weave the miles of data that must be processed to provide an accurate picture of their environment. For those that have neither the capital nor other resources to bring to bear, we propose that *some* process is better then none. Trade organizations, the Internet, industry trade magazines, and research firms with subscription services, to name a few, are relatively inexpensive and readily available. In addition to the data, format is also very import. Start simple and build. Establishing a basic discipline and weaving it into your management meetings and other business sessions will begin a process that by its very nature will support business improvement. The following table (Table 2.4) contains a summary profile of the analysis.[5]

An example of one of the force's influences on a company's strategy is the story of NutraSweet's rise and fall as a powerful supplier of aspartame.[6]

Table 2.3 Market Share Leaders and Competitive Advantages

Rank	Competitor	Market Share Percentage	Competitive Advantage	Weaknesses	Impact on Your Company
1.	Company A				
2.	Company B				
3.	Company C				
4.	Company D				

Table 2.4 Industry and Competitive Analysis Summary Profile

1. Dominant Economic Characteristics of the Industry Environment	• Market growth • Geographic scope • Industry structure • Scale economies • Experience curve effects
2. Competition Analysis	• Competitive rivalry • Threat of potential entrants • Competition from substitutes • Supplier power • Customer power
3. Driving Forces	• Based on industry being analyzed
4. Competitive Position of Major Companies/Strategic Groups	• Favorably positioned, and why • Unfavorably positioned, and why
5. Competitor Analysis	• Strategic approaches/predicted moves of key competitors • Who to watch, and why
6. Key Success Factors	• Specific to targeted industry—see "Key Success Factors" section in this chapter
7. Industry Prospects and Overall Attractiveness	• Factors making the industry attractive • Factors making the industry unattractive • Special industry issues/problems • Profit outlook [favorable/unfavorable]

While holding the patent for NutraSweet, Monsanto could dictate terms to its customers, such as pricing, and displaying the NutraSweet logo. After the patent expired, Monsanto was forced to lower their prices and support their customers' promotional efforts due to the advent of new aspartame suppliers. Monsanto was successful, however, in differentiating NutraSweet among the new entrants by focusing on customers who had high stakes in their customers' brand and taste loyalty. The switching costs for two important customers, Coke and Pepsi, were too high for them to risk replacing a vital ingredient of their products' image and reputation.

Some companies find that market positioning is done so well that it is difficult to change. Harley Davidson enjoys a distinctive definition related to its motorcycle image in *The Wild One*. Its reputation was deliberately cultivated among riders as being rebellious, nasty, and tough. Its definition contrasts sharply with that of Honda's image. In its early motorcycle advertisements, Honda proclaimed, "You meet the nicest people on a Honda." This image persists today, and it has been difficult for Honda to penetrate the "tough guy" market.[7]

Coors Beer once enjoyed the mystique that came from its distribution strategy being limited to the West Coast. Beer drinkers from the eastern and midwestern states would travel back from Colorado with loads of the brew in their trunks. When Coors achieved national distribution, however, some of its distinctiveness and Rocky Mountain image was lost.

Profiling Your Target Customers

"We started thinking about the lifetime value of customers as opposed to their transactional value."—Henry Joyner

Understanding both the needs of your existing customers and prospective customers requires management to invest resources. It's unlikely that the power of the customer is going to diminish anytime soon. Understanding the needs and wants of your customers, and mapping those needs to your products and services, provides an organization with the path of least resistance.

We live in a world where Michael Dell, Bill Gates, Sam Walton, or Hugh McColl can change the landscape of an industry and dominate within 20 years. Think about that. Bill Gates conceived Microsoft in 1976, and today dominates the globe as the common operating system for desktop computing. Michael Dell conceived Dell Computers in 1980, and today controls the number-two or three spot in computer manufacturing. Sam Walton decided to take on Sears and K-Mart. Between 1980 and 1993 he took Wal-Mart from $1.6 billion in sales to $67 billion. From number three to number one, and though Sam is no longer with us, his legacy lives on as the largest retail chain on the planet.

You may not have heard of Hugh McColl, who headed up a regional bank called North Carolina National Bank (NCNB). In 1983, he and his team changed the name of the bank to NationsBank and set the organization on a course to become the "nation's bank." In 1998, they purchased Bank of America, which resulted in becoming the second-largest bank in the United States.

These leaders, in each case, made indelible marks on our business community in less than 20 years. Who will be the next Bill Gates, Michael Dell, Sam Walton, or Hugh McColl? They are among us, looking to seize the opportunity to redefine a market. It may be your market, your industry, your customer. Understanding your market, your customer, and your position puts you in the position to be in front of the next big wave.

Where to begin? A first step is to understand the customer better. What are their needs today, and equally important is what will those needs look like tomorrow? What are the criteria to understand your customer better?

When we evaluate an organization's ability to understand their existing and future customers, we assess the following:

1. Do they clearly define the reasons that customers buy their products/services?
2. Do they clearly define the benefits that customers seek?
3. Do they clearly define the reasons why customers would not buy their products or services?
4. Do they clearly understand and document the bargaining power that their customers possess?
5. Do they clearly define which distribution channel their customers prefer?
6. Do they have the technology, systems, capital, and manpower to support the tracking and monitoring of customer behavior and trends?

The old adage for successful entrepreneurs, "Determine what your customer wants, and then give it to them," is still an effective guideline for strategic success. An organization cannot respond to customer needs until it identifies them. Understanding your customers' buying criteria, nature of demand, points of resistance, and choice of channel is essential to sound product design and development, efficient production, targeted marketing, sales effectiveness, and ultimately, the right customer service model. Standard approaches to profiling customers usually come in one of three forms, as shown in Table 2.5.

Profiling a customer involves more than just informal employee contact with a customer. The challenge becomes to solicit customer feedback while having the organizational systems necessary to route that feedback to the appropriate personnel. Customer feedback was a major influencer to Lands' End's decision to convert from a sailboat equipment company to an outdoor clothing organization.[8] Customer feedback taken by mail-order operators urged them to include the clothing as part of their catalog offering. Soon, the offerings migrated away from equipment and solely to clothing. Today, the

Table 2.5   Standard Customer Profile Approach[9]

1. Demographics	Generally consisting of specific statistics: age, sex, marital status, family size and makeup, residence status (own or rent), ethnicity, education level, employment, and other census-based data.
2. Psychographics	Generally reflect lifestyle or desired lifestyle characteristics. Where the person lives, what they drive, what they wear, where they vacation, where their children are educated, where they retire, and other self-image related information make up a psychographic profile.
3. Psycho-demographics	Generally a hybrid of life stages and corresponding lifestyle choices. Attitudes toward saving, gender roles, leisure time, product quality, and service are among psycho-demographics.

company still solicits customer feedback by printing and distributing customer requests and comments on a monthly basis.

The following table (Table 2.6) represents one approach to clearly defining the primary characteristics of a targeted customer.

Customer groups (segments) generally have common characteristics. Whether you're serving consumers or businesses (B2B), they tend to follow a common path in purchasing products or services. There are organizations that provide proprietary models that articulate the characteristics of customers. Within the consumer markets, the Claritas and Donnelley models are the most widely used. The Claritas model is known as PRIZM (Potential Rating Index by ZIP Markets), and Donnelley has a product known as ClusterPlus. PRIZM profiles 40 different demographic/lifestyle clusters. ClusterPlus classifies all households into 47 different clusters. Both companies can slice and dice and provide segment-specific data to support their clients' needs.

The common characteristics that both companies attempt to profile include:

1. Defining the characteristics of the customer. This would include age, occupation, economic status, ethnic background, size of family, and even lifestyle tendencies.

Table 2.6 Customer Profile Model

Data Requirements	Target Customer A	Target Customer B	Target Customer C	Target Customer D
Buying Characteristics/ Nature of Demand				
Primary Benefits Sought				
Resistance Points to Purchase				
Trends in Buying Patterns, Needs, and Shifts in Habit				
Substitute Products				
Desired Buying Channel or Method of Purchase				

2. Defining the benefits that the customer seeks. For example, a McDonald's customer may seek a reliable, clean, fast, and reasonably priced meal wherever they might travel. A Wal-Mart customer's benefits would include lower price, convenience, selection, and quality for the price.

3. As important as why a customer would purchase is why a customer may not purchase. Resistance points can include price, location, selection, financing, or reputation.

4. Trends in buying patterns tied to existing customers or new customer segments are a dynamic that could affect your relationship with your current customer or the pursuit of a new one. As customers age, or move, or earnings increase, etc., their loyalty to your product or service may change.

5. Substitute products are a constant threat. At one point in time, all a bank had to worry about were banks, savings and loans, and credit unions. In today's market, they can just as easily lose a customer to E*Trade, Prudential Mortgage, or Charles Schwab. The U.S. Post Office is now competing with Internet email services, FedEx, and UPS.

6. The method of delivery or the channel in which a customer chooses to purchase is equally important. A Barnes and Noble customer that

likes to browse through a bookstore and leaf through books is not as likely to purchase from Amazon.com on the Internet. Dell has proven that there is an extraordinarily large market of businesses and consumers who would rather purchase a computer on the Internet than walk into CompUSA. Understanding the form in which your customer chooses to purchase and ultimately be served is crucial.

A good example of responding to a changing customer profile is Yamaha's strategy in the piano industry.[10] With decline in sales approaching 10 percent annually, Yamaha discovered that most pianos in American, European, and Japanese homes were not being used. In most cases, the reasons for the piano's purchase had expired. Children had left home, or opportunities to play were seldom. Yamaha also uncovered the fact that most pianos were being used as fine furniture, and that most purchasers had incomes well above average.

In response to this market opportunity, Yamaha released a converter that would play prerecorded tunes on the pianos. They followed the release of the piano converter with an upright that could play and record tunes on a floppy disk. The sales revived a maturing market and Yamaha enjoyed renewed profitability.

As an organization becomes more proficient at trend analysis, it will become better positioned to anticipate the future needs of its customers, thereby strengthening its customer relationships and impeding the threats posed by the competition.

The position a company takes in the marketplace with regard to its product offerings, proprietary technology, innovations, channel selection, pricing, and promotional strategies plays a major role in its efficiency. *Efficiency* can be described in terms of acquiring and retaining an organization's customer base. An organization that excels in maintaining its market position will have selected a position that contributes to developing customer loyalty while increases switching costs between itself and its competitor.

By retaining its customers, a firm's competitive advantage increases due in part to not having to bear the increased cost of customer acquisition.

Understanding where competitor strengths lie, which market segments are being exploited, and what customer needs are being met, and by what means they are being met, can improve an organization's market position. Selecting a market that is void of leadership, has an underserved customer base, and invites innovation can lead to significant customer acquisition and cost-saving, long-term retention.

Environmental Assessment

"Positive trends in the environment breeds complacency. That underscores a basic point: In change there is both opportunity and challenge."—Clifton Garvin, Chairman of the Board, Exxon, Retired

Now the fun stuff. Macro- and microeconomics, just to mention two. An effective and beneficial process supporting environmental analysis includes assessing and understanding the critical environmental conditions that face a company's industry. This would include assessing economic conditions, technology shifts, demographic shifts, sociocultural values and institutions, regulatory infringement, and vulnerability to unidentified business cycle influences.

The influence of macro- or microeconomics can either be devastating or the greatest thing that has ever happened to an organization. Remember, one person's crisis is another person's opportunity.

The impact that inflation and rising interest rates can have on an industry are significant. Inflation can drive the costs of goods up at a rate faster than the consumer or business can absorb. In fact, many have argued that the recent recession that we've experienced in the United States actually has served as a means to correct an inflated stock market. The chart below (Table 2.7) illustrates an industry-accepted model for examining key economic indices.

Just as inflation can, and does, affect industry, so, of course, does technology. The pace of technology has rapidly accelerated since World War II.

Table 2.7 Blue Chip Consensus External Forecasts[11]

Indices	Actual 1995				Forecast 1996				1997		
	1Q	2Q	3Q	4Q	1Q	2Q	3Q	4Q	1Q	2Q	3Q
Fed Funds	5.79	6.03	5.78	5.72	5.39	5.27	5.40	5.50	5.60	5.50	5.50
3-Mo. T-Bill	5.96	5.79	5.54	5.43	5.07	5.16	5.30	5.40	5.50	5.40	5.40
30-Yr. Treasury	7.64	6.96	6.72	6.23	6.30	7.06	7.10	7.00	6.80	6.80	6.70
Home Mtg. Rate	8.82	7.95	7.70	7.34	7.26	8.11	8.20	8.10	8.10	7.90	7.80
GDP	0.6	0.5	3.6	0.5	2.2	4.2	2.6	2.1	1.9	1.8	2.0
CPI	3.2	3.2	2.1	2.1	2.8	3.9	2.7	2.8	3.1	3.0	3.0
Unemployment	5.5	5.6	5.7	5.6	5.5	5.4	5.5	5.6	5.6	5.6	5.6

Table 2.8 Organization's Technology-Monitoring Process

---

1. What forms of technology are forming, shaping, or influencing the industry?
2. What are the specific threats or opportunities that technology presents to the growth aspects of the business?
3. How do these technologies support or impair the company's competitive advantage?
4. How does technology support and influence the buying patterns and needs of target customers?

Technological advancement can make products and processes obsolete, literally overnight. On the other hand, it can offer new opportunities for business commerce. Organizations' monitoring of technology should address the issues detailed in Table 2.8.

Similarly, the aging of the population, along with a host of other changing demographics, has created threats and opportunities for organizations. Companies catering to needs of seniors have experienced an increased demand, while others have been affected by changing spending habits, income levels, and attitudes. For example, if you consider increased teenage obesity, young Americans as a whole might be becoming less interested in fitness. Companies in this sector, such as Nike, Reebok, and Nordic Track, could experience declines in sales.

Another emerging external variable that can have profound influence on organization performance is ecological concerns. More and more resources are being put into green issues such as air and water pollution, ozone depletion, and waste management. Table 2.9 outlines some important environmental forces.

Environmental analysis can also help a company take advantage of sociocultural forces. Miami-based Knight-Ridder, originally a newspaper company, now a $2.3 billion information industry player, is a good example. Taking advantage of technologies' impact on how its customers gather information, Knight-Ridder owns an on-line newswire service, a cable television channel, and an electronic information retrieval service. Cognizant of changing social and demographic changes in Miami, Knight-Ridder launched a Spanish-language daily newspaper that became the largest of its kind in the United States.

Table 2.9 Macroenvironmental Forces[12]

Political/Legal	Economic	Technological	Sociocultural
Tax laws	Money supply	R&D expenditures	Attitudes toward
International trade	Monetary policy	Rate of new product	lifestyles, innovations,
regulations	Unemployment	introductions	careers, and consumer
Consumer lending	rate	Automation	activism
regulations	Energy costs	Robotics	Life expectancies
Environmental	Disposable	Focus of R&D	Concern with quality
protection laws	personal income	expenditures	of life
Antitrust regulations	Stage of economic		Birth rates
and enforcement	cycle		Population shifts
Hiring, firing,			Shifts in the presence
promotion, and			of women in the
pay laws			workforce
Wage/price controls			

Table 2.10 presents the relative utility of data-gathering and forecasting techniques for analyzing these various environmental segments.[13]

A powerful example of a company that failed to capitalize on its key environmental assessment strengths was Wang Laboratories, Inc.[14] Founded in 1951, the company managed in the early 1970s to find a niche in the word processing industry. By carefully outmaneuvering IBM, the software and hardware manufacturer grew to generate over $92.7 million in after-tax profits on revenues of over $3 billion by 1988. However, by 1992, the company had filed for bankruptcy. The company had lost a total of $1.9 billion since 1988, and its stock market value had fallen from $5.6 billion, had slumped to $70 million. Once trading at $42.50 per share in 1982, Wang's 1992 share price was around $0.37 per share.

Complacent, and even somewhat prideful in their success, Wang had allowed the talents that had brought them so much success to lay dormant. By overlooking the changes in the marketplace, the growing sophistication of the buyer and competitor encroachment, Wang had failed to respond to emerging opportunities to stay ahead of their rivals.

When offered a chance to align with Apple in early 1984, Wang turned their nose up, saying that Apple was too young and unpredictable of a partner. They also failed to take notice of small start-up software competitors such as WordPerfect and WordStar. By assuming that $2 billion was enough of a head start, Wang underestimated the value of routine analysis and response. Consequently, unwatched, unimpeded, small, distant rivals, very much like Wang at their start, have endured and have far surpassed Wang in sales.

Key Success Factors

Organizations utilize "key success factors" when articulating areas of focus within their given industry. This approach requires that management apply a critical thinking process when evaluating all factors that influence business within their sector of commerce. Once evaluated, the factors that drive a successful outcome are identified as "key."

When we evaluate organizations for their ability to understand and tie key success factors to their business, we ask the following:

1. Do they possess and utilize a critical thinking process?
2. Do they clearly measure competitive intensity?
3. Do they clearly define product or service demand within their markets?
4. Do they clearly define key drivers to success within their industry?
5. Do they support a system that consistently monitors key influences within their industry?

Several industries have many characteristics that, although minor when looked at singularly, when taken together are extremely important for gaining and maintaining competitive advantages. *Key* or *critical success factors* are those areas in which all firms must be competent at performing or achieving in order to be successful in that industry. Most of these success factors have a direct bearing on a company's profitability. A sound strategy will usually incorporate the intent to excel in one or more of these critical success factors.

Table 2.10 Environmental Analysis Techniques

	Social			Political			
	Demographics	Lifestyles	Social values	Political milieu	Regulatory	Economic	Technological
Data-gathering methods							
Type of sources	Primarily quantitative Secondary sources	Quantitative and qualitative Secondary and primary	Inferential/ qualitative Primary and secondary	Real-time personal Qualitative	Historical/ real-time Primary and secondary Qualitative	Historical/ real-time Secondary Quantitative	Mostly primary/ qualitative Secondary sources for later stages
Techniques	Market research techniques	Focus groups In-depth interviews Panels	In-depth interviews Panels Content analysis	Content analysis of speeches Lobbying Opinion leaders	Content analysis of legislation Regulatory opinions Expert opinion	Outputs of model	Expert panels Interviews with experts

casting methods and techniques	Simulation (A)	Lifestyle (M) profiling	Analytical (A)	Event history analysis	Network analysis (M)	World and historical dynamics (A-M)	Historical analysis (M)
	Logistics equation models (M) Transition matrices (M) Geographic mobility models (A-M)	Probability-diffusion matrices (A)	Value profile Social pressures, priority analysis (A)	Political risk analysis (M) Networks (M)		Econometric models (A-M) Input-output analysis (M) Simulation models (A) Trend extrapolation (M) Time-series analysis (M)	Probability-diffusion matrices (A-M) Morphological methods (I) Delphi (A) Relevance trees (I) Logistical curves
Characteristics	Generally robust	Variable in robustness	Very variable	Weak in robustness	Moderately robust	Robust in terms of direction of change	Variable/inventive
Integrative forecasting methods	M = mechanistic A = adaptive I = inventive						

45

Many entrepreneurial companies find that in order to maintain their momentum and strengthen their market position, they need to balance their intuitive understanding and implementation of key success factors with certain structural disciplines that must also be adopted.

Robert M. Grant in *Contemporary Strategy Analysis* introduces an effective model to follow for an organization's approach to identifying industry "key success" factors, as illustrated in Figure 2.3.[15]

Determining an organization's industry success factors should be a top priority in light of today's technology-influenced, rapidly changing environment. Prioritizing initiatives and aligning resources on issues that truly influence success is the key to a winning strategy.

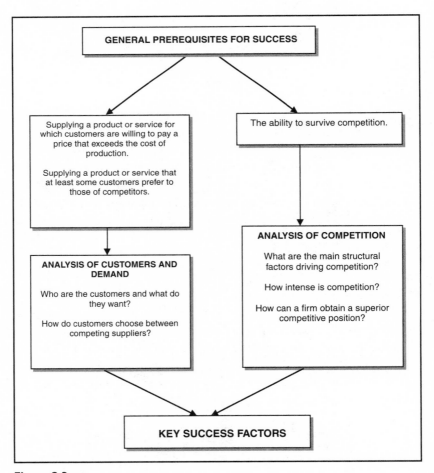

Figure 2.3

Microsoft's efforts to turn "positive feedback" of its operating system into a winning strategy is described in Bill Gates' book, *The Road Ahead*.[16] By focusing on its core technology of operating systems and languages, Microsoft encourages other software application developers to compete with it by developing applications for its operating systems. The key success factor in their business is their installed customer base. By encouraging applications, more businesses will install Microsoft's operating system. With a growing installed base, more software developers will make applications. This positive feedback spiral is a cornerstone of Microsoft's rapid growth strategy.

Table 2.11 illustrates types of key success factors.[17]

Effectively defining your "key success factors" will not only assist you in aligning your resources properly, it will provide you with the foundation for an effective communication platform for your employees and customers.

What to Do

Creating the systems, process, and data to support effective environmental analysis is not for the faint of heart. Building these systems is like owning a boat; it can be an economic bottomless pit. Having said that, having the right business intelligence at your fingertips can ensure a maximum return on your capital. Go into this process with a long-term attitude. Establish a well-thought-out foundation that you can build on over time. The following four steps can be "right-sized" to your organization's manpower and financial resources.

Know Your Industry, Know Your Market(s), Know Your Competition

Porter's model is the best launching ground. It encompasses the multiple dimensions that most organizations compete within. There is a common thread that weaves through Porter's model. That thread is the need for industry-specific data. So, rather than restating within each section, remember, most industries have trade organizations or publications that analyze most aspects of an industry. Start there. Additionally, the Web is a multiple resource. Yahoo's financial site, for example, has a very deep industry knowledge section. Let's review Porter's model in more depth.

1. Identify the main structural features of an industry that influence competitive behavior and profitability and analyze relationships between industry structure, competition, and the level of profitability.

Table 2.11 Types of Key Success Factors

Technology-related KSFs	• Scientific research expertise • Production process innovation capability • Product innovation capability • Expertise in a given technology
Manufacturing-related KSFs	• Low-cost production efficiency • Quality of manufacturing • High utilization of fixed assets • Low-cost plant locations • Access to adequate supplies of skilled labor • High labor productivity • Low-cost product design and engineering • Flexibility to manufacture a range of models and sizes/customization
Distribution-related KSFs	• A strong network of wholesale distributors/dealers • Gaining ample space on retailer shelves • Having company-owned retail outlets • Low distribution costs • Fast delivery
Marketing-related KSFs	• A well-trained, effective sales force • Available, dependable service and technical assistance • Accurate filling of buyer orders • Breadth of product line and product selection • Merchandising skills • Attractive styling/packaging • Customer guarantees and warranties
Skills-related KSFs	• Superior talent • Quality know-how • Design expertise • Expertise in a particular technology • Ability to come up with clever, catchy ads • Ability to get newly developed products out of the R and D phase and into the market very quickly
Organizational capability	• Superior information systems • Ability to respond quickly to shifting market conditions

2. Assess the attractiveness of an industry in terms of the industry's potential for generating above or below-average returns.
3. Use evidence on structural trends within industries to forecast changes in industry profitability in the future. Again, looking to trade organizations, and research-based organizations with specific industry focus provides trend analysis in a broad range of areas. Making calculated or informed decisions based on industry history and informed forecasting is a fundamental responsibility of management.
4. Identify the opportunities available to a firm to influence industry structure in order to moderate the intensity of competition and improve industry profitability. There are several areas in which one company's action can influence an industry. These influences can bring an immediate competitive advantage to an organization, but over time this influence can improve the overall health of the industry. Quick examples would include the work that American Airlines has done in reservation systems and technology; Wal-Mart has done it for its industry in the area of inventory control; Toyota and Nissan did it in the 1970s with work teams to participate in design and production of their automobiles; and the list goes on. You can improve your business as well as serve the greater good of your industry.
5. Analyze competition and customer requirements in an industry in order to identify key success factors—opportunities for competitive advantage within an industry. Identify direct and indirect competitors. List their strengths and weaknesses. Match yours against theirs, and assess how you stand up. Get frequent updates on market shares. The frequency is driven by the age and dynamics of your industry.

Know Your Customer—Be Your Customer

As stated earlier, there are six areas of information that will populate your customer profile. Repeat this process for each customer segment.

1. Define the characteristics of the customer. This would include age, occupation, economic status, ethnic background, size of family, and even lifestyle tendencies. For a business customer, it would include age and size, financial health, ownership type (corporation, family-owned, nonprofit, government agency, etc.), and decision-making process.

2. Define the benefits that the customer seeks. For example, a McDonald's customer may seek a reliable, clean, fast, and reasonably priced meal wherever they might travel. A Wal-Mart customer's benefits would include lower price, convenience, selection, and quality for the price. B2B customer benefits may be price-driven, proprietary (exclusives), speed of delivery, quality, or partner-based.

3. Equally important to why a customer would purchase is why a customer may not purchase. Resistance points can include price, location, selection, financing, or reputation.

4. Trends in buying patterns tied to existing customers or new customer segments are a dynamic that could affect your relationship with your current customer or your pursuit of a new one. As the customers age, move, or earnings increase, etc., their loyalty to your product or service may change. You may have a large corporate client in a declining or mature industry that may not have the demands of your long-term growth.

5. Understand the threat of substitute products. They are a constant threat, and are often overlooked. At one point in time all a bank had to worry about were other banks, savings and loans, and credit unions. In today's market, they can just as easily lose a customer to E*Trade, Prudential Mortgage, or Charles Schwab. The U.S. Post Office is now competing with Internet email services, FedEx, and UPS.

6. Delivery or the channel in which a customer chooses to purchase are equally important. A Barnes and Noble customer that likes to browse through a bookstore and leaf through books is not as likely to want to purchase from Amazaon.com on the Internet. Dell has proven that there is an extraordinary large market of businesses and consumers that would rather purchase a computer on the Internet than walk into CompUSA. Understanding the form in which your customer chooses to purchase and ultimately be served is crucial.

Understand Your Macro- and Microeconomic Conditions

This is your process piece. Creating a reusable model to house the environmental data that you need to analyze enables a broader base of use and application. If the various departments or divisions within your organization understand that there is a common vehicle to gain industry insight, they are less likely to duplicate efforts, and more importantly, if they know the information is available, they are more likely to make informed decisions.

Table 2.10 is the best process model we have found for supporting an organization's environmental analysis process.

Build Your Organization around Your "Key Success Factors"

Articulating your key success factors demonstrates the level of awareness and understanding you have of your industry, markets, and customers. If you follow the previous three steps, you will have sufficient information to define those characteristics that are fundamentally "key" to your success. Key success factors tend to follow a "supply-chain" model. Your key success factors can involve your research and development function, your production function, your marketing and sales functions, and your customer service functions. Review the Robert Grant model (Figure 2.3) to create an information flow chart that will enable you to craft your KSFs.

This chapter is all about understanding the business world around you. Embracing the techniques, systems, and processes outlined in this chapter creates a *fact-based* knowledge system within your organization. This is a powerful tool. Our next chapter focuses on measuring, understanding, and leveraging an organization's capabilities and constraints. Employing lessons learned in this chapter will enable management to determine which capabilities need to exist within the organization in order to compete and grow.

CHAPTER

The Internal Assessment— Dell, Microsoft, Nike, and the Four Seasons Hotels and Resorts

I firmly believe if you're going to do something, you should do it better than anyone else. To copy or emulate a company who's succeeding is a very hard strategy to play.

—Michael Dell

THE INTERNAL ASSESSMENT IS ALL ABOUT two things— capabilities and constraints. Can or can't your business achieve your strategic intent?

A thorough audit of an organization comes only through an objective, sometimes painfully honest approach to evaluating capabilities and constraints. These can include assessing capital, human, and technology resources, operational capacities, and the ability to track and manage these components. Identifying gaps or incongruencies as well as distinctive competencies early in a planning process provides an organization with opportunities to adjust its intent. This helps the organization mitigate weaknesses while leveraging their strengths.

One popular approach to evaluating a company's capabilities and performance is through the use of complimentary perspectives. Authors Kaplan and Norton use the metaphor of flying an airplane to illustrate a need to focus on a broad range of issues when evaluating performance. Just as pilots rely on multiple instruments to monitor their flights, so should managers utilize a variety of perspectives and information sources to develop successful strategies. The Balanced Scorecard approach emphasizes the need to balance each perspective and not allow any one perspective to outweigh any other in evaluating performance. A summary (Table 3.1) of the four perspectives appears below:[1]

Understanding an organization from these interrelated perspectives gives a clearer understanding of the functional areas for improvement, as well as areas of expertise to leverage for competitive advantage.

Robert Grant offers a good example. The Walt Disney Company first identified its strengths in its assets and resources and leveraged them up to gain an advantage in their industry. Under their new CEO's direction in 1984, Disney aggressively licensed their classic film library beyond their traditional periodic rereleases. They revitalized their movie studio and heavily recruited top talent to double their movie title output quickly. In four short years, Disney became America's leading studio in terms of box office receipts.

Coupled with aggressive theme park development in Florida, and their push into cable and network TV, Disney took advantage of their number-one resource and strength, the love of millions of adoring fans of all ages from all nations for Disney characters and the Disney name.

Grant also proposes the idea of identifying strengths or weaknesses by mapping a company's profile by resource. (See Table 3.2)

Table 3.1 Balanced Scorecard Perspectives

Financial Perspective	Does the firm's strategic response and execution contribute to improvement of the bottom line? Most measurements include traditional business financial performance ratios and economic valuation models.
Customer Perspective	Does the firm provide the customer with superior value defined on the customer's terms? Measurements may include, depending on industry, satisfaction, new customer acquisition, retention, profitability, and market share.
Internal Business [Operations] Perspective	Does the firm efficiently and profitably produce the products and/or services that its customers value? Measurements may include time to market, new product innovations, and cost of goods.
Learning and Growth Perspective	Does the firm readily adapt to shifts in strategy? Does its culture support change? Are the employees committed to its strategic intent? Measurements include employee satisfaction, retention, training, and skill sets.

Table 3.2 Assessing a Firm's Resources[2]

Resource	Main Characteristics	Key Indicators
Financial Resources	The firm's borrowing capacity and its internal funds generation determine its investment capacity and its cyclical resilience.	• Debt/equity ratio • Ratio of net cash to capital expenditure • Credit rating
Physical Resources	The size, location, technical sophistication, and flexibility of plant and equipment; location and alternative uses for land and buildings, and reserves of raw materials constrain the firm's set of production possibilities and determine the potential for cost and quality advantage.	• Resale values of fixed assets • Vintage of capital equipment • Scale of plants • Alternative uses of fixed assets
Human Resources	The training and expertise of employees determine the skills available to the firm. The adaptability of employees determines the strategic flexibility of the firm. The commitment and loyalty of the employees determines the firm's ability to maintain competitive advantage.	• Educational, technical, professional qualifications of employees • Pay rates relative to industry average
Technological Resources	Stock of technology including proprietary technology (patents, copyrights, trade secrets) and expertise in its application of know-how. Resources for innovation: research facilities, technical and scientific employees.	• Number and significance of patents • Revenue from patent licenses. • R and D staff as a percentage of total employees
Reputation	Reputation with customers through the ownership of brands, established relationships with customers, the association of the firm's products with quality, reliability, etc. The reputation of the company with the suppliers of components, finance, labor services, and other inputs.	• Brand recognition • Price-premium over competing brands • Percentage of repeat buying • Objective measures of product performance • Level and consistency of company performance

Table 3.3 Organization Dynamic Model—Corporate Edition

• Organization Strategy		• Organization Design		• Organization Culture	
• **Mission, Vision Competitive Advantage**	• Focused Purpose • Future Perspective • Strategic Advantage	• **Basic Structure**	• Structure Criteria • Structure Evolution	• **Values & Beliefs**	• Values Integration • Values Credibility
• **External Assessment**	• Customer Profile • Industry & Competitive Analysis • Environmental Assessment	• **Core Competence**	• Identifying Core • Leveraging Core Competence	• **Leadership**	• Management Modeling • Strategic/Tactical Balance • Empowerment • Developmental Coaching • Building Effective Teams
• **Internal Assessment**	• Finance • Research & Development • Production • Marketing • Sales/Distribution • Customer Service	• **Information, Systems, & Technology**	• Organization Communication • Targeted Information • Enterprising Systems • Applied Technology	• **Human Resource Systems**	• Selective Recruitment • Employee Orientation • Continuous Learning • Performance Management • Reward Systems
• **Objectives, Initiatives, & Goals**	• Vital Direction • Resource Alignment • Organization Accountabilities	• **Organization Efficiency**	• Balanced Oversight & Direction • Synthesized Roles & Responsibilities • Managed Outsource & Strategic Alliances	• **Organization Character**	• Informal Communication • Organizational Feedback • Adaptability to Change

When we developed the Organization Dynamic Model (Table 3.3)[3] we were searching for a means to evaluate all aspects of organization's process, systems, management, and alignment against primary and secondary "Best Practice" research. In addition to internal capabilities and constraints, this model allows an organization to evaluate itself from multiple stakeholder perspectives. In so doing, it can identify those areas that are critical to its success, and immediately seek and implement solutions tied to clearly defined business improvement needs.

Throughout this chapter, we illustrate and document how certain industry leaders and best-practiced companies leverage their capabilities and work around their constraints.

Finance

"Remember, that time is money."—Benjamin Franklin

Financial discipline is certainly one of the most essential skill sets necessary to operate a successful business. Yet, as a discipline, it is one of the least understood and poorly managed areas in business today. Continuing to seek excellence in illustrating strategic disciplines, we found the Dell Computer Corporation to be a model of rapid sustained growth, while demonstrating the highest level of financial management practices.

A Look at Dell

In less then 20 years, Michael Dell has built Dell Computer Corporation into one of the largest computer manufacturers in the world. Wow.

Dell Computer Corporation is a direct computer systems company. The company offers its customers a full range of computer systems, including desktop computer systems, notebook computers, workstations, network servers and storage products, as well as an extended selection of peripheral hardware, computing software, and related services. Additionally, the company offers an array of services to support its customers' on-line initiatives. The company's direct model offers in-person relationships with corporate and institutional customers, as well as telephone and Internet purchasing, build-to-order computer systems, telephone and on-line technical support, and on-site product service. The company sells its products and services to large corporate, government, healthcare, and education customers, small to medium-sized businesses, and individuals.

Table 3.4 Dell Financial Performance—1997–2001[4]

Consideration	2001	2000	1999	1998	1997
Stock Price[*5]	$27.18	$17.44	$51.00	$36.59	$10.50
Total Sales in Millions	$31,168	$31,888	$25,265	$18,243	$12,327
EPS	$.457	$.866	$.657	$.577	$.359

Michael Dell founded Dell Computer Corporation in 1984. He is currently the computer industry's longest-tenured chief executive officer. He had a simple concept: by selling computer systems directly to customers, Dell could best understand their needs and efficiently provide the most effective computing solutions to meet those needs. Dell climbed to market leadership by directly selling computing products and services based on industry-standard technology. Revenue for the last four quarters totaled $31.2 billion (see Table 3.4), and the company employs approximately 34,600 team members around the globe.

Dell's high return to shareholders has been the result of a focused effort over time to balance growth with profitability and liquidity. Dell has consistently led its largest competitors in each of those categories, and did so again in fiscal year 2002.

A bulleted review of the Dell growth curve (Table 3.5) is impressive.[6]

When we evaluate an organization's financial processes and disciplines, we probe the following areas:

1. Do they allocate the necessary financial resources to achieve their strategic intent?
2. Do they utilize a comprehensive pricing model to make informed pricing decisions?
3. Have they consistently performed within a range of targeted financial goals?
4. Does their operating budget reflect the financial allocations that are necessary to achieve their strategic intent?
5. Do they utilize a "cost-benefit" approach when allocating resources for any business opportunity?
6. Do they have a long-term financial plan that identifies the key financial indicators to be used to measure progress against their strategic plan?
7. Does their financial plan contain sufficient flexibility so they can quickly adapt to economic or environmental disruptions?

Table 3.5 Dell's Path to Dominance

Timeline	Events and Milestones
1984	• Michael Dell founds Dell Computer Corporation.
1985	• Company introduces the first computer system of its own design, the Turbo, featuring Intel 8088 processor running at eight megahertz.
1987	• Dell is first computer systems company to offer next-day, on-site product service. • International expansion begins with opening of subsidiary in United Kingdom.
1988	• Dell conducts initial public offering of company stock, 3.5 million shares at $8.50 each.
1990	• Manufacturing center in Limerick, Ireland, opened to serve European, Middle Eastern, and African markets.
1991	• Company introduces its first notebook computer.
1992	• Dell included for first time among Fortune 500 roster of world's largest companies.
1993	• Dell joins ranks of the top-five computer system makers worldwide. • Subsidiaries in Australia and Japan are company's first entries into Asia-Pacific region.
1995	• $8.50 shares of Dell stock worth $100 on presplit basis.
1996	• Dell opens original Asia-Pacific manufacturing center in Penang, Malaysia. • Customers begin buying Dell computers via Internet at www.dell.com. • Dell begins major push into network-server market. • Company added to Standard & Poor's 500 stock index.
1997	• Dell ships its 10-millionth computer system. • Per-share value of common stock reaches $1000 on presplit basis. • Dell introduces its first workstation systems. • Company sales via Internet exceed $4 million per day, from $1 million at the start of the year.
1998	• Company expands manufacturing facilities in the Americas and Europe, and opens a production and customer center in Xiamen, China. • Dell introduces its PowerVault storage products.
1999	• Dell opens second major U.S. location in Nashville, Tenn. • Dell opens manufacturing facility in Eldorado do Sul, Brazil, to Serve Latin America. • Dell introduces "E-Support Direct from Dell" on-line technical support.
2000	• Company sales via Internet reach $50 million per day. • For the first time, Dell is No. 1 in worldwide workstation shipments. • Dell introduces PowerApp appliance servers. • Dell ships its one millionth PowerEdge server.
2001	• For the first time, Dell ranks No. 1 in global market share. • Dell is No. 1 in the United States for standard Intel architecture server shipments. • Dell introduces PowerConnect network switches.

8. Do they utilize an "If/Then" scenario-building exercise when formulating their strategic plan?

Analyzing Dell's path to success, it is clear that they both complied and, in many cases, set the standard for sound financial management. Evaluating Dell against the above criteria underscores that Dell's performance is no accident.

The financial condition of a firm is often thought of as the single best measure of its competitive potential and its attractiveness to investors. Whether it's a sole proprietorship, a privately held enterprise, or a publicly traded corporation, the integrity of an organization's financial performance is critical in the achievement of the firm's strategic intent. A firm's profitability, cash flow, liquidity, working capital, leverage, and asset utilization can either limit or enable strategic options.

The pie chart[7] below (Figure 3.1) provides us with an example of why businesses fail. Thirty-eight percent of the time, it's due to financial trouble. We would argue the some of the other factors reflect indirect financial weakness as well.

Without effective financial management, the ability to raise capital, attract investors, or satisfy regulators can be seriously impaired.

Simply stated, the financial manager's task is to acquire and use funds to maximize the value of the firm. Brigham and Gapenski address the challenge of the finance paradigm and point out four key responsibilities of the financial function within the organization. (See Table 3.6.)

Financial ratio analysis is probably the most commonly used method for assessing an organization's financial strengths and weaknesses. Because financial decisions impact all functional areas of an organization, weak ratios can often indicate issues in management, marketing, production, and information systems.

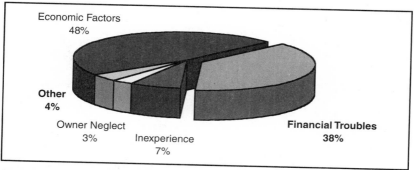

Figure 3.1 Reasons for Business Failure

Table 3.6 Four Key Responsibilities of the Financial Function[8]

1. Forecasting and Planning	The financial manager must interact with other executives as they look ahead and lay the plans, which will shape the firm's future.
2. Major Investments and Financial Decisions	A successful firm usually has rapid growth in sales, which require investments in plant, equipment, and inventory. The company must determine the optimal sales growth rate, they must decide on the specific assets to acquire and the best way to finance those assets.
3. Coordination and Control	Under normal circumstances it is the responsibility of the financial group to insure that the firm is operating as efficiently as possible. All business decisions have financial implications, and all managers—financial and otherwise need to take this into account. For example, marketing decisions affect sales growth, which in turn influences investment requirements. Thus, marketing decision makers must take account of how their actions affect (and are affected by) such factors as the availability of funds, inventory policies, and plant capacity utilization.
4. The Financial Function Deals Directly with Money and Capital Markets	If your organization deals with the capital markets as a financial resource, you are well aware of the impact the markets can have on your ability to raise capital, how your stock may trade, and whether your investors make or lose money.

Ratio analysis does have some limitations, as the ratios are based on accounting data that can differ in treatment of inventory valuation, depreciation, taxes, etc., from firm to firm. Also, like any comparative exercise, industry norms can be affected by seasonal demand, aggressive competition, and the firm's own innovative practices. Like all other evaluative tools, financial ratio analysis should be used in conjunction with other assessment tools and with a holistic view of the organization.

The following (Table 3.7) is a summary of some key financial ratios, how to calculate them, and what they indicate:

Table 3.7 Key Financials Ratios[9]

Profitability Ratios

	Formula	Definition
Gross profit margin	$\dfrac{\text{Sales} - \text{Cost of Goods Sold}}{\text{Sales}}$	An indication of the total margin available to cover operating expenses and yield a profit.
Operating profit margin [or return on sales]	$\dfrac{\text{Profits before taxes and before interest}}{\text{Sales}}$	An indication of the firm's profitability from current operations without regard to the interest charges accruing from the capital structure.
Net profit margin [net return on sales]	$\dfrac{\text{Profits after taxes}}{\text{Sales}}$	Shows after-tax profits per dollar of sales. Subpar profit margins indicate that the firm's sales prices are relatively low or that costs are relatively high, or both.
Return on total assets	$\dfrac{\text{Profits after taxes}}{\text{Total assets}}$ or $\dfrac{\text{Profits after taxes} + \text{interest}}{\text{Total assets}}$	A measure of the return on total investment in the enterprise. It is sometimes desirable to add interest to after-tax profits to form the numerator of the ratio since total assets are financed by creditors as well as by stockholders; hence, it is accurate to measure the productivity of assets by the returns provided to both classes of investors.
Return on stockholder's equity [return on net worth]	$\dfrac{\text{Profits after taxes}}{\text{Total stockholders' equity}}$	A measure of the rate of return on stockholders' investment in the enterprise.
Return on common equity	$\dfrac{\text{Profits after taxes} - \text{Preferred stock dividends}}{\text{Total stockholders' equity} - \text{Par value of preferred stock}}$	A measure of the rate of return on the investment the owners of the common stock have made in the enterprise.
Earnings per share	$\dfrac{\text{Profits after taxes} - \text{Preferred stock dividends}}{\text{Number of shares of common stock outstanding}}$	Shows the earnings available to the owners of each share of common stock.

(continued)

Table 3.7 Key Financials Ratios (*Continued*)

Liquidity Ratios

	Formula	Definition
Current ratio	$\dfrac{\text{Current assets}}{\text{Current liabilities}}$	Indicates the extent to which the claims of short-term creditors are covered by assets that are expected to be converted to cash in a period roughly corresponding to the maturity of the liabilities.
Quick ratio	$\dfrac{\text{Current assets} - \text{Inventory}}{\text{Current liabilities}}$	A measure of the firm's ability to pay off short-term obligations without relying on the sale of its inventories.
Inventory to net working capital	$\dfrac{\text{Inventory}}{\text{Current assets} - \text{Current liabilities}}$	A measure of the extent to which the firm's working capital is tied up in inventory.

Leverage Ratios

	Formula	Definition
Debt-to-asset ratio	$\dfrac{\text{Total debt}}{\text{Total assets}}$	Measures the extent to which borrowed funds have been used to finance the firm's operations.
Debt-to-equity ratio	$\dfrac{\text{Total debt}}{\text{Total stockholders' equity}}$	Provides another measure of the funds provided by creditors versus the funds provided by owners.
Long-term debt-to-equity ratio	$\dfrac{\text{Long-term debt}}{\text{Total stockholders' equity}}$	A widely used measure of the balance between debt and equity in the firm's long-term capital structure.
Times-interest-earned	$\dfrac{\text{Profits before interest \& taxes}}{\text{Total interest charges}}$	Measures the extent to which earnings can decline without the firm becoming unable to meet its annual interest costs.
Fixed-charge coverage	$\dfrac{\text{Profits before interest \& taxes} + \text{Lease obligations}}{\text{Total interest charges} + \text{Lease obligations}}$	A more inclusive indication of the firm's ability to meet all of its fixed-charge obligations.

Activity Ratios

	Formula	Definition
Inventory turnover	$$\frac{\text{Sales}}{\text{Inventory of finished goods}}$$	When compared to industry averages, it provides an indication of whether a company has excessive or perhaps inadequate finished goods inventory.
Fixed assets turnover	$$\frac{\text{Sales}}{\text{Fixed assets}}$$	A measure of the sales productivity and utilization of plant and equipment.
Total assets turnover	$$\frac{\text{Sales}}{\text{Total assets}}$$	A measure of the utilization of all of the firm's assets; a ratio below the industry average indicates the company is not generating a sufficient volume of business, given the size of its asset investment.
Accounts receivable turnover	$$\frac{\text{Annual credit sales}}{\text{Accounts receivable}}$$	A measure of the average length of time it takes the firm to collect the sales made on credit.
Average collection period	$$\frac{\text{Annual credit sales}}{\text{Total sales} \div 365} \quad \text{or} \quad \frac{\text{Accounts receivable}}{\text{Average daily sales}}$$	Indicates the average length of time the firm must wait after making a sale before it receives payment.

Other Ratios

	Formula	Definition
Dividend yield on common stock	$$\frac{\text{Annual dividends per share}}{\text{Current market price per share}}$$	A measure of the return to owners received in the form of dividends.
Price-earnings ratio	$$\frac{\text{Current market price per share}}{\text{After-tax earnings per share}}$$	Faster-growing or less-risky firms tend to have higher price-earnings ratios than slower-growing or more-risky firms, traditionally.
Dividend payout ratio	$$\frac{\text{Annual dividends per share}}{\text{After-tax earnings per share}}$$	Indicates the percentage of profits paid out as dividends.
Cash flow per share	$$\frac{\text{After-tax profits} + \text{depreciation}}{\text{Number of common shares outstanding}}$$	A measure of the discretionary funds over and above the expenses that are available for use by the firm.

One of the biggest factors that can impact the financial performance of an organization is its pricing policy. A comprehensive approach to pricing can serve as an economic benchmark for how your product performs and what ongoing decisions have to be made in order to optimize profitability. The following model (Table 3.8) captures the essence of a comprehensive pricing approach.

It is important to recognize that a firm's financial condition may be impacted not only by functional issues, but by market conditions, environmental issues, and other factors affecting all firms within the industry as well.

Allied Signal is a good example of an organization that puts emphasis on the right measurement of financial performance. Allied, like many organizations, had traditionally relied upon cutting costs through labor reductions. However, since Allied Signal's operations tend to be capital intensive, labor amounted to only 25 percent of their total costs. One manager pointed out that cutting costs through labor reduction would ultimately lead to a plant with no one in it. Instead, they focused on:

1. Total cost productivity calculated as sales,
2. Discounted for price increases due to inflation and not value added,
3. Divided by all costs, including plant, materials, equipment, and labor.
4. Managers were encouraged to look over the broad spectrum of operations for increased productivity.[11]

Practical Applications

Financial management disciplines are some of the best-documented procedures. We encourage all businesses, regardless of size, to adopt fundamental budgeting processes. The activities outlined below are geared toward strategic business execution.

If You Can't Fund It Don't Do It

If a business opportunity is worth pursuing, appropriate funding should be a priority. If funding is scarce, be prudent. Approach the opportunity in a manner that allows you to support your intent adequately.

Don't Guess When It Comes to Pricing—Have a Model

There should be a method to your madness. However, once prices are set, it can be very challenging to make significant adjustments, especially if you have priced too low. Follow the steps set forth in Table 3.8.

Table 3.8 A General Pricing Model[10]

1. Define Market Targets.	All marketing decision making should begin with a definition of segmentation strategy and the identification of potential customers.
2. Estimate Market Potential.	The maximum size of the available market determines what is possible and helps define competitive opportunities.
3. Develop Product Positioning.	The brand image and the desired niche in the competitive marketplace provide important constraints on the pricing decision as the firm attempts to obtain a unique competitive advantage by differentiating its product offering from that of competitors.
4. Design the Marketing Mix.	Design of the marketing mix defines the role to be played by pricing in relation to and in support of their marketing variables, especially distribution and promotional policies.
5. Estimate Price Elasticity of Demand.	The sensitivity of the level of demand to differences in price can be estimated either from past experience or through market tests.
6. Estimate All Relevant Costs.	While straight cost-plus pricing is to be avoided because it is insensitive to demand, pricing decisions must take into account necessary plant investment, investment in R and D, and investment in market development, as well as variable costs of production and marketing.
7. Analyze Environmental Factors.	Pricing decisions are further constrained by industry practices, likely competitive response to alternative pricing strategies, and legal requirements.
8. Set Pricing Objectives.	Pricing decisions must be guided by a clear statement of objectives that recognizes environmental constraints and defines the role of pricing in the marketing strategy, while at the same time relating pricing to the firm's financial objectives.
9. Develop the Price Structure.	The price structure for a given product can now be determined and will define selling prices for the product (perhaps in a variety of styles and sizes) and the discounts from list price to be offered to various kinds of intermediaries and various types of buyers.

- Define market targets.
- Estimate market potential.
- Design the marketing mix.
- Estimate price elasticity of demand.
- Estimate all relevant costs.
- Analyze the environmental factors.
- Set pricing objectives.
- Develop the pricing structure.

Set Achievable Goals and Routinely Track and Report

Financial goals are the easiest to track and monitor. The challenge is to set them correctly. Miscalculated financial goals can result in investor dissatisfaction or a number of other crises.

Adopt a "Cost Benefit" Discipline

Understanding the value of an opportunity prior to committing is essential. Whether you are looking to make a capital investment, hire a consultant, or expand staff—calculate the full cost of the investment and estimate the direct return to the organization if the investment were to be made. You may not always be correct, but not doing it at all significantly increases your chances for misallocated funds and potential loss.

Link Your Financial Plan and Metrics to Your Strategy!

There must be a relationship between measurable financial targets and initiatives within your strategy. If your strategic goal is to add an alternative distribution channel, then there should be specific goals within your budget measuring cost and revenue.

Be Flexible—Model Economic or Other Market Impacts that Can Influence Your Financial Performance

Being aware of potential gain or loss relative to environmental circumstances increases your ability to respond effectively. If the scenario were favorable, then your response would be to harvest the opportunity quickly. Should the scenario be unfavorable, you can respond in a manner that would reduce loss or excess financial exposure. An effective approach to modeling these potential outcomes is utilizing an "If/Then" scenario exercise. Examples include:

- If interest rates go up—then _____.
- If competitors drastically drop their prices—then _____.
- If unemployment rates in my markets go down—then _____.
- If the cost of materials go up 15 percent—then _____.
- Etc., etc.

Financial disciplines, unlike many other aspects of business, are a science. It is acquired learning and is essential to building a sustainable and economically sound business.

Research and Development— a Peek at Microsoft

"Research, I think, is the lifeblood of innovation in the economy. But big companies always have a problem taking their research and making sure it's focused on the problems that count."—Bill Gates[12]

When we reviewed our list of best-practiced companies for an appropriate model for our *research and development* chapter, one company came to mind—Microsoft. Microsoft, since its inception in 1976, has consistently explored their role in the future and crafted a course to fulfill it. The following excerpt is from an internally published book within Microsoft. It was written by Bill Gates and others within the company. It was written for employee consumption and as somewhat of an archive document. We believe that it captures the spirit of an organization that is rooted in sound research and development disciplines. Here it is:

Think it; Build it, Bit by Bit[13]
What does it take to create revolutionary software? Does it mean being first to come up with a new idea, or being first to turn that idea into a product? Does it mean carrying out pioneering research, or making incremental improvements to what's already there until you get it right? Does it mean becoming a giant, or standing on the shoulders of giants? Usually, the answer is a bit of each. Most software blends innovation, inspiration, and incremental improvement in equal measure.

Whatever the blend, great ideas alone don't guarantee success—you have to create an environment where those ideas can be transformed into products and services that are easy to use, a great value, and widely available. You also have to make big, do-or-die bets on the future, committing to technologies and strategies that may not pay off for years. It's easy to spend so much time thinking about today's markets and competitors that you're not ready for those you'll encounter tomorrow. That's why I schedule "think weeks" several times a year—so I can spend time reading up on trends that are just beyond the horizon.

Second-guessing the future isn't easy. Back in 1975, everyone thought the personal computer industry would look very much like the entire computer industry did at the time—you'd buy your software from the company that built your computer. Few people even thought there would be a distinct "software industry." Paul and I disagreed. We believed that computing power would be cheap, that there would be computers everywhere made by lots of different companies, and that software would be needed to take advantage of these trends. So we decided to write and supply software for personal computers without getting involved in making or selling the hardware itself.

Our first product was Microsoft BASIC. The BASIC language was already used on larger computers, but we knew it would also be ideal for the PC—it was simple and easy to learn; yet powerful enough to create complex programs that made the computer do useful things. Once we created a version of BASIC that fit into the limited memory of early PCs, we started extending it—adding new commands to take advantage of the richness of the machine. Today, Visual Basic is the most widely used programming language in the world, and it's just amazing what people have been able to do with it. Over the years, BASIC in all its forms has been the key to much of our success.

Our belief in the potential of the PC also led us to a different licensing approach. Instead of licensing our software to a single hardware vendor at a high price, we licensed software at extremely low prices to all computer makers because we were betting on volume. At the time, most other companies charged high prices, assuming that they would sell very few copies of their products. In addition, when we developed our MS-DOS PC operating system, we worked closely with all the PC makers to ensure that every feature they wanted was incorporated as quickly as possible. We didn't want to lose a single customer.

Developer support for MS-DOS was crucial to bringing the PC into the mainstream. Early on, young PC companies like Compaq understood the need to make computers that were compatible with each other and gave users a familiar and consistent experience. Because MS-DOS helped hide the differences between computers, it rapidly became the most popular operating system for PCs. Software developers who were building applications to run on it knew that their products would run on millions of computers. It started a positive feedback loop: as more and more applications became available for the PC, more and more users had a reason to buy one—and then even more software developers wanted to write applications for PCs. That's what made the PC such a runaway success.

As the PC became powerful enough to handle rich graphics, we saw another opportunity to move computing forward: the graphical user interface. The GUI had been around since the mid-seventies, and some companies had already started building GUI-based computers, but we saw that our experience in building platforms and nurturing standards would be useful in popularizing the GUI—so we bet the company on Windows. At first, people thought we were crazy—after all, why would anyone switch to Windows when everyone had just gotten used to MS-DOS?

But after several years of hard work to improve Windows, we started seeing a repeat of what happened with MS-DOS. Windows made the PC easier to use, which led more people to use it. That combined with Visual Basic, which made it easy to write software for Windows, encouraged developers to create lots of

Windows-based applications. And just as we evolved **BASIC** over the years, we made each new version of **Windows** better and better—we greatly improved its performance and multitasking support, and we continuously added new elements to the **GUI**. This endless evolution—of ideas building on ideas—is what has always set Microsoft apart.

With Microsoft Office, we changed the way people think about business computing by looking at productivity as a whole and developing tools that bring together the many different tasks you do every day. While most software companies were still focusing on stand-alone applications, we realized that most people wanted to be able to share text, data, and graphics across applications. They also wanted those applications to work together seamlessly and have a common look and feel. Office created a whole new product category that met those needs.

At other times, we've bet on totally new concepts. Obviously, one of our biggest bets has been on the Internet. But there have been many others. With Windows NT, we made a huge long-term bet that PCs would become powerful enough to be the backbone of enterprise computing. With our ClearType font technology, we bet that most people would one day read eBooks. And with Microsoft Bob, we bet on a social interface that "humanized" the PC. It was a little ahead of its time, and PCs weren't yet powerful enough to handle what we wanted Bob to do, so the product was a commercial failure. But we learned a huge amount from the experience, and some of the ideas we pioneered with Bob are already appearing in other products.

We're lucky enough to live in an age where the potential of computer technology to change our lives still appears limitless. The combined power of the PC, the Internet, and wireless and broadband technologies is revolutionizing the way we work, learn, and play. We're betting on this revolution with Microsoft.NET, which we hope will do for the next generation of computing what MS-DOS and Windows did for the PC—change our lives through software that's inexpensive, widely available, and easy to use.

Although I sometimes get a little apprehensive when we take big risks like this, I wouldn't do it any other way. I've always enjoyed building new things and coming up with creative solutions to hard problems, so I look forward to the challenge of creating the software that will shape computing in the next 25 years. I'm confident we'll succeed—we've got the people and the skills to make it happen, and we're just as passionate about technology as we were back in 1975.

Clearly, Microsoft's "risks" have paid off more than they haven't. Equally important to an effective R and D process is the culture and guiding principles that support the mission and vision of the organization.

When we evaluate an organization's research and development process, there are three broad elements that we look at:

1. Do they allocate the necessary resources to support a successful research and development process?
2. Is their research and development process innovative and creative?
3. Does their research and development process incorporate the feedback from all appropriate stakeholders (customers, suppliers, employees, etc.)?

With expenditures in research and development for all U.S. firms exceeding $200 billion in 1997, there is an ever-increasing need for organizations to focus their attention on productive R and D operations. Organizations invest in research and development in order to improve their competitive advantage either through product innovation or process improvement.

Effective R and D requires alignment and integration between all other functions of the organization and the R and D function. The best-managed firms today incorporate a cross-functional approach to the R and D process. This has required once-isolated R and D managers to work with other functional managers to prioritize tasks and align resources.

The following model (Table 3.9) reflects key considerations of an effective R and D process.

While most firms have little choice but to invest in R and D due to the dynamics of technology and changing tastes of consumers, some organizations are content to follow market innovations with lower-cost imitations. In this time of technology shifts and strong global competition, the task of innovation is becoming increasingly more difficult. The pharmaceutical industry,

Table 3.9 Evaluating Intellectual Output: R and D as an Output System[14]

R and D Activities	Direct Outputs: Technologies	Opportunities to Exploit	Indirect Outputs: Value Actually Exploited	Goals	Value Created
1. Fundamental Research 2. Applied Research 3. Development 4. Engineering	• Ideas • Theories • Understanding • Consulting • Timing advantages • Designs • Software • Processes • Products • Materials • Devices • Services	• Present value as opportunities to exploit (Net of costs)	• New products or services • Improved products or services • Patent position or salable intelligence • Cost-reducing materials, processes, or software • Flexibility and responsiveness • Image building • Bases for further knowledge building	• Assets • Profits • Jobs • Community contributions • Image • Customer service • Shareholder value	
The source of intellectual output…	…Produces technology as an output…	…Which has value as opportunities to exploit, if taken…	…Which the company may exploit in different forms…	…To support its multiple goals…	Which have value

for example, enjoys only one successful launch out of 10,000 drugs created. Noted strategists Scarpello, Boulton, and Hofer explain that different strategies require different R and D capabilities.[15] For market leaders and innovators, new product launches and innovations are the driving force behind their strategy. R and D must play an integral part in terms of new ideas, technology, and service. Market followers need to focus on making current products in a cost-effective way. Process-oriented R and D must be the driving force.

An organization's understanding of the nature of its product types, its life cycle, and its position in the industry is a key driver of product improvement. The following model (Table 3.10) illustrates several product types.

Table 3.10 Defining the Product or Service Type[16]

Breakthrough	Breakthrough products, as the name implies, depart significantly and fundamentally from existing practice. They may introduce highly innovative product or process technology, open up a new market segment, or take the business into a totally new arena.
Platform	Platform products form the base of a product "family" that can be leveraged over several years and often across multiple market segments. Though not as radically different as a breakthrough, a new platform usually provides a substantial boost in value to customers and to the firm's competitive position. Thus, it may enable the business to address a new distribution channel or may involve a new manufacturing process.
Derivative	Derivative products are derived from other products—usually platforms. They may offer lower cost, enhanced features, or modifications in packaging. They usually extend the product line, fill in gaps in the offerings, exploit a niche, and otherwise leverage investment in a platform.
Support	Support products lie at the very end of the change spectrum, and entail only minor changes in technology, marketing, or processing to support the product line. These minor modifications support the product line by extending the range of its application, correcting a problem in an existing product, keeping it fresh in customers' minds, giving the sales force something "new" to discuss during regular customer visits, or customizing it for a specific customer.

Intel Corporation is the world leader in the development of micro processing chips that play a key role in the computer industry. Competition for controlling the technology is very tight as competitors such as Motorola, Digital Equipment, NEC, and others race to introduce the latest improved-performance chip to the market.

In order to stay ahead of these competitors, Intel has organized its R and D department into work teams. The company has six different teams working on the next generation of chip technology simultaneously. Each team's innovations are often synthesized to make the final product, such as the successful Pentium generation chip unveiled in 1993. Intel, however, has six other teams working on its successor, as well as six more teams on the generations of chip design to follow. To ensure its market leadership, Intel has focused its efforts on R and D, in an effort to control the technology of not only today but tomorrow as well.

Coming back to Microsoft, let's close this section with a strategic and economic view of an organization that has grown and continues to lead, in large part due to its commitment to research and development.

Microsoft Corporation, founded in 1975, develops, manufactures, licenses, and supports a wide range of software products for a multitude of computing devices. Microsoft software includes scalable operating systems for servers, personal computers (PCs), and intelligent devices; server applications for client/server environments; knowledge worker productivity applications; and software development tools. The company's on-line efforts include the MSN network of Internet products and services, and alliances with companies involved with broadband access and various forms of digital interactivity. Microsoft also licenses consumer software programs, sells hardware devices, provides consulting services, trains and certifies system integrators and developers, and researches and develops advanced technologies for future software products. Microsoft has four product segments: Desktop and Enterprise Software and Services; Consumer Software, Services, and Devices; Consumer Commerce Investments; and Others.

Microsoft invested $4.4 billion in fiscal 2001 on research and development. That translates into over 17% of its $25.3 billion in revenue. (See Table 3.11.) It appears that Microsoft not only puts its money where its mouth is, but also intends to continue as an industry leader for as far into the future and as you care to look.

How an organization approaches the function of research and development is as different as there are number of industries. Having said that, there are certain common threads to close with:

Table 3.11 Microsoft's Financial Performance 1997–2001[17]

Consideration	2001	2000	1999	1998	1997
Stock Price	$66.25	$43.38	$116.75	$69.34	$32.31
Total Sales in Billions	$25.3	$22.9	$19.7	$15.3	$11.9
EPS	$1.39	$1.70	$1.42	$.87	$.67

1. R and D must be recognized as a defined discipline within the organization. It may be matrixed among several departments, but the underlying purpose must be funded, managed, and adequately resourced.
2. R and D is your incubator. The underlying philosophy must reflect a creative and innovative sense of purpose.
3. R and D fuels an organization's future.

Production

"Most of what we call management consists of making it difficult for people to get their work done."—Peter F. Drucker

As we examine the internal capabilities of an organization, the first phase is reviewing the financial management capabilities. Research and development is the second phase, and reviewing the production capabilities is the third phase. Organizations with a strong production capability will demonstrate strength in operating efficiency, coordinated third-party agreements, speed, flexibility, and a capacity for continual improvement.

When we evaluate an organization's production capabilities, we ask:

1. Are they effectively coordinating individuals and departments during the production phase of their products or services?
2. Do their strategic partners consistently fulfill their commitments relating to product or service production?
3. Is their product or service production process cost-efficient?
4. Is their product or service production process flexible, fast, and responsive?

The *production* process within the value chain, following the concept and design created in the R and D system, transforms inputs into products and services deliverable to the company's targeted customer. Inputs can include raw materials, labor, capital, plant, and equipment. Often utilizing the largest portion of an organization's human and capital assets, production and operations activities often affect strategic choices in achieving a company's strategic intent. Indeed, limited production capabilities and policies may even dictate corporate strategies if not first considered by management in formulating their strategic intent.

Roger Schroeder suggests that production/operations management has five basic functions. (See Table 3.12.)

In today's highly competitive marketplace, production often holds the key to sustaining an organization's competitive edge or losing it. Slow cycle times have often been to blame for a dominant player's losing ground to competitors.

General Motors is a classic example of a large firm that has been traditionally mired in bureaucracy, resulting in product development cycle times

Table 3.12 Five Functions of Production/Operations Management[18]

1. Process	Process decisions concern the design of the physical production system. Specific decisions include choice of technology, facility layout, process flow analysis, facility location, line balancing, process control, and transportation analysis.
2. Capacity	Capacity decisions concern determination of optimal output levels for the organization—not too much and not too little. Specific decisions include forecasting, facilities planning, aggregate planning, scheduling, capacity planning, and queuing analysis.
3. Inventory	Inventory decisions involve managing the level of raw materials, work in progress, and finished goods. Specific decisions include what to order, when to order, how much to order, and materials handled.
4. Workforce	Workforce decisions are concerned with managing the skilled, unskilled, clerical, and managerial employees. Specific decisions include job design, work measurement, job enrichment, work standards, and motivation techniques.
5. Quality	Quality decisions are aimed at ensuring that high-quality goods and services are produced. Specific decisions include quality control, sampling, testing, quality assurance, and cost control.

of over five years. By the time cars came to market, they were hopelessly outdated by the more innovative cars produced by Ford, Mazda, Toyota, and Honda, all with cycle times of less than four years.

In 1980, Apollo Computer created the market for engineering computer workstations. Experiencing rapid growth and a virtual monopoly for nearly two years, Apollo failed to accelerate their technology capabilities. Unable to adapt their design and production function to keep pace with Sun Microsystems' encroachment, Apollo eventually lost their market lead, dwindling to less than a 20-percent share by 1988. Facing mounting problems brought on by outdated systems, Apollo was acquired by Hewlett-Packard in 1989.[19]

The following model (Table 3.13) illustrates the different strategic concerns that a firm will face depending on its stage of development. Being mindful of an organization's evolution in today's dynamic environment is also a hallmark of good operations management.

Bose Corporation is an example of the impact a good production system can have on sustaining a strategy. Bose is known for manufacturing some of the best speakers in the world. They are best sellers in Japan as well as domestically. In the United States, Bose maintains its speaker manufacturing facilities in Massachusetts, while most of its materials come from the Far East. Strategically committed to meeting its customer demands, even when they change, Bose materials managers have the challenge of maintaining a just-in-time inventory strategy while fulfilling customer demands accurately and on time.

They accomplish this by tracking their inventory, using a strategic partnership with a local freight forwarding company. Using technology to handle their inventory as easily as they would if it were housed in their facilities, Bose works in tandem with their shipping agent to bring in the needed parts on time. Bose is even electronically tied to U.S. Customs, and can often clear their goods electronically, five days before the shipment enters the harbor.

Proof of their success in their materials-handling program came when a large Japanese customer recently doubled their order for a popular speaker system. Bose geared up their facility, and by using the technology of the forwarder/partner, was able to reroute needed parts out of their normal delivery channel and airfreight them in time to meet the customer's delivery date. The system may cost more, but speed plays a vital role in maintaining Bose's image and reputation in the marketplace.

Table 3.13 Product and Cycle-Time Excellence Evolution[20]

Characteristics	Stage 0	Stage 1	Stage 2	Stage 3
Product Development Process (Structure and Definition)	None—Concern about just getting the product out overwhelms any consideration of process. Weak project management discipline.	Distinct functional process. Hard to coordinate. Adherence to process varies widely.	The process is structured and clearly but simply defined. A single overall process integrates all functions. Used on all projects.	Process is integrated in the culture. Product development process is formally linked to product strategy and technologies processes.
Project Team Orientation	Ad hoc. Firefighters often more highly regarded than project managers.	Inconsistent team membership. Functional policies strong. Leadership shifts or is indeterminate.	Small dedicated cross-functional teams similar to Core Team model. Strong project management.	Experienced Core Teams often develop multiple generations of products. Core Teams are used for platform and technology development.
Management Decision Process	Informal and highly reactive. Resources flow to whatever catches management's attention.	Priorities are set through annual budgeting. Project status reporting is initiated but is time-consuming. Functional managers set de facto, often conflicting priorities. Resource allocation is very difficult.	Efficient, event-based Phase Review process is used by a decisive cross-functional management team to set priorities. Priorities are accompanied by resources.	Decisions are based on fully developed product and technology strategies. Priorities set within context of overall pipeline and skill mix plans. Product platform decisions get an increased focus of attention.
Continuous Improvement	Individual learning takes place, but is not captured in a process.	Process elements are owned by individual functions, key skills often known only to certain individuals. It's hard to learn from failed projects because of fear of being blamed.	Full-time process owner in place. Process is evaluated regularly and updated. Opportunities to advance to next stage identified.	Process is "owned" by all who used it. There is a history of process upgrades and extensions. Opportunities to advance the state of the art regularly identified.
Targeted Setting/Metrics	No process targets. Focus is often on survival or financial turnaround.	Overall process targets not set or set by management flat. Currently performance is hard to measure.	Process targets are routinely set and measured against. These include cycle time and quality measures.	Process targets are set based on quantitative benchmarking of world-class companies. Five to fifteen percent in all major metrics routinely planned.

Product Strategy Process	No process in place, only the de facto implications of past decisions. Tendency to follow inconsistent strategies.	Strategic visions inconsistent and not linked with product strategy. Tendency to attempt too much to be all things to all customers.	Focus is on individual products, not platforms. Product strategy is done in annual planning, if at all. Product strategy issues raised in phase reviews tend to be dealt with informally.	Focus is on product platforms, current and new. Product strategy is a formal process. It is linked to technology planning and executed through efficient product development process.
Technology Management Process	No distinction between technology and product development.	This is a functional responsibility. Finger pointing between marketing and technical functions is common. Large resource swings year to year are common.	Typically no formal process for technology planning. Distinction between technology and product development becomes clearer, but not managed.	Technology strategy is linked to product strategy. Technology development is more deliberately managed. Technology transfer to product development process is well defined.
Pipeline Management	Pipeline not managed or balanced. Firefighting gets disproportionate share of resources.	Project proliferation is common. Chronic bottlenecks occur in certain functions.	Distribution of projects by phase is known. Fewer projects staffed. Skill mix problems still common.	The strategic distribution of projects is known and managed. Skill mix management is long term.
Time-to-Market Performance	Not measured or managed. May be infinite.	Inconsistent and unpredictable. Very hard to measure. Tendency to bring many products to market before they are fully debugged, so manufacturing problems or high levels of engineering changes are common.	Forty percent to sixty percent of Stage 1 Cycle times are based on completing development of a quality product, which is manufacturable in volume and at acceptable yields.	Best in industry and declining. Combined with product strategy advantages, which focus effort on right products, the advantage is very hard for competitors to overcome.
Development Productivity	Not measured or managed. Typically very low.	Many projects are canceled late or never brought to market. Slow time to market limits productivity. Revenues from new products lag behind industry leaders.	Reduced time to market greatly increase productivity. Greatly reduced, wasted R and D since phase reviews lead to earlier cancellation. Revenues from new products increasing.	Little wasted R and D. All efforts highly focused by platform, technology, and product. High percentage of sales generated by new products and new platforms.

Bose facilities represent the new age of flexible manufacturing. When polled by *Business Week,* production and operations managers agreed on the following characteristics of the responsive factory of the future. (See Table 3.14.)

Quality

According to *Juran's Quality Handbook,*[22] there are five types of processes that are critical to ensure quality and effective management of the production

Table 3.14   Characteristics of the Truly Reposnsive Factory[21]

Concurrent everything	Enterprisewide computer integration, with electronic links to customers and suppliers, means that transactions occur mostly between computers, which will automatically route information to all proper departments or operations.
Fast development cycles	A real-time database will unite the distributed processing computers used by design, engineering, production, logistics, marketing, and customer service—whether the work is done in-house or is outsourced. All parties will have instant access to the latest information, eliminating the rework now caused by delays in shuffling paper.
Flexible production	Flexibility will be built into all levels of manufacturing, from the controls on each machine to the computers that coordinate work cells and factorywide systems. Products can thus be turned out in greater variety and customized easily, with no cost penalty for small production runs.
Quick response	Dynamic factory-scheduling systems will put production "on call" and thus pare inventories to the bone. Production will begin only after a customer places an order.
Commitment to lifelong quality	Ongoing quality programs will lead to continuous improvement of both processes and products. A primary focus will be to make products easier to recycle or dispose of in environmentally sound ways.

function. *Juran's* stresses that it is not just that these processes work, but that these processes work together properly. The five processes are:

- Production process
- Sampling processes
- Measurement processes
- Decision/control processes
- Computing processes

The Production Process

The production process itself must be consistent, to ensure that the production of a product consistently meets customer requirements. ISO (International Operating Standards) criteria have been established and are now followed by over 60,000 organizations worldwide. These standards set forth the protocols, procedures, and practices that ensure consistency and quality in the production process.

The Sampling Processes

Samplings are taken where variability can occur. Samples must be taken in a way that makes it truly typical of the material that it must represent, so that:

- "Acceptance samples" of incoming materials may be required to verify conformity to their required specifications. In a well-developed quality system, suppliers' measurements can be relied upon, which minimizes the amount of acceptance sampling required, thus reducing redundant costs in the value-added chain from supplier to producer.
- "In-process samples" are needed for production process control.
- "Finished product samples" are needed for production process control, for product characterization, and for product release.
- "Measurement control samples" are needed to keep the measurement process accurate.

The samples that result from these processes must be tagged with identification telling where they came from and how and when they were obtained.

Most quality management procedures are applied to a single property at a time. Although a single physical test sample is, in practice, frequently used to obtain test results for multiple product properties, the term "sample" in this section normally refers to a single product property sample.

The Measurement Processes

The output of the measurement process is numbers (the measured property values for each sample submitted). Some measurement processes are conducted in the laboratory, while others are done on the production floor. Some are highly automated, while others are labor intensive. The measurement processes often are as complex as the production process, and are just as capable of going out of control. If reported test results have large measurement error, they may cause improper actions to be taken in the decision processes. This can cause the product uniformity to be poorer then if the process were left alone.

The Decision/Control Processes

The decision processes are of two types:

- "Process control" decisions leading to actions to maintain the production process and the measurement processes on aim.
- "Accept and release" decisions leading to action regarding product disposition to ensure that only conforming process materials are used and only conforming product is released.

The Computing Processes

Computer hardware and software typically implement parts of all of the preceding processes. Data from the measurement processes may be entered and stored in a computer database, either manually or by automatic instrument data entry. Automated instrumentation may be used to produce sample measurements. Data collected from these processes are then used as input to the control and decision processes. Diagnostics data analysis software may be used to produce graphs, reports, and other quantitative summaries to detect quality problems and monitor quality status.

The computer hardware and software processes involved in these tasks may be complex. The reliability and adequacy of the hardware and software used in these computing systems need to be given attention.

Operating Standards

Whether you provide a product or service, there is a production process that leads to your end product. Your production process in many cases represents your final output to your customer. Five key drivers to keep in the top of your mind include:

1. Production requires input from all departments. Create a system that allows the production group to capture knowledge and other necessary resources from all departments within the organization.
2. If any part of your production process is outsourced, be sure that your partners are held to the same standards that you hold your employees to.
3. More times than not, your production process represents a repetitive process; seek efficiencies as an ongoing discipline.
4. Your production process should always maintain a flexible, fast, and responsive posture within the organization.
5. Maintain quality, as defined by your deliverables and your competitive model.

Marketing: Nike—It's All About Brand!

"The trouble in America is not that we are making too many mistakes, but that we are making too few."—Philip H. Knight, Cofounder, Chairman, CEO, and President, Nike, Inc.

Somehow, when it comes to *marketing*, and specifically talking about "brand" value, inevitably the discussion will turn to Nike. Nike has become the billboard for advertising and marketing agencies when describing a company that "gets it."

Before we review a specific Nike campaign and study how they approach bringing a new product to market, it's worth briefly describing Nike as a corporation. Nike, Inc., incorporated in 1968, is principally engaged in the design, development, and worldwide marketing of footwear, apparel, equipment, and accessory products. Nike sells its products to approximately 17,000 retail accounts in the United States, and through a mix of independent distributors, licensees, and subsidiaries, in approximately 140 countries around the world. Virtually all of the company's products are manufactured by independent contractors. Most of the company's footwear products are produced outside the United States, while apparel products are produced both in the United States and abroad. *(Authors' Note: We are aware that Nike has been strongly criticized for their business practices involving foreign labor. For the purposes of this chapter and this book, we go on record as neither condemning nor condoning Nike's approach to manufacturing their products.)*

Nike's athletic footwear products are designed primarily for specific athletic use, although a large percentage of the products are worn for casual or leisure purposes. The company places considerable emphasis on high-quality construction and innovative design. Running, basketball, children's, cross-training, and women's shoes are currently Nike's top-selling product categories, and the company expects them to continue to lead in product sales in the near future. The company also markets shoes designed for outdoor activities, tennis, golf, soccer, baseball, football, bicycling, volleyball, wrestling, cheerleading, aquatic activities, hiking, and other athletic and recreational uses.

Nike sells active sports apparel covering each of the above categories, as well as athletic bags and accessory items. Nike apparel and accessories are designed to complement its athletic footwear products, feature the same trademarks, and are sold through the same marketing and distribution channels. The company often markets footwear, apparel, and accessories in "collections" of similar design or for specific purposes. The company also markets apparel with licensed college and professional team and league logos.

The company sells a line of performance equipment under the Nike brand name, including sport balls, timepieces, eyewear, skates, bats, gloves, and other equipment designed for sports activities. The company has agreements for licensees to produce and sell Nike brand swimwear, women's sports bras, cycling apparel, children's clothing, posters, school supplies, and electronic media devices. Nike sells a line of dress and casual footwear and accessories for men, women, and children under the brand name Cole Haan through its wholly owned subsidiary, Cole Haan Holdings, Incorporated. The company also sells small amounts of various plastic products to other manufacturers through its wholly owned subsidiary, Nike IHM, Inc.

Nike's wholly owned subsidiary, Bauer Nike Hockey, Inc., manufactures and distributes ice skates, skate blades, in-line roller skates, protective gear, hockey sticks, and hockey jerseys and accessories under the Bauer and Nike brand names. Bauer also offers a full selection of products for street, roller, and field hockey.

Nike competes internationally with an increasing number of athletic and leisure shoe companies, athletic and leisure apparel companies, sports equipment companies, and large companies having diversified lines of athletic and leisure shoes, apparel, and equipment, including Reebok, Adidas, and others.

For the nine months ending February 28, 2002, revenues rose three percent, to $7.21 billion. Net income before accounting change increased eight percent to $459.9 million. Revenues reflect an increase in U.S. apparel and equipment sales, and increased footwear sales in Europe. Earnings also reflect lower interest rates and lower average debt levels.

A Nike Marketing Campaign[23]

When Nike wanted to promote their new cross trainer shoe, the company realized they had to do more than pay a high-profile athlete to run their patented "swoosh" logo across the screen. Nike truly wanted to demonstrate the message of the new footwear: versatility. The sports apparel maker and a team of creative agencies not only developed a Web site that features the cross trainer in all of its colorful glory, they created commercials for TV and the Internet that link content and commerce like never before.

A series of three TV commercials was created to generate awareness of the new shoe, but more significantly, to actually prompt viewers to visit the newly created site whatever.nike.com. Of course, the commercials feature well-known athletes, but they end abruptly with cliffhanger-type situations and the simple tag "continued at whatever.nike.com."

Once on the site, users enter a full brand experience. They can select one of seven endings to the commercial, find out more information about the shoe and the featured athletes, and purchase the shoe.

Succumbing to Network Paranoia

It's true—many ads will indirectly drive viewers to a Web site. However, this commercial was designed to evoke the direct action of moving from TV to the Internet, and it created some controversy.

"There were two of the three major TV networks that threatened not to run the ad at all unless we removed the 'continued at' portion," says Ian Yolles, director of marketing for Nike.com. "They were worried about driving eyes away from their programming, so we only removed that part of the ads running on those networks."

Yolles would not directly reveal the names of the two major networks, however, he did say that ABC did not have a problem with the ads. The fact is, whether TV networks like it or not, Nike believes this is the future of advertising, and they are probably right.

Objective

Like any retailer, the company wanted to sell its products; in this case it was the new Air *Cross Trainer II*. Nike began to sell its products on the Web in June of 1999 and wanted to create an attractive and memorable way to sell this particular piece of footwear. Branding and traffic driving just came with the package.

Table 3.15 Statistics Supporting Nike's Campaign Objectives

- According to *Consumer Insights,* 20 million people currently cross-train in the United States, participating in activities that range from running and aerobics to skateboarding and mountain biking. Sixty-three percent of these people are under the age of 35.
- *NPD Group* surveys indicate that cross-training footwear is a $2.3 billion market in the United States.
- *Consumer Insights* says that on average, American consumers spend $236 and purchase 3.2 pairs of fitness-related shoes (basketball, tennis, aerobics, etc.) per year.

"We're not just sending people to a site; this experience comes out of a specific product with specific aspects," says Yolles. "We are trying to be innovative and at the same time communicate the idea behind cross training, which is 'do whatever you want with this shoe.'" (See Table 3.15.)

Creative Strategy

Nike is once again relying heavily on its long-time agency Wieden & Kennedy, which created the TV spots and SUPERSTITIAL™ rich media ads for the Internet. These ads were created in Macromedia Flash™ and are commercial-like in presentation. They are not the actual TV spots, but Nike used them as teasers for the commercials and to drive traffic to the site.

The TV ads are 30 seconds long, but as the ending tagline indicates, can be continued at whatever.nike.com. The site itself was created by New York-based Web developer one9ine.

The ads feature three world-class athletes—world champion sprinter Marion Jones, major league baseball player Mark McGwire, and snowboarding champ Rob Kingwill. All of the TV spots place these athletes in precarious situations that can be continued by going to the site and selecting one of seven endings by simply dragging and dropping selected icons into an Apple QuickTime™ viewer.

Users can also drag and drop icons of the cross trainer shoe into Apple Quicktime. This will provide more information about the shoe, as well as the ability to buy it. The site also contains icons of the featured athletes so users can learn more about them.

"We have turned what is typically a 30- to 60-second experience into one that can last up to 20 minutes," says Steve Sandoz, interactive creative director at Wieden & Kennedy. "We regret that there was a fundamental denial on the part of those two major TV networks, but I think they will eventually have to see that this is the future of advertising."

Sandoz also admitted that having the Quicktime viewer on the site may seem limiting, since Microsoft's *Windows Media Player* and Real Networks' RealPlayer are more widely installed. He says it was "a quality issue, and a conscious decision" to use Quicktime.

"When we ran the spots and all of the functionality we wanted to have in Media Player and RealPlayer, it just did not look as good, especially with lower speed connections," Sandoz says. "We thought it would be more limiting on our part to sacrifice quality."

QuickTime—version 4 can be installed via the whatever.nike.com site.

Media Buys

Even though this is a "multimillion dollar" campaign and the ads will be seen on all major TV and many cable networks between Jan. 15 and the end of February, the company decided not to run the ad during the Super Bowl.

"This campaign is not about making a big splash and hoping for the best; we have some clear and specific objectives to achieve," says Sandoz. "The Super Bowl just doesn't work that well for advertising anymore and it has become painful to watch all of the dot-coms trying to out-gerbil Outpost.com."

TV Buys

- sports programming on network and cable
- primetime and late night programming on network TV
- youth-oriented cable (including a cosponsorship with MTV's *Web Riot* program)

On-line Buys

Although TV ads will run until the end of February, SUPERSTITIAL ads may run longer. Since Nike is targeting more of a 35 and under demographic, as well as sports enthusiasts, initial buys were made on the following sites:

- Bolt.com
- Alloy.com
- ESPN.com
- MTV's Web Riot

Results/Expectations[24]

Nike's somewhat publicized "whatever.nike.com" campaign did what it set out to do. Through a combination of rich media Web advertising, a cliff-hanger TV spot, and an engaging e-commerce-enabled site, Nike increased sales and created yet another branding experience people would not soon forget... at least, not in the advertising world.

Campaign Recap

The goal: sell the new *Air Cross Trainer II,* drive traffic, and enhance branding.

The Creatives:

- SUPERSTITIAL™ rich media ads were created in Macromedia Flash™ by Nike's AOR Wieden & Kennedy. Commercial-like in presentation, they were used as teasers for the TV commercials and to drive traffic to the site.
- The TV ads were 30 seconds long, but ended with the tagline "continued at whatever.nike.com." Once at the site, users could view or download an Apple QuickTime movie of the TV commercial through which they could choose different endings, find out more about the featured athletes in the commercials, and buy the shoe.

Media Buys

The ads were seen on major TV and many cable networks between Jan. 15 and the end of February. Though they did not run during the Super Bowl, the ads were seen during network and cable sports programming, primetime and late night programming on network TV, and youth-oriented cable (including a cosponsorship with MTV's *Web Riot* program). SUPERSTITIALs and gif ads ran on Bolt.com, Alloy.com, ESPN.com, and MTV's *Web Riot.*

Results

Overall Nike was "very pleased" with the traffic it received during the campaign's short, post-holiday run between January 15 and the end of February.

"We expected that there would be a drop-off in traffic, which is typical of e-commerce after the holidays," says Ian Yolles, Nike.com's director of marketing. "Instead we saw a 50 percent increase in traffic during January and another 50 percent in February."

He also noted a lot of interaction on the whatever.nike site, but declined to release those numbers. Nike's SUPERSTITIAL ads received click-throughs that were "12 times higher than the banners and buttons" they ran, according to a Nike spokesperson.

Shoe Sales Skyrocket

No one at Nike would comment directly about sales. However, in a February article for *Sports Illustrated,* Mike Wilsky, Nike's VP of U.S. marketing mentioned, "After the ads debuted, the shoe immediately shot to number one in Nike sales. It's outselling our second-most-popular shoe 10 to 1."

According to Nike's quarterly earnings report, U.S. footwear revenues continued to grow, with a four percent increase during the first quarter of this year compared to the same quarter last year, and a five percent growth rate year-to-date.

B-ball Ad-venture

The whatever.nike.com site has been taken down, "because they did not want to spend the money to keep a site up to support a commercial," according to Mark Owens, partner at one9ine. However, one9ine did design another site for a similar TV campaign that ran during the college basketball playoffs. The ads featured the fictional town of *Bracketville,* a place where college basketball stars are born. Although the ad did not prompt viewers to "continue" the experience on the Web, per se, one9ine did design a site based on the Bracketville theme. The URL appeared in the commercial, too.

Next Steps

Nike's Yolles admitted that while the whatever.nike campaign was significant, he "does not see this as an isolated example of Nike trying new things." Will we see more ads like whatever.nike? The most information Yolles would volunteer was, "We are always going to try and push the envelope."

Seth Fineberg provides a unique insight to a leader in "brand" strategies and provides us with a glimpse of how Nike conceives, structures, executes, evaluates, and responds to their marketing initiatives. Is there a relationship between Nike's skills as a masterful marketing organization and financial performance? We do not have empirical data to make this case. However, upon review of their numbers, one might argue that the sports shoe company that incorporated some 34 years ago is doing something right. Our guess—it's working. (See Table 3.16.)

Marketing Best Practices and Areas of Focus

We have identified seven best practices (disciplines and characteristics) that existed in the top 10 percent of our research database. There are other areas that we evaluate and study, but it is interesting to review which characteristics stand out. This research included 1460 senior executives representing over 500 companies. The companies ranged from small businesses to Global 50 firms. Industries included technology, aerospace, pharmaceuticals, consulting, government, transportation, and manufacturing, as well as several others. One interesting aspect was that there was little variance between industries. *Marketing* as a discipline seems to transcend industry barriers. Regardless of the age, type, or size of industry, there are specific things that organizations must do from a marketing perspective in order to be successful.

The seven best practices are:[26]

1. The companies identified the critical factors that are required to be successful in their industry.
2. The companies enjoy a higher rate of repeat business, referrals, or customer loyalty than their competitors.
3. Their commitment to customer satisfaction and loyalty is understood and embraced by all employees within their company.

Table 3.16 Nike's Financial Performance 1997–2001[25]

Consideration	2001	2000	1999	1998	1997
Stock Price	$56.24	$55.81	$49.56	$40.56	$39.06
Total Sales in Billions	$9.5	$9.0	$8.8	$9.5	$9.2
EPS	$2.16	$2.06	$1.66	$1.62	$2.68

4. The company leverages its corporate core competencies to increase customer value.
5. Branding is a key element of their marketing process.
6. They measure customer satisfaction by routinely obtaining direct customer feedback.
7. They had well-documented and targeted marketing plans.

There were three common themes that surfaced among the organizations that we studied, and among the identified best practices. The three themes were a clearly defined plan, good information to make decisions, and a strong insight into customers' requirements. The clearly defined plan ensures that all resources are aligned behind the specific product or service offering. The information ensures that they understand the market and industry dynamics in which they compete. A customer-centric approach ensures that they understand what form of marketing (i.e. direct mail, TV, radio, publications, etc.) outreach will result in the most favorable response.

When we reflect on the Nike case, it's fair to say that they line up well against the best-practice criteria. They have demonstrated over time that they know their industry. Though we don't have specifics, we represent one of those repeat customers. Their organization is all about the customer, from Phil Knight down. Leveraging their core competencies is demonstrated through the business lines and acquisition of Cole Hahn. They are all about branding, customer feedback is a core practice, and lastly, they have a clear and targeted marketing plan.

What to Look For in Your Organization

When we evaluate organizations for the effectiveness of their marketing function, we ask:

1. If the company effectively coordinates individuals and departments to ensure successful marketing of their products or services.
2. If the company has a clearly defined marketing plan.
3. If branding is a key element of their marketing process.
4. If the company utilizes a comprehensive marketing database that provides management with detailed customer and market information.
5. If the company employs an effective, comprehensive product or service management process.

6. If *competitive advantage* is a key driver in determining their resource and capital allocations for marketing.
7. If all employees in the company take great pride in their ability to promote their products or services.
8. If the company consistently analyzes the *return-on-investment* tied to their major marketing campaigns.

Take the time to review your business and determine if you can answer affirmatively to the questions above. An organization's approach to its marketing strategy can be very focused, or it can cover a broad range of issues, depending on its strategic intent. At its very basic root, marketing can be defined as "the analysis, planning, implementation, and control of programs designed to bring about desired exchanges with target markets for the purpose of achieving organizational objectives. It relies heavily on designing the organization's offering in terms of the target market's needs and desires, and on using effective pricing, communication, and distribution to inform, motivate, and service the market."[27]

Marketing activities should start with a clear understanding of the organization's mission and objectives. Marketing management must be aware of the firm's direction, targeted market, and method of conducting business.

These marketing activities typically fall into the traditional areas of the marketing mix known as the 4 Ps of marketing: Product, Price, Promotion, and Place or distribution. (See Table 3.17.)

Table 3.17 The Traditional Marketing Mix

Product	Price	Promotion	Place
• Quality	• Level	• Advertising	• Distribution channels
• Features and benefits	• Discounts	• Personal selling	• Distribution coverage
• Style	• Allowances	• Sales promotion	• Outlet locations
• Brand name	• Payment terms	• Publicity	• Sales territories
• Packaging	• Returns	• Investor relations	• Inventory locations
• Product line		• Tradeshows	• Transportation centers
• Warranty			
• Service level			
• Supporting services			

Countless marketing variables can affect the success or failure of strategy implementation. Marketing as a cross-functional discipline integrates with all other areas of organizational performance. For emphasis in this book, many marketing subjects are addressed specifically on their own. These include: industry and competitive analysis, environmental assessment, customer profile, sales effectiveness, and customer service. Additional related points within the book include *targeted information* and *organization communication.*

While volumes have been written on any of these marketing issues, common themes are cross-functional integration and the use of ROI-based benchmarks for success (that is, monitoring marketing activities on their impact on the profitability of the enterprise). The following model (Table 3.18) illustrates ten key principles for marketing success:

Common to all successful marketing campaigns is a focused and strategically aligned marketing plan. A good marketing plan will ensure that branding images will be consistent, the market is clearly defined, and that marketing plays a defined role in product development. Table 3.19 lists key elements that should be addressed when putting together a successful marketing plan.

What to Do

Creating and sustaining a successful marketing function within your organization requires an unwavering commitment from the top. Often, manage-

Table 3.18   Ten Key Principles to Marketing Success[28]

Principle 1.	Create Customer Satisfaction.
Principle 2.	Know Your Buyer Characteristics.
Principle 3.	Divide the Market into Segments.
Principle 4.	Strive for Higher Market Share.
Principle 5.	Develop Deep and Wide Product Lines.
Principle 6.	Price Position Products and Upgrade Markets.
Principle 7.	Treat Channels as Intermediate Buyers.
Principle 8.	Coordinate Elements of Physical Distribution.
Principle 9.	Promote Performance Features.
Principle 10.	Use Information to Improve Decisions.

Table 3.19 Key Elements in the Marketing Plan[29]

People	What is the target market for the firm's product[s]? What is its size and growth potential?
Profit	What is the expected profit from implementing the marketing plan? What are other objectives of the marketing plan, and how will their achievement be evaluated?
Personnel	What personnel will be involved in implementing the marketing plan? Will only intrafirm personnel be involved, or will other firms, such as advertising agencies or marketing research firms, also be employed?
Product	What product[s] will be offered? What variations in the product will be offered in terms of style, features, quality, branding, packaging, and in terms of sale and service. How should products be positioned in the marketplace?
Price	What price or prices will products be sold for?
Promotion	How will information about the firm's offerings be communicated to the target market?
Place	How, when, and where will the firm's offerings be delivered for sale to the target market?
Policy	What is the overall marketing policy for dealing with anticipated problems in the marketing plan? How will unanticipated problems be handled?
Period	For how long a time is the marketing plan to be in effect? When should the plan be implemented, and what is the schedule for executing and evaluating marketing activities?

ment can find themselves caught up in the "flavor of the month" campaigns. Once you've defined your mission, vision, and competitive advantage, bring them to bear when developing your marketing strategy. Marketing is your vehicle to say who you are, what you do, and why you're indispensable to your customer. Be consistent, targeted, and responsive. The following areas of focus will help you navigate through the process of building and sustaining a dynamic and successful marketing organization.

Marketing Is a Team Sport

Be sure you set the foundation to draw support and information from within your entire organization. Marketing requires a cross-functional and interdependent approach. A successful marketing organization draws input from operations, sales, legal, finance, accounting, and outsource partners like advertising agencies, market research firms, and marketing consultants.

Have a Plan

It's pretty tough to market effectively without a clear path to follow. To review your marketing plan will include:

- Target customer(s).
- Timeline.
- Personnel requirements.
- Product(s) description.
- Price.
- Promotion—what form will your message take?
- Channel selection—how and where will your customers make their purchases?
- Establish policies—what process and contingencies are laid out to support a responsive organization?
- Measurement—know when you cross the finish line. This may come in the form of profit, transactions, Web hits, call center activity, sales leads, cross-sell ratio, customer profitability, etc.

Branding Is Everything

Brand management requires discipline. Set up a process to test campaigns and collateral against your brand standards. Your brand is your identity. Inconsistency such as a change in look, message, or market positioning can confuse your customer, resulting in a longer sales cycle or a loss of the customer.

Information Is King

This is a big target and subject in large part to capital budget. To build an effective plan that has a high probability for success, business facts are required. Good customer data, industry and market intelligence, and economic impact are essential. Be creative, use the Web, industry publications, government reporting agencies, market research firms, and trade organizations to capture the necessary information to make fact-based decisions.

Manage Your Products and Services

Once you've defined your value proposition and aligned it against your customer needs, be sure that the organization stays true to these guiding standards. Any number of crises can arise from inefficient or laissez-faire product management. Risks are time-to-market, product reliability, patent or copyright infringement, and financial miscalculations, to name a few.

Test Every Decision Against Your Competitive Advantage

Remember, your point of differentiation can only come in the form of three or four scenarios. You are either a low-cost provider, a product innovator, customer service provider, or a hybrid mixing service with one of the other two. Your marketing message and position must be clearly aligned with your competitive advantage. If your target customers are ultimately driven by price— a compelling service-driven message will most likely fall on deaf ears.

Every Employee Is an Ambassador

Pride. Are your employees proud of what you do? As a key stakeholder, your employees must understand your market position, and more specifically, must be *brand* champions. Pride comes with involvement and appreciation. If all your employees understand how they contribute to the value of the organization, and that their contribution is appreciated, they are more likely to go the extra distance to support the success of the organization.

Measure the Effectiveness of Your Marketing Efforts and Campaigns

It is often difficult, and some would argue impossible, to measure the success or failure of a given marketing effort. Measuring ROI (Return on investment) is a key driver to determine how future marketing dollars will be spent. ROI can be a negotiated measure. Most management teams would prefer to see ROI in the form of profit or growth. However, success can come in the form of lead generation, Web or call center hits, foot traffic, or cross-sell ratio. Management and marketing must negotiate the metrics that each views as instrumental on allocating resources to future marketing investment.

One of the great internal battles in many companies is the conflict between the sales organization and the marketing organization. Depending on your business model, the marketing or the sales group may have the upper hand over the other. A low-cost provider that relies on marketing efforts featuring price as the compelling customer call to action will often place authority and responsibility within the marketing group. However, a service-driven organization that may have a long sales cycle or high-touch approach to selling customers may empower the sales organization to a greater advantage. In short, both departments bring specific skills to the table and are interdependent. The following pages explore how the sales function and organization best serve the company.

Sales Effectiveness

"Just being able to conceive bold new strategies is not enough. The general manager must also be able to translate his or her strategic vision into concrete steps that 'get things done'."—Richard G. Hamermesh

In a growing global economy—with fewer barriers to entry, nontraditional channels, quality wars, price wars, and substitute products—the sales management function has never been more challenging. Many companies have acknowledged this difficulty and have opted to obtain growth through merger or acquisition. At times, it would appear that it is more cost-efficient, more reliable, and much less risky for certain industries to buy market share rather than to capture it. Yet, it still remains true that, in general, successful long-term strategy implementation rests upon the ability of an organization to sell and deliver their products or services.

The sales process includes sales promotion, personal selling, sales force management, and customer relations. The traditional approach to selling has always involved a step-by-step process. This process involved:

1. Getting the customer's attention
2. Arousing the customer's interest
3. Stimulating the customer's desire for the product
4. Getting the customer to buy
5. Building satisfaction into the transaction

In their book, *The Nordstrom Way*,[30] in the chapter titled "The Art of Selling," Robert Spector and Patrick D. McCarthy clearly illustrate how Nordstrom's has distinguished themselves as being a customer-focused, high-touch sales organization. In Table 3.20, they articulate Nordstrom's "Keys to Success" in selling:

We would like to take a moment and elaborate on the level of information a Nordstrom's sales associate has provided to them. The knowledge about each of their customers that they acquire includes:

- Contact information
- Charge account number
- Sizes (apparel, etc.)
- Previous purchases
- Vendor preferences

Table 3.20 Nordstrom's Keys to Sales Success

At Nordstrom, the priority is on selling, and the key to successful selling is providing outstanding customer service. Nordstrom wants to sell everybody, through practice, experience, and commitment. Nordstrom's best associates have learned how *not* to lose a sale because they couldn't satisfy the customer.

- If you treat customers like royalty and let them know that you will take care of them, they usually come back to you.
- Nordstrom's top salespeople don't put things off until the end of the day. They get them out of the way so they can start the next day fresh.
- When customers enter a department, salespeople always make sure they are acknowledged. They are relaxed and unhurried in order to help the customer feel the same way.
- Top salespeople keep the process simple and easy by helping the customers eliminate the things they don't want. They constantly ask for feedback because the more information they have, the better they can serve the customer. Price is never a primary issue.
- "Trust" is the coin of the realm. Salespeople earn the confidence of customers by being well versed in the merchandise they sell. They aren't just selling clothes and shoes, they are also selling service.
- Top salespeople rely on the tools that Nordstrom provides including a personal customer book to keep track of pertinent information on every customer.
- Multiple sales distinguish the top sales performers.
- The telephone is a powerful tool for generating business, improving productivity, and saving time.
- Follow-through is important. Top salespeople aren't looking for the big score. They are committed to nurturing an ongoing business relationship.

- Likes and dislikes
- Special orders
- Other specific characteristics:
  - Difficult fit
  - Time preferences for shopping (i.e., time of day or sales events)

Additionally, sales associates maintain their own calendar of customer activities, to-dos, and other specific contact database applications.

Whether an organization's sales process involves personal selling or mass communication, it is important that messages are congruent with the firm's overall strategic intent. Consistent messages will build durability, market position, and brand identity among potential customers. As companies refocus on more effective sales and customer service, we have identified the following ingredients as keys to selling success:

1. **Rethink training.** Salespeople now require new skills. They must be taught to be advocates of their customers with detailed knowledge of their customers' needs. High-pressure selling tactics and one-time, slam-dunk sales will not be effective.
2. **Total involvement.** Effective salespeople no longer act alone. The efforts of product designers, plant managers, and financial officers must be a part of selling, and serving customers.
3. **Top management support.** CEOs and other top managers must be visibly and frequently involved in any change effort. This often includes regularly making sales calls and leading sales training meetings.
4. **Relating objectives to motivation.** Remove incentives that encourage quick-hit sales. Include measures of long-term customer satisfaction in compensation plans.
5. **Use technology.** Increase responsiveness with marketing and distribution technology. Technology can be used to track customer relationships, to ensure that the right products get to the right place at the right time, and to simplify order taking.
6. **Stay close to the customer.** Pay attention to customers. Call them often or send notes to frequent shoppers. Assign a specific employee to good customers.

In summary, like many organizational disciplines, sales management crosses functional lines. Having trained personnel understand the relationship between their job function and customer service is key to transforming a production-oriented company into a sales-oriented one. The following are fundamentals that all sales-oriented personnel should possess:

1. A thorough knowledge of the company, including its past history, the management philosophy, and its basic operating policies.
2. A thorough technical and commercial knowledge of products and product lines.

3. A good working knowledge of competitors' products, including their costs and benefits, strengths and weaknesses.
4. An in-depth knowledge of the market, including economic and other external issues that may affect demand.
5. A thorough understanding of methods used to locate and qualify prospects. A consistent method of evaluating potential customers' needs, financial resources, and willingness to be approached.
6. An accurate knowledge of the customer's buying profile, including product applications and customer requirements. Be able to describe product benefits as well as understand how the customer makes a buying decision.

There are several good case studies of companies that excel in implementing a good sales process. We have illustrated the Nordstrom approach, which reflects a strong service emphasis along with a very "high-touch" or intimate-relationship management discipline. Amazon.com and Dell have demonstrated how the Internet can become a highly successful sales distribution channel. Amazon.com, like Nordstrom, has a detailed database of customer characteristics and buying habits. They leverage this knowledge to align cross-sell opportunities and other products that fit the customer's purchasing profile. In so doing, they significantly increase the value of each customer and strive to establish a profitable, long-term, and dependent customer relationship.

Dell has perfected the real-time custom order. Through their Web site, and with the support, if needed, of a trained salesperson, the customer can specify exactly what they want their purchased product to do. Not only does Dell ensure that customers are getting exactly what they want, but also that a significant business benefit occurs. Most Dell products are paid for at the time of order, thereby providing Dell with immediate cash flow and one of the most favorable accounts receivable profiles we have ever seen. When we last checked, Dell's aged accounts receivable were −18 days. (We don't mean to get sidetracked from sales effectiveness, however, when we can insert cross-functional business excellence, we cannot let it pass.)

All three, Nordstrom, Amazon.com, and Dell are providing their customers with a *branded* unique sales experience. In all three cases, these organizations have tied their sales process into their overall value proposition, thereby strengthening their barriers to entry.

Direct and Indirect Sales Channels

In addition to quality-trained, sales-oriented employees, an organization needs to evaluate its sales and distribution channels for alignment with its strategic intent. From an operational standpoint, a channel is the path that a product or service takes as it moves from the manufacturer to the ultimate consumer. Whether an organization selects an indirect channel such as Compaq's distribution through CompUSA, Costco, Staples, et al., or a direct channel such as Dell Computer's e-commerce or direct mail catalog process, channel selection is vital to reaching a firm's customer base profitably and efficiently. Table 3.21 illustrates the characteristics of direct and indirect channels.

Good channel management has a number of defining characteristics. First and foremost is the selection of the channels through which the firm does business. The old two-path dichotomy of indirect and direct choices have expanded to include Internet, OEM arrangements, and others that make channel choices more difficult, yet more efficient when targeting a

Table 3.21 Categories of Direct and Indirect Channels[31]

Direct	Indirect	
Product Ownership	**Product Ownership**	**Product Nonownership**
• Direct sales force • National account sales • Direct mail • Telemarketing • Manufacturer's catalog • Internet	• Distributor • Private label • Stocking manufacturer sales representative • Original equipment manufacturer (OEM) • Catalog house • Telemarketing company • Wholesaler • Master distributor • Reseller • Retailer • Dealer • Value-added reseller • System integrator • Phantom channel of distribution	• Manufacturer sales representative • Broker • Independent sales agent • Export management company (EMC) • Synthetic channel of distribution • Fulfillment channel

market segment. When selecting or designing a channel for expansion, a firm can take a number of steps to ensure that its primary channel choice is in alignment with its overall marketing plan. (See Table 3.22.)

There are many companies who have broken away from traditional channels of distribution and added new pathways to new consumers. For example, IBM learned a hard lesson when it found that selling new products to new end users with new requirements could not be done through existing channels. Thus, IBM turned to new indirect channels to sell its microcomputer products to consumers and small businesses rather than rely on its direct staff of sales professionals, who normally handled the company's larger mainframe business. Rubbermaid has made big inroads into Tupperware's market by selling through efficient channels such as Wal-Mart, while Tupperware continues to sell through much more costly, multilevel distribution.

Although a difficult task to master, sales and distribution in today's marketplace offer firms a greater number of options than ever before. Organizations that are customer driven, technology wise, and congruent in their positioning can restructure their channel design to reach their customer base with increasingly more efficient methods.

A word of caution as you explore alternative distribution strategies if you currently rely on a live direct sales force or VARs (Value added resellers). Introducing a direct channel when the bulk of your business has relied on

Table 3.22   The Channel Design Sequence[32]

---

1. Identify the new market you want to penetrate or new product you need to launch.
2. Verify the need for a new channel or distribution or some form of channel reorganization.
3. Evaluate all macro market conditions.
4. Conduct a competitive channel analysis.
5. Research and rank customers/end-user satisfaction requirements.
6. Specify and rank the tasks you want your channel partner to perform.
7. Investigate all possible channels of distribution structures.
8. Decide upon the best channel partners.
9. Obtain internal corporate recommitment.
10. Approach and sign the selected distributors.
11. Monitor and evaluate the channel structure.

---

direct sales forces and VARS can create channel conflict. For example, for years State Farm has relied on its network of independent insurance brokers to drive their business. The advent of the Internet provided a less expensive alternative to meeting the needs of customers who clearly understood their insurance needs. Needless to say, the State Farm agents were less enthusiastic about this approach.

Closing Thoughts

Nordstrom's has built a 100-year-old organization on the simple premise that service and sales are synonymous. Here are their restated "Keys to Sales Success":

1. If you treat customers like royalty and let them know that you will take care of them, they usually come back to you.
2. Nordstrom's top salespeople don't put things off until the end of the day. They get them out of the way so they can start the next day fresh.
3. When customers enter a department, salespeople always make sure they are acknowledged. They are relaxed and unhurried in order to help the customer feel the same way.
4. Top salespeople keep the process simple and easy by helping the customers eliminate the things they don't want. They constantly ask for feedback because the more information they have, the better they can serve the customer. Price is never a primary issue.
5. "Trust" is the coin of the realm. Salespeople earn the confidence of customers by being well versed in the merchandise they sell. They aren't just selling clothes and shoes, they are also selling service.
6. Top salespeople rely on the tools that Nordstrom provides including a personal customer book to keep track of pertinent information on every customer.
7. Multiple sales distinguish the top sales performers.
8. The telephone is a powerful tool for generating business, improving productivity, and saving time.
9. Follow-through is important. Top salespeople aren't looking for the big score. They are committed to nurturing an ongoing business relationship.

Their record for success speaks for itself.

Customer Service—Four Seasons Experience, "Staying Ahead of the Rest"

"We define the experience through the service we provide, and we strive to offer the same high level of personalized service visit to visit and hotel to hotel. It is this quality of service that is so critically important to our guests, and the degree to which we can provide and evolve it, worldwide, is also the degree to which we can differentiate ourselves and stay ahead of the rest."—Isadore ("Issy") Sharp, Founder, Chairman, and CEO Four Seasons Hotels and Resorts

"Not in *my* hotel you won't!" That was the comment a friend of ours received while staying at the Four Seasons Hotel in Carlsbad, California. It was late at night and he stepped out of his room to get some ice. While walking through the hallway, he came across a staff electrician—utility belt and all. The electrician politely asked him how he might be of assistance. He said that he was fine and that he was just retrieving some ice. The electrician replied, "not in *my* hotel you won't," and he politely took the ice bucket, suggested our friend return to his room and the ice would be there immediately.

This "moment of truth" at the Four Seasons Hotel in Carlsbad, California embodies what every service-driven organization strives for: employees that go beyond the scope of their responsibilities and step up to create memorable customer experiences. Experiences that most likely will result in repeat business, and stories shared about the Four Seasons experience.

Having a philosophical commitment to exceeding customer expectations is key. However, not having all the necessary components to create an experience like the one previously mentioned will most likely result in an unsatisfactory outcome. When we evaluate a company's service approach, we test against six attributes across the organization:

1. Their customer service standards are clearly defined and documented.
2. They consistently exceed their customers' expectations.
3. They measure customer satisfaction by routinely obtaining direct customer feedback.
4. Their commitment to customer satisfaction and loyalty is understood and embraced by *all* employees within their company.
5. Their company employs a system to obtain and evaluate customer service information.

6. Their company enjoys a higher rate of repeat business, referrals, or customer loyalty than their competitors.

Four Seasons Hotels and Resorts

Selecting a "Best Practice" organization in the area of customer service is a daunting task. There are a couple of things we've discovered over the last several years of research. One is that there are many definitions of "quality" or "outstanding" customer service. Secondly, within successful service-driven organizations, there is no ambiguity about the role of their service standards and how those standards support a sustainable competitive advantage. Service is at the root of all organizations' value. Establishing a relationship and building it over the lifetime value of the customer influences every aspect of an organization's business. Four Seasons Hotels and Resorts clearly has the customer at the center of their universe, and within their industry, their numbers bear them out. (See Tables 3.23 and 3.24.) Four Seasons' financial performance consistently leads their industry. Even though their industry was significantly impacted by the events of September 11, 2001, they continue to stay focused on their vision and their commitment to their customers.

Founded in 1960 by Chairman and Chief Executive Officer Isadore Sharp, Four Seasons traces it roots to an idea that would prove to be revolutionary: what the global business traveler wanted most was personalized service, available round-the-clock. Frequent international travel, now so commonplace, was an emerging trend in the 1960s and 1970s. It set the stage for a new kind of luxury hotel experience.

Table 3.23 Four Seasons Hotels and Resorts Financial Performance 1997–2001[33]

Consideration	2001	2000	1999	1998	1997
Stock Price	$46.76	$63.63	$53.25	$29.25	$31.63
Total Sales In millions	$194.40	$222.9	$178.0	$159.0	$154.2
EPS	$1.06	$1.50	$1.24	$1.27	$1.17

Table 3.24 Industry Peer Analysis—Four Seasons[34]

Consideration	Four Seasons	Hotel Industry
Price to Earnings	25.44	20.00
Price to Sales (TTM)	8.99	1.76
EPS—5 Yr. Growth	30.94	16.45
Sales—5 yr. Growth	20.71	15.41
Operating Margin (TTM)	41.69	16.19
Operating Margin—5 yr. average	32.79	10.68

After a decade of trial and refinement Mr. Sharp created a single vision that today has made Four Seasons the only operator in the world exclusively focused on mid-size luxury hotels and resorts of exceptional quality. Four Seasons creates properties of enduring value using superior design and finishes, and supports them with a deeply instilled ethic of personal service. Doing so allows Four Seasons to satisfy the needs and tastes of discriminating customers, and to maintain its position as the world's premier luxury hospitality company.

The educational background of Isadore Sharp combined with his design and construction expertise, his single focus on satisfying the customer and his leadership skills have allowed Issy to attract the capital sources and a loyal employee base to create the largest luxury hotel management company in the world.

The Canadian-based company has, over the past forty years, transformed the hospitality industry by combining North American friendliness and efficiency with the finest traditions of international hotel keeping. In the process, Four Seasons has redefined luxury for the modern traveler.

Sharp had the opportunity to capitalize on this trend when the company opened its third hotel, and its first in Europe, the Inn on the Park, now known as Four Seasons Hotel London. In a market dominated by classic, traditional hotels, the new arrival was an instant success. Key features included spacious rooms equipped for business and relaxation, as well as a friendly staff to make every guest wish a reality.

The success of London made Sharp realize that what he enjoyed creating and what was really lacking in the marketplace—was medium-sized hotels of exceptional quality, with exceptional service levels. He decided to focus his efforts on this niche and thus set the future course for the company.

Building on the success of London, Four Seasons then embarked on a targeted course of expansion, which continues to the present time, opening hotels in major city centers across North America and around the world. As the company expanded, Four Seasons became the first in North America to introduce now-standard items such as bath amenities, terry-cloth robes, hairdryers, and multiple, 2-line telephones in the guest room and bath.

Four Seasons was also the first to provide European-style concierge services and room service 24/7 . . . to offer innovative choices in cuisine, taking the hotel dining experience to a new level . . . and to make all of these services available at every hotel it operated. Twice-daily housekeeping service, one-hour pressing and round-the-clock, and four-hour laundry and dry cleaning service are additional brand features, introduced at Four Seasons long before these were introduced by other luxury hotel operators.

"We have aspired to be the best hotel in each location where we operate," says Sharp. "Early in the company's history we decided to focus on redefining luxury as service and that became our strategic edge. And, in order to deliver on that promise, we needed employees who are dedicated, committed, and to harness the 'best of the best' inspired to deliver great service. They are the standard bearers for the intuitive, highly personalized service we aspire to provide."

By pioneering new ways to serve the changing lifestyle of the global traveler, Four Seasons continues to respond to emerging guest needs. Nowhere is this more evident than in the way that in-room services also have evolved. Dining options now include Alternative Cuisine® (an inspired selection of nutritionally balanced healthier fare), and Home Cooking (simple, wholesome recipes that travelers would have at home) as well as the creative dishes of Vegetarian Dining. Today's guest can also choose from an ever-widening array of services that are completely customized to his or her needs, such as massage and aromatherapy, or in-room exercise equipment upon request.

Four Seasons President, Worldwide Hotel Operations Wolf Hengst observes: "Today, more than ever, time is our guests' most precious commodity. What they value are services designed to help them use their time well, whether traveling for business or leisure. We see this with room service breakfast. No longer just for leisurely breakfasts in bed, it is used most by the business traveler to save valuable time. One can check e-mail, watch CNN, scan the *Wall Street Journal,* get dressed and have a full breakfast—all in the comfort of one's room and within the same thirty-minute slot."

During the last five years, Four Seasons' has expanded their competence in to two new offerings, Four Seasons Private Residences and Residence Clubs. Four Seasons Private Residences provide full or fractional ownership of city and vacation homes in some of the most desirable locations around the world. Four Seasons Residence Clubs, a fractional ownership product, offer fully appointed vacation villas and a stress-free, maintenance-free alternative to vacation home ownership.

With the success of Four Seasons private residences as well as Residence Clubs in Aviara and Scottsdale, Four Seasons has demonstrated its ability to set a new service standard level in luxury residential ownership as it has for its hotels and resorts.

Sustaining customer value is an important key to strategic management. Successful strategy formulation involves measuring customer value in order to understand potential problems and emphasize customer service and satisfaction. (See Table 3.25.) Meeting customer expectations is the key to satisfaction, but exceeding expectations is the key to customer loyalty.

Table 3.25   Top Ten Best Practice Customer Service Diagnostic Questions[35]

---

1. What is your customer retention? Does it indicate any trends you can act upon?

2. What is the level of cross-functional communication between your company and its customers?

3. Do you train employees throughout the organization in various tasks so that any of them can handle any problem that arises during the customer cycle?

4. What financial empowerment do you provide to your frontline employees to solve customer problems? Do you give them additional authority to make decisions on the spot?

5. Do those frontline employees have access to executive groups such as IBM's customer action councils where they can receive additional assistance and powers of authority?

6. Do you have in place a cross-functional database to track and analyze customer service highlights and lowlights?

7. How do you explicitly gauge your customer's satisfaction? Do focus groups play a role?

8. Is any portion of your company's merit system based on customer service?

9. Do you have a client advisory board? How often does it meet? What does it accomplish?

10. Do you surprise your customers with great customer service? Do your customers experience a level of service that is beyond their expectations?

There are literally hundreds of good examples of outstanding customer service in business journals and in best practice literature. Companies like Nordstrom, Tiffany's, FAO Schwartz, and American Express are legends of customer service. Most of the time, these best practice stories of customer service are anomalies. They are newsworthy for just that reason: excellent customer service is hard to sustain.

Growing out of these stories of extraordinary customer service are systemic approaches that can change an organization into a more customer-focused enterprise. Metro Bank, for example, defined three key elements of excellent customer relations in their industry:

1. **Knowledgeable People:** Differentiate ourselves through employees capable of recognizing customer needs and possessing the knowledge to proactively satisfy them.

2. **Convenient Access:** Give customers access to banking services or information 24 hours a day.
3. **Responsiveness:** Service customers expediently. The timeliness of the response could meet the customer's perceived sense of urgency.

Although marketing plays a critical role in meeting customer expectations before, during, and after a sales transaction, other functions within the organization also contribute to superior customer responsiveness. (See Table 3.26.)

Measuring customer satisfaction and creating management decision information has become an industry unto itself. Establish a system that can provide reliable decision-driven knowledge over time. In addition to capturing information that tells you what your customers need, it is also helpful to share this data in a manner that ensures common understanding and consistency throughout your organization. Research has proven time and again that knowing what the customer thinks is only part of the job.

Many organizations fall short of achieving desired customer outcomes because they lack alignment among customers, management, and those that serve the customer. The following spider graph (Figure 3.2) illustrates the

Table 3.26 Primary Roles of Different Functions in Achieving Superior Customer Responsiveness[36]

Value-Creation Function	Primary Role
Infrastructure	Through leadership by example, build a companywide commitment to customer service responsiveness.
Manufacturing	Achieving customization by implementing flexible manufacturing.
Marketing	Know the customer. Communicate customer feedback to appropriate functions.
Materials Management	Develop logistics systems capable of responding quickly to unanticipated customer demands.
Research and Development	Bring customers into the product development process.
Human Resources	Develop training programs that make employees think of themselves as customers.

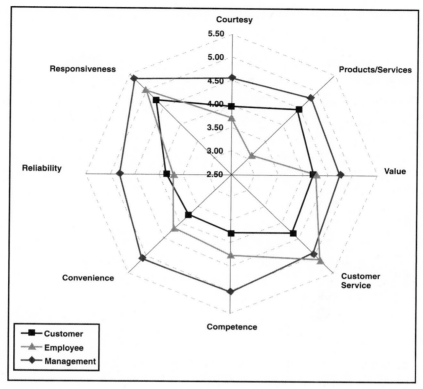

Figure 3.2 Virtual CEO, Inc., Customer Service Alignment Assessment[37]

value of gaining input from primary constituencies and measuring gaps between them. This particular assessment captures the perceptions of customers, management, and line employees tied to common themes and values.

You can quickly identify if management, employees, and customers agree or disagree on what's important and how the organization is performing. Within this illustration, management clearly has a rosier view than the customer or the employees. In short, through this assessment, not only does the company understand how their customers measure their service proposition, but they also are provided with crucial information on the internal view and alignment behind the key issues. Companies routinely break down due to a lack of buy-in or common understanding of the key issues that drive value with their customers. This is one way organizations can ensure that everyone is all on the same page with the customer—good or bad.

What To Do

Clearly Define and Document Your Service Standards

Leave nothing to chance when it comes to serving your customers. Define the standards necessary to support your customers' needs, and document them in a manner that supports decision making and execution.

Exceed Customer Expectations

Develop a culture that lives to surprise and delight. Develop the training, performance management systems, and rewards systems that reinforce exceeding expectations. Management that cannot model the behavior doesn't get to stay.

Measure Customer Satisfaction

Install the necessary systems and skill set to obtain and manage customer "G2." This can come in the form of Web-based surveys, focus groups, feedback cards, or telephone surveys. Third-party providers usually provide the best approach and most accurate data. Customer satisfaction, as set forth by your standards, must be a metric that is as available and current as key financial data such as balance sheet, P and L, and cash flow.

Living the Service Standards Is a Condition of Employment

If employees are not with you on your standards, then they are against you. Don't waste good energy trying to convert the unconvertible!

Measure Your Success!

Track and report repeat business, referrals, and cross-sell. Obtain competitor information to determine the magnitude of your success or failure. Establish the lifetime value of your customers. There is no better tool to work you through a tough spot with customers than knowing exactly what their worth is to you over time!

Execution and Action Plans—the U.S. Army Corps of Engineers, the Huntington District— Leaving Nothing to Chance

"All winning teams are goal-oriented. Teams like these win consistently because everyone connected with them concentrates on specific objectives. They go about their business with blinders on; nothing will distract them from achieving their aims."

—LOU HOLTZ, FORMER NOTRE DAME FOOTBALL COACH

SUCCESS IS GENERALLY MEASURED by an organization's ability to execute against a plan. You could say that without a plan, it would be very difficult to measure how successful a company is. Many organizations do struggle through their business life in an organic fashion or with an implicit approach to managing their business. We would suggest that though short-term success may be experienced through this undisciplined approach, success is not sustainable without a defined explicit plan of action tied directly to the organizations' strategic plan.

The most direct approach to building an executable action plan is to understand the process and adopt a common language tied to plan elements.

We define these elements as objectives, initiatives, and goals. These elements articulate what a company wants to accomplish, how it will to do it, and when it will be achieved. Once defined, the organization can align its resources, including human, financial, technological, and physical, along a distinct path. A targeted action plan with the appropriate resources positions the organization for the highest probability of success.

We have had the good fortune of observing an organization that gets it. Albeit no claims of perfection—yet a consistent and deliberate approach to translating their mission into a clearly defined project plan.

The United States Army Corps of Engineer's, Huntington District, has over 1000 employees, an operating budget over $200 million dollars, and among other things, they are responsible for the safe passage of over 74 million tons of coal and other commodities along the Ohio River. They manage 35 lakes and 9 locks and dams, are on call 24/7 for disaster recovery in three states, and manage close to 100 major infrastructure and environmental restoration projects. Located in Huntington, West Virginia, a community of just over 50,000 citizens and Marshall University, the District has since 1995 aggressively embedded the disciplines and guiding principles of the Malcolm Baldrige criteria. The Huntington District is no stranger to process or management. As engineers, they understand project management techniques and planning a critical path to success. Their challenge is to apply their talents and skills as large project managers to the execution of a targeted business plan.

Though not a for-profit organization, the District demonstrates the intensity and passion that one might find in any Fortune 50 company. Throughout this chapter, we illustrate the variety of systems, tools, and processes that the District applies to get the job done.

Objectives, initiatives, and goals provide a framework for business planners to articulate a company's future plans in concrete terms. Goals are stated outcomes of the strategic planning process, and may be long-term in nature. Goals can address both financial and nonfinancial issues, and cut across functional boundaries. Table 4.1 is a basic example of a strategic decision to increase sales.

The table illustrates the intent and expectation of the sales objective. This organization made the decision to increase sales by creating a new delivery channel that leverages their customers' comfort with the Internet. The goals reflect a desired increase in sales performance, the

Table 4.1   Strategic Objectives, Initiatives, and Goals Summary

Objective	Initiatives	Goals		
Increase product sales volume through the introduction of a new delivery channel.	• Create customer direct delivery channel. • Expand Web site support. • Install "e-commerce" software. • Expand database capabilities to support initiatives.	**Fiscal Year**	**Percent of Total Sales**	**ROI**
		2002	5%	−.65
		2003	12.5%	.75
		2004	18%	2.75

return-on-investment, and when the company intends to realize the increases.

Within objectives, initiatives, and goals, you are developing the communication vehicle that will summarize the critical elements that support your strategic intent, as well as an explicit timeline in which these expectations are to be achieved.

In larger or diversified companies, these may be broad-stroked descriptions, allowing business units or divisions the ability to build their operating plans in a manner that specifically identifies their contribution and role in achieving the organization's strategic intent. These are the tactical plans that provide the muscle necessary for the company to successfully fulfill its plan, and are captured in the fourth and final leg in the strategic planning model.

The management challenge in setting objectives, initiatives, and goals is to align the organization's resources, and to ensure that the plans are prioritized and consistent with the overall strategic intent of the organization. And, upon implementation, it is vital that management shows leadership in communicating roles and responsibilities throughout the organization, assuring that the organization has the appropriate structure and skills to achieve the overall intent.

In short—it's all about execution. And if you want to execute—having a clearly defined action plan is not negotiable.

Vital Direction

"We strategize beautifully, we implement pathetically."—unknown executive

An organization's *vital direction* is nothing more than effectively converting strategic intent into clearly defined, actionable activities. Through prioritizing critical objectives by their strategic importance, aligning these objectives with the necessary resources, and remaining poised to integrate dynamic emerging opportunities, organizations are better positioned to achieve their strategic goals.

Once an organization's management team has crafted a strategy, the next priority is to convert the strategy into complementary actions and measurable results. While successful strategy formulation relies on analysis, assessment, and creativity, establishing and furthering the vital direction of the firm requires leading, motivating, directing change, managing people, and an operations orientation.

To develop an agenda for execution, managers need to assess the gaps between the current organization and the intended strategy. Looking from a value-chain activities perspective, a firm should look for gaps between the new strategic requirements and:

1. **The skills sets of the organization:** additional core competencies, distinctive competencies, or new training curriculum.
2. **The structure of the organization:** reporting responsibilities, policies, information systems, communication, and operating efficiencies.
3. **The culture of the organization:** a nurturing and supportive environment, values communication, empowerment, and appropriate performance measurements.

The following figure (Figure 4.1) is a page from the Huntington District of the U.S. Army Corps of Engineers FY 2003 action plan. The plan outlines several objectives that have been distilled from a strategic planning exercise.

When we evaluate an organization's ability to communicate their vital direction, we review their plans for at least seven critical components. The plan shown illustrates these seven key elements that articulate the organization's vital direction:

1. *Strategic Business Goal* (Invest in People)—This represents the overriding goal that is directly tied to the strategic intent of the organization.

US Army Corps of Engineers
Huntington District

Management Validation & Action Planning

Objectives	Resource Allocation	Ownership	Milestones	Due Date	Goals & Measurement
INVEST IN PEOPLE					
Build Trust Through Communication	PAO IM Supervisors LM HR	Deputy District Engineer	1. Install intercom system (LM)	10/31/2002	Increase Employee satisfaction score
			2. Effective use of monitors (review type, determine current information, possibly add monitors) (PAO)	10/31/2002	Increase scores in Employee Satisfaction Assessment, particularly in the areas of informal Communication and Organization Communication
			3. Develop template for communicating information / initiatives (PAO)	12/31/2002	
			4. Implement Knowledge Dispatch System	12/31/2002	
			PH-1 Create user oriented design (IM)	12/31/2002	Positive feedback from employees regarding Knowledge Dispatch system, intercom system, E-mail Management system and new monitors.
			PH-2 Establish accountability for updates (supervisors)	12/31/2002	
			5. Implement E-mail Management system (IM)	03/31/2003	
			PH-1 Create design	03/31/2003	TAPES results.
			PH-2 Implement E-mail management system	03/31/2003	
			6. Continue and improve implementation of consideration of others (supervisors)	03/31/2003	
			7. Develop a tracking system for TAPES/Appraisals, Awards, and Counseling (HR)	03/31/2003	

Figure 4.1

In this example, the Huntington District of the Army Corps of Engineers believes that the investment in people is central to the successful execution of their long-term strategy. The following components illustrate the steps they feel are necessary to support this overriding goal.

2. *Objective*—This is a key component supporting the strategic business goal. It's a broad description of a specific set of actions that can be measured.

3. *Resources*—These describe what departments, people, or other necessary components are needed to support the objective. This is an area where organizations often make their greatest mistakes. This comes in the form of insufficient or no resources necessary to support the objective or achieve the goal.

4. *Ownership*—Accountability must be embedded in every action plan. The owner accepts responsibility for the objective. It is this person's role to see that timelines are kept, resources are available, communication is maintained, and that the overall goal is achieved.

5. *Milestones*—These represent the mission-critical steps to achieving the goal. These tactical items communicate to the management team and the organization what activities need to take place in order to satisfy the plan and the needs of the company.

6. *Due Dates*—These indicate when each milestone should be completed.

7. *Goals and Measurement*—This column draws the "finish line." When plans are established, there must be a clearly communicated measure

that represents successful completion of the objective. Items in this column can include financial performance, percentage of growth, ROI, or any other quantifiable measure that represents the fulfillment of the objective.

These seven items drawn from a strategic planning exercise are the embodiment of the organization's *vital direction*. A well-developed action plan increases the organization's probability of success, provides an effective means of internal communication, and serves as a means to transfer knowledge of the organization. With communication of the strategy enhanced by this documentation, the necessary resources, personnel training, and organizational processes may be put into place much more effectively.

The Huntington District uses this approach not only to communicate their strategic intent, but to reinforce their commitment to being a fully integrated, cross-functional team. The publishing of the plan within the District illustrates how multiple divisions and individuals are brought together to support numerous objectives.

It is worth noting that the seven items above are labels. Other common terms representing the essence of what we're discussing could be "strategies and initiatives," or "objectives and tactics." The important take-away from this section is leaving little or nothing to chance. A well-developed strategy without a clearly defined vital direction is less likely to be achieved.

Resource Alignment

"No company can afford everything it would like to do. Resources have to be allocated. The essence of strategic planning is to allocate resources to those areas that have the greatest future potential."—Reginald Jones, former chairman of General Electric

This chapter is all about execution. We cannot stress enough the importance of well-thought-out action plans. All too often, management teams become disillusioned with strategic planning not because of the process, but because the strategies rarely become supported by clearly defined and executable action plans. So, with this theme and experience in mind, we continue to peel back the onion of building and executing against clearly defined action plans.

In the previous section, we call out the necessity of clearly defining required resources. To further expand on the subject, think of *resource alignment* when defining resource requirements. Resource alignment is committing the necessary capital, technological, physical, or human resources for key strategic objectives. When focusing on human capital, be careful to evaluate past performance as well as individual or group capacity. The inability to commit the necessary resources to key strategic objectives has historically been the undoing of many organizations.

When we evaluate an organization's resource alignment, we determine if in fact they:

- Have adequate resources aligned with each critical action
- Determine the success and capacity of individuals or groups before expanding their workload
- Have clearly defined roles of individuals or groups within each action

One barrier to implementing strategy is the failure to link action plans and resource allocation to short and long-term strategic priorities.[1] Organizational business units need enough resources to contribute their part to the strategic intent of the firm. Resources include not only having sufficient budget, but also the correct, trained people to perform the tasks. Often, financial budgets are established through totally separate methods outside the strategic planning process. Actual budgets and expenses are often reviewed for variances against budgeted targets without regard for accomplishing the firm's intent.

How well a firm redirects its assets can make or break a strategy. Too little funding can slow or stop any progress made in achieving a firm's strategic intent, while too much allocation can waste precious resources and reduce financial returns. Careful attention must be paid to linking strategic goals with adequate resources needed to accomplish them.

Some strategic initiatives require substantial redirection of investment on the part of the firm. For example, Whirlpool Corporation's "Quality Express" initiatives outlined on-time, prompt delivery of product to 90 percent of Whirlpool's dealers network within 24 hours, and the rest with 48 hours. This initiative, geared towards providing superior customer service and maintaining customer satisfaction, required a huge logistics effort and a shift in capital and resources.

When supporting an increased budget to implement a new initiative, management ought to be prepared to justify any budget allocations in terms of contribution to the overall strategy. A cash flow budget can anticipate any cash shortfalls during the period of the initiative. A sample budget follows (Table 4.2):

Table 4.2 Sample Six-Month Cash Budget

Cash Budget [in 000's]
Desired level
of Cash Balance   5,000

	Month 1	Month 2	Month 3	Month 4	Month 5	Month 6	Total
Income							
Receipts	12,000	21,000	15,000	14,000	9,000	18,000	89,000
Other Income							0
Total Income	12,000	21,000	15,000	14,000	9,000	18,000	89,000
Expenses							
Purchases	10,500	18,000	13,500	12,000	7,000	12,000	73,000
Wages and Salaries	1,500	1,500	1,500	1,500	1,500	1,500	9,000
Rent	500	500	500	500	500	500	3,000
Other Expenses	250	300	350	200	450	125	1,675
Interest	100	100	100	100	100	100	600
Taxes		6				377	383
Total Expenses	12,850	20,406	15,950	14,300	9,550	14,602	87,658
Net Cash Gain [Loss]	(850)	594	(950)	(300)	(550)	3,398	1,342
Beginning Cash Balance	6,000	5,150	5,744	4,794	4,494	3,944	6,000
Cumulative Cash Balance	5,150	5,744	4,794	4,494	3,944	7,342	7,342
Cash Available [Required]	150	744	(206)	(506)	(1,056)	2,342	2,342

In the above example, the unit forecasting the cash flow based on its strategic implementation of the initiatives needs to allocate an additional one million dollars to cover its projected cash shortage during months three, four, and five. At the end of the period, there will be a surplus of cash available to repay the cash investment with a small return, presuming this unit contributes to the overall intent of the company, the investment is well worth the effort.

Another resource often overlooked is the necessary people-and-skills sets required to fulfill the strategic initiative. Too often, rewards and incentives are in direct opposition to strategic intents. No matter how well conceived a strategy may be, without incentives (or consequences) linked to its accomplishment, employees will have difficulty implementing it successfully. Assembling, motivating, and managing human resources is just as critical to a firm in achieving its strategic intent.

Finally, successful implementation requires the appropriate systems support. These systems have to be linked with the overall intent of the strategy. For example, in order to carry out its mission of next-day delivery, FedEx has a communication system that tracks every package in its transit delivery system. It can report instantly the last known whereabouts of any package. The system allows FedEx to coordinate its 21,000 vans nationwide who make an average of 720,000 stops per day.[2] Similarly, Procter & Gamble codes more than 900,000 phone calls it receives annually as an early warning indicator of product problems and changing consumer tastes.[3] No company can expect to execute its strategic intent without sufficient support systems already in place. Moreover, unusually good support systems can strengthen a firm and provide a competitive advantage in the marketplace.

Organization Accountabilities

"I have a duty to the soldiers, their parents, and the country to remove immediately any commander who does not satisfy the highest performance demands. It is a mistake to put a person in a command that is not the right command. It is therefore my job to think through where that person belongs."—General George C. Marshall

Organization accountabilities ensure that individuals and groups within the company have a clear understanding of management's expectations, and that they understand their specific roles in accomplishing critical objectives, initiatives, and goals.

Part of resource allocation is to match the skill sets, attitudes, and experience of the firm's workforce with the challenges and requirements of successfully implementing the organization's strategic intent. Inadequate support for the implementation of the strategic plan can undermine an organization's success. Key management team members must be personally committed to successful execution.

Perhaps the easiest way to overcome resistance to change and other human resource issues is to actively involve as many managers and employees as possible in the planning process. Although time-consuming, this approach builds understanding, trust, commitment, ownership, and cooperation.

Table 4.3 is a basic model that articulates specific accountabilities. It also provides the vehicle to invite participation between managers and employees to craft solutions to strategic requirements. It also serves as an effective communication vehicle for rank and file.

Putting together a strong team to execute the strategy is a fundamental step toward successful execution. Rarely will an organization possess all the skill sets, aptitudes, and experience required to implement a new strategic direction or turn around an existing one. Filling these key positions and delegating ownership of initiatives is part of the strategic process. Recruiting people with the correct mix of culture, experience, expertise, values, and management styles to reinforce and support the strategic goals of the organization is key to success.

Training and retraining are additional options that can reinforce a strategy requiring new skill sets or operating methods. Training budgets, programs, and schedules should be part of the strategic plan for execution. Training needs to begin early in the execution phase and should be a priority objective.

Once they're trained and given a complete understanding of their roles and responsibilities, as they relate to the overall strategic intent of the company, management and employee performance should be tracked against milestones, time frames, and initiatives, established in the action planning process.

Table 4.3 Basic Accountability Model

Goal or Task	Priority	Person(s) or Group Responsible	Begin Date	Milestones or Due Date	Outcome or Results

By reporting progress through an enterprisewide system, an organization can remain responsive and active to changing environmental dynamics while ensuring that performance is aligned with the organization's overall intent.

Measurement

Effective measurement means demonstrating consistency when tracking or reporting performance. Using an effective and uniform measurement process for financial reporting, project management, third-party performance, and operating standards. It ensures that there is an ongoing process for improvement.

Measuring strategic performance provides the mechanism to communicate the degree of success that the company is experiencing as it achieves its strategic intent. Failure to reach certain milestones or performance levels signals a need to reevaluate the organization's assumption base and operating practices of its strategy. External factors, policies, vendors, and ineffective management can all contribute to poor performance.

The Huntington District of the U.S. Army Corps of Engineers values good information through effective measurement. They employ a fully integrated approach to identifying which key metrics are required to measure and report their strategic and operating performance. They have also begun a Web-enabled "dashboard" to visually report and track their business performance. Figure 4.2 is a screen capture of the "dashboard" they selected. While Huntington would be the first to admit that they are still tracking too many business performance numbers, having a common platform and reporting system creates a consistent language and approach to reporting mission-critical business information.

There are several good Web-based business information systems for reporting business and strategic performance. The Huntington District lined up a service provider that listened well to their clients and localized the system to support the District needs. If at all possible, attempt to adopt a common language and format to report cross-department, cross-functional performance. When we evaluate an organization's ability to measure performance effectively, we examine their use of:

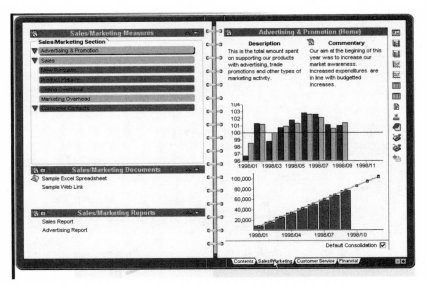

Figure 4.2

- Financial ratios such as return on assets, return on equity, gross profit, gross margin, current ratio, quick ratio, inventory to net working capital, debt to assets, debt to equity, times-interest earned, fixed charge coverage, inventory turnover, fixed asset turnover, total asset turnover, accounts receivable turnover, average collection period, etc. It is important to recognize that many industry verticals have a specific set of metrics.
- Project management and process controls.
- Individual, group, or partner goal setting and management.
- The use of technology-based solutions (i.e., management reporting systems, key performance indicators tied to dashboard, etc.).

The biggest challenge in evaluating performance is ensuring that what is being measured is drawn specifically from the critical success factors of the organization. It is critically important that the company prioritize what it wants to examine, track, and report in terms of having the most significant impact on the enterprise. Aside from financial ratios, other factors, such as work climate, production quality, and customer satisfaction, can all be good indicators of success. Care should be given that dependence on only a few metrics be avoided. Such one-sided metrics can allow a business to show good progress in the measured activity while drifting away from the overall strategy.

Kaplan and Norton[4] give a good example of a firm's using on-time delivery to rate increased customer satisfaction, a direct strategic initiative. By only focusing on OTD, the firm may invest large amounts of capital-producing finished goods to assure customer satisfaction. While pleasing the customer, the firm may encounter higher shipping, storage, and handling expenses, as well as the threat of obsolete inventory.

The following table illustrates one method to summarize the key items to measure against one's strategy (Table 4.4 below). There are multiple subsets that fall under each of the bullet points. However, a company must review these areas and determine whether they are meeting minimum standards of strategic performance measurement.

Table 4.5 illustrates a simplified report that tracks the current status of performance indicators to a firm's strategy.[6] These indicators report progress after two years of a five-year strategy intended to differentiate the firm as a customer-service-oriented provider of high-quality products. When evaluating performance, management should compare expected results with actual progress. Any negative deviations should form the basis of additional action planning or adjustments to the overall initiative.

Table 4.4 Measuring Business Strategy[5]

Perspective	Generic Measures
Financial	• Revenue growth and mix • Cost reduction/productivity improvement • Asset utilization/investment strategy
Customer	• Share • Customer retention • Customer acquisition • Customer satisfaction • Profitability
Internal	• Quality • Response time • Cost • New product introductions
Learning and Growth	• Employee satisfaction • Employee retention • Employee productivity

Table 4.5 Sample Monitoring and Performance Evaluation for a Differentiated Firm

Key Success Factors	Objective, Assumption, or Budget	Forecast Performance at This Time	Current Performance	Current Deviation	Analysis
Cost Control: Ratio of indirect overhead costs to direct field and labor costs	10%	15%	12%	+3% [ahead]	Are we moving too fast, or is there more unnecessary overhead than was originally thought?
Gross Profit	39%	40%	40%	0%	
Customer Service: Installation cycle in days	2.5 days	3.2 days	2.7 days	+0.5 days [ahead]	Can this progress be maintained?
Ratio of service to sales personnel	3.2	2.7	2.1	−0.6 [behind]	Why are we behind here? How can we maintain the installation-cycle progress?
Product Quality: Percentage of products returned	1.0%	2.0%	2.1%	−0.1% [behind]	Why are we behind here? What are the ramifications for other operations?

Measure				Variance	Comments
Product performance versus specification	100%	92%	80%	−12% [behind]	
Marketing: Monthly sales per employee	$12,500	$11,500	$12,100	+$600 [ahead]	Good progress. Is it creating any problems to support?
Expansion of product line	6	3	5	+2 products [ahead]	Are the products ready? Are the perfect standards met?
Employee morale in service area: Absenteeism rate	2.5%	3.0%	3.0%	On target	Looks like a problem! Why are we so far behind?
Turnover rate	5%	10%	15%	−5% [behind]	
Competition: New product introductions [average number]	6	6	3	−3 [behind]	Did we underestimate timing? What are the implications for our basic assumptions?

What to Do

This chapter is all about execution. Once you have determined a strategic direction for your organization, an action plan must be created to provide the organization with a specific course of action.

Set Your Vital Direction

Upon the completion of your strategic planning formulation, you shift to the development of the plan itself. Many companies create a narrative to communicate their process and general sense of where the plan is taking them. For the purpose of our discussion—execution—we suggest that you draft a comprehensive plan that includes seven critical elements:

1. *Strategic Business Goal*—Your strategic business goals represent a high-level component that is tied to the strategic intent of your organization. There may be more than one, but generally not more than six. Your business goals set the overriding direction for your objectives, initiatives, and goals.
2. *Objective*—This is a key component supporting the Strategic Business Goal. Your objectives are broad descriptions of a specific set of actions that can be measured.
3. *Resources*—These articulate which departments, people, or other necessary factors are required to support the objective. This is an area where organizations often make their greatest mistakes. This comes in the form of insufficient or no resources necessary to support the objective or achieve the goal.
4. *Ownership*—Who owns it? Accountability must be embedded in every action plan. The owner accepts responsibility for the objective. It is that person's role to see that timelines are kept, resources are available, communication is maintained, and that the overall goal is achieved.
5. *Milestones*—Milestones are the mission-critical steps to achieving the goal. These tactical items communicate to the management team and the organization what activities need to take place in order to satisfy the plan and the needs of the company.
6. *Due Dates*—Due dates comprise the target completion timeline for each milestone.
7. *Goals and Measurement*—This column draws the "finish line." When plans are established, there must be a clearly communicated measure

that represents successful completion of the objective. Items in this column can include financial performance, percentage of growth, ROI, or any other quantifiable measure that represents the fulfillment of the objective.

Ensure that the Necessary Resources Are Aligned against Each Objective

The key to successful execution is the right resource aligned against the right objective. The first question to be answered is have I identified the appropriate mix of capital, human, technology, and physical resources to support the objective? When the people equation is being determined, be sure not only that the correct skill sets are in place, but equally important is to ensure that the individual or group has the capacity to support the objective given their current workload.

Accountability Must Be a Cornerstone within Your Plan

Each objective must have an owner! Ownership translates into responsibility. An owner provides management with a "go to" person to determine the status of any given objective. The owner is also responsible for managing the resources placed against the objective. They coordinate the corporate effort to achieve all goals related to their piece of the plan. Accountability implies that there are consequences associated with the role. If the objective is met and the goals are achieved, there should be a corresponding reward for success. On the other hand, should the objective not be met and the goals not achieved, there should be a corresponding adverse consequence associated with the lack of success. This is a cultural issue as much as a process and management challenge.

Everything Should Be Measurable

Measurement is your litmus test. If you can't measure it, it should not be in your action plan. Quantifiable measures include financial performance, percentages of growth or reduction, as well as units associated with growth or reduction. Sales efforts, efficiencies, manpower, processes, and leadership can all be measured. Additionally, invest in a mechanism that can report *key performance indicators*. This mechanism can serve as your "dashboard" to track and monitor your progress against your plan. Remember— inspect what you expect.

Our closing thoughts as we wrap up this chapter as well as the section of the book on strategy, is this—forming a successful strategy to achieve your intended business outcomes requires commitment and patience. It may be months or longer before the benefits are realized. Stay the course, but maintain a high level of intensity around the specific actions that were derived from your planning effort. As this chapter has attempted to point out, "it's all about execution."

The next section of this book (Organization Design) challenges you and your management team to determine whether your structure, competence, systems, and processes are aligned with your strategy. No one said that being the best in business is easy—but it sure pays off when you are.

Organization Design

"Organizing is what you do before you do something, so that when you do it, it is not mixed all up."

—A. A. MILNE

Organization Design is the infrastructure imposed by management that employees must contend with in order to do their jobs. *Design elements* include the creation of the organizational hierarchy, development of communication systems, use of technology, crafting policies and procedures, and defining job descriptions. Organizational infrastructures will either facilitate or impede a company's ability to achieve its strategic goals. The challenge for the senior executives of any organization is to combine structure and systems effectively into an efficient, responsive configuration that not only supports but also drives strategic intent.

Organization Design goes well beyond setting up the hierarchical structure. Design also includes establishing controls and protocols, such as how the firm will communicate with its stakeholders, what information technology will be required, what policies and procedures will be enforced, and what roles and responsibilities will be expected from positions throughout the company.

Organization Design also encompasses identifying which competencies will be developed internally and which should be outsourced to strategic partners. With the demands of the current marketplace, it is becoming increasingly difficult to be "all things to all people." Today, it makes more sense for companies to concentrate on developing skills that can truly become organizational core competencies, and to rely on outsourcing for other capabilities that will be necessary to secure an advantage in the marketplace.

An emerging company may have an easier time setting up or revising their organization infrastructure than a mature company. Start-ups have, essentially, a clean slate where they can begin to develop and clarify their strategy, design, and culture. Even the youngest or smallest companies should pay close attention to these factors. In our experience, both as consultants and with our own company, it is surprising how quickly a company can begin to lose focus without the elements of strategy, design, and culture being clearly defined and practiced. When a smaller company elects to outsource its human resources processes, this is not just a financial decision, it is a decision to remain focused on what really matters. The young company is essentially saying, "You prepare the payroll checks. We'll concentrate on creating and selling products."

An established company faces the additional challenge of modifying its existing—and probably deep-rooted—structure and systems in order to adapt and succeed as its industry evolves. But regardless of a company's age, size, or industry, its ability to evaluate and modify its organizational design consistently will impact its success in achieving its strategic intent. Dale McConkey, Professor of Sociology at Berry College in Georgia, states, "A management truism says structure follows strategy. However, this truism is often ignored. Too many organizations attempt to carry out a new strategy with an old structure."

Organization Design is by its nature a work in progress. These days, the competitive landscape changes rapidly. It used to be that if you wanted a home loan, you went to a bank or broker. Now you can have several lenders instantly compete for your business over the Internet. If a lender tried to compete using the same structure they had in place 10 years ago, they would be in serious jeopardy of extinction. Smart senior managers continually monitor their structure and systems to evaluate whether the current design allows them to compete effectively. Management must remain ready and willing to make design changes that support the long-term success of the enterprise.

In 1985, HP began to reverse its long-standing practice of allowing its units to operate as independent companies, each having its own manufacturing, marketing, finance, and other functional departments. By having control at the local level, unit managers could set their own product volume and quality levels. But the downward pressure on prices as the PC market matured made this costly design strategy inappropriate. HP consolidated manufacturing into a few sites and put the entire production department under control of a single manager.

Under their previous design, HP manufactured three different computers that were incompatible with one another, although they were marketed to the same target customer. The three business units acted as if they were competitors. In 1987, HP consolidated these divisions and mandated that all products share technology and be cross-compatible.[1]

The following four guidelines can be helpful in ensuring that design follows strategy:[2]

1. Pinpoint the primary activities and key tasks in the value chain (R and D, production, marketing, sales, and service) that are pivotal to successful strategy execution, and make them the main building blocks in the organizational structure.
2. Whenever it doesn't make organizational sense to group all facets of a strategy-related activity under a single manager, establish ways to bridge departmental lines and achieve the necessary coordination.

3. Determine the degrees of authority needed to manage each organizational unit, endeavoring to strike an effective balance between capturing the advantages of both centralization and decentralization.
4. Determine whether noncritical activities can be outsourced more efficiently or effectively than they can be performed internally.

Without a strategic point of reference, designing the organization would be a meaningless venture. *Organization Design* and everything that goes with it must be crafted to facilitate the strategic pursuit of an organization. Understanding the dynamics of the relationship between design and strategy is a key factor in accomplishing a company's goals.

We explore this content in the following chapters:

Basic Structure:
Does your structure make sense, given your strategic intent?

Core Competence:
What is your organization particularly good at, and how can you leverage this set of skills?

Information, Systems, and Technology:
Are you getting information in the hands of people who need it? Do you have the right technology in place?

Organization Efficiency:
Do you have well-defined policies and procedures? Do your employees understand how their roles contribute to the big picture? Do you manage your strategic partners and outsource relationships with the same high standard with which you manage yourself?

CHAPTER

Basic Structure

"The ideal organizational structure is a place where ideas filter up as well as down, where the merit of the idea carries more weight than their source, and where participation and shared objectives are valued more than executive orders."

—Edson Spencer

Former Honeywell CEO and Rhodes Scholar

DOES YOUR CURRENT structure make sense? This is the central question of this chapter. Do you believe that your company's hierarchy and infrastructure facilitate or impede the pursuit of your strategic intent and organizational excellence? Are divisions and departments reporting to the appropriate managers? What impact does your current structure have on your ability to make quick decisions and to deliver goods or services to the marketplace faster and better than your competition? Are you experiencing any bottlenecks? If you are not sure about the answers to these questions... find out! Ask your customers, your employees, and your managers. It would be foolish to drive critical strategic initiatives through a structure that feels like an obstacle course to your employees.

Basic Structure looks at whether a company's organizational design is conducive to achieving its strategic intent. It evaluates an organization's chain of command, systems, and policies in relation to the demands of its strategic plan. A key factor in this analysis is to take into consideration whether a company's structure is politically or strategically driven.

After formulating an organization's strategy, senior executives must concentrate on designing an organizational structure that supports and advances this strategy. Strategic activities need to be coordinated between functional departments. Effective structures will help to eliminate, or at least reduce, myopic "silo" thinking.

A typical research and development department focuses on creativity and innovation in developing new products or services. Traditional marketing and sales departments are concerned with promoting and selling products and services to the marketplace. If left functionally isolated in their respective silos, these two departments will discover few synergies between themselves. In fact, they may inadvertently work against themselves, which leads to frustration and finger pointing. Marketing and sales departments are notorious for making promises that R and D and production can't fulfill. If, however, organizational design encourages collaboration and effective communication between departments, marketing and sales may be more inclined to keep customer expectations under control, while R and D and production may be more inclined create and deliver products with a greater appreciation of the revenue demands the other departments must deal with.

There is no one correct way to structure an organization. Most organization charts are unique, based on the product or service offering, means of delivery, and the vertical markets the company serves. Structure can be a product of the company's established pattern for doing business. It sometimes reflects past and current bias toward reporting relationships, personnel politics, and other internal circumstances. Because every strategy is conceived amidst its own set of key success factors and own value-chain activities, the company structures that support them will differ as well.

Organizational structures take many forms. They may be organic, evolving without formal design or planning, or they may reflect well-planned and designed architecture. In either case, structures contain mechanisms that facilitate or impede the development and execution of the firm's strategic intent and the means in which the enterprise develops, supports, and coordinates the business of marketing its products or services.

These mechanisms include:[1]

1. Hierarchical reporting relationships
2. Policies, standard operating procedures, and control systems
3. Information systems and flow of information moving through the organization

Depending on the size of the organization, the structural map or organizational chart may illustrate the functional roles of individuals and depart-

Figure 5.1 Basic Organization Chart

ments. The structure above (Figure 5.1) reflects a typical organization chart for most public companies.

Regardless of the size of the enterprise, these basic components are represented to some extent in virtually every company. In smaller companies, many of these functional responsibilities may reside with a single individual or a small number of individuals. As the organization grows, additional functional roles, such as production, purchasing, and so on, might be added. Those responsible for these key functions would in most cases constitute the executive team in the organization. The table below (Table 5.1) highlights some of the activities that fall within the traditional functional areas of an organization.

The appropriate organizational structure will prioritize and support these strategy-related activities. The structure should be flexible enough to yield to new market influences or changes in the operating environment. The right structure will enhance efficiency, reduce costs, promote collaboration and cooperation, and increase shareholder value.

We divide the discussion of *Basic Structure* into two sections:

- **Structure Criteria**
- **Structure Evolution**

Structure Criteria: Form Follows Function

"At about $50 million, I felt I could run it. . . . I could name everybody in the company. But as it grew larger, I found myself stretched. One Friday night at 11 P.M., I realized that if there wasn't a change, I'd have to stop sleeping within six months to keep up the pace.—T. J. Rodgers, President and CEO, Cypress Semiconductor Corp.

Is your current organizational structure conducive to your company's strategy? When a strategic initiative is implemented, does senior management consider how the current organizational infrastructure, systems, and proce-

Table 5.1 Basic Organization Structure Functional Components[2]

Executive Team	Finance	Human Resource	Research and Development	Operations	Marketing/ Sales
• Business Planning	• Financial Management	• Recruitment	• Creativity and Innovation	• Production	• Marketing Research
• Capital Structure	• Capital Acquisition	• Orientation	• Product and Process Design	• Fulfillment	• Collateral Development
• Resource Allocation	• Accounts Payable and Receivable	• Training	• Assess Competitive Research and Development Environment	• Customer Service	• Direct Sales
• Corporate Strategy	• Payroll	• Performance Management		• Purchasing	• Customer Relations
	• Investments	• Reward Systems		• Information Systems	• Channel Management

dures will impact the new strategy, or does management simply force business activities through a structure that may not be designed or positioned to support them?

Does your organizational structure help to facilitate the *value chain* activities of research and development, production, marketing, sales, and service? Does the way in which your company is organized encourage communication and teamwork between employees from different areas who may need to cooperate together on common projects? The answers to these questions will impact your ability to get things done in your organization.

When we evaluate *structure criteria*, we look at an organization's ability to:

1. Recognize that organizational structure impacts implementation and achievement of a strategic plan.
2. Ensure that the organization structure is not influenced by company politics.
3. Establish a chain of command that is conducive to the activities and key tasks associated with the *value chain*.
4. Develop a structure that promotes collaboration and coordination between departments.

There are five formal approaches to structure (Table 5.2): functional, geographic, divisional lines of business or product, strategic business unit, and a matrix structure. In addition, companies can be centralized or decentralized along these traditional lines.

It is important to mention that resource allocation is often dictated by the organization's structure. If an organization is structured along functional lines, resources will usually be deployed within those functional areas. Someone who is in charge of the functional domain will vie for resources during budget time, based on strategic need, and then deploy the budget according to functional needs. The danger here is that the focus shifts towards functional success—meeting divisional goals—which can lead to the "silo" thinking discussed earlier. This can be a tough paradigm to shake if the strategic direction shifts and resources need to be reallocated.

What About Politics?—A Case Study

A financial company had a service center, which was managed by a woman who had been with the company for more than 30 years. In Covey's termi-

Table 5.2 Five Formal Organization Structures[3]

Type	Description
Functional Structure	• Small-size, single product line • Undifferentiated market • Scale or expertise within the function • Long product development and life cycles • Common standards • Hybrids in large organizations may follow structure by division or business unit
Product or Line of Business Structure	• Product focused • Multiple products for separate customers • Short product development and life cycle • Minimum efficient scale for functions or outsourcing
Business Unit Structure	• Important market segments • Product or service unique to segment • Buyer strength • Customer knowledge advantage • Rapid customer service and product cycles • Minimum efficient scale in functions or outsourcing
Geographical Structures	• Low value-to-transport cost ratio • Service delivery on site • Closeness to customer for delivery or support • Perception of the organization as local • Geographical market segments needed
Matrix Structure	• Seen as an alternative to the functional structure • Potential for new processes and radical change to processes • Reduced working capital • Often put in place when there is a need for reducing process cycle times

nology, she was firmly entrenched in the "scientific authoritarian" style of management. (See Chapter 10.) She ran the department with an iron fist. It would never occur to her to say so much as "good morning" to any of her staff of 100—although she did reserve this minor courtesy to her two assistant managers, who, not surprisingly, behaved almost exactly like her. Policies were delivered as impersonal edicts passed out in memo format that inevitably began with the phrase, "Effective immediately..." Over time, the situation deteriorated, resulting in a host of employee relations issues and customer complaints—all related to the hostile work environment. And still the woman was allowed to run her organization without any interference. She was immovable. Why? She was a close friend with a person who over the years had eventually become president of the company. She had friends in high places. Her position and her department had significant strategic impact, yet she and her department were allowed to operate, without change, year after year.

Organizational politics are in plain view. Employees quickly learn who is connected to influential people at a company. Too often, these relationships may alter objectivity. What happens when politics prevent the changes in the organizational hierarchy that are necessary to drive strategic intent? Political influences can lead to poor decisions that decrease the strategic advantages of a well-conceived structure.

Organizational structures must reflect strategic rather than political thinking. Changes in structure that cannot be specifically tied to strategic intent are most likely being driven by personal preferences and politics. These types of structural decisions lead to cynicism and create distractions that erode the organization's focus.

Incidentally, the manager at the service center was eventually replaced with someone much more effective. She was removed shortly after the president retired.

Formal Structures: Advantages and Disadvantages

The five formal organizational structures from earlier in this chapter are used as a reference point for designing an organization. Companies may evolve from one structure to another, either as a product of growth or industry influences. Depending on the new strategic intent or changes in the environment, some of these formal structures can be adopted whenever strategically necessary.

By understanding the relationship of the five structures to a company's strategic intent, senior managers can select the format that they believe will provide them with the greatest chance of success. Each of the structures has inherent advantages and disadvantages. The following table (Table 5.3) illustrates the general pros and cons.

Table 5.3 Five Organization Structures—Advantages/Disadvantages[4]

Type	Strategic Advantages	Strategic Disadvantages
Functional	• Centralized control of strategic results. • Very well suited for structuring a single business. • Structure is linked tightly to strategy by designating key activities as functional departments. • Promotes in-depth functional expertise. • Well suited to developing functional skills and functional-based competencies. • Conducive to exploiting learning/experience curve effects associated with functional specialization. • Enhances operating efficiency where tasks are routine and repetitive.	• Excessive fragmentation of strategy-critical processes. • Can lead to interfunctional rivalry and conflict, rather than team play and cooperation—GM must referee. • Multilayered management bureaucracies and centralized decision making slow response time. • Hinders development of managers with cross-functional experience because the ladder of advancement is up the ranks within the same functional area. • Forces profit responsibility to the top. • Functional specialists often attach more importance to what's best for the functional area than to what's best for the whole business—can lead to functional empire building. • Functional myopia often works against creative entrepreneurship, adapting to change, and attempts to create cross-functional core—functional core competencies.
Decentralized Line of Business [Product or Service]	• Offers a logical and workable means of decentralizing responsibility and delegating authority in diversified organizations. • Puts responsibility for business strategy in closer proximity to each business's unique environment. • Allows each business unit to organize around its own value chain system, key activities, and functional requirements. • Frees CEO to handle corporate strategy issues.	• May lead to costly duplication of staff functions at corporate and business-unit levels, thus raising administrative overhead costs. • Poses a problem of what decisions to centralize and what decisions to decentralize (business managers need enough authority to get the job done, but not so much that corporate management loses control of key business-level decisions). • May lead to excessive division rivalry for corporate resources and attention.

- Business/division autonomy works against achieving coordination of related activities in different business units, thus blocking to some extent the capture of strategic-fit benefits.
- Corporate management becomes heavily dependent on business unit managers.
- Corporate managers can lose touch with business–unit situations, end up surprised when problems arise, and not know much about how to fix such problems.

- Puts clear profit/loss accountability on shoulders of business-unit managers.

Strategic Business Units

- Provides a strategically relevant way to organize the business-unit portfolio of a broadly diversified company.
- Facilitates the coordination of related activities within an SBU, thus helping to capture the benefits of strategic fits in the SBU.
- Promotes more cohesiveness among the new initiatives of separate but related businesses.
- Allows strategic planning to be done at the most relevant level within the total enterprise.
- Makes the task of strategic review by top executives more objective and more effective.
- Helps allocate corporate resources to areas with greatest growth opportunities.

- It is easy for the definition and grouping of businesses into SBUs to be so arbitrary that the SBU serves no other purpose than administrative convenience. If the criteria for defining SBUs are rationalizations and have little to do with the nitty-gritty of strategy coordination, then the groupings lose real strategic significance.
- The SBUs can still be myopic in charting their future direction.
- Adds another layer to top management.
- The roles and authority of the CEO, the group vice president, and the business-unit manager have to be carefully worked out or the group vice president gets trapped in the middle with ill-defined authority.
- Unless the SBU head is strong willed, very little strategy coordination is likely to occur across business units in the SBU.
- Performance recognition gets blurred; credit for successful business units tends to go to corporate CEO, then to business-unit head, last to group vice president.

(*continued*)

Table 5.3 Five Organization Structures—Advantages/Disadvantages[4] (*Continued*)

Type	Strategic Advantages	Strategic Disadvantages
Geographic	• Allows tailoring of strategy to needs of each geographical market. • Delegates profit/loss responsibility to lowest strategic level. • Improves functional coordination within target market. • Takes advantage of economies of local operations. • Area units make an excellent training ground for higher-level general managers.	• Poses a problem of how much geographic uniformity headquarters should impose versus how much geographic diversity should be allowed. • Greater difficulty in maintaining consistent company image/reputation from area to area when area managers exercise much strategic freedom. • Adds another layer of management to run geographic units. • Can result in duplication of staff services at headquarters and district levels, creating cost disadvantages.
Matrix	• Gives formal attention to each dimension of strategic priority. • Creates checks and balances among competing viewpoints. • Facilitates capture of functionally-based strategic fits in diversified companies. • Promotes making trade-off decisions on the basis of "what's best for the organization as a whole." • Encourages cooperation, consensus building, conflict resolution, and coordination of related activities.	• Very complex to manage. • Hard to maintain "balance" between the two lines of authority. • So much shared authority can result in transactions logjam and disproportionate amounts of time being spent on communications. • It is hard to move quickly and decisively without getting clearance from many other people. • Promotes an organizational bureaucracy and hamstrings creative entrepreneurship.

It is important to recognize that these structures are rarely implemented in their purest forms. In practice, each company should adjust, expand, and combine structures to optimize its efficiency. As the organization evolves, growth in the structure can come horizontally or vertically. Horizontal growth is a result of adding and promoting additional functional or divisional responsibilities to the executive level. Vertical growth comes from establishing additional levels in the organizational hierarchy.

Organizations with a relatively large number of reporting levels are described as being relatively tall, and those with fewer levels as relatively flat. Flat organizations traditionally have wide spans of control, are decentralized, and have lower administrative costs. Tall organizations generally have better communication and coordination and are typically centrally directed.

Applying Structure Criteria: Making Strategic Sense

Matching structure to strategy occurs when strategy-critical activities provide the foundation for *organization design*. The measure of effectiveness regarding a company's structure is relatively simple: Does the structure support the strategic direction of the company, or does it get in the way? The following questions (Table 5.4) can assist in assessing the strategic appropriateness of a firm's structure.

Structure Evolution

"The single biggest problem in business is staying with your previously successful business model one year too long."—Lew Platt, Former Chairman of Hewlett-Packard

In their book, *Integrated Strategic Change,* Worley, Hitchin, and Ross explain that as companies move from one strategy to another, they must also shift the organizational format from the current structure to a new structure that is conducive to the new strategy. In other words, any significant movement strategy requires a similar adjustment in organizational structure. (See Figure 5.2.)

Organizations must remain reasonably flexible so that they can react when emerging opportunities or dynamic events within the industry call for change. Is your organizational design flexible? Could you adapt to modified structures like matrixes or self-directed teams to take advantage of a market opportunity or to deal with a threat? Would your senior management team

Table 5.4 Checklist for Determining Appropriateness of Organizational Structure[5]

1. Is the structure compatible with the corporate profile and the corporate strategy?	A single business company can easily adopt a functional structure. As it grows, however, the functional nature of its structure may become limiting. A product or divisional structure would be more appropriate.
2. At the corporate level, is the structure compatible with the outputs of the firm's business units?	The outputs of an organization can influence structure, depending on how customers purchase them. Culturally dependent items such as shoes and clothing would respond to a geographic structure while more universal products such as screws, bolts, and tools could be more suited to a product structure.
3. Are there too few or too many hierarchical levels at either the corporate or business-unit level of analysis?	Flat organizations tend to favor dynamic, fast growing, or changing environments and strategies, while more traditionally tall, multilevel organizations offer more stability and tighter spans of control. For larger corporations, not all divisions need to have the same substructure. Managers should understand that business units can and should respond to their own environments.
4. Does the structure promote coordination among its parts?	Depending on how an organization supports its core competencies, a company may need to coordinate most of its strategy-related activities across functions and divisions. If the company is a small or single business enterprise, then cross-functional coordination may simply involve good information systems. For conglomerates whose businesses are all related to their core business, a matrix or team-oriented structure may be appropriate.
5. Does the structure allow for appropriate centralization or decentralization of authority?	The traditional evolution of a company is from a centralized organization to a decentralized one. Smaller companies tend to make decisions for the entire enterprise from one source, while large corporations with a multidivisional or business-unit structure tend to leave control at the local level. The relative stability of the environment also plays a role in this decision. Stable environments favor centralized structures, while dynamic ones usually require faster decisions facilitated by a decentralized structure.
6. Does the structure permit the appropriate grouping of activities?	The nature of products may affect how a company groups activities. If the firm sells closely related products such as computer products, then it might serve the customer best by grouping the activities around sets of related products. Some would argue that groups should control the entire value chain related to a set of products, claiming it is difficult to hold a product manager responsible if he or she does not control production and design as well.

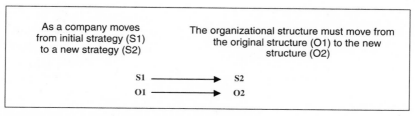

Figure 5.2 Integrated Strategic Change Model[6]

be willing to make structural changes to support and strengthen your company, even if it meant losing some of their corporate empire?

When we evaluate *structure evolution,* we consider an organization's ability to:

1. Modify its organization structure when market factors dictate the need to do so
2. Ensure that the structure supports innovation and change
3. Demonstrate a willingness on the part of management to reorganize divisions or departments, when necessary, to achieve its strategic intent

Although changes in strategy may affect the strategy of an organization, outside forces can also influence the firm's overall design. No organization can be expected to change its structure quickly in response to every market scenario. But organizational structures do not remain static. As strategy shifts render the organization's existing structure ineffective, change becomes imperative. Symptoms of an ineffective structure may include too many levels of management, too much time-resolving conflicts between departments, too many people assigned to one manager, and of course, too many unrealized goals and initiatives.

A company's structure and its ability—or inability—to respond to market change can influence its strategic choices. Say, for example, a company was considering a strategic opportunity, but the opportunity would require a massive reorganization to the information technology division resulting in significant additional costs and delays in current IT projects. This scenario might not represent an attractive or even reasonable choice.

Designing a structure that is flexible enough to grow and evolve with the organization is critically important. As companies develop from small, one-man shops into more complex organizations, their structures tend to evolve from one person with multiple responsibilities, to functional departments, to product or divisional specialization, to decentralized business units. Knowing when to make such changes is an organization's biggest structural challenge.

IBM in the early 1990s is a good example of a firm that had to overcome political and cultural obstacles in order to regain its performance luster. One of the world's largest and most successful firms, IBM recorded its first loss in its history in 1991, $2.8 billion. For years, IBM[7] stuck to its tried and tested structure. The environment had changed, booming with technological discoveries and innovation. IBM's competitors were more flexible, aggressive, and customer oriented. Their margins were high, typical of first-to-market innovators, while IBM was consistently shut out at the gate.

IBM's traditional culture and structure combined to slow the giant down. All major decisions were made at headquarters in New York, which had, as its number one policy, forbidden internal competition with its flagship mainframe business. As a result of this political and culturally inspired policy, IBM was 4 years behind Apple with their personal computers, 5 years behind Toshiba in the laptop market, and 11 years behind Digital Equipment in breaking into the minicomputer market.

To turn the company around, top management restructured the company into semiautonomous profit centers. For the first time in its 70-year history, IBM reduced its workforce by 160,000 and its payroll by 40 percent, with most of the cuts coming in managerial and staff positions. Finally, IBM streamlined its research and development department, reducing the organization's time to market.

W.L. Gore and Associates provides an excellent example of staying flexible and permitting the organization to grow. The company is the maker of Gore-Tex fabric and other laminated materials.[8] The company has no formal structure, choosing instead to enjoy a flexible lattice structure with associates, not employees, who are empowered to make critical decisions. The company has direct lines of communication, no fixed or assigned authority, sponsors rather than bosses, team leadership, and tasks and functions organized through commitments.

Its structure has evolved to include several business units that have grown organically as the market opportunities arose. The lattice structure has been put to the test several times, including during a crisis when the first generation of Gore-Tex failed to keep a mountain climber warm. The company remedied the technical problems in less than a month and recalled all the existing merchandise in their distribution channels to effect the change.

Other structure policies include having not more than 200 associates at any plant. These policies evolved when Bill Gore realized one day while walking around a plant, that he did not know everyone's name. Emphasizing close-knit, flat structures that employ good communication and responsiveness is a hallmark of Gore-Tex's strategy.

Key to Gore-Tex's success, and that of other companies like them, is a culture that promotes willingness to change. Today's fast, demanding marketplace requires an understanding of the strategic need for change. All organizational factors, including structure, must be in place for the organization to take advantage of that changing environment.[9]

Alfred Chandler describes the evolutionary process of structure as a cyclical mechanism triggered by administrative problems arising from implementation of a new strategy. As structural responses are given to ease the implementation, a new formal structure evolves. Figure 5.3 summarizes Chandler's model.

A company's ability to maintain a reasonably flexible, fluid organizational structure has become a key competitive factor. The market demands quick responses to competitive forces. An organizational structure must support strategic intent while remaining flexible enough to deal with emerging trends.

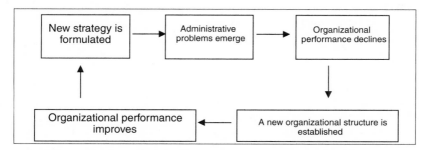

Figure 5.3 Chandler's Stategy Evolution[10]

Every company, no matter its size, must answer the simple question of whether its current structure makes sense. Does the current structure enhance or impede the organization's ability to create, produce, market, sell, and support its goods and services?

In the next chapter, we look at why identifying and leveraging core competencies remain as fundamental steps for creating and sustaining competitive advantage.

Identifying and Leveraging Core Competence

"Perhaps the most important lesson we learned is that mergers are mostly about three things: managing change . . . articulating a vision . . . and inspiring people."

—HUGH L. McCOLL, JR., MARCH 25, 1999,

UNIVERSITY OF TAMPA

WHEN HUGH McCOLL became chief executive of the predecessor of NationsBank in 1983, (NCNB—North Carolina National Bank), which ultimately became Bank of America, the bank had $12 billion in assets, $8 billion in deposits, and a market capitalization of $700 million. The company operated in two states, employed 7600 associates, and generated net income of $92 million.

When he retired in April of 2001, Bank of America had $610 billion in assets, $352 billion in deposits, $48.9 billion in shareholders' equity, operating net income for 2000 of $7.9 billion, and a market capitalization of $87.7 billion, making it one of the most highly valued financial services companies in the country and in the world. The company now operates retail branches in 21 states and the District of Columbia, employs more than 142,000 associates, and has relationships with more than 30 million retail and business customers in the United States and 37 other countries.[1]

We're not sure if Hugh McColl sat down with his management team in 1983 and asked the direct question, "what core competencies do you think we need to become *The Nation's Bank?*" However, we do know that when he crafted the bank's vision, the finish line would be measured by being "the Nation's Bank." This vision put Hugh McColl and his team at NCNB on an 18-year path resulting in the acquisition of Bank of America in 1998. *Who da thunk it?* For those of us who have been close to the banking industry, if you would have told us that Bank of America, one of the United States' largest and oldest financial institutions, was going to be acquired by a bank located in the southeastern part of the states, and that headquarters was going to be moved from San Francisco to Charlotte, North Carolina, we would have all said that you were nuts! But that is exactly what happened. Hugh McColl and his team charted a course in 1983 and realized the vision in 1998.

Where do core competencies tie in to this discussion? First, let's examine the question that Mr. McColl would have asked his team: "We know where we want to go, now, how do we get there?" Potential choices could have been:

1. Organic growth
2. Mergers and acquisitions
3. A combination

Each scenario would call for a defined set of skills or competencies.

Understanding Core Competencies

Core competencies are defined as the skills, knowledge, and special abilities that a company possesses that set it apart from other organizations. By effectively bundling these skills, knowledge, and special abilities, a company can create their competitive advantage, enhance customer value, and expand their market position.

In the case of NationsBank, they clearly chose the mergers and acquisition path. They merged or acquired 52 banks over a 15-year period. Imagine the systems integration challenge alone. Any one bank may have hundreds of different systems supporting lending, bank services, asset management, human resources, etc. This choice represents one formidable challenge.

One of management's most important tasks when executing strategy is to cultivate the necessary skill sets, aptitudes, and capacities that will give the organization a continued competitive advantage. Understanding the vital role that core competencies play in an organization's overall strategy is key to achieving its strategic intent.

Put simply, core competence, sometimes referred to as distinctive competence, is what an organization possesses in terms of skill sets and capabilities—qualities that enable the firm to meet the demands of its market better than its competitors.[2] It is important to distinguish between a company's assets, environmental circumstances, and core competence.

While competitive advantage can certainly arise out of these factors (e.g., close proximity to resources, brand awareness, product quality), none could be called core competence. Certainly, core competence contributes to a company's competitive advantage, but not all competitive advantages are core competencies.

Also called competencies are those basic elements, such as courteous drivers for a delivery company, that a firm may need to possess in order to do business in a particular industry. But not all of those competencies will be critical or core for a firm's success.

A firm's core competence, for example, may be its ability to process and distribute customer-profiling information faster than its competitors, giving it an edge in meeting the customer's high expectations of service. Not only is this competency linked to the abilities of the IT personnel, but the skills of those in customer service, sales, marketing, product design, and manufacturing as well. It is assumed that in this particular example, quality customer service is a critical success factor of the industry.

The root of a firm's core competence rests in its people skills. These skills normally transcend traditional functional silos such as marketing, production, operations, and engineering, and involve knowledge-based activities such as product design, innovation, and customer service. These activities tend to be a big part of the value proposition in both service and manufacturing businesses.

Identifying Core Competencies

Once an organization understands the meaning and importance of core competencies, the next step is to identify those core competencies that enable their strategy and competitive advantage. Also worth noting is the fact that the term "core competencies" seems to mean different things to different people; organizations must adopt a common language and common understanding of core competencies.

Many organizations identify core competencies by reviewing specific departments or divisions for any unique or special capabilities that support that group's function. (See Table 6.1.) Though this method may prove to be

Table 6.1 Capabilities Arranged by Function[3]

Functional Area	Capability	Examples
Corporate Management	• Effective financial control systems • Expertise in strategic control of diversified corporation • Effectiveness in motivating and coordinating divisional and business-unit management • Management of acquisitions • Values-driven, in-touch corporate leadership	• Hanson, Exxon • General Electric, ABB • Shell, in motivating • ConAgra • Wal-Mart, FedEx
Management Information	• Comprehensive and effective MIS network, with strong central coordinator	• American Airlines, L.L. Bean
Research and Development	• Capability in basic research • Ability to develop innovative new products	• Merck, AT&T • Sony, 3M
Manufacturing	• Efficiency in volume manufacturing • Capacity for continual improvements in production processes • Flexibility and speed of response	• Briggs & Stratton • Toyota, Nucor • Benetton, Worthington Industries
Production Design	• Design capability	• Apple
Marketing	• Brand management and brand promotion • Promoting and exploiting reputation for quality • Responsiveness to market trends	• Procter & Gamble, Pepsico • American Express, Mercedes Benz • The Gap, Campbell Soup
Sales and Distribution	• Effectiveness in promoting and executing sales • Efficiency and speed of distribution • Quality and effectiveness of customer service	• Microsoft, Glaxo • FedEx, The Limited • Walt Disney, Marks & Spencer

effective, there is potential for overstated department focus, which can lead to losing sight of the organization's strategic intent. Another method of reviewing an organization's capacities and activities is through "value chain analysis," the sequential chain of activities that includes identifying, fulfilling, and satisfying customer needs.

As illustrated in Figure 6.1, the value-chain components normally include the following:

1. Defining the customer's need
2. Conceptualizing a product or service to satisfy the need
3. Developing the product or service
4. Manufacturing or producing the product or service
5. Selling and distributing the product or service
6. Servicing the product or service

Management should focus on those activities, capacities, and aptitudes that significantly contribute to the organization's overall strategic intent and long-term competitive success. Core competencies ought to be developed not only to sustain the current competitive advantage, but also to open up new opportunities for future markets. Table 6.2 describes the relationship between new and existing competencies and new and existing products and markets.

By carefully identifying current and potential competencies, applying them to existing opportunities, and leveraging them for the future, an organization can enjoy sustained competitive advantages in their markets.

In order to advance your strategy and fulfill your mission, you must get your arms around your core competencies. When we test an organization's ability to identify and understand their core competence, we evaluate them against the following attributes companywide:

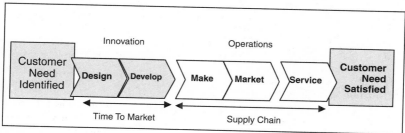

Figure 6.1

Table 6.2 Relationship Between New and Existing Competencies[4]

Competencies	Current Markets	Future Markets
New	What new core competencies will the firm need to build to protect and extend the firm's franchise in current markets?	What new core competencies would the firm need to build to participate in the most exciting markets of the future?
Existing	What is the opportunity to improve the firm's position in existing markets by better leveraging existing core competence?	What new products or services could the firm create by creatively redeploying or recombining the firm's current core competencies?

1. Does management clearly understand what corporate core competence is?
2. Has management identified what their core competence should be in order to fulfill their mission and vision?
3. Has management set a course of action to build their competence in a manner that supports the achievement of their strategic intent?

Returning to the Bank of America/NationsBank case, it is clear that the management team understood what competencies were necessary to pursue their goal. Choosing a course that required significant skills in the mergers-and-acquisition space, they set out systematically to identify clearly the skills, systems, and other traits that would leave nothing to chance.

Which skills would Hugh McColl and his team view to be essential, and bundle as their core competencies?[5]

1. *Financial/Risk Management*—Skills supporting: valuation, accretive nature of the transaction, cost-tied customer retention, cost savings tied to efficiencies, regulatory compliance, profit and loss, and balance sheet treatment.
2. *Systems and Technology*—Skills supporting: operating systems analysis, systems compatibility, systems integration, systems security, etc.
3. *Marketing*—Skills supporting: customer segmentation, aligning customer needs to maximize retention, forecasting probable customer retention, product integration, and value proposition alignment.

4. *Human Resources*—Skills supporting: cultural gap analysis, matching policies and procedures, retention of key personnel, aligning performance management and reward systems, and general employment compliance regulations.

5. *General Management*—Skills supporting: negotiating mergers and acquisitions, large-scale project management, and extraordinary communication skills, both internal and external.

Though this may not represent the entire scope and breadth of mapping NationsBank's core competencies, you can capture the essence and themes of effectively bundling the necessary skills and systems needed to achieve their long-term strategy.

Recognizing the opportunities that the right set of core competencies presents for an organization is part of a leader's focused purpose and future perspective for the company. As we discuss in Chapter 3, Michael Dell, of Dell Computers, identified an opportunity in the PC manufacturing industry that clearly set his company apart from the competition. Dell and his team examined the traditional production and distribution process, and changed their focus to marketing their products through a direct consumer delivery channel.

Not only did Dell revolutionize PC distribution, he put his organization at least one step closer to the customer. This innovative thinking resulted in more direct customer feedback and a better understanding of what their customers wanted to see in the next generation of products. This capacity to break outside the normal parameters of business and implement an innovative distribution strategy was Dell's core competency. This has been the primary driver of Dell's rapid growth, and has given the company a position of industry leadership.

Hamel and Prahalad introduced an effective model to identify whether a capacity is a core competence. (See Table 6.3.)

By utilizing this approach, a company is more likely to identify critical abilities as they relate to their long-term strategic intent. It is important to understand the relationship between identifying core competencies among the firm's human and organizational resources, and not just its products or services per se.

With rare exceptions, products themselves cannot be the source of competitive advantage. It is too easy for some intelligent producer elsewhere to clone, substitute, or improve them.[7] Therefore, it becomes necessary for an

Table 6.3 Defining Core Competencies[6]

Consideration	Proposition	Test
Customer Value	A core competence must make a disproportionate contribution to customer perceived value.	Readily identify a unique benefit that the firm's customers derive from its product or service that is the by-product of a specific skill, collection of skills, or capacity. (The capability itself need not be identifiable by the customer—but in the benefit derived by the capability.)
Competitor Differentiation	A core competence must clearly differentiate itself among competitors.	Through benchmarking or other means, readily identify a unique capability in developing, producing, or servicing the firm's product(s) from those methods deployed by the competitors.
Extendibility	While a particular competence may be "core" in the eyes of a single business, in that it meets the test of customer value and competitive uniqueness, it may not be a core competence from the point of view of the corporation if there is no way of imagining an array of new products or services issuing from the competence.	Readily identify any specific capability that is not only unique today both in terms of customer value and competitive differentiation, but can also form the basis for entry into new or future product markets.

organization to align its core competencies with internal and external resources in order to advance its sustainable competitive advantage. To arrive at a sound diagnosis of a company's competitive capabilities, some managers use a value chain approach, using four steps:

1. Construct a value chain of company activities.
2. Identify the activities and competencies critical to customer satisfaction and market success.
3. Examine the links among internally performed activities, and the links with supplier and customer chains.

4. Establish internal and external benchmarks to determine how well the company compares with competitors in performing activities and structuring its costs. Use this information to determine which activities represent core competencies and which ones are better outsourced.

Whatever approach is taken to identify current core competencies and opportunities for future competencies, it is vitally important that managers share a common view of the firm's current core competencies. While most managers will have some sense of what the organization does best, they may have difficulty specifically linking the competitiveness of the firm or the firm's products with the skill sets of its people.

An analysis of your company's core competence should include:

1. A shared definition of the firm's competitive capabilities
2. A link between competence and customer-perceived value
3. An established benchmark of current and future desired competence

There are inherent dangers in ignoring or minimizing the importance of defining an organization's viability in terms of core competence. Too often, opportunities will be missed when firms focus on the here and now of current products and markets.

For Richard and Maurice McDonald, it took a milkshake salesman, by the name of Ray Kroc, to recognize their expertise in their approach to fast food and its potential for replication and franchising.

EMI's experience with the loss of its leadership in the CAT scan industry is a great example of a firm's not identifying the core competencies required to sustain its competitive advantage. As a result the accomplishment of one of their scientists, who was given the Nobel Prize for his achievement, EMI enjoyed sole ownership of the CAT scan market due to their proprietary position. But failing to recognize the marketing knowledge needed to remain at the top of this industry and build for that competency, EMI was out of the CAT scanner business less than eight years after their product's introduction. General Electric had become the market leader.

Every organization has activities in which they excel or have the potential to excel. McDonald's, FedEx, Procter & Gamble, and General Electric are excellent examples of firms who have recognized what they do best and have built their strategies around these competencies. Recognizing what it takes to be successful in the marketplace is the first step in maintaining a competitive position.

Applying Core Competence

The means by which management demonstrates its understanding of the value and role that core competencies play in achieving the company's strategic intent. It reflects their ability to examine and evaluate their core competencies in relation to creating customer value, expanding competitive advantage, and identifying new business or product opportunities. It reflects their skill in bringing their core competence to enable their strategic intent.

Maintaining a core competence perspective inside the organization is a difficult paradigm to instill. Most organizations are strategically structured to give emphasis to market activities and products. These strategic business units have, at their root, products and services targeted along customer and functional lines.

Having a core competence focus usually involves a cross-functional dialogue and the tendency to view the organization as not only a portfolio of products and services but as a portfolio of competencies as well.

Having this competency perspective makes it easier to integrate core competency into the strategic planning process. Resting on past achievements or inherited positions cannot lead to long market leadership.

Porsche discovered this when their reputation for world-class engineering quality, normally commanding a premium price, was tarnished by their failure to sustain the advantage that this particular competency gave them. It was not that their skill sets eroded; it was the fact that their nearest competitors' skill sets reached a level of parity, or perhaps exceeded them in certain areas of performance. Porsche, blinded by its brand strength and the buying trends of that time, continued to ignore their relative competence and continued to raise their prices.

The savvy consumer soon discovered that paying a premium for Porsche's engineering reputation did not always guarantee a superior performance. In fact, in some instances, the competitors were delivering better-performance cars, for substantially less cost. The result was that Porsche's sales fell from a high of 30,741 vehicles in 1986 to only 3738 in 1993.

Even in today's highly competitive environment and given the continuous evolution of technology, consistency in approach and dedication of resources is the key to success. Such consistency is unlikely unless management is stable and is in agreement on what competencies to build and sustain. Without a consensus, the company may fail in deploying their strategy, because the necessary competencies for success will not be available when needed.

Prahalad and Hamel outline several mistakes an organization may make in the process of building or not building the essential core competencies for success.[8]

1. Too firmly entrenched in current market/product silos to seize new opportunities.
2. Resources imprisoned within departmental channels, difficult to redeploy to take advantage of an emerging opportunity.
3. Fragmented and increasingly smaller business unit boundaries make cross-functional applications difficult.
4. A growing dependence on outsourced competencies.
5. A myopic focus on current end products making future perspective dim and current competencies in danger of obsolescence.
6. Failure to understand the relationship between core competence and market success, providing an opening for new entrants with competencies developed elsewhere to compete.

Most often, an organization's competencies will evolve in response to foreseen customer requirements, competitor encroachment, or the organization's effort to reinforce those skills identified as contributing to the firm's historical success.

Successful companies infuse the organization with these competencies, taking a systemic approach rather than relying on specific personnel. It is important for growing companies to establish the necessary organizational systems that contain the capacity to improve the firm's durability.

This organizational capability is best sustained when it comprises skills and activities from different locations on the value chain. Because core competencies typically emerge from the combined efforts of work groups and departments, department supervisors can't be expected to shoulder the responsibility of building the overall competency on their own.

The multitask, multiskill nature of core competency development requires management expertise in both people skills and knowledge management, and the logistics of networking disciplines.[9] This expertise should be coupled with the necessary authority to encourage cross-discipline cooperation.

Maintaining core competencies is a function of culture, values, structure, and organizational resource commitment. Having the necessary structure and culture to support a flexible, capacity-driven organization is as much a function of empowerment, motivation, values durability, and good-quality information as it is a function of budget.

Finally, while it is not necessary to control all points of capacity along the value chain, it is good practice to focus on the components that add the most value and benefit to the firm's customers. Although Nike outsources its entire shoe manufacturing, it keeps tight control of its core competencies in logistics, design, endorsements, distribution, and merchandising.

Leveraging Core Competence

Organizations cannot be complacent once they have identified and built their core competencies. Indeed, the visionary challenge for management in today's dynamic environment is to broaden the scope of those capacities that have led to the organization's historical success and to find new ways to compete.

Once Amazon.com developed the competency to deliver books efficiently through the Internet, they immediately initiated steps to expand and leverage this capacity to distribute other consumer products, such as music CDs, and power tools.

Amazon.com didn't stop there. In 1999, they leveraged the same strengths to enter the on-line auction market pioneered by such firms as Ebay, and they are on course toward commanding a large share of this market as well.

Clearly, Amazon.com faces the challenge of long-term durability and achieving a level of respectable profitability. However, there is no disputing the fact that they have been relentless in their strategic pursuit to establish their core competence and leverage that competence at every opportunity.

In leveraging knowledge and skill rather than financial or market dominance, firms need a supportive culture, empowerment, values, motivation, efficient structure, short deadlines, great training programs, and efficient organizational systems.

The following is a summary of common characteristics of successfully leveraging and evolving companies:

- *Risk Orientation*—Always seeking expandable opportunities; remaining flexible enough to respond to an unknown future
- *Marketing*—Targeted messages strengthening brand image and awareness to all stakeholders and to potential markets
- *Distribution*—Clearly defined, efficient distribution channel strategies
- *Culture*—Motivated, talented, informed personnel with a high sense of ownership and empowerment
- *Technology*—Investing in and aligning the appropriate technologies to leverage the quality of product, distribution, and service

Let's close by revisiting NationsBank/Bank of America. What do we know?

1. Hugh McColl gathered his team together in 1983 while they were NCNB, and set a vision to become NationsBank.
2. Over an 18-year period, they acquired and/or merged with over 50 financial institutions.
3. The strategy culminated in the acquisition of Bank of America in 1998.

This accomplishment consists of many factors. For the purposes of this chapter, let's zero in on the bank's ability to understand core competence, to identify their core competence, applying their core competence, and ultimately leveraging their core competence. It obviously worked. Where is Bank of America today? The follow table (Table 6.4) illustrates the success this mergers-and-acquisition strategy yielded the NCNB team.

Table 6.4 NCNB—NationsBank—Bank of America Snapshot[10]

Consideration	1983	2002	Growth Percentage
Assets	$12 billion	$642 billion	5,200%
Market Cap	$700 million	$113.8 billion	16,157%
Employees	7,600	137,240	1,705%

Albeit the future of Bank of America is now in the hands of Ken Lewis, the current Chairman, President, and CEO, and his team. The numbers are impressive, and they provide a canvas for the B of A management team to expand their vision and build the competencies necessary to achieve it.

What to Do

An organization's core competencies are the enabling factor to achieve its strategic intent. Understanding, identifying, applying, and leveraging one's core competencies are the key to creating a sustainable competitive advantage. What can you and your management team do, starting tomorrow, to employ lessons learned from this chapter?

Create an Understanding and Common Language around Your Core Competencies

Appoint a "subject" champion from within the management team to provide senior management with a composite definition of "corporate core competencies." Abstracts from C.K. Prahalad and Gary Hamel's work as well as Robert Grant (and the content of this book), should provide the foundation for learning. Remember, *core competencies are defined as the skills, knowledge, and special abilities a company possesses that set it apart from other organizations. By effectively bundling these skills, knowledge, and special abilities, a company can create their competitive advantage, enhance customer value, and expand their market position.*

Test the team's understanding. It is essential that management adopt a common language and understanding prior to moving forward.

Once Understood—Define Your Organization's Core Competencies

Create a small team to evaluate the organization and develop a sample for management to review and validate. The criteria should include how these competencies:

1. Create customer value
2. Differentiate you from your competition
3. Provide extendibility or expansion to your current business

This is an ideal situation to build a cross-functional dialogue among your business groups. The team should have representation from sales, finance, operations, customer service, marketing, and executive management.

Determine the Level to which Your Core Competencies Are Being Applied

First, figure out if your senior managers agree or disagree that your competencies are an integral part of your business performance. Are you serving your customer, clearly differentiating yourself from your competition, and expanding your business at a level that meets or exceeds your plan?

This is a perfect opportunity to evaluate your budget allocations. What are you investing in? Is it consistent, or does it map to your core competencies? Remember, there are traps:[11]

1. Are you too firmly entrenched in current market/product silos to seize new opportunities?
2. Are your resources imprisoned within departmental channels and difficult to redeploy to take advantage of an emerging opportunity?
3. Do fragmented and increasingly smaller business-unit boundaries make cross-functional applications difficult?
4. Do you have a growing dependence on outsourced competencies?
5. Is myopic focus on current end products making future perspective dim and current competencies in danger of obsolescence?
6. Do you recognize that failure to understand the relationship between core competence and market success provides an opening for new entrants with competencies developed elsewhere to compete.

Leverage Your Competencies

Within your strategic planning process, define the course of action to leverage your core competencies. The Bank of America/NationsBank case is one good example. Additional case studies include: Starbucks, Dell, Southwest Airlines, Wal-Mart, Ebay, Corporate Executive Board, Four Seasons Hotel, and Microsoft.

Can you identify any specific capability that is not only unique today both in terms of customer value and competitive differentiation, but can also form the basis for entry into new or future product markets?

Identifying your core competencies, gaining a clear understanding of how they support your competitive advantage, and exploring ways to leverage them to expand and sustain your market position are foundational exercises that every management team must experience.

In the next chapter we explore how information, systems, and technology are integrated to enable strategic performance.

CHAPTER

Information, Systems, and Technology

"To get the full benefit of technology, business leaders will streamline and modernize their processes and their organization. The goal is to make business reflex nearly instantaneous and to make strategic thought an ongoing, iterative process—not something done every 12 to 18 months, separate from the daily flow of business."

—BILL GATES

TODAY'S COMPETITIVE ENVIRONMENT requires organizations to have access to rapid and targeted information, to have their information systems aligned, and to be innovative when selecting and leveraging the appropriate technology.

Information is the glue that binds business operations and provides the basis for all managerial decisions. Although a traditional aim of design has been to organize tasks that need to be accomplished in order to achieve the firm's strategic intent, information and the systems for managing the flow of information through an organization are increasingly playing a larger role in strategic implementation. Indeed, the way an organization acquires, stores, disseminates, and applies information can be a competitive advantage.

Behind this growing dependence on information is the advent and evolution of computer technology. Because of increasing computer power and connectivity, the cost of data retrieval has fallen significantly over recent times. This data output is available quickly in a variety of formats, documents, and combinations. To become useful to management, data must be transformed into information through filtering, screening, comparing, and other methods of analysis and interpretation. When this information is timely, accurate, and shared through an effectively managed system, it can evolve into corporate knowledge.

Knowledge management, like other popular business trends before it, has been described in many ways. The large consulting firm, KPMG, in their 1998 Knowledge Management report defined *knowledge management* as a systematic and organized attempt to use knowledge within an organization to transform its ability to store and use knowledge to improve performance. Knowledge being defined as the information about an organization's customers, products, processes, competitors, and so on, which can be locked away in people's minds or filed on paper or in electronic form. The model below (Figure 7.1) illustrates the flow of normally intangible people-based knowledge, including insights, experiences, interactions, and judgments, as well as the traditional database information about the organization, its environment, competitors, and processes.

An effective knowledge management system will require management's commitment to sharing information, integrating the information in a meaningful way, and getting the right information to the people who need it to make effective business decisions.

The commitment to sharing information begins with an organization's recognition that collaboration between functional departments is more

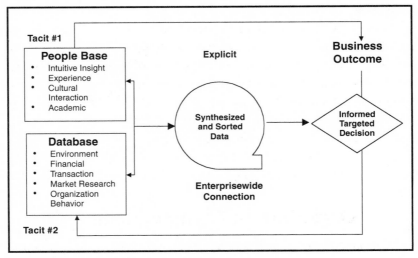

Figure 7.1

effective than data contained solely within functional silos. The strategic benefit of good organizational communication is the alignment of the executive team through integrated thoughts and opinions.

Information becomes useful knowledge when it is linked to the central strategy of the organization. Systems must recognize the individual needs for knowledge within the organization and allow recombining and dissemination of data in a timely fashion to support decision making.

In order to retrieve the data as well as disseminate it efficiently, every component of the organization must participate in the system. Highly sophisticated systems link processes along the entire value chain, increasing an organization's responsiveness.

Several years ago, Frito-Lay gave each of their 10,000 route sales personnel a hand held computer, and in the process transformed them from "laborers" to "knowledge facilitators."[1] Instead of simply ordering and racking merchandise, these employees now play a vital role in Frito-Lay's market research program. Information on sales entered on the portables is fed daily and sent to executives at Frito-Lay's Dallas headquarters. These executives have accurate, up-to-date market share and sales information and can respond to the data much faster.

When numbers were down in a region, careful tracking of the sales data revealed that, in one area of Texas, a local chain of stores had launched their own brands of chips. Frito-Lay was able to respond quickly with a counter-strategy, and sales retuned to previous levels. It had normally taken several months to address a problem of this magnitude. Using technology, this problem was resolved in a matter of days.

Contrast this with the majority of companies with similar resources and opportunities, such as water bottle companies, delivery companies, etc., who surprisingly overlook the cost savings and potential competitive benefits of a knowledge system. How a company uses the data and information it receives is more important than just obtaining it.

In this chapter, we weave together the importance of organization communication, the value of providing targeted information to those who need it, the benefits of aligning knowledge systems, and the importance of applying the correct technology to support your strategic intent.

Organization Communication

"Without credible communication, and lots of it, the hearts and minds of others are never captured."—*John P. Kotter*

One of the most common complaints we hear when dealing with organizations is the lack of communication. Few organizations seem to get this function right. In a cross-cultural study, roughly 74 percent of the managers sampled from companies in Japan, Great Britain, and the United States, cited communication breakdown as the single greatest barrier to corporate excellence.[2]

It is important to note that the frustration is felt not only by the employees, but by management as well. The bigger the organization, the bigger the problem. The idea of keeping employees informed may sound easy enough, but the practice is time-consuming. Every organization understands the importance of communication. Every company intends to communicate with their employees, but the demands of the business—increasing sales, handling customer complaints, dealing with investors, complying with regulations, and so on—can quickly erode this intent. It takes a real commitment on the part of senior leadership to establish a culture in which communication remains a high priority.

Since all management functions involve some type of communication, the ability to communicate effectively might be considered one of a manager's most important skills.[3] The average manager spends 50 to 70 percent of his or her time communicating in some way.[4] Yet few managers engage in improving their own personal communication skills. Effective communication requires speaking, writing, and listening skills; a willingness to inform others; and a desire to foster open communication. When managers master these skills, they harness a great deal of power—the power to get things done through others.[5]

One reason that senior managers get frustrated with communication problems in their companies is that they often rely on middle management to relay important information throughout the organization. If these mid-level managers either do not posses the skills listed above, or are simply unwilling to take the time, communication breaks down mid-stream, and important information is delayed or lost.

Organization communication involves implementing a system to ensure that all primary stakeholders consistently receive the information that they need regarding the organization's vision, mission, and strategy. This requires identifying and satisfying the specific communication needs of all stakeholders. It also means clearly communicating the strategic plan throughout the company and reporting progress in relation to this strategy.

Formal communication within an organization can move downward, forward, and laterally. A study by the Hay Group[6] of 250 firms showed that 54 to 67 percent of employees saw "top-down" communication as positive, but only 30 to 42 percent saw "bottom-up" listening programs as positive. This could imply that most companies are better at giving employees information than they are at soliciting their input. Another independent study[7] indicated that fewer than half of employees felt that their companies were good at letting them know what was going on.

Research shows that only 20 percent of downward-directed information ever reaches the bottom organization level. (Findings in a subsequent study lowered the figure to a mere 5 percent.) Information losses tend to be substantial at each level, from top to bottom.[8] Depending on the size of the organization, messages can be almost unrecognizable by the time they reach lower-level employees.

When we evaluate *organization communication,* we look at an organization's ability to:

1. Keep all stakeholders well informed regarding strategy and current performance
2. Communicate critical organizational objectives throughout the company
3. Clearly identify the primary performance metrics that will be used to gauge progress toward objectives
4. Let employees know how well they and the company are performing in relation to key strategic goals

Analog Devices CEO, Ray Strata, talked about the importance of communication within the organization:[9]

> **There are many impediments to organizational learning, but the most basic is communication . . . Only in recent years have I begun to fully understand how profoundly the words that come out of my mouth and my pen affect organizational performance both for better or for worse. When you think about it, the only thing that a manager does that is visible to the organization is listen and speak . . . We can change each other by what we say and how we listen.**

An individual's position within an organization affects the overall credibility of the information. If a coworker says he heard that the corporate offices are moving, you may not take it as fact. If the president says, "we're moving," you can start packing your desk. In fact, a study by social power theorists, French, Raven, and Kotter contends that *rank* is one of five key factors affecting credibility.[10] (The other four are *goodwill:* personal relationships and track record; *expertise:* knowledge and competence; *image:* attractiveness to an audience; and *shared values:* common values shared with an audience.)

Communication and Culture

Often, what appears to be a communication problem may actually be a symptom of a bigger issue. Communication difficulties are often linked to ineffective or unhealthy cultures. Authors Kolb, Osland, and Rubin, state that, "from a dynamic standpoint, problems of communication in organizations frequently reflect dysfunctions at the level of *corporate climate.* (Emphasis theirs.) The feelings people have about where [they work] or with whom they work—feelings of impotence, distrust, resentment, insecurity, social inconsequence, and all other human emotions—not only define the climate which prevails but the manner in which communications will be managed."[11]

According to studies by Blake and Mouton, when management is effective and relationships are sound, problems of communication tend not to occur. It is only when relationships among members of an organization are unsound and fraught with unarticulated tensions that one hears complaints of communication breakdowns. Thus, the quality of relationships in an organization may dictate to a great extent the level of communication effectiveness that is achieved.[12]

Barriers to Organization Communication:
Knowing What Gets in the Way Is Half the Battle

To be effective, communication in organizations must move downward, upward, and laterally. Barriers to communication differ depending on which direction the information is heading. The following table (Table 7.1) provides a description of typical barriers for each of the three directions, and some pointers for overcoming these barriers.

Finally, communication can break down simply due to lack of the infrastructure required to facilitate the exchange of the desired information. Without investment in the correct technology, information flow is hindered. Information can become obsolete. Important events that drove the information simply run their course. All barriers to exchange of critical information rob the organization of its ability to respond in a timely manner.

Table 7.1 Barriers to Organizational Communication[13]

	Downward Communication	
Barriers	Problem Definition	Solutions
One-Way Communication	Downward communication is often a one-way message from superior to subordinates, providing no opportunity for feedback. This problem is especially severe in written communication and in mechanical communication methods such as cassettes and videotapes. Face-to-face communication allows for continuous correction until the message is understood.	1. Maintain adequate contact with subordinates and encourage two-way communication.
Differences in Values and Perceptions	Superiors tend to be committed to the total organization; subordinates to their department or subgroup. Superiors usually see their performance in terms of long-term goals; subordinates see theirs in terms of immediate outcomes. Superiors typically view their contribution in terms of achievements, while subordinates are more likely to see themselves as contributing long hours and hard work. Such differences in viewpoint can cause subordinates to filter out parts of a downward message.	2. Use multiple channels of communication, including face-to-face conversation, opinion surveys, and periodic group meetings. 3. Keep informed of subordinates' values and perceptions, and share personal points of view with them.
Mistrust	Employees who mistrust a superior may misunderstand or block the relay of downward messages. Reasons for mistrust include lack of frequent boss-subordinate contact and the fact that the superior controls the subordinate's rewards. Employees often feel their boss to be a more biased source of information than their immediate coworkers or the organization's grapevine.	4. Build trust by letting subordinates know how decisions that are important to them are to be made, and by involving them in decision-making when possible.
The Psychic Conflicts of Leadership	The pressures that leaders experience often produce severe inner conflicts. Abraham Zaleznik identifies two such conflicts, **status anxiety and competition anxiety.** Status anxiety affects the leader who is torn between the responsibilities of authority and the desire to be liked. Competition anxiety refers to the fears that arise in those who have trouble dealing with the inevitable fact that managerial work is competitive. These fears may be fears of success as well as fears of failure. Clearly, such inner turmoil can cause a manager to leave out or distort information when communicating with subordinates.	5. Develop a keen sense of his or her own reactions and a firm sense of personal identity.

(continued)

Table 7.1 Barriers to Organizational Communication[13] (*Continued*)

	Upward Communication	
Barriers	**Problem Definition**	**Solutions**
Attitudes of the Subordinate	One reason for the perceptual gap between superiors and subordinates, documented by a long history of research, is the tendency of people at lower hierarchical levels to distort information they communicate to persons of higher rank. Early studies of upward distortion discovered that it is most prevalent in bureaucratic, machinelike organizational climates; these studies also found that the stronger the subordinate's interest in advancement and promotion, the greater the chance for distortion. More recent research concludes that subordinates are least willing to reveal unfavorable information when it reflects negatively on them and when they fear being the bearer of bad news.	1. Subordinates can increase their willingness to build relationships (not simply to register complaints) with their superiors. 2. Superiors can develop skill in sensitive, objective listening in order to reduce subordinates' fear about communicating problems upward. 3. Superiors can work to increase the balance and coverage of upward communication by not allowing aggressive representatives from some departments to monopolize attention, while others get none. 4. Superiors can increase their informal contact with subordinates through, for example, social events, ceremonial occasions, or occasional tours of the plant. 5. Superiors can take action in response to upward messages. Subordinates, in turn, can more persistently seek responses from their superiors.
Attitudes and Actions of the Superior	The research findings just mentioned suggest that superiors may contribute to upward distortion by maintaining mistrustful, intimidating relationships with their subordinates. From a more constructive angle, the same findings suggest that superiors often have the power to help subordinates be more open in their upward communication. By the same token, subordinates do not automatically fall victim to upward distortion. Research by Cal W. Downs and Charles Conrad has found that superiors perceive more effective subordinates as those who are willing to confront their bosses with challenging or unwanted information.	
Characteristics of the Organization	Highly formal organization structures and procedures may also block upward communication. In the Nixon White House, it is said, cabinet officials had to swim through a tight net to get to the president. Typically, the visitor would be ushered into the Oval Office by a top presidential aide who would explain that the visitor's proposal was complex and that the president was studying it but was not yet ready to make a decision. Thus intimidated, the visitor would often exchange brief greetings with Nixon and then leave, so as not to waste the president's time. Meetings that could have provided the president with a wide range of information thus came to naught. Physical distance between superior and subordinates also restricts upward communication, especially in large organizations, where senior executives may work in corporate or divisional headquarters buildings far from their subordinates in factories, retail outlets, or field offices. Even when the whole organization is within one building, managers' offices may not be easily accessible. In some organizations, information-sharing practices inhibit upward flows. One such practice is the MUM effect, identified in research by Sidney Rosen and Abraham Tesser. MUM, which stands for "minimize unpleasant messages," refers to the tendency of subordinates in a given organization to try to create a favorable impression on their superiors by passing only pleasant information up through the organization.	

174

Table 7.1 Barriers to Organizational Communication[13] (*Continued*)

Lateral Communication

Barriers	Problem Definition	Solutions
Increased Specialization	Though it produces a greater need for lateral communication by increasing the need for coordination, specialization simultaneously reduces the extent to which organization members share common interests. Increased specialization is a frequent problem for growing organizations, where rapid growth in lateral communication can dog communication channels.	1. Expand members' awareness of overall organizational goals and of other departments' problems through methods such as training programs, job rotation, social events, or organization development approaches.
Lack of Management Recognition and Reward	Numerous studies have shown that organizations encourage and reward vertical communication, but not lateral communication. Organization members tend to limit behavior that is not rewarded.	2. Augment the structure of the organization by adding "integrative devices," such as liaison roles and interdepartmental task forces, or "integrating departments" to relieve the specialists of the main burden of coordination.
Suppression of Differences	Some people communicate less than candidly with their peers because they are afraid to express rivalry or disagreement. This may stem from childhood training as well as from an idea, common in democratic societies, that everyone is equal. Some adopt bureaucracy as their form of personal defense, doing everything "by the book" and quoting company rules to depersonalize their contacts with others in the organization. Another defense is to be a "good guy"—the one who always goes along with the group and never disagrees.	3. Explicitly encourage and reward effective lateral communication. 4. Encourage constructive confrontation and the full expression and working through of disagreements. 5. Dispel the drone-like myth of equality by rewarding people according to the excellence of their contribution.

Applying Organization Communication: Use a Model

Communication strategies are built around a communication plan. It is tough enough to improve communication with a plan. It is impossible to accomplish this without one. There are just too many ways for managers to get distracted. Just like a strategic plan helps to keep an organization focused on performance, a communication plan keeps an organization focused on the flow of information that supports this performance. A solid communication plan addresses four key areas:

1. The audience
2. The content of the information
3. The media that will be used to disseminate the information
4. The process that will be followed

The following model is useful for considering the components of an effective communication plan (Table 7.2). This model is not intended to indicate the only options. Rather, it can be used as a discussion starter.

Managers must be committed to sharing information that is vital to achieving the organization's strategic intent. This commitment must begin at the top, with the executive team leading by example. Sharing information is a fundamental step to establishing a culture of mutual trust, openness, and active listening that will help erode communication barriers between all stakeholders.

Targeted Information

"To achieve nirvana, you must have perfect information about every customer order [new and old] and every asset in your business [both permanent physical assets and various inventory components]. And guess what? The only way to secure, maintain, and harvest this information is through the aggressive use of technology."—J. William Gurley, "Above the Crowd"

Once an organization is committed to sharing information, the key to knowledge management is identifying the information that is vital to achieving the organization's strategic intent. What is critical to an organization will vary according to key success factors, the nature of the industry, and the type of strategic choices made.

Table 7.3 illustrates some of the different information needs by different levels in an organization.

Table 7.2 Communication Plan Components

Audience	Content	Media	Process		Follow-Up
Who needs to know?	What needs to be communicated?	What are the presentation options?	One-Way	Interactive	Follow-Up
Identify which organizational stakeholders will receive the information. Employees? All or some? Customers? Board of Directors? Investors? Strategic partners? Vendors? Regulators?	Determine the key elements of communication • Be careful of information overload. • If you want people to remember, a few items are better than a laundry list. What significant changes are forthcoming? How will the employees be affected?	Print Media • Brochures • Bulletins • Newsletters • Video • Interviews with senior managers • Group panel discussion (could include selected staff members) Audio Cassettes E-Mails	Distribute print media Video presentation Distribute cassettes Staff meetings • Managers may use a leader's guide to present the information and keep the message consistent.	All of the one-way methods, but include feedback mechanisms: • Written responses from employees • Comments from staff meetings • Employee "hotline" with response from senior management • Written response • Group presentations • Follow-up media	Determine how often the information will be reinforced. What is the follow-up communication schedule? What will be said? How will the information be presented? Include progress reports if appropriate.

This model will help you determine: How information will be communicated. Who will communicate the information. What resources will be required.

Table 7.3 Information Needs by Level of Organization[14]

Characteristic	Top Management	Middle Management	Operating Management
Planning Focus	Heavy	Moderate	Minimum
Control Focus	Moderate	Heavy	Heavy
Time Frame	Long Term	Short term	Day to day
Scope of Activity	Broad	Functional Areas	Single Focus Area
Nature of Activity	Unstructured	Moderately Structured	Highly Structured
Level of Complexity	Many Open Variables, Complex	Better-Defined Variables	Straightforward
Result of Activity	Mission, Goals, Objectives	Action Plans	End Products and Services

Unlike data, information has meaning when applied to an organization's unique strategic situation. Organizations can transform data into useful information by adding value in different ways. The following list shows several methods.[15]

1. *Contextualized:* The firm knows for what purpose the data was gathered.
2. *Categorized:* The firm knows the units of analysis or key components of the data.
3. *Calculated:* The data may have been analyzed mathematically or statistically.
4. *Corrected:* Errors have been removed from the data.
5. *Condensed:* The data may have been summarized in a more concise form.

The key to obtaining good, targeted information is to glean from the information, knowledge that can lead to corporate action. This is possible when management is trained to evaluate the information on the following:[16]

1. *Comparison:* How does the information about this situation compare to other situations the firm has known?

2. *Consequences:* What implications does the information have for decisions and actions?
3. *Connections:* How does this bit of knowledge relate to others?
4. *Conversation:* What do other people think about this organization?

Once information needs have been defined, the next step is to determine how frequently the information needs to be refreshed. Sales and production may require daily or even hourly revitalization. Competitor and environmental data may need to be reviewed weekly, monthly, or quarterly. The drivers within the firm's industry should determine the information frequency required to support its strategy.

When we evaluate how an organization utilizes "targeted information," we review the following:

1. Are managers provided with the information they need to make informed decisions?
2. Are they continually updating environmental factors that affect their business?
3. Are they using an effective system to disseminate important market data?
4. Are managers provided with timely updates regarding the performance of their area of responsibility?
5. Is the quality of their information reliable and accurate in order to support rapid decision making?

Procter & Gamble[17] codes more than 900,000 phone calls it receives annually on its toll-free number to obtain early signals of consumer tastes and product concerns. Mrs. Fields Cookies systems can monitor sales at 15-minute intervals and suggest product mix changes, promotional tactics, and operating changes to improve customer response.[18]

Federal Express can instantly track any given package is in its delivery process through its tracking system. Its communications system tracks its 21,000 trucks and vans nationwide who make over 720,000 stops per day. Its flights operations systems lets a single controller direct as many as 200 FedEx aircraft simultaneously, overriding their flight plans as weather and situations develop. All of these systems are core to FedEx's strategy of next-day delivery. We will further review FedEx's use of information and technology later in this chapter.

Accurate, timely, and *targeted information* is vital for functional heads and executive teams to monitor the organization's progress in taking corrective action as early as possible. Being able to identify variances quickly in expected outcomes is one of the major goals of quality information systems.

Before moving on to the next section of this chapter, take a moment and test your organization against the five evaluation questions that we list on the previous page. We cannot stress enough the value of information that is targeted for specific uses or applications. If your responses are less than favorable, or if you do not know—you have just identified a critical area of focus for you and your organization to address.

Enterprising Systems

"The productivity of knowledge has already become the key to productivity, competitive strength, and economic achievement. Knowledge has already become the primary industry, the industry that supplies the economy, the essential and central resource of production."—Peter F. Drucker

Enterprising systems are the procedures and protocols for allocating and monitoring its human, organizational, and physical resources. Effective systems should be operational through all portions of the value chain. The diagram below (Figure 7.2) illustrates the operational effects of a firm's enterprising systems.

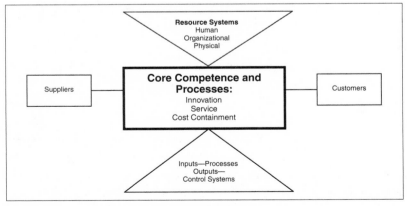

Figure 7.2 Model of Systems within an Organization[19]

The way these processes are managed can affect the organization's ability to sustain, apply, and leverage its core competencies. Information collection, hiring practices, and capital structure practices, for example, can influence the strategic direction of an organization.

When these systems are mismanaged, or misaligned, the organization will face unnecessary obstacles to achieving their strategic intent. A classic example of systems misalignment is the organization that is strategically differentiated in terms of offering superior customer service and high-quality products, but has an information system based on costs.

It is important to point out that systemic issues for a firm do not usually stem from a lack of a significant system, but more from the way critical systems are managed. Even small variances in managing these systems may have considerable impact on the company's ability to implement their strategy successfully.

When we evaluate an organization's systems, we ask:

1. Do their systems facilitate the flow of information across departmental lines to maximize performance and effective decision making?
2. Do the technological aspects of the system allow for the sharing of information from department to department and individual to individual?
3. Does management continually challenge and validate that their current systems met the demands of the organization?

A large government contractor, for example,[20] was concerned about the costs of a particular part of their operations. The engineers in charge knew of several operations overseas that were using similar processes at much lower costs. Although the potential savings to the company over the life of the government contract was several million dollars, the company refused to approve the travel budget for a benchmarking visit, since it could not contractually recover the cost of the international travel from the government agency. The opportunity for increased profitability was lost.

Like all design issues, in order to align better with the firm's intent, enterprise systems normally follow strategic choice. Alignment of systems can be classified in one of three levels (as illustrated in Table 7.4.) The low-

Table 7.4 Degree of Alignment

Low Level of Alignment	Medium Level of Alignment	High Level of Alignment
Strong negative impact.	Neutral impact.	Strong positive impact.
Attributes of system work against achieving the strategic intent of the organization.	Doesn't restrain implementation, but is not suited for it, either.	Tailored to support the firm's strategy. Can deduce intent from system attributes.

est level illustrated above is misalignment, where systems actually operate in opposition to the firm's strategic intent.

At the minimum or medium level of alignment, systems will neither support nor detract from a firm's strategy. Examples of this neutral impact would include systems that are driven by vague initiatives such as "people are our most valuable asset." Without a clear understanding of what constitutes a quality workforce, the company may invest in high-quality training programs without any significant return on their investments.

At the highest level, a study of an organization's systems should lead one to understand clearly the strategic intent of the firm simply by identifying the system's attributes. Such closely aligned systems actually magnify the firm's ability to succeed.

Properly aligned information systems have two purposes:

1. Connectivity, coordination, and integration
2. Providing accurate measurements

Ritz-Carlton[21] is the best-known example of an organization that leverages its information systems into a huge competitive advantage to further the firm's intent. R-C compiles customer profiles on all of their guests. The robust data includes any formal request made during previous stays as well as observations made by the staff during their normal course of duties. Everyone is issued a note pad for recording things such as, "Mr. Smith in room 225 seems to enjoy tennis," after observing the tennis whites, tennis magazine, etc., in the room. The notes are quickly recorded on the enterprisewide database.

Guest recognition coordinators receive advanced lists of incoming guests and link them to all recorded history of the guests' previous stays. Using this enterprisewide information base, should Mr. and Mrs. Jones, who preferred an early dinner and chocolate while staying in Atlanta, check into Laguna, a box of chocolates and a timely dinner reservation will be waiting for them.

R-C integrates this technological system with cross-functional training in hotel services for the staff, and empowers graduates with a "fix-it" budget of up to $2000 to remedy guest problems without prior approval. R-C's guest retention rate since the start of the program has increased 25 percent.

Today's intensely competitive environment places a significant challenge at the feet of management. Possessing the systems to communicate necessary information effectively to every corner of the organization is a nonnegotiable skill if you intend to remain vital.

Applied Technology—the FedEx Way

"There really isn't any right amount to spend on information systems. Many management teams spend too much time thinking about how to beat down the information system's cost, instead of thinking about how to get more value out of the information they could have available and how to link that to strategic goals of the company."—John Young, Former CEO, Hewlett-Packard

Data today is available in more abundant forms and media than ever before. The rate of data availability is increasing exponentially. Technologies that drive this data access are doubling in power within shorter and shorter time frames. Firms that efficiently and quickly acquire, interpret, and respond to information about their business can gain competitive advantage over their rivals. Yet it remains that, while no aggressive company poised for growth would use a 20-year-old marketing approach, many firms choose to operate with 20-year-old computer information systems. Putting priority on maintenance and the status quo rather than innovation and opportunity will leave many of these firms far behind the pace. Many will not recover.

Technological advancement can affect entire industries in several ways. It can:

1. Rejuvenate, render obsolete, and create industries
2. Reconfigure industry boundaries

3. Redefine the way firms do business
4. Bring new substitute products and process innovations into a market, and create new synergies across traditionally separate businesses

Consider the following examples:

- The watch industry has been dramatically rejuvenated by the evolution of new mechanical, electronic, quartz, and digital technologies. The advent of word processing capabilities in personal computers has devastated the typewriter industry.
- Advances in information technologies have rendered old conceptions of the financial services industry obsolete: insurance firms, banks, and brokerage houses can now all be interconnected to provide new financial services, thus blurring long-held distinctions among the services offered by these industries.
- Many U.S. firms have found themselves having to reconfigure their business definitions due to the success of Japanese firms in miniaturizing products, in part, through technological advances. This is the position in which Xerox found itself in the copier business. Because Japanese firms like Canon introduced smaller-sized copiers, Xerox soon found itself selling to different customers with different needs through different distribution channels and competing on a different basis (price was much more important) in order to survive.[22]
- Industries are also affected by product substitutions, such as plastics replacing many uses of steel, and frozen food preparation and microwave ovens frequently being substituted for conventional ovens and cooking. In the VCR industry, firms differentiate their products through the introduction of new technological features, such as longer recording time, longer advanced time setting, sharper picture reproduction, clearer sound, and so on.
- Process innovations such as automation, robotics, and CAD/CAM (computer-aided design/computer-aided manufacturing) have bestowed cost and quality advantages on many firms. Japanese automobile manufacturers have gained a significant competitive edge on their U.S. competitors through the adroit use of this form of technology.

- Advances in telecommunication and computer technologies have made new synergies possible across businesses dealing with computers, television sets, and communications.

When we evaluate an organization's approach to *applied technology,* we ask:

1. Are all stakeholder requirements met with their existing technology?
2. Does management possess and demonstrate a strong commitment to acquiring and integrating the appropriate technology to remain vital?
3. Does the organization have a discipline and process in place to explore new or improved technology solutions?
4. Does the organization have a systematic approach to monitoring the role that technology plays within their industry and tracking the shifts and trends of technology applications?

Technology, in its role as a critical enabler in the fulfillment of a firm's strategic intent, has often been looked at as the ultimate panacea for business performance. It is not technology per se that improves an organization, but the effective use of it. It is the responsibility of IT officers to align their systems with the strategy of the company and allow the firm's intent to drive their technology-use decisions.

There are several organizations today that we could profile to demonstrate how technology enables their position of dominance within their industry. However, there is none better in our opinion then FedEx. Let's explore how FedEx has made technology a strategic ally in their pursuit to a sustained competitive advantage.

A Look at FedEx

FedEx can be viewed as a leader in aligning the appropriate technology for its industry and clients. FedEx provides an excellent brief on its Web site that outlines how technology serves the organization and its stakeholders.

FedEx Technology[23]

"The information about a package is as important as the delivery of the package itself."—Frederick W. Smith, Chairman of the Board, President, and CEO FedEx

FedEx chairman and founder Fred Smith had that vision in 1979, and it remains the heart and soul of the FedEx technology story. It's not about bits and bytes, but about delivering information, and it has revolutionized the way business is conducted in a global economy.

FedEx Corporation is a world leader in technology, setting the industry standard for efficiency and customer service. Its technological advances have always been in response to customers' needs, anticipated future requests, and the demands of an information-driven environment.

fedex.com

FedEx has long been recognized as a trailblazer for harnessing the power of the Internet to provide fast, easy, and convenient service options for its customers. The FedEx Web site made waves when it was launched in 1994 with a bold package-tracking application that was perhaps one of the first true corporate Web services.

A few years later, FedEx became the first transportation company with a Web site offering a feature that allowed customers to generate their own unique bar-coded shipping labels and summon couriers to pick up shipments.

Today, fedex.com hosts more than 3 million unique visitors per month and experiences more than 60 million total page views. On average, the site handles over 1.1 million package-tracking requests daily. More than 2.5 million customers connect with the company electronically every day, and electronic transactions account for almost two-thirds of the 5 million shipments that FedEx delivers daily.

The FedEx Web site is widely recognized for its speed, ease of use, and customer-focused features. The Web Marketing Association recently praised fedex.com as the "Best Transportation Web Site," and *eWeek* recently saluted it as a top e-business innovator.

Duty and Tax Estimator

FedEx is the first company ever to offer a carrier-based "Estimate Duties and Taxes" application on its Web site. This new, revolutionary feature on fedex.com allows shippers instant, round-the-clock, daily access and visibility to the information they need to make important international shipping decisions. This includes customs duties, value added tax (VAT), Most

Favored Nation (MFN) duties, and other governmental fees that are levied on international shipments to and from 42 countries.

This feature was designed as a business-planning tool to help customers obtain this information, before they ship, about charges and fees they can expect in the overseas shipping process, whereas before, that information was only available after the transaction had been completed.

A valuable component of the FedEx duty and tax estimator is the integrated Harmonized System (HS) Code identification. The HS Code is an internationally accepted uniform-description system for classifying goods for customs, statistical reporting, and other purposes. FedEx includes this feature in its service, in contrast to many third-party providers that often charge customers simply to identify the code. In addition, unlike many expensive third-party providers, the FedEx estimator offers customers of any size simple, convenient and affordable transaction-based billing options.

The Estimate Duties and Taxes enhancement to fedex.com is one of several services available through "FedEx Global Trade Manager," which is designed to help small- and medium-size businesses navigate the growing, complex, and fast-paced world of international commerce.

Wireless Solutions

FedEx technology enables customers, couriers, and contract delivery personnel to access wirelessly the company's information systems networks anytime, anywhere. In fact, FedEx was the first transportation company to embrace wireless technology more than two decades ago, and continues to be a leader in the use of innovative wireless solutions.

Customers can access package tracking and drop-off location data for FedEx Express, FedEx Ground, and FedEx Home Delivery via Web-enabled devices such as WAP phones, Personal Digital Assistants, and pagers.

FedEx couriers, contract delivery personnel, and other team members use wireless data collection devices to scan bar codes on shipments. These "magic wands" are a key part of what makes it possible for you to find out where your package is in transit, whether on a FedEx Express jet speeding across the Atlantic Ocean or a FedEx Ground tractor-trailer on the Pennsylvania Turnpike. On average, FedEx Express and FedEx Ground packages are scanned at least a dozen times from pickup to delivery. At pickup, each package's shipping label bar code is immediately scanned to record the pickup time, destination, and delivery commitment. The scanned information is uploaded to the FedEx mainframe. Bar codes are scanned again at every key step of the shipping process, allowing customers to follow the status of their shipments throughout the journey.

FedEx's newest data collection device for couriers incorporates a microradio for hands-free communication with a printer and mobile computer in the courier's delivery vehicle. Called the PowerPad, the devices use Bluetooth wireless technology that allows them to communicate with each other within 30 feet.

FedEx eBusiness Tools

- FedEx eShipping tools provide Internet, desktop, and mailroom solutions to improve the whole shipping process.
- FedEx eCommerce solutions enable customers to integrate FedEx shipping capabilities into their systems.

From Amazon.com to Travelocity, customers of all sizes are using FedEx eBusiness solutions to manage their businesses more effectively. FedEx offers a wealth of electronic tools, applications, and APIs for customers to integrate into their shipping processes to shorten response time, reduce inventory costs, and generate better returns.

FedEx Technology Institute

As a world leader in technological business solutions, who better to learn from than FedEx? Construction recently began on the FedEx Technology Institute at the University of Memphis, a state-of-the-art facility designed to house an educational endeavor teaching the newest technologies using the most advanced learning techniques.

The facility will give faculty and students throughout the university access to cutting-edge information technology for learning and research. The primary objective is to provide an environment that produces graduates prepared for employment in the rapidly changing world of the Internet and information technologies.

The four-story, 92,000-square-foot building will incorporate elements from the most advanced high-tech businesses in Silicon Valley and elsewhere. The facility will contain a 200-seat forum, computer labs, a training room, collaboration suites, an exhibit area, and labs for the development of hardware of software.

FedEx contributed $5 million for the institute, which is a public-private partnership between the company and state and local government.

FedEx Technology Awards

Over the years, FedEx has received much recognition for innovative customer-focused technological advances, including:

- *eWeek:* 2d place, FastTrack 500 ranking of the top e-business innovators
- *Computerworld:* "100 Best Places to Work in IT"
- *InformationWeek:* FedEx CIO Robert Carter named one of the "Chiefs of the Year" in 2001

So when all is said and done, how has Fred Smith's vision, the FedEx management team, and overall organization performed? (See Table 7.5.)

FedEx, through a recession, growing competition, and dealing with the challenges of being an industry leader, consistently posts financial results that are the model of their space.

After reviewing the FedEx approach to bringing the appropriate technology to bear within their industry, what are some closing considerations or standards that you can test within your organization? Some minimal performance standards[24] for information systems include:

- It should facilitate global information consistency.
- Departments should be self-sufficient yet compatible in their information system capabilities.
- It should support cross-functional integration of the firm.
- It should integrate voice and data communications.
- It should make data and information available to anyone who demonstrates a need for it, within security and data integrity parameters.

Table 7.5 FedEx Financial Performance—1997–2001[25]

Consideration	2001	2000	1999	1998	1997
Stock Price	$51.88	$39.96	$40.94	$44.59	$30.53
Total Sales in Billions	$19.629	$18.257	$16.773	$15.873	$14.238
EPS	$1.99	$2.32	$2.10	$1.80	$1.01

- Design should emphasize effectiveness in the business setting over efficiency in the technical environment.

We have reviewed three critical components of organization design. We've explored the importance of having the correct organization structure, understanding and leveraging your core competencies, and in this chapter we zeroed in on information, systems, and technology. In our next chapter, we delve into how efficiency best serves organizations.

Organization Efficiency

"Of all the things I've done, the most vital is coordinating the talents of those who work for us and pointing them to a certain goal."

—Walt Disney

ORGANIZATION EFFICIENCY deals with having the right people focused on doing the right jobs within an optimal work environment. To achieve efficiency, organizations require some degree of simplicity. This involves a number of factors, including useful policies and procedures, clarity of individual and group roles and responsibilities, and being able to rely on vendors and suppliers who contribute to the successful delivery of good and services.

In the best-run companies, policies and procedures facilitate production. They make sense. They act as helpful guidelines that employees use to make good decisions and confidently perform their jobs. Some companies pride themselves in keeping things simple, brief, and to the point. (See the "Employee Handbook" that Nordstrom uses, in Chapter 10.) It seems self-evident, but companies should strive for simplicity and clarity. When policies and procedures are complicated or burdensome, employees will first question the reasoning, and then, barring a logical answer, will eventually grow to resent them. Companies have enough problems dealing with customer demands, strict regulations, and tough competition in tight economies. The last thing they want to do is frustrate and alienate their workforce by imposing rules and regulations that are not clear or understandable.

We worked with one department within a government agency that was completely frustrated by centralized hiring practices. The centralized approach was put in place to ensure that hiring practices were in compliance with Equal Opportunity regulations; however, this policy resulted in long delays in getting job positions filled. This shortage of personnel led to an overtaxed workforce and low morale. The authorities who imposed the policy had no real appreciation of how this approach impacted the productivity of the outlining agencies.

In another example, the operations division at an airline announced a new system for clearing stand-by passengers at the airport. Not only was this edict imposed without input from the airport, but the computer system was changed so that these employees were forced to comply. The new system resulted in long lines at the gates, delayed flights, and very angry customers. The old system was restored in less than 48 hours. Employees need support from the policy makers, not interference.

The speed at which organizations can carry out their initiatives is based solely on the skills and dedication of their workforces. In essence, organizational performance is the sum total of individual contribution. This is the first level of performance efficiency. Since individuals seldom work by themselves, group performance constitutes the next level of efficiency. Sometimes group performance can be seen simply as the total output of individual performances. One example of this is when a group of engineers works on separate projects. Other times, group performance results from the synergistic efforts of individuals, such as those working on an assembly line. In every case, performance is enhanced when individuals understand how their individual jobs contribute to the organization's overall success, when they can see the bigger picture.

Management's role in improving efficiency and effectiveness can be summarized by the following diagram (Figure 8.1).

If a chain is only as strong as its weakest link, so it goes that an organization is only as strong as its weakest contributor. Sometimes that contributor exists outside the organization. For example, Dell relies on Intel to provide the microprocessors for their PCs and laptops. Late-arriving chips mean delayed deliveries to Dell customers. Intel relies on Applied Materials to provide sophisticated equipment that they use to produce computer chips. Incorrectly calibrated equipment could result in substandard chips that Intel cannot sell to Dell. Applied Materials relies on their vendors to supply materials used in constructing their equipment. And so it goes. Relationships likes these are critical to the delivery of good and services. Companies must hold strategic partners to the same high standards that they themselves aspire to.

In order to satisfy the scrutiny of all organization stakeholders, senior managers must coordinate the output of all contributors through planning,

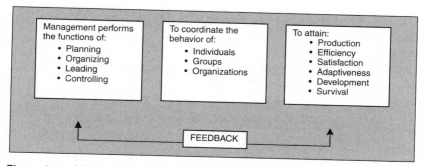

Figure 8.1 Management's Contribution to Effectiveness[1]

organizing, leading, controlling behavior, and designing structures and processes to facilitate communication.[2] These relationships are illustrated in Table 8.1.

Organization efficiency is organized into three sections:

- **Balanced Oversight and Direction:** Writing policies and procedures that facilitate rather than impede productivity
- **Synthesized Roles and Responsibilities:** Creating job descriptions that are clearly tied to strategic intent and that reduce redundancy
- **Managed Outsource and Strategic Alliances:** Establishing standards for outside partners who bring your goods and services to market

Designing an organization to optimize the firm's efficiency includes establishing supportive policies and procedures, implementing effective

Table 8.1 Sources of Efficiency[3]

Management Functions	Individuals	Groups	Organizations
Planning	Objectives	Goals	Mission
Organizing	Job design Delegated authority	Department bases Department size	Integrative methods and processes
Leading	Person-centered influence	Group-centered influence	Entity-centered influence
Controlling	Individual standards of performance	Group standards of performance	Organization standards of performance

control systems, defining specific tasks and responsibilities, and working effectively with strategic partners.

Balanced Oversight and Direction

"You cannot create prosperity by law. But you can easily destroy prosperity by law."—Theodore Roosevelt

Organizations use policies and procedures to maintain control. The question is not whether there should be control, but rather, how much control there should be. Detailed procedures leave little to chance, but also leave no room for personal judgment. As companies continue to downsize, the span of control between supervisor and staff increases. Less layers generally means more staff per manager. If decision making is reserved exclusively for the manager, work slows down.

In 1994, we consulted with the loan services department of one of the country's largest mortgage lenders. The policy at the time required managers to approve any waiving of late fees, regardless of the amount. Whenever the employees in loan services took a call from a customer requesting that a late fee be waived, the employee had to complete a handwritten form, including the basic information associated with the customer's request—the amount of late fee, the 12-month payment record of the customer, the number of days the payment was late, etc. Procedures in place at the time required that employees submit the form to their supervisors for approval. This lender had nearly 200,000 loan customers. It was not unusual for late fee waiver forms to get backlogged in the in-boxes of the bosses. Because it took days to get a response, anxious customers, concerned about getting a black mark on their credit report, would call back second and third times, more agitated each time, causing another manual fee waiver form to be generated.

Here is the irony. Every employee knew from experience that if the late fee was $200 or less and the loan customer had a spotless record of payment for the preceding 12 months, the late fee would *always* be waived. These employees were smart enough to make these decisions on the spot if only the loan services management group would change the policy and the procedure. Earlier in the year, the company had conducted a customer satisfaction survey and discovered that *more than 60 percent* of its current customers would *not* recommend the lender to their friends and associates. The late-fee waiver policy was a key contributor to this reaction.

Think about this for a moment. At the same time that the company was paying millions to advertise on the radio and plaster the boulevards with billboards trying to attract new loan customers, its internal late fee policy was causing such a bad service experience that current customers where telling potential customers to stay away. Finally, the pain of lost customers exceeded the managements' desire for control, and—you guessed it—any time a customer with a solid payment record asked for a late fee of $200 or less to be dismissed, the customer service staff were allowed to reverse the fee on the spot. What policies exist in your organization that are defeating your strategic intent?

When we evaluate *balanced oversight and direction,* we examine a company's ability to:

1. Develop concise policies and procedures that provide clear guidance and direction to all divisions, departments, and individuals
2. Ensure that employees are *not* burdened by an overabundance of policy and procedure
3. Create work environments where managers and employees feel that they can get things done without a lot of "red tape"
4. Establish effective internal processes to monitor compliance with current policies and procedures

Balanced oversight and direction means creating policies and procedures that provide clear guidance without being excessive or overbearing. It is important to distinguish between these two terms. A *policy* is a "predetermined course of action established as a guide toward accepted business strategies and objectives." A *procedure* is a "method by which a policy can be accomplished; it provides the instructions necessary to carry out a policy statement."[4]

Policies can be defined as "a guide to managerial action."[5] An organization may have policies in a number of areas: quality, environment, safety, HR, etc. These policies guide day-to-day decision making. Policies are general statements of how an organization wants things to be managed internally. They become the rules and regulations of the organization. These can include ethics policies, attendance policies, travel policies, grievance policies, substance-abuse policies, and so on. Sometimes the word "policy" is used interchangeably with terms like "standard operating procedures" or "work standards." Once published in manuals or via electronic means, the policies are available for everybody in the organization to refer to. They become the corporate rule of law and the means for clarifying actions and resolving differing opinions within the organization.

To make a policy a working reality, it must have one or more procedures tied to it that define exactly what to do, step by step.[6] This type of guidance is important, particularly as workforces receive more autonomy. Without reasonable controls in place, greater autonomy can result in the organization's being pulled in many conflicting directions to the extent that progress toward achieving a strategy becomes more of a random act rather than a carefully planned event.

Procter & Gamble[7] pioneered empowerment and autonomy 10 years before it became a popular practice. When the company's annual earnings growth fell from 30 percent to nearly zero, the management team realized that there was a need for controls despite all the progressive changes that had taken place at P&G. CEO Edwin Artzt stressed a policy of measuring results and reasserted the need for individual accountability as the key for getting P&G back on track.

Other useful reasons for policies and procedures are:[8]

- New or freshly revised policies and procedures provide top-down guidance to operating managers, supervisory personnel, and employees, regarding how certain things now need to be done and what behavior is expected, thus establishing some degree of regularity, stability, and dependability in how management has decided to execute the strategy and operate business on a daily basis.

- Policies and procedures help align actions and behavior with strategy throughout the organization, placing limits on independent action and channeling individual and group efforts along the intended path of accomplishment. Policies and procedures counteract tendencies for parts of the organization to resist or reject common approaches—most people refrain from ignoring established practices or violating company policy without first gaining clearance or else having strong justification.

- Policies and standardized operating procedures establish and help enforce needed consistency in how strategy-critical activities are performed in geographically scattered operating units. The existence of significant differences in the operating practices and procedures among organizational units performing common functions sends mixed messages to internal personnel about how to do their jobs, and also to customers who do business with the company at multiple locations.

- Because the process of dismantling old policies and procedures and instituting new ones invariably alters the character of the internal work climate, managers charged with implementing strategy can use the policy-changing process as a powerful lever for changing the corporate culture to produce better alignment with the new strategy.

Well-constructed policies and procedures help support the achievement of a organization's strategic intent by channeling actions, behavior, decisions, and practices in directions that improve strategy execution. When policies conflict with a strategic intent, they become obstacles.

Nike[9] decided to focus on its core competencies of advertising, logistics, and outsourcing of its manufacturing. It developed a series of policies aimed at nurturing its relationships with its production partners. With these policies in place, Nike overcame cross-cultural barriers and other long-distance communication obstacles to their low-cost production strategy.

Some of their policies included:

- Having a Nike employee stationed full-time at each manufacturing site to act as liaison with Nike. These employees were expected to remain at site for several years getting to know the key personnel, culture, and operating style of the factory. They matched Nike R and D efforts with factory capabilities and were responsible for keeping monthly orders in line with forecasts.
- Nike worked to minimize variances in production orders for their premium-line exclusive factories. The partnership included the factories' investment in new technology and codeveloping new models.
- For the volume producers of Nike's low- to mid-priced line, factories were expected to balance the variances with the other five to eight buyers and stabilize their own production schedules.
- Finally, it was Nike's strictest policy to pay the factories on time and provide them with predictable cash flows. Such care led to tremendous loyalty and flexibility in production.

This is not meant to suggest that all organizations need vast amounts of policies and procedures to guarantee the achievement of their intent. If anything, we are suggesting the opposite. The amount of oversight and direction will vary based on the complexity and risk associated with each situation and the skills and experience of the members of the organization.

In some situations, having too many policies can stifle the creative and entrepreneurial spirit of managers and employees, and, as a result, may be as costly as having no policies. Often, empowerment and encouragement of initiative and creativity is more instrumental in accomplishing the organization's strategic goals than written rules and regulations. For example, at one point, Dana Corporation's CEO Rene McPherson dramatically threw out the company's 22-inch policy manual and replaced it with a one-page statement focusing on a "productive people" philosophy.[10]

Using Policies and Procedures to Support Good Decisions

Policies and procedures play a strategic role in a company's environment. They dictate how decisions will be made. Policies and procedures provide any organizational decision maker with limits, alternatives, and general guidelines. They help to make instructions definite, provide a common understanding of a policy interpretation, and provide quick settlement of misunderstanding. Policies set boundary conditions so that actions and decisions are channeled along a particular path in pursuit of an objective. Policies allow management to operate with constant intervention and, once established, enable others to work within that framework.[11]

Policies and procedures eliminate the organizational chaos that could occur if every employee made independent decisions with no point of reference. These guidelines reduce the range of individual decisions and encourage management by exception. The decision maker only needs to give special attention to unusual problems not covered by a specific policy or procedure.[12]

Achieving *balanced oversight and direction* is one key to supporting a company's strategic intent. Finding this equilibrium between providing autonomy to individuals so that they can make quick decisions and establishing the right amount of policies and procedures to give them structure and guidance is extremely important, particularly in industries that are changing rapidly. An audit of current policies can take place when new initiatives are generated. Companies must discontinue outdated policies and revise others to ensure that policies and procedures are aligned with the implementation of strategy.

Synthesized Roles and Responsibilities

"You want your people to run the business as if it were their own."—
William Fulmer, Senior Fellow and Senior Vice President, Executive
Development Center of the Harvard Business School

For years, business books by the leading authors have often shared a mutual
theme—the need for all members of an organization to share a common
vision and guiding principles. Porras and Collins refer to this concept as
"preserving the core ideology." Covey talks about having an organization
focused on "true north." Warren Bennis calls it a "guiding purpose." Peter
Senge uses the term "shared vision." The concept is pretty simple when you
get right down to it. The goal is to get everyone in an organization excited
about the potential of the company and being willing—even proud—to
behave in a manner that is consistent with realizing that potential.

A big part of this formula is to explain to employees how their jobs drive
the organization forward—how their contribution lines up with the bigger
picture. *Synthesized Roles and Responsibilities* involves making sure that all managers and employees clearly understand their role and how they fit into the
organizational strategy. Employees also need to understand how their job
integrates with those of other departments. The best-run companies continually reinforce the need for cross-department integration and communication. You won't find silos or organizational "fiefdoms." Instead, you find a real
desire to work together towards a common objective. A good example of this
is what Jack Stack accomplished with his team at the Springfield Remanufacturing Corporation (see Chapter 10); or what Xerox senior executives, managers, and employees did to successfully compete against some very good
Japanese firms, restoring the organization to prominence in the 1980s, and
earn the Malcolm Baldrige award in 1989. (See Chapter 9.)

When we evaluate *synthesized roles and responsibilities,* we look at an organization's ability to:

1. Ensure that all employees clearly understand their roles and responsibilities as they relate to strategic objectives
2. Clearly define the role of management
3. Eliminate or minimize redundant roles and responsibilities
4. Effectively integrate multiple areas or functional disciplines to better
   achieve its strategic intent

One major concern of an organization in executing a new strategy, especially one that is a significant departure from the previous course of action, is defining significant roles and filling them with the most suitable personnel. Having appropriately skilled and experienced personnel occupying key positions within the company is one of the main concerns of CEOs, venture groups, investors, and other closely tied stakeholders. In the end, the degree of confidence that outsiders have regarding top management's ability to achieve its strategic intent can be directly correlated to confidence in the ability and commitment of the people of the organization. After all, except in the smallest companies, it's not the top managers who are delivering the company's goods or services—it's the general workforce.

The more complex an organization becomes, the greater the level of integration needed to make organizational structure work effectively.[13] FedEx, for example, needs a high degree of integration to deliver on its promise of next-day package delivery. From pickup to delivery, the company's service proposition depends completely on the reliable integration of ground and air networks. More recently, sophisticated tracking systems are used to allow customers to determine the status and location of their parcel anywhere along the network.

The higher the degree of integration, the higher the cost. Adding layers of management to supervise and coordinate value-chain or supply-chain activities is expensive. As a company grows, cross-functional dependencies will become more complex. It is important for organizations to consider the risk/reward issues associated with increasingly complex systems. Moving to more complex systems, such as self-directed teams, should only be undertaken if there is a clear indication that: (1) this system will help the organization achieve its strategic objectives; and (2) the organization has the skill and experience to implement the system successfully.

We have, for example, worked with many organizations that have had significant trouble initiating and sustaining matrix teams. Employees who are placed on matrix teams get very frustrated when their matrix "boss" asks them to do one thing, and their functional boss asks them to do something else. The question: "To whom do I really report?" is frequently voiced. Matrix teams look good on paper, but they require significant role clarity and complete management buy-in in order to succeed. And, just as many organizations lack the patience to maintain up-to-date job descriptions, many organizations lack the stamina to coordinate and support matrix teams properly. Ask a random set of employees about their experience with matrix teams and see what reaction you get. This is not always a favorite topic of discussion.

Organizations should graduate carefully from simple to more complex integration mechanisms. There is no value in hastily implementing new systems that have not been examined thoroughly. Instead of increasing productivity, companies run the risk of increasing frustration and cynicism. The following table (Table 8.2) lists types and examples of integrating mechanisms available to an organization. They are listed in order of complexity, from the simplest to the most complex.

The objective is for management to match the level of organizational complexity and differentiation with the necessary level of integration in order to achieve the company's overall strategic intent. It is readily apparent that too much complexity and not enough integration can ultimately lead to poor implementation and a failed strategy. But the reverse is also true. Too much integration for a simple organization is costly and slows down responsive decision making. This organization could become overburdened. The ideal is to optimize the simplest structure needed to carry out the company's mission.

AT&T is a good example of an organization that adjusted its tasks and authority in response to changes within its environment. Before deregulation, AT&T cared little for the speed in which its tall, centralized structure responded to its markets. However, after the markets were forced open, AT&T found itself a poor third to the innovative, highly responsive Japanese telephone equipment manufacturers in terms of phone features and low

Table 8.2   Types and Examples of Integrating Mechanisms[14]

Type	Example
Direct contact	Sales and production managers
Liaison roles	Assistant sales and plant managers
Temporary task forces	Representatives from sales, production, and R and D
Teams	Company executive committee
Integrating roles	Vice president of strategic planning
Integrating departments	Corporate headquarters staff
Matrix	All roles are integrating roles

prices. In response to these threats, AT&T bypassed its traditional functional structure and created cross-functional work teams who were given deadlines for various development phases and then left to do their work. Under this flexible structure, development time dropped by 50 percent, costs went down, and quality went up, with the company regaining some of its product prestige in the marketplace.[15]

Applying Roles and Responsibilities: Clarity and Focus Tied to Strategy

Writing job descriptions is one of the least favorite—and most often avoided—tasks facing any company. It's laborious. Right now, HR departments all over the world are beseeching department heads to complete the process. Yet, the advantages of clarifying job responsibilities and linking each job to the organization's strategy is self-evident. In smaller companies, employees wear many hats. Job descriptions in these companies become, by necessity, more fluid. The focus is more on process than individual tasks. But as companies grow, a lack of clarity can lead to frustration ("I don't know who is supposed to do what.") and redundant jobs ("I thought our department was handling that.").

One key to successful implementation of strategy is not only to have the right personnel in critical roles, but to define those roles and responsibilities in such a way as to promote cross-functional integration of efforts, and eliminate any unnecessary redundancy of effort. Here are five specific activities to keep in mind:[16]

1. **Defining the nature and content of each job in the organization**
   This activity has tangible results: job specifications, position descriptions, or task definitions. These documents describe each position's responsibilities, outcomes, and objectives. In turn, the skills, abilities, and training required to meet the defined expectations are also specified.

2. **Determining the basis for grouping the jobs together**
   The essence of defining jobs is specialization, that is, dividing the work. But once the overall task has been subdivided into jobs, those jobs must be combined into groups or departments. The managerial decision involves the selection of appropriate criteria for grouping. For example, all jobs requiring similar machinery may be grouped together, or the manager may decide to group jobs according to the product or service they produce.

3. **Delegating authority to the assigned manager**

   The preceding activities create groups of jobs with defined tasks. It then becomes necessary to determine to what extent managers of the groups should be able to make decisions and use the resources of the group without higher approval. This right is termed *authority*.

4. **Deciding the size of the group**

   Jobs are grouped to facilitate supervision of the activities. Obviously, there is a limit on the number of jobs that one person can supervise, but the precise number varies, depending on the situation. For example, it is possible to supervise a greater number of similar, simple jobs (such as an airline reservation center) than of dissimilar, complex jobs (such as project manager on a major commercial development). The appropriate span of control is also affected by the group's overall task, the extent of geographic dispersion, and the availability of standardized procedures.

5. **Devising integrative methods and procedures**

   An organization's structure comprises many different parts doing different things. These differences must be integrated into a coordinated whole, and it is management's responsibility to devise integrating methods and processes. If the differences among jobs and departments are not too great, then the simple exercise of authority is sufficient to integrate the differences. For example, the manager of a small yogurt shop can easily integrate the work of the order takers by issuing directives. But the manager of a multiproduct, multidivisional organization will have to rely on more complex, cross-functional teams, product and customer service managers, and electronic communications.

Do employees at your company understand how their positions contribute to your strategic intent? Do they understand how their roles compare or contrast to their colleagues'? Do managers at your company understand the leadership and managerial expectations associated with their positions? Can employees differentiate between the roles and responsibilities associated with one manager as compared to another? Would it be likely or unlikely that employees would discover someone else performing a function that they thought they were solely responsible for? Has your company established a means where different areas of your organization can more effectively collaborate on the same strategic objective?

These are some of the questions that are resolved when organizations take the time to define and synthesize roles and responsibilities properly.

Managed Outsourced and Strategic Alliances

"For most global businesses, the days of flat-out, predatory competition are over.... In place of predation, many multinational companies are learning that they must collaborate to compete."—*Joel Bleeke and David Ernst McKinsey Consultants*

Managers spend a great deal of their time, energy, and resources dealing with nonstrategy-critical activities. These activities generally do not contribute to the firm's competitive advantage, and could be best left to others to do while the company focuses on those vital areas that are critical to its strategic success. Companies like Nike and Liz Claiborne partner with production firms to make all or most of their end products, while focusing on core competencies such as design and logistics.

Managed outsourced and strategic alliances involves holding strategic partners to the same performance standards to which company employees are held. It requires the close monitoring of any provider of a product or service that is critical to the on-time, successful delivery of a company's goods and services. In essence, it means ensuring that partner performance standards are held consistent with internal standards. The working relationship with a strategic partner is, of course, much different than the relationship a company has with its employees. The ability to provide rewards or levy consequences is very different with an outside party. But make no mistake about it, there is leverage.

At a conference sponsored by the Association of Strategic Planners (ASP), the speakers made a very compelling case for how strategic alliances are becoming much more common. Organizations are making a determined effort to keep their costs down. Outsourcing noncore activities, like human resources, ground delivery, security, payroll, and others, has become commonplace. As a result, these types of industries are seeing new entrants join the ranks of providers. Companies have many more providers to choose from. No one is more aware of this competition than the providers themselves. There is no reason for any company to stick with a poor-performing provider. Customers don't care who is at fault if you can't live up to your promises. If a vendor lets you down, you lose the customer regardless of where the process broke down.

When we evaluate *managed outsource and strategic alliances*, we look at an organization's ability to:

1. Outsource activities and initiate strategic alliances, where appropriate, to support the achievement of its strategic intent.
2. Demonstrate a willingness to outsource processes and functions that do not relate to its corporate core competencies.
3. Have an effective process in place that monitors the performance of outsourcing vendors and strategic partners.
4. Hold strategic partners to the same high standard of performance that they expect of themselves.

Outsourcing is defined as: "Identifying and subcontracting to an outside supplier a process currently conducted in house." Outsourcing is undertaken to cut costs, improve quality, or both. Generally, outsourcing is confined to utility processes, (processes that are required but do not provide a competitive advantage, such as security, facility maintenance and repair, laboratory testing, income tax preparation, legal services, and so on.[17]

Many organizations have reduced their total personnel by transferring complete functions to a supplier (outsourcing). In one survey, 86 percent of firms used outsourcing in 1995, compared to 58 percent in 1992.[18] In one financial services company of about 8000 people, 74 percent are "contract" personnel, most of whom come from one supplier.[19]

Extensive steps are taken to ensure the quality of the services. Examples of activities for outsourcing include manufacturing operations, billing, service, and human resource tasks. As a research project, the National Science Foundation is studying the impact of contract workers and outsourcing on quality.[20]

Critics of this growing trend of alliances and outsourcing claim that the process takes the control out of the hands of management and breeds dependency on the organization's vendors and suppliers. Others argue that globalization, limited resources, and spiraling costs make collaboration an eventual imperative. As technology and business practices blur the line between traditional internal processes and a strategic-alliance approach to products and services, organizations will face the challenge of managing their internal and external relationships with equal scrutiny and standards of control.

What About Customer Service?

Would it seem odd to you to outsource your customer service department? How would you feel to be once-removed from your customers? There is perhaps no greater moment of truth regarding the integrity of a company's operating principles than when it deals with customer issues. Should L. L. Bean outsource its customer contact employees? Should The Four Seasons Hotel, Hertz Rental Car, and Southwest Airlines do the same? Does it make sense financially? Operationally? Culturally? Competitively?

This subject has become a corollary issue when the subject of outsourcing is discussed. In the *Juran Quality Handbook, Fifth Edition,* author Edward Fuchs points out that the central question is whether the customer service functions should be handled entirely inside the enterprise, or whether the enterprise should outsource the functions to companies that specialize in performing them. Companies that provide customer service functions on an outsourced basis are prominent in the customer service arena, performing many of the associated functions at superior levels.[21]

Fuchs goes on to say that the conventional wisdom on this question is that, if the customer service functions are strategic to the enterprise's business strategy, then the functions should be performed internally. This is easy to understand, since the functions are part of a strategy to be better than the best competitor in some critical dimensions of service. On the other hand, if the functions are not strategic, then the question of whether they can be performed at levels of quality and at costs that are comparable with those of the outside companies is a valid one. Customer service functions of many quality award-winning companies are provided by outside companies unbeknownst to the customers.[22]

Dartmouth professor James Brian Quinn gives several reasons for outsourcing relationships.[23]

- Intellectual and service activities now occupy the critical spots in most companies' value chains—regardless of whether the company is in the service or manufacturing sector—and if companies are not "best in the world" at these critical intellectual and service activities, then they are sacrificing competitive advantage by performing those activities internally or with their existing levels of expertise.
- Each company should focus its strategic investments and management attention on those capabilities and processes—usually intellectual or

service activities—where it can achieve and maintain "best in world" status.

- The specialized capabilities and efficiency of outside service suppliers have so changed industry boundaries and supplier capabilities that they have substantially diminished the desirability of much vertical integration, and, strategically approached, outsourcing does not "hollow out" a corporation, but can decrease internal bureaucracies, flatten organizations, and give companies heightened strategic focus, vastly improving their competitive responsiveness.

Other reasons and benefits for partnering include:

1. **Improved Business Focus**—Concentrate on core competencies.
2. **Access to World Class Capabilities**—The right partner can offer new technologies, tools, and techniques.
3. **Accelerated Reengineering Benefits**—Having someone already versed in the new process takeover saves time.
4. **Shared Risks**—Become more dynamic, flexible, and adaptable to changing markets.
5. **Free Resources for Other Purposes**—Redirected resources can be applied to leverage core competencies.

Making Alliances Work

The key to every alliance is understanding the value of each organization's contribution to the partnership. Partners must be prepared to renegotiate the alliance, as necessary, should there be significant changes in the industry. In order to remain competitive, a company's focus might shift from current to future alliances. When Barnes and Noble geared up to compete with Amazon to sell books over the Internet, new competencies, including new on-line alliances, were required. Structuring alliances that provide a win-win situation for all partners, although it can be difficult and may require some creative thinking, can significantly enhance performance and increase a company's chances to become or remain one of the top providers in its industry.

Strategic alliances have been a key element in Toshiba's corporate strategy since the early 1900s. Since then, Toshiba has taken advantage of partnerships, licensing agreements, and joint ventures, to become one of the world's leading manufacturers of electronic products.[24]

Table 8.3 Tips for Collaboration[25]

1. Treat the collaboration as a personal commitment. It is people that make the partnerships work.

2. Anticipate that it will take up management time. If you can't spare the time, don't start it.

3. Mutual respect and trust are essential. If you don't trust the people you are negotiating with, forget it.

4. Remember that both partners must get something out of it (money, eventually). Mutual benefit is vital. This will probably mean you've got to give something up. Recognize this from the outset.

5. Make sure you tie up a tight legal contract. Don't put off resolving unpleasant or contentious issues until "later." Once signed, however, the contract should be put away. If you refer to it, something is wrong with the relationship.

6. Recognize that during the course of a collaboration, circumstances and markets change. Recognize your partner's problems and be flexible.

7. Make sure that you and your partner have mutual expectations of the collaboration and its time scale. One happy and one unhappy partner is a formula for failure.

8. Get to know your opposite numbers at all levels socially. Friends take longer to fall out.

9. Appreciate that cultures—both geographic and corporate—are different. Don't expect a partner to act or respond identically to you. Find out the true reason for a particular response.

10. Recognize your partner's interests and independence.

11. Even if the arrangement is tactical in your eyes, make sure you have corporate approval. Your tactical activity may be a key piece in an overall strategic jigsaw puzzle. With corporate commitment to the partnership, you can act with the positive authority needed in these relationships.

12. Celebrate achievement together. It's a shared elation, and you have earned it!

Postscript (from Ohmae)

Two further things to bear in mind:

13. If you're negotiating a product original equipment manufacturer (OEM) deal, look for a quid pro quo. Remember that another product may offer more in return.

14. Joint development agreements must include joint marketing arrangements. You need the largest market possible to recover development costs and to get volume/margin benefits.

Applying Managed Outsourced and Strategic Alliances

Any partnership, from corporate conglomerates, to the military branches of the Department of Defense, to a marriage, requires trust and collaboration. Steven Covey's concept of *emotional bank accounts,* applies to strategic alliances as well. Covey says that whenever someone behaves in a way that that builds trust or respect with another person, this act is essentially a "deposit" in the receiving person's emotional bank account. Likewise an act that leads to distrust or lack of respect is a "withdrawal." Just like standard bank accounts, emotional bank accounts can be overdrawn. A successful partnership requires actions and behaviors that make deposits and not withdrawals.

Kenichi Ohmae, Chairman of McKinsey & Company's Japan offices, lists twelve steps to better collaboration between firms (Table 8.3).

There are a number of examples of firms who engage in excellent strategic partnering. Microsoft's Bill Gates and Intel's Andy Grove meet together periodically to revisit their "Wintel" strategy that has positioned Windows and Intel chips as the standard for business applications.[26] Soft drink and beer producers work closely with their distributor/bottlers, cultivating relationships that strengthen loyalties, local market access, and commitment for co-operative marketing programs. Strategic partnerships, alliances, and close collaboration with suppliers, distributors, the makers of complementary products and services, and competitors make good strategic sense whenever the result is to enhance organizational resources and capabilities.

Do you hold your outsourced vendors and strategic alliances to the same standards you have set for yourself? Companies cannot expect to compete if the strategic partners they count on to deliver goods and services let them down. Customers do not care who caused a late delivery or a billing error. The fact that a problem can be blamed on outsourced activities is no consolation. Satisfying your customers is a holistic process, one that involves many interdependencies that must interact collaboratively and reliably.

3

Organization Culture

"Companies start with a white cloth and dye it in the colors they like."

—Noritake Kobayashi
Director (Ret.) Fuji Xerox Co., Ltd.
Professor Emeritus, Kelo University

Whether they know it or not, every company has a culture. Some companies carefully shape their culture. They figure out what they stand for and communicate these principles explicitly with placards in corporate offices or proclamations in the annual report. Others let their cultures evolve informally. Consciously or unconsciously, they take a more implicit approach. Their cultures form as a result of actions, decisions, and behaviors. Employees in organizations with implicit cultures eventually learn which behaviors get rewarded and which get punished.

Culture establishes company parameters for what is considered acceptable or unacceptable, right or wrong, appropriate or inappropriate. Culture teaches employees what is valued. In this sense, culture becomes a major determinant for shaping employee behavior and performance.

In essence, culture is the outcome of the total set of beliefs, protocols, and practices that an organization maintains for prolonged periods of time. Strong, embedded cultures usually endure much longer than the incumbent CEO who fostered them. Thomas Watson, Jr., discussed IBM's "Respect for the Individual" in his book *A Business and its Beliefs* in the 1960s,[1] but the roots of this guiding principal date back to his father's presidency of the company in the 1920s. Bill Hewlett and Dave Packard first wrote and communicated their seven *Hewlett-Packard Objectives* in 1957.[2]

Culture in an organization evolves first under the influence of the organization's founder. His or her personal values and standards form the foundation of the firm's culture.[3] For example, Ray Kroc and McDonald's, Sam Walton and Wal-Mart, and Bill Gates at Microsoft are all founders with powerful influences over the shaping of each organization's culture.

The culture evolves over time as the environment changes, with new elements added and others discarded to sustain the company's strategic intent. The addition of an influential, transformational leader may also affect the firm's culture. Figure P3.1 below illustrates the evolution of culture.

Although it is common to think of an organization's culture in the singular, most companies have multiple cultures or subcultures.[5] As most employees will tell you, organizational values, beliefs, and practices can vary by department, division, or location. In the mid 1990s, we had the opportunity to work with a major bank in California. In was evident that the culture of individual departments were subject to the dictates of the immediate boss. The result was a "schizophrenic" organization where the work experience in one department could be decidedly different than another. This led to pockets of high or low

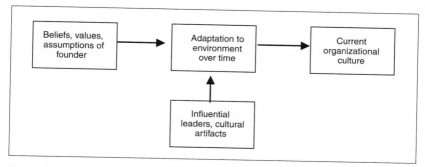

Figure P3.1 Evolution of Organizational Culture[4]

morale within the company. Because of the interdependencies between departments in an organization, low morale in any department can have a negative impact on the overall productivity of the company. We worked with the senior team at this bank to establish four key values and corresponding behaviors. They then communicated and enforced these values throughout the organization, reducing the schizophrenic society.

Whatever its final composition, an organization's culture can hinder or facilitate the company's strategic initiatives. One key to sustaining a competitive advantage is to establish a work environment where the culture fosters conditions for good strategy execution. Strategy-supportive cultures shape the mood, temperament, and motivation of the workforce. In such a culture, approved behavior flourishes, while disapproved behavior is discouraged. Conversely, when culture and strategic direction are misaligned, strategy-supportive behavior can be discouraged, even criticized.

A closely-aligned culture motivates personnel to do their jobs in ways that are conducive to the company's strategy. This provides structure, standards, and a value system in which to operate. It also promotes stronger employee identification with the company's vision, performance targets, and strategy.[6]

To manage this strategy-culture relationship effectively, managers must be sensitive to the compatibility or "fit" between strategic direction and culture. Figure P3.2 provides a framework for managing the strategy-culture relationship by identifying the four basic situations that a firm may face.

The task of aligning culture with the intended strategy of a firm is not a short-term exercise. It takes time for a new culture to evolve and take root in the organization. It is not an overnight phenomenon that can be enforced with a few

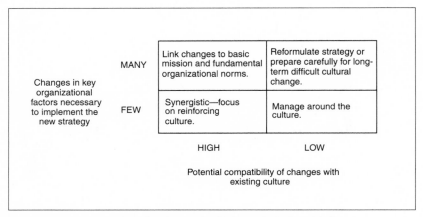

Figure P3.2 Managing the Strategic-Culture Relationship[7]

tertiary workshops and lip service by leadership. The larger the organization, the longer it will take, and the greater the degree of commitment that will be necessary to invoke a change.

It is the leaders of strategy who must consider whether strategies can be successful, given the company's culture. The first step for any leader is to recognize that culture has a powerful influence over strategy implementation. Culture is not some soft or fuzzy phenomenon that high-strung visionaries can ignore in the excitement of taking a company into the stratosphere. It may not seem as apparent, but culture can affect your success as much as finance or technology. Culture, like these factors, can provide the fuel or the brakes.

Organizational culture by itself is not a bottom-line commodity. You won't see it itemized on a balance sheet. But a company with a healthy, adaptive culture will generally outperform a company with an unhealthy, rigid culture, sometimes in dramatic fashion.[8] Simply put, companies with strategically conducive cultures stand a better chance of achieving their goals.

We explore this concept in the following chapters:

Values and Beliefs
Leadership
Human Resources Systems
Organization Character

CHAPTER

9

Values and Beliefs

"The basic philosophy, spirit, and desire of an organization have far more to do with its relative achievements than do technological or economic resources, organization structure, innovation, and timing. All these things weigh heavily on success. But they are, I think, transcended by how strongly the people in the organization believe in its basic precepts and how faithfully they carry them out."

—THOMAS WATSON, JR.

IN ALL ORGANIZATIONS, there are two fundamental factors that impact success: vision, which is the strategic component, and values, which are the behavioral component. Vision statements answer the question: What must we accomplish? Values statements answer the question: How must we behave? Your best performance is achieved with careful consideration of both factors. A strong, clearly worded values statement should be given the same status in the organization as a vision or mission statement.

At the core of an organization's culture are its principles and beliefs. These shared values shape how the work of the organization is done. In much the same way as personality influences the behavior of an individual, shared assumptions about what is valued among a firm's employees and stakeholders influences opinions, attitudes, behaviors, and, ultimately, outcomes within the organization. When the beliefs and practices called for in a strategy are not compatible with a firm's culture, a company usually finds it difficult to implement the strategy successfully.[1]

Employees of an organization can simply be aware of the beliefs and values without necessarily adopting them in a personally significant way.

However, when employees view values and beliefs as genuine guidelines for appropriate behavior within the organization, these values tend to take on a greater personal relevance. If employees simply comply with the standards established and enforced by an organization, corporate goals can still be achieved. Real synergy, however, occurs when managers and employees derive personal satisfaction, or intrinsic rewards, from actions tied to these standards.

Go to Wal-Mart's Web site, and you get the feeling that the employees like being part of a service-driven company. They actually like being greeters or being a part of the company's community activities. In the "Good Works" area of the Web site, the company states: "We live here, too. So we strongly believe in our responsibility to contribute to the well-being of our community. Together with our customers, we know where Wal-Mart can help the most, and we can take great pride in getting involved and seeing the results of our efforts in person."[2] In 1979, Wal-Mart racked up a billion dollars in sales. By 1993 it did that much business in a week.[3]

When organizational values are congruent with employees' personal beliefs, it's just easier to get the job done. Thus, wherever possible, aligning the internalized values of employees with the stated values of the company leads to a stronger and strategically supportive culture.

In a typical evolution, the values and beliefs of the founders of an organization have the greatest influence on the developing culture and the initial set of values and beliefs. These values begin to shape the culture of the organization. They describe the specific attitude and behaviors directed towards each member of the organization, towards the customer, towards suppliers, towards the community, and even towards the competition. This influence on culture was certainly true with Mr. Procter and Mr. Gamble, Mr. Hewlett and Mr. Packard, Mr. Walton, Mr. Watson, and others. These individuals not only spoke about the values, they lived them.

Employees pay more attention to what is modeled than to what is stated. Simply putting placards on the wall won't do the trick. For example, we were working with a large military installation in 1998. This organization had the most beautifully-designed posters you could imagine—lots of eagles, unfurling flags, and gold lettering. Each poster was nicely framed and placed in offices, hallways, and meeting rooms throughout the installation. Among their list of principles was a value that we see just about everywhere we go. It said something to the effect of: "We respect our employees. We believe in an empowered and involved workforce." We had, however, spent some time interviewing employees, and we can say with confidence that the employees were not involved. Some of the managers were extremely autocratic—not much room for empowerment. Instead of having a motivating effect, as senior management had hoped, these beautifully-designed posters only served to build cynicism.

Collins and Porras put it this way: "Hewlett, Packard, Merck, Johnson, and Watson didn't sit down and ask 'What business values would maximize our wealth?' or 'What philosophy would look nice printed on glossy paper?'...No! They articulated what was inside them—what was in their gut, what was bone deep. It was as natural to them as breathing. It's not what they believed as much as *how deeply they believed it* and how consistently their organization lived it."[4]

Xerox rose to legendary status as the fastest company to reach the billion-dollar mark in history. The company's success is due in large part to the influence of founders and charter employees in establishing a benchmark set of enduring values. While rapidly developing its flagship copier, the 914, expenses were high and capital scarce. In order to save money, the company turned off the heat in the winter of 1959–60. Engineers kept bundled in jackets, with blankets draped over their machines that gave off heat, working 24 hours a day, 7 days a week, in order to get the product out on time.

The successful launch of the 914 created an explosion in demand, and parts became scarce. The lack of a critical part, made in Chattanooga, threatened to shut down the entire Rochester production. The director of manufacturing and a purchasing agent decided to fly to Tennessee to get the part, but a snowstorm diverted their plane to Washington, D.C. Nonplussed, the two tried to get train tickets instead, but the railroad would not accept their plane tickets as credit. Lacking cash, the two tracked down a local Xerox employee and borrowed money to take the train. Once in Chattanooga, the two resorted to actually driving a taxi from the station to the vendor, because the regular drivers would not risk it in the storm. The parts were secured. Splitting up to increase their chances of getting back to Rochester, the two traveled a total of 72 hours nonstop, sleeping in their seats and eating peanut butter sandwiches, but the production line never stopped.[5]

Heroic efforts like this become important symbols in establishing an attitude of success in an organization. This can-do spirit was critical to Xerox's early success. It is important to note that these acts were committed not by the founder or CEO. Individuals throughout an organization can exert influence on the firm's values and belief systems through their personal actions.

People have a fundamental need to belong to something they can be proud of. More than any time in the past, employees are demanding operating autonomy while also demanding that the organizations they are connected with stand for something.[6]

We divide the discussion of values and beliefs into two sections:

- Values Integration
- Values Credibility

Values Integration

"It is the consistency of principle that gives us direction. (Certain principles) have been characteristics of P&G ever since our founding in 1837. While Procter & Gamble is oriented to progress and growth, it is vital that employees understand that the company is not only concerned with results, but how the results are obtained."—Ed Harness Former President of P&G

Values Integration is a comprehensive process that begins with a company's clearly defining its core values, and then communicating and reinforcing these values continually throughout the organization. The process includes carefully aligning company practices, systems, and processes to support and sustain core values. Companies who take their values seriously make sure that all employees understand both the content and the spirit of their values and beliefs. Core values are enduring and nonnegotiable.

When we evaluate *Values Integration,* we look at an organization's ability to:

1. Articulate and communicate its core values and beliefs
2. Consider the needs of all key stakeholders as reflected in the values
3. Align all company processes, systems, and practices with core values
4. Reinforce values in all internal communication and company media
5. Ensure that all employees understand the critical importance of rising to the standards set down in the values and beliefs
6. Integrate core values into the strategic planning process

The critical question to ask when identifying core values is, "What values would not be compromised, regardless of external changes in the environment, industry, or market conditions?" Values and beliefs should be distilled from careful consideration and not from shortcut methods of mimicking others, calculating popular positions, or assuming the most profitable short-term stances. Core values are those that are nonnegotiable—even when the environment punishes the firm for having them.

Johnson & Johnson has perhaps one of the most widely publicized and referenced credo or value statements. Written by founder Robert W. Johnson, and modified and expanded over time, the credo has played a very active role in Johnson & Johnson's culture and strategic decision making. The credo establishes the hierarchy of priorities and responsibilities, serving first the customer, then those who work with the company, then management, the community, and finally shareholders, promising them a fair return rather than the often used "maximum profitability."

The differences in the power and influence of a firm's credo were readily apparent in 1982 when Tylenol bottles were tampered with in the Chicago area. Johnson & Johnson immediately responded to the crisis by pulling every bottle of product off the shelves throughout the United States and refitting the product with tamper-fit packaging. The recall alone cost J&J in excess of $100 million dollars. The company also organized a massive communication effort to warn the public and deal with the problem.

Contrast this response with that of Bristol-Myers, who had no credo until 1987 (and which reads like a summary of J&J's credo). A few days after the Tylenol incident, bottles of Excedrin were tampered with in Colorado. The company responded by recalling only the bottles in Colorado and trying to keep the incident quiet. When asked about this approach, Brystol-Myers chairman Richard Gelb was quick to emphasize that the Excedrin incident would have a negative effect on B-M's earnings.[7]

Nokia: Company Ethics Make Good Business Sense

Nokia is a recognized world leader in the telecommunications industry. Around 300 million people are using Nokia phones. The company employs over 50,000 people.

Chairman and CEO, Jorma Ollila, believes that good business sense and sound company ethics are interrelated. (See Table 9.1.) He believes that Nokia stakeholders expect it. He is quoted on their Web site as saying: "It makes business sense to look after the markets we operate in; to anticipate risks; to demonstrate the company values; to work at employee satisfaction; to protect the Nokia brand and build a reputation for citizenship; to improve company efficiency; to meet emerging market needs. As market leader and a

Table 9.1 Nokia Financial Performance 1997–2001[9]

Consideration	2001	2000	1999	1998	1997
Stock Price	24.53	43.50	47.77	15.05	4.34
Total Sales in Millions	27,464.1	26,746.5	17,409.5	11,733.7	7,791.4
EPS	0.405	0.707	0.472	0.317	0.200

leading world brand, Nokia has to earn stakeholders' trust in its company and products in everything it does, throughout the world. The responsibility of a company is of increasing importance for socially responsible investors, environment-conscious consumers, and ethically-aware business partners. And to this end, every single Nokia employee plays his or her part in this challenge."[8]

Can a Steadfast Preoccupation with Values Make a Difference on the Bottom Line?

In a very competitive environment, Nokia's operating margins for the five years ending in 2001 have averaged 16.86 compared to an industry average of just 6.78. The company's net income per employee for the trailing 12 months (as of April 2002) was $37,331, compared to $13,764 for the industry. Nokia's five-year return on investment is 33.22. The industry at large managed only a 5.25 ROI.

A code of conduct was first approved by Nokia's Group Executive Board, and then introduced and reinforced to Nokia employees through recruitment, training, and internal communications. This code of conduct is reflected in the Nokia Values, part of the "Nokia Way," and every Nokia employee is expected to conduct himself or herself, and his or her business, in line with this code without exception. Nokia periodically reviews this code of conduct and is committed to making changes in its content and implementation when changes or further clarification so demand.

The values and principles incorporated in the Nokia Way are at the heart of the organization's culture. They unite the company across the world. Their aim is to create the opportunities for a fluid exchange of ideas—so that employees, customers, suppliers, and partners can feel empowered to develop and deepen their relations.

Nokia's core values are:[10]

Customer satisfaction
We respect and care for our customers, working in partnership with them to satisfy their needs and give them the best possible value.

Respect for the individual
We value people as individuals, whether they are an employee, customer or business partner. This means that trust, openness, fairness, and acceptance, even celebration of diversity—are a given.

Achievement
Our results are achieved because Nokia employees are as familiar with their own well-defined goals as those of the whole company. Our leading position in the industry stems from individual courage, innovation and a constant willingness to learn.

Continuous learning
Entitles everybody at Nokia to develop themselves and find ways to improve their performance. And what's true for the individual is just as true for the company as a whole. We're well aware of the pitfalls of complacency and are committed to keeping our minds open and learning from new developments—wherever they may be.

Core values and beliefs are those underlying assumptions, perceptions, thoughts, and feelings about the way the organization views the world, its members, and the nature and purpose of its existence. These assumptions often go beyond the oft-recited profit motive and enhancement of shareholder wealth.[11]

For value-driven companies, core beliefs are an integral part of strategic thinking. John Young, former CEO at Hewlett-Packard, describes the culture-strategy relationship at H-P and its commitment to its core values, as follows.

> **Our basic principles have endured intact since our founders con-
> ceived them. We distinguish between core values and practices;
> the core values don't change, but the practices might. We've also
> remained clear that profit—as important as it is—is not why the
> Hewlett-Packard Company exists; it exists for more fundamental
> reasons.**[12]

To gain a real foothold with most members of an organization, core values must be self-evident. They must permeate the organization. They must
be timeless in their credibility, and not subject for debate. Because of the
deep personal nature of these ideologies, each organization should strive to
identify its own set of core beliefs and not "borrow" stated values from other
benchmark organizations.

Getting Started

If you have carefully considered, identified, and communicated your core
values to all constituencies, congratulations. You are well on your way to
creating the balance you need as a CEO, business owner, or other executive to increase your chances of achieving whatever it is you hope to
achieve as a company. If not, you have two choices for working towards
this balance:

1. If you have identified your company's core values but they have not
   taken hold . . . kick up the heat. Presuming they are the right values—
   that they address the needs of all stakeholders—find ways to make
   them a real part of the fabric of your company. Refer to them often
   in company meetings and literature. Make sure that they are included
   in your company practices, particularly in the performance management system. (The first time someone does not receive a bonus
   because they violated an operating principle to hit their numbers, the
   word will spread very quickly that the "how" is as important as, if not
   more important than, the "what.")
2. If you have not taken the time to crystallize your values, get you
   senior team together and begin the process. You will be surprised how
   much you can accomplish in just a day.

Here are the steps (Table 9.2):

Table 9.2 Values Identification Exercise

1. Invite everyone to offer ideas for what they believe are (or should be) the overriding principles of the organization.

2. Get everyone's input on flipcharts or some other means of recording. This should be a free exchange with little or no editorial comments or debate.

3. Look for common or similar themes.

4. Discuss these themes and allow them to evolve into a set of care values. (Note: It is better to arrive at a manageable few than a long list of values.

5. Break into groups, one for each of the values.

6. Have each team provide a first draft of their value definition and the expected management and employee behaviors relative to that value.

7. Each group presents their definition and behaviors for adoption or revision by the other senior managers.

8. One person from each team is given the "homework assignment" of incorporating any revisions and distributing the final draft to all participants (after the session).

You might find *Values Formulation Model* (Table 9.3) useful:

This approach is effective because, in addition to clearly defining the value, it provides managers and employees with examples of how they can promote the value inside and outside the organization. Once the values, definitions, and behaviors have been finalized, begin a company-wide communication process. This can be as simple as discussing the values in employee meetings or creating some fanfare around a more formal company event.

One company we worked with added a step between identifying and communicating the values. They conducted several employee focus groups to determine whether employees understood the definitions, whether a significant value had been overlooked, and whether employees felt that the company could live up to the expectations set down in the values. These meetings produced some very interesting exchanges. Based on their personal experiences, some employees put the chances of success of a particular value at less than 10 percent. Needless to say, these meetings were enlightening to management. Fortunately, the reaction by management was to toughen the resolve.

In *Built to Last,* Collins and Porras point out that the 18 "Visionary" companies included in their research tended to have only a few core values, usu-

Table 9.3 Values Formulation Model

Core Value	Definition	Management Behaviors	Employee Behaviors
What is sacred, non-negotiable?	What does it really mean?	How can managers promote this value?	How can employees promote this value?
TEAMWORK (example)	Teamwork is essential to achieving our goals. Capitalizing on the abilities and contributions of individuals across organizational boundaries is vital to our success. We accomplish this by creating an atmosphere of candor and trust between individuals, and treating each other with dignity and respect.	• Facilitate open discussion and an exchange of ideas in group meetings. • Foster interaction among all levels of the organization. • Look for the best resource to achieve goals, regardless of the company structure. • Be tolerant of mistakes. • Wherever possible, empower employees to make things happen.	• Be willing to give 100 percent—all the time. • Treat others with respect. • Be willing to put team rewards ahead of individual rewards. • Think innovatively; don't be afraid to fail. • Be proactive; initiate ideas for improvement.

ally between three and six. In fact, none of the 18 companies has more than six, and most have fewer.[13]

Table 9.4 below lists the kinds of topics that may be included in value and ethics statements. The list is not comprehensive, nor should it be construed that all of these elements ought to be included in a written statement. These are lists that are simply designed to get your thought processes started.

Communicating and reinforcing core values and beliefs is as important as identifying them. By keeping values and beliefs at the center of the radar screen, companies can help employees understand and model the organization's commitment to customers, shareholders, community, and the employees themselves.

The late Mary Kay Ash, founder of Mary Kay Cosmetics, demonstrates one good example of values communication. Ash was frustrated with the fact that she could not find good opportunities for herself and other women in business. This dilemma led to investing in herself and others with the

Table 9.4 Topics Generally Covered in Values Statements and Codes of Ethics[14]

Value Statement Topics	Code of Ethics Topics
• Importance of customers and customer service	• Honesty and observance of the law
• Commitment to quality	• Conflicts of interest
• Commitment to innovation	• Fairness in selling and marketing services
• Respect for the individual employee and the duty the company has to the employee	• Using inside information and securities trading
• Importance of honesty, integrity, and ethical standards	• Supplier relationships and purchasing practices
• Duty to stockholders	• Payments made to obtain business; Foreign Corrupt Practices Act
• Duty to suppliers	• Acquiring and using information about others
• Corporate citizenship	• Political activities
• Importance of protecting the environment	• Use of company assets, resources, and property
	• Protection of proprietary information
	• Pricing, contracting, and billing

forming of Mary Kay Cosmetics. Ash's concern for women's advancement and self-esteem is told over and over again by those who worked for her. These stories promote and sustain the values and norms Mary Kay sought for herself and her associates. She wanted to create a work environment where women could gain self-respect; a motivating environment where performance is rewarded, and where it is clear that management cares about its people. Her ability to communicate and model these behaviors provided a degree of credibility that was infectious. No one could deny that she was serious about these principles.[15]

Disney's use of language, symbolism, ceremonies, and rituals also has solidified a corporate culture admired worldwide. Everyone at Disney is a "cast member," job descriptions are "scripts," a work shift is a "performance," a uniform is a "costume," being on duty is "onstage," and customers are "guests." The special language communicates and reinforces the frame of mind Disney imposes on its employees. In addition, Disney's motto of never being finished as long as there is imagination in the world conveys a feeling of anticipation and innovation.[16]

Organization communication should convey not only an organization's strategic intent, but also the method, atmosphere, and attitude through which the intent may be achieved. This process is vital to gaining the cooperation and commitment of those who will implement the strategy.

Values Credibility

"Numbers and values. We don't have the final answer here—at least I don't. People who make the numbers and share our values go onward and upward. People who miss the numbers and share our values get a second chance. People with no values and no numbers—easy call. The problem is with those who make the numbers, but don't share our value... We try to persuade them, we wrestle with them, we agonize over these people." —Jack Welch

Values Credibility is the outcome of a company's ability to manage performance tied to its values and beliefs. It involves tracking performance against values with the same emphasis as financial or production performance. Credibility comes from creating work environments that are aligned with, and conducive to, core values. This requires rewarding behaviors that model core values, and establishing consequences for the behaviors that could erode these principles. Companies who are serious about the standards they set will take the necessary steps to deal with violations to ensure that values are not compromised.

We evaluate *Values Credibility* by examining an organization's ability to:

1. Maintain a consistency of the culture across all divisions or departments
2. Ensure that no business strategy is ever adopted that might violate the core values and principles
3. Establish a work environment where the day-to-day experience of all employees is consistent with organizational values
4. Rectify circumstances that are inconsistent with these values
5. Reduce or eliminate cynicism throughout the organization

When faced with pressures to perform against increasing competitive intensity, it may be tempting for an organization to compromise core values. Quarterly dividends, earnings per share, competitor encroachment, emerging technology, and the challenge of a global marketplace may affect an organization's commitment to its basic principles.

One only has to look at the recent Enron debacle to realize that the temptation of wealth and greed can corrupt an organization's conscience. Today, there is no telling the degree to which heads of companies will go to conceal problems with the balance sheet. In the Enron case, the victims of this gap of conscience included many loyal employees who literally lost all their savings.

Credibility in values comes from consistency and steadfast, unwavering leadership. In his 1963 booklet, *A Business and Its Beliefs*, Thomas J. Watson, Jr., former CEO of IBM states:

I believe the real difference between success and failure in a corporation can very often be traced to the question of how well the organization brings out the great energies and talents of its people. What does it do to help these people find common cause with each other? . . . And how can it sustain this common cause and sense of direction through the many changes which take place from one generation to another? . . . The answer lies in the power of what we call beliefs and the appeal these beliefs have for its people . . .

I firmly believe that any organization, in order to survive and achieve success, must have a sound set of beliefs on which it premises all its policies and actions. I believe that the most important single factor in corporate success is faithful adherence to those beliefs . . . Beliefs must always come before policies, practices and goals. The latter must always be altered if they are seen to violate fundamental beliefs.[17]

Achieving a durable culture where employee and organizational values are aligned can only be accomplished through the consistent communicating, reviewing, and tracking of these principles throughout the organization.

According to the research conducted by Collins and Porras, "the *authenticity* of the ideology and the extent to which a company attains consistent alignment with the ideology counts more than the *content* of the ideology."[18] They offer the following two-part definition of core ideology (Table 9.5).[19]

Once the values and standards have been established, integrating them into everyday action involves several steps:[20]

- Incorporating the statement of values and the code of ethics into employment orientation, training, and educational programs
- Explicit attention to values and ethics in recruiting and hiring to screen out applicants who lack compatible character traits
- Communication of the values and ethics code to all employees, explaining compliance procedures
- Management involvement and oversight, from the CEO to first line supervisors

Table 9.5   Core Ideology = Core Values + Purpose

Core Values	The organization's essential and enduring tenets—a small set of general guiding principles; not to be confused with specific cultural or operating practices; not to be compromised for financial gain or short-term expediency.
Purpose	The organization's fundamental reasons for existence, beyond just making money—a perpetual guiding star on the horizon; not to be confused with specific goals or business strategies.

- Strong public endorsements by the CEO
- Word-of-mouth indoctrination

Kouzes and Posner provide some practical steps for organizations that are attempting to clarify and renew their shared values:[21]

1. *Participation:* **Solicit feedback from everyone in the organization. An old Chinese proverb applies: "Tell me, I may learn. Teach me, I may remember. Involve me, I will do it."**

2. *Build consensus:* **Focus on understanding shared values. Clarify what is vital and unchangeable as well as secondary and flexible. Solicit responses to hypothetical value dilemmas. Evaluate recent decisions for alignment with agreed-upon values.**

3. *Survey the climate:* **The best way to know what people are thinking is to ask them. Well-designed climate surveys will illuminate which issues and values are clearly understood and which need clarification. They will also measure commitment to established values and allow people to see areas of consistency, change, and improvement.**

4. *Connect values with reasons:* **The importance of certain values may be self-evident. But commitment to values is facilitated when values are traceable to a valid rationale. It also helps people apply the "logic" of that value to new and different situations and promotes consistency in the interpretation and enactment of important principles.**

5. *Structure cooperative goals:* **Encourage cross-functional dialogue and interdisciplinary learning. Members should perceive that they are interconnected, interdependent, and working for the same shared goals.**

6. *Communicate the business:* **Solicit people's responses to the nature of the firm's business, customer profile, revenue streams, and profitability. If members of the organization don't know basic business data, how can they work together to translate shared values and purpose into achieving intent?**

7. *Publicly affirm shared values:* Constituents are filled with energy and enthusiasm when their leaders speak with passion about shared beliefs. Keep people focused by constantly and enthusiastically supporting the process.

8. *Accumulate "yes's":* The key word in agreements is yes. When people say yes to one another, their relationship changes. Look for opportunities to say yes as often as possible. Acknowledge viewpoints and add your own. Don't contradict.

9. *Go slow to go fast:* Start with values and issues easily agreed upon, and move progressively toward more difficult and complex issues. Get people into the habit and role of solving things on a smaller level. Show them that consensus is possible.

10. *Establish a sunset statute:* Rethink your credo or values set periodically. Resist the temptation to rest on your success. Over time, as people leave the organization and new people enter and circumstances change, it would be good practice to review and repeat the process. The outcome may not result in any changes in core values, but the worth of involving people and reinforcing their commitment to the organization will be great.

Social cognition research shows that individuals pick up on all the signals in their work environment—big and small—as cues for how they should behave. Employees notice little things. They want to believe in their company's expressed vision and values, but they are always watchful for those inconsistencies that destroy the credibility of the core ideology.[22]

When people were asked to define credibility in terms of believability of a leader, the two components of almost every definition were what leaders say and what they do.[23] Credibility is about consistency between action and words. People tend to hear the words, observe the actions, and measure the gaps. An individual is deemed credible when the gaps are too small to worry about.

Cynicism, born from consistent disappointment, is virtually nonexistent in a credible organization. Everyone has a voice and acts on behalf of the unit. Credible leaders in credible organizations find unity among diverse interests, points of view, and beliefs. Strengthening the firm's credibility requires clarity, unity, and intensity from its leadership. This process, repeatedly followed, earns the organization credibility and sustains it over time.

Credibility begins with leaders clarifying their own values and modeling these values as they conduct business within an organization and with outside constituencies. When members of an organization understand the guiding principles and core competencies that most directly contribute to the company's success, and when they see these principles in action, a community of shared vision and values is gradually built.

The end result is an organization that lacks cynicism, where employees are engaged in their day-to-day tasks without surprise or frustration. The organization has achieved an important balance between strategy (What will we do?) and culture (How will we behave?).

CHAPTER

Leadership

"Failing organizations are usually over-managed and under-led."

—WARREN BENNIS

No OTHER ELEMENT of a company's culture has a more immediate or sustained impact on an employee attitude, behavior, and performance than how they feel about working for their boss. Want evidence? Just ask employees from two different divisions within the same company how they feel about working for that company. You could get two very different answers. Why? They work for different kinds of bosses with different leadership styles. You remember your best bosses and your worst. So do your employees.

Satisfied employees tend to stick around. Dissatisfied employees hope to leave. Given the cost of training new employees, this is not a trivial issue. Particularly in this time where employees tend to be more transient, keeping talented employees is a challenge that all employers face. Leadership directly impacts the degree of job satisfaction employees experience and their desire to stay.

One of the criteria used to select the *Fortune* magazine 2002 *100 Best Companies to Work For* list is the willingness of these companies to "scramble—to come up with creative ways to keep employees satisfied, and to treat them with respect and dignity."[1] The article goes on to say that no matter how rough the economy—meaning fewer job options for disgruntled employees, "retaining top talent is a huge issue. In fact, losing people in key positions during downturns can be disastrous."[2]

In a poll of 25,000 workers, conducted by the Wilson Learning Corporation, employees said that their managers' leadership skills accounted for 69 percent of their job satisfaction.[3] According to the poll, managers get high ratings when they show employees how their work affects the company's success; when they involve employees in decisions; when they offer developmental opportunities; when they are good coaches and mentors; when they provide frequent performance feedback; and when they recognize and reward achievements.[4]

Leaders create visions. That is their charter. Moses, Abraham Lincoln, Henry Ford, Franklin Roosevelt, Gandhi, Martin Luther King, Gloria Steinem, and Fred Smith have a common trait. They possessed the persuasive skills and the resolve to develop followers who are committed to carrying out a vision. Whether you agree with their agenda is not the point. What is apparent in all these individuals is their ability to set their minds to an outcome and develop a following to help them get there.

Although seemingly obvious, unless a leader has followers that person is not truly a leader. He or she may be a person in authority, but certainly not a leader. "Followers" are defined in a corporate context as those who are influenced into carrying out the activities required to achieve the goals of the organization.

It is important to make the distinction between leaders and managers. Managing your staff is not the same as leading them. A leader defines what the future should look like, aligns people with that vision, and inspires them to make it happen despite the many obstacles that may intervene.[5] Some business thinkers and authors have put it this way: "You manage things. You lead people." Or put another way: "Leadership deals with direction. Management deals with speed."[6]

Stephen Covey offers this insight:

In organizations, people usually perform one of three essential roles: producer, manager, or leader. Each role is vital to the success of the organization ... If there is no producer, great ideas and high resolves are not carried out. The work simply doesn't get done. Where there is no manager, there is role conflict and ambiguity; everyone attempts to be a producer, working independently, with few established systems or procedures. And if there is no leader, there is a lack of vision and direction. People begin to lose sight of their mission ... Although each role is important to the organization, the role of the leader is most important. Without strategic leadership, people may dutifully climb the "ladder of success," but discover, upon reaching the top rung, that the ladder is leaning against the wrong wall.[7]

Management can be defined as dealing with those processes that keep an organization running smoothly. Leadership involves those processes that create organizations or adapt them to changing circumstances. The following table (Figure 10.1)[8] illustrates some of the differences between management and leadership.

Managers who want to become leaders must use their skills to balance the needs of their organization and their followers. Korzes and Posner concluded after much research that to be effective, leaders rely on the following five principles of action:[9]

- Leaders challenge the process. They are pioneers and innovators.
- They encourage those with ideas.
- Leaders inspire a shared vision. They are enthusiastic.
- Leaders enable others to act. They are team players.
- Leaders model the way. They show others how to behave as leaders.
- Leaders "encourage the heart." They openly and often celebrate achievements.

Management	Leadership
Planning and Budgeting: Establishing detailed steps and timetables for achieving needed results, then allocating the resources necessary to make it happen.	**Establishing Direction:** Developing a vision of the future—often the distant future—and strategies for producing the changes needed to achieve that vision.
Organizing and Staffing: Establishing some structure for accomplishing plan requirements, staffing that structure with individuals, delegating responsibility and authority for carrying out the plan, providing policies and procedures to help guide people, and creating methods or systems to monitor implementation.	**Aligning People:** Communicating direction in words and deeds to all those whose cooperation may be needed, so as to influence the creation of teams and coalitions that understand the vision and strategies and that accept their validity.
Controlling and Problem Solving: Monitoring results, identifying deviations from plan, then planning and organizing to solve those problems.	**Motivating and Inspiring:** Energizing people to overcome major political, bureaucratic, and resource barriers to change by satisfying basic, but often unfulfilled, human needs.
↓	↓
Produces a degree of predictability and order, and has the potential to produce consistently the short-term results expected by various stakeholders (e.g., for customers, always being on time; for shareholders, being on budget).	Produces change, often to a dramatic degree, and has the potential to produce extremely useful change (e.g., new products that customers want, new approaches to labor relations that help make a firm more competitive).

Figure 10.1 Management Versus Leadership

One of the best illustrations of the power and impact a leader can have is the concept of "managing by walking around." "MBWA" serves a two-fold purpose—the managing function of observing, communicating, and reviewing performance, and the leadership function of inspiring and modeling behavior.[10]

Bill Hewlett made MBWA a company practice at HP. At the so-called weekly "beer busts" in each division, formal structure yielded to informal socialization as employees were given the opportunity to talk freely with executives at all levels. One symbol of this leadership was the policy to have every employee called by his or her first name.

Roy Kroc regularly visited McDonald's franchises and conducted his own inspections on his four key principles of quality, service, cleanliness, and value. There are stories of his getting out of his limo to pick up litter and lecturing the staff on increased efforts on cleanliness.

Sam Walton had a long-standing reputation for visiting each Wal-Mart store, listening to the customers, store managers, and employees. Sam insisted that the best ideas came from the stockboys and clerks.

GE's Jack Welch not only spent time personally visiting GE operations and talking with major customers, but he arranged his schedule so that he could spend time talking with GE managers taking courses at the company's leadership development center. As Welch put it at the time, "I'm here every day, or out into a factory, smelling it, feeling it, touching it, challenging the people."[11] A. G. Lafley, who has orchestrated the remarkable turnaround at P&G, is another CEO who believes you can learn a lot from walking the floor of a manufacturing plant or visiting stores.

Derailing the Leader: What stops managers from climbing the ladder?

In their book, *The Lessons of Experience,* authors McCall, Lombardo, and Morrison provide a list of "The Ten Fatal Flaws" (Table 10.1) that they contend are key factors that can derail executives. In this chapter, we address several of these flaws and how managers can avoid them.

Leadership can be divided into many specific areas of focus. We have organized the discussion of *leadership* into five sections:

- Management Modeling
- Strategic/Tactical Balance
- Empowerment

Table 10.1 The Ten Fatal Flaws[12]

1. Specific performance problems with the business	Managers run into profit problems, get lazy, or demonstrate that they can't handle certain kinds of jobs (usually new ventures or jobs requiring a lot of persuasion). By failing to admit the problems or covering them up, the managers show they can't change.
2. Insensitivity to others: an abrasive, intimidating, bullying style	*This is the most frequent cause of derailment.* The problem often shows when the manager is under stress.
3. Cold, aloof, arrogant	Some managers are so brilliant that they become arrogant, intimidating others with their knowledge. Managers like this make others feel ignorant, don't listen, think they have all the answers, and don't give people the time of day unless they perceive them to be equally brilliant.
4. Betrayal of trust	This may be a manager's most unforgivable sin. Trust in this context is usually demonstrated in failure to follow through on promises or attempting to "one-up" peers.
5. Overmanaging: failure to delegate or build a team	After a certain point, managers cease to do the work themselves and become executives who see that it is done. Some managers never make this transition, never learning to delegate or build a team beneath them. Overmanaging at any level is frustrating, but at the executive level it can be fatal.
6. Overly ambitious: thinking of the next job, playing politics	Some managers dwell on their advancement, bruising people in their haste and spending too much time trying to please upper management.
7. Failing to staff effectively	Some managers simply pick the wrong people. They create staffs that are too much like them. Therefore, there is no balance of skills.
8. Inability to think strategically	A preoccupation with details and miring in technical problems keeps some executives from grasping the bigger picture. They simply can't go from being doers to being planners.
9. Unable to adapt to a boss with a different style	Successful managers don't always get along with their bosses. But, unlike the derailed manager, they don't get into wars over disagreements, and rarely do they let the issues get personal.
10. Overdependence on a mentor or advocate	Sometimes managers stay with a single advocate or mentor for too long. If the mentor falls from favor, so do they. Even if the mentor remains in power, people begin to question the executive's ability to make independent judgments.

- Developmental Coaching
- Building Effective Teams

Although there are many theories and models about leadership's role in the organization and how leadership style can impact the culture, the leadership characteristics selected are universal in scope and common to most organizations.

Management Modeling

"Example isn't another way to teach, it is the only way to teach."
—Albert Einstein

Management modeling is the means by which leaders demonstrate, through their words and deeds, a genuine commitment to their organization's vision and values. *Management modeling* is "walking the talk." It means behaving the way you want all members of the organization to behave. It means exemplifying company values and beliefs through personal actions. This leadership characteristic requires a real understanding and appreciation of the significant impact that management behavior has on the overall credibility of the company's standards and ideals.

When we assess *management modeling* in an organization, we look at senior management's ability to:

1. Consistently model the behaviors and principles articulated in the company's values and beliefs
2. Ensure that employees across the company experience management styles that are consistent with organizational values and beliefs
3. Instill a sense of confidence in the organization's leadership
4. Demonstrate unwavering ethics and honesty

Effective leaders know that their own visible behavior is the most powerful way to communicate the underlying standards and beliefs of a company to other members of the organization. This requires more than just giving lip service to the firm's stated goals, objectives, and values. It means coming to work every day demonstrating a commitment to strategy through personal actions.[13]

As Gayle Hamilton of Pacific Gas and Electric, a firm known for its strong culture, put it, "You can't follow someone who isn't credible, who doesn't truly believe in what they're doing—and how they are doing it."[14]

A survey was used to ask employees to name characteristics of leaders they most admired. Honesty was selected more often than any other trait.[15] Honesty (and its companion, integrity) is essential to leadership and establishing and maintaining trust within the organization. Nothing will establish that trust more effectively than employees' observing a company's leaders doing the sorts of things that naturally reinforce the principles of the organization.

Applying Management Modeling: Building Credibility at the Top

As the old adage says, "Actions speak louder than words." This has never been more important than when tied to the concept of *management modeling*. Unfortunately, studies indicate that, where many senior executives are concerned, this fundamental advice goes unheeded. The Enron and Adelphia Cable scandals are severe examples of what can happen when an organization loses its conscience. As one leadership expert put it, "Ninety-five percent of American managers today say the right thing. Five percent actually do it."[16] Table 10.2 illustrates what leaders can do to gain credibility.

A study by Booz Allen & Hamilton surveyed management teams at 27 Fortune 500 manufacturing and service firms.[17] They found that although virtually all the companies surveyed paid lip service to quality, customer satisfaction, and maintaining superior service levels, virtually none of the top

Table 10.2 Some Common Actions Leaders Can Do to Build Respect, Trust, and a Willingness to Be Influenced

A Leader Can...

• Have the courage to do the right thing	• Make time for people
• Share the vision, frequently	• Open doors
• Provide support	• Admit mistakes
• Act as a mentor and advisor	• Celebrate success stories
• Listen	• Personally thank someone
• Praise good works	• Empower others
• Follow through on commitments	• Trust others
• Establish personal trustworthiness	• Keep promises
• Exemplify company principles	• Give good service
• Show patience	• Solve problems creatively

executives actually tracked these areas' performances at nearly the level they did for financial indicators such as profitability, costs, and stock performance.

Sound familiar?

It is critically important that leadership behaviors be based on personal convictions rather than on exterior influences. Anyone can tell the difference between someone who is acting on personal beliefs and one who is acting because they are paid to do so—or afraid they won't be paid if they don't. How do your senior managers behave away from work? Are ethics and fairplay in evidence away from the shop? How much do you trust your colleagues to do the right thing? Tsun-Yan Hsieh, a leadership consultant at McKinsey & Company, explains, "Successful leaders...are not deliberately 'acting' as much as they are doing what they believe in, living it, personifying it."[18]

When leaders act contrary to their stated positions and values, in addition to creating an atmosphere of mistrust, they can directly affect the performance of the organization.

Consider this case study: A capital equipment manufacturer had grown to $400 million in eight short years. The company was trying to transform itself from a tightly controlled family-run shop into a fully developed corporation. The management presentations, memos, and events sponsored by the firm all pushed for empowerment and lower-level decision making, particularly in the areas of customer service and sales. The sales group was especially vulnerable to competitor encroachment.

However, in spite of the company's good intentions, the approval process on all activities still required an executive team member's signature. In one instance, a package that was to be sent at the request of a large customer in India was delayed. The international manager missed an important customer deadline and a subsequent chance at getting a very large order in India.

The bottleneck occurred when the CFO held up his approval of sending the package until he had more information. He was concerned about the shipping costs. The CFO waited until he could call the international manager into his office and inquire whether the customer response process could be streamlined to allow the packages in the future to be sent through routine U.S. Postal Service rather than overnight delivery. The international manager assured the CFO that the overnight service was required, not just because of time constraints, but because of the tracking and delivery verification included in the service.

The actual discussion between the CFO and the international manager took 10 minutes. Ironically, the discussion interrupted a meeting the manager was having with his department on improving the company's poor responsiveness to customer requests. It turns out that the cost of the overnight invoice—resulting in a discussion that occupied the time of two executives and kept five others waiting—was $32. Said the international manager, "When measured against the messages delivered that day to not only me, but to all the managers at the meeting and throughout the organization, the cost of that 'savings' was far too high."

Kotter and Heskett's research into adaptive versus unadaptive cultures (see "Adaptability to Change" in Chapter 12) tells us that, in adaptive cultures, most managers care deeply about customers, stockholders, and employees. They also strongly value people and processes that can create useful change throughout the organization. Managers in healthy work environments tend to pay close attention to all their constituencies, especially customers, and initiate change when needed to serve the legitimate interests of these constituencies, even if that entails taking some risks.

However, in unadaptive cultures, managers tend to behave somewhat insularly, politically, and bureaucratically. Most managers in these environments care mainly about themselves, their immediate work group, or some product (or technology) associated with that work group. The drive in these instances is personal gain.[19]

Building trust through *management modeling* promotes open and honest communication and builds solid, productive working relationships. Lack of trust in an organization, brought on by inconsistent or self-serving behaviors, leads to unadaptive cultures where time is spent protecting one's turf, double-checking people's work, questioning colleagues' intentions, looking out for number one, and so on. Lack of trust drains a company of its ability to do the important work of innovating, collaborating, and, ultimately, adding value.

Strategic / Tactical Balance

"Effective managers live in the present but concentrate on the future."
—*James Hayes*

The best-run companies make sure that managers and employees understand both the short- and long-term direction of the organization. *Strategic and tactical balance* is the outcome achieved by organizations that establish and sustain a standard where managers are expected to understand the "big picture." This balance ensures that managers appreciate the impact of their decisions. Educating managers with this approach adjusts their focus from a tactical or departmental view, to a broader, company-wide perspective.

We evaluate a company's *strategic and tactical balance* by looking at its ability to:

1. Establish the importance of a strategic view throughout the organization at all levels
2. Develop an effective balance of strategic skills (vision and planning) and tactical skills (job competence) with its managers
3. Ensure that managers consider the broader, long-term implications of their decisions and actions, not just the short-term gains
4. Make sure that managers at all levels can effectively communicate the strategic plan to their staff

Leadership and management are often an exercise in balance. Allocating limited resources such as time, personnel, budgets, and equipment always involves weighing one priority over the next. Balancing time and energy between long-term strategic thinking and short-term tactical implementation is a perennial business challenge. Too much attention to planning for the future can lead to missing current targets. All one has to do is look at the "dot.com" blow-up of 2001 to see example after example of how long-term strategies never got off the ground because short-term cash needs were insufficient.

On the other hand, too much attention to day-to-day concerns causes managers to become departmentalized and myopic. When tasks in and of themselves become the focal point, managers start to forget why they are completing these tasks to begin with. The balance required in this trade-off between strategy and tactics most often falls on the shoulders of middle managers who have the responsibility for contributing the tangible deliverables that are the milestones of a company's strategic intent.

Leadership requires an ability to see the bigger picture and to maintain a balance between high-level strategies and front-line tactics.

General Electric: Integrity, Performance, and a Thirst for Change

In 2002, for the fifth consecutive year, General Electric was number one on *Fortune* magazine's list of America's Most Admired Companies. GE also sits on top of the *Fortune*'s Global Most Admired list. Candidates for these lists include all companies on the *Fortune* Global 500 list, plus 100 additional companies, with revenues of at least $8 billion, that are leaders in their industries. Over 10,000 executives were asked to rate the companies in their own industries based on eight criteria: innovation, financial soundness, employee talent, use of corporate assets, long-term investment value, social responsibility, quality of management, and quality of products and services.[20]

GE achieved record earnings and cash generation in 2001 with 11-percent increases in earning and earning per share (EPS) as well as 12-percent growth in cash flow from operating activities.[21] GE Chairman and CEO Jeff Immelt stated in the release, "Despite a global recession and the September 11 terrorist attacks, we delivered double-digit earnings growth. This is a tribute to our great global team and the strength of the GE business model." (See Table 10.3.)[22]

Why has GE become so admired over the years? A big part of the reason is the company's legacy of training great managers and its long-standing culture of entrepreneurship and achievement. Achievement is a religion at GE. Life as a manager at GE is all about business performance. In short, this means hitting your numbers. Jack Welch, GE's CEO from 1981 until 2001, is well known for establishing a standard where if a strategic business unit (SBU) is not first or second in its industry, the president may be replaced or the SBU may be sold. At GE, if you are a senior manager and you miss your numbers, you may be paid a personal visit from the CEO.

In Welch's memoir, *Jack: Straight from the Gut,* he remembers cornering Jeffrey Immelt at a company retreat in early 1995. At the time, Immelt was the chief of GE's plastics division. Increased costs led to a revenue amount that was $50 million less than the 1994 target. Welch issued this stern warning to Immelt: "I love you, and I know you can do better. But I'm going to take you out if you can't get it fixed."[23] Obviously, Immelt got it fixed.

That's how things work at GE. Financial targets are set. Some adjustments are made for economic conditions and industry-specific difficulties,

Table 10.3 GE Financial Performance 1997–2001

Consideration	2001	2000	1999	1998	1997
Stock Price	39.89	46.97	50.26	33.13	23.83
Total Sales in Millions	125,913.0	129,853.0	111,630.0	100,469.0	90,840.0
EPS	1.422	1.287	1.090	0.948	0.835

but the true GE heroes are those who make their numbers even when times are tough. And if you're able to help out with something extra to help the company meet its overall goals when other divisions are struggling, well, that's even better.[24]

In order to contribute cross-functionally, managers must be aware of the big picture. They must understand how all the parts come together and how they contribute to the organizational bottom line, not just within their SBU. They must possess the strategic and tactical balance.

GE values are built around what the company refers to as the "Three Traditions of GE:" unyielding integrity, commitment to performance, and a thirst for change. Notice how the values invite participation and involvement from all employees:

- **Passion for Our Customers:** Measuring our success by that of our customers...always driven by Six Sigma quality and a spirit of innovation.
- **Meritocracy:** Creating opportunities for the best people from around the world to grow and live their dreams.
- **Growth Driven, Globally Oriented:** Growing our people, markets, and businesses around the world.
- **Every Person, Every Idea Counts:** Respecting the individual and valuing contributions of each employee.
- **Playing Offense:** Using the advantages of size to take risks and try new things...never allowing size to be a disadvantage.
- **Embracing Speed and Excellence:** Using the benefits of a digital age to accelerate our success and build a faster and smarter GE.
- **Living the Hallmarks of GE Leadership:**
  - Passion for learning and sharing ideas
  - Committed to delivering results in every environment
  - Ability to energize and inspire global, diverse teams
  - Connected to workplace, customers, and communities...in touch with the world

Crotonville: Teaching the Balance

GE backs up these values with a strong commitment to education. The company provides forums where employees can openly discuss strategies. Crotonville, GE's 52-acre corporate campus nestled in the Hudson Valley of

New York, is where GE managers learn to think strategically. This is the home of the famous "Workout" sessions that Welch embraced as far back as 1982. In classrooms such as the main auditorium, often called "The Pit," everyone, from newly hired college graduates to the Chairman, come together to identify opportunities and debate the issues facing GE around the world. This amounts to thousands of people involved in theses discussions each year, which means thousands of managers and employees are encouraged to think outside their immediate departments and discuss the implications of organizational strategy from the 30,000-foot level.

The *Leadership Development Program* at Crotonville brings together leaders from all of the diverse GE businesses around the world. Crotonville serves as a common frame of reference to forge ties that promote the sharing of best practices throughout the company. The *Executive Development Program* emphasizes strategic thinking, executive leadership, and cross-functional integration. Over the years, GE has used Crotonville to introduce landmark programs like Management by Objectives (MBO), SWOT (an analysis of Strengths, Weaknesses, Opportunities and Threats), and more recently, Six Sigma, and Best Practices.[25]

Through Crotonville programs and other means, GE provides forums for employees and managers not only to understand, but also to embrace the strategic thinking process. They meet to work on significant business problems and share their knowledge. These are the types of environments where employees develop a real appreciation for how their efforts are tied to the big picture.

Applying Strategic and Tactical Balance

The best-run companies ensure that all employees understand the strategic direction of the organization, and just as importantly, how their individual contributions are tied to that strategy. In our company, Virtual CEO, Inc., we make a concerted effort to let our employees know, at every opportunity, how their specific actions are tied to the bottom line. We let them know exactly how much revenue was generated at a result of their efforts. We also let them know how this revenue fuels our overall strategic plan.

In his book, *The One Page Business Plan,* Jim Horan offers a simple, straightforward methodology for getting all members of an organization, from the CEO and senior management to the newest employee, focused on the organizational vision and the strategies that will drive that vision. Horan provides

Table 10.4   One Page Business Plan[26]

Vision	**How do you visualize your business?**
	• **What** products and services will you offer?
	• **Where** will you operate? Where are your customers?
	• **Who** are you customers? Your strategic alliances?
	• **When** will you begin? When will systems be functional?
	• **Why** are you creating this business? Why would customers be interested?
	• **How** will you finance the business? What kind of culture will you create? How do you want to interact with employees, suppliers, and customers?
Mission	**Why does your business exist?**
	• **What** is your product or service? What makes you different from the competition?
	• **Describe** your ideal customers.
	• **Why** will customers buy your products and services? What value will they perceive?
	• **What** passions are you trying to satisfy? Who will benefit from this business?
Objectives	**What are the goals? How do you define success?**
	• **What** targets will you set for Finance, Marketing and Sales, Operations, Human Resources, R&D, Manufacturing, etc?
Strategies	**How will you grow and manage the business?**
	What are the strengths and weaknesses of your organization? **What** opportunities and threats do the marketplace provide? **How** do we get there from here?
Plans	**What specific actions will the business implement to achieve its goals?**
	• **What** projects should be undertaken?
	• **How** will you measure the results?
	• **What** are the next steps?

a model (Table 10.4). We have added some information taken from his book to give you an idea of the scope of each of the five components.

Every level in the organization completes a *One Page Business Plan* with their version of the five components. All departmental plans are tied to the organization's master plan. These individual plans describe the profit center, department, project or program being built, why it is being built, how it will be built, and the specific measurable results that will be accomplished.[27]

Here is a quick example of the difference in perspectives of executives at a company with strategic and tactical balance and executives from a company without this balance. A group of executives from a *Fortune 500* firm visited Chaparral Steel to learn how to manage its teams. One executive asked, "How do you schedule coffee breaks in the plant?" The Chaparral manager replied, "The workers decide when they want a cup of coffee." "Yes," said the executive, "but who tells them it's okay to leave the machines?" As the Chaparral manager commented later, "The guy left and still didn't get it."[28]

The Chaparral workers know when to take a break because they were trained to understand how the whole business operates. They know the "big picture." Once trained in the "Chaparral process," workers understand how their jobs relate to the welfare of the entire organization. Financial statements are posted monthly in the mill, including a chart tracking operating profits before taxes—the key measure for profit sharing. Because employees at Chaparral understand the relationship between production and profits, they choose to take their breaks at times that will not negatively impact production. It's not rocket science. It's common-sense thinking brought about by involving employees in understanding how the business works.

Speaking of which, we would be remiss in discussing this idea of involving employees in the big picture if we did not mention Jack Stack's book, *The Great Game of Business.* In 1983, Jack and his team of managers took over a failing International Harvester plant in Springfield, Missouri. The company offered to let Jack and his team purchase the plant. As a result, Springfield Remanufacturing Corporation (SRC) was born. Jack says in his book that SRC couldn't rely on traditional ways of managing because this style of management wouldn't produce the kind of results they needed in time to save the company. As a result, he and his managers developed an "Open Book Management" approach, where all employees have at least a basic understanding of cash flow and the balance sheet. Jack describes what lies at the heart of the concept of *The Great Game of Business:*

The best, most efficient, and most profitable way to operate a business is to give everybody in the company a voice in saying how the company is run and a stake in the financial outcome good or bad.[29]

The essence of the leadership concept of *strategic and tactical balance* is finding ways to ensure that managers and employees truly understand the vision and strategic direction of their company and how their efforts are directly tied to that plan. How many of your employees would be able to answer you with confidence if you asked them to describe your company's strategy and what role they played in that strategy? There is a very simple way to find out... ask.

Empowerment

"The best executive is the one who has enough sense to pick good people to do what he wants done, and self-restraint enough to keep from meddling with them while they do it." —*Theodore Roosevelt*

Empowerment involves sharing decision-making responsibilities throughout all levels in an organization. Companies who empower employees tend to utilize localized rather than centralized control, wherever possible. They attempt to minimize bureaucratic "red tape."

When we evaluate *empowerment*, we look at an organization's ability to:

1. Drive decision making to the lowest appropriate level in the organization
2. Reach decisions without unnecessary "chain of command" approvals
3. Develop managers who know when to manage projects personally and when to let their staff have the authority
4. Consistently encourage employee involvement

Cisco: Letting Employees Discover and Develop Solutions

Cisco Systems, Inc. was founded in 1984 by a group of computer scientists from Stanford University. The San Jose-based company is recognized as a worldwide leader in networking for the Internet. Cisco engineers have been prominent in advancing the development of Internet Protocol-based (IP), the basic language used to communicate over the Internet and in private networks. The company develops products and technologies that are designed to make the Internet more useful now and in the future. These technologies include routing and switching, voice and video over IP, optical networking, wireless, storage networking, security, broadband, and content networking.[30]

Virtually all messages or transactions passing over the Internet are carried through Cisco equipment. As of January 2002, the company had a market cap of $138.3 billion. For the five years ending in 2001, Cisco has enjoyed a High Price Earnings Ratio of 236.05. The same ratio for the communications equipment industry during this time frame was 64.65. For the last five years, Cisco's pre-tax margin has averaged 20.28, compared to 9.50 for the industry as a whole. The company's five-year sales growth rate was 40.33 compared to the industry average of 34.24.[31] (See Table 10.5 below.)[32]

In addition to major operations in California, North Carolina, Massachusetts, and the United Kingdom, Cisco has grown to more than 430 sales and support offices located in 60 countries. As of October of 2001, Cisco had 37,546 employees worldwide, of which approximately 14,800 work in or reside near the California bay area headquarters.

Empowerment as Part of the Culture

According to Peter Senge, in his book *The Fifth Discipline,* "To empower people in an unaligned organization can be counterproductive. If people do not share a common vision, and do not share common 'mental models' about the business reality within which they operate, empowering people will only increase organizational stress and the burden of management to maintain coherence and direction."[33]

Cisco's culture encourages creative thinking tied to a shared vision. They make it easier for employees to contribute. The structure and culture of the company dictate that local decision making be instituted. One of the guiding principles that has allowed Cisco to grow so quickly is the belief that employees must be empowered to find solutions on their own.

Here are some excerpts from Cisco's "Company Overview" on their Web site:

Cisco is unlike most companies you've worked for, or even read about. We do not focus on narrow markets. We focus on creating solutions that offer our customers a tremendous competitive advantage. That takes talented, innovative, and creative people.

Table 10.5 Cisco Financial Performance 1997–2001

Consideration	2001	2000	1999	1998	1997
Stock Price	18.11	38.25	53.56	23.20	9.29
Total Sales in Millions	22,293.0	18,928.0	12,173.0	8,489.0	6,452.0
EPS	(0.141)	0.386	0.304	0.211	0.176

While many companies stifle enthusiasm with a long set of rules, Cisco has a short list of guidelines designed to inspire "out-of-the-box" thinking. Simply put, Cisco creates opportunities and solutions for our customers.

This begins with every employee. At every turn, employees are empowered to discover and develop new solutions. We strive to achieve this goal in product development, selling complete business solutions, after-sale customer care, and across all of our business units and functions.

We rely on teamwork—a collaborative environment that thrives on working across geographical and organizational boundaries, sharing information and finding new and better ways to support each other and our customers.

Empowerment Applies to the Public Sector, Too

The Army Corps of Engineers carries on a proud heritage that began in 1775 when the Continental Congress designated the first Chief Engineer, whose first task was to build fortifications near Boston at Bunker Hill. As commander of the U.S. Army Corps of Engineers, the Chief of Engineers leads a major Army command that is the world's largest public engineering, design, and construction management agency. His office has the overarching responsibility for maintaining the historic high standards of the Corps.

We like the direct and uncomplicated statement of empowerment provided to all members of the Corps by LTG Robert B. Flowers, current Chief of Engineers and Commander, U.S. Army Corps of Engineers. In the "Commitment" section of the Corps Strategic Vision Statement, General Flowers poses a simple set of questions regarding one's ability to take action. He says:

ASK YOURSELF:

- Is it good for the customer?
- Is it legal and ethical?
- Is it something I am willing to be accountable for?

If so, don't ask permission, you already have it.

DO IT!

Many of the same organizational attributes required to develop leadership are also needed to empower employees. These facilitating factors include flatter organizational hierarchies, less bureaucracy, and a greater willingness to take risks.[34] Organizations that thrive in today's intensely competitive marketplaces will usually have flat structures, self-managing workforces, and executives that focus on providing and fostering leadership.

Nordstrom is one of the 18 visionary companies carefully detailed in Collins and Porras' *Built to Last.* Consider the company's "Employee Handbook." It consists of a single five-by-eight-inch card (Figure 10.2) that reads:[35]

WELCOME TO NORDSTROM

We're glad to have you with our Company.
Our number one goal is to provide
outstanding customer service.
Set both your personal and professional goals high.
We have great confidence in your ability to achieve them.

Nordstrom Rules:
Rule #1: **Use your good
judgment in all situations.**
There are no additional rules.

Please feel free to ask your department manager,
store manager or division general manager
any question at any time.

Figure 10.2

It takes a considerable degree of trust and confidence to leave judgment entirely up to your workforce. What degree of autonomy is right for the employees of your organization? How do you know? How do they know? Covey says you can't have empowerment without first having trust.[36] *Trust* in this context is described as a manager having confidence in an employee's skill and judgment. Which of your employees have demonstrated the skill and judgment to take on more responsibility? Are you and your managers paying attention?

It's useful for all managers to remember that each of their employees—even the low performers—take on leadership roles in their lives away from work. They manage households. They sit on homeowners association boards. They lead PTAs or church groups. They run little league and soccer camps. And yet, as managers, we may forget that they may have these skills. We too often insist on taking control, resisting the opportunity to share some of our responsibilities and the authority that comes with them. The result is more work for the manager and a conditioning process in which employees gradually decrease their initiative and involvement. Are your employees given opportunities to demonstrate leadership inside your organization? Or do they have to seek these opportunities elsewhere?

Significant evidence exists to suggest that a participative management style results in greater job satisfaction than an autocratic approach. Leaders who adopt and utilize participative principles create motivational environments that lead to greater employee satisfaction, and ultimately, better job performance.[37] Employees who experience a greater degree of freedom and autonomy, who are consistently recognized for their contributions, and who are involved in the decision-making process are generally more satisfied than employees who do not experience these approaches.[38] The implication is that managers who adopt and utilize participative approaches that encourage employee involvement create motivational work climates that, in turn, lead to higher degrees of job satisfaction.

Yet, despite these outcomes, many companies fail to remove the barriers to employee empowerment. According to change expert John Kotter, there are four key barriers to empowerment (Figure 10.3).

1. **Structural Barriers** can include silos that function independently and thus inhibit communication, layers of middle-level managers who may question or second-guess employee ideas, fragmented resources that make productivity difficult, and corporate headquarters that impose centralized decision making.

2. **Inadequate Training** can inhibit empowerment. Companies must recognize that new behaviors, skills, and attitudes will be needed when major changes are initiated. Without the right skills and attitudes, people feel unempowered. Companies also view the cost of training as a deterrent.

3. **Outmoded Systems** can block action. Human resource systems such as recruitment programs, compensation plans, and performance management programs, as well as company information systems, must be properly aligned to support empowerment.

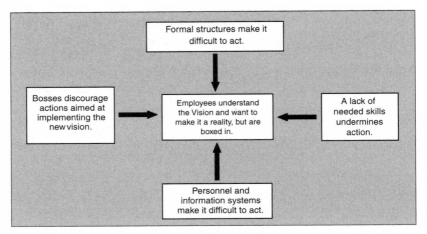

Figure 10.3 Barriers to Empowerment[39]

4. **Ineffective Bosses** can also undercut empowerment. With the right kind of leadership, companies are finding that they can tap into an enormous source of power to improve organizational performance.

An example of the success of empowerment is the case of Scandinavian Air Systems (SAS). Jan Carlzon was named President and CEO of the SAS Group in 1981, after less than a year as Chief Operating Officer and head of the airline. He rapidly turned SAS into a moneymaker and consumer favorite, replacing production orientation with customer focus.

Jan Carlzon created his now-famous "Moments of Truth" referring to the critically important moments when an employee had the opportunity to satisfy a passenger who was upset with some element of SAS's service. These incidents, contended Jan, would make or break the airline's success. Recognizing the need for immediate solutions at moments like this, Jann began empowering his employees to make decisions on their own and not be thwarted by company policy and procedure.[40] At first, Jan's management team expressed their concern that employees would "give away the store." But just the opposite happened. When given the added authority to use company funds to solve passenger problems, employees treated this new authority responsibly. In a few short years, performance steadily improved, and in January 1984, SAS was nominated "Airline of the Year 1983" by *Air Transport World* magazine.[41]

Here is an excerpt from Carlzon's book, *Moments of Truth,* that illustrates how effectively the airline created an empowered workforce:

Rudy Peterson was an American businessman staying at the Grand Hotel in Stockholm. One day he left the hotel and headed for Arlanda Airport, north of Stockholm, to accompany a colleague on a Scandinavian Airlines flight to Copenhagen. The trip was only for the day, but it was important.

When he arrived at the airport, he realized he'd left his ticket back at the hotel. He had set it down on the bureau to don his overcoat and had forgotten to pick it up.

Everyone knows you can't board an airplane without a ticket, so Rudy Peterson had already resigned himself to missing the flight and his business meeting in Copenhagen. But when he explained his dilemma to the ticket agent, he got a pleasant surprise.

"Don't worry, Mr. Peterson," she said with a smile. "Here's your boarding card. I'll insert a temporary ticket in here. If you just tell me your room number at the Grand Hotel and your destination in Copenhagen, I'll take care of the rest."

While Rudy and his colleague waited in the passenger lounge, the ticket agent dialed the hotel. A bellhop checked the room and found the ticket—exactly where Mr. Peterson had said it would be. The ticket agent then sent an SAS limo to retrieve it from the hotel and bring it directly to her. As it happened, they moved so quickly that the ticket arrived before the Copenhagen flight departed. No one was more surprised than Rudy Peterson when the flight attendant approached him and said calmly, "Mr. Peterson? Here's your ticket."

What would have happened at a more traditional airline? Most airline manuals are clear: "No ticket, no flight." At best, the ticket agent would have informed her supervisor of the problem, but Rudy Peterson almost certainly would have missed his flight.

Instead, because of the way SAS handled his situation, he was both impressed and on time for his meeting.[42]

Tim Firnstahl,[43] who owns a chain of restaurants in and around Seattle, discovered the benefits of aligning systems with empowered employees. Tim's market position and overriding ethic is to provide world-class customer service and to make the customer happy. The company motto, "We Always Guarantee Satisfaction" (WAGS), is a shared rallying cry throughout the organization, and the WAGS logo appears on shirts, report forms, menus, nametags, and training manuals.

Some time after opening, however, Tim realized that although employees signed WAGS commitment pledges and were trained on their responsibility to the customer, they had not been taught to make use of their authority to please the customer. The result was finger pointing and abdication of their roles and responsibilities.

Employees were given the authority to correct situations with no delay and with no paperwork. Guidelines were established. Employees were instructed to do whatever possible to ensure the guarantee was in effect. The entire tab could be picked up if necessary without penalties. Although skeptical at first, the employees' power as company representatives increased their pride in the business, and increased motivation.

Creative solutions began to impress the clientele. When the customer ordered a margarita as it was made at another restaurant, the waiter informed the bartender, who called the other restaurant and got the recipe. When an elderly woman who had not been in for a long while ordered breakfast, which was no longer served, the crew went out and bought the required eggs and bacon and prepared the breakfast she wanted.

The end result was increased profits. Customers always ask Tim where he found such wonderful staff. Tim's reply is that his employees are "better than most, because they have power and the obligation to solve customer problems on their own and on the spot. Giving them complete discretion about how they do it has also given them pride ... The people who work for us know we take our guarantee seriously and expect them to do the same."

Applying Empowerment

Ken Blanchard is chairman of Blanchard Training and Development, Inc., a full-service management consulting and training company, which he co-founded in 1979 with his wife Marjorie. Blanchard developed the *Situational Leadership Model* that teaches leaders to diagnose the needs of an individual or a team at a particular point in time and to use the leadership style that matches or responds to the needs of the situation.[44]

Using a quadrant approach, the *Situational Leadership Model* (Figure 10.4) demonstrates how managers have the ability to move from *directing* to *delegating*, depending on the complexity of the task and the maturity and experience of the individual or team.

In essence, the Situational Leadership approach conditions managers to think first before they involve themselves in directing or supervising a project or situation. If managers want to develop better delegation skills, they should begin by understanding their current level of comfort regarding taking or releasing control.

Once, when we were leading executive leadership courses at a large national bank, a substantial number of branch managers in attendance lamented how they had to work long hours just to keep up, many of them staying late on weekdays and coming in on weekends. When pressed to discuss what tasks they were accomplishing during theses long hours, many of them indicated tasks that could have easily been delegated to their staff. In effect, their heavy workload was directly related to their inability or unwillingness to give up control.

The *Leadership Involvement Matrix* (Figure 10.5) shows the four choices available to all managers whenever they are confronted with a project. Although the choices seem evident, a surprising number of managers remain locked in one or two of the choices.

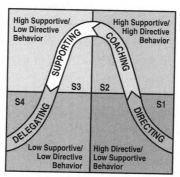

Figure 10.4 Situational Leadership Model—©The Ken Blanchard Companies.[45]

RESPONSIBILITY BELONGS TO:

		THE EMPLOYEE	THE LEADER
INDEPENDENCE IS:	**LOW**	3. YOU'LL DO IT WITH MY INPUT	2. I'LL DO IT WITH YOUR INPUT
	HIGH	4. YOU'LL DO IT	1. I'LL DO IT

Figure 10.5   Leadership Involvement Matrix

When presented with a task, managers can elect to take one of four approaches:

1. They can complete the assignment themselves with no help or input from their staff.
2. They can maintain primary responsibility for the task, but ask for input from their staff.
3. They can give a staff member primary responsibility, but reserve the opportunity to provide input.
4. They can let the staff member complete the assignment independently, with no input.

Each of these choices can be appropriate given the circumstances surrounding the assignment. If there are substantial time restraints, and no individual on their staff has the skill to complete the assignment without significant supervision and guidance, a manager may elect to complete the task independently. If time is less of an issue and the employee is reasonably competent to lead the project, the manager may elect to delegate the assignment, but reserve the right to offer input before the work is completed. The key point here is not to become locked into using the same approach for every situation.

Successful implementation of a strategic plan is best served by a management style that is based on situational leadership practices, where the degree of control or empowerment is determined by the complexity of the task and the skill and maturation of the employee, and not by the personal preferences or habits of the manager. With the right structure, training, systems, and supervision in place, employees can significantly contribute to improving organizational performance.

Developmental Coaching

"Never tell people how to do things. Tell them what to do and they will surprise you with their ingenuity."—General George S. Patton

Developmental coaching is as much an attitude as it is an action. This approach requires more of a manager's time and attention because it involves getting to know the personal aspirations of their staff. *Developmental Coaching* builds upon the skills we learned in our first supervision class—skills like maintaining an employee's self-esteem during counseling, being willing to confront poor performance, showing appreciation for good work, and taking steps to raise the level of employee initiative.

When we assess *developmental coaching,* we consider an organization's ability to:

1. Integrate employees' personal goals with those of the organization
2. Use coaching as a developmental opportunity versus a punitive process
3. Regard delegation as a motivational tool
4. Promote and sustain employee initiative
5. Develop managers who are able and willing to use positive reinforcement

In the book *Becoming a Master Manager,* the authors offer the following observation: "One of the greatest sources of frustration [for managers] is the common misconception that people join organizations to pursue the organization's goals. In fact, most people join organization's to pursue their *own* goals."[46] How do you tap into the potential of employees whose primary sense of motivation is "What's in it for me?" How do you match the work that needs to get done with the work employees want to do?

Delegation has been around since God told Noah to build an ark. Over the centuries, the art of delegation has been analyzed, reengineered, and refined, but even to this day, employees may perceive delegated work as just one more thing on their plate. What makes a new task seem more appealing? Some suggest that this occurs when employees perceive the task as being aligned with their personal development goals.

Does this mean that every time managers delegate tasks, they must first check with employees to see if it fits their personal agenda? Of course not. No one is suggesting that work environments are pure democracies. Still, there is sufficient research to suggest that if employee aspirations are considered in tandem with company objectives, the outcome will be better for all concerned.

Covey talks about breaking the "human barrier," a process where organizations evolve and begin truly to see their employees as assets, not liabilities. He says, "A few well-trained and courageous managers are breaking the mythical human barrier and proving that gains in human performance of 500 percent—not just 5 percent—are possible...People in high-performance organizations tend to be much healthier and happier. Because they are treated as the most valuable resource in the organization, they assist each other in making quantum leaps in quality and productivity."[47]

To explain this perspective more clearly, Covey provides a model (Table 10.6) that describes four management paradigms that have evolved since the industrial age.

Covey explains each paradigm as follows. (Some liberties have been taken with the text for purposes of brevity.)

1. **Scientific Authoritarian (Scientific Management)**: In this paradigm, managers primarily view employees as "economic beings" ("Pay

Table 10.6 Four Paradigms[48]

NEED	METAPHOR	PARADIGM	PRINCIPLE
Physical/Economic	Stomach	Scientific Authoritarian	Fairness
Social/Emotional	Heart	Human Relations	Kindness
Psychological	Mind	Human Resources	Use and Development of Talent
Spiritual	Spirit (whole person)	Principle-Centered Leadership	Meaning

me well."). The authoritarian manager makes the decisions and gives the commands, and workers conform and cooperate, perform and contribute, as requested, to receive the economic rewards of pay and other benefits. The overriding principle is *fairness:* "You put in a day's work and I'll give you a day's pay." We saw this style used almost exclusively in the factories that sprung up during the industrial revolution.

2. **Human Relations:** In this state of mind, managers begin to recognize that employees have social and emotional needs in addition to their economic needs ("Treat me well"). Using this paradigm, managers are still in charge, making all the decisions, but they will at least try to create a more harmonious work environment. Perhaps the manager will say "good morning" or ask about the family. The key principle is *kindness.* But in the end, the manager retains absolute control. Covey likens this manager to the kind father who knows what's best for his children and takes care of them as long as they comply with his wishes. In this sense, you could consider the human relations paradigm as being a "benevolent authoritarian" approach. The human relations paradigm came about, in part, due the rise of unions and strikes in the 1920s and 1930s that resulted from unfair or inhuman work environments in the factories. One could assume that it was easier to "be a nicer boss" than to deal with the problems resulting from union uprisings.

3. **Human Resources:** Managers who adopt this paradigm see that people have minds, in addition to stomachs and hearts ("Use me well."). They begin to find ways to make better use of their talent, creativity, resourcefulness, ingenuity, and imagination. They understand that in addition to the need for economic and social gratification, employees need to grow and develop, and to contribute effectively and creatively to the accomplishment of worthwhile objectives. The main principle here is the *use and development of talent.* Managers who operate under the human resources paradigm create environments in which people can contribute their full range of talents. This is a more involving style of management. The roots are harder to pinpoint, but the attitude of the so-called "baby boom" employees in the 1960s and 1970s give us a clue. These employees were much different than their parents. They were protesting the war in Viet Nam. They were challenging political leadership. They were demanding equality. They wanted more of a say in what was going on around them, including at work.

This is why we saw the rise of suggestion programs, quality circles, and other employee involvement initiatives during this time. Part of this evolution can be tied to enlightened management, but a significant contributing factor was a more demanding workforce.

4. **Principle-Centered Leadership:** Covey encourages managers to take a step beyond the human resources paradigm and learn to consider the employee as a whole person. He contends that all employees are spiritual beings and that they want to have a sense of doing something that matters. The key principle for this paradigm is *meaning*. Managers who adopt principle-centered leadership practices encourage participation in decision making and other important matters. They understand that employees want to be involved in enterprises that lift them, ennoble them, inspire them, empower them, and encourage them to be their best selves. Make no mistake about it, this approach takes longer than the authoritarian approaches, because it takes more time for a manager to involve the ideas of his or her employees than simply to dictate orders. Covey uses this formula: *involvement + patience = commitment.* With this paradigm, the opportunity exists to gain much more commitment on the part of employees, by integrating their personal goals and aspirations with those of the organization, assuming that the organization exists for a meaningful purpose.

Committed employees demonstrate a greater degree of personal initiative towards individual goals and make faster progress against those goals than employees who feel no real attachment to an organization or its objectives. To foster this attitude, managers must be willing to give employees reasonable autonomy in carrying out their tasks. In other words, the supervisor must be willing to give up some control by delegating responsibility to *qualified* members of his or her staff. Employees are motivated by a sense of achievement, recognition, enjoyment of the job, responsibility, and the chance for personal growth.[49] Excessive control stifles employee initiative and motivation.

Managers who are committed to developing their employees will take the time to be good coaches and advisors. William McKnight, CEO of the 3M Company from its beginnings in 1914 until he retired in 1966, was a strong advocate for allowing employees to develop their initiative without fear of reprisal:

Mistakes will be made (by giving the freedom and encouragement to act autonomously), but . . . the mistakes he or she makes are not as serious in the long run as the mistakes management will make if it is dictatorial and undertakes to tell those under its authority exactly how they must do their job. Management that is destructively critical when mistakes are made kills initiative and it's essential that we have many people with initiative if we are to continue to grow.[50]

Applying Development Coaching: Involvement + Patience = Commitment[51]

How can managers learn to give up some of their control and begin to share responsibility with those employees who have demonstrated competency and good judgment? Kouzes and Posner offer 10 practical steps to providing people with opportunities to develop their capacities.[52]

1. Stop making decisions. See to it that the people responsible for implementing decisions get a chance to make them. Make sure they have the necessary information to make smart decisions and the training and experience to recognize good and bad decision criteria. Ask them if they feel ready to make the decisions and if they are willing to bear the consequences of their decisions.

2. Stop talking at meetings. Managers cannot listen if they are doing all the talking. One-way communication can be perceived as an indication that other people's contributions aren't valuable. The best meetings are those where people are talking to each another, instead of just one person talking . . . the boss.

3. Set up coaching opportunities. Putting staff members in situations of responsibility with no training or support could be disastrous. The chance to lead must be coupled with adequate support. Coaching gives employees confidence and a much greater chance for success. Positive experiences increase the appetite for more opportunities.

4. Invite people to assume responsibility. Look for opportunities to ask employees, "What would you do if you were me?" This approach

generates good ideas and conditions employees to think of solutions rather than just announcing problems. Go one step further by inviting people to implement their suggestions. Be there to back them up.

5. Give everyone a customer. Make certain that whatever their job function, every employee has an individual or group that they perceive as their personal customer. Customers can be internal or external. Having a customer focus creates a stronger business paradigm. Employees become more like owners.

6. Have an open house. Invite customers, suppliers, and vendors to visit your facilities. Expand the guest list to include family, friends, and, neighbors. Foster pride and self-respect among your staff by informing customers and significant others about the jobs your staff does and why they're important. Share success stories. Talk about significant accomplishments.

7. Share the big picture. Giving someone an assignment without explaining how the assignment contributes to larger corporate initiatives is like asking someone to assemble a jigsaw puzzle without a picture of the finished product. Sometimes, in order to be fully engaged, people need to see the picture on the box.

8. Enrich people's jobs. Wherever possible, allow employees to experience a variety of task assignments and opportunities. Involve them in programs, meetings, and decisions that have direct impact on their job performance. Get an idea of their personal areas of interest within the organization and make an attempt to line up opportunities with those interests.

9. Let people teach. Peter Drucker points out, "Knowledge workers and service workers learn most when they teach."[53] He finds the best way to improve productivity is to have people instruct their peers and others. Schoolteachers have known this for years. They have older students tutor the younger ones. This way both are enlightened.

10. Use modeling to develop competencies. First think about and write down the competencies each employee will need to develop if they hope to advance in the organization. Then separate these abilities into skill sets, such as decision-making, problem-solving, presentation skills, meeting management, and so on. Whenever the opportunity arises, give employees a chance to watch others (managers or peers) who have developed the skill they need to acquire. As employees begin to work on their skills, provide feedback to build their confidence and fine-tune their skills.

Achievement: Who Is Able and Willing?

Development coaching includes promoting and sustaining employee initiative. In the preceding section, we talked about how managers can learn to release some control. Now we focus on the other half of the productivity equation: the employees' willingness to take on additional responsibility. Simply put, achievement occurs when people are both able and willing to contribute. If an employee is willing but not able, training and development may be the solution. If the employee is able but not willing, counseling is required.

The *Achievement Potential Matrix* (Figure 10.6) is a useful way to identify which members of your staff are likely or unlikely to perform, given their current aptitude and attitude, and which actions might be required to raise the overall level of achievement in your department.

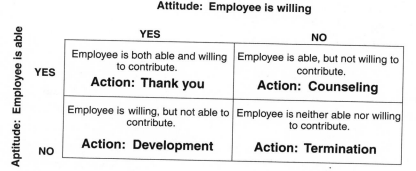

Figure 10.6 Achievement Potential Matrix.

Let's call the employee who is both able and willing to contribute to organizational objectives the "Yes-Yes" employee. Managers love "Yes-Yes" employees. We often count on them to manage important tasks. We are relieved to know that they are in the office when we are away on business or on vacation. We think of the "Yes-Yes" employee as our "go-to" player. Sometimes we forget that there is an action plan for these employees as well. It's called appreciation. There is a very real risk of burnout for "Yes-Yes" employees, either because they take on too much or because their manager gives them too much, or both. Letting a top performer know that they are appreciated is vitally important. Don't let these individuals think, even for a minute, that their commitment and contributions are unnoticed.

If more than 30 percent of your staff are true "Yes-Yes" employees, consider yourself fortunate. In our experience working with dozens of companies over the years, if a managers has a staff of 10, 1 or 2 employees might be considered their "go-to" players. The others are generally a mix of good to poor performers with varying degrees of ability and desire.

One of the more foolish things a manager can do is to ask repeatedly the same one or two chosen employees to take on major projects. Two very counterproductive outcomes are possible. First, the other employees will "mentally atrophy" and lose their initiative due to a lack of interesting tasks; and second, these precious but overwhelmed "Yes-Yes" employees may present you with a resignation letter. Now you're in real trouble. One of your best employees is gone, and you have no bench strength. Guess who gets to work longer hours until you find a substitute.

To avoid this scenario, managers must increase the contribution of the other members of their staff. One place to start is with employees who are willing, but not yet able to contribute. Let's call these people the "No-Yes" employees (no I can't; yes I would). These employees are eager for the chance to learn. Sometimes managers overlook these employees because developing them is time-consuming. Plus, it's a whole lot easier to keep dumping on the "Yes-Yes" people. "No-Yes" employees are also a manager's bench strength. They want to join the "Yes-Yes" group. They are waiting for their opportunity to take on more responsibility. Some make it clear that they want more growth and development. Others aren't as assertive. It is the manager's responsibility to find out. Developing these employees is an investment in time that could pay big dividends for a manager in the future. Left underutilized, these employees may opt to transfer to another department or leave the company altogether. When they do, they take their sparkling attitudes and their potential with them.

What about those members on your staff who have the ability, but are unwilling to contribute more than the bare minimum? Let's call these folks the "Yes-No" employees (yes I can; no I won't). These folks really annoy the "Yes-Yes" employees because they always leave right at five o'clock and seldom offer to help. "Yes-No" employees enjoy being invisible. It is the manager's responsibility to remove that option. Counseling is never the most popular aspect of a manager's job, but it is a very important one. Remember that, whether they tell you or not, your top employees are wondering when you are going to do something about the low performers. **If you avoid counseling poor performers, you run the risk of losing your best employees.**

The last category of employee is the "No-No" group (no I can't; no I won't). These are chronic nonperformers. These folks have flunked the counseling sessions. It is our sincere hope that you have few, if any, of these types on your staff. If you do, the action is clear. Get rid of them as fast as you possibly can!

The following exercise, *Analyzing Staff Potential* (Table 10.7), is offered to managers who would like to get a better idea of the percentages of top performers, potential performers, and low performers they currently have on staff. This could be a very interesting exercise to go through at performance review time, possibly division-wide.

Before you complete this exercise, please give some thought to how you rate the overall performance of each person. What criteria are you using to define their competence? What skills and attitudes have they demonstrated?

Remember that exercises like these are intended to avoid the risk of losing your best performers while, at the same time, raising the initiative of the remaining staff. The idea is to create a work environment where achievement is fostered and rewarded, and where invisibility is not tolerated.

Building Effective Teams

"The way a team plays together as a whole determines its success. You may have the greatest bunch of individual stars in the world, but if they don't play together, the club won't be worth a dime."—Babe Ruth

Leaders develop coalitions to further their visions. Teams are a part of this coalition. *Building effective teams* is an ongoing process where managers learn

Table 10.7 Analyzing Staff Potential

Total number of employees in my department:	
Yes—Yes	*Yes—No*
(I can. I will.)	**(I can. I won't.)**
Staff I need to *thank:*	Staff I need to *counsel:*
1.	1.
2.	2.
3.	3.
4.	4.
5.	5.
No—Yes	*No—No*
(I can't. I will)	**(I can't. I won't.)**
Staff I need to *develop:*	Staff I need to *terminate:*
1.	1.
2.	2.
3.	3.
4.	4.
5.	5.

% I can/I will:	% I can't/I will:	% I can/I won't:	% I can't/I won't:

to foster cooperation and collaboration among staff members, where they generate genuine enthusiasm, loyalty, and commitment for the work that is generated by their departments. The process entails rewarding team performance and encouraging cross-functional collaboration. It also involves managing meetings that are crisp, well disciplined, and productive.

When we examine a company's skill at *building effective teams,* we note their ability to:

1. Develop managers who can create team environments
2. Obtain employee support around goals and objectives
3. Effectively integrate multiple areas or functional disciplines to better achieve the company's strategic intent
4. Use meetings as a means to advance team performance

You will recall from earlier in this chapter the list of *The Ten Fatal Flaws* (see Table 10.1) that can potentially derail a manager, in other words, prevent him or her from achieving that next level of management up to and including executive managements and CEO. Number five on this list (items are not listed in order of importance) was: "Overmanaging: failing to delegate or build a team."[54]

Even the most controlling, workaholic managers realize at some point in their careers that they can't do the work by themselves. They need to count on their staff as much as a CEO counts on his or her senior managers. In both cases, the leader must be able to develop a genuine sense of excitement and commitment regarding the mission of the company or the department. This means creating an unwavering spirit around the products or services the manager and staff are being called on to deliver.

This may seem like an unrealistic expectation, especially if the work produced by a department may appear to be repetitive or routine. For example, working in a department store may not seem particularly motivating. There must be hundreds of thousands of employees who go to work in department stores every day with little or no sense of excitement. You might imagine that this reaction is just the nature of working in this type of job. You might even conclude that a manager in a department store could never create the same level of job enthusiasm as, say, a project leader for the latest pharmaceutical advancement at Merck or the latest chip technology at Intel.

You might think this way until you learn about the "Wal-Mart cheer."[55] Enthusiastic Wal-Mart employees in stores all over the country and the world shout this cheer. It goes like this:

Give me a W!

Give me an A!

Give me an L!

Give me a Squiggly!

Give me an M!

Give me an A!

Give me an R!

Give me a T!

What's that spell?

Wal-Mart!

Who's number one?

The Customer! Always!

What is the origin of the Wal-Mart cheer? Sam Walton was visiting a tennis ball factory in Korea, where the workers did a company cheer and calisthenics together every morning. He liked the idea and couldn't wait to get back home to try it with his associates. He said, "My feeling is that just because we work so hard, we don't have to go around with long faces all the time—while we're doing all of this work, we like to have a good time. It's sort of a 'whistle while you work' philosophy, and we not only have a heck of a good time with it, we work better because of it." Visit the Wal-Mart Web site and you see a picture of the late Sam Walton, performing the "squiggly" during the cheer at one of his stores.[56]

Could Sam build effective teams? During his many store visits, he encouraged associates to take a pledge with him: "... I want you to promise that whenever you come within 10 feet of a customer, you will look him in the eye, greet him and ask him if you can help him." This has now become known as the "Ten Foot Rule," and it remains a steadfast principle of the company. The tremendous success of Sam's company has been well documented. For the fiscal year ending January 31, 2002, revenues rose 14 percent to $219.81 billion.[57] At the time of this writing, the company's market cap is $262.3 billion.

Katzenbach and Smith, consultants at McKinsey & Company, define teams as "a small number of people with complementary skills who are committed to a common purpose, performance goals, and approach, for which they hold themselves accountable."[58] They offer the useful pointers to managers or anyone who aspires to lead teams (Table 10.8).

Esprit de corps among team members is not automatic, nor is it established easily or quickly. As teams form, there is a series of phases they generally experience en route to becoming collaborative, efficient, and high performing. In order to minimize the adverse effects of this adjustment, many new teams, particularly those who are likely to be together for a while, engage in some form of team-building exercises during early formation. Outdoor activities like ropes courses, repelling, and sailing are a few examples.

The Four Phases of Team Development (Figure 10.7) illustrates the evolutionary process as a group of individuals transition into a high-performing team.

During the "forming" phase, the team members get to know each other (presuming that they are from different departments). They attempt to define their mission, the tasks associated with that mission, and the skills and experience required to accomplish the mission. This requires that the team take inventory of each member's skills. If the manager or team leader has done an effective job of recruitment, the skills represented by the group

Table 10.8 What Team Leaders Do and Do Not Do[59]

1. Keep the purpose, goals, and approach relevant and meaningful.	Team members expect the leader to have clarity of mission and goals. Leaders should be careful not to appear rigid. They need to demonstrate patience and be willing to be silent at times during team discussions. Be there to guide the team, but do not be overbearing.
2. Build commitment and confidence.	Leaders should keep both the individuals and the team in mind and try to provide positive, constructive reinforcement while avoiding intimidation. This is where leaders introduce slogans, cheers, songs, even team costumes to create energy and esprit de corps. (Remember Sam Walton and the Wal-Mart cheer.)
3. Strengthen the mix and level of skills.	Top-performing teams consist of people with all the necessary technical, functional, problem-solving, decision-making, interpersonal, and teamwork skills needed to succeed.
4. Manage relationships with outsiders, including removing obstacles.	Team leaders manage the team's relationship with the rest of the organization. They must have the courage to intercede on the team's behalf when obstacles that might cripple or demoralize the team get placed in their way.
5. Create opportunities for others.	Team performance is simply not possible if managers grab all the best opportunities, assignments, and credit for themselves. Stepping aside to allow others to share the spotlight, however, does not mean abdicating responsibility for guidance, monitoring, or control.
6. Do real work.	Everyone on a real team, including the team leader, should do real work in roughly equal amounts. Managers must contribute to their team's goals by whatever means their staff needs.

should be conducive to the goals of the team. At this stage, teams also begin to set some ground rules regarding how they will relate to each other. During the forming phase, team member emotions can range from enthusiastic participation to anxiety regarding the personal skills and time demands that will be required.

During the "storming" phase, members may begin to posture and compete for control. This is natural. If talented employees have been recruited, there will be ample egos in the room. Many of these individuals are already

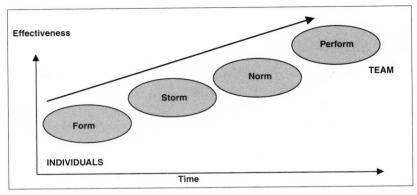

Figure 10.7 Four Phases of Team Development

accustomed to leading. Some time has to be spent figuring out how best to use all that talent and confidence. Progress can get bogged down during the storming phase as team members try to establish an effective means of working together. The planners will want to plan. The implementers will want to get started. Participation may be unbalanced. The talkative types may begin to overpower the quiet types. Concern may develop regarding the inequities of individual involvement and influence. Eventually, the team will establish a hierarchy within the group and a task list that makes sense for all members. Managers should stay in relatively close contact with the team at this phase to make sure that the level of frustration does not become intolerable.

During "norming," members accept the fact that they must work as a team, reconcile competing interests, and begin acting in line with the ground rules or norms by which the team members agreed to cooperate. Work methods begin to get ironed out. The process becomes more efficient. Meetings are better managed and stay on track. There is greater comfort and acceptance with giving and receiving feedback and positive reinforcement. Team members begin to feel safer. Risk-taking increases. Overall, there is greater satisfaction regarding team progress.

In the "performing" phase, the team's work methods are followed with speed and efficiency. Problems are handled with confidence and with the full participation of the group. A win-win spirit has fully developed. Team relationships have been solidified. There is a strong sense of accomplishment as the team successfully meets project milestones. There is a shared commitment to the importance of all team objectives. Everyone is on track. At this stage, the team has become capable of more work in concert than the sum of their individual efforts would have produced.[60]

Self-Managed Teams: How Are They Different from Other Teams?

Over the last 10 to 15 years, there has been growing interest in the concept of self-managed work groups. As far back as 1986, *Business Week* reported that plants using self-directed work teams were, on average, 30 to 50 percent more productive than their counterparts.[61] The change is also taking place because more managers are realizing that empowered teams provide a way to meet the needs of a changing workforce. Remember Stephen Covey's discussion of "Principle-Centered Leadership," in which he contends that leaders must understand and appreciate their employees' need to become a part of something meaningful.

In their book, *Empowered Teams,* Wellins, Byham, and Wilson clarify the difference between a true self-managed team and a team that is brought together for a specific task. They state, "A self-directed work team is an intact group of employees who are responsible for a "whole" work process or segment that delivers a product or service to an internal or external customer... [This] is not a group brought together for a special purpose, such as a product-launch team [or] a quality action team..."[62] According to the authors, self-directed teams share the following characteristics:[63]

- They are empowered to share various management and leadership functions.
- They plan, control, and improve their own processes.
- They set their goals and inspect their own work.
- They often create their own schedules and review their performance as a group.
- They may prepare their own budgets and coordinate their work with other departments.
- They usually order materials, keep inventories, and deal with suppliers.
- They are frequently responsible for acquiring any new training they might need.
- They may hire their own replacements or assume responsibility for disciplining their own members.
- They—not others outside the team—take responsibility for the quality of their products and services.

The transition to self-managing teams is at least as challenging for the managers as for the team members. Managers are likely to experience four stages:[64]

1. Initial suspicion, uncertainty, and resistance. The move to teams may be viewed as an indication of ineffectiveness in the manager's previous behavior. Also, teams are seen as benefiting someone else (such as an internal champion or an external consultant) and ultimately destined to fail.
2. Gradual realization of the positive possibilities and benefits offered by self-directed teams. Employee development of empathy for the customer, constructive peer pressure within teams, and freed-up managerial time for developing key people.
3. Understanding of their new leadership role. Struggling with questions such as, "What is a facilitator versus a manager?" "How does self-management influence managerial behavior?"
4. Learning a new language. Managers identify and develop the verbal skills, vocabulary, and communication scripts that form the core of their new leadership roles.

Building successful teams requires patience, time, and continuous effort. Thermos used teams effectively to recover their ailing grilling products unit. The $225 million division depended largely on its grilling products for a significant portion of its sales. The markets for these products went flat, and the entire industry began to cut prices to almost commodity levels.

The bureaucratic functional structure at Thermos seemed unable to respond to this crisis. CEO Monte Peterson formed a cross-functional team to develop new products and bring them to market. After the initial resistance, the team evolved to design, build, market, and sell a series of revolutionary grills. The products won four design awards and boosted Thermos' market share from 2 percent to 20 percent.[65]

Meetings that Matter

There are 11 million business meetings each and every day in the United States.[66] People don't like to waste their time in a meeting that is poorly organized and managed. Everyone is just too busy these days to have their time disrespected in this fashion. Although the guidelines for running a crisp, disciplined meeting are for the most part common sense, it is surprising how often people call meetings and then take no real responsibility for the time spent or for the outcomes.

Here are some pointers (Table 10.9) that will help you manage the kind of meeting that attendees will appreciate.

Application: Have You Created a Team Environment?

There are hundreds of great books regarding teamwork. We have discussed several leadership qualities and initiatives in this chapter. Getting to know more about the art of team building is always a good idea for any manager, especially those of you who are smart enough admit that you don't possess this skill naturally. You can begin by using the following *Team Effectiveness Checklist* (Table 10.10) to see how you stack up against the suggested practices:

Leadership is the outcome of a number of characteristics. We believe that leaders earn their stripes through:

- **Management Modeling:** walking the talk
- **Strategic/Tactical Balance:** ensuring that the vision and mission is communicated throughout the organization
- **Empowerment:** driving autonomy and decision making to the lowest appropriate level in the organization.

Table 10.9 Six Tips for More Effective Meetings[67]

1. Don't meet.	Avoid a meeting if the same information could be covered in a memo, e-mail, or brief report.
2. Set objectives for the meeting.	Before planning the agenda, determine the objective of the meeting. The more concrete your objectives, the more focused your agenda will be.
3. Provide an agenda beforehand.	Your agenda needs to include a one-sentence description of the meeting objectives, a list of the topics to be covered, and a list stating who will address each topic for how long. Follow the agenda closely during the meeting.
4. Assign meeting preparation.	Give all participants something to prepare for the meeting, and that meeting will take on a new significance to each group member.
5. Assign action items.	Don't finish any discussion in the meeting without deciding how to act on it.
6. Examine your meeting process.	Don't leave the meeting without assessing what took place and making a plan to improve the next meeting.

- **Developmental Coaching:** consistently developing the competencies and experience of the organization
- **Building Effective Teams:** creating a work environment where people can cooperate and collaborate

Table 10.10 Team Effectiveness Checklist

CHARAC- TERISTIC	DESCRIPTION	YOUR SCORE (using a 10 pt. scale)
1. Suitable Membership	Your team members are individually qualified and capable of contributing the necessary mix of skills.	
2. Clear Mission and Objectives	Every member understands the primary team objectives and can visualize the desired outcome.	
3. Team Values Honored	The principles of good teamwork, such as cooperation and respect, are being practiced uniformly by all team members.	
4. Constructive Climate	Team members feel comfortable in dealing candidly and directly with issues and with each other. Feelings are expressed respectfully and openly without fear of reprisal.	
5. Commitment Is Evident	There is active participation, synergy, and the shared, passionate belief that the team's purpose and goals are important.	
6. Focus Is on Achievement	The team is results-oriented. Milestones are scheduled and achieved. Progress is measured.	
7. Work Methods Are Effective	Roles are clearly defined. Communication is frequent and effective. Processes are clear.	
8. Team Is Empowered	Individuals generally feel that they can influence outcomes. They believe that the effort is worth it.	
9. Creativity Is Encouraged	Innovation is encouraged. Ideas are welcome. Judgment is withheld until the full idea is communicated and developed.	
10. Regular Team Activities	A conscious effort is made to get the team together away from work so that members can get to know each other on a more personal level.	
	TOTAL SCORE (out of a possible 100)	

General H. Norman Schwarzkopf once said, "Leadership is a combination of strategy and character. If you must be without one, be without the strategy." The traits and characteristics outlined in this chapter are intended to help leaders—at all levels of an organization—develop a balance between strategic thinking and personal character.

In the next chapter, we discuss how human resource systems can assist these leaders by finding, hiring, and developing the talented individuals they hope to lead.

CHAPTER

Human Resources Systems

"We try not to hire people who are humorless, self-centered, or complacent. When they come to work, we want them, not their corporate clones. They are what makes us different, and in most enterprises, different is better."

—HERB KELLEHER

HUMAN RESOURCES SYSTEMS deal with attracting, engaging, developing, and keeping skilled individuals. These systems define how a company recruits, involves, trains, challenges, and rewards its employees in the pursuit of its strategic intent.

The ability to manage its human resources effectively is consistently identified as a critical element to an organization's success.[1] Over the last 20 years or more, HR departments have been transitioning from the traditional role of a personnel department to the role of strategic partner with their internal customers. In fact, many of the deliverables of a personnel department—payroll, benefits, performance records, compliance, and so on—are frequently being outsourced. If you have any doubt that outsourced HR functions is a growing industry, try a search entering "Outsourcing Human Resources" in the Internet search engine of your choice. We did, and received a listing of 426 individual companies, each one eager to provide your HR functions, from staff administration to benefits, payroll, performance management, and relocation. Another quick search on the Internet provided a list so long, we had to scroll through more than 15 screens.[2]

Outsourcing personnel services frees the internal human resources group to focus on providing services that are directly aligned with the business needs of their company clients. Some would argue that the emphasis is shifting from HR processes to the development of "human capital." Advocates of the human capital paradigm contend that "human resources" provides the same or greater impact on achieving strategic intent as any other strategic element of an organization, such as capital resources, R and D, marketing, or technology.

Changes in the way human resources are being managed are being driven by the strategic business needs from other parts of the organization.[3] An aggressive or adversarial approach to managing human resources—getting the most performance for the lowest wages and benefits—is giving way to a recognition that the workforce can be a source of competitive advantage.[4] In fact, many contend that human capital is the only true differentiator.

As part of a company-wide quality-improvement effort, Texas Instruments implemented a pilot program calling for each and every one of its employees to come up with ideas for improvement, and then to implement them.[5] They were not required to justify their ideas in terms of cost savings in order to implement them. In one plant in the program, over 60 percent of the workforce had implemented 10 or more ideas for better performance.

While only half of the 7000 ideas implemented at TI were tied to actual cost savings, those that were provided more than $7 million of additional profits. The significance of this program was that the $7 million in additional profits resulted from the ideas of just one plant in one year. Texas Instruments employs nearly 35,000 employees in over 30 manufacturing locations worldwide.[6]

This human capital perspective is changing the way organizations manage their human resources. Some of the traditional and emerging trends are listed in Table 11.1 below:

The *human resource systems* value chain can be broken down into five components:

1. **Selective Recruitment:** a process that screens available candidates to evaluate both their skills and their compatibility with the organizational culture.
2. **Employee Orientation:** a forum to communicate the strategic intent of the company firsthand to new recruits, and to clarify and emphasize organizational values and beliefs.

Table 11.1 Traditional and Emerging Ideas of Human Resource Management[7]

Traditional	*Emerging*
Labor force seen as a necessary expense	Labor force seen as a critical investment
Workforce is management's adversary	Management and workforce are partners
Functional and subfunctional specialization	Cross-functional integration
Emphasis solely on physical skills	Emphasis on total contribution to the firm
Expectation of predictable, repetitious behavior	Expectation of innovative and creative behavior
Comfort with stability and conformity	Tolerance of ambiguity and change
Avoidance of responsibility and decision making	Accepting responsibility for making decisions
Training covering only specific tasks	Open-ended commitment: broad, continuous development
Emphasis placed on outcomes and results	Emphasis placed on process and means
High concern for quality and throughput	High concern for total customer value
Concern for individual efficiency	Concern for overall effectiveness
Evaluation and rewards focused narrowly on work output	Evaluation and rewards defined broadly, depending on the strategy

3. **Continuous Learning:** developing the capacity and competency of the workforce, in alignment with strategic goals, in order to achieve and maintain a competitive advantage.

4. **Performance Management:** a process that evaluates the quality of the skills and behaviors of the workforce relative to strategic intent. Performance standards should focus on behaviors and skills that are required for successful strategic implementation.

5. **Reward Systems:** economic and psychological rewards designed to provide incentive for strategically important skills and behaviors. Rewards must be fair, impartial, and worthy of the effort expended to achieve them.

Organizations stand little chance of successfully implementing their strategies without first possessing the skills required to do so. Companies can accumulate talent in two ways. They can recruit it, and they can develop it. George Moore, President of Citicorp from 1959 until 1967, focused first and foremost on making Citicorp an institution built largely around procedures for finding, training, and promoting personnel. He sums up the benefit of aligned human resource systems: "Without the capable people these procedures developed, none of our goals would have been attainable."[8]

Selective Recruitment: Getting the Right People on the Bus[9]

"Organization doesn't really accomplish anything. Plans don't accomplish anything, either. Theories of management don't much matter. Endeavors succeed or fail because of the people involved. Only by attracting the best people will you accomplish great deeds." — *General Colin Powell, Chairman (Ret.) Joint Chiefs of Staff*

Selective recruitment is a process in which companies screen, evaluate, and select job candidates based on their skills and their compatibility with the organizational culture.

When we evaluate the recruitment process, we look at an organization's ability to:

1. Design and implement a targeted recruitment and selection process to ensure that only high-caliber candidates are considered for open positions
2. Evaluate whether outside candidates are compatible with the company culture
3. Develop their managers' interviewing skills
4. Share opinions between colleagues in pursuit of the best candidates
5. Evaluate managers on their success at recruiting top talent

Southwest Airlines: Having Fun at 30,000 Feet

Less than three percent of the candidates applying for jobs at Southwest Airlines are hired. Southwest reviewed 216,000 resumes to find the 5134 new employees they hired in 2000.[10] Why so many resumes? Because Southwest goes to considerable lengths to hire people who can both have fun and *be* fun on the job. The airline uses specially developed methods, including interviews with customers, to determine whether applicants for customer-contact jobs have the outgoing personality traits that match its strategy of creating a high-spirited, fun-loving in-flight atmosphere for passengers. Southwest goes all out to make flying a pleasant experience.[11]

Does it make a difference to have the right people? In fiscal year 2001, Southwest Airlines had total operating revenue of $5.6 billion, and carried over 63 million passengers. The airline's net income was $625.2 million. Southwest's total debt-to-equity ratio is a paltry .31 compared to an industry standard of 1.07. Their five-year sales growth rate is 14.48 compared to the industry average of 11.71.[12]

Success has become the norm for the airline. Year-end results for 2000 marked Southwest Airlines' twenty-eighth consecutive year of profitability, and ninth year of increased profits. (see Table 11.2 below) The airline has ranked number one in fewest customer complaints for the last 10 consecutive years, as published in the Department of Transportation's Air Travel Consumer Report.

Since 1997, *Fortune* magazine has ranked Southwest Airlines in the top five of the magazine's annual list of 100 Best Companies to Work for in America. In the magazine's Jan. 8, 2001 issue, Southwest was ranked as the number-four company to work for in America. Southwest was ranked number two for 1999, and was number one for 1997 and 1998. Business journalists Robert Levering and Milton Moskowitz compiled the list, using methodology similar to that used for their 1993 bestseller, *The 100 Best Companies to Work For in America,* in which Southwest was named one of the "Top Ten" companies.[13] In 2002, Southwest was ranked number two on Fortune's *America's Most Admired Companies* list.

Candidate Compatibility with Culture

The Southwest case study points out a very important point concerning the interviewing and selection of job candidates: Hiring someone who has the

Table 11.2 Southwest Airlines Financial Performance 1997–2001[14]

Consideration	2001	2000	1999	1998	1997
Stock Price	18.48	22.35	10.75	10.08	7.30
Total Sales in Millions	5,555.2	5,649.6	4,735.6	4,164.0	3,816.8
EPS	0.633	0.785	0.590	0.545	0.414

skills to fulfill the job requirements is only half the equation. Employees must also possess the work ethic, attitude, and behavior that are in line with the company's culture. In other words, in addition to being competent in the position, *the candidate must be able to model and promote the organization's core values.* Therefore, interviewing techniques must include some elements of discovery regarding the candidate's character, personality, and work habits.

An excerpt from *The 100 Best Companies to Work for in American* states:

Competition to get into P&G is tough . . . Recruits, when they sign on, may feel like they have joined an institution rather than a company[15] . . . There is a P&G way of doing things, and if you don't master it or at least feel comfortable with it, you're not going to be happy here, not to speak of being successful.[16]

When George Cain became CEO of Abbott Laboratories, he set in place some very high standards. He could not stand mediocrity in any form, and he was intolerant of anyone who would accept the idea that good is good enough. (This included family members, by the way.) All managers who worked for Abbott would have to demonstrate that they had the capacity to become the best executives in the industry for their particular position.[17] During the pivotal transition time for Abbott from 1974 to 1989, the company's overall performance was nearly four times that of the market, based on a ratio of cumulative stock returns relative to the general stock market.[18]

Before candidates are allowed to complete an application at Disney, potential recruits are required to view a video called "Backstage." This video emphasizes the company's dedication to its ideals of fun, fantasy, and entertainment. The video also clearly illustrates ideals like proper grooming standards, a Disney hallmark, as well as expected guest service standards, attitude, and self-image. The approach is an effective means to screen out applicants who may not be able to live up to the high standards required to be a successful "cast member" of the Magic Kingdom. About 20 percent of applicants at Disney theme parks and resorts disqualify themselves during the application process.[19]

If you have a young, start-up company, you need people with a unique set of skills and attributes suited to an entrepreneurial environment. These companies need individuals who are not only willing, but *expect* to work long hours. They must be resilient enough to deal with the trials and tribulations of a company that is continually evolving. In 1979, during the very early days of creation of the MacIntosh computer, the small Mac development team of about five dedicated people had to compete within Apple for funding designated for the new "Lisa" computer. At the time, Lisa had a team of 200 engineers and significantly more company support. These Mac team members needed tons of ingenuity and tenacity to conceive, design, and develop a truly revolutionary product in a sometimes-unsupportive environment. The project was almost killed several times.[20] You know how the story ends. The Macintosh lives on today. The Lisa is a very distant memory.

How do you think a person with a "9:00 to 5:00" mentality would have faired in the Mac thinktank? An individual who has difficulty working in a constantly changing environment had better stay away from the start-ups. Managers in these companies can do themselves a huge favor by taking the time to find individuals with an entrepreneurial mindset, strong work ethics, an independent spirit, and a pretty tough skin. Managers and employees who join start-ups have to be comfortable working without a net. In fact, they have to be excited by the prospect.

As best-selling author, Jim Collins, points out in his book *Good to Great:* "In a good-to-great company, people are not your most important asset. The *right* people are."[21] Using Tom Wolfe's book, *The Electric Kool-Acid Test*, as the backdrop, Collins emphasizes the importance of "getting the right people on the bus (and the wrong people off the bus)."[22] "Effective recruiting means more than just hiring the highest-skilled talent. It means hiring the most *suitable* talent. A company must be careful to select candidates who not only possess the right technical skill sets, but who are compatible with, or better yet, can flourish in the company's work environment.

The recruitment process can be divided into two actions:

1. Establishing the correct hiring criteria for each position in the company
2. Perfecting the interview process so that the match to this criteria is realized

The Hiring Criteria: Setting the Target

Has your company identified the skills and attributes required for each of your job positions? Probably not. It is a daunting task to maintain up-to-date job descriptions, particularly those that include the so-called "soft skills" required to do the job in addition to the technical know-how. But how can you aim for a target without the target? Developing complete job profiles provides the target.

Most managers would agree that identifying the full job criteria is important, including behavioral characteristics. Matching a candidate against these criteria is the ideal outcome. However, due to the challenge of exploring and assessing an individual's overall character, these qualities may be overlooked or treated in a superficial fashion during an interview. Unfortunately, the softer skills often play a less significant role in the hiring decision.

Evaluating character attributes is less tangible, and therefore more difficult than, for example, evaluating a person's sales background. However, if you accept the premise of industry leaders like Procter and Gamble,[23] that a candidate's compatibility with the culture is of paramount importance, you will take the time to develop comprehensive job profiles, particularly for high-profile or highly influential positions. There are companies, as we have seen with Southwest Airlines and Disney, who have developed their manager's competencies in judging an applicant's personality or temperament to the same level as assessing mathematical skills, sales expertise, or computer proficiency. For these companies, it has been a matter of carefully isolating those qualities and then crafting the right questions to probe for character traits and predictive behaviors.

Tom Melohn, co-owner of North American Tool & Die[24] interviewed several applicants for a clerical position. Most of the applicants began by asking about tasks, money, hours, and other job mechanics. The one he hired, however, asked questions about the nature of the business.

Perfecting the Interview Process: Hitting the Target

How many times have you been on an interview where the interviewer did all the talking, or, worse yet, asked questions that were inappropriate or illegal? We live in a more transient society than previous generations. With all of the downsizing, rightsizing, mergers, and acquisitions, people interview for jobs more frequently. Candidates have become better *interviewees*. Your managers need to be better *interviewers*. Table 11.3 provides a few pointers to help prepare for and conduct a first-rate interview:

Some positions have more organizational impact than others. Hiring a bank teller is important, but the job itself has less impact than hiring a CFO. For high-profile positions that have significant influence over a company or division, consider using a peer review process where these candidates are interviewed by a team of managers who will interact with this position. Again, it becomes a matter of effectiveness versus efficiency. Obviously, a single interview is much more time-efficient than a series of interviews. However, the chances of finding the *optimum* person for a position increases with the input of colleagues.

Table 11.3 Interviewer Techniques

Interviewers must manage the interview process. You must be in control and yet create a comfortable environment where the candidate is encouraged to talk freely. Generally speaking, an interview will include the following 5 steps:

1. Preparation	• Review the applicant's resume. You can save yourself some time by not asking questions that are already answered to your satisfaction on paper. Get a sense of the candidate's strengths and weaknesses relative to the position. This will help you focus on the important elements of the interview.
	• Select and rehearse a list of questions you intend to use relative to the open position. (See the list of suggested questions in this chapter.)
	• Figure out where you are going to conduct the interview long before the candidate arrives. Running around at the last minute to find an available office or conference room, with the candidate waiting in the lobby, is not a good way to begin an interview.
	• Make sure you choose a noninterruptive environment. No ringing phones or people barging in.
	• Clear your head and get in the right frame of mind to conduct the interview. Forget the fact that your Web site just went down. Now is the time to focus on the candidate. The person you are about to interview could be that dream employee that every manager searches for. Give him or her your complete attention.
	• Be ready!
2. Setting the Tone	• Open the interview with a sincere welcome. The applicant has just rearranged his or her schedule to meet with you at your convenience. Thank candidates for taking an interest in the job and your company.
	• Introduce yourself and explain how your position relates to the job opening.
	• Let the candidate know that the primary objective of the interview is to determine whether the job is right for the candidate and the candidate is right for the job. In other words, would offering the candidate the job be mutually beneficial to both parties?
	• Ask the candidate if he or she understands the full scope and responsibilities that are related to the job for which he or she is applying. The last thing you want is to waste your time interviewing someone who ultimately is not interested in the job. Take a moment to make sure that you are on the same page. Often, job applicant screeners (possibly from HR or on your staff) will have ensured that the job applicant is a viable candidate...but it doesn't hurt to make sure before you get to far along in the interview.

Table 11.3 Interviewer Techniques (*Continued*)

3. Discovery	• Explore the applicant's technical skills as they relate to the job, and behavioral attributes as they relate to your organization's culture. Ask questions that will provide the evidence that he or she can do the job and, just as importantly, adapt well to the work environment. (You can choose from the list of questions in this chapter.) • Conduct a balanced interview. Don't just ask questions that allow job applicants to pontificate about their talents. Ask them questions that cause them to indicate areas they need to develop: "What was the most useful criticism you ever received and why?" • If you uncover an aspect of the candidate that is particularly interesting (good or bad), ask them to elaborate: "Tell me more about how that situation evolved." • Don't end this part of the interview process until you are satisfied that you have enough information to make an informed decision.
4. Provide Information	• Ask the candidate if he or she has any questions about the position. • Describe the full expectations of the position. Include any relevant information: possibility of long hours, working on nights or weekends, travel requirements, working with other teams, sales expectations, budget responsibilities, and so on. • Talk about your organizational culture. Let the candidate know what it is like to work for your company. • Offer any relative information about the company (entry into new markets, new product launches, strategic alliances, etc.). • Ask the interviewee if he or she has any additional questions.
5. Close the Interview	• Give the candidate some idea of when a decision will be made and how he or she will be informed. • Thank the candidate for his or her time.

Interview Questions

Table 11.4 offers some excellent interview questions that will help you explore a broad scope of the candidate's skills and character.[25]

By using preselected questions to interview applicants, the danger of asking potentially illegal or discriminatory questions is greatly reduced (Table 11.5).

Table 11.4   Interview Questions

1. Why are you interested in working for our organization?
2. Tell me about yourself.
3. What personal and professional goals have you set for yourself?
4. What kind of work do you like to do?
5. What are your greatest strengths?
6. What was the most useful criticism you ever received and why?
7. What work experience has been the most valuable to you and why?
8. Tell me about a project you managed.
9. Tell me about a problem you solved and how you solved it.
10. What comes to mind if I ask you about your greatest challenge?
11. Describe a situation where you had a conflict with someone. How did you deal with it?
12. What would your former bosses say about your abilities to work as a team player?
13. What does "leadership" mean to you? How would you describe your leadership style?
14. Tell me about an idea you developed and implemented that was particularly creative or innovative.
15. What characteristics do *you* think are important for this position?
16. How do you motivate people?
17. What types of situations put you under pressure? How do you deal with the pressure?
18. Tell me about a difficult decision you have made. How did it turn out?
19. Give an example of a situation in which you failed and how you handled it.
20. Tell me about a situation when you had to persuade another person to your point of view.
21. What frustrates you the most?
22. What characteristics are most important in a good manager? Tell me how you have incorporated one or more of these characteristics in your career.
23. What challenges are you looking for in a position?
24. Are you willing to relocate or travel?
25. What two or three accomplishments have given you the most satisfaction?
26. Describe a leadership role of yours professionally or personally and tell me why you committed your time to it.
27. What is the most important lesson you have learned in or out of school?
28. We are looking at many great candidates. Why are you the best person for this position?
29. How would your friends describe you?
30. What else should I know about you?

Table 11.5 Common Unlawful Interview Questions

Are you married?	Have you ever worked under another name?
Are you pregnant?	Have you ever had your wages garnished?
How old are you?	What is your religious affiliation?
Where were you born?	What is your political affiliation?
Do you have any children?	Tell me about organizations to which you belong.
Do you own a home?	What is your maiden name?
Have you ever been arrested?	What is your wife's maiden name?
How tall are you?	What type of work does your spouse do?
How much do you weigh?	What is the lowest salary you would accept?
Please supply a list of three relatives.	Do you have a photo of yourself?

These are examples of interview questions that could be reasonably construed to be discriminatory.

For companies that recruit carefully, line managers share the responsibility of successfully matching a candidate with both the job requirements and the culture. It is their judgment, not those of the professionals in the HR department, that is on the line. Having managers interview and hire their own candidate makes sense, especially for key positions.

The recruiting processes demonstrated by Southwest, Disney, P&G, and other successful companies are important for many reasons. A carefully-planned interview process, which may include additional interviews by appropriate colleagues, unmistakably demonstrates a firm's concern for both the candidate and the company. Since these organizations demonstrate their values so openly, job candidates will either enthusiastically pursue the relationship, or eliminate themselves from consideration. Those who are hired will appreciate the organization's key values, starting with the recruiting process itself.

Employee Orientation: Passion or Paperwork?

"Yesterday's idea of the boss, who became the boss because he or she knew one more fact than the person working for them, is yesterday's manager. Tomorrow's person needs to envision a shared set of values, a shared objective."—Jack Welch

Employee orientation is often an overlooked opportunity. Here is a chance to get new employees on board when their enthusiasm is high and their eagerness to learn more about the company is peaked. Yet the orientation programs most employees experience consist of an overview of benefits and a shuffle of paperwork to make sure they get their first paycheck. We have all suffered through these types of orientations. We sat in a room with strangers watching some outdated videotape of the history of the company, while some efficient but lackluster HR staff member, who presumably drew the short straw for that month, takes us through mounds of paper and pamphlets designed to get us employed, but not engaged.

The better-run companies don't make this mistake. They understand that the best time to impress employees with the vision, mission, and values of their organization is day one. Senior managers at these companies see the orientation process as a chance to build excitement and dedication around the shared goals of the company. While at other companies, managers seem to prefer that someone else meet the new recruits.

Employee Orientation is about getting new employees off to the right start. These programs should capitalize on the natural enthusiasm of these employees. Orientations provide a forum for senior managers to explain where the company is headed, underscore core values and beliefs, and clarify how these new members will be contributing to the organization's strategy. Don't reduce orientation to an administrative event. Also, the orientation process should include ongoing follow-up and support activities, particularly during the employee's first year.

When we evaluate *employee orientation* programs, we look at an organization's ability to:

1. Design and implement a comprehensive process that gets employees involved early.
2. Passionately instill company vision and goals.
3. Underscore organizational values and beliefs and clearly explain why these principles are sacred and nonnegotiable.
4. Ensure that senior managers participate and that they do so willingly and enthusiastically.

In the previous chapter, we discuss how the selection process should focus as much on an individual's compatibility with the organization's culture as is does on the candidate's job competencies. Once the person is hired, companies must effectively acclimate the employee to the culture. And, since each employee is hired to contribute to the achievement of the company's strategic intent, the orientation should include an overview of how each department and the employees in these departments contribute to the organization's success.

The two-day orientation at Disney is an excellent case study for establishing shared values from the very start of an employee's career. At Disney, every new hire, including the "ninety-day" summer employee, goes to "Disney Traditions." The list of attendees can include vice presidents, popcorn vendors, and housekeepers, all of whom share seats in the same classroom.

Class size is held to forty and rank is unrecognized. Everyone wears a nametag with only their first name on it. The only special people, they are told, are the guests. Split into smaller groups, the rookies are taken into the Magic Kingdom to observe veterans working at their posts. Occasionally one of the veterans will give a scenario to a rookie and ask how they would respond. The goal is to get their people connected and comfortable as soon as possible.[26]

During this process, new hires learn Disney's four cardinal principles of guest relations—safety, courtesy, show, and efficiency—which together provide a framework for all decisions made in the operating areas. Faced with a dilemma of conflicting values, safety always comes first.

Disney is also a good example of how the orientation process for new recruits extends well beyond their first day. After their orientation, new hires begin to work at their assigned locations. They meet their supervisors as well as their Disney Qualified Trainer, a veteran at the same job always available to answer questions. With an outline and a checklist, new employees start training programs of various lengths, monitored by human resources managers, to ensure a smooth transition.

Disney is often cited when discussing employee orientation, because they pay close attention to the real-time, day-to-day values and behaviors that consistently communicate the high ideals that Walt Disney, himself, established when he opened for business.

Another example of an orientation program being used to its full capabilities is General Electric's Crotonville Management Development Institute. The 31-year-old institution spreads the company's vision to over 2500 new MBA recruits per year. Each of these recruits participates in a comprehensive two-and-one-half-day orientation.

It is through intensive orientation programs such as these examples that employees get acquainted with the core values of the firm. In addition to gaining insight into the strategic intent of the organization, these new hires begin to understand the relationship between their individual roles and responsibilities and the company's success.

These programs also clearly identify expectations. The orientation program is essentially the final screening process for new recruits. If these new hires have any doubts about their ability to conform to the core values of the organization, orientation provides the opportunity to either make a solid personal commitment or select themselves out of the organization. Employee expectations at the best-run companies are very clear. If you don't think business environments should be fun, don't work for Southwest Airlines. If you think calling employees "cast members" is corny, don't work for Disney. If you can't see yourself joining in for the Wal-Mart Cheer, work someplace else. These cultures are very clearly defined and have had many years of durability. They don't adapt to you. You adapt to them.

In the most effective orientation programs, senior managers demonstrate their support by simply spending some time with the new employees. P&G inducts new employees into the company with training and orientation sessions and expects them to read its official biography *Eyes on Tomorrow* (known to insiders as "The Book") that describes the company as an integral part of the nation's history with "a spiritual inheritance" and "unchanging character." Talks by executives and formal orientation materials stress P&G's history, values, and traditions.[27]

Applying Employee Orientation: Get Them While They're Hot

A few relatively simple ingredients can make the difference between an orientation program that is engaging, not just efficient. Table 11.6 provides some guiding principles of an effective orientation program:

A Stanford MBA who spent a summer at Disney doing financial analysis, strategic planning, and other similar work described his experience at the Disney Traditions class:[28]

"I recognized the magic of Walt's vision on my first day at the Walt Disney Company...At Disney University, through videos and "pixie dust," Walt shared his dream and the magic of Disney's 'world.' After orientation, I stopped at the corner of Mickey Avenue and Dopey Drive—I felt the magic, the sentimentality, the history. I believed in Walt's dream and shared this belief with others in the organization."

Does your employee orientation program—large or small—evoke a sense of spirit and commitment to your company's vision?

Table 11.6 Employee Orientation Guidelines

1. Make it inspiring.	The program must be more than just an exchange of paperwork. Use this time to create a sense of direction. If your company or organization has been around a while, give new employees a sense of the legacy of the company. Create a sense of spirit. These new hires should leave the orientation event with a feeling that they joined an outstanding, unique company.
2. Let them know they are important.	Show a willingness to invest in "human capital" (employee satisfaction and well-being) as much as in hardware.[32] Get senior managers involved in the program.
3. Build trust right from the beginning.	Be candid and forthcoming regarding the successes and challenges facing the company.
4. Explain how they contribute to the big picture.	Connect the individual's role and responsibility with the strategic intent of the organization.
5. Set very clear expectations.	Explain not only how they are to contribute to the success of the company but how they are expected to behave en route to that success. Talk about the culture … not just the strategy.
6. Check in on them occasionally.	Schedule some form of contact with each new employee at the 30-day and 60-day marks. Check on how they are adjusting to working at your company. Help them effectively navigate this new terrain. In reality, employee orientation lasts much longer than one day.

Continuous Learning: Giving Employees the Tools to Contribute

"Each of us brings to our job, whatever it is, our lifetime of experience and our values."—Sandra Day O'Connor, Supreme Court Justice

Continuous learning encompasses the training and development opportunities an organization provides to its managers and employees. In addition to classroom training, these opportunities can take the form of self-study mentoring, and other "on-the-job" alternatives. Companies who make employee development a high priority ensure that educational programs are of high quality and that they are directly aligned with the organization's strategic objectives.

When we evaluate *continuous learning,* we look at an organization's ability to:

1. Maintain training and development as an organizational imperative
2. Provide educational programs to ensure that managers and employees have the necessary skills to work at their optimum levels
3. Ensure that training programs are aligned with and directly support strategic goals
4. Offer training programs that are well designed and structured
5. Provide comprehensive leadership and management development courses
6. Develop future leaders through a well-designed succession-planning program

According to Peter Senge in his book, *The Fifth Discipline,* "Organizations learn only through individuals who learn. Individual learning does not guarantee organizational learning. But without it, no organizational learning occurs."[29]

McDonald's: Burgers, Books, and Best Practices

McDonald's trains so many people each year that they have surpassed the U.S. Army as the nation's largest training organization.[30] The company views the training and development of its employees and managers as a strategic imperative. McDonald's Hamburger University, a 130,000-square-foot facility on an 80-acre campus located at McDonald's headquarters in Oak Brook, IL, was actually founded in 1961 in the basement of the McDonald's restaurant located in Elk Grove, IL. Nearly 6000 students attend the university each year.

Hamburger University was built on the foundation of helping McDonald's employees take advantage of each other's knowledge, gathering best practices and key learnings to achieve the McDonald's vision to be the best quick-service restaurant experience in the world.

Here are some additional facts regarding the university:[31]

- 22 full-time international resident professors teach students from more than 119 countries.
- There are 17 state-of-the-art classrooms, a 300-seat auditorium, and four special team rooms for interactive education.

- Translators can provide simultaneous translation of more than 27 different languages.
- Restaurant employees receive about 32 hours of training in their first month with McDonald's.
- There were 85 weeks of classes conducted in 2000.
- More than 70,000 students have graduated from Hamburger University.
- Much of the training that's taught all over the world originates from Hamburger University's field implementation and design departments.

While attending university courses, employees learn about founder Ray Kroc's four core principles of *quality, service, cleanliness, and value.* The company has written a simple and direct "People Promise" dedicated to its employees:

To the 1.5 million people who work at McDonald's in 119 countries around the world, and to all future employees, we want you to know that: We Value You, Your Growth, and Your Contributions. This is our People Promise.

At year-end 2000, systemwide sales exceeded $40 billion for the first time in the company's history.[32] As of January 2002, McDonald's market cap had grown to nearly $33 billion. For the last five years, McDonald's average earnings margin before interest, taxes, and depreciation (EBITD) has been 31.04. The EBITD ratio for the restaurant sector during this timeframe was 21.46. For the last five years, McDonald's pretax margin has averaged 20.55, compared to 12.43 for the sector as a whole. (See Table 11.7.)

Successful companies invest aggressively in employee training and professional development programs. Merck, 3M, P&G, Motorola, GE, Disney, Marriott, and IBM have all made significant investments in company "uni-

Table 11.7 McDonald's Financial Performance 1997–2001[33]

Consideration	2001	2000	1999	1998	1997
Stock Price	26.47	34.00	40.31	38.41	23.88
Total Sales in Millions	14,243.0	13,259.3	12,421.4	11,408.8	10,686.5
EPS	1.458	1.387	1.103	1.147	1.078

versities" and "educational centers." At one point, Motorola targeted 40 hours of training per employee per year and required that every division spend 1.5 percent of payroll on training.

Such a formalized training program requires a firm commitment from the senior managers of an organization. Training can be expensive, not only in terms of dollars spent, but also in time. Training classes may require employees to be off the job for days, weeks, or more. One government course we know of focuses on managing the acquisition and logistics process for large government programs. Managers who enroll in this class will be gone for nearly 14 weeks. You can imagine that before their bosses suffer the loss of a key manager for over three months, they need to be convinced of the value.

To go forward with regular training opportunities in light of these cost obstacles, companies must have a real commitment to educating their people. In a case like McDonald's, the educational process is built into the fabric of the culture. It simply becomes a way of life. In other cases, the impetus to train employees may be linked to outside forces, such as competitive pressures.

From 1976 to 1982, Xerox saw their market share in the copier business shrink from 80 percent to 13 percent, due in part to the encroachment of higher-quality, lower-cost machines from Japan. To increase quality and to gain back lost customers, Xerox began a quality improvement program that included six full days of training for *each* of the company's more than 100,000 employees.

The program took four years to complete and cost millions of dollars. Why did Xerox decide to make this huge investment in time and money at a time when they were losing revenue? It was a simple case of return on investment. They estimated that the problems associated with the lack of quality were costing the company $1.4 billion dollars a year.[34] Did it work? The answer is an unqualified "yes." The quality improvement program eventually led to winning the Malcolm Baldrige Award and restored Xerox to a leadership role in the industry.

Management Development: Giving Managers a Boost Up the Ladder

To take the helm of a McDonald's restaurant, managers must complete a comprehensive training program that consists of self-study and classroom work, capped off with a leadership course at the headquarters Hamburger University campus or at one of the other six campuses in Australia, Brazil, Germany, Hong Kong, Japan, and the U.K.[35]

As early as the 1970s, Marriott was spending up to five percent of its pre-tax profits on management development.

General Electric has long been known for developing some of the best leaders in business, and some of the most widely practiced business techniques. GE invests about $500 million annually on training and education programs around the world—from assembly lines to corporate classrooms to boardrooms. GE's commitment to excellence in leadership development starts at Crotonville, the world's first major corporate business school.[36]

Organizations have a two-fold training mission. The first is to train employees in the specific skill sets they will need to effectively perform their duties. The second and more far-reaching mission is to develop employees over the long-term so that they can advance in their careers. Naturally, companies will be selective in whom they invest these educational dollars. Not everyone is management material. But to hold on to exceptionally talented people in today's transient business society, organizations must provide opportunities for advancement. This means they must be willing to develop the skills that high-potential employees and managers need to advance.

A side benefit of management development programs is that smart managers congregate together for training. These managers not only get the training they need, they also develop personal relationships and informal contacts that can help them navigate the formal systems and structure within an organization. They can learn from each other's stories, both successes and failures. In the more than 20 years in which we have facilitated management development classes, one very consistent advantage to these courses, as stated by managers on the course evaluation forms, is the opportunity to meet with other managers to discuss common problems and issues.

Succession Planning: Who's on Your Bench?

Who will take over the reigns at your company or organization after the current guard steps down? Who on your senior management team is likely to leave or retire in the next five years? If you expect to maintain some level of performance continuity, you need to know who can step up when you or your seasoned executives leave.

In 1991, Robert Galvin, CEO of Motorola and son of the founder, Paul Galvin, said the following: "One responsibility [we] considered paramount is seeing to the continuity of capable senior leadership. We have always striven to have proven back-up candidates available, employed transition training programs to best prepare the prime candidates, and have been very open about [succession planning]...We believe that continuity is immensely valuable."[37]

Wall Street increasingly values the bench strength behind the CEO, something that companies often overlook until they need a successor. Depth of management is one reason why GE, Southwest Airlines, Wal-Mart, and Home Depot are still hitting the top 10 after their famous CEOs have stepped aside.[38]

Collins and Porras state that visionary companies develop, promote, and carefully select managerial talent grown from within the company. Out of hundreds years of combined history of the companies they categorize as visionary, there were only four cases where an outsider took over the role of CEO.[39] These 18 time-honored companies have "preserved the core" as they put it. In other words, over time, and through the transitioning of CEO to CEO, these companies have maintained their core ideologies.

The authors provide a model known as the "Leadership Continuity Loop" (Figure 11.1 below) to demonstrate how promoting from within can maintain this continuity of the "core."

Applying Continuous Learning

When do you train and when do you let managers manage? Too often, managers will send a problem employee to training in the hope that the capable folks in the training department will fix the employee as if the person was a broken appliance in for repair. The *only* time that training is

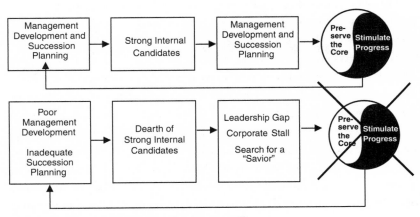

Figure 11.1   Leadership Continuity Loop[40]

the proper course of action is when there is a clear *skill or knowledge deficiency*. Training fills the void. If an employee wants to contribute but can't because he doesn't know how, send him to training. If he knows how to contribute, but won't, send him to his supervisor. Training is not an alternative to managing.

Training courses must be tied to the organizational strategy. Why else would you offer a course? Simply to agree to deliver a training program because someone requested it, without relating the outcomes to strategic intent, is a *training* paradigm, not a *business* paradigm. One reason that training departments lose their budgets during times of financial crises is that the decision makers can't see a direct relationship between the training courses and the bottom line. For their own survival, when training directors or their staff get a request for a course, they must probe for more information and find out what business need is driving the request.

A training need occurs only when a gap exists in job performance for which a lack of skill or knowledge is at least one cause.

A Training Effectiveness Plan (Table 11.8), if followed properly, will lead to targeted training courses that are directly aligned with key organizational objectives:

Trainers are always interested in reading course evaluations. Sometimes they read them to see if they can improve the course based on the participants' comments. Other times they read them to see if anyone said anything that might get them in trouble with their boss. In any event, these course evaluations—sometimes called "happy sheets" because participants usually bond with their instructor, and as a result they are generous with their praise—are only the start of the evaluation analysis.

These days, managers often work short-handed in order to send an employee to class. They are far less concerned about whether an employee *liked* the course. What really matters to them is whether the employee can *apply* the skills back on the job.

To truly evaluate the usefulness of a training program, you must determine if the skills and knowledge learned in class are being used, and if so, whether they are having the desired impact. In his book *A Practical Guide for Supervisory Training and Development*, Donald Kirkpatrick defines four levels of evaluation. To achieve the return on investment desired from any training course, all four levels must be realized. (See Table 11.9.)

Table 11.8   Training Effectiveness Plan

The focus of this plan is to link training programs to specific business needs. The objective is to understand the business context for developing and implementing corporate training courses.

1. Clarify the business need.	• Make sure the performance problem has something to do with a skill or knowledge deficiency and not just an unwillingness on the part of the employee(s) to perform. • Figure out how the training will help the company financially. What is the ROI? • Start thinking about the metrics you might use to determine the overall value of a training class.
2. Conduct a cause analysis.	• What factors have contributed to the problem? • Are there conditions outside the company that are contributing to the problem? Could the lack of sales have something do with competitive pricing and not the lack of sales skills?
3. Design the program.	• Create a program that gets to the heart of the matter. • Finalize the metrics that will be used to determine the effectiveness of the program. • In the course introduction, tell participants what they will learn and *why* they are learning it. What is the intended outcome, not just for the class but for the company?
4. Evaluate the program.	• Go beyond the "happy sheets" turned in at the end of the class and figure out if the skills are being applied. (See the following Table 11.9.) • Be prepared to tell your internal client the benefits that have been derived from the company's investment.
5. Report the outcomes.	• Let your client know how the course has impacted the performance issue. • Use the metrics identified in the previous steps to report all tangible benefits.

Table 11.9 The Kirkpatrick Model Four Levels of Course Evaluation[41]

Use these four steps to determine if a course was effective:	
Level One: Reaction Evaluation	This is sometimes called the "happy sheet." It is typically a questionnaire, which is distributed and completed at the conclusion of a training program. These forms are very useful for determining how a course can be improved.
Level Two: Learning Evaluation	This level reveals whether participants have actually learned what you intended them to learn. Competency checks and other tests fall into this category. These evaluations are used to determine if a participant has developed sufficient competency. For an airline, it might take the form of a safety exam. For a bank, it might be a test of a teller's ability to balance his or her daily transactions.
Level Three: Skill Application Evaluation	This level gets us to the real issue: Are people applying the skills they learned? These types of evaluations are used to gather evidence that course participants have adopted the skills or behaviors covered in the course. Usually, these types of assessments occur after the participant has had sufficient time back on the job—generally three to six months after class. These postclass evaluations also have the added benefit of reinforcing the topics presented in the classroom.
Level Four: Impact or Results Evaluation	Now we get to the bottom-line impact. Level Four evaluations collect verifiable examples of how the participants' improved skills and knowledge have positively impacted their personal performance, and just as importantly, the performance of their department. What turned out to be the true value of the program? Can you tie increased sales, better reliability, or lower attrition rates to the course? How do the outcomes relate to the performance metrics you developed for the program? This analysis is sometimes integrated with Level Three analysis on the same form.

Here is an idea. What if no one actually "graduated" from a course until they could demonstrate that they have used the skills successfully on the job? In one company we know, graduates of their leadership program do not get their certificates until they submit a form that describes at least two or three scenarios they handled using the skills taught in the program. They are asked to discuss three points briefly:

1. Describe the situation.
2. How did you handle it?
3. What was the outcome?

In *Thriving on Chaos,* Tom Peters offers 10 components of a successful organizational approach to training (Table 11.10).

Table 11.10 Elements of a Successful Training Program[42]

- Extensive entry-level training that focuses on exactly the skills the firm wants to use to differentiate itself.
- All employees are treated as potential career employees.
- Regular retraining is required.
- Both time and money are generously expended.
- On-the-job training counts too.
- There are no limits to the skills that can profitably be taught to everyone.
- Training is used to herald a commitment to a new strategic intent.
- Training is emphasized at a time of crisis.
- All training is line driven.
- Training is used to teach the organization's vision and values.

Finally, training is truly developmental when an employee's career goals are taken into consideration. Stephen Covey asserts that employees want to make a meaningful contribution. He contends that companies who want to get the highest level of performance from their employees must first see these employees as more than just resources or assets. As mentioned earlier, Covey maintains that employees are "spiritual beings," not just economic or social beings, and that they want meaning, a sense of doing something that matters.[43] For these reasons, both corporate needs and employee aspirations should be considered when designing training programs.

Performance Management: Building Resumes

"Good management consists in showing average people how to do the work of superior people."—John D. Rockefeller

Back in 1994, we had the opportunity to listen to Tom Peters address an audience in Los Angeles. Peters was in his usual form—chastising the audience for a number of organizational sins, speaking like someone possessed, raising his voice a few octaves to make his points and then settling in quietly with carefully-placed pauses to let the message sink in. He was masterful and compelling. One point he made in that presentation that has stuck with us over these years was his suggestion for "fixing" the current state of performance management programs. In his trademark "pull no punches" style, he suggested that we "blow up" our performance management programs, and instead think of the process as an opportunity to build employee resumes. This is not a trivial distinction.

Organizational performance management programs tend to be more historical than forward-looking. Managers run the risk of spending a disproportionate amount of time addressing past performance rather than thinking about the future. Emphasis is placed more on the last 12 months than on the next 12 months. As a result, the developmental needs of the employee may be neglected.

The temptation is understandable. Performance reviews swoop down on managers, sometimes all at once. Often, overburdened managers have to take the time to complete several pages of performance information at times when they are already dealing with work schedules, budgets, customer issues, orders from their bosses, and a host of other demands. Retracing performance over the last 12 months is easier than thinking about the next 12. It is tempting to fill in only the minimum necessary rating information and move on to the next review. However, the time saved is also an opportunity lost.

You will recall in the *Development Coaching* section of Chapter 10, we point out the advantages of integrating employee goals and aspirations with those of the organizations they work for. The performance review meeting with your employee is an ideal time to talk about this integration. This type of discussion takes a little longer, but the outcomes are much more satisfying for both manager and employee. It is better for employees because they develop new skills and build their resumes. It is better for the manager because he or she increases bench strength. Managers can delegate some of that over-burdensome workload only if they have a staff that is skilled enough to take on new responsibilities. Building those skills begins with a solid performance management program.

When we evaluate *performance management*, we look at a company's ability to:

1. Develop and employ a result-oriented performance management process
2. Involve employees in the goal-setting process
3. Hold people accountable for their work
4. Establish clear performance expectations and timelines
5. Conduct interim performance reviews—not just an annual review
6. Set a standard that performance appraisals must be complete and well substantiated
7. Conduct performance reviews in appropriate settings with no interruptions

Strategic plans provide the criteria for macro views of organizational performance. Performance plans provide the micro view. Simply put, organizational performance is the outcome of contributions made by every individual in the company. As Senge says, without individual performance, there would be no organization performance. This is a universal truth that applies to every organization, unless, of course, your company has found a way of getting things done without any human intervention. For the rest of us, we need to effectively manage individual performance if we have any hope of achieving optimum organizational performance. Individual performance plans are the fuel injectors, spark plugs, and pistons that ignite a company's performance engine.

From the moment we first sat up in the crib, we learned that is was smart to do the things that got rewarded and not so smart to do the things that got punished. It is a natural act of human behavior to modify our behavior according the rewards and consequences of our actions. *Performance management* is another occasion where these principles apply. Evaluating an employee's performance leads to moments of truth where managers determine whether rewards—or consequences—are appropriate, based on the goals agreed to by the employee and the degree to which these goals have or have not be achieved.

This leads us to a discussion of the employee's role in goal setting. Should managers set performance expectations, or should this be a participative exercise with input from the employee? Well-designed performance management programs are built on a foundation of establishing clear, results-oriented goals that are tied to strategic intent. The most effective systems include employee feedback in the goal-setting process. This is not a democracy where employees have carte blanche to set the performance standards. It should be, however, a meritocracy, where employees have the opportunity, in conjunction with their manager, to set challenging but realistic goals and be rewarded for achieving those goals. This approach satisfies organizational objectives while developing the employee's personal skill set.

Performance Evaluations "Underwhelm" Employees

According to a recent study,[44] 52 percent of workers want their supervisors to state performance goals more clearly. Nearly 40 percent want the issue of their performance on the job tied more closely to both their development plans and their compensation outcomes. The survey also found that 42 percent of workers were at least moderately dissatisfied with their employer's system of performance evaluation.

There are many reasons for this widespread feeling of dissatisfaction. Says one source, "A lot of employers still use it [appraisal] to punish workers instead of helping them develop." Another common complaint is that managers "... fail to explain to employees what they expect from them or clearly define the standards and criteria they use to evaluate performance... This just sets up employees—and the process—for failure."

Strategy-supportive performance management systems define job expectations in terms of *the desired outcomes*, not just the duties and functions to be performed. Working hard, staying busy, and diligently performing assigned tasks does not guarantee results. Stressing *what to accomplish* instead of *what to do*, encourages employees to focus on results rather than just doing their job. Start by making sure that all employees understand what they are expected to contribute to the bigger picture. Tie their outcomes to broader organizational objectives so that it is clear how their results impact bottom-line performance. After all, if an employee's contribution to a company's strategic objectives can't be quantified, the job may not be necessary.

In general, the steps to establishing an effective performance management system include the following:

1. Determine key outcomes necessary to achieve strategic intent.
2. Identify the cross-functional output that will be necessary to produce these outcomes.
3. Identify the critical activities and capabilities within these cross-functional areas that are required to carry out the processes.
4. Translate these activities and capabilities into departmental and individual performance plans.
5. Develop a means of tracking and measuring individual and departmental performance.
6. Focus on future development of employees, not just past performance.

Table 11.11 Examples of Unintended Consequences[45]

Intended Consequences	Measure	Potential for Unintended Consequences
Sustained levels of innovation and growth	Sales of new products	Lack of attention to and early abandonment of older products leads to sales decline
Focused attention to market standing relative to the competition	Growth of market share	Increasingly narrow definition of the market, leading the organization to ignore valuable market segments
Lowering labor costs	Employee turnover	Workforce ages, which drives up health care costs
Improved level of stockholder value	Cash flow from operations	Managers consistently underinvest in order to conserve cash in the short run, weakening the value of the company
Improved working capital productivity and cash flow	Accounts receivable turnover	Heavy-handed collections techniques drive off customers and lower future sales, limiting future cash flow
Improved competitiveness through speed	Cycle time for new product development	Corners are cut, leading to massive returns, huge warranty costs
Increased earning potential	Sales growth	Sales force accepts orders at levels too low to allow a profit
Expansion of quality improvement efforts	Number of active quality improvement teams	Numerous shell teams are created, making a mockery out of the quality program, and damaging morale
Performance of the order fulfillment process	Number of inventory stock outs	Overstocking drives up inventory costs, making the order fulfillment process less competitive
Lowered production costs	Cost variance reports	Fear of not meeting standard costs limits experimentation, and costs fail to improve significantly

But be careful what you measure! Unintended consequences may result from even the best intentions and actions. Table 11.11 lists some of these unintended outcomes:

We would like to emphasize that performance management is *not* an annual event. One common complaint we hear from employees is that they receive very little feedback on their performance during the year. Providing this feedback, even if only informally, on an interim basis is extremely important. This approach not only helps to keep employee performance on track, but also assists the manager in more accurately evaluating yearlong performance. Regular contact with employees eliminates those ineffective annual appraisals that account for the last three months of performance—because that's all the manager can remember.

Table 11.12 Comparing Performance Management with Performance Appraisal

Performance Management	Performance Appraisal
Focus on planning and managing (the future)	Focus on judging after the fact (the past)
Emphasizes the process	Emphasizes the form
Measures are consistently revised to fit the changing times and direction of the business	Evaluation of a constant and standard set of measures over an extended period of time
Performance expectations are linked to the business plan, tracking progress toward strategic goals	Evaluation factors are subjectively identified, tracking performance against set plans
Measures not only work contributions, but also capabilities, knowledge, experience, personal characteristics, and style	Measurement is often a simplistic evaluation of recent performance of designated tasks in a narrowly-defined job
Includes both results and behavioral skills equally (the *how* in addition to the *what*)	Tends to emphasize results over traits
Review of performance is a participative conversation between manager and employee	One-way delivery of information to the employee via the appraisal form
A responsibility of line management	A human resources department procedure

Applying Performance Management: Establishing a Credible Approach

While we are on the subject, Table 11.12 distinguishes *performance management* from performance appraisal.

Conducting a Substantial and Effective Performance Review

There are some guidelines to consider before you step into a conference room to conduct a performance review with an employee. Remember that this employee may have been anticipating this moment for a better part of a year. There could be a significant morale drain if it appears that whole event was just thrown together at the last minute. A well-substantiated, comprehensive review demonstrates respect for the employee—a standard we have seen on more company placards than we can recall. Table 11.13 offers some pointers:

Table 11.13 Performance Review Guidelines

1. Before the review	Plan in advance what you are going to say at each stage of the review. Be ready to substantiate each aspect of the review, both the favorable and the unfavorable. Anticipate employee reaction.
	Schedule the review well in advance and use an office or conference room where you will not be interrupted.
2. Begin the session	Welcome the employee. Try to put him or her at ease. Explain how the review will be conducted and how he or she will participate.
3. Review the employee's performance	Discuss your observation of the employee's performance and behavior for each of his or her key objectives. Substantiate your evaluation with information that you have either personally observed or have been able to verify through other reliable means. Invite the employee to take notes so that they can respond after you have had a chance to complete the review.
	Compliment the employee for areas that meet or exceed expectations. Provide constructive feedback for areas that have fallen short of expectations. Remember to be specific. Don't say, "You have done a great job." Instead say something like, "The positive comments we have received from customers you have helped have been outstanding!" Along the same lines,

Table 11.13   Performance Review Guidelines (*Continued*)

	don't say, "You have a bad attitude." Instead say, "I have witnessed several occasions where you acted impatiently with customers."
	Provide an overall performance rating, based on the system in use by your organization.
4. Ask for feedback	Give the employee an opportunity to offer his or her perspective regarding performance. If the review has been primarily positive, the employee's feedback may amount to nothing more than a "thank you." If however, there have been some critical issues, be prepared for a rebuttal. This is why having well-substantiated information is so important.
	Listen attentively until the employee has finished. If the employee has offered additional information or extenuating circumstances that legitimately alter your opinion for any aspect of the review, be willing to make a change. Reviews should not be egocentric. The goal is employee development, not being right. If, on the other hand, the employee's feedback does not change your view, stick to your opinion and leave the review as is.
5. Suggest development opportunities	Discuss what the employee can do over the next several months to develop his or her skills. Consideration should be given to both organizational need and individual aspirations. Remember…Build their resume!
6. Discuss salary implications	If there is an increase in the employee's salary tied to the review, indicate the amount of increase and when it will become effective.
7. Closing	As with any coaching session, try to end this review on an encouraging note. If the review has been mostly favorable, this will be easy. If the review has been critical, reaffirm your confidence in the employee's ability to improve. Refer back to the development plan.
	Thank the employee for his or her time.

Performance Management Roles

Where performance management programs are concerned, there are very clear roles for each level in the organizational hierarchy (see Figure 11.2).

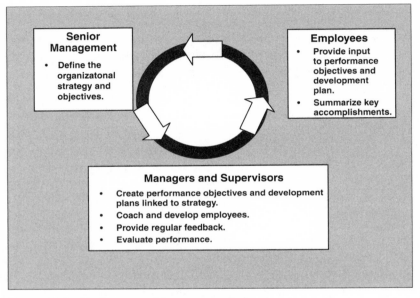

Figure 11.2 Performance Management Roles

In closing, we get back to this concept of building resumes. These days it is impossible for any organization, regardless of its size, to guarantee employment. Layoffs are very common events in the American business economy. In fact, this has become much more of a global condition.

According to author Nakato Hirakubo in a 1999 article for *Business Horizons*, "Today, because of the recent economic downturn in Asia, Japanese companies are having a hard time providing lifetime job security and creating enough middle management positions. Risutora (restructuring) is the buzzword in the Japanese business community. An estimated two million or more jobs must be cut to make Japanese companies profitable. As a result, the unemployment rate will soar to 8 percent from 4.8 percent, which is already the highest in the country's modern history."[46]

Given the constant threat of staff reductions, employers cannot guarantee employment. However, employers can go a long way to guarantee **employability**—by helping their employees build their resumes.

Reward Systems

"If you talk about change but don't change the reward and recognition system, nothing changes."—*Paul Allaire, Former Chairman of the Board and CEO of Xerox*

If you were offered a million dollars to accomplish something, your obvious question would be "accomplish what?" If the answer was, "cross the road," you would question the intention to pay. If the answer was, "climb Mount Everest," you would question your ability to complete the task. This, in essence, is the basic premise of a concept known as "The Expectancy Theory," first developed in 1964 by Victor Vroom.[47] This motivational theory is based on the belief that, given any risk/reward opportunity, employees will ask themselves three questions: (1) Can I achieve it? (2) What positive or negative outcomes will occur if I put out the effort? and (3) Given these possible outcomes, what is the real value of the opportunity? Vroom defines these elements as *Expectancy, Instrumentality,* and *Valence* (Figure 11.3).

We mention this theory because before you can design reward systems, you must first understand some basics of human motivation. Organizational rewards are generally thought to be economic in nature—pay increases, bonuses, and so on. But rewards can also exist on a psychological level, such as recognition, advancement, or just plain appreciation. Economic and psychological rewards can be used in tandem with excellent results.

As we have seen with all the other elements of human resources, to be effective, *reward systems* must be aligned with an organization's strategic intent. In other words, once the strategic direction of a company is determined, recruitment, orientation, training, performance management, and rewards must each be specifically designed to locate, engage, teach, coach, and motivate employees in order to increase the chances of achieving this strategic intent.

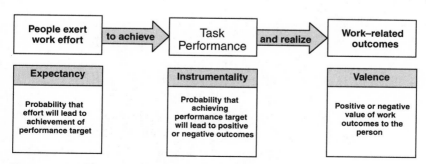

Figure 11.3 Elements of the Expectancy Theory[48]

A key element in this pursuit is to make sure that employees are being rewarded for the specific skills and behaviors that will advance a company's strategy. These rewards must be fair, equitable, and worthy of the effort required to earn them. In other words, to be attractive, rewards must pass the scrutiny of employees who, consciously or otherwise, will evaluate the value of the reward through the lens of something like The Expectancy Theory.

When we evaluate *reward systems,* we consider an organization's ability to:

1. Identify and reward the appropriate skills and behaviors
2. Reward employees in a manner that is fair and equitable to all
3. Develop programs where employees believe that the rewards for achieving their goals are proportionate to the effort
4. Ensure that promotions are deserved and are based on the individual's competence and performance
5. Reward team performance at a level equal to or greater than individual performance

The execution of strategy ultimately depends on the contribution of individuals within an organization. Organizations strive to shape employee skills and behavior by linking rewards for these attributes to their performance management system. The incentive structure is a vital element in an organization's strategic process, because, properly designed, this system will positively impact the values, skills, and behaviors throughout the organization.

Rewarding the wrong behavior while hoping for a positive outcome is both shortsighted and foolish. Here is an example: After establishing a good customer base, a large furniture company wants to increase its sales revenues. Rewarding the sales staff for every increased sales transaction soon leads the firm to higher sales, but ultimately drives the company into bankruptcy. Why? With rewards based on sales, all efforts had focused on the transaction. The sales staff was quick to finance sales transactions in the quest for numbers. Little attention was paid to cash flow and profitability. The overriding assumption was more sales, more money. However, after a few months of offering long-term financing, the firm's cash reserves dried up, and they were out of business.

If the achievement of the firm's strategic intent is top priority, then the reward system should reflect it. Designers of reward systems can utilize many incentive and consequences mechanisms, including compensation, raises, bonuses, stock options, incentives, benefits, promotions, demotions, recognition, praise and criticism, group norms, performance appraisal, tension, and fear.

Psychological Rewards

During the 1950s and 1960s, theoretician Fredrick Hertzberg decided to carefully study and research the key factors affecting a worker's performance. During his research, he found that certain factors tended to cause a worker to feel unsatisfied with his or her job. These factors seemed to relate directly to the employee's environment, such as the physical surroundings, supervisors, and even the company itself. He developed a theory based on this observation, naming it the "Hygiene Theory."

According to his theory, for a worker to be happy and therefore productive, these environmental factors must not cause discomfort. An interesting aspect of Hertzberg's research was that, although the elimination of the environmental problems may make workers productive, it will not necessarily motivate them. The question remains, "How can managers motivate employees?"

Many managers believe that motivating employees requires giving rewards. Hertzberg, however, contends that the workers get motivated through feeling responsible for and connected to their work. In this case, the work itself is rewarding. Managers can help the employees connect to their work by giving them more authority over the job, as well as by offering direct and individual feedback.[49]

Hertzberg provided an early look at motivation and job satisfaction. He developed two theories of organizational motivation:

1. Hygiene Factors
2. Motivation Factors

Hygiene factors can maintain employee satisfaction, but cannot serve to motivate. Hertzberg called these factors "dissatisfiers" because although they

Table 11.14 Hertzberg Motivation Factors[50]

Motivation Factors/Satisfiers	Hygiene Factors/Dissatisfiers
Recognition	Salary
Advancement	Working Conditions
Achievement	Supervisory Relationships
Additional Opportunities	Interpersonal Relationships
The Work Itself	Security

Table 11.15 Reward Systems Guidelines[51]

1. Link rewards tightly to the strategic plan.	Rewards linked to the accomplishment of strategic objectives, milestones, completion of key projects, or actions that sustain competitive advantage keep people energized and focused on the right things and on doing them right.
2. Use variable incentives and make them a major part of everyone's compensation.	If a significant portion of a person's compensation (20 to 60 percent) varies with performance, then a person should be inclined to perform well. This guideline can backfire if the reward system is not fair, not understood, or not consistent with the next guideline.
3. Rewards and incentives must be linked to an individual's job and the outcomes the individual can personally affect.	People are more accepting of incentive programs when they feel that they control those things being measured. (This does not exclude the value of team-based rewards.)
4. Reward performance and link value to success, rather than to a position in the organizational hierarchy.	While seniority has its place, and positions of responsibility often correlate with contribution to results, progressive managers focus on the skill sets and expertise essential for success.
5. Reward everyone and be sensitive to discrepancies between the top and bottom of the organization.	Incentive-based systems should include programs wherein every member of the firm participates in some fashion. And while varying skill sets, responsibilities, and roles must be recognized with different rewards, extremely high rewards out of sync with everyone else can erode confidence and commitment.
6. Be scrupulously fair, accurate, and informative.	Reward systems that are perceived to be fair work better than those that are not. Accurate measurements of the outcomes triggering the rewards play a key role in perceived fairness.
7. Reward generously when successful; minimally when not.	Reward systems that reinforce success do just that. Systems that reward with no link to performance can send a message that effort does not matter.
8. Don't underestimate the value of a rewarding and motivational environment.	While cash, stock, and perks get people's attention, a motivating environment is a very important part of any effective reward system. Increased responsibility, autonomy, recognition, and opportunity for growth are all proven "rewards" that motivate people.
9. Be open to changing the reward systems.	Strategies and tactics change. Situations change. Organization members encounter different needs. Certain aspects of a reward system may no longer be appropriate. Managers should regard reward systems as evolving, rather than permanent. Avoid confusion and unfairness when changing the rules.

do not motivate employees, they can become "demotivators" if they are not present in the work environment.

Motivation factors, on the other hand, are those that can motivate employees to demonstrate positive attitude and achieve results. He called these "satisfiers." Table 11.14 lists examples of satisfiers and dissatisfiers.

Applying Reward Systems: Strategic Motivation

Managers at every level can improve the effectiveness of their reward system by following nine guidelines (Table 11.15).

In summary, *human resource systems* are designed to attract talented people (*selective recruitment*); make them feel like they are a part of something exciting (*employee orientation*); give them the training they need to contribute (*continuous learning*); manage individual performance with substance and credibility (*performance management*); and establish rewards that are fair and worthy of the effort (*reward systems*).

Organization Character

"There is a gap between what the organization says it wants and what it feels like to work there. Those gaps between what you say and what you do erode trust in the enterprise and in the leadership, and they inhibit action. The more you can narrow that gap, the more people's energies can be released toward company purposes."

—ROBERT HASS, U.S. POET LAUREATE, LECTURER

VALUES AND BELIEFS (discussed in Chapter 9) represent the *explicit* nature of a company's culture. *Organization character* reflects the *implicit* nature of this culture. Outcomes associated with identifying and communicating values and beliefs generally result in some form of printed media—usually value statements or operating principles that are proudly displayed on posters, placards, or in company newsletters, Web sites, or annual reports.

Organization character is not overt. It is not publicized with colorful media. Rather, it is experienced, first hand, by employees, customers, vendors, partners, and anyone else who may have repetitive dealings with the organization. In essence, *organization character* is the "behind-the-scenes personality" of a company. This is the real nature of the work environment that soon becomes apparent to all employees. Employees' perception of their company is shaped far more by their day-to-day experiences than by any print media, no matter how inspiring the words may read. *Organization character* defines the true nature of a company, stripped of any pretenses.

This topic includes an organization's informal communication practices, for example, whether there is an open or closed-door policy, how conflict is resolved, whether the company is receptive to employee feedback (and willing to respond to this feedback), and how the organization deals with events requiring significant change.

Formal communication includes all structured processes that have been organized to provide information exchange within the organization and between the organization and outside constituencies. This could include newsletters, corporate memos, video productions, Webcasts, management forums, shareholder meetings, annual reports, Web site content, and other media.

Informal communication refers to the way managers and peers communicate outside this formal structure of the organization. It occurs continuously within the organization and includes impromptu meetings, so-called "water cooler" conversations, social engagements, discussions over lunch or dinner, employee conversations in the breakroom, or any other time where information exchange occurs outside the formal communication methods.

Feedback systems work in a similar fashion. Credibility and trust are important components in the free flow of information throughout an organization. Managers and employees should be encouraged to exchange ideas and opinions openly, to offer constructive feedback, and to provide improvement suggestions. The atmosphere and climate of the organization must support this idea exchange without fear of reprisals.

Sharing information is critical in developing people's capacities. As we pointed out in Chapters 10 and 11, employees who see and experience the merit of their contribution are more committed. Members of any organization perform more effectively when they believe that they are part of a community, with common values and shared interests. Leaders who solicit feedback help to create this community. As a result, they are much more in touch with the climate and character of their company.

Finally, the character of the organization is expressed in its ability and willingness to change. Never is there a more important time for communication than when an organization is undergoing significant change. It is critically important for employees to understand both the compelling reasons for change and how the change will impact them personally. This can be accomplished much more effectively in an atmosphere with open channels of communication, where trust exists between management and employees, due in no small part to the free flow of information. Try implementing a major change in an environment of mistrust, closed minds, and one-way communication. If there are any results at all, they are likely to be slow and frustrating.

An organization suffering from diminished character is likely to commit many of the mistakes companies make when faced with change imperatives:[1]

- The organization that cannot communicate feedback, good or bad, will sink into complacency. Without feedback, it is perceived that all is well, therefore urgency is lost and change cannot happen.
- Without strong, respected champions leading the way, any change initiative will fail due to the amount of inertia required to overcome potential resistance.
- Lack of good communication will dampen efforts to communicate the new corporate vision, rendering change impossible.
- People will not make sacrifices for an organization to change if they do not trust the organization to recognize that sacrifice and to respond in kind.
- Changing is difficult with little or no feedback or trust.
- Real change or transformation takes time.
- Without clear communication and trust in leadership and systems, change may only be temporary.
- Without proper communication of the company's strategy and how it fits with the organizational culture, employees may misinterpret the strategy and credibility and performance will be [negatively] affected further.

Testing Organization Character

In the early 1940s, Kathryn Briggs and her daughter Isabel Briggs Myers expanded on the psychological theories first developed by Swiss psychiatrist Carl Jung (1875–1961). Their research eventually led to the creation of the Myers-Briggs Type Indicator (MBTI), a self-reporting, personality inventory diagnostic that has been used for nearly 60 years to provide people with information regarding which of 16 personality types they may fall into. This information helps individuals understand why they and others behave in certain ways under certain conditions.

Author William Bridges proposes that organizations differ in character in the same way that individuals do. Through this analogy, he is able to explain why organizations act as they do and why they are so hard to change. He groups organizations into the same personality aspects covered in the MBTI (Figure 12.1).

Extroverted		Introverted	
Focuses outward; responds to external stimuli.	Vs.	Takes cues and draws power from within; is fairly closed.	
Example: Are decisions more often made because of market data or because of internal factors like the beliefs of the leaders or the capacities of the facilities?			
Sensing		Intuition	
Concerns itself with actualities; attends to details.	Vs.	Concerns itself with possibilities; attends to the big picture.	
Example: Does the leadership base its decisions on detailed information about situations or on general trends and a big picture concept of what is going on?			
Thinking		Feeling	
Depends on impersonal procedures and principles.	Vs.	Reaches conclusions on the basis of values and beliefs.	
Example: How are organizational decisions really made? More from the head (and then tempered by humanity) or more from the heart (and then balanced by information)?			
Judging		Perceiving	
Likes things spelled out and definite; seeks closure.	Vs.	Likes to keep options open; distrusts too much definition.	
Example: Does the organization more often choose to reach a decision or look for more options?			

Figure 12.1 Organizational Character Index (OCI)[2]

We have organized the discussion of *organization character* into three sections:

- Informal Communication
- Organization Feedback
- Adaptability to Change

Organizations with deficient organizational character, loaded with issues of poor communication, lack of feedback, and the inability to change will, simply put, be less competitive, primarily because the very individuals they count on to get the job done will have become disenfranchised. Frustrated employees are resistant to change because they view the latest change as just another one in a series of unexplained changes. Being kept in the dark fuels this frustration resulting in resistance that can slow progress to the point of failure. Sales may fall, budgets are likely to get pinched, and the organization is left to struggle.

These errors are not inevitable. They can be avoided by promoting *organizational character.*

Informal Communication

"Nobody tells you to be a customer service hero; it's just sort of expected."—Nordstrom Employee

Within 90 days of so after they have completed their orientation, after they have read all about the exploits of the company, learned about the rich heritage, gained some knowledge of past and present executives, and settled into their jobs, employees begin to discover what the company is really like.

If an enthusiastic new employee sat in a lunchroom and told long-term employees how happy he or she was to be with your company or how fantastic your company is, would these seasoned employees agree or would they roll their eyes? These perceptions are built over time. Every employee judges the credibility of their company through their personal experiences. *Informal communication* is key contributor to this perception.

We evaluate an organization's *informal communication* by looking at a its ability to:

1. Exchange ideas and opinions openly, regardless of position or title, and without fear of reprisal
2. Resolve conflict or disagreement constructively to achieve more complete solutions
3. Establish an "open door" policy, where employees feel comfortable contacting any person in this company regardless of position or title
4. Create a balance between "high-tech" communication (e-mail, voice-mail, etc.) and face-to-face conversations

Informal communication includes impromptu dialogues, e-mails, and other messages that pass between members of the organization through informal channels. An informal channel could be employees on break, conversations at lunch, or simply observations of managers and employees regarding organizational behavior.

There is an old adage in business that says something like, "Satisfy a customer and 3 other customers find out. Dissatisfy a customer and 10 or more other customers find out." Why? Because we human beings talk more about times when we have been wronged than when things go as expected. If the dry cleaners have your clothes ready as planned, there is no compelling reason to share this outcome with friends. The event is not particularly interesting to you or your friends. But if that same cleaner not only can't deliver your best suit for this weekend's wedding, but also informs you that they have somehow torn the sleeve, you are much more compelled to share this outcome with a few friends—maybe more than a few.

When things go as expected, we tell almost no one. But when we have experienced something distressing, we usually pass along the story. *Informal communication* in organizations follows the same pattern. Employees will be disinterested in scenarios that have little or no impact on their work lives. But these same employees will quickly beat the jungle drums and alert their associates when they feel that the company has mistreated them, or if they have witnessed the mistreatment of others. *Informal communication* is viral…it spreads quickly and takes root in the system.

But keep in mind that this network can work in an organization's favor as well. What if an employee witnessed something that was totally unexpected in a positive way? What if the president called an employee out of the blue to thank him or her for receiving an appreciative letter from a customer? What if the benefits department went the extra mile to deal with a medical issue? What if a manager took the time to make sure that his employee received credit for a project completed by his department? These actions could lead to that same viral impact, but with much more positive outcomes. Companies who work hard to build organizational character understand this.

When *informal communication* is consistent with the assertions an organization makes through its formal communication—for example, values statements and operating principles—the workforce develops a sense of trust, and as a result, is in a better frame of mind to deliver. When it becomes clear that the character of the organization is inconsistent with values and beliefs, or worse, is in violation of those values, the informal network will rapidly communicate these undesirable work conditions. The discrepancies between what is expected and what actually transpires will quickly become known to even the newest employees.

The Grapevine: Is it Working for You or against You?

Organizations should be tuned to the "grapevine" and its capacity to transmit free-flowing information quickly. Although the information on an informal network is usually fairly accurate, the more emotionally charged the information, the more likely it will become inaccurate. Since inaccurate information can lead to mistrust and loss of credibility, all attempts should be made to correct misinformation.

Keith Davis has studied the organizational grapevine for more than 30 years. "With the rapidity of a burning powder train," Davis claims, "information flows out of the woodwork, past the manager's door and the janitor's closet, through the steel walls or glass partitions." The messages are often "symbolic expressions of feelings." For example, if a rumor says the boss may quit, and he or she is not going to, it may be that the employees wish it were true. So misinformation gets spread around due to the emotion tied to the potential outcome.

One frequent rumor is the threat of layoffs. We know of one company who elected to outsource most of their information services. The plan was to have the outsource firm hire nearly all of the company's technical staff. The layoffs would be comparatively minimal. The pay would be the same at the new company. The benefits would actually be a little better. But because the issue was so emotionally charged, the rumor spread that everyone in the information services division was going to lose their jobs. Morale sank and productivity decreased dramatically. Finally, the president visited with the technology staff and set them straight. But for at least three weeks, the informal communication network made up its own story and threw the division into a tailspin.

Among Davis' findings are the following:[3]

- Grapevines are accurate 75 to 95 percent of the time.
- There are only a few sources that supply the entire formal network.
- There are not many other channels of communication as capable of supplying the entire formal network.
- Admittedly, the grapevine can have some dramatic failures in accuracy.
- The grapevine is a psychological reflection of employee interest in the organization or its members.
- Levels of activity in the informal network parallel those in the formal network.
- Troublemakers sometimes use the grapevine. All untrue rumors, whether started by troublemakers or not, are best countered by truth told directly by management to employees early in the situation in question.

Davis concludes that wise managers "feed, water, and cultivate the grapevine," because it "cannot be abolished, rubbed out, hidden under a basket, chopped down, tied up, or stopped. It is as hard to kill as the mythical glass snake which when struck, broke into fragments and grew a new snake out of each piece."

Applying Informal Communication

There are a few aspects of the informal communication network that are fundamental to a healthy work environment. Table 12.1 lists some of these aspects and provides you with an opportunity to quickly evaluate them within your organization.

Give yourself one point for a "Strongly Disagree" response moving up to six points for a "Strongly Agree" response. No points for "Don't Know" responses.

At your company, is it natural for people to have candid discussions without regard to who is in the room? Is it understood that all parties have the best interests of your company in mind and that position or title is irrelevant? Is conflict viewed as a constructive means to arrive at the best answer or solution, or is it viewed more as an attack or threat? Do you feel that, when disagreements arise, individuals at your company act in a secure or insecure manner? Is there a collegial atmosphere at your company across all levels? Would senior managers at your company welcome a phone call or an unannounced visit from an employee who may be several rungs down the corporate ladder, or would they be surprised or even annoyed? Has your company remained "high touch" in spite of all the "high tech?" Does your company encourage a more social work environment where people on related projects get to know each other?

These are important questions to ask regarding your informal communication network. Knowing the answers can help you foster management styles that promote open communication and credibility throughout the organization. It is important for senior managers to have their fingers on the pulse of the organization. When this happens, information can be properly clarified, the grapevine can be accessed and managed, and the facts—positive or negative—can be communicated and dealt with in the most effective manner.

Organization Feedback

"There's a big difference between showing interest and really taking interest."—Michael P. Nichols, Ph.D., Department of Psychology, College of William and Mary

Table 12.1 Evaluating Informal Communication Processes

Aspect	Evaluation							
	Don't Know	Strongly Disagree	Disagree	Somewhat Disagree	Somewhat Agree	Agree	Strongly Agree	
At our company, ideas and opinions are exchanged openly, regardless of position or title, and without fear of reprisal.								
Conflict or disagreement is used productively to achieve more complete solutions.								
We have an "open door" policy. Employees feel comfortable contacting any person in this company regardless of position or title.								
We encourage cross-functional communication, where employees in one department are free to collaborate with employees in another department.								
Although we use e-mail and voicemail to communicate, we encourage face-to-face conversations, wherever possible.								
							TOTAL SCORE	

If there is one key piece of advice we can offer you regarding obtaining feedback from your organization, it is this: ***Don't ask unless you intend to answer.*** You may reduce cynicism by asking for employee input and then responding honestly to the feedback. But you will surely *increase* cynicism by inducing employees to complete a survey and then doing nothing with the results. Do not undertake a process to gather input unless you intend to close the loop properly.

Assuming that there is an interest in gaining useful input from members of your company and then responding candidly to the input, we offer some pointers regarding how this can be best accomplished.

Organization feedback involves implementing methods or forums to solicit employee feedback; encouraging employees to offer their input openly and honestly; and acting on the feedback by communicating the results.

When we evaluate *organization feedback,* we look at an organization's ability to:

1. Embrace the value of feedback
2. Regularly solicit feedback from its employees
3. Implement communication vehicles that encourage employee feedback as it relates to organizational performance and the work environment
4. Take the time to communicate the results of employee feedback and the actions, if any, that will be taken

Our company, Virtual CEO, Inc., develops researched-based organizational-performance assessments. We have used our diagnostics with more than 2000 companies. From personal experience, we can tell you that there are essentially two types of managers: those that want to know and those that would rather not know. It may or may not surprise you to learn that there are a number of managers at all levels of the hierarchy who view organizational feedback as a potential headache. These managers are like people who never undergo a physical examination because they would rather not know if something is wrong.

Organization feedback is one of many sources of fact-based information that leaders use to manage their organizations effectively. Employee feedback is no less important than customer or competitor information.

Feedback systems not only help employees alert management to work environment and performance issues, these systems—and the cross-functional communication they encourage—also help employees understand the organizational interdependencies that drive performance. As CEO Jack Stack of Springfield Remanufacturing Corporation points out, at most companies, "No one explains how one person's actions affect another's, how each department depends on the others, what impact they all have on the company as a whole."[4]

Sharing information rather than guarding it facilitates dialogue and helps everyone understand how decisions are made and how these decisions are linked to strategy. Employee inclination to improve their productivity on a task increases when they have a challenging goal and receive feedback on their progress.[5] Goals without feedback and feedback without goals have little effect on motivation.

Has senior management in your organization communicated a strong commitment to employee feedback? Have there been material improvements within your company that can be tracked back to employee feedback? Is there an internal communication device that provides your employees with an unimpeded means of providing management with direct feedback? Can your employees make company improvement suggestions in a manner that gets directly to a decision maker? Does your company act on the feedback given by employees and communicate the results (even if the response is a "no")?

The following diagram (Figure 12.2), based on Demming's work with quality, represents an abstract process that drives input through a particular

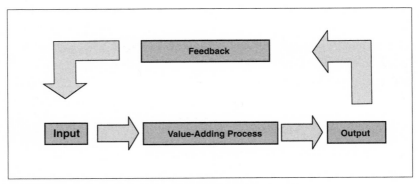

Figure 12.2   Feedback and the Value-Adding Process[6]

value-adding process and produces an output. Feedback is an important factor in addressing ways to improve output.

Organization Feedback as a Part of History

According to author Robert Cutler, western specialists on the Soviet Union during the Cold War encountered, without realizing it, many issues that are studied as part of management sciences. He states that the political disintegration of the USSR can be regarded as a failure of the Soviet system to adapt successfully to demands from increasingly complex international and domestic environments. As such, he says, there is direct relevance to the situation encountered by managers in complex bureaucracies today.

In a nutshell, as the organizations in the Soviet establishment become more bureaucratic, constituent parts within the USSR began to self-organize their own foreign policies independent of Moscow. At the time, there was actually a pre-existing doctrine that prohibited citizens of the USSR from even saying they *saw* things that, according to the doctrine, were not permitted to exist. In other words, feedback was shut down by law. The resulting failure of the USSR to receive and properly interpret feedback meant that their internal control systems were increasingly fallible and unable to respond to demands emanating from the society at large. This blocking of communications ultimately led to collapse.

Cutler goes on to say the collapse of the USSR, resulting from a breakdown in feedback, holds lessons for the modern North American corporation. IBM's failure to exploit the personal computer, American auto manufacturers' inability to deal with Japanese imports, Apple's failure to develop market share, Microsoft's initial response to the Internet, and even the quick demise of "New Coke" are all such examples resulting from the lack of feedback coming from different organizational levels. Without feedback, what management understands as "fact" may mean little to the employees in the field, and vice versa.[7]

Applying Organizational Feedback

There are many excellent instruments for collecting feedback. Some are completed manually. Others are completed on-line via the Internet. Some are created in-house, while others are developed by external companies who specialize in building these diagnostics based on best practices. The employee feedback process has become so simplified and convenient that deploying an assessment throughout an organization is unlikely to cause any significant interruption in productivity. With today's technology, survey results can be compiled in a matter of hours rather than days.

Figure 12.3 is a sample of "ClimatePlus," an on-line employment satisfaction survey, delivered by Virtual CEO, Inc.

Six Common Trouble Signs for Organizational Feedback Systems[8]

Some employees avoid providing feedback either because they are afraid of reprisals or they don't feel that the outcomes warrant the time it takes to complete the survey. If you address and prevent the following mistakes, your feedback processes will have a far better chance of succeeding:

1. Feedback is used to punish, embarrass, or put down employees.
2. Those receiving the feedback see it as irrelevant to their work.
3. Feedback information is provided too late to do any good.
4. People receiving feedback believe it relates to matters beyond their control.

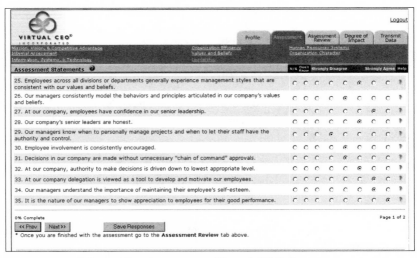

Figure 12.3 ClimatePlus Assessment, Virtual CEO, Inc.

5. Employees complain about wasting too much time collecting and recording feedback data.
6. Feedback recipients complain about feedback being too complex or difficult to understand.

Leaders encourage employees to voice their concerns, ideas, and suggestions. Sam Goldwyn, legendary President of Metro Goldwyn Mayer studios during the golden era of Hollywood, had a philosophy about feedback. After a series of box office losers, Mr. Goldwyn called his brain trust together and told them, "I want you to tell me exactly what's wrong with MGM, even if it means losing your job." Goldwyn was looking for some strong opinions, not "yes men." [9]

Providing a forum for an honest and candid exchange of ideas and opinions is vital if an organization is going to learn to improve. This can be accomplished by asking employees to speak up and tell it like it is.

Adaptability to Change

"The rate of change is not going to slow down anytime soon. If anything, competition in most industries will probably speed up even more in the next few decades."—John Kotter, Professor of Leadership at the Harvard Business School

Adaptability to change involves the designing and implementing of change management processes. It involves effectively communicating the need or rationale for change while determining organizational tolerance for change. By evaluating the overall level of employee acceptance or resistance to change, a company can begin to assess its ability to respond quickly to opportunities or threats.

When we evaluate *adaptability to change,* we look at an organization's ability to:

1. Respond and adapt to change
2. Effectively negotiate a significant change event
3. Communicate the compelling reasons for change to its employees
4. Ensure that all employees understand the process and methods that will be used to implement change, and how they will be individually impacted
5. Establish a culture where employees learn to expect change

Why Change?

Not everyone looks forward to change in the workplace. Consistency and predictability can be very comforting. In many cases, we may see change as loss: *I had something and now it's gone.* It could be job responsibilities and processes to which I have become accustomed and accomplished. It could be a relationship with a long-standing customer that will no longer be my account. Or I could simply disagree with the way the company wants to conduct business going forward.

In his book, *Managing at the Speed of Change,* Darryl Conner offers two prerequisites for major organizational change:

1. *Pain:* There must be a critical mass of information that justifies breaking from the status quo.
2. *Remedy:* It must be clear that the change strategy presents desirable, accessible actions that will either solve the problem or take advantage of an opportunity afforded by the current situation.[10]

In 1998, we were working with a major utility in California, who, like most utilities at that time, was grappling with the need to reinvent themselves due to significant changes in deregulation. In this new market, their long-standing empire was about to be invaded by lower-cost competitors. To become more competitive, they had to explore and resolve inefficiencies in their entire operation, including their call centers. Lengthy customer calls require more staff, which drives up general and administrative expenses, and reduces the ability to compete.

So, the question was raised: How long should the average commercial or consumer call take? This was a question that had never really been asked before. When you are the only game in town, customers have no choice but to wait their turn and hang on the line for however long it takes. But when competitors are saying they can provide more convenient service, the game changes. This utility was having significant difficulty in imposing new call standards on supervisors and employees who, for many years, had taken "as long as was necessary" to handle each call.

Why the resistance to change? One key factor was that the compelling reason for the change was not sinking in. It had definitely sunk in at the senior management level. (By the way, this was years before California's infamous energy crisis.) But somehow, the employee population either did not understand or accept the threat of competition or simply believed the threat was too distant to worry about.

To be fair, these employees did take a great deal of pride in providing good service, which they defined as taking the time necessary to make sure that each customer was fully satisfied. This tradition created a service paradigm that was very difficult to revise. To a large extent, employees were unwilling or unready to rethink how they could deliver good service more efficiently. As Spencer Johnson, M.D., states in his very popular book, *Who Moved My Cheese?*, "The more important your cheese is to you, the more you want to hold on to it."[11]

Deal and Kennedy emphasize that making strategic changes in an organization always threatens a culture: "People form strong attachments to heroes, legends, the rituals of daily life, the hoopla extravaganza and ceremonies, and all the symbols of the workplace. Change strips relationships and leaves employees confused, insecure, and often angry. Unless something can be done to provide support for transitions from old to new, the force of a culture can neutralize and emasculate strategy changes."[12]

For more than 20 years, John Kotter, who teaches Leadership at Harvard Business School, has focused on the study of both the success and failure of change initiatives in business. In *Leading Change*, he points out how complacency will always undermine a change effort: "Establishing a sense of urgency is crucial to gaining needed cooperation...No matter how hard [executives] push, no matter how much they threaten, if others don't feel the same sense of urgency, the momentum for change will probably die far short of the finish line. People will find a thousand ingenious ways to withhold cooperation from a process that they sincerely think is unnecessary or wrong."[13]

In their definitive book, *Corporate Culture and Performance*, Kotter, along with co-author James Heskett, argues that the primary function of leadership is to produce change. If a culture encourages this activity, it will foster risk taking, initiative, communication, and motivation.[14]

In spite of the sensibility of this advice, many companies have trouble adopting change, particularly when they have been perennially successful. McDonald's is the largest restaurant chain in the world and enjoys some tremendous business strengths. Yet, despite all of its strengths, McDonald's share began declining in 1998. Its stock performance lagged. Its industry experienced shifts in customer tastes. What went wrong at McDonald's? First and foremost was top management's resistance to recognize the need for change. In the face of these industry shifts and competitor encroachment, McDonald's chairman at the time was quoted as saying, "Do we have to change? No, we don't have to change. We have the most successful brand in the world." As the company's performance deteriorated, top executives tended to blame others. They publicly blasted dissident franchises and negative news accounts that were chalked up to misperceptions by the media. One particular reporter was barred from the biennial briefing.[15]

Adaptive vs. Unadaptive Cultures

In *Corporate Culture and Performance,* Kotter and Heskett make a strong case for the advantages of an adaptive culture when change is required. They say, "In the firms with more adaptive cultures, the cultural ideal is that managers throughout the hierarchy should provide leadership to initiate change in strategies and tactics whenever necessary to satisfy the legitimate interests of

Table 12.2 Adaptive versus Unadaptive Corporate Cultures[16]

	Adaptive Corporate Cultures	Unadaptive Corporate Cultures
Core Values	Most managers care deeply about customers, stockholders, and employees. They also strongly value people and processes that can create useful change.	Most managers care mainly about themselves, their immediate work group, or some product (or technology) associated with that work group. They value the orderly and risk-reducing management process much more highly than leadership initiatives.
Common Behavior	Managers pay close attention to all their constituencies, especially customers, and initiate change when needed to serve their legitimate interests, even if that entails taking some risks.	Managers tend to behave somewhat insularly, politically, and bureaucratically. As a result, they do not change their strategies quickly, or adjust to or take advantage of changes in their business environments.

not just the stockholder, or customers or employees, but all three. In less adaptive cultures, the norm is that the managers behave cautiously and politically to protect or advance themselves, their product, or their immediate work groups."[17]

Ralph Kilmann describes an adaptive culture as "a culture that entails a risk-taking, trusting, and proactive approach to organizational as well as individual life. Members actively support one another's efforts to identify all problems and implement workable solutions. There is a shared feeling of confidence: the members believe, without a doubt, that they can effectively manage whatever new problems and opportunities will come their way. There is widespread enthusiasm, a spirit of doing whatever it takes to achieve organizational success. The members are receptive to change and innovation."[18]

Rosabeth Kanter adds that adaptive cultures favor entrepreneurship, which can help a firm adapt to a changing environment by allowing it to identify and exploit new opportunities.[19] Table 12.2 offers a comparison between adaptive and unadaptive cultures:

Does it Really Matter?

Kotter and Heskett's study provides compelling evidence that healthy, adaptive cultures can have a dramatic impact on the bottom line (Table 12.3):

Although this study is now more than 10 years old, one could deduce that, given the collaborative advantages of an adaptive culture, similar results could be expected in today's market. (Cisco is a current example of what can happen when employees not only embrace change, but help to drive it. See *Empowerment*, in Chapter 10: Leadership.)

Table 12.3 Performance Comparisons between Adaptive versus Unadaptive Cultures[20]

1979–1990	Adaptive Cultures	Unadaptive Cultures
Increased Revenues	682%	166%
Expanded Workforce	282%	36%
Stock Price	901%	74%
Net Incomes	756%	1%

Resistance to Change

Even the clear evidence of the need for change may not provoke senior executives into action. Why? Robert Quinn offers some reasons why in his book, *Deep Change*. He says that with all the challenges that occur in our lives and in our organizations, executives lose the internal drive necessary to lead and manage change.[21] He quotes several executives who, for the most part, have lost this drive: "If I can hang around just a couple of more years, this problem will belong to someone else."

Quinn describes three ways in which people deal with what he calls "The Slow Death Dilemma." This is a phenomenon where someone who is confronted with the need to implement deep organizational change versus living with the status quo, rejects the option for change. The three reactions are:

1. **Peace and Pay:** Characterized by a "don't rock the boat" attitude. Simply maintain the status quo; come in at 8:00 and leave at 5:00. Quinn calls this reaction a form of mental illness where individuals actually cope with the slow death by choosing slow death.

2. **Active Exit:** In this mode, individuals spend their time thinking about leaving. They stay in touch with the market, think creatively about alternate career paths, and, when it becomes feasible, they change jobs. Although this is a less passive approach than "peace and pay," individuals who choose this strategy are also contributing to the slow death of the company because, as they begin to check out, problems are likely to get worse for their peers and subordinates.

3. **Deep Change:** This paradigm comes from the realization that if you're not continually growing, you're continually dying. This revelation leads to increased discipline, courage, and motivation, all of which create a better foundation for change. As one of Quinn's students said, "To choose death is to choose to cease to be. Such a choice is a horror to contemplate."[22]

Applying Adaptability to Change

Successful organizational change involves two key factors:

1. Having an effective change process
2. Knowing how to deal with resistance to change

1. **Establishing a Sense of Urgency**
   - Examining the market and competitive realities
   - Identifying and discussing crises, potential crises, or major opportunities

2. **Creating the Guiding Coalition**
   - Putting together a group with enough power to lead the change
   - Getting the group to work together like a team

3. **Developing a Vision and Strategy**
   - Creating a vision to help direct the change effort
   - Developing strategies for achieving that vision

4. **Communicating the Change Vision**
   - Using every vehicle possible to constantly communicate the new vision and strategies
   - Having the guiding coalition role model the behavior expected of employees

5. **Empowering Broad-Based Action**
   - Getting rid of obstacles
   - Changing systems or structures that undermine the change vision
   - Encouraging risk taking and nontraditional ideas, activities, and actions

6. **Generating Short-Term Wins**
   - Planning for visible improvements in performance, or "wins"
   - Creating those wins
   - Visibly recognizing and rewarding people who made the wins possible

7. **Consolidating Gains and Producing More Changes**
   - Using increased credibility to change all systems, structures, and policies that don't fit together and don't fit the transformation vision
   - Hiring, promoting, and developing people who can implement the change vision
   - Reinvigorating the process with new projects, themes, and change agents

8. **Anchoring New Approaches in the Culture**
   - Creating better performance through customer- and productivity-oriented behavior, more better leadership and more effective management
   - Articulating the connection between new behaviors and organizational success
   - Developing the means to ensure leadership development and succession

Figure 12.4   The Eight-Stage Process of Creating Major Change[23]

After years of study with many companies, change expert John Kotter suggests an eight-stage methodology (Fig. 12.4):

Table 12.4 below lists several change approaches that can be taken to reduce resistance to change and establish a more adaptive culture.

Remember that, even for those who get bored without some degree of change, the act of changing is uncomfortable. Learning new ways to do a job, reporting to a different boss, taking on new clients, dealing with new regulations,

Table 12.4 Approaches to Lessening Resistance to Change[24]

Approach	Commonly Used When...	Advantages	Disadvantages
Education and Communication	There is a lack of information or inaccurate information and analysis.	Once persuaded, people will often help implement the change.	Can be very time-consuming if many people are involved.
Participation and Involvement	The initiators do not have all the information they need to design the change, and others have considerable power to resist.	People who participate will be committed to implementing the change, and any relevant information they have will be integrated into the change plan.	Can be very time-consuming if many participants design an appropriate change plan.
Facilitation and Support	People are resisting because of adjustment problems.	No other approach works as well with adjustment problems.	Can be time-consuming, expensive, and still fail.
Negotiation and Agreement	Some person or group with considerable power to resist will clearly lose out in a change.	Sometimes it is a relatively quick and inexpensive solution to resistance problems.	Can be too expensive if it alerts others to negotiate for compliance.
Manipulation and Co-optation	Other tactics will not work or are too expensive.	It can be a relatively quick and inexpensive solution to resistance problems.	Can lead to future problems if people feel manipulated.
Explicit and Implicit Coercion	Speed is essential, and the change initiators possess considerable power.	It is speedy and can overcome any kind of resistance.	Can be risky if it leaves people angry with the initiators.

or having new work rules (as we have seen imposed on airline employees many times), will always require some degree of adjustment even for the most nimble employee.

When organizations take the time to explain clearly the compelling reasons for the change and to describe carefully how the change will affect each employee, the chances of success increase substantially.

Endnotes

Part I

1. Bill Gates, *Business @ the Speed of Thought,* Warner Books, 1999; p. 3.
2. Henry Mintzberg, "The Fall and Rise of Strategic Planning" The Free Press. 1994, page 324.
3. Donald Beal, Former Chairman and CEO, Rockwell International, *Internal Report,* 1990.
4. Michael E. Porter. *Competitive Strategy. Free Press,* 1980, p. xix–xx.

Chapter I

1. Harley-Davidson Annual Reports 1999–2001.
2. Excerpt from Harley-Davidson Corporation Mission Statement.
3. Excerpt from Harley-Davidson Corporation Vision Statement.
4. W. R. King and D. I. Cleland. *Strategic Planning and Policy.* McGraw-Hill, 1979, p. 124–125.
5. Peter Drucker. *Management: Tasks, Responsibilities, and Practices.* Harper and Row, 1974, p. 61.
6. Derek F. Abell, *Defining the Business: The Starting Point of Strategic Planning* (Englewood Cliffs, NJ: Prentice-Hall, 1980) p. 17.
7. Fred R. David. *Strategic Management, 7th Edition.* Prentice-Hall, 1998, p. 91.
8. Oxford Dictionary. AskOxford.com. 2002.
9. John P. Kotter. *Leading Change.* Harvard Business School Press, 1996, p. 72.
10. Burt Nanus. *Visionary Leadership.* 1992, p. 30–32.
11. Peter Schultz. *Business Week.* September 14, 1987, p. 120.
12. SEC filings and NYSE 1998–2002.
13. A direct extract from the Wal-Mart Web site, January 2002.
14. A. A. Thompson and K. Pinegar, and T. R. Kramer. "Wal-Mart Stores Case Study," 1994.
15. Market Guide, January 2002.
16. Michael Treacy and Frederik D. Wiersema. *Disciplines of Market Leaders.* Addison-Wesley, 1995.
17. Gary Hamel and C. K. Prahalad, "Strategic Intent," *Harvard Business Review,* (May–June 1989), p. 64.
18. J. B. Barney. "Firm Resources and Sustained Competitive Advantage." *Journal of Management,* 17, p. 99–120.

19. Stratford P. Sherman. "The Secret to Intel's Success." *Fortune,* 1994, p. 14.
20. G. Hamel and C. K. Prahalad. *Competing for the Future.* 1994:129.

Chapter 2

1. John A. Pierce II and Richard B. Robinson. *Strategic Management: Formulation, Implementation, and Control.* Irwin, 1997, p. 62.
2. Arthur A. Thompson, Jr. and A. J. Strickland III. *Strategic Management: Concepts and Cases.* Tenth Edition, Irwin, McGraw-Hill, 1998, p. 70–71.
3. Charlotte Thompson. Southwest Airlines. Case Study, University of Virginia, 1993.
4. Michael E. Porter. *Competitive Strategy.* Free Press, 1980, p. 4.
5. Arthur A. Thompson, Jr. and A. J. Strickland III. *Strategic Management: Concepts and Cases.* Tenth Edition, Irwin McGraw-Hill, 1998, p. 90.
6. M. Wilke. "Sweetener Battle Could Fizz Up." Advertising Age. 1 May 1995, p. 39.—"America's Most Valuable Companies." *Business Week,* 28 March 1994, p. 72.—Therrien, P. Oster, and C. Hawkins, "How Sweet It Isn't at NutraSweet." *Business Week,* 14 Dec. 1992, p. 42.—M. J. McCarthy. "Pepsi, Coke Say They're Loyal to NutraSweet." *Wall Street Journal,* 22 April 1992.
7. Henry Mintzberg, James Brian Quinn, and John Voyer. *The Strategy Process.* Prentice Hall, 1995, p. 120–121.
8. A. A. Thompson and A. J. Strickland. *Crafting and Implementing Strategy.* Irwin, 1995, p. 154.
9. A. B. Blankenship and George E. Breen. *State of the Art Marketing Research.* American Marketing Association, 1995, p. 389–390.
10. A. A. Thompson and A. J. Strickland. *Crafting and Implementing Strategy.* Irwin, 1995, p. 154.
11. Economic forecast as of August 10, 1996 and Financial forecast as of August 1, 1996.
12. Peter Wright, Mark J. Kroll, and John Parnell. *Strategic Management,* 4th Edition. Prentice-Hall, 1998, p. 31.
13. Macro environmental Analysis for Strategic Management, Liam Fahey & V. K. Narayanan, West, 1986, p. 212.
14. P. Andrews, "Wrong Turns on the Road to Pcdom Come Back to Haunt Wang." *Seattle Times,* 25 August 1992, p. D3.—W. M. Bulkeley and J. R. Wilkes. "Steep Slide: Filing in Chapter 11, Wang Sends Warning to High Tech Circles." *Wall Street Journal,* 19 August 1992, p. A1.
15. Robert M. Grant. *Contemporary Strategy Analysis.* Blackwell, 1995, p. 76.
16. Bill Gates. *The Road Ahead,* Penguin, 1996, p. 50–52.
17. A. A. Thompson and A. J. Strickland. *Crafting and Implementing Strategy.* Irwin, 1995, p. 87.

Chapter 3

1. Kaplan, Norton, Balanced scorecard. page 2.
2. *Contemporary Strategy Analysis,* Robert M. Grant, 1995, pp. 120–122.

3. Jeffrey Rigsby and Guy Greco, *Virtual CEO Strategic Business Disciplines.* 1999.
4. SEC filings and NYSE 1998–2002.
5. Not adjusted for four stock splits, 1 in 1997, 2 in 1998, and 1 in 1999.
6. www.dell.com. Dell History, 2002.
7. *Wall Street Journal,* October 16, 1992, p. R7.
8. *Financial Management—Theory and Practice,* Eugene F. Brigham & Louis C. Gapenski, 1994, pp. 9–10.
9. A.A. Thompson and A.J. Strickland. *Strategic Management, 10th Edition.* Irwin McGraw-Hill, 1998, p. 36.
10. Fredrick E. Webster. *Marketing for Managers.* 1974, pp. 178–179.
11. Thomas a. Stewart. "Allied Signal's Turnaround Blitz." *Fortune,* 30 November 1992, pp. 72–75.
12. CNN Interview. March 1, 2002.
13. *Microsoft. Inside Out: Microsoft: In Its Own Words.* Time Warner, 2002.
14. James Brian Quinn. *Intelligent Enterprise.* Free Press, 1992, p. 250.
15. Vida Scarpello, William Boulton. and Charles Hofer, "Reintegrating R&D into Business Strategy." *Journal of Business Strategy* 6:4 Sp, 1986, p. 50.
16. Steven C. Wheelwright & Kim B. Clark. *Leading Product Development,* Free Press, 1995, pp. 51–52.
17. *Market Guide,* June 2002.
18. R. Schroeder, Operations Management (New York: McGraw-Hill Book Co., 1981), p. 160.
19. B. Buell and R. D. Hof, "HP rethinks itself" *Business Week* 4.1.91 pp. 76–79 [hill p155#40].
20. *Setting the PACE in Product Development,* Michael E. McGrath, BH, 1996, pp. 150–151.
21. John A. Pearce II and Richard B. Robinson. "Strategic Management: Formulation, Implementation, and Control." Irwin, 1997, p. 313; originally appeared in *Business Week,* 22 October 1993.
22. Joseph M. Juran and A. Blanton Godfrey. *Juran's Quality Handbook,* Fifth Edition. McGraw-Hill, 1999, pp. 27.11–27.13.
23. Seth Fineberg. "Choose Your Own Adventure, Swoosh Style: Orcs and Trolls Need Not Apply," 18 Jan 00, ChannelSeven.com.
24. Seth Fineberg. "Swoosh Sequel," 2 May 00, ChannelSeven.com.
25. *Market Guide,* June 2002.
26. Virtual CEO, Inc. "Marketing Best Practice Study." 12 June 02.
27. Philip Kotler, *Marketing Management,* Prentice-Hall, 1984, p. 14.
28. Fred C. Allvine. *Marketing: Principles and Practices.* Harcourt Brace Jovanovich, 1987, p. viii.
29. John J. Peter and James H. Donnelly, Jr. *A Preface to Marketing Management, 6th edition,* page 24.
30. Robert Spector and Patrick D. McCarthy. *The Nordstrom Way.* John Wiley & Sons, Inc., 1995, p. 202.
31. Kenneth Rolnicki. *Channels of Distribution.* AMACOM, 1998, pp. 11.
32. Kenneth Rolnicki, *Channels of Distribution,* AMACOM, 1998, pp. 11.
33. *Market Guide,* January 6, 2002.
34. *Market Guide,* January 6, 2002.
35. *Best Practices: Building Your Business with Customer-Focused Solutions,* (Arthur Andersen), Hiebler, Kelly, & Ketteman, Simon & Schuster, 1998, pp. 199–200.

36. Charles W. L. Hill and Gareth R. Jones. *Strategic Management Theory: An Integrated Approach.* Houghton Mifflin, 1995, p. 162.
37. Virtual CEO, Inc. Customer Service—Gap Analysis Report.

Chapter 4

1. Robert S. Kaplan and David P. Norton. *The Balanced Scorecard.* Harvard Business School Press, 1996, p. 195.
2. FedX Web site, Feb. 2002.
3. James Brian Quinn. *Intelligent Enterprise.* NY Free Press, 1992, p. 181 [T/S p. 273].
4. Robert S. Kaplan and David P. Norton. *The Balanced Scorecard.* Harvard Business School Press, 1996, p. 164.
5. Robert S. Kaplan and David P. Norton. *The Balanced Scorecard.* Harvard Business School Press, 1996, pp. 43–44.
6. Pearce & Robinson, *Strategic Management,* p. 390.

Part 2

1. "IBM's Plan to Decentralize May Set a Trend—But Imitation Has a Price." *Wall Street Journal,* 19 Feb 1988, p. 17.
2. A. A. Thompson and A. J. Strickland, *Crafting and Implementing Strategy,* Irwin, 1995.

Chapter 5

1. L. J. Bourgeois, Irene M. Duhaime, and J. L. Stimpert, *Strategic Management: A Managerial Perspective,* Dryden, 1999.
2. Virtual CEO, Inc.
3. Jay R. Galbraith, *Designing Organizations,* Jossey-Bass, 1995.
4. A. A. Thompson and A. J. Strickland, *Strategic Management,* 6th Edition, Irwin, 1995.
5. Peter Wright, Mark J. Kroll, and John Parnell, *Strategic Management,* 4th Edition, Prentice-Hall, 1998.
6. Christopher Worley, David E. Hitchin, and Walter L. Ross, *Integrated Strategic Change,* Addison-Wesley, 1996.
7. B. Ziegler, "IBM is Growing Again: 'Fires Are Out,' Chief Says. *Wall Street Journal Interactive,* May 1, 1996—L. Hayes, "Gerstner Is Struggling as He Tries to Change Ingrained IBM Culture." *Wall Street Journal,* May 13, 1994, pp. A1, A8—D. Moreau, "From Big Bust to Big Blue: IBM and Its Vigorous Rebirth." *Kiplinger's Personal Finance Magazine,* July 1995, pp. 34–35.
8. Charles C. Manz and Henry P. Sims, Jr., *Business Without Bosses,* Wiley & Sons, 1993.
9. For more information regarding change strategies, see "Adaptability to Change" in Chapter 12.
10. Adapted from Alfred Chandler, *Strategy and Structure,* MIT Press, 1962.

Chapter 6

1. Hugh L. McColl, Jr. Bio, Bank of America Archives, 2002.
2. Gary Hamel and C. K. Prahalad. *Competing for the Future.* Harvard Business School Press, 1994, p. 199.
3. Robert M. Grant. *Contemporary Strategy Analysis.* Blackwell, 1995, p. 76.
4. Gary Hamel and C. K. Prahalad. *Competing for the Future.* Harvard Business School Press, 1994, p. 227.
5. These views are the opinion of the authors and may not reflect the approach deployed at NationsBank.
6. Gary Hamel and C. K. Prahalad. *Competing for the Future.* Harvard Business School Press, 1994, pp. 202–207.
7. James Brian Quinn. *Intelligent Enterprise.* 1993, p. 54.
8. Gary Hamel and C. K. Prahalad. *Competing for the Future.* Harvard Business School Press, 1994, pp. 202–207.
9. Arthur A. Thompson, Jr. and A. J. Strickland III. *Strategic management: Concept and Cases.* Tenth Edition, Irwin McGraw-Hill, 1998, p. 237.
10. *Market Guide,* March 30, 2002.
11. Gary Hamel and C. K. Prahalad. *Competing for the Future.* Harvard Business School Press, 1994, pp. 202–207.

Chapter 7

1. R. H. Beeby. "How to Crunch a Bunch of Figures." *The Wall Street Journal,* 11 June 1990, p. A14
2. R.R. Blake and Jane S. Mouton, *Corporate Excellence Through Grid Organization Development,* Gulf Publishing Co., 1968.
3. Daniel R. Boyd, Stephen D. Lewis, and Grady L. Butler. "Getting Your Message Across." *Management Review,* Jul.–Aug. 1998, pp. 7–10.
4. William V. Harvey. *Communication and Interpersonal Relations,* Irwin, 1979, p. 3.
5. Brian L. Davis, Susan H. Gebelein, Lowell W. Hellervik, James L. Sheard, and Carol J. Skube, *Successful Manager's Handbook.* Personnel Decisions, Inc. 1992.
6. "Labor Letter, Dialogues with Workers Gained Increased Employer Attention," *The Wall Street Journal,* Jan. 3, 1986, p. A1.
7. Walter Kiechell III. "Now Word from Up High," *Fortune,* Jan. 6, 1986, pp. 125–126.
8. Dalmar Fisher. *Communication in Organizations.* West Publishing, 1993.
9. Ray Strata. "Organizational Learning in Practice." *McKinsey Quarterly,* Winter 1992, pp. 79–82.
10. Mary Munter. *Guide to Managerial Communication, Third Edition.* Prentice-Hall, 1992.
11. David A. Kolb, Joyce S. Osland, and Irwin M. Rubin. *The Organizational Behavior Reader, Sixth Edition.* Prentice Hall, 1995.
12. R.R. Blake and Jane S. Mouton. *Corporate Excellence Through Grid Organization Development.* Gulf Publishing Co., 1968.
13. Dalmar Fisher, *Communication in Organizations.* West Publishing, 1993.
14. Adapted from Jerome Kantor. *Management Information Systems,* 3rd Edition. Prentice-Hall, 1984, p. 6.

15. Thomas H. Davenport and Laurence Prusak. *Working Knowledge.* Harvard Business Press, 1998, p. 4.
16. Thomas H. Davenport and Laurence Prusak. *Working Knowledge.* Harvard Business Press, 1998, p. 6.
17. James Brian Quinn. *Intelligent Enterprise.* Free Press, 1992, p. 186.
18. A.A. Thompson and A. J. Strickland. *Strategic Management,* 10th Edition. Irwin, McGraw-Hill, 1998, p. 675.
19. Adapted from Alex Miller. *Strategic Management.* Irwin, McGraw-Hill, 1998, p. 385.
20. Alex Miller. *Strategic Management.* Irwin, McGraw-Hill, 1998, pp. 387–388.
21. Robert Hiebler, Thomas B. Kelly, and Charles Ketterman. *Best Practices: Building Your Business with Customer-Focused Solutions.* Simon & Schuster, 1998, p. 208.
22. David T. Kearns and David A. Nadler. *Prophets in the Dark—How Xerox Reinvented Itself and Beat Back the Japanese.* Harper Business, 1992, p. 89.
23. FedEx Web site—12 July 2002.
24. Thomas H. Davenport, Michael Hammer, and Tauno Metsisto. "How Executives Can Shape Their Company's Information Systems." *Harvard Business Review* 67, Mar–Apr 1989, p. 131.
25. SEC filings and NYSE, 1998–2002.

Chapter 8

1. James L. Gibson, John M. Ivancevich, and James H. Donnelly, Jr., *Organizations: Behavior, Structure, Processes,* Irwin, 1991.
2. Gregory H. Gaertner and S. Ramnarayan, "Organizational Effectiveness: An Alternative Perspective." *Academy of Management Review,* Jan. 1983, pp. 97–107.
3. James L. Gibson, John M. Ivancevich, and James H. Donnelly, Jr., *Organizations: Behavior, Structure, Processes,* Irwin, 1991.
4. Steve Page, *Establishing a System of Policies and Procedures,* BookMasters, Inc., 1998.
5. Joseph A. DeFeo, *Strategic Deployment,* taken from *Juran's Quality Handbook,* Fifth Edition, McGraw-Hill, 1999, p. 13.7.
6. http://www.io.com/~hcexres/tcm1603/acchtml/orgpols.html
7. Zachary Schiller, "No More Mr. Nice Guy at P&G." *Business Week,* Feb. 3, 1992, pp. 54–56.
8. A. A. Thompson and A. J. Strickland, *Crafting and Implementing Strategy,* Irwin, 1995.
9. James Brian Quinn, *Intelligent Enterprise,* Free Press, 1992.
10. Thomas Peters and Robert Waterman, *In Search of Excellence,* Harper and Row, 1980.
11. Steve Page, *Establishing a System of Policies and Procedures,* BookMasters, Inc., 1998.
12. Ibid.
13. P. R. Lawrence and J. Lorach, *Organization and Environment,* Harvard Business School, 1967, pp. 50–55.
14. Charles W.L. Hill and Gareth R. Jones, *Strategic Management Theory: An Integrated Approach,* Houghton Mifflin, 1995.

15. James L. Gibson, John M. Ivancevich, and James H. Donnelly, Jr., *Organizations: Behavior, Structure, Processes,* Irwin, 2000.
16. Henry Mintzberg, "Organization Design: Fashion or Fit?" *Harvard Business Review,* Jan.–Feb. 1981, pp. 103–106.
17. J.A Donovan, *Supplier Relations,* taken from *Juran's Quality Handbook,* Fifth Edition, McGraw-Hill, 1999, p. 21.15.
18. *Business Week,* April, 1, 1996.
19. Frank M. Gryna, *Operations,* taken from *Juran's Quality Handbook,* Fifth Edition, McGraw-Hill, 1999, p. 22.3.
20. Ibid.
21. Edward Fuchs, "Customer Service," taken from *Juran's Quality Handbook,* Fifth Edition, McGraw-Hill, 1999, pp. 25.17–25.18.
22. Ibid.
23. James Brian Quinn, *Intelligent Enterprise,* Free Press, 1992.
24. Richard L. Daft, *Organization Theory and Design,* Southwest Publishing, 1998.
25. Kenichi Ohmae, "The Global Logic of Strategic Alliances." *Harvard Business Review,* Mar.–Apr. 1998, p. 148.
26. A. A. Thompson and A. J. Strickland, *Strategic Management Concepts and Cases,* 10th Edition, Irwin, McGraw-Hill, 1998.

Part 3

1. Thomas J. Peters and Robert H. Waterman, *In Search of Excellence,* Warner Books, 1982, p. 15.
2. Hewlett-Packard Website.
3. Edgar H. Stein, "The Role of the Founder in Creating Organizational Culture." *Organizational Dynamics,* Summer 1983, p. 14.
4. Unknown author.
5. John P. Kotter and James L. Heskett, *Corporate Culture and Performance,* Free Press, 1992, p. 5.
6. John Alexander and Meena S. Wilson, "Leading Across Cultures: Five Verbal Capabilities" (In *The Organization of the Future,* Frances Hesselbein, Marshall Goldsmith, and Richard Beckard, Jossey-Bass, 1997, pp. 291–92.)
7. John A Pearce and Richard B. Robinson, *Strategic Management: Formulation, Implementation, and Control,* Irwin, 1997, p. 359.
8. John P. Kotter and James L. Heskett, *Corporate Culture and Performance,* Free Press, 1992, p. 11.

Chapter 9

1. John P. Kotter and James L. Heskett, *Corporate Culture and Performance,* Free Press, 1992, p. 42.
2. http://www.walmartfoundation.org/wmstore/goodworks/scripts/Community
3. http://www.fortune.com/April 15, 2002.
4. James C. Collins and Jerry I. Porras, *Built to Last,* HarperCollins, 1994, p. 76.
5. David T. Kearns and David A. Nadler, *Prophets in the Dark—How Xerox Reinvented Itself and Beat Back the Japanese,* Harper Business, 1992.

6. James C. Collins and Jerry I. Porras, *Built to Last*, HarperCollins, 1994.
7. "Bristol-Meyers Prescription for Profits," *Dun's Business Month*, December 1982.
8. http://www.nokia.com/aboutnokia/inbrief/corporate_responsibility.html
9. *Market Guide*, April 6, 2002.
10. http://www.nokia.com/aboutnokia/inbrief/nokia_way.html
11. Edgar H. Schein, *Organizational Culture and Leadership*, Jossey-Bass, 1993, pp. 16–25.
12. Interview with James C. Collins and Jerry I. Porras, 17 April 1992. Documented in *Built to Last*, HarperCollins, 1994.
13. James C. Collins and Jerry I. Porras, *Built to Last*, HarperCollins, 1994, p. 74.
14. A.A. Thompson and A. J. Strickland, *Crafting and Implementing Strategy*, Irwin, 1995, p. 291.
15. A.A. Thompson and A. J. Strickland, *Strategic Management: Concepts and Cases*, 8th Edition, Irwin McGraw-Hill, 1995, p. 898.
16. James C. Collins and Jerry I. Porras, *Built to Last*, HarperCollins, 1994, p. 128.
17. Thomas J. Watson, Jr., *A Business and Its Beliefs*, New York Columbia University Press, 1963.
18. James C. Collins and Jerry I. Porras, *Built to Last*, HarperCollins, 1994, p. 87.
19. Ibid, p. 73.
20. A.A. Thompson and A. J. Strickland, *Strategic Management: Concepts and Cases*, 8th Edition, Irwin, McGraw-Hill, 1995, p. 301.
21. James M. Kouzes and Barry Z. Posner, *Credibility: How Leaders Gain and Lose It, Why People Demand It*, Jossey-Bass, 1993, pp. 145–152.
22. James C. Collins and Jerry I. Porras, *Built to Last*, HarperCollins, 1994.
23. James M. Kouzes and Barry Z. Posner, *Credibility: How Leaders Gain and Lose It, Why People Demand It*, Jossey-Bass, 1993, p. 47.

Chapter 10

1. http://www.fortune.com/lists/bestcompanies/April 15, 2002.
2. Ibid.
3. Anonymous. "Effective Managers, Happy Employees" *Small Business Reports* 18, May 1994: 19.
4. Ibid.
5. John P. Kotter, *Leading Change*, Harvard Business School Press, 1996, p. 25.
6. Stephen R. Covey, *Principle-Centered Leadership*, Summit Books, 1990, p. 246.
7. Ibid, p. 244.
8. John Kotter, *A Force for Change: How Leadership Differs from Management*, Free Press, 1990.
9. James M. Kouzes and Barry Z. Posner, *The Leadership Challenge*, Jossey-Bass, 1987.
10. Thomas Peters and Robert H. Waterman, Jr., *In Search of Excellence*, Warner Books, 1982.
11. Remarks made to Ann M. Morrison, "Trying to Bring GE to Life," *Fortune*, 25 Jan., 1982, p. 52.
12. Morgan W. McCall, Jr., Michael M. Lombardo, and Ann M. Morrison, *The*

Lesson of Experience: How Successful Executives Develop on the Job, Lexington Books, 1988, pp. 168–169.

13. Alex Miller, *Strategic Management,* Irwin McGraw-Hill, 1998.
14. James M. Kouzes and Barry Z. Posner, *Credibility: How Leaders Gain and Lose It, Why People Demand It,* Jossey-Bass, 1993.
15. Ibid.
16. John Huey, "The New Post-Heroic Leadership," *Fortune,* Apr. 18, 1994, pp. 14–15.
17. Ronald Henkoff, "CEO's Still Don't Walk the Talk," *Fortune,* Apr. 18, 1994, pp. 14–15.
18. Tsun-Yan Hsieh, "Leadership Actions," *McKinsey Quarterly,* Fall 1990, pp. 42–58.
19. John P. Kotter and James L. Heskett, *Corporate Culture and Performance,* The Free Press, New York, 1992, p. 51.
20. http://www.fortune.com.
21. GE Press Release, Fairfield, CT, April, 11, 2002.
22. *Market Guide,* April 14, 2002.
23. Jack Welch and John A. Byrne, *Jack: Straight from the Gut,* Warner Books, Sep. 2001.
24. http://www.fortune.com, March 4, 2002.
25. http://www.ge.com/news/podium_papers.html.
26. Jim Horan, *The One Page Business Plan,* 1998, p. 18.
27. http://www.onepageplanning.com/system_tour2.html
28. Brian Dumaine, "Who Needs a Boss?" *Fortune,* May 7, 1990.
29. Jack Stack with Bo Burlingham, *The Great Game of Business,* Doubleday & Company, Inc, 1994, p. 3.
30. *Market Guide,* January 20, 2002.
31. Ibid.
32. Ibid.
33. Peter Senge, *The Fifth Discipline,* Doubleday, 1990, p. 146.
34. John P. Kotter, *Leading Change,* Harvard Business School, 1996, p. 167.
35. Robert Levering and Milton Moskowitz, *The 100 Best Companies to Work for in America,* Doubleday Currency, 1993.
36. Stephen R. Covey, *Principle-Centered Leadership,* Summit Books, 1990, p. 65.
37. Lawson K. Savery, "Attitudes to Work: The Influence of Perceived Styles of Leadership on a Group of Workers." *Leadership and Development Journal,* 15, 1994, p. 17.
38. Charles C. Manz and Henry P. Sims, *Business Without Bosses,* John Wiley & Sons, 1993.
39. John P. Kotter, *Leading Change,* Harvard Business School, 1996, p. 102.
40. Jan Carlzon, *Moments of Truth,* HarperTrade, 1989.
41. http//:www.scandinavian.net/company/newsfacts/facts/historyinbrief.
42. Jan Carlzon, *Moments of Truth,* HarperTrade, 1989.
43. T.W. Firnstahl, *"My Employees Are My Service Guarantee,"* Harvard Business Review, Jul–Aug, 1989, pp. 28–31, 34.
44. www.kenblanchardcompanies.com.
45. Ken Blanchard, *Leadership and The One-Minute Manager,* William Morrow and Company, 1985, p. 68.
46. Robert E. Quinn, Sue R. Faerman, Michael Thompson, and Michael R. McGrath, *Becoming a Master Manager,* John Wiley & Sons, 1990, p. 62.

47. Stephen R. Covey, *Principle-Centered Leadership*, Summit Books, 1990, p. 72.
48. Stephen R. Covey, *Principle-Centered Leadership*, Summit Books, 1990, p. 176.
49. John W., Kennish, CPP, "Motivating with a Positive, Participatory Policy," *Security Management* 38, August, 1994: 22.
50. *Our Story So Far*, The 3M Company, 1977.
51. Stephen R. Covey, *Principle-Centered Leadership*, Summit Books, 1990, p. 179.
52. James M. Kouzes and Barry Z. Posner, *Credibility: How Leaders Gain and Lose It, Why People Demand It*, Jossey-Bass, 1993.
53. Peter F. Drucker, "The New Productivity Challenge," *Harvard Business Review*, 69(6), Nov–Dec. 1991, pp. 69–79.
54. Morgan W. McCall, Jr., Michael M. Lombardo, and Ann M. Morrison, *The Lesson of Experience: How Successful Executives Develop on the Job*, Lexington Books, 1988, p. 169.
55. http://www.walmart.com/.
56. Ibid.
57. http://biz.yahoo.com/p/w/wmt.html.
58. Jon R. Katzenbach and Douglas K. Smith, *The Wisdom of Teams*, Harvard Business School Press, 1993, p. 45.
59. Ibid, p. 137.
60. Based in part on *The Team Handbook* by Peter R. Scholtes, Joiner Associates, 1988.
61. Richard S. Wellins, William C. Byham, and Jeanne M. Wilson, *Empowered Teams*, Jossey-Bass, 1991, pp. 13–14.
62. Ibid, p. 3.
63. Ibid, pp. 4–5.
64. Charles C. Manz and Henry P. Sims, *Business Without Bosses*, John Wiley & Sons, 1993.
65. Brian Dumaine, "Payoff from the New Management," *Fortune*, Dec. 13, 1993, pp. 103–110 and Fara Warner, "Message in a Bottle: Thermos Updates Its Image," *Brandweek*, 35, Jan. 31, 1994, p. 32.
66. *Meetings in America: A study of trends, costs and attitudes toward business travel, teleconferencing, and their impact on productivity*. A network MCI Conferencing White Paper, 1998.
67. http://www.effectivemeetings.com/meetingbasics/6tips.asp.

Chapter 11

1. C.A. Lengnick-Hall and M.I. Lengnick-Hall, "Strategic Human Resources Management: A Review of the Literature and Proposed Typology," *Academy of Management Review*, Jul 1988, pp. 454–470—L. Baird and I. Meshoulam, "Managing Two Fits of Strategic Human Resource Management Practices," *Academy of Management Executive*, Aug. 1987, pp. 207–219.
2. http://www.business.com/directory/human_resources/outsourcing.
3. R.H. Killman, *Beyond the Quick Fix: Managing Five Tracks to Organizational Success*, Jossey-Bass, 1984.
4. D. Ulrich and D. Lake, "Organization Capability: Creating Competitive Advantage," *Academy of Management Executive*, 5, 1991, pp. 77–92.

5. A. Smith, "The 'People Factor' in Competitive Advantage," *Academy of Management Executive*, 5, 1991, pp. 77–92.
6. http://www.ti.com/corp/docs/company/factsheet.shtml#map.
7. Alex Miller, *Strategic Management*, Irwin, McGraw-Hill, 1998.
8. James C. Collins and Jerry I. Porras, *Built to Last*, Harper Collins, 1994, p. 109.
9. A reference to Jim Collins, *Good to Great*, HarperCollins, 2001.
10. *Market Guide*, January 7, 2002.
11. James L. Gibson, John M. Ivancevich, and James H. Donnelly, Jr., *Organizations: Behavior, Implementation and Control*, Irwin, 1997, p. 84.
12. *Market Guide*, January 7, 2002.
13. Southwest Airlines Web site, "About SWA," "Southwest Airlines Distinctions," January 7, 2002.
14. *Market Guide*, January 7, 2002.
15. Robert Levering, Milton Moskowitz, *The 100 Best Companies to Work for in America*, Doubleday Currency, 1993.
16. Robert Levering, Milton Moskowitz, and Michael Katz, *The 100 Best Companies to Work for in America*, New American Library, 1985.
17. Jim Collins, *Good to Great*, HarperCollins, 2001.
18. Ibid.
19. "Selecting the Best: Casting for a Role in Our Show." Walt Disney World Workshop in Interviewing, p. 35.
20. Interview with Jef Raskin, first manager of the Macintosh project; Making the Macintosh: Technology and Culture in Silicon Valley; http://library.stanford.edu/mac/.
21. Jim Collins, *Good to Great*, HarperCollins, 2001, p. 51.
22. Ibid, p. 41.
23. James C. Collins and Jerry Porras, *Built to Last*, Harper Collins, 1994, pp. 131–132.
24. Tom Peters, *Thriving on Chaos*, Knopf, 1988, p. 316.
25. Selected in part from the *Northwestern Lindquist-Endicott Report*, The Placement Center, Northwestern University, Evanston, IL. 1991.
26. Robert Hiebler, Thomas B. Kelly, and Charles Ketterman, *Best Practices: Building Your Business with Customer-Focused Solutions*, Simon & Schuster, 1998.
27. James C. Collins and Jerry I. Porras, *Built to Last*, Harper-Collins, 1994, p. 132.
28. Student paper on Walt Disney, Stanford University.
29. Peter Senge, *The Fifth Discipline*, Doubleday, 1990, p. 139.
30. http://www.media.mcdonalds.com/secured/company/training/.
31. Ibid.
32. McDonald's 2000 Annual Report.
33. *Market Guide*, January 2002.
34. David T. Kearns and David A. Nadler. *Prophets in the Dark: How XEROX Reinvented Itself and Beat Back the Japanese*. New York: Harper-Collins, 1992, p. 177.
35. http://www.mcdonalds.com/corporate/investor/financialinfo/annual/annualreport/index.html.
36. http://www.ge.com/news/podium_papers/geleadtrain.htm.
37. Robert W. Galvin, *The Idea of Ideas*, Motorola University Press, 1991; James C. Collins and Jerry I. Porras, *Built to Last*, HarperCollins, 1994, p. 169.
38. http://www.fortune.com, April 15, 2002.

39. James C. Collins and Jerry I. Porras, *Built to Last,* HarperCollins, 1994, p. 173.

40. Ibid, p. 174–175.

41. Donald Kirkpatrick, *A Practical Guide for Supervisory Training and Development,* Addison-Wesley Longman, 1983.

42. Tom Peters, *Thriving on Chaos,* Knopf, 1988, pp. 326–328.

43. Stephen R. Covey, *Principled-Centered Leadership,* Simon and Schuster, 1991, p. 128.

44. http://www.performance-appraisal.com/news.htm.

45. Alex Miller, *Strategic Management,* Irwin McGraw-Hill, 1998.

46. http://www.findarticles.com/m1038/6_42/58381519/p1/article.jhtml.

47. V.H. Vroom, *Work and Motivation,* John Wiley and Sons, 1964.

48. John R. Schermerhorn, Jr., *Management for Productivity,* 3rd ed., John Wiley and Sons, 1989, p. 365.

49. http://www.skymark.com/resources/leaders/herzberg.asp.

50. Frederick Hertzberg, *Motivation to Work,* John Wiley & Sons, 1959.

51. John A. Pearce II and Richard B. Robinson, *Strategic Management: Formulation, Implementation, and Control,* Irwin, 1997.

Chapter 12

1. Based on John P. Kotter, *Leading Change,* Harvard Business School, 1996, pp. 4–16.

2. William Bridges, *The Character of Organizations: Using Personality Type in Organizational Development,* Davies-Black Publishing, Updated edition 2000.

3. Keith Davis, "Cut Those Rumors Down to Size." *Supervisory Management,* June 1975, pp. 2–6.—"The Care and Cultivation of the Corporate Grapevine." *Dun's Review,* July 1973, pp. 44–47.—"Management Communication and the Grapevine." *Harvard Business Review,* Sept–Oct, 1953, pp. 43–49.

4. Jack Stack, *The Great Game of Business,* Doubleday, 1992, p. 5.

5. A. Bandura and D. Cervone, "Self-Evaluative and Self-Efficacy Mechanisms Governing the Motivational Effects of Goal Systems." *Journal of Personality and Social Psychology,* 45, 1983, pp. 1017–1028.

6. From Robert M. Cutler, "Gorbachev as CEO Road Kill: Lessons for the Modern Corporation from the Soviet Foreign Policy Establishment's Failure to Manage Complexity," located at: http://www.cu.edu/~irm/about_irm/self_study/96_commdata.ht.

7. Ibid.

8. www.mcgraw-hill.co.uk/he/web_sites/business/organizational_behaviour.

9. Warren Bennis, "Followers Make Good Leaders Good." *New York Times,* Dec. 31, 1989, p. 3.

10. Darryl R. Connor, *Managing at the Speed of Change,* Random House, 1992, p. 97.

11. Spencer Johnson, MD, *Who Moved My Cheese?,* G.P. Putnam's Sons, 1998, p. 36.

12. T. Deal and A. Kennedy, *Corporate Cultures: The Rites and Rituals of Corporate Life,* Addison-Wesley, 1982.

13. John P. Kotter, *Leading Change,* Harvard Business School Press, Boston, 1996, p. 36.

14. John P. Kotter and James L. Heskett, *Corporate Culture and Performance,* The Free Press, New York, 1992, p. 45.
15. David Leonhardt, "McDonald's: Can It Regain Its Golden Touch?" *Business Week,* 9 Mar 1998, p. 72.
16. John P. Kotter and James L. Heskett, *Corporate Culture and Performance,* The Free Press, New York, 1992, p. 143.
17. David Leonhardt, "MacDonald's: Can It Regain Its Golden Touch?" *Business Week,* 9 Mar 1998, p. 72.
18. Ralph H. Killman, Mary J. Saxton, and Roy Serpa, editors, *Gaining Control of the Corporate Culture,* Jossey-Bass, 1986.
19. Rosabeth Kanter, *The Change Masters,* Simon & Schuster, 1983.
20. John P. Kotter and James L. Heskett, *Corporate Culture and Performance,* The Free Press, New York, 1992, p. 11.
21. Robert E. Quinn, *Deep Change,* Jossey-Bass, 1996, p. 15.
22. Ibid, pp. 20–24.
23. John P. Kotter, *Leading Change,* Harvard Business School Press, Boston, 1996, p. 21.
24. P.R. Lawrence, "How to Deal with Resistance to Change," *Harvard Business Review,* Jan–Feb 1969, pp. 4–12.

Index

Business Enterprise
in its Social Setting

Business Enterprise
in its Social Setting

by ARTHUR H. COLE

HARVARD University Press

Cambridge, Massachusetts

338.72
C689

This book has been aided by a grant from the Ford Foundation.

© *1959 by the President and Fellows of Harvard College*

Second Printing, 1971

Distributed in Great Britain by Oxford University Press, London

Library of Congress Catalog Card Number 59–7649

SBN 674–08751–8

Printed in the United States of America

TO EDWIN F. GAY AND JOSEPH H. WILLITS

THEY HELPED BY PUSHING

PREFACE

The ensuing volume has a Janus quality: it looks in two directions. On the one hand, it looks backward, and so in major fashion reveals my indebtedness to the group of rather exceptional individuals who collaborated with me at the Research Center in Entrepreneurial History here at Harvard over appreciable periods until the Center closed its doors at the end of the academic year 1957–58. I have in mind such mature scholars as Thomas C. Cochran, Leland H. Jenks, Fritz L. Redlich, and Joseph A. Schumpeter, who helped me to set up the Center or held my hand in the early days, and the group of adventurous younger folk who threw in their lot with us for longer or shorter periods, some of them venturing to write their doctoral dissertations in the new field: folk such as Hugh G. J. Aitken, Sigmund Diamond, David S. Landes, Harold C. Passer, Henry Rosovsky, and R. Richard Wohl. William Miller and John E. Sawyer were less committed but exceedingly helpful. We all were particularly beholden to Messrs. Aitken, Rosovsky, and Wohl, who launched and maintained our journal of discussion, *Explorations in Entrepreneurial History,* over ten volumes of real "exploratory" writing. My intellectual debt to one or more of these erstwhile associates is evident on nearly every ensuing page, being especially great — and obvious — to the senior quartet of Cochran, Jenks, Redlich, and Schumpeter. In addition, I should state that Aitken, Cochran, and Redlich were good enough to examine the manuscript of the present book at an early stage of its preparation, and to give me the benefit of their criticisms. I fear that they will still find numerous points at which their heads will shake in disapproval.

The ensuing volume has linkage with the past also as a sort of fruit — perhaps a belated fruit and surely an inadequate return — deriving from significant acts of generosity displayed to the Research Center in the decade after 1948, and filtering through to me as a variety of residuary legatee. The Center was launched and sustained by important grants from the Rockefeller Foundation, while we benefited also from a special gift from the Carnegie Corporation of New York. The latter permitted us to undertake an inquiry into entrepreneurship in a foreign country — Brazil — which Stanley J. Stein prosecuted with real valor. Another source of very welcome assistance came from individuals of the Harvard family. Provost Paul H. Buck and subsequently Dean McGeorge Bundy extended protecting hands over our small unit standing unattached to any of the older and larger divisions of the University, while Professors Alexander Gerschenkron and Oscar Handlin bolstered the unit with their prestige and gave me always the advantage of their counsels. When account is also taken of the space and the services supplied by the University, it becomes obvious that the Harvard community contributed much to our welfare. Without such sustenance and security, the Center would have shriveled — and then I would not have had the opportunity to learn from my associates there.

In a broader way, my book looks back on many significant developments outside of Harvard, which have taken place in the past decade or so. The study of entrepreneurial history and of matters closely connected with the latter has spread rather widely in these years, the Center at Harvard serving in considerable measure merely as a vehicle of communication among individuals and institutions dispersed in many regions, from W. T. Easterbrook at Toronto to Noel G. Butlin in Canberra, who, like scores of other scholars, were interested in the subject and enrolled soon as contributors to our efforts at exploration. The Committee on Research in Economic History may well take pride in giving an initial impetus to inquiries in the subject through the outline of the field which it published in 1944; but to a greater degree, it was the importance and intellectual challenge of the topic itself that attracted the attention and provoked the endeavors of such American scholars as G. Heberton Evans, Jr., of Johns Hopkins or Bert F. Hoselitz of Chicago, and such distinguished foreign historians as Ludwig Beutin of Cologne, H. J. Habakkuk of Oxford, and Charles Wilson of Cambridge. The contributions of all such men were incitements to further debates at the Center, and so ultimately grist for my mill.

Last but not least, I would acknowledge certain personal obligations which also look backward. There is my longstanding indebtedness to Edwin F. Gay, my sponsor in the field of economic history, who, as I have stated in my dedication, "pushed" me into responsible activities with both the International Scientific Committee on Price History and later the above-mentioned Committee on Research in Economic History. Following hard on the foregoing, there is my debt to Joseph H. Willits, then attached to the Rockefeller Foundation, who not only acted to create the Research Committee and to sustain both it and the Research Center, but initially "pushed" me into attempting to develop the latter when I was timid of success. I am likewise beholden to the deans of the Harvard Business School under whom I served — Deans Donham, David, and Teele — for allowing me to take time and to expend efforts in the affairs first of the Research Committee and later of the Research Center as well, sometimes, I fear, at an appreciable cost to the Library at the School over which I was supposed to be the chief officer. And quite recently I became indebted to Miss Ruth Crandall and Mrs. Andrew B. Jack, who came to my rescue when my eyes began to fail me, and who both saw the manuscript completed for submission to the printer and subsequently guided the document through the trials of actual publication. In the case of Miss Crandall I was merely adding to a chain of indebtedness that stretches back continuously to work on my first book thirty years ago. Finally, I would extend my thanks to my many friends at the Harvard University Press, both for their kindnesses in connection with the issuance of the Center's several monographs, and now in helping with my own small endeavor.

The present volume, however, looks forward also. In both construction and objectives, I hope it to be new; while I have borrowed heavily from the output and spoken ideas of my erstwhile associates at the Center and from friends elsewhere, I must exonerate them from the uses to which their data and concepts have been put. Stimulated by the example and words of my friends Oswald Knauth and Robert L. Masson, I have ventured to attempt to be creative, especially to attempt to point out uniformities and to formulate generalizations — at least low-order generalizations — in and about historical materials. I was warmly spurred in this direction by the assertion of my ever-provocative colleague in explorations, Thomas Cochran, who complained a couple of years ago that social scientists in general, and economists in particular, took little interest in what we were doing, indeed, had been offered no help in grasping hold of what we believed to be important in entrepreneurial history. I felt it my duty to try to remedy the deficiency.

The book looks forward in the sense that it is related intimately to the problem which has latterly been disturbing

economists and which threatens to continue disturbing them
for some time to come, economists and indeed many social
scientists and governmental administrators — the problem
of economic growth. Economic historians have long been
studying economic growth, including that of "underdeveloped countries" such as England or the United States in
times past, but they have not put their findings into forms
which attracted the attention of theorists. Similarly, students
of business and entrepreneurial history have long appreciated
that — as in the 19th-century case cited by Leland Jenks —
it was not the supply of capital in England that was important, it was the horde of American would-be borrowers
who pounded the doors of potential British lenders. Yet such
historians have also failed to make up packages for the theorists. Perhaps the latter should have read more history and
developed their own generalizations, but theorists have never
read extensively in historical materials. Perhaps if they did
do so, they would become enamored of the facts — and so
be lost to the world of theory! Anyway, there has long been
a notion prevalent in academic circles that a theoretical
hypothesis, however shaky its bases, is somehow superior in
intellectual quality to a historical finding, however broad
and well supported by evidence; and the deduction has followed that historians should study theory, but theorists may
be excused from immersing themselves in facts.

At all events, I have attempted to extend a bridge between
history and theory, slight though it may be in this noteworthy area — a bridge that is evolved from historical materials, not derived from assumptions. (So also in some
measure had been the theory with which Professor
Schumpeter's name is associated and to which, obviously,
I owe much.) And I am encouraged the more to make
public my rash ideas by recent remarks of my similarly
minded friend, Walt W. Rostow. He believes to see a direct

positive correlation between advances in economic theorizing and economists' confrontations with practical problems; now, in the post-World War II period, they have been attempting to deal with economic growth (although, as it seems to a historian, under procedures transferred from the handling of statical affairs); and so Rostow is hopeful for the future. Also my friend goes on to urge economists to take account of "the biological strains" in their intellectual "heritage"; and conceivably economists may be forced in the end into the study of economic evolution, and much more deeply than the present-day computation of historical time-series. Perhaps they may yet return to the problem of "the trees in the forest" which Marshall mentioned fifty or seventy-five years ago. In the subsequent complex of theory, stocks of capital and labor, now so precious in economists' model-building, may come to be viewed as no more significant — though no less so — than stocks of finished goods in manufacturers' hands.

The present volume looks forward in yet another way. Economics has been, it seems, wandering ever further during recent decades from most other social sciences. In the present dosage type of economic theorizing, books of theory can be written with scarcely a mention of businessmen, indeed, with human beings noted only under such vague agglomerations as "labor" or possibly "management." And I offer the present book in the exalted hope — perhaps permitted of a professor emeritus, no longer responsible to dean, faculty or students — that it may serve as a first stone in yet another bridge (or possibly better the first section in a traffic circle) to bring together economics, business administration, sociology, and history, and incidentally, in a sense, to restore economics to the rubric of the "social" sciences. In fact, if economics takes on an evolutionary cast, there seems no area so central for the scientific handling of economic change — stagnation and decline as well as growth — with all relevant factors brought into the models, as entrepreneurial history — business administration dealing with economic forces over time within a framework of social institutions and cultural themes. It would not be economics reduced to a series of algebraic formulae, but it might well be economics more useful to decision-makers concerned with long-run problems in business, in government, and in society.

The study of variant entrepreneurship and of the same "economic factor" changing over time is just beginning. We can as yet attempt no entrepreneurial history of a single country, and we can scarcely compare entrepreneurship qualities in any two countries at any given point in time. Correspondingly, any effort to see uniformities in historical details is younger still. Changing and variant quality in entrepreneurship has found no place in the theorizing about economic productivity, movements of international trade, and the like. Yet nothing seems closer to many questions of economic and social policy, while entrepreneurial history seems the most "practical" of all segments in that discipline. The area of entrepreneurship and its evolution calls out for continued research and for more sustained speculation about relationships of changing flows of information, changing social structures, changing economic conditions, and other forces upon entrepreneurial character and performance.

Arthur H. Cole

Harvard University

CONTENTS

PART ONE·
THE CONCEPTUAL PROBLEM

Chapter I ·

THE NATURE OF
ENTREPRENEURSHIP

THE LATE Professor Harold A. Innis of Toronto used to speak
in the most serious terms of the problem of time in economics. There was the problem of horizons for businessmen, governments, perhaps civilizations; there was the problem of changing perspectives of young folks, of consumers,
of public censors; and, not least, there was the problem of
historical depth in economics — or the question, at least in
his mind, of the competence of contemporary economic
theory to deal with changes through time.[1] Not all economic
historians have been as perturbed as Professor Innis, but all
quite surely would be happy to contribute to the approach
to economics which is not content to consider static or
artificially restricted conditions alone. Perhaps it is possible,
in fact, to build on certain ideas to be found in Marshall,
which in turn hark back to the pre-Ricardian days, and to
bring closer together the disciplines of economics and history.

After all, there is a good deal of history in economics already, if one may be liberal in one's interpretation of that
word. The ideas of going wage, standard practice, consumer
habits, price trends, and many others in the field have historical bases. The business cycle has a time dimension; so
have the readjustments in international trade. All that the

economic or social historian proposes is that a somewhat greater variety of *all* pertinent historical facts should be brought into the purview of economists as they evolve their theories of change.

To be sure, economists and historians usually have different concepts of the nature of the time useful for scientific purposes. I have in mind especially the tempo of movement. Economists, at least those of recent generations, have been thinking of short-run movements and adjustments. Even economists who now seek to deal with economic development seem to dislike to change the level of their expectations; they want to find their familiar short-term adjustments. On the other hand, historians, at least those who concern themselves with economic and social change, have to do mainly with alterations that require substantial periods to occur. And many problems of entrepreneurship, even some not directly related to economic development, are matters of slow change. Thus, as Professor Thomas S. Ashton points out, the closeness of the rungs in the English social ladder, which was so important an element in England's eighteenth-century economic success, was the product of centuries of history, a fact that this eminent scholar declares "has not been sufficiently appreciated by those who, looking at English progress in technology and wealth, lightly assume that similar results can be obtained with equal speed (and less social disharmony) in communities of undifferentiated peasants today." [2]

There is a second major divergence relative to time and movement in the attitudes of the two types of student. The economist looks frequently for a terminal point — an equilibrium restored, a readjustment achieved, a limited change previsioned, or "stagnation" or a stationary state attained. The writers on economic development again seem sometimes to speak of that desirable phenomenon as a "one-shot" problem: let's get Indonesia or the Argentine developed and then turn to something else. But historians have open-ended concepts. They look backward to times that are open because the data become so misty; and they look forward to change proceeding continuingly into an indefinite future.

There is also the important difference between the two groups that they do not usually utilize the same raw materials in their labors. The economist feels uneasy, if not baffled, if among the variables which he can imprison within his *ceteris paribus* he cannot place all alterations in the society (or societies) under consideration, even modifications of technology. When economists find themselves required by their specific problem to deal with matters of culture and cultural change, they are likely to regard themselves as "stepping out of their depth"; and they may attempt to limit the problem to something with which they can deal by contending that, for the economist, the question of the process of cultural change is "summed up concretely and fully in the rate of capital accumulation required to effect the cultural changes necessary for development." [3] Other ways of stating the economists' general position is that they want to deal with changes within a given economic and social structure; or they seek to discover fixed relationships between variables in order that forecasting and the further evolution of theory may be promoted. On the other hand, the historian draws no lines around the proper area or "depth" of his considerations. He follows where his problem takes him, if necessary to esthetic appreciation, religious convictions, or philosophic beliefs. Accordingly, he is much readier than the economist to make table companions, if not bedfellows, of social psychologists and anthropologists and all sorts of peculiar citizens. And such will be raising their tousled heads in the ensuing study of entrepreneurship and entrepreneurial history.

5

It does appear essential to specify at the start that the examination of data in this entrepreneurial field, like the examination of data in other areas of economics or economic history, should involve a perspective, a tempo, and a set of apparatus appropriate to the endeavor. Such was allowed the study of bimetallism in the past, or that of the business cycle, or even monopolistic competition. It is especially worth noting that in these several cases variant dredgings of historical facts were allowed. In the study of entrepreneurship, rather extreme degrees of dredging seem essential; that particular research excursion becomes blended with an exploration of entrepreneurial history. Accordingly, one may not inappropriately contend that we, as economists, who quite properly are interested in entrepreneurship, are not "as economists" really out of our depth in pursuing the inquiry into whatever territories it may lead us. There is no logical requirement that economics be limited to the handling of data of today and this week, or the phenomena merely of the market place.

The Concept of Entrepreneurship

Entrepreneurship has enjoyed a number of definitions which have varied to some extent according to time and place. In the days when the creative aspects of the entrepreneur were first being recognized, he was referred to as a "projector." [4] The modern term came into use in England only in 1878, when it signified a "director or manager of a public musical institution" or "one who gets up entertainments," [5] although thirty years earlier John Stuart Mill had actually mentioned the word as a French term in a footnote to his *Principles*, in which he expressed regret at the lack of an English equivalent. [6] Recently the word has frequently been employed to differentiate an active businessman from a slow-moving one. Thus, in his description of the bazaars at Beirut, Professor Dalton Potter of American University introduces the dichotomy of "chandler" and "entrepreneur" (not hesitating to draft the latter term), the former to cover the retail dealer who carries on a passive trade in traditional goods and the latter one who "makes a market" for new varieties of items.[7] This last practice approaches a distinction which Dr. Redlich and others are disposed to make between "entrepreneur" or "enterpriser" and "manager" — of which more shortly.

In this book, entrepreneurship will be used in two senses, although the context of each use should make the particular meaning obvious. Usually, the word will be employed to mean the function or activity. Here I shall have in mind the purposeful activity (including an integrated sequence of decisions) of an individual or group of associated individuals, undertaken to initiate, maintain, or aggrandize a profit-oriented business unit for the production or distribution of economic goods and services. The aggregate of individuals which together and cooperatively develop the decisions might perhaps be denominated the "entrepreneurial team." It is really a team in the senses (a) that each person or officer plays a particular position or represents a particular aspect of the total enterprise, and (b) that each such person or officer is in some measure a complement of the others as far as the total purposes of the unit are concerned. The team feature is observed when individuals in such a group have to be replaced. If a weak sales manager is succeeded by one quite capable of expressing his division's interest, all the other members of the group shift their positions to some extent. For instance, the chief executive may give hitherto unknown support to the production chief or the personnel manager. A balance is reasserted.

In such activity the goal or measure of success will ordinarily be pecuniary, but that basis may be supplemented by other yardsticks of appraisal. Again, it should be specified that this entrepreneurial activity proceeds in relationship to the situation internal to the unit itself, the social group that really constitutes the unit, and to the economic, political, and social circumstances — institutions, practices, and ideas which surround the unit.[8]

Perhaps it should be pointed out here that while there are a number of people involved in the development of a decision, and while the group may be looked upon as a team, there is no escaping the fact that all the members of such a team are not equals in any administrative sense. The effective element is to some extent compensated for by shifts in the actions, perhaps in the informal subgroupings, of the remaining members. There remains, however, the chief executive, president, or chairman of the board, who undoubtedly exerts more influence than any other individual in the team, and sometimes, depending on personality or force of character, may have almost the power of veto over all the rest. Mr. Chester I. Barnard, president of the New Jersey Bell Telephone Company for many years as well as being a distinguished scholar, once was belittling the real contribution of top executives, asserting that in his job all that he did was to say "Yes" and "No"; but I noted that it was he who did the saying of "Yes" and "No."

Some observers have been inclined, it seems, to take the easy road of identifying the latter variety of figure as "the entrepreneur" of economic theory, even if they have to dip down in corporate hierarchies sometimes to take a powerful vice-president or "take-over" comptroller as the entrepreneur of specific enterprises. I am disposed rather to lean to the other extreme and doubt whether the economists' entrepreneur ever existed in reality. To my way of thinking, when an enterprise had grown large enough or the period of operation extended long enough so that the head of the unit had to share his duties of observation, planning, and execution with one or more other persons, he was in effect sharing his entrepreneurial function; he was moving toward the "multiple" entrepreneur of which I have spoken above. And with the increase in the complexity of relationships surrounding business institutions and an increase in the complexity of data needed to operate such units successfully, the multiple or divided quality of entrepreneurship becomes the most important element.

Although the word "entrepreneurship" will usually be used to indicate function or activity, occasionally I may use it to signify the commonalty of entrepreneurs. By this I have in mind the aggregate of individuals performing that function or carrying on that activity in a given time and place, or even over considerable periods of time, just as one might speak of "knighthood" or "the ministry." Thus, I might remark that entrepreneurship in England has been drawn lately from certain classes of society.

It is obvious here that with the first effort at definition we run into complexities. I am attempting to grasp the economic significance of certain aspects, at least, of business enterprise conceived as social phenomena, and, as will appear more clearly in a moment, I wish to view these social elements as in a state of constant change. In other words, I seek to merge some aspects of the supposedly distinct disciplines of business administration, economics, sociology, and history. In such fearful circumstances, it will surely be wise for me to try to make clear what I believe the operational limitations and implications of the definition to be.

For example, brief reflection suggests the notion that entrepreneurship can be viewed by such a person as a social psychologist as similar to other forms of activity in somewhat comparable relations, such as the statesman in connection with the economic development of a region or a college president in the up-building of his institution. Of the first category, one could cite Alexander Hamilton operating in the early days under the American Constitution, or Julius Vogel in connection with the upsurge of New Zealand in the 1870's and 1880's; of the second, Charles W. Eliot at Harvard or William R. Harper at Chicago.[9] However, limitation of the term "entrepreneurship" to the purveyance of economic goods and services on certain terms seems necessary for purposes of clear analysis, especially relative to motivations and to sources of power.

Cursory examination of phenomena in the area suggests that the term "the entrepreneur" may be construed occasionally in the singular, but usually in the plural — and for two reasons. The first is that decision-making is the critical or key operation in entrepreneurship, and even in single-man proprietorships the head of the enterprise rarely decides by himself, that is, under circumstances where the original suggestion or some later advice has not come from subordinates or staff. Effective administration is a necessary condition for innovation or other creative action by businessmen; and it is true that usually administrative activity must also be shared by the individual entrepreneur. The second reason is that frequently nowadays decision-making in companies is purposefully plural. A president may exist, but he is only one among equals.

Mr. Barnard, Professor Marshall E. Dimock, and others have pointed out the complexities of decision-development in sizable organizations, and the nature of the administrative delegation of powers. It becomes necessary in entrepreneurial study — which is concerned with the business type of enterprise — to keep in mind the two related, really interdependent phenomena. There may be a broad participation in the formation of decision, and there is usually a delegation and dispersal (through the organization) of various types of decision-making, but there is also a seat of major policy decision-making, and decisions from this last source over-rule all others insofar as there is any conflict. Nevertheless, all varieties of other decisions are necessary to interpret those that deal with policy as well as routine decisions that repeat interpretations.

Professor Karl W. Deutsch then at Massachusetts Institute of Technology once proposed that entrepreneurial decisions be defined as those made at the risk of not being able to make the same or similar ones again. No doubt decisions of this quality are the most important ones — those which give entrepreneurs sleepless nights and stomach ulcers — but surely decisions of other sorts are essential to the "initiation, maintenance, and aggrandizement" of business institutions. Similarly, the establishment, and change, of an administrative organization for the proper execution of decisions, and the supervision of subordinate units, are necessary for the "maintenance" of entrepreneurship. Hence, as I have suggested, the entrepreneurial function is both dispersed and concentrated. Usually, in speaking hereafter of decision-making and of entrepreneurship, I shall have in mind the "concentrated" or "policy" aspect, sometimes designated as "coordinating" operations, but I shall not mean to imply that the top executive, like the proverbial professor, arrives at decisions in an ivory tower, insulated from ideas that come up from members of their staffs, or that decisions get executed from a single center by some omniscient, omnipresent boss.

This explanation, however, gives rise to another sort of question: what is the difference between entrepreneurship and business in real life and between the study of entrepreneurship and that of business administration? Of the former it may be asserted quickly that the two areas are substantially coterminous. I do believe it economically and socially important to emphasize the time element in the phenomena common to the two concepts, the potentiality of indefinite continuance and of persisting innovational action. These features subsume a multipersonal organization of some sort; and this latter circumstance in turn spells social elements of leadership, effective coordination, human relations, and the like.

Put in concrete terms, my contention is that the individual peddler was a businessman but not an entrepreneur. So also is the man who sits in a stockbroker's office all day, buying and selling shares on his own account; likewise the "dickerer" of Maine record, who, at least in the past, started from Portland or Bangor with money, bought goods from one farmer, and proceeded to swap goods for other goods, until in the end he wound up with a supply of butter or some other commodity easily salable in the city, and hopefully salable for a sum of money greater than that with which he launched the series of transactions! Obviously, however, the actual number of individuals (at any one time-period) who would be businessmen but not entrepreneurs in my differentiation would be small. The corner druggist or any such type of small businessman becomes, to my mind, an entrepreneur as soon as he has to rely on a night clerk to help carry the enterprise, try to satisfy customers, note what customers ask for and cannot purchase, make the right change, endeavor to outdo the store down the street, and so on.[10]

Between studies of entrepreneurship and of business administration as bodies of thought, there are, I believe, two important differences. First is the fact that entrepreneurship is interested in the economic and social significance of business procedures and institutions, whereas business administration must also give attention to their instrumental qualities. For example, scholars in the latter area must consider the best ways of measuring advertising effort, not merely the economic and social consequences of that effort.

And the same sort of distinction would hold true of fitting the best cost-accounting system to given situations, the best procedures for operating advancement from within the organization, and the like.

Second, students of business administration usually accept the nature of the businessman as given, as indeed do most economists. Typically, in both disciplines, the implication holds that the businessman in all cultures and countries now and throughout history has always been, and is, the same. Students of entrepreneurship, on the other hand, are interested in discovering why the American or any other businessman of 1959 has the character that he has, and operates in the manner in which he does; and almost inevitably such students become enmeshed in history, at least to some degree. Here again the inquirer is involved with time: he cannot understand the current businessman in any country — that is, why he behaves as he does — wholly in terms of current fact. He must search into the past for the formative, slowly changing forces. "Entrepreneurial history" is a term convenient for designating that aspect of thought or writing about entrepreneurship, which does not necessarily carry the inquiry up to the time of observation, although it may do so. Business administration, on the other hand, may be looked upon as an operational discipline related primarily to the self-generated policies and procedures of the private enterprises, while entrepreneurship is at best advisory and interpretive. It forms part of a social-cultural area, coordinate with the study of religion or politics or art.

I have, however, ventured down a convenient side road. The point from which I turned was the nature of entrepreneurship within the business unit. I should now point out that decisions are integrated, and that one decision becomes in some measure the basis for subsequent ones. This is an important specific phase of the open-endedness men-

13

tioned above. The entrepreneur looks toward an indefinite future, to a growth, a development, at least a continuation. This integrated quality is especially significant because it suggests that the business institution with which entrepreneurship is concerned has a certain organic quality. And quite surely the growth and survival of the individual enterprise must form an element in the biological schema, which Professor Rostow of the Massachusetts Institute of Technology recently commended to our brother economists.[11]

It should be noted again, moreover, that there is nothing in the definition given above that requires the employment of innovation in the activities of entrepreneurship, at least innovation in the usual sense. A business unit may be "initiated," but that is all. However, innovation is not excluded, and I am inclined to believe that business activity is shot through with novelty — local, industry, individual-plant novelty — and that novelty is unsuccessful in the business world unless the institution introducing it is being maintained effectively. The whole area of invention, innovation, adaptation, and so on, is filled with difficulties, both of concept and of application.[12] Is every child innovating when, for the first time, at least for him, he learns to walk? Was each act an innovation when the steam engine was applied to cotton spinning, to wool spinning, to linen spinning, to silk throwing, et cetera? What is the rise of soft-drink bottling in Iran: an innovation, an imitation, an adaptation?

For our present purposes, however, it will suffice to insist on a few, rather self-evident propositions. Innovations are often unrecognized as such at the time of their introduction, since the innovators are usually attempting to meet a specific situation, and anyway would have little opportunity to survey all comparable situations even in their own industries, let alone throughout the world; accordingly, the intellectual process of spotting and appraising innovations is a *post hoc,* historical one, not one that could have value in the world of business action. The introduction of an innovation in a specific business enterprise at a specific time is often merely one course among several open to the entrepreneur to meet a recognized competitive situation. Whether it is called innovation, imitation, or adaptation, the spread among business institutions of new ways of doing things, from one location to others, from industry to industry, and from plant to plant, is much more important for economic growth than the initiation of such new ways at specific points in space and time. (There is also the effect of an innovation in the proliferation of new business institutions, a multiplier effect, of which more will be said later.) [13]

For my second point concerning innovation, namely, that novelty is successful in the business world only if the institution introducing it is being effectively maintained, I need make no long argument. To be sure, I have to admit that there have been cases where adequate capital or exceptional circumstances allowed invasion of new business forms, new processes of production, and the like. However, the costs of getting the "bugs" out of new machinery are well recognized; the trials of introducing a new product or new system of selling or other major change are no less expensive; and a solidly based enterprise is abler to bear such costs, even more inclined to risk the consequences of incurring them. [14]

Another element in the definition of entrepreneurship presented above relates to motivation. That business institutions should be concerned with money-making need not be elaborated. But it is important to notice, especially over the past two or three decades, how considerably American corporations have modified any rule of financial maximization that may have existed, so that corporate longevity, community relations, or public responsibilities might be taken into account. Especially significant has been the trend over an even longer period in the United States toward a reduction in the sovereignty of the stockholder.

Nor is there need any longer to emphasize, at least in the United States, the existence of non-pecuniary incentives among modern business executives. A score of writers — Robert A. Gordon, Oswald Knauth, Thomas C. Cochran, among others — have expressed concurrent views on this matter;[15] and a goodly amount of thought and writing in the field of business administration is going, and has gone, into the problem of finding substitutes in large business organizations for the older pecuniary stimulus. The unit in General Electric devoting full time to the subject seems inclined to phrase its aim as making entrepreneurs out of managers.

Whatever the immediate motivations, those potent in business seem related to one or another of the psychological incentives of search for security, prestige, power, and social service. Professor Marshall E. Dimock expresses the idea that these incentives form a sequence in the attitudes of individual men through their business lives.[16] They also have some value as a historical series. It may suffice here, however, to point out, as Professor Clarence H. Danhof has done in the case of the search for prestige, that such stimuli or incentives are shared at least through most strata of Western society.[17]

Perhaps, thanks to the existence of the institution of inheritance, security for one's family has counted for more in entrepreneurial circles than many other lines of activity in recent societies. I am thinking of the numberless cases in European experience where business activity has been pursued, sometimes "endured," with the purpose of founding a family. Professor Frederic C. Lane in his *Andrea Barbarigo* gives the impression of return to business every three or four generations in fourteenth- and fifteenth-century Venice in order that family fortunes, diminished by government service and by life on landed estates, might be recouped.[18] Much of the nobility in England and Sweden and Germany stemmed from successful business performance. But neither ennoblement nor landed property is necessary. It is alleged of Latin American businessmen that they persist in business even after one line has been successfully established, taking on successively different lines for the supposed reason of being able to leave a separate factory or store to each child in their families.

To be sure, concern for one's family is not an attitude shown exclusively by businessmen. Other sorts of men from the manorial lord or guild handicraftsman down to the modern factory employee or college professor have shared in this interest. In the family enterprise, however, and in the freedom to divert sizable incomes into sources of security (over time), prestige, and even power of a sort, the entrepreneur has perhaps enjoyed a measure of opportunity that has not been available in most other walks of life.

Internal and External Relationships

The specification that entrepreneurial activity "proceeds in relationship to the situation internal to the [business] unit itself" covers at least three somewhat variant elements. First, there is the legal and managerial form. Quite obviously the form of organization, whether it be proprietorship, partnership, or corporation, makes a considerable difference in the manner in which the entrepreneurial function is carried on, as do also the legal requirements and limitations upon the action of company officers. More important perhaps is the operating form, through which management seeks to attain its objectives. At least this is true: the legal form, and the privileges granted under it, are little affected by the desires of the operating managers of an enterprise; and these legal elements change slowly, usually not in response to managerial needs. The operating framework, however, does lie within the jurisdiction of top management. It can be altered to fit the requirements of the situation; and, actually, it has changed in important parts of various business worlds, especially those of advanced industrial nations.[19]

Second, it is worth noting that the entrepreneurial element in an enterprise forms a team; and no two teams are alike. In fact, individual enterprises have varied characters that change slowly — one strong in a given direction, another strong otherwise. The accession of a Henry Ford II was an event that obviously created a new and different team, but so did the acquisition of Alfred P. Sloan in a less conspicuous spot by a burgeoning General Motors a generation or more earlier. Also, in further relationship to the evolutionary character of entrepreneurial institutions, attention may be drawn to the proposition that no alteration takes place in the higher echelons of management without a reshuffling of the duties and activities of all other members of the team. This is clearly the case when a public-relations director is newly added, or when a somnolent sales manager is replaced by one of vigor and aggressiveness. In any such situation the team, like the bits of glass in a kaleidoscope, becomes something novel. Thus, new features are injected into entrepreneurial practices without an overturn of existing forms, and human groups adjust to change.

Third, and perhaps most important for our present consideration, the "internal" situation within an enterprise is to be viewed chiefly as a group of individuals who, like members of other social groups, interact with one another. In this network of interaction are to be found the elements of role and sanction which provide the mode through which economico-business action takes place, and which, changing over time, constitute a major thread in the history of entrepreneurship. In an appreciable measure, expectations of behavior — what the directors expect of the treasurer, what the production vice-president expects of employees, and so on — become incorporated into company regulations. Other expectations, such as that of his staff anent the behavior of the president, and certain expectations relative to behavior of other individuals, remain outside rule books and company manuals. And both categories, quickly or slowly, are subject to change in response to changing social thought. The proprietor of a department store told me privately that he did things for his employees, and they did things for or to him, which his father, retired but still observant, considered quite shocking.

The relations to entrepreneurial performance of economic, political, and social forces external to individual enterprises are manifold. One phase of the political connection was mentioned above: the legal framework within which enterprises function. The economic situation affects the entrepreneurial aspect in two major ways. That situation defines the entrepreneurial problem through the relative scarcities of the productive factors; and the change in relative scarcities over time, of course, does in fact alter that problem. At one time in the United States, management had to get along primarily with the suppliers of capital or their representatives; more recently it has had to establish improved relations with employees and *their* representatives.

While economic conditions may define the problem for the entrepreneurial actors, they do not necessarily decide it. The latitude of potential, even of likely action, for the entrepreneur is considerable. One aspect is the question of action or no action. When my friend Philip D. Bradley taught South American economic development at Harvard, he used to say that an entrepreneur of that area, at least of some of the countries there, could sit on a mountain of iron ore — and go to sleep! A North American entrepreneur, finding himself in the equivalent situation, would presumably not take rest until he had floated a company to exploit his discovery. As Professors J. Keith Butters and John Lintner of the Harvard Business School pointed out a few years ago, there seems to be a considerable number of people in the United States who annually set about trying their fortunes in businesses when they have much less than a mountain of iron ore to back up their aspirations.[20]

It also appears to be true that entrepreneurs are disposed to set about changing the economic situation as much as they can. Entrepreneurial advantage will tend to impel them in that type of action. The same group of men who established cotton mills at Lowell set up a company, called the Proprietors of the Locks and Canals of the Merrimack River, to develop and distribute water power (which enterprise, interestingly enough, is still going). The Weyerhaeuser Company and other large lumbering enterprises have altered their policies of cutting and conservation so that a limited asset has been changed into substantially an inexhaustible one. Again, our early cotton manufacturers, besides welcoming skilled foreign operatives who could be induced to immigrate, set about training people for the varieties of labor that were scarce. And the same was always true of capital shortage. As my friend Professor Jenks used sometimes to remark about the inflow of foreign capital into the United States, one would think from reading about the export of this capital from Europe that somehow the British and Dutch and Germans were thrusting it down our throats; whereas the important fact is that Americans almost assaulted the foreigners in their countinghouses in order to try to get hands on the funds. In sum, then, not only does entrepreneurial advantage tend to alter the existing complements of the productive factors, each entrepreneur seeking thereby a differential advantage over his competitors, but, over the decades, by dint of individual actions and enforced imitations, it seems probable that the combined effect has been considerable.

Economic forces also have, and have had over the past, an indirect effect. A rising level of economic productivity has meant a higher level of education for management, staff, and employees. It has meant the opportunity to utilize more "unproductive" labor, both white-collar within the plant and expert advisers outside it; and it has meant improved libraries, more professional literature, larger staffs, and more leisure for the staff to take advantage of these opportunities.

These "external" forces offer a particularly important challenge in connection with the launching of entrepreneurial endeavor in specific areas such as underdeveloped countries. Professor W. Thomas Easterbrook speaks of the minimum security elements that entrepreneurship seems to require. A region hazardous to life is likely to be exploited by governmental rather than private enterprise.[21] In addition, a society which from religious or other causes finds material welfare unimportant or money-making improper is hardly a good nursery for entrepreneurship. The theocracy of Massachusetts Bay, for example, was positively hostile to mercantile activities.[22] Professor Alexander Gerschenkron has spoken of the low social status of money-making in eighteenth- and nineteenth-century Russia, and Professor Cochran seems to think that the lack in Spanish countries of the really hearty appeal of getting ahead materially may affect the quality of entrepreneurial performance there.[23]

Moreover, there can be no doubt that changes over time in these external elements have altered the entrepreneurial way of life. Sometimes it has been a lag that has mattered, such as the retention among French business circles of attitudes derived from earlier social regimes.[24] Sometimes it has been an intensification of a pre-existent force, as in the cult of wealth that affected the United States especially in the late nineteenth century.[25]

These external factors yield in large measure the sanctions to which the entrepreneur responds. They condition his psychological development in early life; they sustain his activities throughout his career; they give check to some possible actions and give blessings upon others; and they supply the psychic rewards when retirement comes. These are the elements, much more than physical divergences, that differentiate such a country as the United States or Germany from underdeveloped New Guinea or Paraguay. And they constitute a major line of differentiation between twentieth-century Germany, England, or other countries, and these countries in early times.

In sum, the study of entrepreneurship, especially when viewed as a changing phenomenon, parallels or overlaps studies of various sorts in the social sciences, those of leadership, group dynamics, business operations, prestigious symbols, economic productivity, and the like. It seems to require particular attention to the flow of social thought and the activities of social institutions, which help to shape the form and quality of entrepreneurial performance. It demands the adoption of a pace, or rate of change, and of an open-end path of development that are not common in economics; and it counsels a regard for social, differentiating factors and for economic and social meaning that is usually absent in the study of business administration.

Yet there appears to be an area of inquiry in historical entrepreneurship — an inquiry that carries up to the present day — which does not necessitate the spreading of effort over an unmanageable field, and which can be fenced off in an operational manner. And the area has several attractive features. It deals with phenomena basic to an understanding of the characteristic Western organization of society, which is usually labeled "capitalistic" but more properly should be called "entrepreneurial." The changes in entrepreneurial performance over time, isolated as far as possible from the effects of economic resources, constitute as scientific a basis as we shall secure for the appraisal of the private-enterprise system; and the lessons deducible from the study of nascent and immature economies of the Western past, perhaps even the examination of some aspects of our mature economies, may be of value in the determination of practical policies for the so-called "underdeveloped" areas of the world.[26]

The Entrepreneurial World

Even as a professional musician finds important the appearance of new symphonies or sonatas, the resignations of orchestral conductors, and perhaps the activities of booking agents for winter tours, so the entrepreneurial actors live to a considerable extent in a world of their own. It is not an unintellectual world, at least nowadays, but it will seem strange and perhaps Philistine to those whose worlds are differently oriented — towards the fortunes of Grandma Moses or of mobiles, towards the last novel of William Faulkner, or the new cyclotron at Berkeley.

The elements in the entrepreneurs' world present great variety among themselves, from the officers of labor unions to the effort of certain writers to introduce the term "agribusiness," and from the new rulings of the Federal Trade Commission on unethical advertising practices to the echoes from the nineteenth century which occur in the complaints of discontented stockholders. These different elements impinge upon entrepreneurs in varying degrees at different times, conditioning entrepreneurial decisions, molding entrepreneurial characters, and so on. They also react upon one another in some measure, and the entrepreneurs in turn react upon the forces and institutions that condition their decisions or mold their attitudes. Yet, for purposes of exposition, it may be useful to think of such elements as forming classes or unities, however intermixed they may be in reality.

The outstanding, inherent feature of such elements which has inevitably crept into the foregoing description is that of change: the idea of a *novel* term or *new* rulings, the fact that a critical feature of entrepreneurial life itself is change. The entrepreneur looks back into the past to learn the bases of his successes or failures. He is particularly conscious of what his competitors are doing or have just done and he is constantly planning ahead, what to do tomorrow, next month, ten years from now, and what is likely to have happened in government, in the policies of his trade association, in the capacities of statistical analysis to give him help in forecasting sales. For him life is a flow, and for us the representation of the breakdown of the elements impinging upon him must take the form of a composite of flows, perhaps currents in a stream, except that some of these currents became almost motionless, as it were, for varying periods of time: such currents as rulings of the tax authorities, attitudes of columnists, institutions such as professional associations within business that, at least for some years or decades, take on lives of their own. The image which on the whole seems to me to represent the nature of entrepreneurial experience vis-à-vis the various other elements in our society, elements that are sometimes solidified social units and sometimes mere courses of thought, is that of the logger riding a drive of logs down a stream of numerous currents, which in turn are twisted at times by a curving shore line and broken up by protruding rocks and an uneven river bottom. The rider makes his decisions as to the course to be taken by the leading logs, the mass of logs to be kept from jamming, to be kept away from the shore, all almost literally in accordance with Professor Deutsch's definition, namely, at the risk of not being in a position to make further decisions. Here also every decision conditions every subsequent one, and each is made under new, different, and currently changing circumstances.

For heuristic purposes it is convenient and logical to think of the entrepreneurial main current, the sequence of decisions and actions, as affected in its nature by nearby currents of informational and ideational character. By "informational" I have in mind the constantly changing element of technological and professional data, on the basis of which decisions are made, all that the Germans call *fachmässig*. These data change at quite different rates of speed, from the minute-to-minute reportings of moving prices on commodity or stock exchanges to the almost constant understanding of the nature of the wool fiber. In large measure the data become incorporated into printed documents of one type or another, predominantly periodical articles, annual reports, or books, and these come to rest in libraries. Thus the flow of technical data becomes affected by the semirigidities of reporting agencies and business educational institutions. However, the main point is the continuous stream of data, on the basis of which decisions are reached and policies are executed. All is flux.

Behind the flow of technical data lie the slower wellings of concepts and "sentiments." Thus in the intellectual climate in America of the late nineteenth century and particularly with the leadership of Frederick W. Taylor, individuals of unusual apperception in business and in educational institutions began to believe that "right" or "best" ways of doing things in business could be found, that business procedures need not remain the products of trial and error, rules of thumb, each man to learn only by personal experience. Something approaching a scientific business literature could be initiated. And later came beliefs in special portions of the business field: capacity for forecasting changes in the volume of business, the wisdom of "full disclosure," or the desirability of emphasizing human relations.

Associated with such ideas, and to some extent lying behind them, are yet more general notions, many of them deriving from the more or less distant past, but all being modified as they flow along and interact with other more recent ideas and with the circumstances of modern life. I have in mind such concepts as the dignity of the individual, the desirability of material progress, the commendability of personal achievement, and the like.

Such social motivations — what Professor Cochran calls "cultural themes" — are ordinarily not conscious parts of the entrepreneur's world, but they constitute a portion of his social education, and, in a sense, they all condition each entrepreneurial decision at any given time. Even as the past is summed up in the present, and a man is at least in part a creature of his inheritance, so some fragments of relevant history — the lessons of Christianity, the adventurous spirit of the Renaissance, the objectivity of scientific findings, an intolerance of monopolists — are elements in current decisions. These decisions, in turn, may strengthen the force of such ideas, and so the concepts continue to flow and to condition entrepreneurial life. Of course, the interaction of the ideas with circumstances of the modern world may also weaken the power that they had previously exerted. The force of the stream is somewhat altered.

These cultural themes have a consequence other than affecting the character of individual decisions directly. They exert an indirect influence through institutions which they help to bring into existence; indeed, an important segment of the complex of institutions which I shall later include under the term, "the entrepreneurial stream." In the rise of public accounting firms, counselors in industrial relations, even the internal corporate arrangements of line and staff or of co-ordinating committees, ethical principles or cultural themes have play. And the evolution and increased use of such instrumentalities in turn affect the empirical situation. One stream acts upon another, and indeed reacts upon the first.

Basic in the entrepreneurial world, then, as in the world of art or literature or education, are ideas and ideals, themselves a changing flow, far removed from what is usually regarded as the field of business. Out of such concepts and social themes, with conditioning supplied by the techniques of business operations, derives a changing complement of technical and operating institutions, from schools of business to put-and-call brokers, some of them entrepreneurial units ancillary to larger ones. With the aid of these institutions, and responding in part to the preceding centuries of cultural change, a constantly changing body of entrepreneurs makes linked chains of decisions concerned with the "initiation, maintenance, and aggrandizement" of profit-oriented social units, decisions that attempt to relate the changing supplies of productive factors to the changing requirements of the societies (consumers and governments) within which they are allowed to perform their functions. Obviously, the simile of riders of drives of logs, even riders trying to judge the currents in rivers swollen by spring freshets, is no exaggeration.

Conclusion

Entrepreneurship, at least in all nonauthoritarian societies, constitutes a bridge between society as a whole, especially the noneconomic aspects of that society, and the profit-oriented institutions established to take advantage of its economic endowments and to satisfy, as best they can, its economic desires. What talent will be attracted into entrepreneurial activity, how well this talent will perform its function, and, to a considerable extent in modern societies, even how the national product will be shared — all of these questions are determined by the combination of social and technical forces, most of them changing with more or less rapidity, and all having initial impingement upon, or receiving initial impetus from, the entrepreneurial actors. Nothing that I have learned since 1946 has led me to alter the view which I expressed then: namely, that to study the entrepreneur is to study the central figure in modern economic development, and, to my way of thinking, the central figure in economics.[27]

Chapter II·

THE NEED OF A POSITIVE VIEW

LIKE EVERY TOPIC in the social sciences, entrepreneurship, if viewed historically and if analyzed deeply enough, leads one into nearly all fields of knowledge. One could speculate with Pareto whether mankind is divisible, as it were, into those whose complements of "residues" and whose other endowments destine them to be leaders, and into those whose natures make them content to be lead. One could explore with the aid of anthropologists whether the endeavor to get ahead, to improve one's status in some manner, if not in the ways we know best, is universal in human societies. Or, nearer to home, one might examine by the study of the history of economic thought how it came about that the entrepreneur became almost wholly squeezed out of economic theory.

The student of entrepreneurship who himself carries a historical bias must take note of the rather progressive negation and neglect with which economists of the twentieth century have treated the entrepreneur. Marshall found room for such a figure, even elaborated a particular function that he felt to be dominant in the activities of "the undertaker." Taussig gave evidence of a realization that human beings had something to do with directing the productive process. But as the decades rolled by, only such special areas as monopolistic competition or business-cycle analysis knew the enterpriser or even the businessman.[1] Even as much economic history could be written in the same period with no more than picturesque figures on its pages — railroads "were built" and banks "were organized" — so such a highly regarded text in economics as Professor Paul A. Samuelson's could come to be written without use by the author of actors in this drama, at least in the private section.

Profit-Maximization

The foundation on which modern economists have based their analyses dominated by impersonal forces is essentially that of the "economic man" who "naturally" seeks in an entrepreneurial role to maximize profits. Thoughtful theorists have admitted that this proposition is hypothetical, but they have not called upon other social scientists to prove or disprove the assumption; instead they contend that, if not substantiated by facts, it could be employed safely *as if* true — as a book-publisher might elaborate his publishing list *as if* all of us loved poetry.

The only point that needs to be made in this connection is that this belief in profit-maximization was, after all, only a belief. It was launched, indeed, under somewhat suspicious circumstances, for the author who gave greatest currency to the notion of "self-interest" as influencing "the nature and causes of the wealth of nations" had written a book only twenty years earlier in which he stressed the dominance of "sympathy" in social relations. And, if never supported in the minds of theorists by more than "common observation," or at most a willingness to interpret the course of specific events as sufficiently explicable by the use of this hypothesis, it is entirely logical to contend that this prime foundation of recent economic analysis *could* be supplanted by another

30

contention, the latter based on "common observation," or perhaps now on data derived from research.

Such a transition appears to be under way. Professor Joel Dean has summarized the condition of the basic assumption of profit-maximization as follows: the contention has been "qualified . . . to refer to the long run; to refer to management's rather than to owners' income; to include non-financial income such as increased leisure for highstrung executives and more congenial relations between executive levels within the firm; and to make allowance for special considerations such as restraining competition, maintaining management control, holding off wage demands, and forestalling antitrust suits." The concept has, he says, "become so general and hazy that it seems to encompass most of man's aims in life." [2]

A president of the American Economic Association finds the "generally recognized development of a managerial class" — and the rise of an "organizational economy" — to occasion a reappraisal of the "profit maximization" principle.[3] Professor Andreas G. Papandreou raises similar doubts, and former Dean Edward S. Mason's only reply is the expression of a hope that economists will not have to abandon their very useful theorem. These and numerous other expressions of skepticism, uncertainty, and outright rejection leave the observer with the unavoidable conclusion that some fundamental modification of this basic concept is in gestation.[4]

Students of entrepreneurship and entrepreneurial history may well regard this development as an essential first step in the construction of a "positive" theory; it helps to clear the ground. While the hypothesis of profit-maximization commands the allegiance of economists, the latter have a strong logical basis for emasculating the entrepreneur. They may well reason: (a) economic conditions determine the level

31

and variations of profits; (b) entrepreneurs follow the lines defined by the attractiveness of profits; (c) therefore, we need look only at the basic economic conditions; we do not need to concern ourselves with the men who run business enterprises; if John Smith does not have a keen nose for exceptional profits, Bill Jones will have. Hugh G. J. Aitken, one of the originators of *Explorations in Entrepreneurial History,* saw this situation early in his studies, when he restrainedly wrote, "It just is not helpful in economic history to regard business men as mere agents of economic forces . . . It seems to me that this rejection of the impersonality assumption must be one of the basic postulates of entrepreneurial history." [5]

To be sure, such a rejection, even if supported by facts, is only half of the story. It merely opens up a possibility. There remains the obligation upon students of entrepreneurship and entrepreneurial history to demonstrate that acknowledgment of the existence of the entrepreneur has important consequences. Indeed, Professor H. J. Habbakuk once posed the direct question: "What difference does it make that economists and historians pay attention to the entrepreneur?"

Efforts at Reconstruction

One consequence of such attention is to be seen in the endeavors of a few current economists to fit somehow the direction of enterprise, the businessman, the entrepreneur, whatever the agent may be called, into the pre-existing pattern of economic theory. The efforts also seem to show the futility of halfway measures. The recognition of the entrepreneurial function as not determined in character by economic forces causes numerous cracks in the current theoretical structure. Two illustrations will perhaps suffice.

One may be drawn from the highly provocative efforts

that a group at the Carnegie Institute of Technology has been making: Professors William W. Cooper, Richard M. Cyert, and their associates. Professor Cooper raises the criticism of "traditional theory," that, like classical physics vis-à-vis the nature of the atom, no effort was made to pierce the interior of the firm:

Under the Marshallian and later versions of this theory, the entrepreneur is regarded as operating directly on (more or less) "will-less" factors of production. No method of communication is specified. The "factors" are assumed to know immediately what is expected of them and to adjust themselves without further ado; the entrepreneur is assumed to know instantly what is being done and how he should respond in the face of market criteria. Misinformation, conflict of information, and lack of information are all absent. Nor are there intermediaries present to consult and advise, or to transmit information.[6]

Pursuing the thesis, which he had stated earlier,[7] that "control considerations need to be built into the theory" of the firm, Professor Cooper elaborates a construct of a control system. It is somewhat similar to the circular schema sketched by Professor George Albert Smith some years ago (and reported in *Change and the Entrepreneur*, pp. 13 ff.), and to that more specifically pictured by Professor Kenneth E. Boulding shortly thereafter. Professor Cooper's model, however, contains significant advances over preceding efforts. I venture to present it here.[8]

The nature of the process, as described by Professor Cooper, is fairly obvious. Objectives are stated by the entrepreneur and worked out on the basis of observed (reported?) market conditions; a prediction — a "budget" — is developed; men and processes are selected to carry through the envisaged operations; reporting of intermediate results is launched at once and continued. These reports may lead to a redefinition of objectives, an amended budget, and all this takes place on the basis of standards established by management, the entrepreneur. Redefinition is stated to be "necessary if the organization is to adjust to changing conditions";[9] and presumably so also could the process of prediction, the method of reporting. Even the standards themselves could be revised "to adjust to changing conditions."

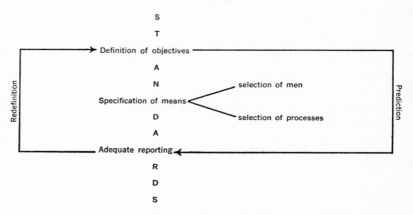

One interesting conclusion which Professor Cooper draws is that the presence of controls "acting through the media of 'willful' agents rather than 'will-less' factors may result in quite different observational behavior than that expected by the economist conducting investigations of business behavior with a model which does not allow for such conditions." [10] The author is particularly concerned with conditions of cost, "administration of equity accounts," and the like; and therefore, he asseverates that costs "may not be allowed to behave; they may, within certain limits, be made to behave." Perhaps others, interested in different aspects of enterprise performances, might wonder whether labor conditions, consumer relations, even natural resources "may be allowed to behave," and whether they may not, "within certain limits, be made to behave."

Professor Cooper was not making a plea for the study of entrepreneurship and entrepreneurial evolution.

Professors Cyert and J. G. March carry the analysis further.[11] For example, they find enterprises to have communication patterns, with "relay points," and that it makes a difference how many such points there are, how long the chain through which communications have to pass, and even the order in which particular pieces of information proceed: for example, data about costs going through a "relay point" occupied by a sales-oriented executive. They hold that the mere size of the decision-making unit is of importance. For example, in a multiple-man unit, each man will tend to hold the belief that the others will conform to known company policies; and therefore innovations have a poorer chance of adoption than in a one-man deciding unit.

They find the use of the budget in businesses important to a proper concept of enterprise behavior. And they see the annual budget not merely as a "prediction," a "schedule," and a "control device," but also as a "precedent." By defining decisions in many features of company action over the succeeding twelve months, the budget thereby establishes "a prima facie case for continuing [the] existing expenditures." There is a sort of dead hand of past budgets!

They also see the existence of "organizational slack" in any sizable business institution. Employees carry various roles other than those for which they are paid: roles of membership in cliques, in their respective families, and so on — and employees, not the company, define the minimum attention that they will give to these other roles. Anyway, here is slack which the enterprise can use to withstand the pressure of unfavorable circumstances and thus bear down upon its costs of operation.

In short, when one looks inside the business unit, one finds reasons to make allowance for willful factors, and really to cast doubts upon the traditional assumptions of rapid, automatic adjustments to profit advantages.

The Endeavor of Professor Burton S. Keirstead

Analysis of a different type is carried in Professor Keirstead's *Essay in the Theory of Profits and Income Distribution* (1953), but some of the same logical features appear: criticisms of previous theories and the elaboration of new ideas pertinent to the field of entrepreneurship, even to entrepreneurship as a historical phenomenon.

Professor Keirstead is concerned primarily with uncertainty and how the entrepreneur can deal over time with that unpleasant feature of business life. He admits that, when one leaves the static model, "the problem of profit maximization becomes more complicated." [12] He sees two sources of profit due to changing circumstances. One is the movement of general conditions, economic and political changes, which, if favorable to the enterprise, result in windfall profits. The other source lies in particular or company conditions; and here profits may arise either from a favorable change in the market for the goods of the enterprise, or from the introduction of innovations, either new processes or new products.

Now uncertainty affects all of these situations; but the author sees experts helping the entrepreneur to prevail against such difficulties. His forecasters can give him a good line on general conditions for something like 12 months in advance, and on particular conditions as much as "100 to 150 months ahead." In the case of large enterprises, with which alone Professor Keirstead deals, the marketing profits seem to him those of an oligopolist, and those arising from innovations to be (temporary) monopoly profits. In general, the author's conclusion seems to be that the entrepreneur may proceed, by aid of his expert advisors, *"as though he were certain,"* even if there really is "objective" uncertainty in the situation.[13]

There are, however, curious lapses in the whole argument, sometimes curious failures to prosecute an admitted limitation. For instance, general conditions are alleged to give occasion for windfall profits in consequence of their influence upon prices; but does this relationship exhaust the situation? The author includes political as well as economic factors in his general conditions, and, if political, why not social and all elements external to the enterprise? Also, whether the general conditions be limited to political and economic alone or more broadly extended, why do the consequences need to be restricted to the effects upon prices? Why are they not regarded as conditioning the whole conduct of the business institution?

Again, the company's experts are viewed as able to help the entrepreneur with respect to market forecasts, but apparently not with regard to accounting procedures, labor relations, public relations, and the like. Why is it not appropriate to corral the company's whole executive team into a relationship with "general" conditions, as apparently Professors Cooper, Cyert, *et al.*, are willing to do?

At one point, Professor Keirstead suggests that with respect to innovations the entrepreneur may well find himself in "unique" situations, where "there is no calculable probability of the hypotheses about the future that he may form." [14] However, are not novel situations, for the particular enterprise or particular region, if not for the business world as a whole, pretty frequent affairs in an entrepreneurial system? Are not many situations more or less unique? Are there really many situations relative to which top executive decisions are called for, for which the entrepreneur can envisage a "calculable probability of the hypotheses about the future," even with the aid of his experts?

The foregoing writers are representatives of the avant garde among economic theorists who, confronted with the world conditions of the postwar years, especially the re-awakened interest in economic development, are currently struggling to convert the pre-existent, predominantly static analysis to a really dynamic form.[15]

A call for such a formulation, made recently by Professor Guy H. Orcutt, a well-regarded Harvard economist, indeed carries a framework in which entrepreneurial activity is most readily fitted. Professor Orcutt wants place for "decision-making units," to be sure, families and governments as well as business enterprises — with the decisions conditioned by historically derived elements. As he puts it, "the probabilities associated with alternative behaviors or responses are treated as dependent on conditions or events prior to the behavior." No wonder that he has to label his proposed construction "a new type of socio-economic system."[16]

Where the unhappy theorists may land is no immediate concern of entrepreneurial historians. The chief point for us is that whether the reformers abandon the notion of profit-maximization or not — and Professor Keirstead quite surely does not — they seem bound to become involved more and more with entrepreneurial problems; conditions internal to the business units, the nature and competence of the staff departments, the launching of given activities which ad-mittedly will not mature until a subsequent time-period, and so on. In other words, the new theory promises to take on major features of history; that is, dynamics, and entrepre-neurship. When one tries to come to grips with economic change or economic development in a free (entrepreneurial) system, one can hardly avoid paying some attention to the entrepreneur.

The Influence of Economic Development

Quite surely, as an Oxonian recently put it, "economic growth is beginning to reoccupy a central position in economics . . . [a position] that it has not had since Adam Smith." [17] And in such a reorganization of economics, the entrepreneur cannot be neglected.

Certain aspects of entrepreneurial performance seem particularly significant for a form of economics that is really dynamic, and is concerned with unlimited economic growth: open-ended economic development. It is noteworthy, for example, that enterprises which escape "infant mortality" — disaster in their earliest years — may well acquire a zest for survival, perhaps a drive for success, which has but loose correlation with profit conditions. As Professor Cooper remarked vis-à-vis costs, the business unit may be made to behave in a manner that economic conditions alone could not guarantee. An extreme case was brought recently to my attention — that of an enterprise currently brewing beer, although it began life manufacturing automobiles.

Again, business decisions, when not concerned with routine affairs, are not unitary in character, but, as already suggested, are likely to be cumulative or at least linked, each major decision conditioning all subsequent ones, each decision, when carried into effect, being a commitment of some sort. Growth of the individual enterprise is the consequence of a succession of successful, linked decisions. For the decision-makers, especially in an economy where the owner-manager is an unusual figure in the larger enterprises, a number of incentives other than profit-maximization come to influence their actions: aggrandizement of the business unit by strategic moves, achievement, power, public service.

Even as the men who write the books or design the buildings of a given society are the children of many diverse influences, and not infrequently persons inexplicable in terms of existing social forces, so also the operators of the larger business enterprises may not be understood without regard to much more than the existing "complement of the productive factors." They are the products of the culture in which they matured and are currently operating, plus idiosyncratic elements that may lead them to deviate from any norm of their time and environment. Moreover, as Mr. Noel G. Butlin once enjoined the Research Center for Entrepreneurial History, "Whether we are dealing with economic or any other type of change, we need also to recognize the moving character of the entire society and to cast our concepts . . . with this fact firmly in the foreground." [18]

Perhaps ultimately a prediction of Saint-Simon made as early as 1814 will be justified; that the science of society would be evolutionary and historical rather than mechanistic.[19] Surely economists will be driven more and more like Cooper, Cyert, and their friends to study business units as social institutions possessed not merely of communication systems, but of role structures, informal organizations, diversities of group interactions, and the like. And they will come to recognize that, with an ever-moving character of the external society, the social organization that is the business enterprise will also be ever-changing.

The aspiration of the theorists of the current generation endeavoring to deal with economic growth, the difficulties that confront them, and the present state of the relevant theories are revealed in the latest book on the subject by two able young economists, Gerald M. Meier and Robert E. Baldwin, entitled *Economic Development: Theory,*

History, Policy.[20] The authors were trained at Harvard, show a familiarity with relevant modern theoretical materials, and the volume is, indeed, the most historical of the treatises that have appeared on the topic.

Professors Meier and Baldwin are engagingly frank. They offer three major propositions which make evident the magnitude of the task which they and indeed all similarly minded adventurers must face when they explore this territory so long a puzzle to historians.

1. Within the economist's usual framework, the rate of economic development is held to be determined by "the degree of utilization and the rate of increase of the various productive means." The authors have no more to say about the degree of utilization of the factors, although that matter might be of interest to those concerned with entrepreneurship; but they do go forward to remark that "when one attempts to trace the causes of changes among the productive factors, he becomes enmeshed in a myriad of social, political, and economic forces. These forces, moreover, cannot be arranged in any neat hierarchy of cause and effect. All of them are interrelated." [21]

2. After a survey of writers of the past who have paid some attention to problems of economic change from the classical school through the neoclassical, Marx, Schumpeter, and the post-Keynesian analysts, Messrs. Meier and Baldwin reach the view that, except on rare occasions, all these writers manifest quite limited visions: "they limit their analyses to the economic performance of Western capitalism," and, "for this purpose, they make many assumptions about the general sociological, political, and economic nature of this society." [22]

3. Despite the need for an extensive rethinking of appropriate economic analysis, and the drawing upon writers such as Max Weber, Pareto, Sombart, and Veblen, "the

widening of the traditional boundaries of economics, so far, has proceeded only very slowly." [23]

Actually, Professors Meier and Baldwin do little to alter the picture. In considering the "basic characteristics of poor countries," they utilize the four rubrics of "underdevelopment," "backwardness," "capital deficiency," and "foreign trade orientation." They do pay passing attention to the entrepreneur, recognizing that in such backward areas he is operating under conditions of insecurity; but they seem to regard him as essentially a twentieth-century, at least a nineteenth-century, American entrepreneur who chances to have been born in some strange foreign land. And when the authors come to deal with "maintaining development in such countries" — which, incidentally, is a notable section of their volume — they make use of concepts all familiar to recent economic literature: population, capital accumulation, technological discoveries, investment, and the like. Investment takes place without borrowing; changes of all sorts, of which actually only technological ones are mentioned, come into use automatically. Even the problem of "resource flexibility" can apparently be surmounted without human intervention. All rich countries — France, Canada, Brazil, Japan, Germany, and others — seem to be regarded as falling into a single category, and their businessmen all to be cast in the American model.

Still this book and others of its class are noteworthy both for their evident recognition of a dynamic situation and for their attempts to suggest the changes in modern economic thinking necessary to analyze it properly, the requirement of dealing with "a myriad of social, political, and economic forces" of which Messrs. Meier and Baldwin speak. In addition, the volumes are important for their attention to flows. It is the increase of population, the rate of technological advance, the accumulation of capital, and so on, that concern them mostly. Equilibrium is hardly mentioned. Perhaps in the end economists' eyes will come to fix upon the business institutions which themselves are changing and which are the principal channels of economic change, as well as upon the individuals who direct their decisions.

A Place for the Entrepreneur

The validity of the thought that the entrepreneur may properly be regarded as the central figure in economics[24] is subject to argument on the grounds of both logic and fact. In logic the question takes the form: what specific contribution in production is attributable to the activities or ideas of the entrepreneur? And the answer clearly will vary according to the depth of analysis. Superficially, it would appear that there is no net product specifically and separately attributable to the entrepreneur. The contribution of the entrepreneur flows out through the actions of labor, the movements of capital goods, and the conversion of raw materials, even as the contribution of an orchestral leader flows out through the singing of the violins or the beating of the kettledrums. Yet no one would doubt that the conductor contributes something, and that the contribution of one conductor is different from that of another. So, too, with the entrepreneur.

If one examines the situation more fully, however, one finds that, in fact, distinct embodiments of entrepreneurial activity do exist, or may be unmistakably discerned to have existed. The mark of the entrepreneur is shown, and always has appeared, in the organization of enterprises under conditions of economic freedom. Occasionally, economists have not been too clear in their handling of this element in production. For example, Marshall held that organization was an important part of capital, and that "it seems best sometimes to reckon [it] . . . as a distinct agent of production." [25] But clearly there is good reason to view the external and internal forms of operating arrangements, especially the latter, as choices of the entrepreneurial actors, not as determined by the supplies of capital, labor, or land. Sometimes the forms and even the procedures remain oddly constant despite appreciable increases in scope of activities. Thus, Professor Stuart W. Bruchey asserts that a fifteenth-century Italian merchant would have felt quite at home if he had dropped into the countinghouse of Robert Oliver of Baltimore, whose business life covered the years 1783–1810.[26] At other times patterns change rather rapidly, even among business institutions of similar size.[27]

Specific cases dot the histories of companies and the biographies of businessmen, offering the analyst almost unmanageable materials: for example, the well-known cases of Standard Oil's experiments with legal forms, U.S. Steel's endeavors to control the supply of its chief raw materials, or Ford's use of the assembly line. Other data, new but typical, have appeared in publications of the Center, of which several may be adduced here.

1. An analysis of the unsuccessful career of the Stanley Steamer automobile and the relation of the Stanley brothers to the events led a recent investigator to conclude that the failure of this motor vehicle in competition with those driven by the internal combustion engine was not "solely or even principally the result of [the latter's] inherent superiority as a form of motive power." The Stanley brothers were craftsmen and were not interested in production volume.[28] The author concludes that "in this case at least the relative success of the rival innovations depended as much upon the managerial abilities of the entrepreneurs reponsible as upon the technical merits of the alternative forms of power." [29]

2. An investigator looking at the rise of the large "first-

class" hotels prior to the Civil War finds that their appearance in the more important commercial centers was due to various forces and to various types of people. No simple formula of businessman's response to profit opportunities summarizes the facts. Instead, the inquirer finds that "the imaginative, bold hotel-keeper, the civic-minded merchant, the architect eager to experiment, the guest who dealt out both praise and adverse criticism — all these have had an important part in the development of the modern hotel." [30]

3. Professor John E. Sawyer of Yale contends that the course of economic development in this country would have differed in timing and probably in significant directions if entrepreneurs had not been susceptible to creative errors, if I may label what he describes as a perfectly logical development out of nineteenth-century American conditions.

Professor Sawyer starts with the two premises "that — leaving the sports aside — most entrepreneurs, like all other social actors, tend to act and react in terms of the social frame in which they are raised and in which they live; and, second, that the American scene [of the nineteenth century] *defined* the entrepreneurial norm in terms of aggressive and creative performance; that it tended to make ceaseless drive and innovation, not deviant behavior, but ideal performance of the [entrepreneurial] role." [31]

To these two basic contentions he adds a third which can be best reproduced in his own words:

. . . in the context suggested, and urged on by the pressures and momentum, even the illusions of the culture, past experience of growth and further real prospects gave rise to exaggerated anticipations of future growth that repeatedly induced entrepreneurs and investors to over-respond to existing market stimuli and in effect over-leap existing economic realities in the scale of their plans and in the scope and timing of investment decisions;

and that in the special circumstances of 19th century America their individual and collective over-estimations operated to accelerate the processes of growth and often, in varying measure, produced the results that, *ex post,* made "economic" their initial over-estimates.[32]

The *kinds* of effects in which I believe its presence may be seen vary widely:
— the *timing* of the building of basic facilities, such as transportation, in advance of demand;
— the *magnitude* both of the investment input and the resulting facility available;
— the premature introduction of economies of scale in earlier stages of manufacturing, etc.;
— the resulting lessening of bottleneck limitations in the succeeding phase of growth;
— the tendency to maximize the credit flow and make maximum use of credit available;
— the pressure upon technology — hastening adoption of the new and development of the better;
— the planning and building of organizations in terms of expansion potentialities;
— the quick response available to recovery from the bottom of a cycle (and even the policy of a Frick, investing in depression on faith in future growth);
— perhaps above all the endless daily decisions to buy a tool or make a plan or hire a man, in which the major premise of growth determined the course of action.[33]

To the extent that it worked in an economic sense — that an over-anticipation of prospects in fact paid off in either a private or social balance sheet, we find ourselves on the perilous edge of an "economics of euphoria" — a dizzy world in which if enough people make parallel errors of over-estimation, and their resulting investment decisions fall in reasonable approximation to the course of growth, they may collectively generate the conditions of realizing their original vision. It suggests, historically, a sort of self-fulfilling prophecy, in which the generalized belief in growth operated to shift the marginal efficiency of capital schedule to the right, and in which the multiple centers of initiative, acting in terms of exaggerated prospects of growth, pulled capital and labor from home and from the available reservoirs abroad, and so acted as to create the conditions on which their initial decisions were predicated.[34]

4. Mr. Charles Wilson of Jesus College, Cambridge, finds in William Lever a splendid exemplar of the concept of the entrepreneur which he favors and which was noted earlier: the possessor of "a sense of market opportunity combined with the capacity needed to exploit it."[35] Rarely has there been a career which was so largely determined by the decisions of the actor, and rarely one of which the consequences were more diverse.

To be sure, Lever as a youth found himself in a small soap works operated unprofitably by his father. However, there was no necessity of his adopting and pushing "every kind of advertising — mostly borrowed from North America"; it was his own choice to continue in existence, operating under their own names and often under the direction of their previous owners, the numerous competing plants that he bought out as he prospered, and thereby retained good will in a market where irrationality has always played a considerable part. It was this English-born and English-bred man who wrote at middle age, "I don't work at business only for the sake of money. I am not a lover of money as money and never have been. I work at business because business is life. It enables me to do things."

And in the end the "things" that he brought into existence embraced a model village in a country where they were unknown, a substantial monopoly of soap production in Great Britain, an international consortium in fats and oils, and new imperial relations of the British government with sources of oil-bearing natural products over a good part of the globe.

Statistical Evidence

A more general appraisal of the contribution of entrepreneurship is to be found in a comparison of inputs and outputs in the American economy over the period from 1869–78 to 1944–53, made recently by Professor Moses Abramovitz.[36] It appears that over these decades the input of labor services, including those of salaried management, and measured in man-hours, declined slightly, that the input per capita of capital increased something like threefold but that the national product per capita increased approximately fourfold.

In explaining this discrepancy Professor Abramovitz turns to "the gradual growth of applied knowledge which is, no doubt, the result of human activity, and not of that kind of activity involving costly choice which we think of as economic input." Some of this growth, apparently, is viewed as a derivative of general social change, as through broader education, but in first place appears "knowledge concerning the organization and technique of production," the use of resources, and the like, all of which are features of entrepreneurial character.[37]

Some part of the explanation might well run in terms of the changes (through time) of the entrepreneurial "stream" — to which attention will be given below, in Chapter IV — as well as to the more nebulous matter of the reaction of that "stream" upon society as a whole, that is, upon its mode of thinking, its standards of value, and the like.

Conclusion

In brief, a new era in economic theorizing seems to be dawning, without the fanfare that accompanied the advent of the institutionalists or the lesser breed of "technocrats." The way had been cleared by the decline, prior to World

War II, in the attractiveness under modern conditions of the profit-maximization thesis. With the coming of peace and the need of paying attention to underdeveloped countries, the replacement of the static type of theory with some form of dynamic concept — mock or truly dynamic — became pressing. Already theorists are moving to fill the gap, and, as they do so, they find it useful or essential to make a place for the entrepreneur or the institutions which he utilizes and directs.

The introduction of change through time, however, and particularly of the agent most productive of change, threatens to upset traditional theory in a far-reaching manner. When the tempo of the theory is altered from that of short-run "adjustment," the entrepreneur with his living enterprise, his "creative responses," his capacity to alter the course of economic development by idiosyncratic performances — these all enter the picture and must be taken care of by the theorists. It is possible that an analysis of entrepreneurial phenomena can make a contribution to the evolution of a new concatenation of theories — which would include, perhaps, some elements of Adam Smith, Alfred Marshall, and those in between, together with others directly related to the social milieu in which the economic process takes place. The elaboration of the latter relationships — what Professor Boulding characterized as the "larger" economics — seems to that eminent scholar a "most challenging" proposition.[38]

Chapter III·

THE ELEMENTS IN A POSITIVE VIEW: THE ENTREPRENEUR AND HIS ORGANIZATION

FOR A PROPER UNDERSTANDING of entrepreneurship, it is essential to keep in mind that it is a social phenomenon in several dimensions, if not in several senses.[1] One dimension relates the bearers of that function to the other human members of the groups that make up their particular enterprises, as well as to different persons more or less loosely connected with these institutions. Another relates entrepreneurial units to one another, to form a sort of constellation of entrepreneurship in which individual enterprises constitute the separate stars. And the third dimension relates the bearers of the entrepreneurial function to the economic and cultural milieus in which they chance to be operating, and this may involve relationships indirectly with cultural milieus of the past. Perhaps these three groupings may be thought of as a set of concentric circles, the second enclosing the first, and the third encompassing the prior two. Such a figure is all the more appropriate since the groupings are to an appreciable degree interconnecting, if not interacting, the first even directly with the third as well as with the second. I propose to discuss the first of these relationships in the current chapter.

Certain sources of possible misconception may well be considered at the start. For one thing, an effort to split an enterprise into the entrepreneur and his organization is recognized as bound to result in difficulties. If, as already proposed, an essential element in entrepreneurship is decision-making, and if that process be held to embrace all steps from the initiation of an idea to the implementation of its official reception, obviously the entrepreneurial function becomes diffused through various strata, as has been suggested above.[2] An innovation may have its origin in a suggestion-box or in a president's office. Also, decisions of sorts are made all down the line, even by the surly gateman who fails to pay proper respect to an unexpected director and gets the president into trouble with his board. And, insofar as the entrepreneurial function extends to the execution of decisions and the maintenance of the profit-oriented institution — and surely one cannot leave the entrepreneur in an ivory tower of merely conceiving the possibilities of innovations — that function becomes diffused through the various layers of the establishment. Mary Parker Follett, for example, studied business administration essentially as a form of government,[3] and probably this approach is sound. Accordingly, just as one should not survey the King or Cabinet without including Parliament, or the President without Congress (and perhaps other parts of the whole governmental structure), so one must, at least for some purposes, include the whole administrative business organization when speaking primarily of the top executives. It should also be recognized, however, that in routine matters hierarchies do exist in business institutions, and that, even in large corporations, there is an individual or a group above whom (or which) appeals cannot be made for change or reversal of decisions. For purposes of the current analysis, this individual or group may be taken as *the* entrepreneur, and an effort will be made to examine the relations of this individual or group with the rest of the social unit.[4] Such relations are important. The exertion of leadership toward determined goals, the taking of blame for failures en route, the absorption of pressures to favor one or another of the participants in the joint enterprise — these and other less critical elements are involved in the activities of the policy-clinching, policy-administering center of the organization relative to the remainder of the group.[5]

Second, the term "organization" also stands in need of clarification. One may conceive of sets of relationships involving the entrepreneur and his organization almost as varied (among different cases) and as complex as the structure of physical atoms. However, perhaps a series of concentric circles will again be enough to portray the typical situations. In the first surrounding circle would perhaps be the board of directors or the executive officers of any wholly-owned subsidiary concerns that existed. Farther out would be the suppliers of materials, the sellers of finished products, the officials of related labor unions, the leaders in the local charities, and the like. Somewhere at about this distance would also fall the various governmental units with which the enterprise has relations. Still farther may be the consumers of its products, and beyond them the general public that may have more or less precise opinions regarding the worthwhileness of the particular enterprise. Here any or all of these elements in the organization may come into the discussion, but chiefly attention will be devoted to the individuals concerned directly with the day-by-day operations of the unit.

Third, and perhaps most important, a limitation of the

area of survey must be proclaimed — and for two reasons: the phrase "entrepreneur and his organization" really covers the whole field of business administration, and there is as yet no history of business management in any country. Having had something to do with the 300,000 books on that subject, past and present, that now exist in the Harvard Business School Library, I am all the more disinclined to attempt a summary of the evolution of that management even in one country within a few pages of a single study.[6] It seems necessary here merely to relate certain groups of facts on which historians are pretty well agreed, to the phenomenon of entrepreneurship as viewed by social scientists. I shall then look only at the developments flowing from changes in financial control, at consequences of the increase in complexity of business units, and the evidences of a rising sense of public and of a social responsibility among business executives.

Role and Sanction in Entrepreneurship

It is enlightening to think of the relationships existing between the entrepreneur and the various elements of his organization in the terms provided by sociology.[7] The bearers of the entrepreneurial function are viewed as playing a role in the Lintonian sense; and the execution of the several aspects of the role is stimulated by positive and negative sanctions exercised by the various individuals and groups with which these role bearers have relationships.

Professor Leland Jenks elaborated a schema of this character with special relevance to entrepreneurship in *Change and the Entrepreneur*, which R. Richard Wohl, then a graduate student at Harvard, summarized in the following fashion:

Every sanction defines a status and a corresponding role. The sanction is aimed to regulate a pattern of social relationships. All types of social relationships are structures, and every sanction relates to a particular type of social structuring. It establishes and regulates certain types of expected behavior, and assesses the rewards and punishments that attach to them. It thus creates a typical organization of the motivational structure of individuals. A given individual occupying a position in the social system (status) is presumed to behave in certain fairly set ways in carrying out the functions that attach to his position (role); he suffers consequences (set by sanctions) in the form of changed attitudes and action on the part of those to whom he is bound by social relationships.[8]

And it may be noted that such structures, behavior, and the like apply to economic and instrumental as well as other social relationships. Here, as I see it, is where economics and business administration, sociology and social psychology converge — with a significant admixture of history. The quality of acquired and currently-flowing communication is also important.[9]

A phenomenon such as the preference for short-term commercial paper in the American banking system, the use of pauper children in the early English cotton mills, or the Burlington strike of 1888 can each be analyzed from nearly all the approaches just suggested. The primary questions become: under the existing conditions of technical knowledge, especially the knowledge which the actors in the specific case might reasonably be expected to possess, given the prevailing state of education, literature, and libraries, what economic advantages and disadvantages were believed by the actors to attach, and to have attached to the specific action, and what did the censors of the actors (that is, their fellow entrepreneurs, the political and religious leaders, and so on) think the right action to be — "right" in both the pragmatic and ethical senses? As the performance of an economy in the past can properly be assessed only on the basis of the natural resources and productive techniques known to have been available at that period, so a business practice or attitude of a given situation can fairly be appraised only on the basis of the body of knowledge and the cultural themes known to have existed at the time. A historian, more than an economist or sociologist, is disinclined to deal in absolutes. He is ever expectant of change. But the historian will place the specific event in the stream of changing social institutions and social thought.

Essential Features of Control

A major factor in determining the relations between an entrepreneur and his organization is the nature of the power that put him into his post and that holds him there. Of course, proprietorships and partnerships wherein the entrepreneurial function is linked to financial involvement are the basic and still the most numerous type of business unit here or abroad. They have appeared so commonly in industrially young economies, or in parts of economies where risks were considerable, that some writers (such as Professor Reinhard Bendix in his *Work and Authority*)[10] have given them the label of "entrepreneur" and used other terms, such as "managers" or "bureaucrats," to designate the executive heads of large enterprises.

Such units have ever served as fields of opportunity for the many entrepreneurial aspirants that seemingly develop — and have always developed — rather widely in Western societies. Recent inquiries have shown that not a few men move back and forth, into and out of their own enterprises, as fortune smiles and refuses to smile! Proprietorships and partnerships are also training grounds for men to become officers of large business institutions. I suspect that this is a more common phenomenon than is generally recognized. Apparently, through past decades, many top executives of large corporations have always been sons of businessmen;

and the latter were, I believe, the proprietors and partners of business units just mentioned. In other words, small businesses have served as steppingstones for the rise of families from farmer or mechanic or clerk to high business positions.

Enterprises of the independent sort have ever given opportunity to men who were restive under authority. The relations of such individuals to subordinates, work force, customers, et cetera, come closer to being authoritarian than anywhere else in business. Here was the home of the man who as a Colonial merchant did not hesitate to embark in privateering when opportunity offered, or, like Morgan in 1907, could take control of a national financial crisis, and — more recently — threatened to close down his plant rather than try to do business under conditions set by "that man Roosevelt"! Under any conditions, however, mortality is high among such units, and individually they do not survive long. Concrete evidence of the life experience of these enterprises in America is provided by the scarcity of records of goods-distributive houses, from village stores to city wholesalers. Few sets of such records survive in any library or other depository; and yet they have existed in this country by the hundreds of thousands.

A common development from the simple proprietorship is the creation of a family firm. The first step may be the addition of the phrase "and son" when the first new generation is taken into the enterprise. However, many family firms lack revealing names. Such firms have advantages and disadvantages from the entrepreneurial point of view. They sometimes command a loyalty from the active members of the family that adds to their economic strength. Sir Henry Clay reported that family concerns in the English textile trades came through the trials of the 1920's and 1930's better than the nonfamily enterprises of comparable size and type. When the mill was in danger of having to close its doors, all members of a family rallied to support the show. Moreover, there seem to have been circumstances of international trading or finance, where supervision from any single point was difficult, and where devotion to the common family venture may have taken its place. This was true of the Italian banking enterprises, the Rothschilds, the eighteenth-century merchants of London or the American colonies, even some of the twentieth-century international. margarine firms described by Mr. Charles Wilson.[11]

It appears that the family firm was most prevalent in France, less so in England, and probably still less in Germany. They are rare in the United States, and perhaps only those of the du Ponts and Fords attract broad attention. Professor David S. Landes indicates that anyhow the family counts for much in French industry and trade, and that, at least in some cases, procedures have been worked out informally within families whereby some of the weaknesses of family succession and family dominance are avoided. The family is sufficiently unified in aspirations so that the ablest, or at least the best available representative, of each successive generation is supported as effective head of the institution; and if there are disgruntled or spendthrift members of that generation, they are persuaded or dragooned into selling their stock to the new head of the show or at least to those who are willing to support the latter's hand. Thus, there is no loss of family control by reason of the sale of stock to strangers, while management is not allowed to deteriorate more than is unavoidable and still maintain the family traditions.

The weaknesses of family firms, enterpreneurially speaking, are the failure of talent to be regularly inherited on the male side, and the likelihood that sons of businessmen, especially successful businessmen, will prefer to pursue careers apart from business — in the professions or in the arts, perhaps. Biological and social forces are antagonistic to the family enterprise. Sometimes, to be sure, marriage helps out. The Whitin Machine Works seems to have prospered in the hands of sons-in-law,[12] and men in the same relation to du Ponts appear recently to have contributed much. But balancing such good fortunes is likely to be the drag on such institutions arising from the necessity of taking care of ineffective members of the family group or of getting members launched in the professions. And then there is always the economic problem that, in cases of distress or of the expansion that competition may make essential, the enterprise can be saved only by giving up financial control.

A successful argument might be presented on the basis that the family enterprise is genetically anterior to the single proprietorship. The former seems essentially a vehicle for the intrusion of an older and more basic social organization, the biological group, into the realm of economic action. In various parts of the world today, from the Near East to Korea, business activity is still severely handicapped by the demands of family obligations. In at least the common Western form of proprietorship, from the medieval itinerant peddler to the present-day corner druggist, the entrepreneur may be looked upon as having shaken free of a normal earlier attachment.

Sometimes, of course, the single proprietorship is extended by the formation of a partnership, while some family firms also take this legal form. But the partnership need not detain us long although it does give some opportunity for the acquisition of added talent. I once knew of a successful wool-selling enterprise in which a Jew and an Irishman were joined. The Jewish partner bought the stock, and the Irish one sold it! A partnership also gives some promise of greater effective longevity, even of continuity, than a single proprietorship if the surviving partner (or partners) take in new, younger folk.[13] And, third, there is surely some added power of sanction from within the enterprise. Economically advantageous or socially meritorious actions are likely to be applauded, and socially disapproved ones curbed. The single proprietorship is the better home for the willful tyrant or headstrong individualist — for the Napoleon or the Hitler.

The Coming of Professional Management

The owner-manager variety of entrepreneurship in its several forms, while increasing numerically, has lost economic dominance pretty well throughout the Western world in what Professor Boulding calls an "organizational" revolution. The facts about the separation of management and ownership, of the rise of salaried executives, even perhaps the mode of life in the large bureaucratic organization with which managers' management is particularly associated, are so well-known that they need not be recounted here.[14] Certain features especially significant for entrepreneurial development, however, need to be noted.

"Professional" management in the sense of effective control by executives with small stockholdings is not limited to large or very large corporations. It will be found in many medium-sized firms, particularly family enterprises that have been converted to "public" ones.

This form of management, at least in the United States, has shown a bias toward the attainment of professional qualities very broadly defined. With less direct involvement in financial results, the professional manager, like the medical man in his hospital, has had an incentive to seek the scientifically best, at least the most broadly approved, methods of operating his adopted establishment. And it may be added that inasmuch as the more narrowly defined professional entrepreneurship that is concerned with stock ownership has penetrated to the stratum of medium-sized enterprises, the more broadly defined professional entrepreneurship has tended also to spread over a considerable portion of the American business system. No change in the entrepreneurial role in America carries as much social significance as this spreading belief in the existence of good ways of carrying through business operations, and the belief that it is the duty of first-class business administrators to discover or learn and to apply such ways.

The rule of professional managers (in the technical sense) has expanded considerably in American industry, beginning with the banks and railroads before the Civil War. There has been some similar development in Germany, to a lesser extent in England, and still less in France. Perhaps it is no coincidence that the progress of an intellectually professional attitude has been registered in about the same proportions.

Surely conditions in the capital market constituted an important factor in the promotion of professional management. In this country the early banks, insurance companies, even cotton mills could be set going through the cooperative efforts of a few merchants or other men of means; but even there professionalism of a sort soon raised its head. The presidency of the commercial banks was usually an honorary position, sometimes carrying no salary at all; the board of directors as a whole or through a committee continued to pass upon investments; but otherwise the cashier came to be the chief executive officer. There is evidence too that as early as the 1840's the stock of such institutions had become widely distributed, and that the officers by no means held control through ownership of shares. The process was, if anything, more rapid in the case of the railroads. To be sure, there was a period in the 1870's and 1880's when certain lines were controlled by such persons as Forbes or

Vanderbilt or Gould through sizable financial investments in the stock of the roads; but these were distinctly the exceptions. The stock of the New England roads was rather quickly dispersed. Even Erastus Corning had little financial commitment in the New York Central or its constituent lines; and any number of roads seem to have taken on early what might be considered a natural American pattern — natural, that is, in the light of underlying economic and technical conditions. There were few men with large personal fortunes, and few of those who wanted to learn to operate so complicated an enterprise as a railroad or other sizable business unit. The trend toward professional management may have had play in the cases of British support of various American railroads, by stock purchase and by loans, when no effort was made, at least in most cases, to try to exercise control over the use of the money committed to the American projects. In many other underdeveloped countries, the British did send managers along with their capital.

The scarcity of capital operated indirectly also in the United States to bring professional management and a separation of ownership from management. Under "general entrepreneurs," of whom Professor Cochran has written,[15] professional managers were a logical development. Later, when investment bankers came to play a prominent role in the procurement of funds, first for railroads and later for the rapidly expanding industrial and commercial enterprises, their intervention was likely to produce the sort of separation of which we are speaking. This was especially true in the hectic 1890's and subsequent years, while the predisposition of the investment-banking houses, feeling themselves to some degree trustees on behalf of the investors whom they had persuaded to place their funds in specific companies, was to seek the best available manager, not to be content with the chance abilities of a large stockholder, let alone the scion of one. In the institutional system of American finance there was a built-in bias in favor of professional management. Perhaps here one should also include the bias supplied by the development of the stock exchange and that of the trend of savings within the country.

The scarcity of capital had affected other relationships in times past. For example, it was fairly common in our pre-Civil War period for the state governments to demand, and receive, the right to appoint government directors to the boards of directors of banks, railroads, or other concerns in which they had invested state funds. Later there were federal government directors on interstate railroads to which the federal government had made land grants. Again, in receiverships the courts of the country appointed trustees to conserve the assets of railroad enterprises; sometimes, in fact, such trustees or receivers operated the lines for years or even decades.

Out of the scarcity of capital also grew the system of affiliations between specific railroads and specific investment-banking houses which was a notable feature of the years between about 1880 and 1930 (and on which the federal Department of Justice largely based its unsuccessful suit against these bankers for violation of the Sherman Act). Pecuniary and other advantages quite as much as pressure or moral compunction kept the ties strong over considerable periods of time. Indeed, the role of the financial houses vis-à-vis all types of American business enterprises seemed so vigorous and promised at the time of his writing to last so long that Professor N. S. B. Gras erected this era as a distinct stage in the evolution of the American economy.

Increase in Complexity

Without stretching the meaning too far, one is probably justified in saying that complexity in business life has increased in the two directions of institutions and ideas. The nature of the former trend is indicated by two facts: a large metropolitan department store buys from something like 20,000 suppliers, while General Motors has 12,000 suppliers who in turn have scores or hundreds of their own. General Motors does its selling through more than 18,000 dealers.[16]

It is revealed also by a recollection of the simplicity of the business life of the American Colonial merchant, who actually did not differ greatly from merchants of that era all over the world. (Perhaps conditions in London were somewhat more complex.) The merchant of that time would probably have *complained* at the paucity of institutions on which he could lean for help, if he could have looked into a reliable crystal ball: banks, insurance companies, freight forwarders, labor exchanges, and scores of other ancillary and service units — of which more will be said in another connection.[17]

Similarly, for the larger enterprises, internal complexity has increased with growth. And this increased complexity of departments and divisions, sales manager and chief accountant and the like, has brought a new creative element into the organization. Typically in the smaller, earlier business unit, the few white-collar people in the office were folk who merely took orders as to what to do. But one does not hire a comptroller or a purchasing specialist or their compeers merely to give them directions; nor would men study to become such specialists if they were to have no initiative. This creativity is strengthened by the greater role of planning in modern business: budgeting, forecasting of sales, training of future executives, the formation of professional associations for accountants, personnel directors, and the like.

To the relatively new notions just mentioned may be added those of market research, inventory control, contingency reserves, incentive wages and whatnot, all of which from time to time come to count in executives' decisions, and all of which change sufficiently with continuing investigations so that the ideas must, as it were, be kept up-to-date. The "advanced management" sessions at schools of business are designed in large part to supply this refurbishing of concepts.

All these types of increased — and increasing — complexities have an important two-dimensional effect. The entrepreneurial function becomes much more that of a coordinator than it was earlier, even in medium-sized business enterprises, calling perhaps for the talents of an Eisenhower rather than those of a Napoleon. To be sure, this variety of entrepreneur would do well for his company if he encouraged communication from his subordinates, and if he on his side communicated downward his ideas as to objectives of the business unit. At all events, the increased and increasing complexity of business connections and operations has been a potent force in altering the role of the entrepreneur toward his organization.

Recognition of Public Responsibility

To a degree that is rather surprising on second thoughts, the social responsibilities of business are self-enforcing, that is, through imitation. The economy of any country probably would have progressed less rapidly, and along different paths, if business processes had been patentable: processes such as installment selling, the issuance of company manuals, assembly-line production, the introduction of new forms of depreciation allowances, and the like. And it is also surprising, even astonishing, how many improvements in business procedures are constantly being devised and imitated — and superseded! — inspired in part by the "instinct of contrivance" (which surely Veblen would not have credited to businessmen) and in part by the desire to gain a differential advantage or to meet competitors' prices. A good deal of the purely instrumental aspect of public responsibility, the acceptance of technical as well as technological change, is forced upon entrepreneurs.

Of somewhat similar character, but not quite, are certain new-blown relationships toward consumers. Beginning apparently with the sewing machine, and spreading with the spread of "consumer durables," producers and distributors have provided ever-improving service to purchasers. Again, the rule of *caveat emptor*, and the attitude of sellers deriving from that legalism, have been modified in practice by the concept that "the consumer is always right," by the institution of complaint bureaus in retail stores, by the grant of liberal return privileges, and the like. To some extent, to be sure, these measures have an instrumental quality, as first indicated: service on electric refrigerators and the rest is merely an imitative gesture, inspired by a desire to secure one's share of the market, while it is indeed somewhat more expensive for a retailer to stand up for his rights than to let the consumers sometimes make false claims. Businessmen have found that there is a financial restraint upon perfection. Still, the role of the entrepreneur in many lines of business has been modified over the decades. As he has become less arbitrary with his staff, so has he developed new attitudes towards consumers.

A development of the twentieth century in the public relations of the larger corporations, especially in the United States, has also affected the entrepreneurial role. I have in mind the so-called "full disclosure." Company reports in the United States, especially the annual type, have always been more revealing of company performance than similar documents of other lands. Perhaps our greater geographical distances which made chummy stockholder meetings relatively unthinkable were a factor. Perhaps in railroad matters, American managers had to keep in mind the European investor, actual or potential. In any case, financial revelation was not universal in the nineteenth century, nor persistently on the same level.

A step in a new direction was initiated by a public accountant of English origin, Mr. A. Lowes Dickinson of Price, Waterhouse and Company, at the time of the first reporting from the United States Steel Corporation. Influenced no doubt by the professional status of public accountants in England, Mr. Dickinson urged a generous disclosure of both physical and financial results of the corporation's first year of operations. Judge Elbert H. Gary agreed and carried the question to Mr. J. P. Morgan, who, having in mind his sponsorship of the sale of many million dollars' worth of securities, gave his approval. The example of the Steel Corporation has been widely, although gradually, followed. The New York Stock Exchange has given support to this same practice. Accordingly, more than ever before, American entrepreneurs manifest at least a modest sense of obligation to the public and to public authorities.

The larger area of "public relations" has shown a modicum of adjustment to the same ideas, and this too is a phenomenon of the twentieth century. However, the early version of such relations even in that century was that of attempting to explain, if not to excuse, public misfortunes such as train wrecks or violent strikes. Subsequently came an endeavor to create favorable publicity for companies and their doings. But some public-relations counselors, such as the important Mr. Edward L. Bernays, have tried to make the relationship of corporations to the public a "two-way street": if the companies wished to create a favorable attitude toward them on the part of the public, they should see to it that they had something to communicate that would be accorded a favorable reception.

The increasing regard which American corporations have

recently displayed toward the communities in which they exist, and the greater willingness of enterprises to accept governmental intervention of various sorts, in order to check inflation, to combat depressions, even to prevent monopoly, are also evidences of a greater degree of public responsibility on the part of American entrepreneurial actors.

Changes in Social Responsibilities

Social sanctions playing upon American entrepreneurship have been evident in various relationships over past decades. The general storekeeper was supposed by his customers to run a sort of social club around the well-known cracker barrel, at least in the winter time. From an early period the banker seems to have been under the virtual obligation to dress soberly, to attend church, and to be conservative in his opinions. As late as the 1920's, the sales representatives of Boston investment bankers were expected to wear vests through the hottest days in summer when calling upon clients.

More significant, of course, was the attitude toward employees taken by employing entrepreneurs, and sanctioned by the censors who were important for them: members of the communities in which they lived, their peers in industry or trade, the forceful members of Congress, leaders in the churches, and so on. To be sure, the history of personnel management, broadly interpreted, is yet to be written; what an employee expected to be required to deliver when he took a job from a factory owner or from a "gang-boss," what the employer or boss expected to be delivered, and how rules were changed from time to time by reason of pressures of one sort or another so that satisfactions were increased on one side or the other or on both.

From what we know at present, it seems as though the relations of employer and employee — if one may venture to average out all the employments in all the corners of the country — have come pretty nearly a full turn. At the start, the employees were members of the same communities as the employers, perhaps members of the same churches, or even distant relatives. The mores and protection of the community prevailed, the relations of one human being to other human beings. Today, employer-employee relations, while on a less personal basis, are no less important.

Human relations have followed various patterns in the past. On shipboard, for example, special relationships existed, and before people were long ashore the management of groups was often necessarily conceived in terms of discipline, perhaps as a "residue" from days of slavery, a "transfer" from military practices, or perhaps as an obvious necessity when workers — quite understandably — put their own convenience above coordination of group efforts. The career of William Austin was perhaps a bit extreme but not wholly atypical. At an early age he achieved the captaincy of a sailing vessel, but he was lured to solid ground and placed in charge of the Charlestown jail. From there he moved to head the operations of a New England cotton mill, and finally wound up as a manager of a southern plantation. No doubt the cotton-mill agent was usually a kindly person, perhaps fatherly, towards the individuals of his organization — at least, outside the mill — but he believed in the necessity of discipline within the establishment, discipline trimmed with fines, discharges, blacklisting, and the like.

In time another primary element in employee-employer relations arose, that of loyalty. In an era when business success was believed to hinge much on secret formulae or individual ways of handling materials — a belief that went back into handicraft days, at least as between guild members and the outside world — it was easy for employers to come to think that workmen ought not to move into the employ of competitors. But the notion spread into nonindustrial areas. Charles E. Perkins and his contemporaries were dismayed at the advent of railroad brotherhoods in considerable part because they saw a conflict in loyalties. A workman could not be loyal to his railroad *and* to his union. And this notion of worker-company attachment, if not allegiance, has persisted into modern decades, now converted into pecuniary or quasi-pecuniary terms. Contentment will reduce labor turnover; and so the costs of worker training, loyalty deriving from an appreciation of the purposes of the enterprise, the sense of sharing, will make for greater worker satisfactions and greater productivity.

Dr. Oscar W. Nestor showed in his doctoral thesis that before the twentieth century little was being done for employees in American industry, even in the fields of safety and sanitation. One Alfred Dolge, trying to introduce into this country some of the social insurance schemes that he had known in Germany, did not have much effect. Nor did other employers with modern beliefs succeed much better.[18]

We know that there was considerable subcontracting within producing establishments, especially in the metal trades, and we can guess that one reason for its elimination was the desire on the part of the heads of the enterprises to introduce uniformity of labor conditions, and perhaps to try to increase the sense of "belonging" mentioned above. We can also suspect that employers in the last decades of the nineteenth and the first of the twentieth centuries took from the nativist movement, which goes back at least to the Know-Nothing political activities of the 1840's, some notions about the immutability of the characters of the recently-arrived immigrants. The concept can well have been widely held that the "Wops," the "Hunks," the "blockheaded Swedes," and the like were incapable of intellectual and social improvement themselves, and their children and children's children likewise. Why try to make it possible for their offspring to become doctors or scientists or business executives?

In any case, it appears clear that the first real change in attitude came with World War I and the accompanying shortage of labor. Most of the schemes then devised, from personnel manuals to baseball teams, were abandoned in the postwar depression, but a new start was made in the 1920's, an effort to find out *What's on the Worker's Mind* (as Whiting Williams' book of the period was called), which in turn led to the Western Electric experiment and contemporary concepts.

The major alteration from the practices and ideas of the nineteenth century, no doubt in high measure imposed by changes in labor supply and the growth in strength of labor unions, and probably facilitated both by periods of prosperity and by the somewhat common cause of paid executives and paid employees, has been the development in entrepreneurs of a much greater sensitivity to the aspirations or demands of their human partners in enterprise. As a result of the new dispensation, entrepreneurship in America is in fact called upon to make rulings in social justice — the distribution of the national income — for which its authority seems merely to be the negative circumstance of inaction elsewhere in society.[19]

The quality of social decision to which I refer is highlighted by the data on cotton-mill earnings in New England over the 1825–1914 period, brought together laboriously by Professor Robert G. Layer.[20] The general picture is that production of fabrics per man per hour rose substantially and pretty steadily in the decades before 1860, but mill-workers' earnings increased little. The workers secured the benefit of the enhanced productivity, which was, of course, not due to proportionately increased exertions on their part, through the lowered cloth prices which they shared with other consumers, and perhaps in somewhat increased stability of employment which the lowered cotton-goods prices helped to assure them through improved competition for the consumer's dollar. On the other hand, earnings and productivity seem to have moved more closely together in the post-Civil War era, especially after 1880, although the basic data on productivity here must be admitted to be much less satisfactory than those for the pre-1860 decades. All one can say is that it *looks* as if the workers in the later period were awarded an important share of the increased productivity that came from technical advances of all sorts.[21]

Something of the same situation obtains relative to the yet more recent "productivity increases" of wages covered in various union-management agreements. Perhaps management in some or all of these cases has the blessing of federal government conciliators, and of course they yield largely because of union pressures. They may actually have the tacit endorsement of our present public censors and public opinion, but concretely they are placed in a position where they are saying in substance that the needs of the workers are greater than those of the consuming public, our export position, the stockholders, or the managers themselves!

To be sure, entrepreneurs have always had some share in the making of such decisions. The New England cotton-mill operators, for example, were participating in the years before 1860. It appears, however, that the "productivity" angle of the recent wage bargains is in large measure fictitious, at best perhaps a hoped-for incentive. There is the difference that, whereas competition among cotton mills prevented much of the gains due to enhanced productivity from sticking to the fingers of the mill owners, today there is less competition among wage-earner groups, and enhanced "productivity" wages do stick to the fingers of the beneficiaries. Presumably, this is all to the good. I am not arguing the merits; I am merely pointing out that management has become a vehicle or agency for the improvement of labor conditions in a degree not evident earlier.

The Nature of Roles and Decisions

Two general features of the relations of entrepreneurs to their organizations deserve special note: the influence of history, and the degree of flexibility. One impact of history upon the role and sanction system is evident in phraseology used by Jenks or Wohl.[22] "Status," "expected behavior," "bound by social relationship," and the like all imply existence and activity in the past, like the businessman's "standard practice" or the economist's "consumption habits." Past years or decades or even centuries have established a pattern of mutual expectations — actions, rewards, punishments — which constitutes a social structure; and social structures permit the entrepreneur to function, and allow production and distribution to proceed.

History is involved in another way as social patterns are worked out. As already suggested, decisions by entrepreneurs are reflections of the experiences which, over the past, have impinged upon the decision-maker or decision-making group.[23] Thus, the Quaker merchants who determined on a one-price system of retailing were summing up a specific religious development. Mr. Frank W. Abrams, who did much for the employees of the Standard Oil Company (New Jersey) during his administration as president of the company, is likewise reflecting the ideas and aspirations which from the Pilgrims down have helped to establish American cultural themes, and are now still molding them.[24] Therefore, it can be said that 1959 decisions are never made on the basis of 1959 data alone; the hand of history rests on each decision-maker, in part by reason of his direct relations with a given culture, and in part, at least, by reason of his connections with a specific system of entrepreneurial roles and sanctions. The entrepreneur is a social animal, not a machine to calculate the probabilities of profits.

If this role and sanction structure is historically based, it is also to some degree flexible. After all, it is man-made, except insofar as the limitations of man's basic nature and the world's limited resources play a part; and what man has put together, he can alter. The notion of "law," reasonably common in economics, is foreign to this approach.

Change and the potentiality of further change are implicit assumptions of the philosophers of business who observe and comment upon the current trends. Thus the thoughtful Charles C. Abbott, dean of the graduate school of business of the University of Virginia, recently laid out a program for businessmen:

> The administrator must seek to serve the people for whom he is responsible. If he is to accomplish things through people, if — in Lord Beveridge's phrase — he is to get "common men to do uncommon things," he must try to supply them with goals they are willing to accept. He must endeavor to furnish them with what they need to do their jobs — whether tools, policies, or attitudes. He must seek to remove their frustrations. He must seek to give them the satisfaction of accomplishment. He must search for ways by which they can advance and develop their potentialities.[25]

Professor Peter F. Drucker places even heavier burdens upon entrepreneurs of the current and future generations. "It is management's public responsibility," he writes, "to *make* whatever is genuinely in the public good *become* the enterprise's own self interest";[26] or, as Adolf A. Berle, Jr., interprets Professor Drucker, the corporation must solve "two combined enigmas, both political: that of achieving functional harmony between the corporation and society and that of achieving harmony between the corporate activities and prevailing ethical ideas."[27]

Mr. Berle himself sees a social "revolution" already well forward to fulfillment. Competition now operates, he believes, "within far narrower limits than classical economics contemplated." And the reason is clear, "at least to political scientists":

Few of the major segments in a community really want a regime of unlimited competition in the modern community — neither the great corporations, nor their labor, nor their supplier. Fundamentally, they all want, not a perpetual struggle, but a steady job — a job of producing goods at a roughly predictable cost under roughly predictable conditions, so that the goods may be sold in the market at a roughly predictable price.[28]

And Professor Thomas C. Cochran, a business historian turned philosopher, gives the most complete analysis:

The managerial ideology [of the earlier 1950's] so emphasized education, cooperation, and success through personal relations, and disapproved so strongly of egotistic individualism, ruthless dealings with competitors, and any quest for high profits dangerous to long-run security, that the managerial creed . . . [of the period] seemed to be in a transition stage toward a rationale for a political rather than an acquisitive culture, toward a doctrine in which the goal was to achieve a position that conferred power and prestige, rather than personal wealth.[29]

Cochran correctly deduced the consequences of such changes:

Once the *major* aim is transferred from extra profits for stockholders to the welfare of the organization, the critical step has been taken in the direction of a new social adjustment. Planning comes to be in terms of how the organization can best adjust to general social trends so as to insure survival over many years, how it can continually raise the compensation of its employees to sustain loyalty and morale.[30]

He observes a noteworthy parallelism in the goals of modern "managerial enterprise" and the modern welfare state; and he ventures the prediction that future historians looking back on the course of the movements of these two trends in the first half of the twentieth century may find the change as important as the end of feudalism, the rise of world trade, or the beginnings of industrialism.

Conclusion

The relationships of the entrepreneur to his organization may advantageously be construed in terms of role structure. To do so confers at least two major gains. For one thing, the technical, economic, ideational, or other elements concerned in the "initiation, maintenance, and aggrandizement" of profit-oriented enterprises, which constitute an area of primary interest to the economist, can be reduced to the same denomination, as it were. The factors of economic growth — discovery of mineral resources, investment of capital, and social approval of money-making — are conveniently located in one and the same model. Again, there is a merging of "micro-" and "macro-economics." The ideas and conditions that characterize the whole society are seen to penetrate and affect the individual enterpriser. And, perhaps as an extra dividend, the forces important in both society and a single plant are notable as heavily freighted with history. An understanding of the economic system, at least in its realistic, evolving character, and through the creative responses of its chief Western actor, the entrepreneur, must be interdisciplinary, involving both social science *and* history.

Chapter IV·

THE ELEMENTS IN A POSITIVE VIEW: THE ENTREPRENEURIAL STREAM

MATURE ENTREPRENEURSHIP is likely to conduce to an economico-social situation which affects more than the "initiation, maintenance, and aggrandizement" of individual business enterprises. And the situation is not readily subordinated to a consideration of entrepreneurial actors responding individually to the social milieu — men, institutions, and ideas — in which they chance to be located, a subject that will concern us in the succeeding chapter. What I have in mind here is, primarily, the interaction of entrepreneurial units.

Perhaps a simile will help to convey my meaning. A composer or a baseball player might possess exceptional talent, but his contribution to the entertainment of the nation would remain rather minor if his performances were restricted, respectively, to his family parlor or his own sand-lot. Music as a social phenomenon nowadays means, when viewed realistically, everything from symphony orchestras to arrangers of FM broadcasts, and from publishers of musical scores to manufacturers of disc recording apparatus. And correspondingly baseball means all sorts of supporting and fulfilling elements: producers of equipment, talent scouts, architects of baseball parks, schools for umpires, and what-not. So, likewise, with entrepreneurship.

I have chosen to call the entrepreneurial concatenation of this sort a "stream." I have done so to emphasize the circumstance that, predominantly, the actors in the various actions are endeavoring to produce changes in the pre-existing situation. We are concerned with individuals caught up in a flow, not men performing repetitive actions in a static system. We want to learn, as it were, how the whole fraternity of log-riders manages to perform in a manner more productive than if each rode alone, relying solely on his hands and his native instincts.

The Elements of the Entrepreneurial Stream

Of primary importance for the proper functioning of an entrepreneurial flow is a beneficent climate of social opinion, a changing climate, to be sure, but one that does not discourage the flotation of new enterprises, especially enterprises that can reasonably anticipate an expanding desire for their goods or services, and a climate that still attracts talent into the area. Desirable also, of course, is relative freedom from government intervention in the form of favoritism, government monopolies, and the like, even freedom from major monopolistic conditions within the private sector.

For purposes of exposition, it is convenient to conceive of business institutions as forming a hierarchy based on function. Colin Clark publicized the threefold division of primary, secondary, and tertiary; that is, extractive, manufacturing, and service industries. This breakdown may be useful for some purposes but not particularly for ours. Utilizing more fully a functional analysis, one can make the divisions of primary productive, ancillary, and service industries. In the first category would be lumped those in-

77

dustries that are usually labeled extractive, manufacturing, and construction. In the second would be mainly the purveyors of equipment, providers of information, disposers of waste products, and so on, for the first. And in the third would fall transportation, marketing, financing, and advice. (For completeness of coverage, one would have to make a place for establishments that serve consumers at the latter's instance: automobile repair shops, cobblers, and the like; but they are negligible for our present purposes.) For other ends, other schema may be preferable. For our analysis, it appears best to conceive the extractive, the consumer-goods manufacturing, and the construction industries as the main stem, and the other industries and professions as ancillary or secondary to them. In turn, of course, a railroad company, a department store, or a management counselor has a network of relationships: suppliers, advisors, et cetera.

Beyond business enterprises, one must take account of affiliated institutions that not only increase the complexity of entrepreneurial relationships but also make a contribution to entrepreneurial performance; for example, trade associations, schools of business, libraries, even governments in their promotive activities. Insofar as these associations, schools, and so forth, provide avenues of communication, means of joint public relations, or the like, they are tantamount, logically, to service institutions.

As a contrast to the stream or system that I have in mind, one need merely look at the American Colonial merchant-manufacturer (for example, the Browns of Providence) from the vantage point of the sophisticated present. We find that they had to assemble their raw materials and equipment themselves from farmers and local handicraftsmen; they did their own banking, carried their own insurance, often provided their own transportation facilities; they had to rig up their own private network of correspondents to gather news of markets and prices; and they had to get along without libraries or schools for the training of either staff or successors. And if there were two, three, or a half-dozen manufacturers, or two, three, or a dozen merchants, they provided little more than duplicate units of self-sustaining operations; there was no system of *other-supporting* relationships, no creatively related hierarchy of business institutions.

In a modest degree, it may also be useful in the ensuing analysis to have in mind the sort of breakdown by qualities which Professor Danhof suggested some years ago and to which further reference will be made: innovators, imitators, Fabians, and drones.[1] I would be inclined to use a somewhat broader basis for classification than that which Professor Danhof employed, that is, readiness to accept new procedures and new lines of production. However, the notion of variant grades or qualities of entrepreneurial capacities is the important feature.

The Contributions from Structure

While an appraisal of the entrepreneurial stream could proceed on several bases, its relationship to long-run economics, especially to economic growth, seems most important. Here one may subdivide the evidence into two types; that concerned primarily with entrepreneurial structure, and that concerned especially with the flow of information.

In the first category, the play of entrepreneurial initiative may first be noted. With young men acquiring as they mature the conditioning of a permissive, even encouraging, culture, there will always be entrepreneurs waiting to take advantage of new opportunities, from the largely imitative effort of starting a new drugstore in a burgeoning suburban center to the setting up of a specialized counseling firm for hotel management. The lure of accomplishment or of the dollar is by no means wholly in the direction of higher profits of established enterprises; it also stimulates the invention of new links in the entrepreneurial network. (The projector of supermarkets kept trying even though his idea caught hold slowly.) The evolution of the economy does not have to await a decision by the central planning soviet. Also the new producing or ancillary institutions will probably come under the guiding hand of *young* men, operating their own small or medium-sized enterprises and eager to make their mark.

Economic growth is promoted also by the organic character of the entrepreneurial institution — that is, that the latter has some similarities to a "tree," as Alfred Marshall remarked, and not to a machine or an algebraic formula. A recognized quality of chemical manufacturing establishments is their bias toward expansion. At the end of the processes necessary for the production of item A, there are waste elements. By adding a little in the way of new raw materials, and carrying out a few further processes, item B can be produced; but there still are waste elements that can be used up by adding, and so on and so forth. In other manufacturing activities, the steps in change may take the form of developing new, and sometimes unanticipated, products like the famous Scotch tape or the Polaroid camera. An unusually interesting case was that of the Lever soap people when they set up a subsidiary in Africa to supply the English establishments with groundnuts. After a few years the subsidiary had elaborated a life of its own: plantations, steamships, import trading into Africa, and the like. And our large corporations manifest similar characteristics. When Frigidaire makes electric stoves, Hotpoint makes refrigerators, et cetera.

Another way in which economic growth is promoted through entrepreneurial action is in the propulsion of a form of multiplier. For example, a shoe manufacturer decides that, instead of tying together pairs of shoes and throwing them into gunny sacks, he will put each pair into a cardboard box. His innovation pleases retailers and customers; he needs more boxes than can be turned out by the old processes; new machinery is devised, perhaps new machines to make the new machinery; possibly a new trade magazine to serve the makers of shoeboxes, or the makers of shoebox-making machinery; and so on. Or, to take another example: the growth of a railroad system promotes a whole circle of chain reactions running off in a number of directions: production of rails, development of special equipment to roll the rails, development of special equipment to test the state of rails that have been a considerable time in use; production of ties, or special track- and tie-laying apparatus, or special tars for variant soils; railroad magazines; compilations like Poor's *Manual of Railroad Securities;* and so on.

And, if entrepreneurship supplies a device for the seizing of opportunities, it also furnishes a mattress on which unwise adventurers may fall. In a way of speaking, enterprises hardly ever die completely! Or, to put it another way, "new" enterprises are hardly ever wholly new! When a hotel changes hands, there may be nothing novel under the new management but a new face in the back office and silverware with new initials. When a cotton mill is sold, it may appear as a statistical unit in a reporting of new establishments, but there may be the same machinery, same employees, same bankers, and same selling connections. Entrepreneurship provides a built-in conservation of trained capacities, sunk capital, and implemented business relationships.

This sort of exfoliation seems more than the economist's "division of labor" or his "external economies." The significance is perhaps best grasped by contrasting a primitive entrepreneurial economy, where each tub stands on its own bottom, with a mature entrepreneurial one with a structure of mutually supporting institutions, in addition to those that compete directly and indirectly. Possibly the significance may also be grasped by contrasting the concept of strata of mutually supporting business institutions with the arena or pit of cutthroat contention, which is often the picture conveyed by nonbusiness observers as valid for all the business world as, of course, it is for some segments at some times.

There is an interaction between institutions which seems to me circular or cumulative in character. Take the case of a management advisory unit. Some enterprising person has the courage, probably based on his particular personal experience, to set himself up as a counselor on marketing or labor relations, perhaps on management problems of all descriptions. He secures some clients who prosper as a result of his advice and, in consequence, they tell their friends. To supplement his talents the expert brings in new men. They give even better advice to clients, who turn out more or better goods thereby and tell more friends, and so on. The same may well be true of any ancillary institution: for example, an advertising agency, a credit-reporting enterprise, or an industrial research bureau.[2]

Quite similar are the relationships that can come to exist between business units and educational or information-purveying institutions: schools of business, business-reference libraries, publishers of business journals and business books. It seems worthwhile to separate this fourth element from the third because of the nature of the data which are interchanged. In an adequate degree, the difference is between business units being aided to do better what they had been trying to do before, and their being urged to do things because they *ought* to do them, or to do things in new ways because this is how these things *ought* to be done.

Here again, there is circular action. An instructor from

a school discovers a novel practice or attitude in a given concern and he writes up the situation, or persuades the businessman to do so, for a business periodical. Other businessmen contribute ideas, their friends on the business-school faculties modify the notions, and gradually an improved practice becomes established and instruction at the business schools becomes improved, so that *future* practitioners of business will learn one more "right" way to perform.

A similar circular action could be elaborated (a) between business executives and their trade associations and (b) between company specialists — controllers, time and motion engineers, and so on — and their professional organizations. The latter type may have the greater long-run influences, since the impact is upon individuals at least one remove from the pressure of financial return.

Two features of the foregoing circular or cumulative interactions deserve special note. One is that these interactions are for the most part "built-in." They are not the sort, like technological innovation or courtesy to consumers, that take their initiation from the free-will decisions of individual businessmen. The interactions mentioned above are in the nature of propensities internal to the system, the type of situation analogous to that which Adam Smith had in mind when he wrote about an "invisible hand."

Second, these interactions seem to constitute relationships in which business is enabled to "lift itself by its own bootstraps," as it were, almost to create something out of nothing! Actually, of course, they are merely instances, like so many in science and art, of the creativity of the human mind.

This aspect of the matter seems to me theoretically very important. If these concepts are valid, there is here a variable acting through time which is not encompassed in the economist's "productive factors" as usually elaborated. It is something that the evolution of the entrepreneurial system brings incidentally into existence, a sort of Archimedean screw spontaneously devised.

I venture to think that Professor Allyn A. Young had something like these phenomena in mind when, writing many years ago in one of his best essays which is, in fact, concerned with economic growth, he said:

The mechanism of increasing returns is not to be discerned adequately by observing the effects of variations in the size of an individual firm or *of a particular industry* [italics mine], for the progressive division and specialization of industries is an essential part of the process by which increasing returns are realized. What is required is that industrial operations be seen as an interrelated whole . . . The division of labour depends upon the extent of the market, but the extent of the market also depends upon the division of labour. In this circumstance lies the possibility of economic progress, apart from the progress which comes as a result of the new knowledge . . .[3]

If Professor Young did not indeed have auxiliary business institutions in mind, his concept does seem to fit the case. Advertising agencies, personnel advisors, machine builders, producers of office equipment, and the rest may be regarded as forming "specialized" industries. They do represent the investment of considerable capital, even when there is little to show in the way of physical assets, and in the aggregate they do provide a considerable market for the products of the primary industries. I would merely add to Professor Young's analysis that, when the "progressive division and specialization" of industries are viewed from the higher level of social action and when these developments are conceived — and properly conceived — as normal elements in a mature entrepreneurial system, these developments will be seen to be built into the system. One can expect such exfoliation in business structure just as one can anticipate exfoliation in botanical specimens. Such an evolution is natural to an entrepreneurial system; and this potentiality is one important element which differentiates such a system from a governmental one. Birth in governmental bodies is a difficult and slow process.

Finally, and especially significant for our particular purposes, it may be noted that the evolution of the "stream" (or perhaps system of interrelated flows) outlined above has altered somewhat, and undoubtedly complicated, the role structure of entrepreneurial actors. Now such actors cannot concentrate their attention upon their own staffs and their own enterprises. They must take proper advantage of, but not be misled by, counseling "experts": machine builders, bankers, comptrollers' institutes, college professors. And insofar as they do seek and accept aid from outside specialists, particularly from outside advisors, they are — as suggested above — putting aside the role of Napoleons vis-à-vis the members of their organizations.

The Gain from Communication

A second feature of interunit interaction is the communication apparatus among entrepreneurial units, a feature that has also played an important part in the promotion of economic growth in Western economies, especially in the United States. This is not the place to attempt to frame a history of economico-business literature, even for the United States alone, where the output has been largest, or of the institutions which have served as channels for the dissemination of business thought.[4]

Briefly, it can be reported that in the experience of the United States there have been three distinguishable eras since the country gained its political independence. Over the first fifty or seventy-five years there was precious little business literature of any sort issuing from the country's presses: a few manuals on bookkeeping, often reprintings of

English texts; a few vade mecums on commercial law; and Niles' *Weekly Register* which, for the most part, informed the businessman merely about what was going on in Washington. Of institutions there were only the coffeehouses, a few mercantile reading rooms, and the stock exchanges in various cities.

If we disregard the growth of organs purveying business "intelligence," such as the prices-currents, the *Journal of Commerce*, and similar newspapers, we find in the next period (from about 1825 to 1885) mostly the rise of industry literature. *Hunt's Merchants' Magazine, The Bankers' Magazine*, and the *Railroad Gazette* were just about what their names betokened. So also were the *Iron Age*, the *Textile World*, and the like, which were launched by publishing entrepreneurs in the years just before or the decades after the Civil War. This was an era when knowledge was, in a sense, partitioned off by industry. To be sure, these periodicals indulged in few interpretive articles about their particular industries. At best they were *fachmässig* — professional, in a way of speaking, concerned with technological changes, new products, alterations in the tariff, new establishments, and not much else. Such monographic literature as appeared was also industry-bound, if I may use the expression, chiefly books on materials and processes in industry.[5] There were, moreover, few institutions to facilitate communication: young trade associations, local chambers of commerce in the older cities, subscription and a few public libraries (although I fear that these institutions paid little attention to the "professional" needs of businessmen), and, toward the very end of this period, the social science associations. Accordingly, such progress as occurred in management, and such progress of this type as was reported, could not very easily move from one segment of business to another.

It is the last fifty years that have been productive in the improvement of media of communication within business. The evolution should perhaps be recognized to have begun in the 1880's or thereabouts, when certain speculative thinkers, American and English, and engineers in particular, began to grasp the notion that there were uniformities in business, maybe "laws" of a sort. "Natural law" was then a dominant element in at least American idea patterns,[6] and its influence may have provided ready acceptance of the notion stemming largely from engineering circles, even if the engineers were not directly affected by it. Curiously enough, the Industrial Revolution in England had not provoked ideas about the uniformities of business. The country seems to have maintained the mercantile, if not the artisan, point of view, the basis of success being the learning of a certain skill or the tricks of a certain branch of trading. An English author has asserted that, even in the primary field of accounting, the mercantile form of double-entry bookkeeping was not converted to industrial purposes until the closing decades of the nineteenth century. In cost accounting, the French appear to have made starts in the earlier part of that century, before the British, although they too did not carry the study far.

At all events, general business periodicals such as *System* and functional ones such as *Industrial Management* or *Marketing* arose, while books took on similar objectives, thereby expanding the horizons of businessmen. A wholesaler in leather need no longer think his vocation to be primarily confined to the recognition of differences among skins of different origins and divergent treatment; he had common ground with the wholesalers of paper or textiles or other commodities. So also with the accountants and the purchasers, those responsible for advertising or the forecasting of business conditions. There was opportunity for what more recently has come in the social sciences to be labeled "cross-fertilization."

In this period came also the institutions which, better than those which had preceded them, could serve as vehicles for the cross-industrial transmission of thought. There were the professional associations, and there were the schools of business. Probably one should add the large corporation, since here were, in daily communication, people trained in marketing, production, accountancy, and the rest; and, with the tendency of the large modern corporation to overleap industrial lines, there was less likelihood of limitations arising out of industrial conditions, supposedly peculiar industrial circumstances. However, perhaps the professional associations and the schools of business were the most influential instruments for the dispersion of knowledge.

Because no one had cast business operations into terms of functions, the earliest professional bodies were connected with activities ancillary to the main lines of primary producers: for example, engineering and banking. Even in the accounting field the first group to organize was that of the public-accounting practitioners. But in the twentieth century all sorts of functional experts have coalesced into such professional associations: purchasing, advertising, credit analyzing, controlling. These institutions have generally possessed two characteristics: they have been compounded of local units which, in addition to the national body, have held meetings for the reading of papers and discussion; and usually the national organization has published proceedings of meetings, a regular periodical, or both, while sometimes a large local unit has distributed material presented before its members. Inevitably industrial or local provincialisms have been broken down, and a more or less abstract "business-ism" or business-administrational point of view has been promoted.

The schools of business have contributed to the same result, although, of course, in a different way. Their graduates have carried such a point of view out into business, proclaimed it in their own activities, and — as another type of built-in, circular action — have tended to look with favor upon other graduates of the same sort of school coming into business with similar prepossessions as to the nature of business operations. Again, the research and writing of professors and doctoral candidates of these schools have extended the influence of this approach to business administration. Indeed, one of the early creative thinkers in this field, Arch W. Shaw, was a businessman who came to Harvard in 1910 to see what Harvard's new school of business was all about, and stayed to assist Dean Gay and to write on the functional analysis of business procedures. And periodicals such as the *Harvard Business Review* and the business research studies from almost every school of business have universally contributed to the same end. Finally, the professors in such schools have been called by "practicing" businessmen to give advice upon specific business problems. Here, through direct contacts, the academic approach of generalizing about all branches and operations of business could have immediate consequences upon the thinking of business managers and their staffs.

Third, but not unimportant in their own right, have been the publishing houses. The contribution of some such institutions has been implied in the references to prices-currents, commercial newspapers, and trade journals. Beyond the establishments that initiated and issued such periodicals I have in mind the publishers of business monographs: McGraw-Hill, Ronald Press, and the like. These houses, which would analytically fall into the category of "service" institutions in the classification proposed above, have actually been creative in this "service." They have sought out possible authors; they have proposed and produced new varieties of books; and they have tried to sell their business books as widely as possible among businessmen. Of course they did, but obviously here again has been a "built-in" promotion of economic progress. What was good business for these publishers was socially advantageous — at least insofar as they did not oversell their clients(!) and insofar as their books proved to carry sound counsel to businessmen.

If one adds the growing volume of government publications useful to business practitioners, the large body of financial "services," the specialized organs such as Dun & Bradstreet reports or the *Official Airline Guide,* and the rest, it becomes apparent that modern entrepreneurship, at least in a mature economy such as the United States, is almost literally floating on a stream of literature! One sometimes wonders how the top executives in America find time to do anything but read!!

At all events, the growth of an entrepreneurial system in a country may lead to the evolution of a business literature of manifold elements. The latter development will, in turn, exert a constructive power, abetted by the entrepreneurial ambitions of periodical and book publishers in the field, and by the professional associations that transmit information about such literature or information from it.

A further process by which this flow of information may have significant impact is through the "leveling-up" in the quality of business units. If, to employ the Danhof terminology, more of drone character can be converted into Fabian, more Fabian into imitative, and so on, the general average of productivity would be raised, and output per entrepreneur or per employee man-hour increased.

90

Finally, and as a sort of footnote, I should add that the evolution of business literature has brought a considerable change in the entrepreneurial role, at least in mature entrepreneurial societies. Professor Danhof says that one class of early American agricultural enterprisers was derided as "book farmers." Probably early railroad operators or early industrialists would have been similarly held up to scorn if they had utilized data out of printed sources. Surely the American entrepreneurs throughout the nineteenth century wished to be known as practical men. In the railroad field, for which alone we have any substantial survey, Professor Cochran found little evidence that his "railroad leaders" of the 1845–1890 period utilized the professional literature of their day, even the *American Railroad Journal*.[7]

Today a real entrepreneurial problem is the control and proper utilization of the ever-swelling flood of business information of all types, from changes in international competition to possible uses of electronic computers. The role of the businessman is coming dangerously close to that of an academic scholar, except that the former still "has to meet a payroll"!

Competition and Monopoly

Not all relationships among entrepreneurial units are socially advantageous, of course, even when they may hold advantages of greater or less duration for the enterprises involved. Almost all of the actions taken have at least a partial motivation in the general desire among business units, as indeed among human beings, to control the environment with which they must interact.[8] Almost all of the leaders in business units also make manifest the interpretation of their social role made by the then-existent group of entrepreneurs in the particular region or country. Some types of action have only minor effects upon the production stream, though they may be fairly widespread. In the early days of industrialization in England and the United States, for example, employers in various segments of industry proclaimed the enticing of skilled workers from one another to be one of the cardinal sins. We have no evidence about the extent to which the employers lived up to their self-inspired ordinance; but the formulation of the concept is interesting as one of the earliest spontaneous structurings of the entrepreneurial role among industrial leaders. Of late years, at least in the United States, there appears to have been no such condemnation of enticement relative to any type of employee from engineer or atomic physicist to company president.

Another variety of self-imposed rule among entrepreneurs of nearly all countries is that one may speak enthusiastically, if not ecstatically, about one's own products, but should not denigrate or belittle the products of one's competitors. It is not good form even to attempt to lure purchasers from possible outlays that are only indirectly competitive: for example, "Reach for a Lucky instead of a sweet." A recent effort by the manufacturer of a cigarette without a filter-tip to combat all varieties with the latter equipment with the slogan, "Smoke for real," did not last long. At all events, advertising has always and universally — or almost so — been single-directional, if I may use the term: it has spoken well of Antony, not ill of Caesar.

A third matter is perhaps, strictly speaking, an internal policy — internal to the individual enterprise — but it is a policy adopted largely with other, possibly competitive, enterprises in mind. I refer to the efforts of corporations over recent decades to keep executives from leaving their doors by the grant of pensions or stock-purchases contingent upon the officers remaining with the company. Often such rights are forfeited by withdrawal of the executive on his own initiative. To be sure, devices of this sort may be looked upon as mere substitutes for the family or blood ties that once helped to keep an executive staff together; but, insofar as they immobilize talent and prevent it from moving to a situation where it would be economically more productive, as might be indicated by the current salary and not be mirrored in the accumulated benefits, the practice is socially disadvantageous. Perhaps, with the attraction of much young talent into the field of business and with the leveling-up of the quality of instruction in the numerous schools of business, it is not of much real social consequence that interunit executive mobility has been cut back over recent decades. The anchoring of executives to specific enterprises, to be sure, does have effects upon the phrasing of the entrepreneurial role. The professional manager, no less than the erstwhile family executive, becomes a one-enterprise man. (And perhaps entrepreneurial monogamy is good.)

Actions of a different sort have to do with the endeavors of entrepreneurs to secure preferred positions in their industries, perhaps partially or fully monopolistic places. Of course, it would be inappropriate here even to attempt to suggest all the types and varieties of efforts that are related more or less closely to such activities: exclusive rights to specific lines of trade or manufacture, privileges as "purveyors to His Majesty," patent rights, monopolistic and oligopolistic situations, and the rest. A library of books has been written on the different aspects of the subject. A few comments will have to suffice.

One important element is the almost universal endeavor of entrepreneurs to acquire a quasi-monopolistic, if only temporarily quasi-monopolistic, position. Businessmen are not unique in this characteristic, of course. When Dame Myra Hess with her piano or Cary Grant with merely his mobile face strives for artistic excellence, they are in reality trying to secure such a quasi-monopolistic position. They desire to be preferred — and perhaps secure larger compensation — when, respectively, a pianist or an adult male motion-picture actor is demanded. The same is true of Emerson's imaginary entrepreneur who made the "better mouse-trap," the Carrier Corporation when it brings out improved air-conditioning apparatus, or the Narragansett Brewing Company when it begins to sell its beer in "king-sized" bottles. Innovations are often introduced in efforts to secure a differential — that is, a temporarily quasi-monopolistic — position and, as Mr. Knauth has said, "Innovation is nearly constant in business." Since innovations, especially if they are imitated, contribute to economic development, it seems to follow that the striving for monopoly is socially advantageous.

Such activity is one facet of entrepreneurship's effort to control its environment. Perhaps one could even go so far as to say that there are two varieties of response by entrepreneurs to the uncertainties imposed by increasing competition; one is to gain ascendancy (that is, control) over one's competitors, and the other is to let them live and arrange for a sharing of the market. Vigorous entrepreneurship is like the man who, confronted with disease, says in substance, "They can't do this to me," while the weak type may be compared with the man, similarly attacked, who calls in nurses and doctors and medicines and tries to lean on others in his illness. In the experience of American business, entrepreneurs have sought monopoly at many times; in the spermaceti-candle manufacture of Colonial days, in the salt mining of western Virginia, in getting the best (and first) railroad line into Chicago. Even in the "combination movement" of the late nineteenth and early twentieth centuries, an effort to get into control of supply rather than to divide the market seems to have been dominant. Industrial pools or cartels represent the alternative form, sometimes carried, it seems, to the form that the most disadvantageously located and the least efficient unit of the industry is allowed to make a profit.

If endeavor for differential, quasi-, or fully monopolistic position be regarded as a normal element in the phrasing of the entrepreneurial role in a fluid economy, it does not follow that free and unlimited exercise of this effort will be socially desirable. Only in the most primitive societies is the sex instinct not curbed by law or custom or both, even though that instinct is rather useful for the continuance of the unit. In the United States it took some time to develop a philosophy and a technique of control over business. As Dr. Lee Benson has pointed out, there were precious few persons, even as late as the 1880's, who pretended themselves or could be looked upon by others as possessing expert knowledge of the "railroad question" of those decades.[9] So also the Sherman Act was a crude instrument for the settlement of the "trust problem." Not unnaturally in the circumstances, businessmen reacted in a rebellious manner.

I believe it to have been a sound development of the last few decades that leading businessmen, all who really count in the monopoly question, have come to accept limitation upon monopolistic conditions as a permanent and socially advantageous phase of governmental activity. They resist extensions of the government's concepts — for example, that mere bigness is evil — but they have come a long way since 1890. Acquiescing in governmental "interference" has become a normal element in the role of the American entrepreneur.

Conclusion

Appreciation of the significance of the entrepreneurial stream, especially the potentialities of creative action within it, seems essential for an understanding of entrepreneurship viewed as a changing phenomenon. The entrepreneur cannot be studied merely within his own enterprise, nor can the social meaning of entrepreneurship as a whole be appraised properly if inquiry is similarly restricted.

To historians and economists, the notion of such a stream offers a variant element in helping to explain economic change. The "structure of the economy" may be viewed, not as such-and-such industries of such-and-such magnitudes, or as equivalent bodies of matter that mysteriously do move, but as a fecundly built, interacting complex of largely self-serving, profit-oriented business institutions, with service attachments not necessarily self-seeking. And this complex, which is, of course, always a changing one, seems to have importance for the explanation of economic growth. The degree of its evolution in various countries may help to make evident the basis for differences in national productivity.

Chapter V·

THE ELEMENTS IN A POSITIVE VIEW: THE SOCIAL CONDITIONING OF ENTREPRENEURSHIP

THE ACTIVITIES of the individual entrepreneurial unit have a separateness, a life of their own, to a far greater extent than could be exposed in the foregoing discussion (Chapter III). These activities constitute the whole area of business administration, about which whole libraries of books and magazines containing discussions of accountancy and bank management, advertising, public relations, and a thousand other themes have been assembled. Yet into these operations, and the changes in their character, forces from outside the field of business seemed to penetrate, and quite naturally, since business is a social phenomenon and could hardly fail to be affected by the society in which it thrives.

Similarly, the concatenation of entrepreneurial units, moving through time and changes, was seen (Chapter IV) to have an instrumental character of its own, indeed to suggest that the whole is greater than the sum of its parts. Yet here too the analysis could not be completed without paying attention to influences from the whole societies, influences that modified the forces or altered the direction of these superunit interrelations.

There is good reason, therefore, to turn one's eyes to the more general, the broader-ranging, elements in human societies to see how they affect entrepreneurship in all its forms and relationships. We shall be concerned primarily with three problems.

First, we must consider the circumstances under which entrepreneurship comes into existence. Societies have carried on quite well without the use of entrepreneurs, and some do still. We need to look at the conditions that are conducive and those that are retardative to the appearance of the entrepreneurial form of production. We should study also the circumstances that favor and those that check the extension of the scope of entrepreneurship within economies. Professor Gay thought at one time that there was a "rhythm of history": that there were periods of increasing "freedom" for entrepreneurship, followed by periods of increasing restraint upon its activities.

Second, we must note that just as there is no necessity in any society's choice of the entrepreneurial form of productive organization, so there is, of course, no necessity in the choice by individuals in a given society of the role of entrepreneur. The institutions of entrepreneurship must compete for talent with other social institutions, the entrepreneurial role with other roles of that society; and it may well be that the performance of individual economies under the entrepreneurial system is in no small way affected by the quality of talent that is attracted into business.

In the third place, we must be concerned with the manifold relationships of the rest of a given society with the entrepreneurial segment, and with the changes in these relationships through time. These connections pertain to the motivations, the modes of conduct, and the effectiveness of entrepreneurs — the "why," the "how," and the "how well" of their actions. And the connections take one into religious, educational, political, and other phases of life in the given societies.

The Appearance of Entrepreneurship

Professor Easterbrook has contended that entrepreneurship as society's chosen instrument of production is the exception in the world's history, really pretty new when projected against the centuries of household, communal, and state enterprise. Professor Gay, in his "rhythm of history" just mentioned, implied that at neither point of the oscillation between state and free enterprise did the alternate form wholly disappear. Professor Gerschenkron is disposed to think of economic development first, and then of the entrepreneur as the child of that development; and he finds the Parsons-Jenks scheme ineffectual in explaining origins, having in mind his native Russia, where the intellectual, social climate was always hostile, but where, nevertheless, entrepreneurs appeared and flourished.

Little research, even by anthropologists, has gone into the matter of origins. Professor Cyril S. Belshaw does report from his examination of South Sea folk that "where indigenous peoples feel that it is in their capacity to produce for a market that is within their reach, without domination or double-dealing by outsiders, and with every step of the process reasonably well delineated, it is seldom that they do not take up the opportunity." [1] Dr. Redlich has suggested the possibility of entrepreneurs appearing in the agents connecting two nonentrepreneurial systems: for example, the serfs who transported surplus grain from the manor to the burgeoning town. Professor Sylvia L. Thrupp finds opportunities for the advent of entrepreneurs in the existence of famine conditions, the fiscal problems of princes, and the need for more or better sacramental wine. [2]

Rarely have entrepreneurs had to struggle against more

adverse forces than in seventeenth-century New England and in nineteenth-century Russia. Professor Bernard Bailyn describes the conflict of the Massachusetts merchants against the theocracy that then controlled the young colony — and the 158-page will of one merchant, Robert Keayne, who tries there to defend himself from the attacks upon him during his lifetime, essentially for embracing mercantile pursuits.[3] In Russia the entrepreneur was "despised by the nobility and the intelligentsia." The good life implied "tilling the land, which belongs to God, and receiving the divine blessing of its fruit" — not craving for riches and laying up treasures on earth. "In innumerable adages, fairy tales, and songs, the wisdom of folklore insisted upon the unrighteous origin of wealth." [4] But, in both instances, entrepreneurship took root and grew.

Since Weber it has been common practice to look to Calvinism as a factor particularly favorable to the introduction and increase of entrepreneurs, at least at one remove: Calvinism encouraged the accumulation of capital, and capital is prerequisite to entrepreneurship. Calvinism was viewed also as directly promotive insofar as it adjured men to be zealous in their "calling" and encouraged them to look on achievement as indicative of their favored place in God's sight.

Calvinism, however, does seem to have counseled a cautious form of entrepreneurship, careful and pedantic, hardly the seedbed of great changes. Professor James S. Duesenberry finds nothing in the Protestant ethic to account for the innovational activity which is characteristic of Western capitalism, and he expresses the belief that entrepreneurship of that sort was an offspring of the Renaissance.[5] And Dr. Jelle C. Riemersma reports findings in his research that give circumstantial support to Professor Duesenberry's conjecture. The strictly Calvinist Dutch merchants who launched the East and West India Companies of the early seventeenth century did not, in their personalities, "conform to the type of the ascetic, frugal, and calculating Protestant." They were instead "men of splendor and bold action." Moreover, Dr. Riemersma cites the German writer, Paul Koch, as having found similar traits among the entrepreneurs of Basel and of Frankfurt-am-Main.[6] A broad effort to explain the rise and expansion of entrepreneurship would probably be couched in terms of promotive and retardative forces, with a further breakdown of minimal and superminimal conditions.

Professor Gerschenkron is surely correct in stressing the primary requirement of economic opportunity. Entrepreneurship did not flourish in the hard conditions of the Middle Ages; it was peripheral to other forms of economic organization. It does not flourish today among primitive peoples living near the margin of subsistence. Production and distribution there must be closely controlled by those who clearly have only the welfare of the community at heart. Even where entrepreneurship has evolved, to some extent, as with the merchants of various Middle Eastern countries, economic conditions must at least be permissive before the phenomenon spreads to other lines of business activity. To be sure, the situation need be no more than permissive; one quality of the entrepreneur is his ability to perceive latent economic opportunities and to devise their exploitation. Typical among nineteenth-century cases is that of Charlemagne Tower, who saw the potentialities of the iron deposits of northern Minnesota and, at the risk of personal bankruptcy, succeeded in bringing them into production.[7]

Similarly, social toleration is important as a minimal condition. In France the nobility of the sixteenth and seventeenth centuries were permitted to engage in trade under specific rules without the loss of their status.[8] Serfs in nineteenth-century Russia were allowed to leave the estates to which they were legally attached, and to carry on various sorts of entrepreneurial activity.[9] However, as in the case of economic opportunity, the minimal conditions were not too restraining. Here personality factors seem sometimes to have "cut through the cake" of customary disapproval. Such factors are said to have accounted in part for the innovations of the Industrial Revolution in England. In somewhat similar fashion, Lebanese merchants in Jamaica are reported to have shrugged their shoulders at public obloquy and led the way to economic revival in the face of disapproval by the old aristocracy and its followers.[10] Innovators are sometimes represented as lonely men who, by their "hard cutting edge" or their boldness, have isolated themselves, at least temporarily, from their fellows.

Entrepreneurs must also be provided with minimum securities of various sorts, as Professor Easterbrook has contended. Perhaps such securities of person and property are the concrete evidences of the minimum of social toleration just mentioned. Andrea Barbarigo and other Venetian merchants of the fourteenth century sailed on trading voyages only under governmental protection.[11] So also did the Spanish galleons that traded between Cadiz and the New World in later centuries. Business in nineteenth-century England was under a handicap because, in the law of libel, statements of businessmen's financial positions could not be broadcast as were their American equivalents in Dun & Bradstreet's reports. The broadcaster was liable for damage if his statement, though true, caused loss to the person reported on. Again, English merchants have, in the post-World War II years, proceeded with some hesitation in their exports to the United States because the import regulations of the latter country were so complex, and so often executed with seeming arbitrariness.

However, the minimal conditions of encouragement and of security are appraised, and have always been appraised, by individuals with different inheritances and different experiences in life. Perhaps there are, and always have been, individuals with a propensity to entrepreneurship, men to whom the support of hazards is an exhilaration, who place exceptionally high values on accomplishment or on the "carrot" of monies to be spent in conspicuous consumption, who find a challenge in leadership, and so on. Quite likely the variation among men in these entrepreneurial qualities is not sufficient to cancel all the difficulties noted above, but those with the strongest propensity in this direction may well place a considerable discount on the supposed obstacles.[12] For them the threshold will be low. They will appear as the innovators, the "sports," the "deviants," the breakers of customary habits of thought and behavior.[13]

Incentives in Entrepreneurship

Above the minimal conditions range circumstances that are more promotive of entrepreneurial zest and capacity. The economic environment may be especially favorable. Such seems to have been the situation at various points in the world's history: when the Italians were exploiting the Mediterranean basin; when the discoverers had opened the New World; when the technological improvements of England's eighteenth century put her temporarily in a cost-differential position; or when American merchants turned their backs to the sea and began to taste the sweets of our western resources. Quite obviously a large carrot had effects.

So also did numerous other circumstances. "Pax Britannica" reduced various uncertainties. The adaptation of corporate organization to trade, and much later the introduction of limited liability, helped to smooth the path. The Heralds' College in England is alleged to have been pliant in the registration of coats-of-arms submitted by rising business-men who desired such a symbol of distinction. In Sweden the prospering group of iron masters actually were unable to break through the more rigid social organization of the country, but, as elsewhere, they at least gained the position of a distinct upper class.[14]

This matter of noneconomic stimuli to entrepreneurial achievement is very important. It can be regarded as an expression of the almost universal human desire for prestige. This brings us close to the anthropologists, to some ideas in Thorstein Veblen's writings, and to all who seek social progress in any line through the erection of a "Hall of Fame." [15]

A different, somewhat broader construct is supplied by Professor Parsons, writing as a sociologist. As phrased by Professor Duesenberry, the position is as follows:

The unique force of money income as a motivation in our society appears to arise from the fact that the social recognition and the self-respect achieved by an individual are largely dependent on the degree of occupational success which he achieves . . .

It follows that a society can achieve a high degree of economic efficiency only if its social structure is such that a very high degree of social recognition is bestowed on the achievement of occupational success . . .

An ethic which places a high valuation on occupational achievement is a necessary condition for economic development but it is not a sufficient one. The criteria for occupational success must be such as to encourage the active searching after new ways of doing things.[16]

One cannot properly contend that social esteem is the only impelling force. The Calvinist leaders in Amsterdam's mercantile world around 1600 — men like Uselinx — were not accepted as social equals by the established Northern merchants, but they persisted. And perhaps it is no coincidence that they were chiefly responsible for launching the East and West India companies in Holland, that is, that they became business "mavericks." [17] The record of the Jews in business is sparkling evidence to the same proposition. So also was the white man in many yellow, black, or brown communities, although here perhaps the exploiter from Europe or America might be regarded as one living by values imported in his person rather than by those that were prevalent in the land of his activities.

Yet social ideas congruent with entrepreneurial aspirations and social structures respondent to entrepreneurial success must be given great weight in an analysis of the operation of entrepreneurial systems. For Europe the residual elements of the older social system, and the diversions of ambitions and efforts which such residues provoke seem to be of major importance to such observers as Professors Tibor de Scitovszky,[18] John E. Sawyer, David S. Landes, and William N. Parker.[19]

Professor de Scitovszky draws a contrast between the situations in Europe, especially England, and in the United States. In the former areas, "the existence of a feudal aristocracy and landed gentry set a social pattern, which to achieve was the ambition of the newly rising capitalist [entrepreneurial] class." The British entrepreneur of the nineteenth century "wanted to outdo his rivals, not in the scale of his business or wealth, but by being admitted to high society and by becoming a member of Parliament or alderman in his native town. Such ambitions restrained the ruthlessness of industrial warfare and diverted a good deal of time, energy, and money from business."

On the other hand, the landed aristocracy of the eastern

United States, such as it was, lacked both the wealth and importance "to set social standards; politics . . . carried little social distinction and could not satisfy social ambition either; and society life, set up in a few Eastern cities by the business class itself, encouraged . . . money-making by adopting wealth as its sole ranking principle." So the American businessman found in money-making, besting his rivals, and enlarging his business "his only ambition and pastime. Only when he was already a spent man would he turn his energies to spending and enjoying his wealth." [20]

Professors Sawyer and Landes have dealt mainly with France. There they find the residues from pre-Revolutionary times to affect various elements in the entrepreneurial world: the tastes of consumers, the attitudes of owner-managers to employees, or the hopes of businessmen for early retirement and devotion to things of the spirit.

Professor Parker observes that in Germany business achievement commands respect only when attained on a large scale, where it will be rather obviously comparable with the contributions to the welfare of the nation, of the army officers, or the bureaucrats.[21]

An entrepreneurial history of the United States would need more strands of analysis than those suggested by Professor de Scitovszky, and some of these additional elements will appear in subsequent discussions. For the present purpose, however, certain forces appear worth specific mention.

One is the religious situation. The struggle in New England, to which reference has already been made, settled one aspect of American business life: it would be secular in character. Perhaps it is important that thereafter there was an increasing number of competing sects, or that these sects were mainly those called "Protestant" in Anglo-American terminology. Quite conceivably our economico-business evolution would have been appreciably different if we had chanced to have secured an official church and if that organ had emphasized the inconsequential character or riches on earth. But that is all speculation.

Surely a dominant folk hero in the United States has been the man who gets ahead, and of such persons no one has outranked the man who rose from rags to riches by his business operations. This social skewness was not any American invention. Literature issued in England from the seventeenth century onward carried the same theme: for example, Thomas Powell's *Tom, of all Trades* (1631), James Donaldson's *Undoubted Art of Thriving* (1700), or later merely *The Art of Growing Rich* (1796).[22] There were perhaps English antecedents of the Horatio Alger type of fiction, even the type with which Alger's name has been allied, although he did not actually follow the formula.[23] However, the American infection with the disease was deeper, and the zest to excel in business success has nowhere been more intense.

In addition to circumstances deriving from economic, religious, or psychological factors, there are developments within the area of business operations and perhaps some political elements, which should be taken into account in explaining conditions within entrepreneurship that conduce to better-than-minimum performance. In other words, there are various influences playing upon the entrepreneurial actors of any period in almost any land, to which the individual performers respond in varying degrees according to their inheritance and previous training.

Out of these circumstances, Professor Danhof drew his classification of entrepreneurs already noted: innovating, imitative, Fabian, and drone.[24] He was examining merely commercial farmers of the 1820–1870 decades, and he used principally the test of speed in innovation to establish his classes. However, numerous social "themes" — to use Professor Cochran's term — affected the farmer's attitude toward the adoption of new methods of cultivation, new crops, et cetera; and classes of roughly corresponding character could be rather readily conceived that would take more elements into consideration.

The main points here, however, are that we are dealing not with an either-or phenomenon but with a more-or-less. That the more-or-less performances derive from a number of elements, of which the talents attracted into business and the relation of the possessors of such talents to the surrounding society, are the most important factors. Such variations in endowments and responses are a sufficient explanation of variant business success, and an alteration in the ratios among such classes of entrepreneurs as innovators, imitators, sluggards, and sloths through education or better communication is one means of raising the aggregate production of an economy, one means of attaining economic progress.

Development of Variant Types

Even if economic and social conditions may be generally favorable, and at least some entrepreneurs are willing to battle the hazards, not all such promoters of economic change turn out alike. There are, and always have been, certain forces that condition the character of such bearers of the entrepreneurial role.

Sometimes it has been governmental intervention that helped to establish the pattern. In the French printing trade of the sixteenth and seventeenth centuries, for example, the number of opportunities was limited by guild decree, and one qualification for entrepreneurial action seemed often to be a willingness to marry a deceased printer's widow! But happily such monopoly conditions, with such dire consequences, did not widely prevail.[25]

In Canada in the early nineteenth century, success seemed to require a combination of political and business skills, at least in canal construction.[26] In the United States throughout that century, many industrialists had to know how to secure support of congressmen in tariff matters; and, even more recently, the businessman in many Latin American countries is supposed to rest easy only if he has a relative in the top echelons of government.

A different type of entrepreneur may be observed in a number of cases of frontier economy, a type which is rarely found elsewhere. A man may reach a primitive community almost accidentally. Having launched one business enterprise, he becomes involved in the economic development of the town or region, and to facilitate the operations of the first line of business, he enters a second line, then a third, until he winds up with a diversity of enterprises under his control. Such a person was Cadwallader Washburn of Minneapolis. He moved from Maine to Minnesota to seek profits in the virgin forests there, but, having started lumbering, he soon found it advantageous to control the water powers at St. Mary's Falls. Next he saw the opportunity to establish a gristmill and supply the growing population of the region with flour, and before long he needed a bank to help in financing his undertakings. Finally, when the existing railroads threatened to raise rates inordinately — at least as he saw the situation — he started the construction of a railroad of his own.

Certain eastern areas provided examples of the phenomenon in our Colonial period, perhaps the Pepperells of New Hampshire, surely the Browns of Providence Plantations.[27] Men or families operating in this manner appear in a number of communities as economic development moved west: for example, the Pillsburys, also of Minneapolis and the McGees of Kansas City. Sometimes the type reappears in a newly expanding community of the East. Such were the Bordens of Fall River, Massachusetts, whose history was traced by Professor Robert K. Lamb in his doctoral dissertation.[28]

One is even tempted to think of a sort of "intensive" frontier, if one may borrow a term from the economists. What I am suggesting is that the frontier entrepreneur, like other frontier characters examined by students such as Professor Samuel D. Clark of Toronto, exhibited a considerable degree of individuality.[29] They were innovating, at least in a territorial sense; they followed no observable pattern of proceedings; and sometimes they won the disapprobation of their fellow townsmen or their equivalent — as, for example, when some of the Browns hoarded wheat at the start of the Revolution or the Bordens sought to monopolize the economic opportunities of Fall River. So, likewise, one could contend that when railroad men or industrialists began to break contracts with their local communities and commenced to employ practices that, to say the least, were arbitrary and self-centered: for example, instituting blacklists against undesirable workers, such entrepreneurs were isolated from their fellows, enjoying the anomie of frontier conditions. They had moved out of the controlling influence of one set of sanctioning individuals and had not yet come into the circle of influence of a new set. To some extent also, the robber baron variety of entrepreneur resembled the frontier enterpreneur in a propensity to spread his activities into numerous lines and to need no one to tell him right from wrong. Jay Gould was no pale shadow of Cadwallader Washburn.[30]

The evolution of a somewhat complex economy (foreign commerce, sizable coastal towns, opportunity for the sale of foodstuffs in the latter) led to the rise of agricultural entrepreneurs. By the close of the second war with Britain, there was a considerable body of farmers in the eastern states whose chief objective was the preparation of cash crops; they had become commercial farmers. It was in connection with the study of these producers that Professor Danhof presented the classification of entrepreneurs noted above; but at least two or three specific peculiarities of these entrepreneurial figures deserve mention. First is the origin of innovations.[31] Almost wholly new tools and apparatus, new farm animals, and new field crops were presented to the farmers, not originated by them. Occasionally, as in the case of merino sheep, a novelty was brought to the country by a person who, although in government service, chanced also to be interested in agriculture. Sometimes American farmers traveled abroad and brought back knowledge of foreign agricultural practices and the like. Chiefly, improvements in farming in this country came from builders of agricultural equipment, seed or plant importers, and editors of agricultural journals. At most, the farmer entrepreneurs helped in the improvement of the equipment or the testing of new crops after the initial steps had been taken.

Second, these agricultural entrepreneurs were extraordinarily subject to delusions of a speculative character, delusions that can readily be named "agricultural crazes" or "fevers." The "merino mania," the curious efforts in the 1830's to grow the *moris multicaulis* tree (for the feeding of silkworms) as far north as Maine, and the "hen fever" of the 1850's are typical of a number of quasi-hysterias that swept the country in the pre-Civil War decades.[32] While the movements did not lack beneficial results to American agriculture (since not only merino sheep but Berkshire hogs, broom corn, and various varieties of wheat reached the country's farms in this manner), they are significant in the present connection for two reasons: they indicate the breadth and intensity with which the cultural theme of getting ahead and seizing the main chance had come to dominate the country; and they point to the importance of information, or its lack, in affecting the decisions of entrepreneurs. There were "crazes" in American agriculture after 1860 — the Belgian hare, the silver fox, various types of wheat — but the epidemics were less prolonged and less severe, and the difference may be attributed to the influence of the national Department of Agriculture, its agencies, and the corresponding state units.

In the third place, agricultural entrepreneurship is noteworthy in that interunit cooperation instead of interunit rivalry tended to prevail. Manufacturing industry, at least through the nineteenth century, put much store by its patents and by its secret processes; but, typically, agriculture shared its successes. A farmer who had secured good crops by use of a certain rotation did not hesitate to spread the good word at the county fair or, if he were literarily inclined, through his favorite agricultural periodical; and so also with the use of a new seed, and so forth. Perhaps the bent toward secrecy on the industrial side was a nonrational residue from the earlier form of manufacturing organization, the handicraft system with its guilds, imported with the earlier skilled factory workers, if not with the hand workers who came over in our Colonial days, but the bent may have had a perfectly rational base. In most manufacturing lines, there was an advantage to the individual enterprise if it could protect a differential in costs deriving from an innovation, whether the innovation was really new or was one borrowed from another economy, which could be preserved through secrecy. In agricultural enterprise there was no such advantage. The individual farmer could secure a differential cost position through innovational activity, but in most agricultural situations no local group of producers would turn out enough of any crop to affect the price in the market. Hence, the advantage in costs secured by one farmer could be shared freely with his neighbors without loss to himself. In any case, the difference in entrepreneurial objectives between farm and industrial units is worth noting.

Some of the foregoing features seem to have characterized European agriculture in the nineteenth century, although from the entrepreneurship point of view European agriculture has been studied less than American. To be sure, the agricultural holding in Europe has always been closely involved with the family system of the several countries, while, with the wider dominance of tradition, there has been less room for fevers. Yet on the whole conditions seem to have been similar: improved agricultural implements have come from the machine-building industry; there have been some "crazes"; and the agricultural producers have been willing to share experiences with their "competitors."

If anything, this similarity has tended to diminish over recent decades. American "commercial" farming has tended to become ever more commercial, really industrial in character. There have been rather numerous cases of the use of the corporate form in agricultural production. Capital in the form of agricultural equipment, irrigation works, and fertilizers has been ever more heavily utilized. Not long after the arrival of "steam on the farm," organized labor made its appearance there. And information in the form of market reports and the trends of legislation began to flow more regularly and more abundantly to the farm. The larger agricultural units (for example, wheat farms run by graduates of agricultural colleges), getting market and other information at least daily by radio, and equipped to handle their operations with scarcely any "hired hands," are not essentially different in form from the "push-button" factory of manufacturing industry. Progressive entrepreneurship can be found in either area.

Evolution of Industrial Entrepreneurship

The examination of the advent of industrial entrepreneurship in communities that had previously been agricultural or commercial or a mixture of these two presents considerable difficulties. The process has been going on for so many centuries in so many circumstances that generalizations must be rather limited in character. Thanks to the research work of Dr. Redlich, it has now become clear that European nobility, far from being an indolent group everywhere and always, saw many of its members active in introducing both mining and manufacturing industry into their territories. It is possible that this was the manner in which a development policy of a Maria Theresa or a Frederick the Great became implemented, at least among a portion of their subjects. The monarch would express the thought that fulling mills or added nail production would be good for his country; nobles desiring to curry favor with their sovereign would hear such opinions expressed; and at least some of them might have the resources and the enterprise to erect the mill or the nailery in the hope of a smile or some more substantial favor from their king or queen.[33]

Another source of entrepreneurial talent or direction in industry was surely the merchant groups in a number of countries. It was this group in England that reached back, as it were, from their selling offices to gain some control of the manufacturing process through the putting-out system. Nearly everywhere it seems to have been the merchants who took active parts in the development and operation of railways, especially as investors and as members of boards of directors; and frequently in England and the United States it was the mercantile persuasion that put its capital into factories and gave its talents to their direction.

The commercial influence may perhaps be held responsible

for a number of specific developments. For instance, the peculiar form of organization in the New England cotton-textile industry seems to have a strong mercantile flavor. The real control of the factories was in the typical case not exerted at the mill itself but in the office of the "treasurer" in Boston. The treasurer did have charge of the financial affairs of the company, sometimes of several mills, but he also was responsible for the purchase of raw materials and the sale of the products, obviously mercantile operations.

Dr. Lee Benson has contended that the practice of the American railroads of charging what the traffic would bear, of giving rebates, et cetera, derived from the fact that merchants of the seaboard were so important in the development of the railways of that area.[34] And the railroad practices were, in part, imitated in the public-utility industries.

One might also suggest that the banking entrepreneurs of the eastern cities, and subsequently their fellow bankers of the western cities, were strongly influenced in their ideas of sound banking practice by the merchants who often collaborated in the founding of such institutions and often dominated on their "discount committees" and boards of directors. Commercial banks were assuredly commercial, at any rate in the eastern cities; and once institutions of this character were given public sanction, they could be utilized for the needs of farmers and small manufacturers only at risk to their solvency in "bad times." "Intermediate credit" and federal land banks came only in the twentieth century.

There is also evidence pointing to the early dominance of the mercantile group in all forms of business, even after industrialization had made considerable progress, and of the continuance of a mental attitude, subsequently still, in the curious history of cost accounting. Bookkeeping on commercial transactions by double entry dates as far back as

115

the fifteenth century, perhaps the fourteenth; a description of it was printed in 1494, and the first exposition of the mystery in English came before the end of the sixteenth century. Some industrial development was already under way in England. There was a further, rather notable expansion — usually spoken of as the Industrial Revolution — in the eighteenth century; but there was no book published in England that gave a conversion of double-entry bookkeeping for industrial cost purposes until the end of the nineteenth century! Actually, there appears to have been some employment of cost accounting in English (as well as in American) manufacturing industry before that time, and it is also noteworthy that the United States took the lead in the development of thought in the field of cost accounting. The circumstance is, indeed, peculiar that commercial accounting should have dominated the business world for so long a period after manufacturing, mining, and various forms of transportation had grown important in economic output.

As manufactures spread, a new element entered entrepreneurship, when men with technical skills set up shops — enterprises that often grew into sizable factories. These men were usually neither engineers nor academically trained. They possessed useful instincts or had acquired a practical skill. Boulton knew how to work iron; much later Michael J. Owens had a way of handling molten glass, while Samuel Slater, the Scholfields, and numerous other mechanics had learned the tricks of the new textile machinery in England, and were minded to set up their own mills in America. A large majority of the individual small establishments launched in England, on the Continent, and in the United States during the early phases of industrialization were quite surely the projects of mechanic entrepreneurs.[35]

Not infrequently, however, the mechanic was aided by association with a businessman. Partnerships (real, although not always following the legal form) between an inventor and a person familiar with manufacturing and especially with commercial matters were often arranged and often successful. Such was the collaboration of Boulton and Watt; likewise that between Lowell and Moody, in the American cotton manufacture; and there have been many others in British and American industry. Inventors have been rather notoriously poor businessmen, especially in the marketing aspects of their operations. A merchant or someone with commercial abilities often could complement the imaginative work of an inventor.[36]

Another organizational form by which the earlier merchants, at least in the United States, could influence the course of industrialization, indirectly if not directly, was that which Professor Cochran has called "general entrepreneurship." With funds assembled by successful mercantile ventures, individuals such as Nathan Appleton or John Murray Forbes made investments in cotton manufacture or the railroad world. But they had a controlling interest in more than one enterprise in the field of their selection. The operating decisions, many of which were by no means unimportant, were left to the heads of the mills or railroads, but the "general entrepreneur" kept in his own hands what might be called the strategic decisions, especially those involving important commitments of capital or the distribution of dividends: whether to expand production for the oncoming season, whether to purchase a connecting railroad line, and so forth.[37]

Professor Cochran seemed disposed to think of the general entrepreneur as shortly yielding place to the investment banker. It appears, in fact, as though this type of entrepreneur has returned. For a while men in business tended to remain within single industries — W. H. Vanderbilt in railroads, Carnegie in steel — although, even in that generation of men there were exceptions, such as the senior Rockefeller, who bought iron mountains in Minnesota. More recently, however, both here and abroad, the activities of Howard Hughes, John Hay Whitney, the notorious match king Krueger, and others offer the implication that the general entrepreneur may be a recurring type.

Still another type of entrepreneurial actor has been the engineer.[38] It appears that for a number of decades men with engineering training were by no means convinced that they ought to turn their hands to the mere making of money; they were professional men like doctors or clergy. This attitude, however, did not prevent some engineers like Whistler's father, for example, from entering the business of managing railroads, and apparently a goodly number broke away in the last years of the nineteenth century and in the twentieth. A typical case was that of Mr. William E. Nickerson, a graduate of the Massachusetts Institute of Technology, who took the idea of a safety razor when it was hardly more than an image in the mind of King C. Gillette and converted the dream into a reality. He thought through and worked through the practical problems of manufacturing a satisfying, foolproof article for world-wide consumption.[39]

More recently engineers have seemingly become still more common in the ranks of top management in all sorts of enterprises, but chiefly in manufacturing, transportation, and public utilities. Possibly the modern bias toward industrial research and toward an increase in output has derived in part from the presence in high places of men with such training. Surely, Thorstein Veblen would have expected such a development.[40]

Migration of Entrepreneurship

The geographical movement of entrepreneurship raises a host of interesting problems on which relatively few data are as yet available. The earliest form of movement was undoubtedly that of commercial entrepreneurship out of Italy or Flanders to various points of the Mediterranean basin, to towns along the Baltic, even to the underdeveloped area of England. Some forms of financial entrepreneurship tended to follow. And at a later date there was a somewhat similar movement out of Europe to India, America, and points around the newly-opened world. While such developments meant much economically, it is uncertain whether they meant much entrepreneurially. There were undoubtedly some converts to entrepreneurial life among the peoples into whose countries the merchants moved — Germans, Swedes, Englishmen, Indians — but neither forms of organization nor manners of doing business seem to have been much affected. Presumably, the first type of business literature can be credited to the expansion of commerce, the mercantile manual such as Pegelotti's of the fourteenth century, and numerous others after printing was invented. And there were indirect effects — for example, the extension of the silk and wool manufactures in Italy, tin mining in Wales — with some consequences upon entrepreneurial techniques. It is just impossible yet to generalize.

More important, at least to us in America, was the transfer of skills and procedures across the Atlantic in our early days, but thus far it is not clear just how and by what notable steps the American entrepreneur became significantly different from the English, or different from what the English entrepreneur had become in the decades since we attained our economic (perhaps our entrepreneurial) independence. There had also been some transfers of entrepreneurial skills to French, Spanish, and other colonies, but less than from England to North America.[41]

The United States, Canada, Brazil, and other parts of the New World benefited in the nineteenth and twentieth centuries from other transfers such as the migration of European talents, or what Professor Oscar Handlin might label "ethnic" factors in entrepreneurial change.[42] Here one runs into uncertainties when attempting to suggest the results of such movements. It does seem probable that the German immigrants to the United States, who brought with them the production of scientific instruments, optical glass, and the like, injected an appreciation of exactitude into American manufacturing methods which had previously been lacking. Perhaps the machine-tool and the automobile industries benefited greatly. I have sometimes thought that the developments in the Passaic wool manufacture were symbolic of the merger of German and American procedures and ideas. There were two firms set up there by German manufacturers, Forstmann & Huffmann and the Botany Worsted. They desired to produce fine worsted cloths especially for women's wear. In Europe such goods were turned out with much hand labor, but labor was expensive in America, so German persistency, German fondness for high-grade, nicely-made goods, and American facility with machine tools yielded a combination factory where goods as fine as the handmade were manufactured by predominantly machine methods.

The influence of the German immigrants — manufacturers and workers — remains largely conjectural, however, and we can speculate with even fewer facts with regard to the contributions of the Dutch and the Italians, the Jews and the Greeks.

No less uncertain have been the experiences of other countries of the Western Hemisphere. If the Germans imparted a notion of accuracy to United States manufactures, did they make the same contribution to the Brazilian? Or was industry there not sufficiently advanced? And did the Italian immigrants into Brazil remain Italian, or did they become Brazilians in entrepreneurial characteristics?

It is alleged that when one goes to Morocco or Iran or even France, one does business on terms imposed by the local businessmen; in Iran, for example, only after several calls and several cups of coffee. How long, then, can an American firm proceed in a pattern devised by American entrepreneurship, after it has tried to settle into French or Scandinavian or Venezuelan business life? Is entrepreneurship transferable between nations? If so, to what extent and under what conditions?

The transfer of entrepreneurship from West to East has, oddly enough, attracted more attention than that of movements within the West itself. We are beginning to know something of what was involved in the industrialization of Japan[43] and what has been happening in India. The latter case is perhaps the clearer and neater. In brief, the course seems to have been as follows: management skill was scarce; capital came almost wholly from England; Englishmen of executive ability were placed in charge of "management agencies," which by stock ownership controlled several manufacturing or marketing enterprises; native Indians began before separation to imitate the British, especially the Parsis in Bombay; and now a large part of Indian business is operated by management agencies staffed and owned by Indians.[44]

Stages of Entrepreneurship

It is a common practice among economists, and not uncommon among historians, to treat the entrepreneur or the businessman as if he were always the same sort of person reacting to changed conditions always in the same manner, and there are a few not unimportant instances where change has been slow indeed, such as the foreign merchant over the centuries or all proprietors of small shops in any country. Note has already been made of differences among entrepreneurial actors of various countries operating at given periods. I have given implications also of changes in the character of performance through time. At least in a country such as the United States, these changes have really been important for appraising the character of the entrepreneurial system. We know that science and medicine, even teaching, have improved over the decades and centuries. Has entrepreneurship?

It is obvious that divergencies in character among entrepreneurial figures in so large a country and over so many different industries, including those of immigrants whose length of residence in the United States varies tremendously, must be considerable even over a brief period. However, I believe that typical characters can be observed in the relevant data, rough "averages" of a sort, if not "ideal types." [45] Indeed, I venture to offer two sets of composite characterizations.

In the first series of figures, particular emphasis is placed upon the quantity and quality of information on the basis of which entrepreneurs of successive time-periods made their decisions, decisions on whether to go into business, what to buy, sell, or produce, how to do it; and second, upon the complexity of the web of institutions and personalities with relation to which they had to move. Accordingly, three types or grades of entrepreneurial characters can be distinguished, which may be labeled rule-of-thumb, informed, and sophisticated, or, in more elegant terms: empirical, rational, and cognitive.[46]

Once thus stated, the trichotomy will be hardly more than

common sense to a business or economic historian. A couple of illustrations will demonstrate the very ordinary character of the concept. At one stage the merchant had to operate on price data supplied him by some more or less reliable correspondent, data which might be anywhere from a week to three or four months old. At a later period he had "prices-currents" to rely upon, and, if he took the trouble, a series of prices of related commodities and of his primary interests extending back in the files of the *New York Shipping List* or equivalent local periodical. Still later he could secure for many goods prices transmitted by telegraph, perhaps presented in the form of an index with secular trend and seasonal variation eliminated. Again, in the matter of techniques: at one time it was the entrepreneur's own bent as a tinkerer, or the skill of the local blacksmith, that both promoted and limited the design of apparatus. Then came the period when foreign machinery tried out abroad was imported, sometimes in the minds of immigrating workmen, or later when apparatus was described in trade periodicals and purveyed by specializing machine-builders. More recently the layout of the producing unit with a preconceived rate of output will first be envisioned, and then machinery, assembly lines, and so on, designed to suit the planned production.

I have also proposed a variant scheme of "stages." [47] Here I tried to add elements that I had not previously utilized as bases for differentiation: namely, the horizon which the entrepreneur seems to have had in his mind, and the location of the effective sanctioning bodies. (To be sure, as the economy expands in complexity and in territory, the "fit" of any single term as descriptive of the whole becomes steadily poorer, as I have just suggested. All the thirteen states were nearer alike economically in 1790 than Pennsylvania is akin to Nevada at the present time. Also, there has come an increasing diversity in the size of business enterprises.)

At all events, I now suggest that we think of entrepreneurs at successive periods as being predominantly community-focused, industry-focused, and nation-focused. As already intimated, the sources of information can be readily cast into categories consonant with this threefold breakdown. For the importing and exporting merchant as well as for the small manufacturer, the bulk of information came from the community in which he carried on his business, if, against the news that he received from his foreign correspondents, we take account of the gossip that he picked up from other merchants,[48] the data that he needed to plan the import side of his business, and the information on ups and downs of trade, methods for collecting foreign debts, and the like, all of which he needed to conduct his enterprise. In later decades information tended to become channeled into industry streams, both technical books and, particularly, the technical, commercial, and personal news carried in the *American Railroad Journal,* the *Iron Age,* and similar trade journals. Professor W. Rupert Maclaurin has sought to establish that the success of specific groups of entrepreneurs has been no little affected by the circumstance that they were operating in an industry which chanced to be open-ended or chanced to be closed. He has in mind that certain industries happened to receive the names of processes (for example, "chemical" or "electrical") whereas others happened to become labeled as "cotton textile" or "coal mining." The first type has tended to expand into a greater variety of product lines and to invest more heavily in technological research. They have manifested stronger and more continued growth potentials.[49] It is obvious that recent decades have brought increasing interest in the national market and a corresponding advance in the number and importance of such periodicals as *Business Week, Fortune, Tide,* and the like, while counseling organizations, schools of business, and the information services of the federal government aim predominantly toward purveying data of national import. While most enterprises, to be sure, continue to produce for and, especially, to sell to a local or at best regional market, still, to a greater extent than ever before, information about national conditions is available to the local operators, styles are national and no longer local, and a national credit structure ties together all parts of the country.

When I suggested the new trilogy, however, I had in mind more than the stream of information. I was thinking also of the changing locus of effective sanctions. In the early days of handicraftsman, general storekeeper, or substantial town merchant, the people that counted for him, in commendation or criticism, were undoubtedly his neighbors, especially perhaps the local minister, school teacher, lawyer, and those of his own vocation who had retired from business life before him. Robert Keayne wrote his long will in an effort to justify his commercial career to his neighbors in Boston. When Nicholas Brown thought to forestall on flour at the commencement of the Revolutionary War, he hid his stock over the state line in Massachusetts. Eli Whitney seems to have been nearly as pleased at the effects of his manufacturing operations upon New Haven as the consequences of his invention upon the whole South.

Subsequently, it seems to me, there was a period when the man's enterprise and the industry of which it was a part bulked largest in his thoughts. The head of a mill or mine, even if it was a small establishment, was more withdrawn from his neighbors than the local handicraftsman or merchant, and as manufacturing enterprises grew larger and sought new sources of water power, their proprietors became yet more isolated from their kind. These entrepreneurs became conscious of themselves not merely as businessmen but as railroad men, cotton manufacturers, or coal-mine operators. In part this consciousness was promoted by the exigencies of the pertinent techniques and of the particularized marketing operations, but also soon by the specialized trade periodicals that conveyed predominantly industry, not national news. Accordingly, there tended to be "in" and "out" groups. A person might excuse himself for an action as the head of a manufacturing enterprise which he would not think of taking as a citizen of his community: for example, allow workmen in a men's hat factory to breathe the air laden with rabbit's fur, even though he realized that they would succumb to tuberculosis within a few years. And the head of a railroad or a bank would look to other railroad men or bankers for approbation, not to businessmen in general, let alone other civilians. From such circumstances arose blacklist practices of early manufacturers, the robber-baron features of railroading, even the high-handed financial practices of the insurance companies as late as 1905. For some decades, partly because of the wide public approval of wealth-getting and of wealthy individuals, of which mention has been made above, there was no adversely critical censor group. Critics there were, of course, such as Henry Demarest Lloyd or Henry George, but they failed to develop a sufficiently large following, especially among the elite groups of the country.

Already in the later decades of the nineteenth century, agencies of the national government from Congress to the Bureau of Corporations were taking interest in domestic business affairs to a degree hitherto unknown (the possible regulation of railroads, the possible curbing of monopoly, the possible reduction in producers' freedom to market any sort of food and drug), because internal commerce had become national; state lines had become unimportant in that regard, and state governments were powerless to promote adequately the general good. Also, with the muckrakers had sprung up a group of public censors, more numerous and more widely heralded than ever before; and, for the most part, these writers and later-day columnists spoke for the nation, not for the city in which particular newspapers chanced to appear or certain evils chanced to be observed. Journalism had become nationalized. Correspondingly, businessmen came more and more to judge their fellows by something more than industry standards. Tom Girdler, Colonel Sewell Avery, and Mr. Frederick C. Crawford of the Thompson Products Company were appraised on some such abstract basis as what was good for business in general. And leaders in business might look, perhaps hope, for recognition from national institutions: the National Association of Manufacturers, the United States Chamber of Commerce, the Committee for Economic Development, the advisory board to the Secretary of Commerce, even a place on the Board of Governors of the Federal Reserve System or a Cabinet post. With many enterprises aiming at a national market and indulging in national advertising, with their executive talent drawn from all quarters of the country, surely the larger concerns were nation-oriented; and these larger companies set the tone for many enterprises of lesser size.

A reflection of the foregoing changes may, I think, be seen in the conclusions drawn by Professor Sigmund Diamond in his *Reputation of the American Businessman* (1955) — a book of value in various connections.[50] He found the successful business leader of the early nineteenth century appraised at his death in terms of such homely virtues as hard work, thrift, and ambition: in other words, the virtues appropriate to the community. On the other hand, he was drawn to see corresponding business leaders a century later appraised in terms of the economic system; in other words, in terms of the whole nation. To be sure, more than this single shift in spatial basis is involved, and Diamond does not find men extolled or condemned in terms of specific industries. (Perhaps the latter connection would have appeared if the author had handled more cases.) At all events, I venture to see confirmation of my own hypothesis in a study pursued with quite a different objective.

Doubtless a sequence of stages could be worked out for England, France, or Germany when we know more of the entrepreneurial histories of these countries. For the moment, however, it is sufficient to realize that entrepreneurs in probably every area have changed in character over decades or over centuries. It may be convenient for historians to have such shorthand designations as I have tried to provide for the handling of American data; but it is a matter of convenience only. The important element is a realization of a continued and continuing change over time. To be sure, it is also possible to use concepts such as those described above for purposes of international comparison; for example, one might place certain countries in the "rule-of-thumb" or the "community-focused" category, others in the "sophisticated" or "nation-focused." It is possible, however, that inaccuracies would develop in international comparisons since one country's rule-of-thumb entrepreneurship might be much more primitive than another's; and so for other stages. Classifications can be put under too much pressure.

Nonetheless, an analysis of the evolution of any economically mature nation will quite surely reveal that entrepreneurship has not stood still. In ways not related to the supply of the economist's "productive factors," at least in any close manner, but in ways that have relevance for expanding national income and for economic development, entrepreneurship has advanced, even as medicine or mathematics. The creative force of human intelligence has not been screened off from the area of business.

The Other Side of the Coin

No one whose memory runs back two or three decades will labor under a belief that business was ever perfect. Of course, neither is the law or medicine, even the ministry; but business has had a disproportionate share of actors who, even by the standards of their times and discounting the occasions when they were merely outwitting one another, must be set down as performing society a disservice, if not behaving as outright rascals. The question here, however, is how and in what degree the entrepreneurial system as such promoted or contributed to this condition, perhaps after an indeterminate discount for the average weaknesses of human nature, in the face of the institution of private property. After all, there have always been robberies elsewhere in Western societies other than those that took place in business.

The combination of a monetary basis for appraising success, the differential operating advantage to the individual entrepreneur in having net profits larger than those of his competitors (enabling him to shade his prices, inaugurate a special service to customers, et cetera), and the prestige deriving from higher than average profits both as regards plant expansion and as gained through personal expenditure weighs heavily upon the individual proprietor or the members of a partnership, perhaps a bit less so in the latter case, as suggested elsewhere.[51] As businesses increase in size, these forces appear to become less vigorous, especially if the executive office becomes, in fact, multiple and if it turns professional. When the concern grows large enough, quite surely all ordinary forms of dishonesty just do not pay. There is still the occasional Krueger or Coster, and there are searches, at least by ambitious members of company teams, for special advantages with governments of local or larger scope; but it appears to be the general opinion of people who have been close to business over recent decades that morals within business have been steadily rising. This could be due in part to institutions within business itself; for example, the public accountants who, employed by the corporations themselves or egged on sometimes by the stock exchange or the investment bankers, inspect the books of enterprises and actually bring pressure — direct pressure on behalf of financial improvements, but indirect pressure in favor of other reforms. We have no reliable data, however, on what Professor Edwin H. Sutherland has labeled "white-collar crime," no data on any variety of entrepreneurial sins, especially no time-series, and one can merely report impressions.

Another charge of considerable age pertains to the supposed influence of business life upon the nonmoral elements in the businessman's character. He was charged with being ignorant of all but his business, yet domineering and self-satisfied, a man ranked low on the basis of "culture." Perhaps through the decades businessmen have typically been more Philistine, more interested in their own narrow path of life than some other groups in their contemporary societies; but no more interested than musicians in theirs, or artists in theirs. We have no objective standards and no objective data. All that appears reasonably certain is that the entrepreneurial mode of economic organization has not made businessmen more Philistine. Perhaps, even by the literati's standards over recent decades, it has given the typical businessman indirect encouragement to become less so. Not much more can be, or perhaps needs to be, said.

The entrepreneurial system may be subject to hostile criticism on account of its deprivation of freedom, although whether it is more restricting than other modes of economic organization may probably be doubtful. I have in mind two features of modern business life, especially in the United States. One is the effort of corporations to check the movement of executives from their ranks. They do not want to lose a good comptroller or a good vice-president in charge of sales; indeed, any officers in whom they have invested time and money for their training. So pension plans, stock-purchase schemes, and the like, in part recently promoted by high personal income taxes, are evolved in the effort to buy loyalty, at least to make certain that loyalty will not lack proper reward. With the diminution of movement, there may be some economic loss in that men do not move to positions where they might make larger contributions to the national dividend; and with this same diminution of movement, there may be some personal frustrations, even despite the carrots of future enjoyment held out by the various retirement rewards.

Another sort of restriction derives from the sanctions of an entrepreneurial system that is, as it were, "laced" with zeal of one sort or another. Apparently the Latin Americans, to some extent the French and English — but probably not the Germans — have escaped the increased tempo and rising pressures of American business life. There was a time, even in this country, when business pace was leisurely. My notion of the Colonial merchant of Boston, Philadelphia, or Charleston is that he walked down to his countinghouse about ten in the forenoon, spent a couple of hours gossiping with friends, repaired home for a midday dinner and nap, and, unless he had a ship in port, did not bother to return to his shop. Also a typical merchant would retire from trading as he reached forty or thereabouts and devote himself to good works and his family, as long as his doctors could keep him alive (which, of course, was not too long, on the average). I fancy that some fragments of this mode of life persisted down perhaps until the 1880's, even on the east coast, and perhaps a little longer in some parts of the west. At all events, it seems that over the past seventy-five years businessmen have been prisoners of their own ideologies: they ought to work hard; they ought to keep busy as long as they physically could; and so on. Perhaps businessmen have gained real satisfaction in doing what gave them a sense of accomplishment, if only by acting as their peers expected them to act; but there may have been some frustration, and there may have been some economic loss. The compulsory retirement plans instituted by the larger corporations, and the programs in the same type of enterprise to conserve the health of their executives, seem to argue that American businessmen carried "the strenuous life" to excess, from their own, their companies', and the economy's points of view.

Frustrations, even wide-flung grief, seem an inevitable feature of interenterprise relations in an entrepreneurial economy. Dr. Redlich has written of this feature as the "daemonic" quality in entrepreneurship: commercial farmers in one region ruining commercial farmers in another, one corner druggist driving his competitor across the street into bankruptcy, the entrepreneurs in the trucking business performing so effectively as to occasion distress among entrepreneurs of the railroad industry, and so on throughout the length and breadth of the economy. As I have suggested elsewhere,[52] the entrepreneurial system operates to minimize the economic loss; but there are undoubtedly heartaches and worse, as the lesson of personal failure is driven home. Indeed, this phenomenon has been so widespread and long-continued, that we all speak of cutthroat competition as if we took life as lightly as Benevenuto Cellini of a fine spring morning.

Finally, we should perhaps note the serious problem of bureaucratic rigidities in business. It is quite possible that entrepreneurs may be held partly accountable for the evolution of large business units; the pursuit of differential advantage led them progressively into operations of increasing scope. And in such organizations the benumbing effect of size can be seen. Men lose their initiative and drive because sooner or later most of them see the dimming of prospects of substantial advancement, although, of course, others find comfort in being taken care of throughout their lives, as some men do in the army. Men become motivated by rivalries and politics within the organization rather than zeal for effective performance in service of the whole enterprise, while as a result of advancement by seniority, a logical development of bureaucratic life, men reach the high points in their careers at ages when they have already begun to lose some of their intellectual keenness and surely have lost much of their zest for reform, with all the headaches that reforms inevitably bring. Large corporations are alive to this problem; their stock-purchase plans for executives, their health programs, and the like constitute one means of combating the evils. Outside of individual companies, the policy of the American government against bigness in our enterprises operates to limit the difficulties, although it was not formulated with that result in mind. Entrepreneurial zest thrives best in small business units.

Conclusion

Economics has always claimed to be a social science. A brand of economics that paid adequate attention to entrepreneurship would be such a science par excellence. The entrepreneur's relations to his organization constitute one level of social phenomena; the interconnections of various entrepreneurial units in a stream of activities involve another level; and here in the "social conditioning of entrepreneurship" we have glimpses of an over-all, interpenetrating relationship. For those who like similes, one might think of a river vessel. Groups of people are busy in the several salons and cabins; the passengers and the crew form a unit of sorts; while the natural elements — water, wind, and sun — exert their respective influences upon all.

Obviously, this social conditioning involves a variety of factors, from education to economic resources, and from governmental administration to ethnic coherences. We are concerned with the impact of cultural forces upon the formation and performance of social groups out of which flow the goods and services desired by society. Our procedures and range of considerations would not be different if we were trying to account for the evolution of our educational system with its state universities and its Fulbright fellowships, its honorary degrees and its parochial schools.

However, it is only by giving attention to such a broad assemblage of factors that one can hope to give answers to such questions of prime importance for a study of economic development as: how did the system of production get into its present form? What makes it operate in the way that it does? Is the performance getting better or worse? What is likely to happen in the future? Present-day economics is not geared by its traditions, its methods, or its objectives to deal with such questions. In a Western world devoted dominantly to private enterprise, only a type of economics with a time dimension in which entrepreneurial activity is the central thread can hope to render enlightening answers.

PART TWO·
ENTREPRENEURIAL REALITIES

INTRODUCTION

THE EXPLORATION of a new field in the social sciences, at least of a field with a historical dimension, proceeds by alternate steps of empirical inquiry and tentative generalization. Thus it has been with entrepreneurial history. Prior to the drafting of *Change and the Entrepreneur,* there had been a sizable amount of empirical research, much of it in Germany, some in the United States, some elsewhere. Very little of it, other than that of Sombart and Weber, utilized hypotheses or employed frameworks appropriate to our study.[1] Generally, it took the form of company histories, businessmen's biographies, and industrial or local histories with many personal data.

This body of information was subject to interpretation by the first endeavors at generalization, those of the German writers, and particularly that of Schumpeter, who had built a theory of economic development on the nature of entrepreneurship as he conceived the latter. The work of Barnard and Parsons in sociology was also available and useful, and to this mass it was possible to add comments offered by speakers at meetings of the Research Center in Entrepreneurial History at Harvard, including some by Mr. Barnard himself. Data from these several sources formed the basis for the first tentative findings in *Change and the Entrepreneur.* This volume, issued in a form that manifests its preliminary nature, was published in 1949.

In the meantime, *Explorations in Entrepreneurial History* had been launched, through the initiative of two young men connected with the Center, Hugh G. J. Aitken and R. Richard Wohl. The periodical was intended as an organ of discussion for the relatively small group of scholars, some in Cambridge and some elsewhere, who had displayed interest in the subject. Before long, however, it came to publish reports of research findings, not merely theoretical speculations derived from previously available data. In the years since 1949 there has been a host of other publications more or less concerned with our themes: from Charles Wilson's study of Unilever to Miss Mabel Newcomer's statistical data upon the social and educational backgrounds of American business leaders, and from Gordon's *Business Leadership in the Large Corporation* to the articles in the new *Business History Review*. Not least important have been the volumes sponsored by the Center and the written or verbal communications of individuals who have been connected with that institution: Redlich, Landes, Sawyer, Easterbrook, Rosovsky, the young men mentioned above and the senior members, past and present. Now appears a proper and convenient time once more to survey the field, and I have ventured above to give what seems to me the theoretical structure of the subject.

In contrast with the situation in 1949, it is now also possible to present concrete data upon entrepreneurial history, the analysis of actual occurrences, selected to illustrate various phases of the whole experience. To be sure, the material must be condensed into vignettes, but it is hoped that the portrayals remain accurate ones. While I have drawn much of the data for the ensuing vignettes from books or periodical articles, many of them written by persons connected with the Center, I have frequently put my own construction upon events or conditions elaborated by these authors, seeking to relate their findings to the entrepreneurial theory presented here. Much of the material comes out of *Explorations*. There are four or five divisions of the descriptive essays: the relations of entrepreneurship to social classes, relations to primitive economic conditions, to technological change, to the different forms of business organization, and to government.

In the actual exploration of any scientific area, endeavors to discover and state uniformities observed in the concrete data — generalizations of greater or less magnitude, typical situations, or noteworthy representative personalities — become appropriate and useful for further exploration. Such is the major purpose of these vignettes.

Section 1 ·

ENTREPRENEURSHIP AND
THE SOCIAL ORDER

VIGNETTE 1: THE ARISTOCRATIC ENTREPRENEUR

Prefatory note: The development of the research activities summarized in the ensuing essay is almost wholly a contribution of Dr. Redlich, who inspired and supplied an introductory statement to an issue of *Explorations*[2] devoted solely to this theme. In addition to encouraging others to put together their thoughts or to launch new inquiries in the area, he has made investigations himself, and prepared précis of his findings. Others had done work earlier on portions of the field, but in no systematic fashion and without the concepts stemming from an appreciation of entrepreneurship. A particularly useful study, despite such limitations, is that of Dr. Charles A. Foster, entitled "Honoring Commerce and Industry in Eighteenth-Century France," which was presented as a doctoral dissertation in history at Harvard in 1950.[3]

The image of the businessman prevalent in the United States is so strictly that of a man of middle-class origins, if indeed he did not rise in the Alger tradition from "poor but honest parents," that there is a danger of entrepreneurship being viewed in such terms. It is useful, therefore, to inquire whether entrepreneurs have always been, or really need to

140

be, of that stamp. European economic development in the early modern period has been couched so largely in terms of burghers, guilds, and town activities that one is tempted to ask whether other elements should not be introduced, especially with respect to mining, agriculture, the iron industry, and the like, which evolved outside the towns. A contribution to better understanding in both fields derives from an appreciation of the aristocratic entrepreneur.

As the student of entrepreneurial history examines data from the late medieval period onward relative to super-burgher cases of entrepreneurial action, he finds in fact that he must put bounds to his observations in order to secure sufficient focus. He must set aside consideration of kingly entrepreneurs — such heads of states as Gustavus Vasa, Peter the Great, or even Duke Julius of Braunschweig.[4] Again, it is unnecessary here to consider the ups and downs of noble fortunes. Professor Lane mentions such movements in fourteenth- and fifteenth-century Venetian life (see his *Andrea Barbarigo*) and Dr. Foster speaks of the same phenomenon in connection with seventeenth- and eighteenth-century French nobility. Nor need one take notice of the important phenomenon of the ennobling of successful entrepreneurs of the bourgeois class. Finally, we may set aside those noblemen who functioned as military enterprisers — organizers, equippers, and managers of aggregations of armed men that could be hired for the making of war.

That entrepreneurs of noble lineage were important to economic development cannot be doubted when the relevant data begin to be rounded up; moreover, the lines of activity in which they were engaged from about the fourteenth to the eighteenth centuries are surprisingly diverse. Many nobles, of course, lived on country estates, but they sometimes also had town properties. In any case, they did not confine their activities to the exploitation of natural resources that chanced to be in their possession. Quite a few appear to have taken active roles in wholesale commerce, often foreign trade. Others carried on manufacturing in the towns, although perhaps less often than in the country.

Dr. Foster notes that as early as the tenth century four noble families seem to have had a monopoly of glass-making in Brittany. Those with landed properties advantageously situated for water shipment often turned their attention to commercial agriculture. For example, Dr. Redlich mentions the evolution of the *Gutswirtschaft* in eastern Germany which shipped grain to the growing towns of western Europe. Professor H. J. Habakkuk writes of the "improving" noble landowners of England in the seventeenth and eighteenth centuries when the towns provided a nicely expanding market. Those with landed properties were also likely to take up mining if their lands contained minerals or coal underground. The counts of Mansfeld, for instance, had almost a monopoly of the mining and smelting of copper in Germany in the sixteenth century, and Dr. Hermann Kellenbenz speaks of the notable Holstein entrepreneur, Henrich Rantzau, who owned no less than thirty-nine mills, establishments that produced lumber, paper, flour, oil, and powder, and manufactured articles from iron, copper, and brass. In Spain, Portugal, Sweden, Germany, Poland, and Italy there were others.[5]

It will be recognized as not unnatural that the degree of activity, and success, among the nobility of a given country differed markedly. Of course, there was at any one time in such a country as France a very considerable diversity in the economic positions of individuals who could claim noble status. There were nobles with extensive lands and with monies available to loan, and there were nobles who, perhaps with a sword around their waists, walked sadly behind the plough on their small plots of land. Undoubtedly, also, there was something of the diversity of initiative that Professor Danhof thinks to see among the American commercial farmers of the early nineteenth century.

On second thoughts, if not on first, it seems quite logical and natural that the nobility should engage in actions of the foregoing types, particularly under monarchs who were interested in strengthening economically their kingdoms or dukedoms or empires. "Sanctions" of effect were chiefly those exerted by such a monarch, and they were perhaps more effective with the nobility than with the burghers of the towns. If the king of Sweden suggested that it would be a good thing for the country to have more powder mills, what would be more natural than for some nobles to seek royal favor by attempting to set up powder mills? Or as I suggested above, if Maria Theresa chanced to mouth the hope for more cotton-cloth production within her empire, would not some nobles be likely to seek to satisfy the Empress in this regard? Thus perhaps mercantilistic or cameralistic policies with respect to domestic manufactures were carried out administratively.

Entrepreneurs among the nobility seem to have had two types of advantage, although these appear to have varied considerably from place to place and from time to time. One was exemption from the payment of certain taxes; and the other was the possession of rights to serf labor. The importance of these conditions would, of course, depend upon the degree of internal or international competition in the commodities produced by the nobility in their enterprises or on their properties. Perhaps it was on account of such circumstances that everywhere the nobility was forbidden to engage in handicraft activities and in retail trade.

One difficulty was that shared by all who sought to promote or execute economic advance in these decades — the paucity of information as to what to produce, how to produce it, what to try to sell abroad, how to get it there, and how to get payment. Probably it is appropriate to speak of these noble entrepreneurs of the early modern period as "community-bound" — at any rate, "locality-bound" — as one might also speak of the Colonial merchants of New England. A few books on mining had appeared in the sixteenth and seventeenth centuries; very little on manufacturing of any sort; some manuals on commercial practices, weights, measures, and monies of European countries; no current commercial journals or the like.

Presumably information of varied sorts was purveyed by travelers. One type of traveler has interested Professor Karl F. Helleiner of Toronto as a possible source of innovations, at least of ideas new to particular areas. This is the quasi-scholar, quasi-humbug, such as the self-styled Count de Saint Germain, who moved from court to court in the seventeenth century, living by his wits, proposing economic changes, spreading ideas. Dr. Redlich suggests also that the alchemists as a group (of whom the Count was one), who likewise moved about more than most men of the period, could supply considerable technological knowledge. And the higher ministers of the several courts could have taken upon themselves to provide both basic and current data. There is, for example, the case of the travels of a son of Count Karl Otto Haugwitz of Austria in 1754 and 1755 through Italy, Hungary, and most of Germany, accompanied by a technical assistant.

One further source of information or perhaps one further medium of information has been suggested by Dr. Redlich as interesting in itself but particularly significant as evidence of one peculiarity of aristocratic entrepreneurship. This is communication among the nobility itself. Apparently, like commercial farmers almost everywhere around the world, they had no practice of secrecy about methods or processes or successful innovations as was true in the same period, and at other times, among handicraftsmen and manufacturers, even to a considerable extent among merchants. The "improving" landowners and farmers of England or the United States reported their crop achievements in agricultural journals and broadcast how they thought that they had accomplished the noteworthy gains. So also presumably an aristocratic owner of a copper smelter or slitting mill would quite surely find pleasure in telling a visiting aristocrat how he operated, what processes he employed, where the skilled workmen were to be procured, and so on. Practices of this sort cannot, of course, be proven, but surely they correlate with the sanctions evident in other aspects of aristocratic behavior.

Beyond the matter of technical and commercial information — to say nothing also about the problems of executing the actions called for by such data — there were at certain times and places legal restrictions to be overcome, hostilities to be surmounted, perhaps particular social roles to be carried through because of public prejudices or anticipations. (In the present state of our knowledge, we can hardly be more specific.) Apparently, the nobility everywhere in Europe was free of legal restraints until the sixteenth century or thereabouts. Outside of France the members of the class could do what they wished in business, except handicraft work and retail trade. Perhaps, on the other hand, the latter restraints derived solely from moral considerations, things that fighting men should not demean themselves to do. Quite generally, the aristocracy lost status if it soiled its hands in work.

The times of change in France seem to have been different from those elsewhere in Europe. Moreover, the data supplied by Dr. Charles A. Foster enable one to trace the nature of the experiences more closely than in any other country (except England, to which none of these matters applies). Briefly it may be stated that after a gradual expansion of noble activities in various lines of business, Louis XI, the great bourgeois king reigning in the fifteenth century, confirmed to the nobility freedom to engage in any activity of a commercial or mechanical nature. With his death, however, a reaction set in which before the end of the sixteenth century had interdicted practically all forms of business to members of the noble class.

Another reversal took place in the seventeenth century, partly in procedure and partly in reality. Quite surely both Richelieu and Colbert encouraged the nobility to take active roles in the economic upbuilding of the nation. Quite surely also there was some evasion or disregard of such decrees as still stood on the statute books, with public sentiments on the subject varying appreciably from region to region of the country. In the meantime, a system of official relaxation of laws in specific cases had grown up. In this manner the noble could escape *dérogeance,* that is, action by which he would lose the rights and privileges attaching to the nobility as such, especially, it seems, the exemption from certain taxation. At the beginning of the new century, specifically in 1701, an act was passed especially concerned with wholesale commerce. Immunity from *dérogeance* was assured to all nobility that chose to engage in such commerce by land or sea.

Despite the apparent general and special relaxations of the rules, French aristocrats going into business in the eighteenth century went to troubles that seem to reflect fears of being subject to *dérogeance.* They would insist that there be written specifically into *lettres-patentes* a clause covering avoidance of such a state. Again, the practice became quite common for nobles to use straw men or false names — *hommes de paille, prête-noms* — in partnership agreements and subscriptions to stock. While a vagueness appears to have persisted in the law, the noble still feared to find himself in a stultifying position. As Dr. Foster remarks, the noble would have to base his case for greater freedom "either actively or passively upon the principles of economic liberalism, which in the last analysis would spell the end of the system of privileges, and indeed of an essential element of the organization of society of which he was a member." [6]

The aristocratic entrepreneur, then, flourished rather widely for some centuries in Europe; he was active in a number of important lines of economic action; and he undoubtedly contributed to the economic development of the area. Despite support at times and in varying degrees from chiefs of state, the form of entrepreneurship did remain primitive in character. Its position at law and in public opinion was clouded over from time to time; frequently, if not usually, the business activity was incidental or distinctly secondary to other roles; and it never grew vigorous enough to promote or devise vehicles of information flow that manifested any substantial advance toward the sophisticated forms of the nineteenth and twentieth centuries.

VIGNETTE 2: THE PERSISTENCE OF SOCIAL RESIDUES

No one has seen more clearly the relations of entrepreneurial character to the nature and operations of the particular social system in which it exists than Professor Sawyer.[7] There are, he writes, "observable national differences in entrepreneurial activity," which he feels "cannot be accounted for in terms of economic factors alone, or in terms of the hero in history, the distribution of genes, or any simple psychological reductionism." In seeking explanation, one must turn to "the system of goals and values, the scale of social rankings, and the pattern of conduct that are 'institutionalized' in the particular society." [8] To be sure, these social elements change through time; for example, when a successful or unsuccessful war gives its backlash, when a Colbert or an Alexander Hamilton influences governmental attitudes, or when a group of robber barons makes manifest how unpleasant some varieties of businessmen can be. So also do the economic circumstances change — the domestic market, the international connections, and the technological situation, any of which may themselves stimulate entrepreneurial action. And again there seem to be social institutions and habits of thought, hierarchies of status, educational practices, et cetera, which last beyond the economic situation that gave them birth (or that at least found them innocuous in terms of economic welfare), and which become deterrents upon the business change that altered economic opportunities would otherwise have encouraged.

Analytically there are three or four elements to be considered separately in a discussion of the impact upon entrepreneurial performance of social systems of variant characters. One of these elements is the acceptance of change. Here one must turn to the anthropologist for the full story, but it appears that societies could be rated variantly, from reluctance to accept economic change to eagerness to promote that change. A society will not tolerate entrepreneurs if it objects to innovations and novelties.

A special form of change important for entrepreneurial performance is that of social mobility. To be sure, a sort of crypto-mobility may suffice for a time, as when a Russian serf accumulated money in the hope of buying his freedom or when he could employ free men to do his bidding. But a greater degree of persistent recognition was better. The Heralds' College in England is alleged to have stimulated entrepreneurial action in that country by providing heraldic shields for successful businessmen who desired to possess coats-of-arms. And in a society such as the United States where wealth opened practically all social doors, entrepreneurs and social movement were found together.

A third element is the toleration of making money, of activity in business. In various societies of the past, the merchant or the businessman in general has ranked below such social figures as the clergy, the soldiers, the teachers, and the professional men as a whole. In other societies, activity in business suffered qualitatively. Men in business maintained low thresholds for the frequent or continual intrusion of art or literature, family pleasures, or just long daily siestas. They sought to retire as early as possible in their lives to participate in "more worthwhile" actions, and tried to make possible the movement of their children into the more honorific posts and activities.

Fourth, one might differentiate materialism, conspicuous consumption, obvious accumulation of property, and the like. A society might tolerate a wealthy class if quite unmistakably on the whole it used its wealth in the service of the country; it might adopt a different attitude toward the activity that brought such wealth into private hands if the possessors built themselves gaudy palaces or indulged in conspicuous profligacy.

And there are still further factors that must be taken into account in explaining such phenomena as an Oriental entrepreneur strongly preferring relatives as members of his staff, a French industrialist disliking to drive competitors out of business, or an American entrepreneur being content to assert that business is his life, really a soul-satisfying career.

Professors Sawyer and Landes have independently examined the situation in France and given substantially comparable reports of their findings. It is unnecessary here to attempt to reproduce their materials.[9] A few fragments from their analyses will serve to illustrate the diversity of the forces involved.

Professor Sawyer finds present-day survivals or residues from the "formally stratified hereditary social order" of earlier days, a society based on a seigneurial, agricultural economy, in which property was tied to family and status, political and legal authority tended to be personal and particularistic, and communal relationships counted for much.[10] And Professor Landes finds that business enterprise in France typically "is not an end in itself, nor is its purpose to be found in any such independent ideal as production or service. It exists by and for the family, and the honor, reputation, and wealth of the one are the honor, wealth, and reputation of the other."[11] Something of the dominant attitudes of the earlier period seems to have persisted also in consumption habits: while the American consumer is characteristically content to secure merely more goods, whether similar to his neighbor's or not, the Frenchman's conspicuous consumption takes the form of individualized items — as if he were feeling, "These were prepared according to my orders for my particular pleasure." In short, the French business world, at least that of larger units, would ideally be constituted along the lines of an aggregate of manorial estates with loyalties, personal responsibilities, and community dominance, largely unchanged.

But Professor Sawyer finds French entrepreneurship conditioned also by another set of residues, those of a society that drew its inspiration from "Liberty, Equality, Fraternity." Out of this complex, seemingly, certain tendencies derive which support predispositions of the earlier society: a higher valuation on personal relationships than on material advantage, as revealed in the French system of goods distribution; or the willingness to "live and let live" in the relations among competing enterprises.[12]

All in all, one gains the impression of substantial variance between French and American entrepreneurship in just the elements that make for creativeness, vigor, long-range planning, and the like: that is, in "the system of goals and values, the scale of social rankings, and the pattern of conduct," that are institutionalized in the two countries.

Somewhat comparable studies have more recently been made of Germany and India, Japan and Jamaica.[13] I venture to call attention to the situation in England. Already I have cited Professor de Scitovszky's appraisal of the influence upon entrepreneurship in England of objectives derived from the hierarchical structure of English society with its important bases or manifestation in land-holding.[14] I would add a second influence.

If the country in England was dominated by king and aristocracy, the towns were not; and the merchant power in the towns persisted over so long a period as to leave its stamp upon modes of English thinking — to bequeath residues that affect present-day entrepreneurial performance in that nation. Professor Thrupp has portrayed vividly the position of the merchant class in medieval London. The economico-business literature from the fifteenth century onward reveals the hegemony of commerce, even above agriculture or finance. It is perhaps significant that even through the nineteenth century "commerce" was a term much more common than "business," and signifying the same thing; that the first books that attempted to deal scientifically with business carried the word "commercial" in their titles; even that Charles Wilson's recent definition of entrepreneurship turns on the ability of a businessman to recognize a market opportunity and to have the ability to exploit that chance.

That Englishmen should have taken a hundred years after the industrial changes of the eighteenth century to convert commercial accounting to industrial uses might be viewed as a not unnatural result of the mercantile domination. So also might be the slowness with which advanced education for business has taken hold in England, and writing in the field also. In commercial life, the size of units is typically small, and success depends greatly upon personal contacts and upon intimate knowledge of goods. One could not really "teach" business; it was necessary for each apprentice to "learn" it for himself. Even the dominant character of English banking, with its reliance largely on short-term commercial paper, and the tardy development of a universalistic investment banking system may, likewise, be conceived as consequences of the socio-economic order of English urban communities.

Perhaps with Professor Danhof one may pursue the analysis in terms of prestigious evaluations.[15] One may prefer to utilize the "structural-functional" approach that stems from Professor Parsons. Or, indeed, one may select to "look merely at the facts," as in Dr. Redlich's essay on the many paths to entrepreneurship. There can be no doubt that "observable national differences in entrepreneurial activity" at any one time — or for that matter changes in entrepreneurial activity in a given nation through time — "cannot be accounted for in terms of economic factors alone" or in any other simple "reductionism," and that most widely potent is (and has been) the "social order" of thought and institutions.

VIGNETTE 3: THE SERF ENTREPRENEUR

As Henry Rosovsky suggests in his excellent article on the Russian serf as entrepreneur,[16] the phenomenon is likely at first blush to seem a paradox. "The serf and the entrepreneur are rarely coupled, and most frequently orthodox economic theory almost separates them by definition. Serfdom implies a condition which ties the individual to the soil and makes him subject, more or less, to the will of his owner. The entrepreneur is thought of in terms of activity, courage, and enterprise — a Schumpeterian figure, not a carry-over from mediaeval times." Yet Rosovsky finds thousands of serf-entrepreneurs in Russia at the time of emancipation (1861), with no few playing rather important roles in the industrial development of the nineteenth century, and many thousands more being useful in the operation of the Russian economy of those decades.

Among the individually more prominent serf entrepreneurs might be specified men by the names of Grachev and Garelin, who were resident in the village of Ivanovo, which is located about 180 miles north of Moscow. This village had been a center of linen-cloth manufacture from the early seventeenth century — an activity promoted by city merchants. Serfs became operatives in these establishments, and out of these workers, perhaps particularly out of the skilled printers, arose men "touched by the entrepreneurial spirit," as Rosovsky puts it. By 1798 Grachev was employing 120 persons in his cotton-cloth plants. In addition he was engaged in the older linen-cloth manufacture, having 90 looms in his village establishments and keeping another 400 busy on a putting-out basis. Garelin was similarly occupied, but seemingly on a somewhat less extensive scale. A goodly number of the employees, incidentally, were also serfs, so that we have the curious combination of serf entrepreneur commanding serf workers!

Compared with such men as Grachev and Garelin, the thousands mentioned above were individually unimportant. They seem to have been largely self-employed: tailors and candlemakers, storekeepers, locksmiths, and free-lance carriage drivers. If inconsequential individually, nevertheless they counted for much in the aggregate, as noted above, in making the economy operative. To be sure, Rosovsky does not hold that, even adding all grades of serf entrepreneur together, one could claim that they bulked large in the Russian economy of the preliberation decades. The economy was very heavily agricultural, and the chief urban element was the group of merchants. It is noteworthy, however, that a few of the serf entrepreneurs prospered enough to be reckoned millionaires, and that in some cases they had free merchants working for them, occasionally holding property for them in areas where ownership by serfs was forbidden. The phenomenon reached fairly deep.

How can one explain such a development? Rosovsky suggests the impact of several factors, most of them noneconomic. There *was* an expanding market for manufactured items in Russia, with the growth of population and the improvements, however slow, in transportation facilities, while, for such men as those specifically named above, a special advantage derived from Napoleon's sack of Moscow: Ivanovo was far enough away, but not too far. Again, the expansion of the towns and cities, in part the result of the inflow of other serfs, constituted part of the increased market for goods.

Serfs were allowed off the properties to which they belonged — in some degree, it seems, were encouraged to leave — by reason of the commutation of labor dues, which by the eighteenth century had become common in certain parts of the country, in the area north of Moscow in a ratio of three to two. Under the straight labor-dues system, the serf had no incentive beyond getting through his obligations to his lord as quickly and easily as possible, and returning to his own small plot, if he had such. Under commutation, there was opportunity, at least for ambitious serfs. They might work off their money payment quickly and have any further earnings for themselves. Indeed, they might dare to look forward to purchasing their freedom from savings out of their activities, and, if not for themselves, then perhaps for their sons.

The ambitions of money-paying serfs were doubtlessly aided by the upward trend in commodity prices which occurred in western Europe in the eighteenth century, and probably affected Russia in the same period, as well as by the special advance in prices over the French Revolution and Napoleonic years. Money dues set at one date could become less burdensome at a later one, and the serf payer would have more of his income left in his hands.

The agreement of lords to commutation of labor dues appears to have stemmed from two or three elements. Certain lands, such as those north of Moscow, were ill-suited to agricultural activities, especially under the inefficient serf system. There was a possibility that some other mode of using the serfs might prove more advantageous. Moreover, in the eighteenth and nineteenth centuries the lords found their expenses rising, perhaps in part as a result of the increasing commodity prices mentioned above, probably more as a consequence of changes in urban and especially court life. As a result they needed more available cash. Some of them had tried to utilize serfs in manufacturing units set up on their estates, but this arrangement had proven futile. The serfs selected to work in the shops were no more efficient than on the land, probably less so because they disliked the requirement of learning something new, and the denial of work that all the others in their status were performing.

Finally, a sort of negative factor should be noted. Serf entrepreneurship sometimes continued to exist, after it had once evolved, because particular lords refused to release serfs even after the latter had become capable of paying liberally for their freedom. The wealthier nobles found less advantage in accepting such payment than the less well-to-do. And there were some who refused release because that act would serve only to lower their own status. Such a lord was the member of the Sheremetev family who owned Ivanovo and controlled many serfs, including Grachev and Garelin.

Perhaps there was even an administrative element involved for some nobles. A serf entrepreneur who took other serfs into his industrial establishment, or even engaged them to work for him on a putting-out basis, frequently undertook to cover the money payments which these other serfs had committed themselves to pay the lord. The serf entrepreneur became in substance a dues collector.

In short, it appears that, given the various circumstances of eighteenth- and early nineteenth-century Russia, the advent and continuance of serf entrepreneurship constituted a "natural," at least a wholly expectable, phenomenon. Indeed, it seems that the phenomenon may not have been restricted to Russia. Dr. Redlich reports the discovery of evidence that serf entrepreneurs existed in parts of Austria and in German Silesia.

These cases do give support to two features of entrepreneurial thought in general: (a) talent for entrepreneurship will be found in all strata of individual societies, a conclusion that is supported by the data already presented upon aristocratic experience, and those offered elsewhere concerning handicraftsmen, merchants, occasionally professional men; and (b) entrepreneurial endeavors will rise through crevices in societies made rigid by tradition or force. The NEP episode in Soviet Russia tends to support this view.

Actually there appear to be aspects of the earlier Russian experience that convey color or overtones to what seem normal social manifestations of entrepreneurial life, at least in communities that are not heavily weighted with Calvinistic values. For example, the successful serf entrepreneurs indulged in "conspicuous consumption," as have newly risen entrepreneurs elsewhere. Turgenev tells of such a serf, who possessed a two-story brick residence — rarely to be found in a Russian village — and who served good dinners, at least on occasion, complete with champagne. These entrepreneurs also, again like new bearers of the role, could become severe disciplinarians. They bore down hard upon other serfs who had not been so fortunate (or so ambitious) as they. They seem even to have attempted to put obstacles in the way of others following in their footsteps. The Russian serf entrepreneur, then, may be accepted as truly a species of the same genus as the Dutch merchants with their lovely town houses, the first large American industrialists who desired to impress their contemporaries in almost all ways, or the early English cotton-mill owners who could be cruel toward orphan children.

Section 2 ·

ENTREPRENEURSHIP AND UNDERDEVELOPED AREAS

VIGNETTE 4: ENTREPRENEURSHIP IN PRIMITIVE CONDITIONS

Perhaps some day scholars will think it worthwhile to spend time in attempting to trace and catalog all sources of entrepreneurship, all the situations in which the activity has taken first root. As already indicated, Professor Thrupp has suggested three possibilities as common in western Europe: local famines, the financial necessities of princes, and the provision of sacramental wine; and Dr. Redlich has thought of the opportunity of becoming business intermediaries that came to serfs or other peasants who transported grain or other goods from manors to the rising towns.

Whatever the initial impulse, there seems to be a period in the economic development of most areas when entrepreneurship lacked the strength to stand alone. Professor Easterbrook would say that the minimum measures of security had not yet been provided.[17] Actually, the phenomenon seems more general in character. Sometimes it appears that the uncertainties of financial return yield consequences not essentially different from the hazards of life, theft, or similar misfortune. At any rate, there are numerous cases in history where the state has stepped in to provide securities that appeared to be necessary to induce entrepreneurial action. It might take the form of naval escort to Venetian merchant vessels of the fourteenth century; it might involve the release to such an entrepreneurial organization as the British East India Company of powers that in most other situations the government kept in its own hands;[18] or, in nineteenth-century America, it might take the aspect of "mixed" enterprise, the state furnishing some of the capital, all of which might be lost.

The Canadian fur trade offers an excellent example of the impact of hazards of various sorts upon the mold in which entrepreneurial endeavor was carried on. Here the evidence was assembled in Professor Innis' *Fur Trade in Canada,* and analyzed anew in Professors Easterbrook's and Aitken's *Canadian Economic History.*

From the earliest days of French possession, merchants of Quebec and Montreal were desirous of dealing in the commodity. Indeed, furs constituted practically the sole item that could be exported from the interior of the country. And it was a commodity with some fortunate characteristics: it enjoyed a steady, if somewhat inelastic, demand in Europe — a demand that grew continuously, it seems, but could not be made to expand by modest price reductions; and it was an item that provided relatively high value in relatively small bulk, a fact that had influence in more than one direction. It facilitated the movement of the goods once they had been secured, but it also encouraged the continued spread of trapping activities over more extended areas of the wilderness.

On the whole, the marketing elements in the trade were difficult for the Quebec and Montreal merchants to overcome. The turnover was slow. A couple of years might well be needed between the assembling of goods to be exchanged for furs, and actual realization from the sale. The friendly

Huron tribe of Indians had initially been utilized as collectors of the furs, but they soon had to become middlemen between the merchants and tribes more remote. In repeated warfare, the Iroquois disputed the role of middleman with the Hurons, and the Indians resented in some measure the efforts of the white men to introduce greater system into the business, especially when *coureurs du bois* and *voyageurs* began to reach back closer to the sources of supply. Occasionally movement of furs was impeded by the unwillingness of a given tribe of Indians — a settled plains group, for example — to participate in the transportation of their catch.

By the eighteenth century, moreover, the British traders operating from Albany, New York, were cutting into the business of the Canadian French. They had support from the Iroquois. Also the British possessed the advantages of shorter lines of communication with Europe, cheaper manufactured goods to barter with the Indians, and West Indian rum, which was not only less costly than French brandy, but widely preferred by the Indians over the latter form of liquor.

Last, but not least, the French government recognized, quite as well as the local merchants, that furs were the only immediately available source of income from its North American hinterland. Therefore, it sought to use the commerce in furs somehow as a source of government revenue.

An important consequence of all these circumstances was that the trade in Canadian furs was free of government or other control only over short intervals. Licenses to engage in the business were usually required; the government endeavored to enforce a monopoly of purchase from dealers; it undertook military action in support of its plans; and the like. Moreover, when the British essayed an attack on the French hunting grounds more direct and more organized than that maintained by a few merchants in Albany, it took the form of the chartered Hudson's Bay Company, although at the time (1670) English public opinion was turning vigorously against such enterprises with exclusive privileges. Perhaps the form was justified in this case; at least it is true that the company declared no dividend for seven years. Again, it is noteworthy that, after 1763 and the reorganization of the trade under the British flag, it was not long before the fur-trading firms of Montreal were agreeing to "join their stock" and soon were setting up a "North West Company," which exercised over much of the next decades an effective monopoly of the business. In 1821 the Hudson's Bay Company absorbed the North West Company and again secured a substantially monopolistic position.

In short, the physical and economic conditions of the Canadian fur trade fostered a relationship to government and a type of entrepreneurial organization quite different from that which was common in the more southerly thirteen colonies. The elements of insecurity in these conditions seem to have been most decisive. The manner in which entrepreneurial activity is carried out — to some extent the manner in which it *can* be carried out — is a derivation of many forces. Sometimes a "free" entrepreneurial system is feasible; often it is not.

VIGNETTE 5: THE PIONEER ENTREPRENEUR

The "underdeveloped," but rapidly expanding, areas of the United States produced the jack-of-all-trades and the "tinkerer" in its handicraftsmen; they stimulated also the blacksmith who could turn his hand to a considerable variety of tasks; and a somewhat comparable entrepreneur arose in the same regions. This pioneer entrepreneur is to be found in eighteenth-century New England and progressively across the country with the opening-up of successive regions.

The Browns of Providence Plantations, as Professor

Hedges has labeled the family, constitute a striking case.[19] The first Brown of note was a merchant of Providence, dealing at wholesale and retail in a diversity of goods. He trained four nephews, John, James, Nicholas, and Moses, in whose hands the family's fortunes rose. Soon they had a distillery to manufacture rum out of the molasses which they were importing from the West Indies; they set up a ropewalk to supply their ships with cordage; they took a brief interest in the slave trade; they were leading figures in the manufacture of spermaceti candles and in the creation and operation of the "trust" that attempted to control the market for such candles. In addition, they established the Hope Iron Furnace nearby, and in fact provided the metal for the iron railing that for decades surrounded the Battery at the tip of Manhattan Island. Before the close of the century, they were in the China trade, owned cotton mills, and had at least a finger, probably more, in banking and insurance. To be sure, they were not active in all of these lines of business at any one time, and some of their operations may be viewed as steps in the transference of mercantile capital to domestic manufacture. There were four brothers, and later their sons and partners, involved in the total experience, although for the most part the brothers went into activities jointly; but the record is a notable one. The entrepreneurship was diversified in objectives, or perhaps subjectives!

A few decades later the case of Erastus Corning could be cited.[20] Admittedly there was some connection between his two major lines of activity, his hardware business and his interest in the railroads stretching westerly from his home-town of Albany, New York: his store sold rails to the railroad companies. However, he seems to have taken a creative attitude toward the railroads, much more than was necessary to foster the market for his iron, and in the end expended much time and energy as president of the New York Central Railroad. In addition, he invested in western lands, became involved in the construction of the canal at Sault St. Marie, helped to create and then served as president of a savings bank, and was concerned in local charities.

Further west, and later, Cadwallader Washburn will serve as an example.[21] Washburn came from Maine to Minnesota in the 1850's, together with a number of other men interested in lumbering.[22] Successively he became interested in lumbering, in the operation of sawmills and the sale of their output, in the waterfalls at Minneapolis, in flour-milling machinery, in banking, and in the development of the rapidly growing city. At one stage he set about the planning and construction of a railroad, because he thought that those then serving Minneapolis were conspiring to exact excessive rates on his goods and those of his fellow citizens.

The McGees of Kansas City, thriving especially in the 1860's, will serve as my final example.[23] The first real blooming seems to have been connected with the outfitting business in the 1850's, but previously the family had had contacts with a flour mill, a distillery, a sawmill, a tavern, and a general store as well as the almost inevitable land speculation. Later the McGees apparently had fingers in many lines of business development in the thriving city.

Actually, one encounters this phenomenon fairly late in the evolution of the eastern United States, as new centers rose. One such case was investigated years ago by Robert K. Lamb, who studied the development of Fall River. This advance did not really get launched until the founding of the Fall River Iron Works in 1825. From that base the intertwined Borden and Durfee families expanded into cotton textiles, commercial banking, the railroads that touched Fall River, and real estate. Professor Lamb came to argue the

163

importance of the group as the source from which individual entrepreneurs often seem to derive much of their strength, and the importance of the community.[24]

The phenomena described above relate to the phase or stage of entrepreneurial evolution that I have ventured to denominate "community-focused." [25] Here it seems to have been the opportunities offered by the area of residence that tended to condition the bearers of the entrepreneurial role. Also these pioneer entrepreneurs frequently became leaders in the business evolution of the city, identifying themselves with the community and finding satisfaction in its prosperity. At a later date businessmen were led to specialize in given industries, and to think of themselves as primarily associated with the rest of that industry, less with the community in which they were located and less with such unexploited opportunities as it offered.

VIGNETTE 6: THE OVERSANGUINE ENTREPRENEUR

Professor Sawyer has called attention to the contribution of error to economic development, although he used rather more careful language.[26] Professors J. Keith Butters and John Lintner spoke a few years ago of the sort of psychological compulsion that spurred men to set up their own enterprises;[27] and the statistics of concerns that do not survive their first birthdays appear to confirm such a hypothesis. Anyway, it seems that cold, rational calculation of risks and chances of success has never controlled the launching of business enterprises, especially in economies that have been undergoing rapid or reasonably rapid growth under conditions of free enterprise. To be sure, there undoubtedly have been numerous businesses begun under unsound economic conditions which have survived and prospered by dint of supernormal exertions and ingenuities of their entrepreneurs.

In Professor William W. Cooper's phrase, they have been "made to behave."

Henry Noble Day's career will serve to illustrate the sort of "error" in business mentioned above. Perhaps because his contribution to American economic evolution was slight, and because little remained behind after his business activities to mark his passage, he is all the more valuable to us. The record is not distorted by subsequent reconstructions deriving from successful achievement. The case is the more important to us, however, by reason of the imaginative and painstaking work of research that his biographer, Professor R. Richard Wohl, carried through. As a result of his labors we are able to see Day the promoter projected against the background of the social thought and sanction patterns of his era and community. No biographical sketch, at least in the field of entrepreneurial history, more fully interweaves historical data and sociological theory.[28]

The chief events in Henry Day's life are rather quickly told. He was born in a small town in Connecticut in 1808, and spent his youth in New Haven, living in the house of his uncle, who was the president of Yale. Henry attended the college, graduating in the class of 1828. After sampling the professions of teaching and law, he turned to the ministry, studied further at Yale, and ultimately wandered almost by chance to Hudson, Ohio, a small town thirty miles south of Cleveland, which was then the seat of Western Reserve University. Henry Day was to teach sacred rhetoric at the university.

Now at Hudson in the 1840's two things happened to Day. He found his duties at the university so simple that he had time for journalism, and soon took responsibility for the local newspaper. Second, and partly as an indirect result of the first circumstance, he was caught up in the railroad fever that was then afflicting that portion of the country. In fact, he rose swiftly to become the promoter of a group of railroad lines that should convert Hudson into an important rail center, tying the roads of the East with other lines that would sooner or later reach the Pacific Coast, and a promoter of stores and other business structures that would be appropriate for such a transportation center. Perhaps it was inevitable in all the circumstances that this delightful dream should not last long. The bubble broke in 1854. It required a year or two, even with Day's help, for the interested parties — and the courts — to distribute such assets as survived. Once this was accomplished Henry Day accepted the headship of a "female seminary" at College Hill, near Cincinnati, and did not touch business again.

Now, there are actually many interesting facets of this story, even if Henry Noble Day cannot be regarded as important by most standards and even if Hudson never has grown to be a Chicago or even a Cleveland. For one thing, it will be obvious to all who know American history passably well that Henry Day was the prototype of "boosters" and local promoters who appeared — and disappeared — in thousands of American communities over the decades of the nineteenth century. It was in part by reason of these Henry Days that the country grew.

With most such individuals, however, it is impossible to reconstruct with even plausible evidence the thoughts and emotions with which they carried through their self-imposed tasks. It is fortunate that a satisfactory documentation does exist in the case of Henry Day, and happily Professor Wohl recognized its unusual quality. I venture to introduce my own interpretations of certain conditions and developments, but essentially the events may be recorded succinctly as follows.

Henry Day grew up in a relatively well-settled area, where

economic opportunity still knocked on doors, but less loudly than elsewhere in the nation, and where the making of money had become subject to socially approved expectancies, if not rules. He matured also in a region which was still heavily permeated with religious thought and religious specification of conduct. The uncle in whose house Henry Day lived through his college years could write to his son, "The acquisition of property will not compensate for the neglect of the great interests of eternity." [29] Third, it will be noted that Henry Day was a member of a leading family of Connecticut. Among his uncles, a distinguished lawyer, who was for years the secretary of state for Connecticut, can be added to the president of Yale. On all these counts it is small wonder that Henry Day sought a professional career of some stripe, and decided to settle upon that of the ministry.

There were also idiosyncratic elements in the whole picture. One quite surely was the "poor relation" circumstance in which the lad grew up. Another, hinted at by Professor Wohl, is the interest of Day in the "revival" or more emotional facet of the religious life of his era. His biographer goes further to suggest that the lack of decisiveness in his choice of career implies a measure of instability in Day's character.[30]

Before he left New Haven for the West, his hostages to a circumspect and perhaps circumscribed life had been enhanced by marriage to the daughter of the leading banker. But also one of the supports to his chosen role of religious teacher had been somewhat undercut. A brother of his, Jeremiah, had avoided college and had gone south, where he prospered in the very new but thriving town of Apalachicola. Henry sent small sums to his brother to commit to southern speculations, profits accrued excellently, but the young man was so eager for financial success that even his brother, located in a bubbling community, felt moved to write him, "You are a little too hasty to get rich." [31]

Then Henry moved to what was essentially frontier. Numerous observers have remarked on the tendency of such regions to loosen the social bonds that invisibly but effectively tie men to patterns of moral behavior approved in their older areas of residence. There is likely to be more of heavy drinking, cheating, homicides in frontier communities, at least until law and order have again been restored. Quite surely social roles of less violent character might be modified in such regions. Henry Day did alter his ways. He had not been in Hudson more than a couple of years when, although sitting in a chair of "sacred rhetoric" at the theological seminary, he projected himself into a world of different nature, that of newspaper publishing. Soon he had allowed himself to be carried even further — into railroad promotion, the building of warehouses and commercial structures, the setting-up of businesses such as a general store and a drugstore, and the borrowing of monies wherever he could find investors.

A technical factor in Henry Day's entrepreneurial performance — and we are interested in the how as well as the why of such activity — was something that Day seems to have picked up from President Pierce of Western Reserve University. The institution was young; there were other, competing theological schools in the neighborhood; and anyway funds for the support of higher education were hard to find in that region in the 1840's. Accordingly, the president did not hesitate to budget a deficit, or utilize such credit as he could discover, and hope to come out "in the black" at the end of the fiscal year. Of course, Western Reserve was not the only institution, and probably not the only educational institution, in the Middle West of that period that made use of credit or lived from year to year "on a shoestring." Nor was it the last such in more parts of the country than Ohio! However, this example of "risk-bearing" right under his nose, as it were, and on the part of a respectable institution may well have had a direct and potent effect on Henry Day's concept of the entrepreneurial role.

By a most happy chance, we are able to apprehend how Henry Day justified to himself the changes that he had introduced into his roles. In 1850, before the crash of his hopes, he preached a sermon, the text of which has been preserved. Building from the base out of Daniel, "In the night I saw visions," he evolved the thesis in substance that, from the nature of the extensive country, the character of its political institutions, and the endowments of its people, there was clearly to be seen the handiwork of God; economic development was obviously a directive upon Americans. Day found an "expression of our national life" to lie "in our industry and in our arts."

> The characteristics which Christianity at its present stage seems to require are chiefly vigor of invention, skill in execution and subscribing to the true trend of industrial arts — utility. In the activity and vigor of inventive talent and in the general success of mechanical enterprise, the docility with which foreign arts are studied and apprehended, and the restless ambition to press on from present achievements to higher stages of perfection give our countrymen advantages over those countries in which a narrow conservatism veils existing defects and indisposes to further improvements . . .
>
> We must despise all nature's influence, if we be not . . . a united, self-relying, powerful, enterprising and magnanimous people — such a people as the advance of Christianity now calls to its service, such a people, in these respects, as a millennial sun will not blush to look upon.[32]

Professor Thomas N. Carver in his *Religion Worth Having* seventy-five years later could hardly do better. Obviously, it was a Christian's obligation to be productive economically

— and how better than in the promotion of railroads and the reorganization of the local economy?

As a final note to this whole episode, it may be observed that one feature of the disturbing influence was its "foreign" character: the railroad was not a community affair. Perhaps Henry Day would not have been led into so much error if he had limited himself to publishing the local newspaper, even to attempting to erect local stores of various sorts. With the external, regional, even national phenomenon, major uncertainties flowing from "misinformation, conflicts of information and lack of information" entered the picture. Sometimes surely this sort of error — as well as the "constructive" error of which Professor Sawyer has spoken — derived from this transition from community-bound to industry- or nation-bound activity.

Section 3 ·

ENTREPRENEURSHIP AND TECHNOLOGICAL CHANGE

VIGNETTE 7: "LINES OF FORCE" IN TECHNOLOGICAL DIFFUSION

Almost from time immemorial, the man who chanced to possess a special handicraft skill could set himself up as a small-scale entrepreneur. Sometimes he possessed a unique talent, or desired to establish a personal monopoly, as it were, such as the father and son who produced the glass flowers now in the Agassiz Museum at Harvard. Customarily they trained successors, often became units in an organized system, and under guild rules or more modern apprenticeship arrangements exercised and taught their skills. With the breakup of the guild form of entrepreneurial order, the mode of transmission of technological knowledge became irregular. This was especially true of the geographical transmission of such knowledge in a growing country like the United States. Undoubtedly, thousands of small businesses in this country, from the grist mills of Colonial days to the automobile repair shops of the twentieth century, have been founded on, and have flourished by reason of, technological competence on the part of the proprietors.

In most such cases the trails of movement have been lost, and imitation appears automatic in quality. In a few instances the data have chanced to be preserved or have been put together by students. When I was working on the American wool manufacture thirty years ago, I stumbled upon an episode that involved a family.[33] John and Arthur Scholfield came from Yorkshire in 1793. These brothers landed in Boston, accompanied by John's wife and six children, and by a certain John Shaw, a spinner and weaver. They brought with them knowledge of the carding and spinning devices that had come into use in the north of England.

The spread of such information began with the connection made by the brothers in 1793 with the Newbury-Port Woolen Manufactory. Shortly — as I wrote in the 1920's — "John Scholfield, in one of his wool-purchasing trips for the Byfield ["Newbury-Port"] factory, became interested in a water-power site at Montville, Connecticut; and there the Scholfields went in 1799, after selling out their interest in the Byfield concern. In 1801 Arthur parted from his brother and moved to Pittsfield, Massachusetts; while John, after staying in Montville until 1806, sold out and purchased a mill-site at Stonington, Connecticut. Subsequently (1814), John set up another plant at Waterford, near New London, which he placed in charge of his son Thomas. Meanwhile, John's oldest son, John Scholfield, Jr., after being in Colchester, Connecticut, for a time, in 1804 or 1805 set up a wool-carding shop in Jewett City, then a part of Preston, Connecticut. This business seems to have grown into a regular woolen mill, and by 1816 contained a full complement of machinery. Another son, Joseph, became interested in the Merino Woolen Factory at Dudley, Massachusetts, in 1817.

In yet another direction the influence of the family was felt. A third brother, James Scholfield, who had been called from England as soon as John and Arthur had made a place for themselves, in 1802 bought a mill privilege and fulling mill at North Andover, with the financial assistance of Arthur. Here for ten years he carded wool for customers, adding in time the manufacture of broadcloth. For this purpose he used machinery, spinning jennies and looms, operated by hand, which he placed in his house. In 1812 he sold out this business, becoming thereafter superintendent in Mr. Nathaniel Stevens's mill, which was erected the following year.

Finally, of yet greater influence, it seems — though of course one cannot estimate the stimulus given by force of example in the cases above mentioned, — was the activity of Arthur Scholfield, who left his brother John in 1801 (apparently because the latter did not like Arthur's newly wedded wife) and went to Pittsfield, Massachusetts. Upon his arrival, Mr. Scholfield, joined soon by his nephew Isaac, also set up a carding machine and for a few years did carding for customers, until in 1804 he began the manufacture of broadcloth on a small scale. But his main contribution was in another line: the manufacture of carding machines. He seems to have built a few almost from the beginning of his residence in Pittsfield. The first advertisement of machines for sale appeared in the *Pittsfield Sun* of September 12, 1803; and in the next year (May 14, 1804) he informed the public that besides having machines to sell, "built under his immediate inspection," he "will give drafts and other instructions to those who wish to build themselves." The terms of these services are not stated; nor is the reason clear, although reading between the lines suggests the competition which was already developing. He gives warning against imposition "by uninformed, speculating companies, who demand more than twice as much for their machines as they are really worth." However, by 1806 the demand for his products was so great that he sold out his carding business and devoted himself solely to the manufacture of machines for sale. Then, and indeed in after years, no more frequent recommendation of a carding machine was made than that it came from Arthur Scholfield's workshop, and evidently it was believed that none higher could be made.

Incidentally it may be noted that Arthur Scholfield's activities were not confined to carding machines. In 1806 he was manufacturing picking machines, — machines for loosening the matted locks of wool in preparation for carding, and used then in conjunction with the carding machine at the mill of the custom-carder; and by 1809 he was constructing spinning jennies. Finally

173

he was concerned with the manufacture of cloth during the embargo and war periods, for a time by himself, but in 1814 as next to the largest subscriber to the Pittsfield Woolen and Cotton Factory, launched in that year. Like others he suffered from the revulsion and depression that followed the advent of peace, for a while went back to wool-carding, and later acted as superintendent in one of the surviving mills. He died in 1827, apparently little richer than when he came to Pittsfield a quarter of a century before.

When it is recalled that good carding of wool is fundamental to good wool-cloth construction, and that in this country the combined carding-fulling mills frequently became the nuclei of wool-cloth factories, it will be recognized that the contribution of the Scholfield family to technological change — and such change on an entrepreneurial level — was highly important.

Somewhat similar cases can be cited out of other industries. In textile-machinery construction, Samuel Slater's brother-in-law, David Wilkinson (not Slater himself) is noteworthy. Wilkinson's shop "became the training school for many machinists who later were important figures in the history of machine-building in America. With one or two notable exceptions, all the textile-machine companies . . . owe their origin in some measure to the skill imparted by David Wilkinson." [34]

Dr. Redlich presents a somewhat comparable situation relative to the spread of steam-engine construction in Germany. There were a half-dozen pioneers, many of whom had English connections, such as Dinnendahl, Jacobi, and Harkort in the western part of the country, and Freund and Egells in the eastern part. Then of the next generation, three of the most important — Borsig, Wöhlert, and Hoppe — had received training in Egell's plant, Paucksch had worked in Freund's, and so on; and the connections can be carried down into the third generations. In fact, Dr. Redlich exhibits the "lines of descent," as it were, in diagrammatic form.[35]

Correspondingly, Thomas Scott, president of the Pennsylvania Railroad, is given credit for training a number of young railroad managers in the 1850–1875 period, men who later headed other railway lines in the expanding American network; Westinghouse is supposed to have trained men in the electrical-apparatus manufacture, et cetera. In short, one may well contend that in the intermediate period between the reign of individual inventors and the dominance of schools of technology, there was a period when temporary and informal organizations had appreciable influence. Evolution was not random nor wholly unstructured. Entrepreneurs arose who helped to inspire other entrepreneurs, and the direction and rapidity of change were surely affected by the character of these trainers of men.

VIGNETTE 8: THE PARTNERSHIP OF INVENTOR AND BUSINESSMAN

If local environments are conditioning forces in early technological development and adoption, there comes a time when the introduction of technological improvements requires a wider entrepreneurial perspective, at first perhaps a whole industry and later the markets of various industries in a whole nation. The first of these two stages was signaled when textile-machine building moved out of the textile mills and became a separate industry. And the same was later true in the locomotive-building in this country; it moved out of a variety of temporary homes and established itself as a separate manufacture purveying to the whole industry of railroad transportation.

When an inventor could look to sales over a whole industry, and perhaps an industry scattered geographically over a goodly part of the industrial East, he seems often to have been fortunate if he had a businessman to aid him in

the adaptation of his device to actual manufacturing operations, in providing finance over such a trial period, and in
"making a market" for the apparatus, perhaps in a field which
was already reasonably well satisfied with what it already
possessed. To be sure, there have been a really surprising
number of inventors of important apparatus who have proven
good also at entrepreneurial performance, men like Cyrus
McCormick or Erastus B. Bigelow or Henry Ford. But there
were others not so well endowed — probably thousands if we
could make a count of the failures which never overpassed
the threshold of historical record. One such case has already
been noted above: the failure of the Stanley steam-driven
automobile to succeed in the early competition with the
gasoline-driven type.[36]

The partnership of Edward D. Libbey and Michael J.
Owens was romantic, improbable, stormy, and yet very
profitable.[37] Its history throws into sharp relief a phase of innovation that is often overlooked: that novelties of apparatus,
processes, or products are likely to be successfully introduced
into an economy only if their introduction takes place on
the basis of a firm operating foundation. In this particular
case, the "firm foundation" was supplied by the two elements,
Mr. Libbey's personal character and the enterprise with
which he was first associated. Let me tell the story briefly.
Professor Warren C. Scoville made a splendid presentation
himself in his *Revolution in Glassmaking*.

Libbey, born in Massachusetts in 1854, had inherited from
his father in 1883 ownership of a small glass manufactory
which had ceased to be promising of financial returns, and
indeed was on the brink of bankruptcy. Just before his father's
death, young Libbey had been able to save the enterprise
only by a bold marketing stroke. With a promissory note due
shortly, he took to the famous Tiffany Company — which
had in fact been one of the concern's best customers — a

sample case full of some peculiarly colored tableware which had been put aside as unmarketable and which only chanced to have been preserved. Libbey thought up the new name of "amberina," was able to impress the Tiffany buyer with the virtues of this new color, and did enough business in this novel line to pull the company around the financial corner.

Within a few years, however, the demands of the skilled glassblowers for higher wages threatened to make thoroughly impossible the continuance of the New England Glass Company in a region which had already lost most of the competitive advantages that it had ever possessed. Libbey again was bold. He picked up his enterprise, shepherded such workers as would accompany him, and moved his business to Toledo, Ohio, where he would secure the advantage of low fuel costs (from the natural gas resources of that region) for a branch of manufacture in which fuel costs always counted for much in total manufacturing costs. Curiously enough, one of the representatives of the American Flint Glass Workers' Union who went to Boston to try to strengthen the resistance of the strikers against Libbey and his company was Michael J. Owens, at the time a worker in a glass house in Wheeling, West Virginia. From 1888, when the move was effected, the Libbey Glass Company, as the new enterprise was named, enjoyed financial success. The glass industry was expanding, in part because of rising American standards of living and in part because of the increased use of glass containers for foods. Factories in Ohio probably enjoyed differential advantages in costs, and the Toledo company was enterprising enough to purchase or develop glass-manipulating apparatus, the products from which were required by the electrical industry, which was also expanding at that time.

And a third bold stroke of Libbey's should be mentioned. Despite objections from most of his associates, he set up a sizable exhibit of glass blowing at the Columbian Exposition in Chicago in 1893, only five years after he had established his plant in Toledo. (By this time, incidentally, Owens had become superintendent of Libbey's factory, and supervised this exhibition at the fair.) The experiment was a conspicuous success, attracting thousands of the visitors to the exposition, and doubtless resulted in giving the Libbey company a position of some prominence in the minds of consumers, again a differential advantage which would make for financial soundness.[38]

Owens was distinctly improbable as a great inventor. Son of an immigrant coal miner of West Virginia, and under the necessity of going to work at the age of ten, he always labored under handicaps: it was near to the end of his life that he mastered the use of decimals, and he seems never to have learned to read mechanical drawings. The basis of his inventions appears to have been mainly a sense or uncommunicable impression of what molten glass may be made to do, and what not. He was a difficult man in his interpersonal relations, at least relations with his business associates but he did "get on well" with workingmen, although he never returned emotionally to the point where he could support labor organizations. And he was improvident, and jealous of those, like Libbey, who were provident. At a time when the latter was collecting paintings for his private art gallery and enjoying the pleasures of a California ranch, special arrangements had to be made whereby Owens was compensated for an action that had happened twenty years earlier, and provision established for a royalty payment on his bottle-blowing apparatus, that had not been contemplated when the invention was turned over to the "partnership."

Yet Owens had a flair for handling hot glass, a quasi-passion for the improvement of technological procedures, and an inner compulsion for accomplishment that Libbey recognized as extraordinary among men. He supported

Owens' experiments with his own money or saw to it that funds were forthcoming from some source; he went to considerable lengths to avoid personal disputes with his quick-tempered, frequently stubborn associate; and he gave Owens his loyal endorsement on many occasions even against the other men in the Toledo group, who were inclined generally to think and feel as did calm, suave, cultured, men of substance. The patience and the loyalty which Libbey displayed may be regarded as a special sort of foundation on which Owens could erect the devices of his imaginings. They were fit and fruitful complements to the pecuniary support that Libbey derived from the glass-working enterprise, the Libbey Glass Company, itself founded upon sound economic rocks and favored by potent economic trends.

The joint endeavors of Libbey and Owens in inventing labor-saving devices for glass-working, and introducing them into general use, began almost immediately after the successful display of processes at the World's Fair at Chicago. In almost a torrent, inventions to make semiautomatically or wholly automatically such items as electric light bulbs, lamp chimneys, tumblers, bottles, and the like flowed from Owens' laboratory or workshop, or he was improving the inventions of others, as in the case of the Colburn sheet-glass machine. A modern touch was given to the mode of capitalizing on these developments by the formation of companies, the function of which was to sell rights to utilize the inventions. This was particularly true of the bottle-machine patents. But in almost all instances the entrepreneurs found themselves drawn sooner or later into actual manufacture of products which were turned out by the use of their patented apparatus. On the whole, this latter phase of their operations seems to have been less profitable than the invention and leasing one, even less profitable — at least relative to the capital involved — than the original Libbey Glass Company.

Libbey appears to have been too much preoccupied with too many ventures to take continuing charge of these manufacturing enterprises; and Owens was not a good executive. He would probably have wound up in a bankruptcy court if he had tried to operate the concerns by himself. He never had operating charge of the Libbey company, and seems to have been kept at arm's length by those who did take charge of it in the middle 1890's, when Owens turned his attention to full-time invention.

The cooperation of the two principal characters occurred within the structures of business corporations. Always they were the principal figures, but they did have support from some individuals, some men with good judgment and some with willingness to carry routine administrative tasks; and these latter contributed to the total success. As Professor Scoville suggests, there was something of a fairly effective entrepreneurial team, with Libbey and Owens the provocative leaders, and not always leading in the same direction! Yet the aggregate result was startling. Libbey had come to Toledo with something like $100,000, and Owens with practically nothing. By 1920 both were millionaires, although one cannot be more precise. We do know that the enterprises over which they then exercised control possessed a value in excess of $50 million, and this had been accomplished in something like twenty-five years. Joint inventor-businessman entrepreneurship paid handsomely under some conditions.

VIGNETTE 9: VARIETY IN PATTERN

Thanks to the extraordinary path-breaking contributions of Professor Schumpeter, entrepreneurship has tended to be made synonymous with the introduction of technological innovations, especially innovations of a momentous character. I believe this identification to be an error, and that Schumpeter came in his latter years to take a broader view.

In his *History of Economic Analysis,* he stated that entrepreneurial gains emerge each time that "an entrepreneur's decision in conditions of uncertainty proves successful and have no definite relation to the size of the capital employed." [39] At another point he seemed to assert that he had placed himself beside Maurice Dobb in defining entrepreneurs as "the people 'who take the ruling decisions' of economic life." [40]

The research which Dr. Harold C. Passer carried through on the evolution of the American electrical manufacturing industry serves to illustrate the variety of performances that fall clearly within the borders of entrepreneurial activity.[41] Among the men who come under his analysis are four that I venture to label the calculating inventor, the inspirational innovator, the overoptimistic promoter, and the builder of a strong enterprise. All four types — and others — can be found in industry, probably in any old industrial country.

Edison was the calculating inventor. There had been arc lighting before he began experimenting with incandescent lights, but he deduced from his study of the former, and deduced rightly, that it could not reach the big market, that of the individual home. Then, having settled on incandescent lighting, he reflected on the existing situation and decided that he should try to "effect exact imitation of all done by gas so as to replace lighting by gas by lighting by electricity." He recognized that gas lighting had secured consumer acceptance as to devices, methods, and practices; and saw an advantage in capitalizing on that fact. His technical problem, then, was to develop a superior and more desirable light which should be delivered to the consumer in much the same manner as gas. His business problem was to be able to deliver that better light at no more than the consumer was already paying for his gas. Such ends became his goal, and such were in fact his achievements. Not the least of his intermediate accomplishments was the invention of a meter by means of which electricity consumption could be measured just as well as a gas meter measured gas consumption.

To be sure, perhaps, cautious calculation exacts its penalty — or the personality that operates in the manner of careful planning will let matters once decided stay decided. At all events, Edison pioneered with a direct-current system, a technique that entailed scattered power stations with short transmission lines. Such installations were set up in lower New York City — and, incidentally, are still there. Not long thereafter Westinghouse came along with an alternating-current system, one which permitted safe transmission at considerable distances. But Edison did not — or could not — change.

Again, Edison had framed his original conception around the notion of household use, imitating the gas utilization in residences. Having achieved a workable system for that purpose, which was, of course, a tremendous accomplishment, he seems to have retired from the field. The development of motors for industrial uses — indeed, the whole exploitation of electricity for power — was left for others to carry through.

The innovator who seems to have been able to rely much on inspiration was Frank Julian Sprague (1857–1934), who may be credited with the adaptation of electrical power to urban transportation. The crucial test came at Richmond, Virginia, in 1887–88. In May, 1887, Sprague entered into a contract to install an electric railroad, at a time when he had had no experience in the field, and when, as he said later, he "had only a blueprint of a machine, and some rough experimental apparatus." Yet by the fall of 1888, despite an intervening bout with typhoid fever that laid Sprague up for more than two months, the railroad was running satisfactorily; and this demonstration of the practicality of electric traction launched a new industry which at its height ranked with the largest in the country in size and in social effects.

To be sure, Sprague had had scientific training at Annapolis and he had pursued some experiments on his own after graduation. Resigning his commission in 1883, he worked for a year or two with Edison; he designed and sold industrial motors; and in 1885–86 he had conducted experiments in New York City, looking toward the replacement of steam trains on the elevated lines with electrically driven ones. (A minor accident may have moved the locus of Sprague's initial triumph from New York to Richmond. Jay Gould had financial control of the Manhattan Elevated Railroad Company, which in turn controlled four leading lines. He chanced to be riding on one of Sprague's experimental cars when a fuse blew out with a frightening detonation. Gould was prevented from jumping off the moving car; but he lost interest in electric traction!)

Actually Sprague took on major technical as well as financial risks at Richmond. He was supposed to produce a forty-car system, with thirty cars to operate at any one time, when the largest existing railway had no more than ten cars all told. And his cars were to surmount grades of 8 per cent, which were considered too great for horses or mules! It is true that Sprague could not meet the original completion date, and true that he lost heavily in unanticipated costs. But his system proved successful without much delay, and with that success his financial future was well assured. His services were much in demand.

One subsequent occasion for his services involved an episode almost identical with the foregoing. It concerned the electric railways of Chicago, and the multiple-unit system of control: a system whereby each car in a train was to be equipped with a motor adequate to start and move it, not have all the power generated or applied in a front-running locomotive.

Sprague sought a contract, and secured it in April, 1897 — as Dr. Passer says, "by agreeing to take upon himself all risk that his plan might fail . . . and the railway company, for its protection, required him to furnish a $100,000 bond for penalties in case he did not fulfill the terms. He agreed to have six cars completely equipped and ready for test on or before July 15 on a standard track, at least one mile long, to be supplied by him at his own expense." Yet, at this time his scheme "existed only on paper"! Actually, Sprague left shortly for London to see about a large contract there, and did not reach New York again until June. He was ten days late in putting on his six-car demonstration, but by that time he had so simplified the apparatus that he allowed his ten-year-old son to handle the controls! And the major installation on the whole South Side system gave efficient and safe service at reduced cost. Net earnings of the line increased nearly fourfold.

The third type mentioned above, that of the overoptimistic promoter, was E. H. Goff. He differs from Edison and Sprague in entering the industry from the sales end, being, in fact, one of the few early figures in the industry who lacked an engineering or scientific background. He differs also in being financially unsuccessful. He appears first in 1881 as sales agent for arc-lighting apparatus of an early concern, the American Electric Company, and by mid-1887, he had lost control of the company which he had set up, but which shortly closed its doors.

Goff's difficulties appear to have derived from the haste with which he pushed an essentially sound scheme. Other early sellers of arc-light equipment had followed the practice of organizing the citizens of a community into a company which then bought the apparatus, ran it as best they could, and hoped to make a profit in the process. Goff chose to set up his own companies in communities which he believed to have need of arc lighting, to get the equipment going properly and giving satisfaction — and profits — and then to sell the concern to the local citizenry.

While this procedure would seem to be one that should have gained him much business in the end, unhappily it did call for the temporary commitment of considerable capital, and apparently the industry was too young to gain the nod of commercial banks. The first successful installation of arc lighting having been made only in 1879, Goff's sole source of funds was the sale of stock in his enterprise; and to sell stock he had to pay generous dividends. He did resort to publicity in his stock-selling endeavors — from a display of lighting on Tremont Street, Boston, to the donation of equipment to illuminate the Statue of Liberty. But cash failed to come in fast enough, and some that did come in was drained out by needs of the manufacturing establishment that he had erected. A couple of adverse patent decisions in the courts came just when the enterprise was shaking, and they precipitated the wreck. Goff was finished — and actually was dead by 1891.

Charles A. Coffin, who had been a top salesman for a Lynn shoe manufacturer, was the first all-round company-builder in the industry. His introduction to the manufacture had been almost casual, since in 1881 he was appointed a member of a committee set up in Lynn, Massachusetts, to select arc-lighting apparatus for the local Grand Army Hall. Coffin chanced also to have encountered the equipment produced under Thomson-Houston patents.

From that point, however, Coffin was on his own. He was impressed by the apparatus; perhaps he was moved by the fact that both Thomson and Houston had scientific backgrounds. At all events, he raised money in Lynn to buy up the enterprise with which the two men were associated, the American Electric Company, renamed it the Thomson-Houston Company, and moved it to Lynn.

With scientists in charge of experiments and research, and with good present apparatus to sell, Coffin could give his attention to the financial, production, and marketing aspects of the concern. Perhaps he would qualify as one of the earliest professional managers in manufacturing industry, although of course he had some financial stake in the company from the outset.

No detailed account of his stewardship should be attempted here. Suffice it to say that he avoided Goff's mistake. Coffin followed the more general practice of encouraging the formation of local companies to buy equipment. His enterprise did accept securities sometimes in part payment, but he was able in effect to pass them along through the formation of "trusts," which held stocks and bonds of several local companies, and which attracted investors. He also rationalized the manufacturing side of the business, being one of the first to organize operations on a functional base. About 1885 he established separate departments of purchasing, production, accounting, et cetera, and with his own skills in marketing, he succeeded in providing all-round competence for the enterprise. Dr. Passer calls him "the leader of the industry by 1890."

Section 4 ·

ENTREPRENEURSHIP
AND BUSINESS ORGANIZATION

In analyzing the economic and social activities of the
merchant in the seaboard towns of the American colonies
and early post-Revolutionary decades, one is in reality dealing with a species of an extensive genus. Professor Stuart W.
Bruchey makes a nice point when, in summarizing the career
of the Baltimore merchant Robert Oliver, who was active
from 1783 to 1819, he draws a comparison with that of
Andrea Barbarigo, Venetian merchant of the fifteenth century.[42] The latter's activities reach back toward the beginnings of the era of "commercial capitalism" or dominating
commercial entrepreneurship, and yet Professor Bruchey
points out how similarly the two merchants acted. Barbarigo
would have almost immediately understood Oliver's form of
organization and his methods of managing men, records, and
investments. In looking at the early American merchant,
then, one is in a sense examining the entrepreneurial figure
that dominated urban life in the Western world for something like five hundred years.

In a broad frame, the social function of the entrepreneur

generally is to provide goods or services to his community or market in such a manner as satisfies its moral sense, at least does not violate that sense too blatantly. In other words, there is a technical or economico-business aspect, and there is a moral one. It seems valid to hold that the American merchant of early decades performed the first function rather poorly, but he sustained the moral relationship very well. Let us look at both, with special reference to the case of Robert Oliver, since only in connection with him has a biographer pursued certain important inquiries.

The operations of Oliver and his predecessors and contemporaries in mercantile life must be considered as wholes, including both export and import activities. In terms of a merchant's relation to his community, either from the point of view of business or morals, his import activities may seem more significant, yet exports were necessary to sustain imports, and the exportation of goods had to be carried out in a manner that was reasonably satisfactory to the communities or markets to which goods were sent. Two elements were important in the performance of these tasks: the acquisition of information about wants, and the expeditious satisfaction of those wants. In both these features the early merchant encountered difficulties.

Beyond the merchant himself the key figures in the operations were his correspondents in the foreign ports, and the supercargo (or the captain of the ship carrying the goods, acting as supercargo). Problems arose almost inevitably with respect to both parties. Correspondents of reliable character had to be located; then they went out of business, or they turned unreliable, and I suspect that those in the smaller ports accumulated conflicting loyalties. Some American merchants sought partial relief from such difficulties by encouraging relatives to settle in foreign commercial centers, at least for a while, or by making good use of those who did live abroad. The Hutchinson family, centered in Boston, had a very good organization in the late seventeenth century. One brother was a prosperous London merchant, two brothers and two nephews carried on trade in the thriving New England port, another nephew — and so a cousin of the Boston nephews — resided in Portsmouth, Rhode Island, where he traded as far west as Hartford, Connecticut, and from which he pushed a considerable commerce with the West Indies, and two brothers of his carried on the latter business from Barbados.[43] Robert Oliver enjoyed communications from his brothers, John and Thomas, one or the other of whom was visiting in Europe almost continuously from 1796 to about 1803. He also had a valuable ally in Philadelphia, a brother-in-law who was a prominent merchant there. However, relatives surely did not suffice to cover even the most important foreign spots for most merchants; and the complaints about correspondents in general, sometimes relatives also, lead one to conclude that the actions of the agent were quite often indifferent reflections of the desires of the principal.

Time and uncertainties of communication were factors in the situation. A voyage to the West Indies required three or four weeks each way around the turn of the eighteenth century, and might take nearly twice that time under unfavorable weather conditions. A voyage to London or Hamburg demanded five or six weeks each way, while one to the Far East could consume four or five months in either direction, often longer. During such periods of transit the conditions in the market of destination could well change as compared with the merchant's anticipations, and the home market for which he had planned purchases in the foreign ports might well move contrary to his expectations. All the time his ship's captain, his supercargo, and his foreign correspondents were really at arm's length from him, subject to the vagaries of unorganized, informal transmission of letters.

Writing about the New England merchants of approximately the same period, Professor Kenneth W. Porter had some rather unpleasant things to say about this mail service, some merchants accommodating other merchants. Ships' captains would accept letters but be curiously tardy in delivering them; they would insist on the letters being given over unsealed, or would not hesitate to open them surreptitiously. Sometimes they refused to take letters of competing merchants. And, of course, sometimes vessels were lost or they changed their course while at sea.

In a recent study of "Merchant Shipping in the [English] Economy of the Late Seventeenth Century," Mr. Ralph Davis states that the charter parties covering voyages to Portugal or the Canary Islands made allowance for forty to forty-five working days for loading in port, while those covering voyages to Virginia allowed for a hundred working days for such loading in port.[44] Butel-Dumont, in describing the conditions in the American tobacco trade of the mid-eighteenth century, talks of ships staying "three or four months, often six months" in Chesapeake Bay collecting a load, while an unusually large vessel might have to spend a whole winter there.[45] Professor James B. Hedges of Brown, who has studied the shipping experience of the Brown family of Providence in the latter Colonial and early national periods, writes me that turn-around in Providence for the Brown ships would average around three months, but this time could on occasion be shortened if news of conditions in a foreign port — for example, a shortage of flour in Surinam — could be sent ahead by another ship. A return cargo might be made ready.[46] However, all these data point to a slow pace of commercial interchange. I wonder how well, indeed, the individual merchant of pre-steamship, pre-cable days could rationally adjust his activities to the needs of his community. I am even tempted to draw inferences from the language in which "sedentary" merchants in Boston or other Atlantic ports were likely to couch their advertising in the daily or weekly newspaper: "J. and H. Perkins announce that they have received a shipment of linens." Did Boston (or the other subject ports) *lack* linens until Messrs. Perkins received their supply?

Finally, it may be noted that purchases had often to be left largely to the discretion of the agent, correspondent, or supercargo. Orders from the principal had to be couched in terms that carried the qualifications: "if prices are not too high," "if the quality is good," "if not too many other ships have loaded up with the item." And, as I have implied already, once the ship had left Baltimore or Salem or Charleston, there was small chance of changing the statement of desires. The lengthening of the lanes of American commerce after 1790, especially the evolution of the trade with the Far East, promoted an alteration in organization. Now the importance of the non-American offices grew. Young Forbeses and the sons in other merchant families served their apprenticeships in Hong Kong or Manila; until, at a still later date, the principal offices of houses, English as well as American, came to be located in the Far Eastern areas. (The English and other East India companies had encountered a similar administrative or control problem earlier.)

A modern observer looking back from days of almost universal airmail, radiograms, and often overseas telephonic communication, and from days when supervision of correspondents or wholly-owned agencies is relatively easy, may perhaps be pardoned for conceiving the older mercantile system as hardly better than a vehicle that wobbled and creaked as it slowly got over the ground. We should probably marvel that, technically, it did as well as it did.

On the other hand, the moral relationship appears to have been quite satisfactorily maintained. I am disposed, with Professor Porter, to relate business ethics to no transcendental criteria. "Ethics, like international law," says Porter, "is a matter of precedent, and the individual who conforms to the standards of his group [of his day and generation] has done all that his biographer [and presumably any other appraiser] can reasonably expect from him."[47] Dr. Redlich would complain — and rightly — that this definition fails to cover the possibility of variant standards of action as between dealings with members of the merchant's "in-group," and those with other members of the whole society.

This situation did occur in the early days of Massachusetts Bay, and may have become briefly manifest in certain other colonies, such as Pennsylvania or Georgia. In the first case, considerable evidence has come down to us, especially the 158-page will of Robert Keayne, a merchant of London. Keayne came to Boston in 1635, and three years later was in trouble with church and state "for selling his wares at excessive Rates, to the Dishonor of Gods name, the Offence of the Generall Cort, and the Publique scandall of the Cuntry." Fourteen years later still, he drew up a will as a "demand that justice be done him even if only in memory." He died in 1657.[48]

With the subsidence of religious controversies, a condition of relative calm seems to have evolved in the colonies, at least as far as the merchants' actions as merchants were concerned. To be sure there were divisions among the merchants, at least in Massachusetts, as Professor Bailyn has shown.[49] These disputes involved matters of public policy and preferments among their own group, and these controversies continued into the Revolutionary period. But the activities of merchants in their business roles did not provoke controversy. Even those who took a larger or smaller share in the slave trade, in smuggling, or in privateering appear to have done so with the acquiescence of their fellow citizens. Nor is this situation surprising. The urban communities were still small enough for communication among the dominant members to be relatively effective. The merchants had not developed a zest for business that made it plausibly a self-sufficient calling; and, despite the decline in the Massachusetts theocracy, the colonies were dominated by unity in a Christian philosophy. Merchants were responsible members of the closely knit Christian societies; there was every reason why they and their communities should think alike; and there was no sufficient reason why the mercantile segment should not *act* in a manner that would receive the approval of their fellow citizens as far as their role performance as merchants was concerned.

VIGNETTE 11: THE "GENERAL ENTREPRENEUR"

A historical view of entrepreneurship is bound to be closely concerned with business forms and their evolution through time. As already indicated, one must have regard for the process or manner of entrepreneurial action as well as its motivation and conditioning. The "regulated company," the joint-stock limited-liability form of enterprise, the partnership, the "public" company — all of these have importance in our field insofar as they have contributed to shaping the economic and social aspects of entrepreneurial performance.

It is to Professor Cochran that we owe the discovery and delineation of the "general entrepreneur."[50] He describes the phenomenon only in relation to the railroad industry, but he recognizes that this type of entrepreneurial actor, at least, had occurred somewhat more widely.

By the term "general entrepreneur," Professor Cochran seeks to differentiate the financier of the mid-nineteenth century in this country who had effective, if not absolute, financial control over several business concerns usually in a single industry, did not typically attempt actually to manage any of them, and yet, by reason of his financial position, did possess final power over the formulation and change of general corporate policy. In historical sequence he represents a business form lying between the individual proprietorship or partnership of the earlier decades of the nineteenth century and the investment bankers of the last decades.

John Murray Forbes's career did not differ markedly from that of men like Israel Thorndike, Nathan Appleton, Erastus Corning, or Nathaniel Thayer, all of whom could be catalogued as general entrepreneurs, at least in the essential element of having made money in mercantile operations — incidentally as had Forbes. They all chose to dominate manufacturing or transportation enterprises through the direct or indirect influence of their possession of wealth. Forbes himself was born in 1813, started apprenticeship in trade at the age of fifteen, went to China at seventeen to serve with his uncles' enterprise of Russell and Company, made the lasting friendship of a wealthy merchant of that country, and, returning to Boston, carried on commercial activities there for the decade 1836–1846. Then with his own money, with that of his friend Houqua, and later with funds secured from family and friends, he began to invest in western railroads: the Michigan Central, the Chicago, Burlington & Quincy, the Hannibal & St. Joseph. He did serve as president of the Michigan Central for the years 1846–1855, and of the Chicago, Burlington & Quincy for the briefer period, 1878–1881, but he did not attempt to manage the properties. That is the important characteristic of the general entrepreneur. Nathan Appleton might have large or controlling financial interests in certain cotton mills, but he did not pretend to operate them. So likewise with Forbes or Thayer or others concerned with railroad lines. The latter men remained typically in the East and constituted the court of last resort relative to decisions on western railroads that contained a significant financial aspect. And it need hardly be asserted that the combination of such discriminating purveyors of funds with the technically trained, carefully selected managers of the enterprises contributed much to the economic development of the country beyond the Appalachians. Here a business form, not determined by, or necessary in, contemporary social, political, or economic conditions, had an important economic effect.

Professor Cochran makes the point that the role of general entrepreneur in such a case as that of Forbes was perfectly consonant with the social concepts of the era. Not only was property protected at law and unquestioningly respected in the public view, but the possession of much property — wealth — had itself a power of command. The boards of directors of the companies should, of course, be made up of representatives of investment groups; the operating heads of the lines in the West should naturally turn to Forbes and his ilk for policy decisions, since hardly any of the latter failed to have a financial feature.

One element in the structuring of this role is a sort of residue from earlier days. Men like Forbes "wanted to live in east-coast civilization," [51] and they were willing to assume executive posts only when their sense of obligation to their fellow investors overcame their disinclination to leave Boston or other eastern cities. Merchants of the Colonial period had retired in middle life to give themselves over to community and family life. Even in the 1840's and 1850's it was not essential, in order to command the favorable regard of their peers and social censors, that they put first and always the making of money, of arranging their lives to that end.

Another element in the role manifests its intermediate character. At an early time proposals for the formation of companies were not uncommonly posted in coffeehouses or similar public places, with blank space below the terms of the proposal, on which the names of interested parties, together with the number of shares which they desired to secure, could be "underwritten." Capital, like other components of entrepreneurship, was at this period community-bound in large measure.

When projects requiring larger amounts of capital — for example, railroads — began to be launched, promoters frequently made journeys about the various centers of potential investors and personally solicited subscriptions. Forbes and his type acted in much this fashion, except that now — at least more than ever before — they spontaneously conceived a responsibility to their friends and neighbors and other investors for the safety of the monies invested in projects of their promotion. There is a particularistic feature and a public-responsibility one. And, when subsequently the particularistic element of soliciting subscription from among friends, family, and social acquaintances pretty much ceased with the rise of investment-banking firms, the latter still retained in some measure the responsibility aspect. The better investment houses "stood behind" the issues of stock that they sponsored, indeed, frequently sought membership on boards of directors of railroad or other enterprises in order that they might "carry through" on the obligation implied by their issuance of the securities of such business units.

Obviously, the roles of general entrepreneur and operating manager were mutually complementary; they each supplied functions necessary to the "initiation, maintenance, and aggrandizement" of the enterprise which the other could not supply, or could have supplied much less effectively. It was a form of the division of labor. There were, to be sure, limitations to the "separation of powers." One was the fact that a general entrepreneur was not always available when he was needed or had other affairs in hand that distracted him from the prompt performance of his duties in his chosen role. For example, Forbes was in Europe when the important Burlington strike broke out in 1879, and Charles E. Perkins, the president, had to make the decisions. At another point, Forbes wrote to his operating president that he could not "attend systematically to the business of the road," that the best that he could do was "perhaps at midnight as now . . . to write a private letter with such hasty suggestions as occur to me." [52]

There seems also to have been some change in the degree of complementary activity over time. For one thing, as the railroad grew longer and its relationships became more complex and numerous, it grew more and more necessary, and common, for subordinates in the growing hierarchy to make important decisions and then turn to their superiors, to the board of directors, and to the general entrepreneur for confirmation. And the operating heads of railroad lines came increasingly to take more and more initiative in at least the framing of alternatives in decisions. Again, the rise in the post-Civil War era of investment-banking enterprises meant inevitably a weakening of the business requirements of the general entrepreneur and his functions. The managers of railroads could surely perform their functions and could maintain and expand their companies much more readily without dependence upon such men as Forbes than they could have in earlier decades.

The complemental quality just mentioned stemmed in part from the intellectual, social, and economic conditions of the period. One way of phrasing the matter is to say that the industry was gaining importance relative to the community. The railroad was a particularly effective instrument in this separation because of its geographical extension. However, it also required an expertness of management that could not be found as a normal element in community life. As early as 1856 William Osborn, president of the Illinois Central, complained of his directors, "I do not think any of them are aware of what an immense machine this is to handle." [53] Education for administrative duties was possible only through apprenticeship; and, given the state of conceptualization regarding management and given the state of railroad literature, it would have been impossible for a general entrepreneur to have learned the "railroad game" except through such a schooling. Those who had grown up in mercantile pursuits would have had to study long to have equipped themselves for railroad management in its totality.

On the other hand, there existed at this period special demands and special opportunities for those who had wealth or had contacts with potential investors, particularly in the railroad world. One peculiar feature of that world was the need of chunks of capital, sizable chunks. As the canal builders had learned earlier, a transportation facility aimed to link two places was not of much value monetarily until the two places *had* been linked. A canal halfway to a coal mine was not really worth much; and, by the same token, neither was a railroad halfway from New York to Buffalo. Given the rather common entrepreneurial (and engineering) tendencies to minimize anticipated costs of construction and to inflate potential earning powers of any such facility,[54] it was just as well if the person taking responsibility for a railroad had a long money pocket, and those possessing contacts with potential investors had relations with a considerable elastic supply of funds.

The last consideration is connected with a more general phenomenon that should not only be specified as a peculiar feature of the experiences now under view but as an integral element in entrepreneurship. I have in mind the apparent capacity of a business unit to take on a life of its own —

198

really, of course, that of the human individuals that from time to time make up its directing personnel — and to grow in various ways differently from the way its projectors had envisaged. Mr. Charles Wilson presents cases in the West African trading and nut-collecting institutions that Lord Leverhulme set up to provide a dependable source of raw materials for his expanding soap and margarine empire. Soon the trading companies had lands of their own, possessed steamships, were looking around for freight to fill these vessels on their return voyages, became involved in quasi-political relations with the local tribes, and so on.[55]

The general entrepreneurs and the railroad industry went through quite as extensive an evolution. Beyond the formation of the transportation enterprise, there was the development of the construction company, after a time the appearance of a conflict between the objectives of the two institutions, and, as Professor Cochran points out, an alteration in the role structure of the railroad executive in the degree that he must put the interests of his company unmistakably first. There were chances to participate in city real-estate dealings and in the erection of commercial buildings. There was the particularly important development of new extension of track to be considered, the building of strategic lines ahead of economic need in order to forestall competitors; and there was the evolution of community and political relationships until the original enterprise was to be seen in the midst of a network of connections, rights, duties, and opportunities, a situation far removed from the simple pair of rails from one city to another with which it might often have begun in men's minds.

Professor Cochran seems wholly justified in paying as much attention as he does to the railroad general entrepreneur in the economic and social setting of the 1845–1890 period. In this kind of entrepreneurial situation, the problems of communication and control that are to be observed in the operations of the Colonial merchants (and their post-Revolutionary successors) became intensified by the change in the time-horizons relative to most managerial operations in variant industries. If the Colonial mercantile system could be said to be like a poorly constructed carriage that wobbled a good deal as it went along, the railroad enterprise was at least a well-turned vehicle, if still horse-drawn and not quite so responsive to external forces as the twentieth-century equivalent. The railroad-plus-general-entrepreneur combination was also noteworthy as one of the first business situations that was, as it were, open-ended [56] and thus capable of promoting company growth. It was, likewise, notable as presenting cases of the separation of ownership and management long before the dawn of the twentieth century. The combination offers in a way a transitional form between the earlier world of proprietary and that of the more modern corporate entrepreneurship.

VIGNETTE 12: THE CORPORATE EXECUTIVE

The members of a corporate executive team would form a multiple entrepreneur, according to the contentions presented above. It appears to me, however, that the members of an executive committee comprise even more clearly a multiple entrepreneur. However, the fact must be faced that the president of a corporation or the chairman of the board of directors, or both, will usually be found to possess somewhat more influence than other members of the whole "top management" or the other members of an executive committee. In some cases, as in that of Mr. Sewell Avery of Montgomery Ward, the differential may be so great that the president or chairman seems closely akin to the traditional entrepreneur. But these cases have now become exceptional among large American companies.

Still the normal differential is adequate to validate the preparation of a brief sketch of the career of Mr. Frank W. Abrams as a typical leader in an entrepreneurial group. The honors which Mr. Abrams has received both within "his" enterprise and outside it lead one to think that he may in quality lie in the top stratum of his category, but an excellent ballplayer is still a ballplayer!

Information about Mr. Abrams after he became an executive is meager — which is just what one should expect: he had been made a member of a team, and only the action of the group was recorded. However, one can learn something.

Let us first look at his initiation. From a home in Rockville Center, Long Island, he went to Syracuse University, and received a civil engineering degree in 1912. He began work with a subsidiary of the Standard Oil Company (New Jersey) almost at once, and almost at the bottom, namely as draftsman in the Eagle Works in Jersey City. By 1917 he was assistant superintendent and by 1922 manager. And at this period he distinguished himself, with the company and ultimately with the industry, by a notable feat of organizational placation which, in a sense, laid the foundation of his subsequent career. This was the period when university-trained engineers like himself were coming into the employ of the company. They found themselves working beside men who had learned their skills merely from experience, and it was Mr. Abrams's task not only to keep the peace, but to preserve the preexisting relationships, intangible but important, of an operating team. He manifested an ability to work with men, but also an interest in trying to make men want to work together.

At about the same time, according to his own admission, a session of self-appraisal convinced him that he possessed no special talent in engineering or executive experience which would give him any peculiar value in the eyes of company officials, and decided that his only chance of advancement lay in making people like him. I suspect that a psychiatrist would readily explain this decision as merely a revelation that Mr. Abrams himself liked people and sought to understand them as brother human beings.

However, the course of Mr. Abrams's career with the enterprise was not immediately altered. In the mid-1920's he performed his stint of foreign service (which is common with "Jersey" for rising young executives) by supervising the construction of a large refinery in Sumatra. Returning to this country in 1926, he was placed in charge of all the refining carried on in the New Jersey area. But by that time Mr. Abrams had apparently served his apprenticeship; indeed, he had almost completed all the administrative work that would be required of him. He had shown that he could think new thoughts, and that he could direct groups of men in several types of operations. Thereafter his posts became more specifically consultative.

In 1927 he was elected to the board, presumably an administrative board, of what is now the Esso Standard Company; in 1933 he was made its president; seven years later he had moved to the top administrative unit, the Standard Oil Company (New Jersey), at first as one of the directors, in 1944 as a vice-president, and the next year as chairman of the board. He remained in the last office until his retirement from the company in 1954.

This is a thoroughly typical bureaucratic career, such as William Miller traced among the top executives whom he studied in his research.[57] Probably the period of operating work, only fifteen years, was on the short side, but the period which he enjoyed in the topmost place, a decade or so, is not far from normal.

Within the administrative groups, Mr. Abrams's personal

qualities seem to have counted heavily in his further advancement because of their correlation with the trend of the times in social relations. According to reports he was what the Spanish call "simpático," an informal man who preferred to persuade and suggest, rather than to criticize harshly, let alone issue orders. His strength derived from his reservoirs of patience and from his social philosophy. The former lack formal recording but are remembered by those who worked with him. His philosophy is exhibited in an article published in 1951 in the *Harvard Business Review*.[58] Briefly, it is founded on the belief that, as a result of the machine age, men are brought ever nearer to one another, and so must learn to get along together — to which Mr. Abrams adds merely the specialized conclusion: that it is the duty of business management to facilitate the process.

It has become more important for us to live in harmony in a new kind of world. People are now more concerned with each other and much less with the mastery of their physical environment. The importance of faith in our fellow men, and understanding among men is thereby made the greater.[59]

The job of professional management, as I see it, is to conduct the affairs of the enterprise in its charge in such a way as to maintain an equitable and workable balance among the claims of the various directly interested groups. Business firms are manmade instruments of society. They can be made to achieve their greatest social usefulness — and thus their future can be best assured — when management succeeds in finding a harmonious balance among the claims of the various interested groups: the stockholders, employees, customers, and the public at large. But management's responsibility, in the broadest sense, extends beyond the search for a balance among respective claims. Management, as a good citizen, and because it cannot properly function in an acrimonious and contentious atmosphere, has the positive duty to work for peaceful relations and understanding among men — for a restoration of faith of men in each other in all walks of life.[60]

The citation which New York University prepared when it was conferring upon him an honorary degree in 1950 gives the right flavor:

For his significant achievements as engineer and administrator, for the part he has played in the evolution of oil refining from a limited mechanical method to the chemically precise process it has become today, for his sincere interest in the welfare of employees and his many benefactions on their behalf, for his forthright assumption of industry's responsibilities to the community and the nation, for his inspired crusading as a champion of institutions of learning, for his personification of the conscience of American business, we bestow upon him with esteem and admiration the degree of Doctor of Commercial Science, *honoris causa.*

Mr. Abrams has gone on to public service of various sorts — as trustee of Syracuse University, as member of the National Planning Association, as a member of Mr. Hoover's task force, as advisor (and sometimes administrator) with the Ford Foundation, the Alfred P. Sloan Foundation, and the Industrial Relations Counselors, among others. He has been a man much sought after by institutions of such character. Perhaps most noteworthy and characteristic of Mr. Abrams' later activities — even before he retired from office with the Standard Oil Company — with his sponsorship and support of the Council for Financial Aid to Education, through which corporations may contribute funds for the maintenance of schools and colleges. He even helped to secure a judicial decision on the legality of such gifts by corporations. (Incidentally, he has had the cooperation of many American businessmen in this project, including such leaders as Mr. Irving S. Olds of the United States Steel Corporation and Mr. Alfred P. Sloan of General Motors.)

For entrepreneurship, however, it is evident that, in sociological terms, Mr. Abrams constituted a deviant whose modification of the role of major entrepreneur proved congruent with the emergent ideas of his peers and with those of public censors. As a result, the alteration in the role may be regarded as incorporated into the total behavior pattern, at least for the current era.

Mr. Abrams's experience is noteworthy in yet another regard, significant at least for American entrepreneurial life. Not alone did his views correlate with the contemporary trend in social thought, but the record of his speeches and actions makes manifest that he was a force himself in accelerating these trends. This is as it should be: a business institution as powerful and extensive as the Standard Oil Company (New Jersey) should be conversant with and conscious of the emergent tendencies in national thought, should select top executives with knowledge of their competence in such expanding fields, and should encourage these executives to seek leadership in the new movements. It was in this correlation of actions that Mr. Abrams himself asserted in substance that what was good for the country should be made good for "Jersey."

Section 5 ·

ENTREPRENEURSHIP AND THE STATE

Economic development, so universally desired in the Western world, at least since the Renaissance, has been propelled along divers paths according to the various combinations of economic, political, and personal factors that chanced at the divers times to obtain. It might occur through the action of a monarch. Such was the contribution of Gustavus Adolphus (1523–1560), whom Professor Eli F. Heckscher describes as "a great business manager in control of the Swedish economy." He was particularly important for launching the Swedish iron industry on its long career, and his endeavors in all directions resulted in "a remarkable increase in the prosperity of the Swedish people." [61] It might take place through the self-inspired efforts of forceful statesmen — Colbert or Hamilton or Peel, Julius Vogel of New Zealand, or Macdonald of Canada.

Not infrequently entrepreneurs have been involved as the instruments through which a monarch or an economic statesman or even a democratic state may choose to act. The East India companies of England or Holland, perhaps the landgrant railroads of the United States, or the "chosen instru-

206

ment" airlines in various modern states may be suggested as typical cases from a large population.

Two representative cases are worth presentation in some detail, to illustrate how the collaboration of state and entrepreneur rises, and how it develops in different situations. One case pertains to eighteenth-century France and becomes available through the research of Professor Paul W. Bamford; and the other relates to nineteenth-century Belgium and derives from investigations of Richard M. Westebbe, erstwhile a research fellow attached to the Center in Entrepreneurial History at Harvard.[62]

Professor Frederic C. Lane once gave a paper to the entrepreneurial history group at Harvard of which the main thesis, based on his research in early modern commerce, was to the effect that in times of uncertainty the businessman sought the protection of the state. Such seems to have been a principal ambition of Pierre Babaud, later Pierre Babaud de la Chaussade, whose career in eighteenth-century France interested Professor Bamford as a particularly neat case illustrating the problems of the French navy vis-à-vis the whole economic and political situation of the *ancien régime.*

Actually, it is almost impossible to digest Babaud's career beyond the point which Professor Bamford squeezed the data in his essay in *Explorations in Entrepreneurial History,* since there are so many special circumstances of the government or the society or the period which conditioned the performance of this entrepreneur. Thus the *contrôleur général* to the Duke of Lorraine could be a secret partner in Babaud's exploitation of the Duke's forests for nearly a decade without knowledge of the latter — and so there might have been other deficiencies of communication; Pierre could purchase the post of *Secrétaire du Roy* and thereby secure privileges and exemptions not available to competitors; and, since most of his workers in the iron as well as in the lumbering business lived on land which he owned, they were, in a sense, dependent upon his political authority as they were upon his economic. By reason of these latter elements, Professor Bamford says that "Chaussade can rightly be called an industrial lord, or feudal industrialist."

Chaussade chose to link his fortunes with those of the French navy by contracting to supply anchors and other iron parts for ships. Not every aspect of this relationship proved fortunate. He had difficulties in securing payment; shipments of products across certain territories were subject to tolls which individuals more privileged than he kept collecting; and the business was hardly steady in volume — in part because France at this period had only a second-class navy, and therefore had poor success against England's first-class service. As a result it was condemned to further second-class treatment by the French government.

However, Chaussade's activity on government contracts did yield numerous advantages. For example, other landowners of the nearby provinces were obliged to transport coal and wool for him at fixed prices; navy inspectors resident at his plants became partisans with him in his efforts to gain even greater privileges and exemptions; while the nature of his work enabled him in effect to put his employees into slavery: if any left his establishments, they could be forcibly returned.

The balance between such advantages and the foregoing disadvantages is indicated perhaps by two circumstances: when in his later decades he tried to sell his products to civilian ship-builders or ship-owners, he found that he could not begin to compete with English ship-iron brought in over the existing tariff duties. According to Bamford, Chaussade wound up as "one of the richest industrialists in France."

But Chaussade was more than a mere governmental dependent. Like all true entrepreneurial actors, he had to be concerned with managing the flow of goods and managing costs. In furtherance of the flow, he tried to assure himself of adequate capital. Relative to working capital, he seems to have gone to quite considerable trouble to convince leaders that he was always liquid. At least there appears to be no other explanation of his persistent borrowing from one person to pay his debt to another. He also kept his hands on his accumulated wealth in part by arranging to turn over dowries for his daughters only at his death, and meanwhile paying his sons-in-law interest on the promised amount!

More importantly, he did introduce technological improvements in the treatment of iron, such as the use of reverberatory furnaces fired with mineral fuel. He built nearby housing for his workers, with at least one building equipped with a clock, since, as he said, it was "extremely desirable that all be on hand to receive quickly the orders of the directors of the forges." In addition, he devised at least two procedures appropriate to large-scale operations anywhere at any time: he delegated the actual management of his numerous and geographically scattered enterprises to such supervisors as the "directors of the forges," reserving to himself the policy decisions; and he "contracted out" the maintenance of his buildings, and again the maintenance in repair of his industrial equipment, to individuals who received annual fees.

Babaud de la Chaussade is really a most interesting figure, and none the less so because Professor Bamford puts him forward as a not-untypical specimen of the eighteenth-century French entrepreneurship. In character Babaud would seem a worthy predecessor of the St. Simonists under the Second Republic and Empire. In method he appears to manifest the pliancy of entrepreneurs elsewhere and at other periods to take advantage of conjunctures, even decadent governmental conditions. Professor Bamford is quite sure that Babaud did not purchase his royal secretaryship solely or principally for the distinction that it gave him; Babaud was intent on using the privileges of nobility to compete in an economy which was shot through with noble privileges. The status was for him a tool, not an end in itself. A way could be found through the tangle of privileges and exemptions — a person with some funds could "buy into" the show!

The case of John Cockerill, like that of Babaud, concerns, at least in part, the development of the iron industry in what eventually became Belgium. Actually, the Cockerills had begun smelting iron ore with charcoal, as had the Frenchman earlier.

The Cockerills are akin to the Scholfields considered above.[63] They were mechanics, familiar with the front-running English technology, who migrated to underdeveloped countries with the purpose of capitalizing on their advanced knowledge. They were the bearers of technological change, the agents of technological diffusion.

William Cockerill, the father, had left England in 1797, a year of business depression in that country, and some time between 1798 and 1800 had settled with his family at Verviers on the Continent. The family contained three sons, of whom John was the youngest. William, like the Scholfields, became a figure in the wool manufacture. He manufactured textile machinery at Verviers, and is credited with reforming the production methods in the Belgian wool manufacture.

Before the close of the Napoleonic period, the three sons had all grown to manhood, and had enlarged the family operations. The Peace of Vienna found them producing steam engines and hydraulic presses at Liège. In the new organization of Europe, what is now Belgium, the Netherlands, and Luxemburg were united, with Willem I as king, but the area was largely shut off — through high customs duties — from the market of almost the whole Continent, for which it had been producing before 1815. There was need for a positive developmental policy, and Willem embraced a program of that character. Support of the entrepreneurial ambitions of John Cockerill came to form an important part of that program.

From the point of view of the King and the nation, there seem to have been several purposes in the support of Cockerill. Initially, the Belgian machine-building should be brought up to the level of the British industry; and obviously the ex-Britishers were well circumstanced to do that. Again, the country should not be dependent upon foreign makers for certain types of machines, especially marine engines for both the new navy and the contemplated fleet of steamships for the Rhine traffic. Third, it appears that the national policy contemplated Belgium's becoming a builder of steam engines and machinery for much of Europe. The country could build on the foundations laid by the Cockerills over the 1800–1815 period.

The part in the drama played by John Cockerill is more difficult to assess. Westebbe portrays him as an indifferent financier, perhaps an indifferent technician, and not a very good manager. Surely he was continually in financial hot water and surely he underestimated the difficulties of constructing marine engines. Westebbe thinks that Cockerill did not appreciate "the real problems of dealing with an unskilled labor force, underdeveloped markets, and large-scale concentrated output." Even a government report not long before the Revolution of 1830 advocated a more aggressive sales policy.

However, the events of the years 1815–1830 are subject to a rather different interpretation. Here are the more striking ones: Cockerill made the first move in attaching himself to the King, when in 1816 he sought to acquire control of a sizable royal estate at Seraing, to be used for industrial purposes. He is alleged to have been persuasive in conversation or argument inducing the government to take half the stock in his enterprise. (Cockerill was always "needing" more money, and getting it — more or less fully — from the government, but he seems to have remained wealthy.) At one time he tried to get the government to take more than 50 per cent control of the establishment; the only other prominent entrepreneur of the young nation threatened to leave the country unless he could have his way with government policy. When Cockerill determined to set up cotton manufacturing, and asked governmental support, his petition was turned down, but he went right ahead anyhow, and soon the government was making a contribution.

The whole sequence need not have been contrived, but I am reminded of a Harvard student who one June told me that he was leaving that day for New York to "sell a monopoly" — namely, his services. Westebbe intimates that entrepreneurial talent was scarce in the Low Countries at this period. Quite obviously Cockerill, as a result of his family's and his own endeavors, enjoyed a differential advantage over the others. And seemingly he understood, and acted consciously or unconsciously to take advantage of a conjuncture. A state policy of economic development can sometimes be made to yield private returns. In this particular case returns appear to have been put to good use: the *Société Anonyme John Cockerill* survives to this day.

VIGNETTE 14: THE STATE TAKES OVER

The notion that entrepreneurship (or private enterprise) formed the all-prevailing element in the economic development of the United States before 1860, that those decades can be accurately labeled a laissez-faire period, has been pretty severely mauled by the series of studies promoted since 1940 by the Committee on Research in Economic History, and is in process of complete demolition at the hands of Professor Carter Goodrich of Columbia.[64] In the period with which we are chiefly concerned, however, 1818–1841, no clear decision had been reached as to whether private or public auspices should prevail in the construction and operation of public works: highways, canals, and railroads. Common roads and town streets were government affairs; turnpikes private; bridges divided, but chiefly public; canals, earlier private and not very successful, more recently public; and railroads private but with some indirect aid. In 1818 the principal item of interest was the successful launching of the Erie Canal, to run more than 350 miles across New York State, with the planning and carrying through in state hands, and the construction scheduled for the same auspices. With the stirrings in Pennsylvania, Massachusetts, and elsewhere along the Atlantic Coast for potentially competing facilities, quite surely at government expense, and with the Cumberland Road authorized by the federal government, there seemed the prospect of a swing toward greater participation of the state in transportation affairs.

It was at the close of the summer of 1818 that William H. Merritt made a survey with such instruments as he found available in the locality, and it was on October 14 of that year that he made the first public presentation of the scheme which later blossomed into the Welland Canal.[65] These events were critical for determining the auspices under which this new enterprise should be initiated, and they reveal aspects peculiarly interesting to the study of entrepreneurship and of economic change.

There was the circumstance that Merritt had connections

south of the border. His father had been a Loyalist at the time of the American Revolution, and had moved from Connecticut to the Niagara peninsula, which was in fact a haven for numerous men of similar sentiments. William Merritt had volunteered for the war that broke out in 1812, had been captured in the battle of Lundy's Lane, and had spent an appreciable period in a prisoners' camp in Massachusetts. He could have learned there of the Middlesex Canal, while, with the proposed terminus of the Erie Canal at Buffalo, it is highly probable that he knew of that project as well.

The original objective of Merritt and his immediate associates was merely a minor addition to activities in which they, and especially Merritt, were engaged already. Merritt was, if you will, acting in a manner typical of a frontier-type entrepreneur. Building on the start which his father had achieved at St. Catharines, William Merritt had successively established a flour mill, a sawmill, a potashery, a distillery, a cooper's shop, and a smithy. The success of these enterprises was in considerable part dependent upon a steady year-round flow of water; but the lumbering of the peninsula — to produce building materials for the growing population of the region — had rendered uncertain the water supply in the local Twelve Mile Creek, especially in the summer months. Merritt's surveying excursion was in search of a means to improve that water flow, just as Nicholas and Moses Brown might help to found the Bank of Providence the better to finance their enterprises of that region. Merritt found no supplemental source short of Lake Erie; but, with the difference in the height of water in Lakes Erie and Ontario spectacularly illustrated by the falls at Niagara, it was easy for Merritt to conceive of a ditch between the two lakes, a mere twenty-eight miles, which could indeed give a steady water flow to his creek. To be sure, a ridge or escarpment stood in the way, but Merritt estimated the ridge to be only thirty feet high.

Here in the study comes an instance of the "locally-oriented" or limited enterprise, of which I have spoken above.[66] The surveying instruments that the locality boasted were in fact defective. The aforesaid ridge was sixty feet high, not thirty; and Professor Aitken speculates that quite conceivably Merritt would not have had the temerity himself to proceed further, and he would not have succeeded in persuading his neighbors to join with him, if he had gotten a true measure of the physical difficulties that confronted construction gangs. Probably Professor John E. Sawyer would classify this episode as a case of constructive error.[67]

The meeting on October 14 reveals finally the elaboration of plans through which an originally simple scheme may go when application succeeds upon initial conception. Now the ditch for the conveyance of water had become a "canal" for the transportation of boats; the advantage which a few mill owners on Twelve Mile Creek might secure had expanded to "the great benefits [that] these provinces will derive"; and the provision of a steady supply of water to a few mills had given way to the capability of this new canal to "counteract" the possible influence of the projected Erie Canal, especially being able to "take down the whole of the produce of the western country." [68] One is led to think of Professor Daniel R. Fusfeld's "Heterogony of Entrepreneurial Goals," [69] to wonder whether this is not a case of the same genus as those which have begun to interest Professor Diamond, where the implementation or carrying-into-effect of a concept has inevitably brought with it a reorganization and redirection of the program.[70]

Many years ago, Charles W. Moulton analyzed several well-known plays of Shakespeare in terms of inevitableness of the subsequent action given the situation exposed by the dramatist in his early scenes: Caesar, Othello, King Lear, et cetera, were, as it were, doomed from the start.[71] Similarly, the subsequent experience of Merritt and the Welland Canal Company were largely contained in the circumstances of its origination. Surely the element that became ever more crucial, the difficulty of securing capital, might be deduced from the location of the project on a frontier of civilization. On the other hand, a reason for governmental interest existed in 1818 but was not specifically mentioned by the petition to the legislature which was drawn up by the meeting of October 14 of that year. I have in mind the military argument. In the war just concluded, the Canadian government had found it necessary to maintain two fleets with no communication between them, one on Lake Erie and one on Lake Ontario. There was continuing danger of attack from the wild men below the border, and thus a sizable canal between the two lakes would be very welcome by those charged with the defense of Canada. (Actually the government went forward with the survey for the construction of the Rideau Canal, which had almost exclusively a military objective.)

The barest facts of this subsequent development are as follows: the company was chartered in January, 1824; it had the outward aspects of a wholly private enterprise, although it did have the right to seize land for its proper purposes (but paying indemnity), and the government had the right of purchase after a thirty-year period (but that was common practice in charters pertaining to enterprise with monopolistic power).[72] Capital proved persistently difficult to secure, although one John B. Yates, who, in today's parlance might be called the "king" of the contemporary American lotteries, was induced to make substantial investment in the stock of the Company. Planning of construction and the execution of plans, the search for capital, and relations with the Canadian legislature came almost exclusively into the hands of William Merritt, largely because he wished it that way, but partly because of the lack in Upper Canada at that time of competent assistants. The administration was not efficient; public money became ever more essential to maintain construction; to some extent the project became a football of politics in a Canadian domestic "revolution" which seems to have had some of the character of Jefferson's struggle with the Federalists around 1800 in the United States. Financial conditions in England and the United States after 1836 added to the pressure, and the canal was forcibly purchased by the government in 1841. The relative stakes of government and private enterprise at a fairly mature date are indicated by a record of stock ownership as of December, 1836:

	Number	Percentage
Government of Upper Canada	8,600	43.0
Government of Lower Canada	2,000	10.0
Individuals in Upper Canada	297	1.5
Individuals in Lower Canada	1,106	5.5
Individuals in New Brunswick	40	0.2
Individuals in New York	5,570	27.8
Individuals in England	2,411	12.0
Total	20,024	100.0

At this time, William Merritt himself owned 38 shares, or less than 0.2 per cent of the total number outstanding.

Professor Aitken gives the mature situation among the interested parties in terms that are somewhat reminiscent of Wellington's illuminating treatment of sectional issues in the United States in the 1828–1842 period: cheap public lands, the protective tariff, and public improvements at governmental expense.[73] Here one might differentiate three principal parties. First, and ultimately the most powerful, was the government. (One should perhaps distinguish two governments: the English and the Canadian. At one stage it seemed possible that the English government might take a larger share of responsibility than it actually did. At all events, the interests of the two governments were parallel in most regards.) The Canadian government did take an increasingly positive view of the canal as a public utility, a means of improving its military defense, and one of challenging the waxing economic power of the United States, while at the same time benefiting its citizens. It manifested, on the whole, less of the desire for rapid completion of the scheme than did the other two chief participants; and surely it welcomed any opportunity to economize on the investment of its own scarce funds.

The attitudes of these other parties, Merritt and Yates, who seem to have carried the entrepreneurial responsibilities, are skillfully sketched by Professor Aitken.

Merritt had taken the lead in the launching of the enterprise primarily as a means of increasing the value of his properties, but gradually, perhaps as a result of the financial and technical difficulties of getting the work completed, he became more and more concerned merely in bringing the job to completion at almost any cost.

Yates began and ended a financial man. He had been involved in the lottery business in New York State, at that period a large-scale affair, and had become interested in the canal as an investment or, perhaps better, a speculation. He was also eager that the waterway be completed, but not as a means for the aggrandizement of St. Catharines, or indeed, the whole of Canada, but as a source of profits which in turn would make marketable — hopefully at a profit also

— the shares of the canal company in which he had placed his money.

The paths of the two men diverged when, viewing the advancing activity of the Canadian government, they saw their respective primary objectives promoted or submerged. Professor Aitken puts the situation thus:

Merritt regarded with equanimity, and indeed welcomed, each successive government grant and subscription. He saw no threat either to his own interests or to those of the Company in dependence on the legislature as a source of capital. The prospect of eventual government purchase he found by no means unattractive. After all, what did "the government" mean to him, if not the Executive Council, composed largely of his friends and fellow directors, the Legislative Council, dominated by the same group, and the Assembly, which might indeed prove bothersome on occasion but which could generally be counted on to grant what was requested? "The government" to Merritt was not an institution existing over and against the Company, but rather an instrument which the Company might use for its own purposes. Just as in his speeches and public papers he portrayed himself and his colleagues as acting *for* the province, so he expected the political leaders of the province to act *for* the Company. And until Mackenzie demonstrated that "the government" could be used as an instrument to destroy the Company as effectively as it formerly had given support, his expectations were not disappointed.

John B. Yates seems to have found this attitude hard to understand and harder still to accept. As a major stockholder, he was by no means content to let the government have the canal, even with repayment of principal and interest, unless complete and final bankruptcy were the only alternative. It was in the expectation of profits — large profits — that he had bought the stock, and that these profits, given time, would be realized he never doubted. To be sure, in the early years he had been as anxious as Merritt that the government should take an interest in the canal and demonstrate that interest by financial aid. But the successive encroachments of the legislature upon the Company's freedom of action he resented and feared. Earlier than any of the directors he recognized the danger implicit in Mackenzie's appointment to the board, suspecting (correctly, as it turned out) the imminence of the kind of organized political attack which he had learned to dread and respect in the lottery business. "The Government" for him was not *his* government; with the office-holders and Councillors whom Merritt admired and attempted to emulate he coöperated because there was no alternative. But he had little confidence in their ability and less in their willingness to put the interests of the stockholders first and their own careers and reputations second.[74]

Economic circumstances in Upper Canada in the 1818–1841 period did not permit the efflorescence of the sort of single-headed, innovating entrepreneurship with which Merritt launched the Welland Canal enterprise, and of which he seems to have been both desirous and capable. Conditions were also unfavorable for the sort of high-profit, quick-return operation which to Yates seemed the only worthwhile form of entrepreneurial performance. Merritt appears to have accommodated himself rather readily to the changes in fortunes. The achievement of construction — construction under almost any circumstances — came to supersede any ideas of the better and worse means of effecting that achievement. The circumstances surrounding the enterprise — economic, political, and to some extent personal — all favored the ultimate eventuality that the state should "take over."

VIGNETTE 15: LONG-TERM SUPPORT OF ENTREPRENEURSHIP

The promotion of industrialization is, of course, an old story, even if it has acquired a new name. The English from Tudor times on, the French under Colbert, the United States under Hamilton, Carey, Clay, and others, the Germans, the Russians — almost every nation has sought to encourage the introduction or expansion of young industries by protection. Economists realize that such state aid may be dangerous. It can become infectious. Manufacturers other than the original ones may be tempted to apply — and have at least a precedent in their favor — and farmers, miners, even organized labor may seek corresponding protection. However, there is often, if not usually, trouble even in the best cases. The "young" industries never grow up. Part of the explanation may be in the variant moods of entrepreneurship, and here we can draw data from a study of Brazilian experience with the cotton manufacture over a century of trial, a study made in large part on the ground by Professor Stanley J. Stein.[75]

The employment of this particular case to illustrate general points may not be appropriate. Possibly Brazil is not a propitious country for the development of industries. Surely Professor Stein shares the view of observers in a number of South American countries, that the market is inelastic; "the problem of cotton textile entrepreneurs was indissolubly linked with the national economy; a sound cotton manufacture could not exist alongside a sick rural economy." This seems to be the situation elsewhere on the continent. As Professor Henry G. Aubrey once put it, unlike the North American industrialist, a South American one does not presume that a reduction in the price of his product will increase the volume of his sales.[76] And a report of the United Nations on economic development in Latin America spoke mainly of overcoming the uncertainties of export volumes.[77]

Perhaps there is something odd about entrepreneurship in Latin America, at least something destructive enough to make unwarranted deductions based on North American data. More than one observer, surely, has commented on the greater measure of fatalism evident among Latin Americans in general. They seem to think that if the good Lord gives wealth, that is fine; if he does not, that is all right too — after all, life is short and not very important. Perhaps financial success, even accomplishment of any sort, counts for less than it does north of the Rio Grande.

There is also a question whether the position of industrialist, even large-scale or successful industrialist, carries the prestige that it does farther north. Professor Stein finds "a landholding aristocracy and a merchant oligarchy" to have constituted the elite group in Brazilian society at least through 1914, and that even now politically "a rural oligarchy and an impoverished rural electorate" are dominant. It is possible that the industrialist's prestige varies among the regions of the very large country, is high in such an industrialized area as São Paulo and lower elsewhere. Brazil was after all, predominantly an agricultural country until World War I, and is still largely so.

At all events, the cotton manufacture in Brazil made slow, although persistent, progress through the second half of the nineteenth century. During this period production was limited pretty much to coarse fabrics for rural consumption — and this despite a rising degree of tariff protection. The industry had attracted the support of well-heeled and influential Portuguese importers in the 1880's. They contributed capital, marketing skill, and presumably political connections. At any rate, the manufacture had reached a reasonable state of maturity around 1890, and secured a tariff wall that was held constant — and rather high — for forty years. Thereafter, administrative measures taken to combat the depression, or the conditions of World War II, made tariff protection less important.

Two developments occurred; one that is rather common under protectionism — although apparently not recognized by so eminent a writer on tariff matters as Taussig — and the other perhaps more noteworthy in Brazil than elsewhere. The first phenomenon is the tendency of entrepreneurs behind tariff walls or their equivalent to "edge up" on the quality of their productions. The Brazilian manufacturers did so before 1934 in a modest degree, and more extensively in the period of World War II. There is a competitive advantage in pressing costs down, and raising the quality of the output. There is probably some "psychic income" also; one has risen a bit in the scale of things, become more akin to the superior foreign producer. At all events, the point which I wish to make is that by reason of this propensity "infant industries" in a sense never grow up; the elevation in quality of output means that there is always some portion of the industry on "the margin," as it were, still as dependent on the same amount of protection as the portion originally sheltered — at least until all qualities of all varieties of the product which can be sold in the domestic market come to be manufactured in domestic mills more cheaply than they can be produced in any other competing country.

The second feature, not peculiar to Brazilian cotton manufactures, but seemingly more noteworthy in their case than in other somewhat comparable affairs, is the persistent and varied reliance on government for aid. Industrialists and farmers in the United States, France, Germany, indeed, in many countries, have gone to considerable lengths to keep a protective umbrella over their heads, and some sorts of farmers in more than one country have sought and accepted other forms of financial aid, usually subsidies of some type. In Brazil aid from the state is allegedly a spontaneous first thought of the cotton manufacturers in time of trouble. Not merely tariff increases, but special loans, or prohibition on the erection of additional mills, or restriction on the import of new machinery — all these have been advocated or accepted.

An explanation is offered by Professor Stein after his scholarly survey of the facts:

As early as the 1890's, the leaders of the Brazilian cotton manufacture advocated practices which converted them forty years later into a business oligarchy operating closely with government. The frontier between industrialization in the national interest and legalized favoritism for a minority of cotton industrialists was vague and easily passed. Here the cotton manufacturers merely followed the traditional patterns of planters and merchants who demanded and received from the state both concessions and privileges in the nineteenth and twentieth centuries.

The rise of rival groups "equally vociferous and influential" in the decades after 1930 made the acquisition of special favor more difficult to secure, but even after 1945 the effects of "government intervention in various forms, the absence of effective competition, and a rapidly growing population" were clearly to be seen: they were evident in a failure to maintain technological and managerial advance.

Professor Stein reaches the conclusion, valuable in other situations, that what Brazil has secured after a century of effort is "a developed segment of an underdeveloped economy," and seemingly an entrepreneurial group that appreciates its somewhat unfortunate situation and, for the most part, merely continues to look toward the state for support. Entrepreneurship does not necessarily grow vigorous with age.

PART THREE·
POSTLUDE: PROCESS OF
ENTREPRENEURIAL CHANGE

THE CHARACTER OF KNOWLEDGE or research in entrepreneurial history is evident in the foregoing parts. It represents a commingling of economics and history, sociology and business administration, technology and social psychology; it constitutes an interdisciplinary inquiry. Obviously, it is "behavioristic," has a good deal to do with communication, and comes close to concerning itself with forecasting, because the forces with which it deals are largely slow-acting and slow-changing, since "history" continues up to the present moment. Again, it is a meeting ground of many varieties of history: economic, social, intellectual, institutional, and technological, with a little religious and philosophical history thrown in. It is international in its scope, and cultural in its focus.

Most practically, the study of entrepreneurial phenomena offers economics on a time dimension, and economics stripped of its *mutatis mutandis,* its assumptions, and its caveats. Its pursuit would constitute in part a return to a range of questions and problems that interested economists of earlier generations: matters of progress, improvement of mankind, the trend toward a "stationary state," and the like.

Alfred Marshall was still influenced by such considerations. In his *Principles,* he mentions the problem of the competitive growth of business units, "trees" in his "forest," but he turns to other matters when he observes that the trees do not last forever. Of course, there are three ripostes to such an argument. When he wrote, there were actually in Britain a number of enterprises that could trace back continuous ex-

227

istence a couple of centuries; second, we should have no study of forestry or even botany in general if scientists were discouraged by the mortality of their specimens; and, anyway, nothing much in economics remains valid much longer than an oak, let alone a redwood, not even the whole economic system which Marshall took for granted.[1]

On the other hand, Marshall does recognize specifically that there are long-run considerations that differ from those pertinent to the short run; and he was prepared to admit that "even indirect influences may produce great effects in the course of a generation, if they happen to act cumulatively," and accordingly, "violence is required for keeping broad forces in the pound of *caeteris paribus*" over any such period.

Marshall in his *Principles* seemed to take fright when he looked into the "pound" of long-run forces. "A theoretically perfect long period," he writes, "must give time enough to enable not only the factors of production of the commodity to be adjusted to the demand, but also the factors of production of those factors of production to be adjusted, and so on." This process perturbed him the more since, as he saw it, "when carried to its logical consequences, [it] will be found to involve the supposition of a stationary state of industry, in which the requirements of a future age can be anticipated an indefinite time beforehand." [2] Obviously, this is not the place to argue scientific procedure in economic research, but it should be clear that, if it is logical for some purposes to stop at the stage of the action of one set of productive factors, it is equally logical for other purposes to stop at one stage removed. And, as a matter of record, Marshall attempted a consideration of once-removed forces in the international comparisons contained in his *Industry and Trade*. Here national aptitudes, national experiences, and the like are called upon to explain economic trends.

Studies of population are, for the most part, good examples of long-run economics. They contain everything from the effects of marriage customs today or in Roman times upon the birth rates of the respective eras to the rate of the communication of medical knowledge upon the death rate, now as compared with a century ago. In fact, thoughtful students do not hesitate to carry the analysis "logically" a step further, concerning themselves not merely with what happened, but what the events meant for the thinking of the people to whom the events related! Such is the contribution of Professor Helleiner to the study of the "vital revolution" of the eighteenth century in Europe. As he states it: the disappearance of the black rat should be given its due "not merely in the sense that it helped to eliminate the greatest single agent of mortality [by the spreading of the plague], but in the sense that perhaps only a society freed from the fear as well as from the material and spiritual consequences of sudden death was able to achieve that high rate of intellectual and technical progress without which population growth could never have been sustained." [3]

The evolution of economico-business literature is a further case in point. I have attempted to outline the more important changes that have occurred in the printed materials since Gutenberg, with some effort at examining the changes, in an essay entitled, "Conspectus for a History of Economic and Business Literature." [4]

So also are the efforts to discover periods of broadly running secular change such as that recently elaborated by Professor Herbert Heaton on the basis of changes in standards of living, or the earlier one of Professor Edwin F. Gay relative to degrees of economic freedom and restraint.[5] Such interpreters of history do not hesitate to bring into their arguments anything from religious and political beliefs to the impact of improved education.

229

Economics on a time scale will always draw heavily from the facts and theories adduced by economic historians. That form of economics would fail to reach its potential, however, if, as one author lately phrased the relationship, economic history should be "based on economic theory." [6] It would seem a mistake also for economic historians to follow too slavishly the admonitions of well-intentioned advisors and use more economic theory in their work — if they were to consider themselves limited by the current body of economic theory.[7]

The point that I am making is an obvious one, really: theory is based on facts, including many historical ones, not facts on theory. Economics on a time dimension may well make use of certain dynamic propositions of current economic theory — such as the Malthusian law (in some form), Gresham's law, and the like — and may wish to employ for its convenience such static notions as noncompeting groups or consumer's surplus. But it may well look to the theorist to provide theories to explain the facts, as indeed they did in the case of business cycles or changing location of industries. Theories important for historical economics need not be the same as those for short-run matters, any more than macro-economics should cover the same topics as micro-economics.

Historical economics would necessarily have a tempo or "time horizon" appropriate to its materials and purposes, just as the tempo of the geologist is different from that of the botanist, and that of the latter different from that of the present-day economist. Yet it does seem important that some branch or section of the social sciences (including analytical history) should pay concentrated and continuous attention to the theoretical explanation, limited though such explanations may be in many cases, of the rise and decline of economies, of the speed in the spread of technical or business knowledge, of the significance of education (of various sorts) upon economic productivity, and — not least — of the consequences upon national income of the changing role, changing proficiency, and changing motivations of entrepreneurs. When economists more generally adopt longer time perspectives, and when they venture to open the "pound" of factors that condition the changing complements of the productive factors, it may well prove convenient — at least for relatively modern Western economies — to make entrepreneurship the central focus. A whole gamut of dynamic flows would be encompassed thereby: relations to the discovery and tapping of new natural resources, relations to the implementation of capital and of labor, relations to the introduction of technological or intellectual innovations, even relations to the circumambient society. It was in the context of economics of this character that, a decade ago, I ventured to speak of "the entrepreneur" as indeed "the central figure." Since doctors should in theory take their own medicine, I venture to elaborate a "model" of the nature of entrepreneurial change.

Entrepreneurial Change

At the outset of an explanation of entrepreneurial change, it will be useful to make manifest what the exposition aims to do, and what it does not attempt. I do think that the analysis should have in mind changes of all sorts, those that seem connected with economic decline of areas or nations as well as those that seem associated with economic development.[8] The explication should perhaps be flexible enough to fit the exigencies of the case of a "moving equilibrium" of entrepreneurial character and performance — a rather improbable situation over any period of time that would be significant for studies other than short-run adjustments.

On the other hand, we are not directly concerned with

the whole subject of economic change. We believe the two to be interrelated, indeed, that the real availability of natural resources, the flow of capital, the improvement in quality of labor, the generation of consumer demand, and the like are much affected by the changing quality of entrepreneurship. Yet the sources and process of economic change are by no means identical with those of entrepreneurial alteration.

"Change" in this whole connection does comprehend the degree to which entrepreneurs take advantage of the total economic situation, but it also comprehends the entrepreneur's interaction with the total cultural situation. The willingness to grasp the possibilities of professional education as well as to accept new and improved machinery must be included. And change is constituted of innovations that alter pre-existing entrepreneurial behavior. The innovation may be largely ceremonial, as when New York bankers ceased to wear cutaway coats to their offices; they may be *fachmässig*, such as the inauguration of a cost-accounting system or — operating in the direction of decreased effectiveness — the acceptance of longer week ends at country houses. And they may be affective (if I may employ this term in the current connection), as when Frederick W. Taylor and his followers promoted the notion of *right* ways of doing things in business, or when businessmen in America took seriously the ideas of natural selection as voiced by Herbert Spencer. At all events, change may be conceived as innovations of thought, procedures, or instruments, initiated at any of several possible points in the entrepreneurial world, and spread among entrepreneurial actors by imitation of one man or institution by others.

The explanation of enterpreneurial change may best be elaborated in three stages: that of entrepreneurial structure, that of motivation, and that of process or course of movement.

The nature of the entrepreneurial world, in terms of structure, has been examined in foregoing chapters.[9] A brief résumé will suffice at this point. I conceive the entrepreneur or entrepreneurial team — those who make, execute, and are responsible for the strategic decisions of a profit-oriented enterprise — as located in the center of a series of concentric circles, or riding a log in the grip of a set of close and distant forces. Nearest to him (or it) is the personnel of the business unit for the "maintenance and aggrandizement" of which the decisions are made. Indeed, I have conceived of this personnel as constituted of two circles or layers, the individuals responsible (with the entrepreneur) for the conduct of the enterprise, and those only indirectly associated, such as the stockholders, bankers, suppliers, and the like.

The latter congeries merges with the next external group, which I have denominated the entrepreneurial stream. Here would be the service institutions, the ancillary units, the purveyors of business information, the schools of business, and the like.

Still further removed, at least in the aggregate, from the decision-making center would be the entrepreneurial world, which I conceive as those facets of the total culture that have relevance for entrepreneurial character and performance; for example, ministers giving their interpretations of proper business conduct, but not the same men calling upon the sick, or an engineering school in its "applied" instruction, but not in its prosecution of basic research. Here would fall the public censors as a whole, the consumers affiliated and potential, the educational system, the governmental organizations, et cetera.

It will become obvious on second thought that while "in the aggregate," as I said immediately above, one circle, or one current in a stream, may be conceived to lie at one or more "removes" from the entrepreneurial center, actually the entrepreneurial actors have in major or minor degree direct interaction with all such circles or currents. These actors read the general literature of their culture, see its motion pictures, and hears its sermons. Similarly, they may well have direct contacts with the theory of games, with Keynesian economics, or other bodies of thought not directly concerned with business administration. And I speak of interaction, since quite obviously businessmen are not passive recipients of social forces; they help to mold those forces.

From time to time in the foregoing exposition I have mentioned various incentives to action on the part of entrepreneurial figures: financial reward, prestige, rise in a business hierarchy, sense of power, sense of public service, and the like. Professor David C. McClelland has coined the general term "need for achievement," [10] although I would be disposed to give the phrase a slight twist, to become the "need for recognition of achievement." There may be some entrepreneurs so "inner-directed" as to gain complete satisfaction in their contemplation of their own work well done; and surely such contemplation constitutes part of most businessmen's flow of psychic income. But achievement is generally a social event; and indeed Professor Drucker has indicated his belief in a report that business executives in America are not so much concerned over the absolute size of their salaries as in the *relationship* of their salaries to those of comparable officers.[11]

I have noted elsewhere that a "need for achievement" or something similar acts as the motive force for the erection of service institutions, and the propagation of a sort of circular action.[12] I would suggest here that the same need operates to galvanize the executives of management advisory enterprises, trade associations, and so on, even deans of business schools or ministers of the gospel, at least in some measure. Before his recent, untimely death, Professor R. Richard Wohl had almost, if not fully, completed a study of the success theme in American life. I believe that it would have carried further the data offered by Professor Irvin G. Wyllie in his book, *The Self-made Man in America*.[13]

A corresponding examination of English, French, Italian, or other experience, and the relevant literary expressions, might reveal a less vigorous growth, but the evidence of the "need for achievement" as well as the social recognition of accomplishment will not be found wholly absent from any of these countries, while the record in Germany and the Netherlands might well rival that of the United States.

It is noteworthy, however, that in entrepreneurial life more than in most other pursuits of achievement, the business unit counts for much, more than in most other social institutions; chambers of commerce, scientific associations, even political parties and most churches. The entrepreneurial actors find themselves compelled to share responsibilities with others; and the instillation of company loyalty forms a protection against too great inefficiency. Competition among business units, where alone the action is alleged sometimes to be "cutthroat," helps to increase the feeling of loyalty, by virtue of the need for individual security. So also does the endeavor of the individual actor in large business organizations to rise in the hierarchy. But surely not least is the entrepreneur's acceptance of the measure, even the reality of his achievement in the aggrandizement of the business unit with which he is affiliated.

Thus, the development of business enterprises comes to support the incentive of personal need for achievement, at least in most cases. The latter qualification is necessary because of the possibility, deriving from features of corporate finance, that a Jay Gould or his ilk may "achieve" the financial wreckage of the enterprise for which he is the effective entrepreneur, in order that through short selling of its stock in the public market, he may secure personal profit. Fortunately for society, most entrepreneurial actors envisage achievement in the shape of company expansion and institutional growth.

Beyond incentive to entrepreneurial change, there must be opportunity. The latter arises chiefly in the circumstance noted by Professor Cochran in *Change and the Entrepreneur,* that the entrepreneurial role is not closely defined. (Professor Cochran was writing about the United States, but his assertion would seem to be true in other Western countries.) Within the individual enterprise, there are in some measure "natural" contenders — the selling versus the production divisions, the stockholders versus the labor unions — each endeavoring to push the entrepreneurial actors in one direction or another.[14] Outside these institutions, in the entrepreneurial stream, lies also the potentiality of contending pressures. The organizations themselves — trade associations, management counselors, public accountants, and the like — may each represent a pull or push in a given direction, the stronger because of the very organization itself (with personnel also concerned with achievement); but they severally oppose one another in many relationships. For instance, the trade association secretary may counsel direct selling — for example, from factory to retailer — but the management adviser may argue against alienation of the traditional agents of distribution.

Insofar as elements of the whole culture may be involved, general social perspectives, what Professor Cochran called "cultural themes," there is even greater latitude of action permissible to entrepreneurial actors. For one thing, cultural themes are not always concurrent in their admonitions. For instance, one strand of social thought may encourage entrepreneurs to be bold, to crash ahead and do new things, but another strand may lay upon his shoulders at least decent care for his work, for people, and for the community in which he is, or has been, located. Again, many elements of social thought are but floating ideas — honorable conduct, respect for the dignity of others, the insurance of real freedom — many of them inheritances from the past. Even fewer of these cultural themes form the basis of social institutions by force of which they may be propagated and their values be continuously driven home. Those stemming from the Christian faith do enjoy the support of the churches, but the latter do not in fact speak with wholly uniform admonitions. And the precepts supported by schools and brotherhoods, Better Business Bureaus, and the editorials of the *New York Times* are by no means always uniform, and, for the most part, given to the expression of pious hopes. In such circumstances, entrepreneurs have considerable freedom in the shaping of their roles. There is much opportunity for change.

Parenthetically, it may be observed that the element of time makes itself noteworthy at various points. We are indeed concerned here with a set of flows also. I have spoken of the cultural themes as often being inheritances from the past. In fact such themes have sometimes varied in force from era to era and place to place. For example, an inventor of a textile spinning machine or apparatus was drowned in Danzig harbor in the seventeenth century, but another somewhat equivalent person was knighted in England in the eighteenth century. In the United States, "tied" houses for the distribution of malt liquors (saloons owned or financially aided by brewing companies in return for agreement to dispense only the products of the particular supporting brewer) threatened to become a common phenomenon in the nineteenth century. The practice aroused public disapproval, largely in consequence of the whole prohibition campaign, and now the local bar or tavern is free, both in the sense of being under no financial obligation to suppliers and in being able to dispense more than one brand of beverage, and of course to switch from one supplier to another. In England, on the other hand, "tied" houses arose in the early nineteenth century, and still flourish. The "free" house is the exception.

Time is involved also through the circumstance that entrepreneurial practices, like other human actions, tend to harden into conventions or thought-patterns that possess force in part because "the memory of man runneth not to the contrary," as was said in English manorial courts. The French local baker produces fresh loaves several times a day, and the French housewife goes to his shop as often in a day as she runs out of bread. The reception clerks in an English automobile-repair shop appear in cutaway coats and striped trousers — as have those in English retail stores since time immemorial. American banks must always be housed in edifices that look substantial. Correspondingly, an old enterprise, industry, or industrialized country possesses less flexibility than its younger equivalents, in entrepreneurial attitudes as in other features, such as the more familiar industrial technology.

A dynamic or growth element is provided within the individual enterprise by what may be called trading on experience — or trading upon history, if you will — provided an active entrepreneurial system exists in the society. W. Hastings Lyon gave an illustration of this factor forty years ago in his "trading on equity" in the financial aspect of corporate life. Lyon's illustrative or ideal case is that of a company that gets started on the capital secured through the issuance of common stock; when the concern has established earning power of adequate proportions and stability, it may secure added capital by issuing preferred stock; that is, trading on its relatively assured income; and then, later still, it could, as it were, give away more of its security in return for capital acquired through the issuance of bonds, capital that would not have been attracted into the enterprise until the concern had demonstrated a substantial and steady "equity" and become willing to "trade" upon the latter.

The same notion can be extended, even in the financial area. Proven stability of net earnings encourages commercial and investment bankers to take a friendlier view of the enterprise; and the same set of circumstances will permit the professional managers of the company to attain a greater degree of freedom from stockholder inspection and "interference." Such managers are enabled to engage the concern in projects of longer incubation than stockholders might contemplate agreeably, at least if a goodly sized regular dividend were not quite reasonably assured.

Processes of similar character are visible in other segments of company operations. In employee relations, for example, it seems clear that good relationships proceed step by step, each favorable move being prepared by the favorable acceptance of the previous action. The same is true in the extension of the line of goods that a concern produces or sells. The "equity" or good repute gained by Hotpoint stoves led the General Electric Company to add Hotpoint refrigerators, despite the incongruity of name; the American Telephone and Telegraph Company is engrossed in a number of electrical activities that have nothing to do with either "telegraph" or "telephone"; and so it goes with many other enterprises.

At one time American corporations used frequently to exhibit an appreciation of the foregoing conditions, at least in a vague sort of way, by carrying a substantial sum on the asset side of their balance sheets under the rubric of "good will." Accounting houses, typically conservative in outlook and apperceptive particularly of the short-run phenomena of the business cycle, have persuaded most concerns to eliminate this item or to carry it at a nominal figure. However, what may be good accounting practice may be inadequate long-term business theory. The good repute of a company and its products (or the quality of its services), its demonstrated earning power in various sets of circumstances, its apparent capacity for survival cannot be shrugged aside as valueless, especially when assessing the potentialities of growth of the institution. In the simpler, slower-moving conditions of eighteenth-century foreign mercantile operations, it seems evident that not a few houses expanded, as well as survived, on a modest supply of ability but a large quantity of integrity. Such intangible elements have not ceased to be of importance in company growth in later times. And the important socio-economic point is that here, "built into" the individual unit of a properly oriented business system, is a propensity, as it were, to lift one's self by one's bootstraps, and a method for accomplishing that feat. A somewhat similar condition will shortly be shown to exist for the business system as a whole.

The introduction of a new feature in entrepreneurial practice in a given area or industry — the inauguration of a public-relations department, the initiation of an executive training program, or the determination to take a firmer attitude vis-à-vis labor unions — is the act of an individual (or group of individuals) taken, in most cases, on behalf of the business enterprise with which they chance to be associated. The basic psychological impulse may be self-aggrandizement, the need for achievement, but the form is usually betterment of the individual's enterprise.

Entrepreneurial actors, like college presidents or managers of baseball teams, are all individual in the sense that for each the physical inheritance, the nurture, and the experiences in early life have been variant, even though the young men of a given "generation" may share many sentiments.[15]

Robert Owen had the misfortune in his youth to burn his stomach severely with hot porridge; and ever after he grew to think of himself as different from other men; Charlemagne Tower chanced to be christened with a name that never ceased to stir his ambitions; and Erastus B. Bigelow happened to be born with an unusual instinct for contrivance. Each business situation, a brief conjuncture, as it were, in a time-bound flow, is also individual, for each enterprise has its own evolved past. Accordingly, a man of perhaps peculiar acquired characteristics, confronted with a hitherto-unknown situation, may well exhibit what Professor Schumpeter called the "creative response."[16] An innovation in entrepreneurial behavior is born. What could not be anticipated from the precedent material conditions does in fact occur. Thus, Jay Cooke in the 1860's and J. P. Morgan in the early 1890's rendered valuable support to the federal treasury, and gave new stature to investment banking in this country; John Murray Forbes imparted a fresh impetus toward higher business ethics among top executives, a step toward the idea of trusteeship, when he refused to allow his railroad officers to participate in railroad construction companies concerned with their own railroad enterprises; and Frank W. Abrams appears possibly to have added almost a whole new facet to American entrepreneurial responsibilities when he advocated, and subsequently helped to implement, corporate aid to education.

However, many innovations in enterpreneurial behavior

241

are, in a sense, successful orphans. So many people, within enterprises, in service organizations, or elsewhere, have participated in the evolution of the idea that no one deserves the title of parent. Surely there is in each instance a first exponent of a new attitude, the first user of a new practice, but the last step in the process of change may be a small one and frequently — indeed in entrepreneurial history one can say "usually" — this true innovator passed unnoticed. An illustrative case is that related to the proper preservation of company records. One can trace the original impulse back at least to the practices of English and German scholars to uncover various phases of medieval and early modern history by the examination of municipal, guild, manorial, and other primary manuscript records. The first two deans of the Harvard Business School, Gay and Donham, were instrumental in the promotion of business history in the United States on a basis comparable with this European practice. Dr. Joseph H. Willits of the Rockefeller Foundation was interested in promoting historical research in this country. Finally, Emmet J. Leahy had had experience during World War II in the handling of U. S. Navy records. Out of this convergence arose the National Records Management Council, and out of the Council stemmed the modern professionalized treatment of corporate archives. And if it had not chanced that Professor Cochran, Professor Shepard B. Clough, and I had been mixed up in the whole development, this significant evolution in entrepreneurial practice would probably never have been recorded.

As will have appeared already, at least by implication, many, if not most, innovations in entrepreneurial behavior are evolutionary in character, whether they be instrumental or affective in nature. I mean that they are constituted chiefly of carrying somewhat further some idea or aspiration already entertained in enterpreneurial life. Thus, Filene's "bargain basement" was in large measure merely a development from well-known bargain sales; and the commuter's ticket was the old railroad "pass" with places for the conductor to punch.

The path of progress, however, is not always as smooth as the foregoing would tend to indicate. Human beings are variable; indeed, there appears even to be a small group that revels in being contrary or rebellious. I know an academic man who admitted that he had unwittingly picked up the mental habit of challenging any generalization: that Sundays in London were dull; that country-bred men were healthier than city-bred ones; and so on. Some businessmen are reportedly of similar character. An episode will illustrate what I mean. Mr. Richard Lenihan, the manager of a Toledo department store, and an old friend of mine, found his fur sales slumping during the war and early postwar years. As everywhere else, fur coats there were sold in "salons" with the help of "models," of course, but the people with the newly-expanded purses were not used to sitting in salons and looking at models; at most their daughters might *aspire* to becoming models. So Dick broke with tradition, put his mink and other coats on racks on the ground floor of his establishment where the women could handle the "goods," and found that the garments sold "like hotcakes."

Once a new practice or attitude has been initiated — by the action of an individual entrepreneur, by a writer in *Fortune,* or the counsel of a management consultant — the novelty is bound to be copied, if it is of the instrumental variety. The innovating enterprise, through the introduction of the new process or product, has gained a differential advantage; and its competitors are moved by the desire for profits, if not for survival, to recapture a position of equivalence. Even in the case of "affective" innovations, there may be competitive pressure promotive of imitation: public approval of such measures as a complaint section in a department store, a helpful housing program for employees, or a real effort to install a nondiscriminatory labor policy, so that institutions comparably situated have to follow suit.

But the speed of imitation may vary widely. The rapidity of spread, and, therefore, the degree and speed of its general impact would seem, indeed, to depend on a number of variables. One is the quality of the entrepreneurial talent in the economy in question. The higher the percentage of top-caliber men, in the Danhof or any similar classification, and the smaller proportion of "Fabians" and "drones," the more rapid and enthusiastic is likely to be the reception of the new notion or technique.

Innovation, however, occurs in the whole system as well as within the individual enterprise. Stimulated by progress in the "arts," the advent of a new intellectual concept, even the prior expansion of the economy itself, entrepreneurs will find it alluring to attempt to establish a new ancillary or service institution — a credit-reporting agency, a counseling bureau in public relations, or just a means of preserving outgoing correspondence simpler than copying the messages into a letter-book. And, of course, here also there is imitation — Dun was followed by Bradstreet, Bernays by a host of others — while improvement in the conduct of such institutions over time, partly the consequence of competition between the first and the later arrivals, will have its own effect: the net contribution of the whole system to economic productiveness will be enhanced.

Another factor is the presence, perhaps the proportion, of new industries, with more flexible entrepreneurs. Erik Dahmen seems to have found a difference in the response of the entrepreneurs in old and in new industries to the pressures of the interwar period in Sweden.[17] In the United States the leaders in the electrical and chemical industries have manifested the quickest appreciation of scientific research. Again, it was the airplane and petroleum companies that responded first to the opportunity for better records management.

Surely a third factor could be the quality of the communication media. In an economically immature area, old or modern, efforts at secrecy of operations and paucity of public vehicles of communication are usual conditions. The gossip of the Rialto, the marketplace, or the coffeehouse had to suffice the early merchants. Early industrial entrepreneurs lived in even greater isolation. In the United States only the rise of first the commercial and then the industrial press gave motion to new ideas. More recently, professional associations, advisory organizations, teaching in schools of business, services of business libraries, and so forth, have speeded the course of new ideas.

Finally, there is the circumstance which might be called sympathetic alignment of institutions. (Here again the basic idea has been contributed by Professor Cochran, while I have obviously also borrowed a notion from Professor Cyert.) My idea is that maximum spread and maximum speed in entrepreneurial change will be found to come, and to have come in the past, where the various elements in the concentric circles of our imagined entrepreneurial world are all, as it were, pointing in the same direction, or charged with the same brand of electricity. A crop of unusually able leaders, business institutions flexible enough to respond to new developments, ancillary and service organizations tuned to encourage novelty and transmit knowledge of them, and an outside society friendly, if not forthrightly beneficent. Under such conditions, the "need for achievement" or "need of recognition" will bloom and thrive; improvement in entrepreneurial quality and resources will be stimulated; and the fruits of such striving will be given recognition of a wide character. An able young entrepreneur's program of cost reduction will "die aborning" if his board of directors and the association of his fellow industrialists frown on any exploitation of the notions which would drive marginal producers out of business. At times in the past the difficulties of New England manufacturers have been laid at the doors of unsympathetic bankers, uncooperative labor unions, overzealous tax authorities, and surely the endeavors of innovation-riding entrepreneurs would not have much effect if the consumers of the relevant economy were habit-bound. The appeal of "streamlined" refrigerators or "1959 model" beds would hardly overreach the threshold of consciousness in a consuming public where cold cellars and durable consumers' goods were expected to serve generation after generation. At all events, there have been occasions in American experience, and there seem to have been rather more frequent occasions in foreign economies, where one or more of the elements was "out of line," as it were, or negative when it might better (for this purpose) have been positive; — a family content with high current income, whatever the future; a society that did (or does not) give adequate recognition to entrepreneurial achievement; or a political system that thrives on the baiting of businessmen.

Entrepreneurial change is rather obviously an important phenomenon. The higher the quality of entrepreneurial talent, the greater the zeal of that talent for achievement, the more developed the ancillary and service institutions, and the more parallel the outlook of the whole entrepreneurial world, the greater will be the likelihood of higher productivity in the economy, and a higher national income, provided, of course, that the easy course of monopolistic control is effectively blocked, and provided the corruption of a cult of wealth can be moderated, if not replaced, by the valuation of other indicia of achievement.

The course of entrepreneurial change, however, is a complicated matter. Obviously it is a social phenomenon, and social in various ways: the innovating entrepreneur is in part a product of his society; he operates through and is operated upon by social organizations; and he and the personnel of these social bodies are influenced by waves of social thought, past and current.

Social change is also a phenomenon of communication. Specific individual changes are rarely of importance, each by itself; the economic or social value comes through imitation, and often also through a continuance of the trend which the specific change signalizes.

The change is usually a deviation from the pre-existing role, and entrepreneurial roles are "prescription-slack" in a degree adequate to permit, if not to encourage, deviation. Such deviation is likely to be progressive, in the sense of continuing a trend already begun and proved acceptable to at least some important censors. However, there are also occasional deviations that seem to run counter to pre-existent and prevailing thought.

The propagation of an entrepreneurial change will be promoted if it takes place in an entrepreneurial world wherein all the elements are beneficent: alert potential imitators; sclerosis-free industries and geographical areas that are not tradition-bound but are sophisticated and alert enough to make effective use of appropriate institutions available in the entrepreneurial stream; and a climate of cultural themes that is beneficent, tolerating, if not encouraging, changes that promise increased entrepreneurial effectiveness.

Obviously, as far as this exposition of entrepreneurial change is concerned, there is point in taking seriously Professor Rostow's reference to the biological antecedents of present-day economics. Long-term economics — which, it seems, can hardly overlook entrepreneurship, social institutions, and cultural themes — appears likely to resemble botany, perhaps, indeed, the "trees of the forest" to which Marshall referred more than a half-century ago.

WORKS CITED

NOTES

INDEX

WORKS CITED

Abbott, Charles C. "Broad View of Administration," University of Virginia *Alumni News*. October, 1956.

Abramovitz, Moses. *Resource and Output Trends in the United States since 1870*. New York, 1956. 23 pp.

Abrams, Frank W. "Management's Responsibilities in a Complex World," in *Harvard Business Review*, 29: 29–34 (1951).

Aitken, Hugh G. J. "Entrepreneurial Biography: A Symposium, Part III," in *Explorations in Entrepreneurial History*, 2: 230–232 (1949–50).

—— *The Welland Canal Company: A Study in Canadian Enterprise*. Cambridge, Mass., 1954. 178 pp.

The Art of Growing Rich. London, 1796. 31 pp.

L'Artisan de la fortune, ou les moyens de s'avancer dans le monde. Toulouse, 1691. 188 pp.

Ashton, Thomas S. *Economic History of England: The Eighteenth Century*. London, 1955. 257 pp.

Aubrey, Henry G. "Investment Decisions in Underdeveloped Countries," in *Capital Formation and Economic Growth*, Princeton, 1955, pp. 397–440.

Bailyn, Bernard. *The New England Merchants in the Seventeenth Century*. Cambridge, Mass., 1955. 249 pp.

—— "The *Apologia* of Robert Keayne," in *William and Mary Quarterly*, 3d ser., 7: 568–587 (1950).

Baldwin, George B. "The Invention of the Modern Safety Razor," in *Explorations in Entrepreneurial History*, 4: 73–102 (1950–51).

Bamford, Paul W. "Entrepreneurship in Seventeenth and Eighteenth Century France: Some General Conditions and a Case Study," in *Explorations in Entrepreneurial History*, 9: 204–213 (1956–57).

Belshaw, Cyril S. "The Cultural Milieu of the Entrepreneur: A Critical Essay," in *Explorations in Entrepreneurial History*, 7: 146–163 (1954–55).

Bendix, Reinhard. *Work and Authority in Industry: Ideologies of*

WORKS CITED

Management in the Course of Industrialization. New York, 1956. 466 pp.

Benson, Lee. *Merchants, Farmers & Railroads: Railroad Regulation and New York Politics.* Cambridge, Mass., 1955. 310 pp.

Berle, Adolf A., Jr. *The 20th Century Capitalist Revolution.* New York, 1954. 192 pp.

Bernstein, Peter L. "Profit Theory — Where do We Go from Here?" in *Quarterly Journal of Economics,* 67: 407–422 (1953).

Boulding, Kenneth E. *The Organizational Revolution. A Study in the Ethics of Economic Organization.* New York, 1953. 286 pp.

—— "Religious Foundations of Economic Progress," in *Harvard Business Review,* 30: 33–40 (1952).

Bowen, Howard R. *Social Responsibilities of the Businessman.* New York, 1953. 276 pp.

Bridges, Hal. *Iron Millionaire: Life of Charlemagne Tower.* Philadelphia, 1952. 322 pp.

Bruchey, Stuart W. *Robert Oliver, Merchant of Baltimore, 1783–1819.* Baltimore, 1956. 411 pp.

Buchanan, Norman S., and Howard S. Ellis. *Approaches to Economic Development.* New York, 1955. 494 pp.

Burnham, James. *Management Revolution: What is Happening in the World.* New York, 1941. 285 pp.

Butel-Dumont, Georges Marie. *Histoire et commerce des colonies angloises . . .* La Haye, 1755.

Butlin, Noel G. "Borderlands or Badlands," in *Explorations in Entrepreneurial History,* 3: 44–50 (1950–51).

Butters, J. Keith, and John Lintner. *Effect of Federal Taxes on Growing Enterprises.* Boston, 1945. 226 pp.

Chandler, Alfred D., Jr. "Management Decentralization: An Historical Analysis," in *Business History Review,* 30: 111–174 (1956–57).

Change and the Entrepreneur. Cambridge, Mass., 1949. 200 pp.

Choi, Kee Il. "Tokugawa Feudalism and the Emergence of the New Leaders of Early Modern Japan," in *Explorations in Entrepreneurial History,* 9: 72–90 (1956–57).

Clark, Samuel D. *The Social Development of Canada.* Toronto, 1942. 484 pp.

Cochran, Thomas C. *The American Business System: A Historical Perspective, 1900–1955.* Cambridge, Mass., 1957. 227 pp.

—— "The Organization Man in Historical Perspective," in *Pennsylvania History,* 25: 9–24 (1958).

—— *Railroad Leaders, 1845–1890: The Business Mind in Action.* Cambridge, Mass., 1953. 564 pp.

Cochran, Thomas C., and William Miller. *The Age of Enterprise: A Social History of Industrial America.* New York, 1942. 394 pp.

WORKS CITED

Cole, Arthur H. "Agricultural Crazes: A Neglected Chapter in American Economic History," in *American Economic Review*, 16: 622–639 (1926).

—— *The American Wool Manufacture*. Cambridge, Mass., 1926. 2 vols.

—— "An Appraisal of Economic Change; Twentieth-Century Entrepreneurship in the United States and Economic Growth," in *American Economic Review*, 40: No. 2: 35–50 (1954).

—— "An Approach to the Study of Entrepreneurship," in *Journal of Economic History*, 6, Suppl.: 1–15 (1946).

—— "Conspectus for a History of Economic and Business Literature," in *Journal of Economic History*, 17: 333–388 (1957).

—— "Entrepreneurship and Entrepreneurial History: The Institutional Setting," in *Change and the Entrepreneur* (1949), pp. 85–107.

—— "A New Set of Stages," in *Explorations in Entrepreneurial History*, 8: 99–107 (1955–56).

Cooper, William W. "A Proposal for Extending the Theory of the Firm," in *Quarterly Journal of Economics*, 65: 87–109 (1951).

—— "Theory of the Firm: Some Suggestions for Revision," in *American Economic Review*, 39: 1204–1222 (1949).

Cyert, Richard M., and J. G. March. "Organizational Factors in the Theory of Oligopoly," in *Quarterly Journal of Economics*, 70: 44–64 (1956).

—— "Organizational Structure and Pricing Behavior in an Oligopolistic Market," in *American Economic Review*, 45: 129–139 (1955).

Dahmen, Erik. *Svensk industriell företagarverksamhet: Kausalanalys av den industriella utvecklingen 1919–1939* (with an English summary). Stockholm, 1950. 2 vols.

Danhof, Clarence H. "Economic Values in Cultural Perspective," in *Goals of Economic Life*, A. Dudley Ward, ed., pp. 84–117. New York, 1953.

Davis, Ralph. "Merchant Shipping in the Economy of the Late Seventeenth Century," in *Economic History Review*, 2d. ser., 9: 59–73 (1956).

Dean, Joel. *Managerial Economics*. New York, 1951. 621 pp.

Diamond, Sigmund. "From Organization to Society: Virginia in the Seventeenth Century," in *American Journal of Sociology*, 63: 457–475 (1957–58).

—— *The Reputation of the American Businessman*. Cambridge, Mass., 1955. 209 pp.

Dimock, Marshall E. *The Executive in Action*. New York, 1945. 276 pp.

Donaldson, James. *The Undoubted Art of Thriving*. Edinburgh, 1700. 135 pp.

WORKS CITED

Drucker, Peter F. *The Practice of Management*. New York, 1954. 404 pp.

Duesenberry, James S. "Some Aspects of the Theory of Economic Development," in *Explorations in Entrepreneurial History*, 3: 63–102 (1950–51).

Easterbrook, William T. "The Climate of Enterprise," in *American Economic Review*, 39: 322–335 (1949) Suppl.

Follett, Mary Parker. *Dynamic Administration: The Collected Papers . . .* , edited by Henry C. Metcalf and L. Urwick. New York, 1943. 320 pp.

Foster, Charles A. "Honoring Commerce and Industry in 18th Century France." Unpublished Ph.D. thesis, Harvard University, 1950.

Fusfeld, Daniel R. "Heterogony of Entrepreneurial Goals," in *Explorations in Entrepreneurial History*, 9: 8–18 (1956–57).

Gay, Edwin F. "The Rhythm of History," in *Harvard Graduates' Magazine*, 32: 1–16 (1923–24).

General Motors Builds its First Fifty Million Cars. Pamphlet issued by the company, 1954.

Goodrich, Carter, "Local Planning of Internal Improvements," in *Political Science Quarterly*, 66: 411–445 (1951).

—— "National Planning of Internal Improvements," in *Political Science Quarterly*, 63: 16–44 (1948).

—— "Public Spirit and American Improvements," in *Proceedings of the American Philosophical Society*, 92: 305–309 (1948).

—— "The Revulsion against Internal Improvements," in *Journal of Economic History*, 10: 145–169 (1950).

—— "The Virginia System of Mixed Enterprise. A Study of State Planning of Internal Improvements," in *Political Science Quarterly*, 64: 355–387 (1949).

Goodrich, Carter, and Harvey H. Segal. "Baltimore's Aid to Railroads. A Study in the Municipal Planning of Internal Improvements," in *Journal of Economic History*, 13: 2–35 (1953).

Gordon, Robert A. *Business Leadership in the Large Corporation*. Washington, D.C., 1945. 369 pp.

Habakkuk, H. J. "Economic Functions of English Landowners in the Seventeenth and Eighteenth Centuries," in *Explorations in Entrepreneurial History*, 6: 92–102 (1953–54).

Handlin, Oscar, and Mary F. Handlin. *Commonwealth: A Study of the Role of Government in the American Economy. Massachusetts, 1774–1861*. New York, 1947. 364 pp.

—— "Ethnic Factors in Social Mobility," in *Explorations in Entrepreneurial History*, 9: 1–7 (1956–57).

Hartz, Louis. *Economic Policy and Democratic Thought: Pennsylvania, 1776–1860*. Cambridge, Mass., 1948. 366 pp.

WORKS CITED

Heath, Milton S. *Constructive Liberalism: The Role of the State in Economic Development in Georgia to 1860.* Cambridge, Mass., 1954. 448 pp.

Heaton, Herbert. "An Economic Historian's View of Enterprise." A Summary of Lectures. Claremont Men's College, Institute on Freedom and Competitive Enterprise, June, 1956. Mimeographed. 20 pp.

Heckscher, Eli F. *An Economic History of Sweden.* Trans. by Göran Ohlin. Cambridge, Mass., 1954. 308 pp.

Hedges, James B. *The Browns of Providence Plantations. Colonial Years.* Cambridge, Mass., 1952. 379 pp.

Helleiner, Karl F. "The Vital Revolution Reconsidered," in *Canadian Journal of Economics and Political Science,* 23: 1–9 (1957).

Hoover, Calvin B. "Institutional and Theoretical Implications of Economic Change," in *American Economic Review,* 44: 1–14 (1954).

Hoselitz, Bert F. "The Early History of Entrepreneurial Theory," in *Explorations in Entrepreneurial History,* 3: 193–220 (1950–51).

Jenks, Leland H. "The Role Structure of Entrepreneurial Personality," in *Change and the Entrepreneur* (1949), pp. 108–152.

Keirstead, Burton S. *An Essay in the Theory of Profits and Income Distribution.* Oxford, 1953. 110 pp.

Kellenbenz, Hermann. "German Aristocratic Entrepreneurship: Economic Activities of the Holstein Nobility in the Sixteenth and Seventeenth Centuries," in *Explorations in Entrepreneurial History,* 6: 103–114 (1953–54).

King, Doris E. "Early Hotel Entrepreneurs and Promoters, 1793–1860," in *Explorations in Entrepreneurial History,* 8: 148–160 (1955–56).

Kirkland, Edward C. *Dream and Thought in the Business Community, 1800–1900.* Ithaca, N.Y., 1956. 175 pp.

Knauth, Oswald. *Business Practices, Trade Position, and Competition.* New York, 1956. 181 pp.

—— *Managerial Enterprise, its Growth and Methods of Operation.* New York, 1948. 224 pp.

Konetzke, Richard. "Entrepreneurial Activities of Spanish and Portuguese Noblemen in Medieval Times," in *Explorations in Entrepreneurial History,* 6: 115–120 (1953–54).

Lamb, Helen B. "Business Organization and Leadership in India Today," prepared for the Seminar on Leadership and Political Institutions in India, University of California, Berkeley, August, 1956. Mimeographed.

—— "Development of Modern Business Communities in India," in *Labor Management and Economic Growth,* in *Proceedings of a*

255

WORKS CITED

Conference on Human Resources and Labor Relations in Under-developed Countries. Ithaca, N.Y., 1954.
—— "The Indian Business Communities and the Evolution of an Industrial Class," in *Pacific Affairs,* 28: 101–116 (1955).
Lamb, Robert K. "The Development of Entrepreneurship in Fall River, Massachusetts, 1813–1859." Unpublished Ph.D. thesis, Harvard University, 1935.
—— "The Entrepreneur and the Community," in *Men in Business* (1952), pp. 91–119.
—— "Entrepreneurship in the Community," in *Explorations in Entrepreneurial History,* 2: 114–127 (1949–50).
Landes, David S. "Business and the Businessman in France," in *Modern France: Problems of the Third and Fourth Republics,* Edward Meade Earle, ed., pp. 334–353. Princeton, 1951.
—— "French Entrepreneurship and Industrial Growth in the Nineteenth Century," in *Journal of Economic History,* 9: 45–61 (1949).
—— "Observations on France: Economy, Society, and Polity," in *World Politics,* 9: 329–349 (1956–57).
Lane, Frederic C. *Andrea Barbarigo, Merchant of Venice, 1418–1449.* Baltimore, 1944. 224 pp.
Larson, Agnes M. *History of the White-pine Industry in Minnesota.* Minneapolis, 1949. 432 pp.
Layer, Robert G. *Earnings of Cotton Mill Operatives, 1825–1914.* Cambridge, Mass., 1955. 71 pp.
Lincoln, Jonathan Thayer. "Material for a History of American Textile Machinery: The Kilburn-Lincoln Papers," in *Journal of Economic and Business History,* 4: 259–280 (1931–32).
Littleton, A. C. *Accounting Evolution to 1900.* New York, 1933. 373 pp.
Lively, Robert A. "The American System," in *Business History Review,* 29: 81–96 (1955).
McClelland, David C. "The Psychology of Mental Content Reconsidered," in *Psychological Review,* 62: 297–303 (1955).
—— "Some Social Consequences of Achievement Motivation," in *Nebraska Symposium on Motivation III,* Lincoln, Nebraska, 1955.
—— *Studies in Motivation.* New York, 1955. 552 pp.
McClelland, David C., and others. *The Achievement Motive.* New York, 1953. 384 pp.
McLaughlin, Charles C. "The Stanley Steamer: A Study in Unsuccessful Innovation," in *Explorations in Entrepreneurial History,* 7: 37–47 (1954–55).
Maclaurin, W. Rupert. *Invention & Innovation in the Radio Industry.* New York, 1949. 304 pp.

WORKS CITED

Manuel, Frank E. *The New World of Henri Saint-Simon.* Cambridge, Mass., 1956. 433 pp.

Marquette, Clare L. "The Business Activities of C. C. Washburn." Unpublished Ph.D. thesis, University of Wisconsin, 1940.

Marshall, Alfred. *Principles of Economics.* 6th ed. London, 1910. 871 pp.

Meany, Edmond S. "History of the Lumber Industry in the Pacific Northwest to 1917." Unpublished Ph.D. thesis, Harvard University, 1935.

Meier, Gerald M., and Robert E. Baldwin. *Economic Development: Theory, History, Policy.* New York, 1957. 588 pp.

Merton, Robert K. "The Role-Set: Problems in Sociological Theory," in *British Journal of Sociology,* 8: 106–120 (1957).

Mill, John Stuart. *Principles of Political Economy.* Boston, 1848. 2 vols.

Miller, William. "The Business Elite in Business Bureaucracies," in *Men in Business* (1952), pp. 286–305.

Moulton, Charles W. *The Library of Literary Criticism.* Vol I. Buffalo, N.Y., 1901.

Muir, Valerie. "The Emergence of State Enterprise in New Zealand in the Nineteenth Century," in *Explorations in Entrepreneurial History,* 5: 186–192 (1952–53).

Navin, Thomas R. *The Whitin Machine Works since 1831.* Cambridge, Mass., 1950. 654 pp.

Nestor, Oscar W. "History of Personnel Administration, 1890–1910." Unpublished Ph.D. thesis, University of Pennsylvania, 1954.

Neu, Irene D. "A Business Biography of Erastus Corning." Unpublished Ph.D. thesis, Cornell University, 1950.

Orcutt, Guy H. "A New Type of Socio-Economic System," in *Review of Economics and Statistics,* 39: 116–123 (1957).

Parker, William N. "Coal and Steel Output Movements in Western Europe, 1880–1956," in *Explorations in Entrepreneurial History,* 9: 214–230 (1956–57).

—— "Entrepreneurial Opportunities and Response in the German Economy," in *Explorations in Entrepreneurial History,* 7: 26–36 (1954–55).

Parsons, Talcott, and Neil J. Smelser. "A Sociological Model for Economic Development," in *Explorations in Entrepreneurial History,* 8: 181–204 (1955–56).

Passer, Harold C. "E. H. Goff: An Entrepreneur Who Failed," in *Explorations in Entrepreneurial History,* 1, No. 5: 17–25 (1949).

—— *The Electrical Manufacturers, 1875–1900. A Study in Competition, Entrepreneurship, Technical Change, and Economic Growth.* Cambridge. Mass., 1953. 412 pp.

WORKS CITED

Pelzel, John. "The Small Industrialist in Japan," in *Explorations in Entrepreneurial History*, 7: 79–93 (1954–55).

Porter, Kenneth W. *The Jacksons and the Lees. Two Generations of Massachusetts Merchants, 1765–1844.* Cambridge, Mass., 1937. 2 vols.

Potter, Dalton. "The Bazaar Merchant," in *Social Forces in the Middle East*, ed. by Sydney N. Fisher. Ithaca, N.Y., 1955, pp. 99–115.

Powell, Thomas. *Tom, of All Trades.* London, 1631. 49 pp.

Primm, James N. *Economic Policy in the Development of a Western State. Missouri, 1820–1860.* Cambridge, Mass., 1954. 174 pp.

Quandt, Richard E. "Review of *Capital Formation and Economic Growth*," in *Review of Economics and Statistics*, 39: 480–481 (1957).

Rae, John B. "The Engineer as Business Man in American Industry," in *Explorations in Entrepreneurial History*, 7: 94–104 (1954–55).

Ranis, Gustav. "The Community-Centered Entrepreneur in Japanese Development," in *Explorations in Entrepreneurial History*, 8: 80–98 (1955–56).

Redlich, Fritz L. "European Aristocracy and Economic Development," in *Explorations in Entrepreneurial History*, 6: 78–91 (1953–54).

—— "Der fürstliche Unternehmer: eine typische Erschunung des 16. Jahrhunderts," in *Tradition*, 3: 17–34, 98–112 (1958).

—— *History of American Business Leaders.* Vol. I. Ann Arbor, 1940. 185 pp.

—— "The Leaders of the German Steam-Engine Industry during the First Hundred Years," in *Journal of Economic History*, 4: 121–148 (1944).

—— "The Origin of the Concepts of 'Entrepreneur' and 'Creative Entrepreneur,'" in *Explorations in Entrepreneurial History*, 1, No. 2: 1–7 (1949).

Riemersma, Jelle C. "The Role of Religion in Economic Development," in *Explorations in Entrepreneurial History*, 2: 297–303 (1949–50).

Ripley, William Z. *Main Street to Wall Street.* Boston, 1927. 359 pp.

Rosovsky, Henry. "The Serf Entrepreneur in Russia," in *Explorations in Entrepreneurial History*, 6: 207–233 (1953–54).

Rostow, Walt W. "The Interrelation of Theory and Economic History," in *Journal of Economic History*, 17: 509–523 (1957).

Rottenberg, Simon. "Entrepreneurship and Economic Progress in Jamaica," in *Inter-American Economic Affairs*, 7: 74–79 (1953–54).

Sawyer, John E. "The Entrepreneur and the Social Order: France and the United States," in *Men in Business* (1952), pp. 7–22.

—— "Entrepreneurial Error and Economic Growth," in *Explorations in Entrepreneurial History*, 4: 199–204 (1951–52).

——"Entrepreneurship in Periods of Rapid Growth: The United

WORKS CITED

States in the 19th Century." A paper presented at a conference on Entrepreneurship and Economic Growth in Cambridge, Massachusetts, November 12 and 13, 1954, Part C. 7 pp.

—— "Strains in the Social Structure of Modern France," in *Modern France: Problems of the Third and Fourth Republics*, Edward Meade Earle, ed., pp. 293–312. Princeton, 1951.

Schumpeter, Joseph A. "The Creative Response in Economic History," in *Journal of Economic History*, 7: 149–159 (1947).

—— *History of Economic Analysis*. New York, 1954. 1260 pp.

Scitovszky, Tibor de. "On the Decline of Competition," in *Social Change*, 3: 28–36 (1941).

Scoville, Warren C. *Revolution in Glassmaking: Entrepreneurship and Technological Change in the American Industry, 1880–1920*. Cambridge, Mass., 1948. 398 pp.

Smith, Roderick H. *The Science of Business*. New York & London, 1885.

Solomons, David, ed. *Studies in Costing*. London, 1952. 643 pp.

Stein, Stanley J. *The Brazilian Cotton Manufacture. Textile Enterprise in an Underdeveloped Area, 1850–1950*. Cambridge, Mass., 1957. 273 pp.

Thrupp, Sylvia L. "Entrepreneurial Theory and the Middle Ages," in *Explorations in Entrepreneurial History*, 2: 160–165 (1949–50).

Tosdal, Harry R. *Selling in Our Economy: An Economic and Social Analysis of Selling and Advertising*. Chicago, 1957. 333 pp.

United Nations Economic and Social Council. Economic Commission for Latin America. Economic Development of Latin America and Its Principal Problems. 1950. (UN. E/CN.12/89/Rev. 1). 49 pp.

Usher, Abbott P. *History of Mechanical Inventions*. Rev. ed. Cambridge, Mass., 1954. 450 pp.

Veblen, Thorstein. *The Engineer and the Price System*. New York, 1921. 169 pp.

Wellington, Raynor G. *The Political and Sectional Influence of the Public Lands, 1828–1842*. N.p., 1914. 131 pp.

Westebbe, Richard M. "State Entrepreneurship: King Willem I, John Cockerill, and the Seraing Engineering Works, 1815–1840," in *Explorations in Entrepreneurial History*, 8: 205–232 (1955–56).

Wiles, P. "Growth versus Choice," in *Economic Journal*, 66: 244–255 (1956).

Wilson, Charles. "The Entrepreneur in the Industrial Revolution in Britain." A paper presented at a conference on Entrepreneurship and Economic Growth in Cambridge, Massachusetts, November 12 and 13, 1954, Part A. 17 pp.

——*The History of Unilever: A Study in Economic Growth and Social Change*. London, 1954. 2 vols.

WORKS CITED

Wohl, R. Richard. "An Historical Context for Entrepreneurship," in *Explorations in Entrepreneurial History*, 1, No. 2: 8–16 (1949).
—— "Henry Noble Day, the Development of an Entrepreneurial Role." Unpublished Ph.D. thesis, Harvard University, 1951.
—— "Henry Noble Day. A Study in Good Works, 1808–1890," in *Men in Business* (1952), pp. 153–192.
—— "The 'Rags to Riches Story': An Episode of Secular Idealism," in *Class, Status, and Power*, ed. by Reinhard Bendix and Seymour M. Lipsit. Glencoe, Ill., 1953, pp. 388–395.
—— "Three Generations of Business Enterprise in a Midwestern City: the McGees of Kansas City," in *Journal of Economic History*, 16: 514–528 (1956).
Wood, Richard G. *History of Lumbering in Maine, 1820–61*. Orono, Me., 1935. 267 pp.
Wyllie, Irvin G. *The Self-made Man in America: The Myth of Rags to Riches*. New Brunswick, N.J., 1954. 210 pp.
Young, Allyn A. "Increasing Returns and Economic Progress," in *Economic Journal*, 38: 527–542 (1928).

NOTES

CHAPTER I
The Nature of Entrepreneurship

1. Professor Innis served with me for more than a decade on the Committee on Research in Economic History. His concern with time is reflected in the title of one of his last books, *Changing Concepts of Time*.

2. T. S. Ashton, *Economic History of England: The Eighteenth Century* (1955), p. 22.

3. N. S. Buchanan and H. S. Ellis, *Approaches to Economic Development* (1955), pp. 74, 87. No more economistic statement could be found. It seems to envisage a one-punch set of "cultural changes," and it surely suggests that a dosage of capital is, to some extent, required in all alterations of social thought and practices.

4. See B. F. Hoselitz, "The Early History of Entrepreneurial Theory," *Explorations in Entrepreneurial History*, 3: 193–220 (1950–51), and F. L. Redlich, "The Origin of the Concepts of 'Entrepreneur' and 'Creative Entrepreneur,'" *Explorations*, 1 (no. 2): 1–7 (1949). This publication of the Center will be referred to hereafter as *Explorations*.

5. "Entrepreneur" in *Shorter Oxford Dictionary on Historical Principles* (1955).

6. J. S. Mill, *Principles of Political Economy* (1848), I, 485.

7. D. Potter, in *Social Forces in the Middle East* (1955), p. 112.

8. A. H. Cole, in *Change and the Entrepreneur* (1949), p. 88.

9. See an essay by Mrs. Valerie Muir on Julius Vogel, entitled "The Emergence of State Enterprise in New Zealand in the Nineteenth Century," *Explorations*, 5: 186–197 (1952–53).

10. There is also an important difference in the value in exposition of the two sets of terms; "entrepreneurship" and "entrepreneur," on the one hand, and "business" and "businessman" on the other. One phase of this matter is pure linguistics. "Business," as a word, does not lend itself to the permutation that "entrepreneur" does in the adjectival form "entrepreneurial." More importantly, the latter group of terms carries a smaller load of connotation. The terms "business"

and "businessman" signify mere money-making to most people; the phrase "social responsibility of business," for example, seems an internal contradiction. The other set of terms conveys fewer "sentiments," and so may be employed with greater hope of scientific precision. For somewhat similar reasons, I have, on the whole, chosen to avoid the terms "enterpriser" and "enterprise." There is no satisfactory adjectival form, and surely an enterpriser would be conceived to be, by nature, enterprising. I do frequently use the term "enterprise" to mean business unit.

I call "entrepreneur" only such businessmen who make decisions within a formal organization called a business enterprise, which is itself a unit in a group of social institutions. My friend Mr. LaFrance, who has operated a stationery store in Brattle Square, Cambridge, for many years all by himself, or Mr. William Harnden, who started the express business in this country by carrying valuable papers from New York to Boston in a half-bushel carpetbag, or the proprietors of thousands of boutiques scattered over the world, have made or do make decisions and they have had (or have) some sorts of social relations. But I choose not to become involved in psychology in thought processes and emotions and perhaps Freudian "compensations." Someone may want to cover this area, which might be looked upon as primitive entrepreneurship, and try to draw a logical line among individuals more or less involved in pecuniary pursuits, from the itinerant peddler down through the widow who invests her funds to provide her with the maximum income.

11. Professor Rostow made an address before the Economic History Association in September, 1957. His paper appeared in the *Journal of Economic History*, 17: 509–23 (1957), entitled "The Interrelation of Theory and Economic History."

12. A recent effort to deal with the problems of invention, innovation, and the like is to be found in the early chapters of A. P. Usher's second edition of his *History of Mechanical Inventions* (1954).

13. Obviously, the foregoing is, in part, restatement of what is to be found in Professor Schumpeter's "novel" and "innovating" ideas; in part revision and in part criticism. And there is this much more to be added, although it is tangential to my argument. The essential element in the tactics of entrepreneurship is the attainment of a differential cost or profit position; the effort to gain such a position is not necessarily coincident with the promotion of economic growth, as, for example, in a case where a manufacturer imitates his neighbors as far as the adoption of the steam engine is concerned, but goes ahead with what is at the moment *more* important to him, the use of a particular dyestuff or the signing up of a particular sales agency. As a result, the "economic development" in which Schumpeter (and

we) are interested must be viewed as a mere incident in entrepreneurial life—a sort of "built-in" feature—with the real entrepreneurial
action pointed in another direction, especially the maintenance and
aggrandizement of the relevant profit-oriented enterprise.

14. I am reminded of the agriculturalist connected with the Bureau
of Agricultural Economics who complained to me many years ago
that the economic theorists were all wrong: shifting of process or
product did not take place at the margin of cultivation; only infra-
marginal farmers could afford to shift into new methods or the production of new crops.

15. R. A. Gordon, *Business Leadership in the Large Corporation*
(1945); M. E. Dimock, *The Executive in Action* (1945); O. Knauth,
Managerial Enterprise, Its Growth and Methods of Operation (1948);
T. C. Cochran, *The American Business System: A Historical Perspec-
tive, 1900–1955* (1957); H. R. Bowen, *Social Responsibilities of the
Businessman* (1953), etc.

16. Dimock, *The Executive in Action.*

17. C. H. Danhof, "Economic Values in Cultural Perspective," in
Goals of Economic Life (1953).

18. F. C. Lane, *Andrea Barbarigo* (1944).

19. Relative to changes in the United States over recent decades,
see the path-breaking essay by Alfred D. Chandler, Jr., "Management
Decentralization," *Business History Review*, 30: 111–174 (1956–57).

20. J. K. Butters and J. Lintner, *Effects of Federal Taxes on Growing Enterprises* (1946).

21. W. T. Easterbrook, "The Climate of Enterprise," *American
Economic Review*, 39: 322–335 (1949), Supp. Another form in past
centuries was a specially chartered company, usually with monopoly
privileges which contributed a variant sort of "security."

22. B. Bailyn, *The New England Merchants in the Seventeenth
Century* (1955).

23. A. Gerschenkron, quoted by H. Rosovsky in *Explorations*, 6:
208 (1953–54).

24. J. E. Sawyer, "Strains in the Social Structure of Modern France,"
in *Modern France: Problems of the Third and Fourth Republics*
(1951), pp. 293–312; D. S. Landes, "Business and the Businessman
in France," *ibid.*, pp. 334–353.

25. T. C. Cochran and W. Miller, *The Age of Enterprise* (1942);
A. H. Cole, "An Appraisal of Economic Change," *American Economic
Review*, 44 (No. 2): 35–50 (1954).

26. In view of the purposes of the present volume as indicated in
the Preface, I believe it inappropriate that I should take up space in
an effort to compare the foregoing ideas with all those respecting the
essential characteristics of entrepreneurs and entrepreneurship that

writers of all nations, living and dead, have put on paper at one time or another. The catalogue of such concepts is a long one, as can be gained from the excellent surveys and special studies of Messrs. Hoselitz and Redlich, cited above, n. 4. However, a few brief comments may be in order. For example, for purposes of empirical research I found rather futile the concept, with which the name of Professor Frank H. Knight is usually associated, of the entrepreneur as the bearer of risks. The bearing of risks or uncertainties is a negative element and does not tell one what the actor contributes. A definition in terms of function is more useful.

A somewhat similar objection can be made to the ideas of Professor Schumpeter. One could not study paintings by looking only for indications of genius; and, in the case of innovations, the practical research worker is confronted, as already indicated above (p. 14) with the difficulty of defining the phenomenon in real life, of pinning it down so that he can separate innovations from noninnovations. He finds a myriad of innovations from the railroad and the electric motor down to a machine for laying new rails on old railroads, and to plastic handles for electric switches, and many applications of new gadgets and new business methods. The best that one can do is to recognize that the search for novelties has always been a feature of business life, that this element has become increasingly prominent as the tempo of business has changed, and that the installation of novelties of equipment or mode of operation constitutes one means of the preservation of business enterprises in the face of competition.

In the third place, I would protest against the dichotomy between "entrepreneur" and "manager," which is found often in economic and sociological literature. (See, for example, R. Bendix's valuable study, *Work and Authority in Industry* [1956].) The dichotomy is just unrealistic and inoperable in research. One cannot study women by first setting up the categories of beautiful and homely. All businessmen have some elements of both characteristics or qualities. They are imaginative, innovating, vigorous, etc., sometimes and to some degree; and they are unimaginative, traditionally minded, lazy, etc., also sometimes and in some degree. And most of the discussions overlook what Professor Schumpeter once stressed. At a luncheon at the Harvard Business School Dean Wallace B. Donham asked him what he thought to be the most important element in business success, and Professor Schumpeter replied, without a moment's hesitation, "Why, to be sure, good health!"

27. A. H. Cole, "An Approach to the Study of Entrepreneurship," *Journal of Economic History*, 6, Suppl.: 8 (1946).

CHAPTER II
The Need of a Positive View

1. Actually, in the theory of monopolistic competition, the entrepreneur can hardly be distinguished from the enterprise. The assumption of profit-maximization as the sole rule of action in the formation of business policy made further thought on these matters seem unnecessary, as will be suggested in a moment.

2. J. Dean, *Managerial Economics* (1951), p. 28.

3. C. B. Hoover, "Institutional and Theoretical Implications of Economic Change," *American Economic Review*, 44: 11, 12 (1954).

4. One can add testimony of other writers. Mr. Peter L. Bernstein, himself associated with business, asserts that because "a very large proportion of business capital" today is economically or institutionally immobile, the tendency of profits to be equalized in the economy would be appropriate only to "long period analysis," when the period was conceived to be "very, very long indeed." See Bernstein's article, "Profit Theory—Where Do We Go From Here?" *Quarterly Journal of Economics*, 67: 419 (1953). With an even somewhat broader sweep A. A. Berle, Jr., writes, "It is indefensibly disingenuous to assert that these operations [those of modern large-scale corporations] are primarily following economic laws more or less accurately outlined by the classic economists a century ago when the fact appears to be that they are following a slowly emerging pattern of sociological and political laws, relevant to the rather different community demands of our time." *The 20th Century Capitalist Revolution* (1954), p. 12.

5. H. G. J. Aitken, "Entrepreneurial Biography: A Symposium," Part III, *Explorations*, 2: 231 (1949–50).

6. W. W. Cooper, "A Proposal for Extending the Theory of the Firm," *Quarterly Journal of Economics*, 65: 90 (1951).

7. W. W. Cooper, "Theory of the Firm," *American Economic Review*, 39: 1207 (1949).

8. Cooper, "A Proposal . . . ," p. 92.

9. *Ibid.*, p. 92.

10. *Ibid.*, p. 91.

11. R. M. Cyert and J. G. March, "Organizational Structure and Pricing Behavior in an Oligopolistic Market," *American Economic Review*, 45: 129–139 (1955) and "Organizational Factors in the Theory of Oligopoly," *Quarterly Journal of Economics*, 70: 44–64 (1956).

12. B. S. Keirstead, *An Essay in the Theory of Profits and Income Distribution* (1953), p. 44.

13. *Ibid.*, p. 28.

14. *Ibid.*, p. 29.

15. Unhappily, the term "dynamic" has been purloined to the labeling of a form of analysis which is dynamic only in a very limited degree: the shift from one equilibrium to another. Obviously, this is not the place to argue the propriety of names, or even the utility or disutility of the notion of an equilibrium; but perhaps one may properly note that to the economic historian "dynamic" connotes something more extensive than short-run or medium-run adjustment, and that to him the appearance of an equilibrium in the historical record is, indeed, a very rare occurrence. Given a tempo or metronome appropriate to economic or social change, everything is in process of flux. It is clear that the foregoing is in strong disagreement with Professor Parsons and Mr. Neil Smelser, who in a recent essay stated categorically, "Like any system, a going economy tends to equilibrium." *Explorations*, 8: 193 (1955–56). Historically, it seems more accurate to assert that for the Western world since the twelfth century no appreciable periods of equilibrium have been observable in any "going economy."

16. G. H. Orcutt, "A New Type of Socio-economic System," *Review of Economics and Statistics*, 39: 116–123 (1957).

17. P. Wiles, "Growth versus Choice," *Economic Journal*, 66: 244 (1956).

18. N. G. Butlin, "Borderlands or Badlands?" *Explorations*, 3: 50 (1950–51).

19. F. E. Manuel, *The New World of Henri Saint-Simon* (1956), p. 137.

20. G. M. Meier and R. E. Baldwin, *Economic Development* (1957).

21. *Ibid.*, p. 120.

22. *Ibid.*, p. 121.

23. *Ibid.*, p. 123. I should like to call attention to a recent independent appraisal of the situation: "One finds it difficult to relate them [the factors of income distribution, the propensity to save, the role of capital intensity, the significance of channels of finance, etc.] to each other because no theoretical framework exists within which these factors could find a comfortable niche. This is not to say that there exists no theory at all: Ricardo or Weber or Schumpeter or Harrod-Domar represent some possible approaches. But none of these really fulfils the need. Information about particular countries, particular eras, particular factors accumulates rapidly but no strides seem to be made toward establishing relationships between the various factors." R. E. Quandt's review of *Capital Formation and Economic Growth* (1955) in *The Review of Economics and Statistics*, 39: 480–481 (1957).

24. See above, p. 28.

25. A. Marshall, *Principles of Economics* (1910), pp. 138–139.

26. S. W. Bruchey, *Robert Oliver* (1956), p. 370.

27. Chandler, "Management Decentralization."

28. When I knew one of the brothers in his later years, he was interested in the construction of fine violins fabricated in a shop attached to his house in Newton, Mass.

29. C. C. McLaughlin, "The Stanley Steamer," *Explorations*, 7: 46 (1954–55).

30. D. E. King, "Early Hotel Entrepreneurs and Promoters, 1793–1860," *Explorations*, 8: 156 (1955–56).

31. Professor Sawyer's comments are contained in a research note entitled, "Entrepreneurial Error and Economic Growth," *Explorations*, 4: 199–204 (1951–52) and in a paper, "Entrepreneurship in Periods of Rapid Growth: The United States in the 19th Century," presented at a conference on Entrepreneurship and Economic Growth in Cambridge, Mass., November 12 and 13, Part C, p. 3 (1954).

32. Sawyer, "Entrepreneurship in Periods of Rapid Growth," p. 3.

33. *Ibid.*, pp. 5–6.

34. *Ibid.*, p. 6.

35. C. Wilson, "The Entrepreneur in the Industrial Revolution in Britain," a paper presented at the conference (1954) just mentioned (see n. 31), Part A, pp. 5, 11, 17; and *The History of Unilever* (1954).

36. M. Abramovitz, *Resource and Output Trends in the United States since 1870* (1956).

37. *Ibid.*, p. 13.

38. K. E. Boulding, "Religious Foundations of Economic Progress," *Harvard Business Review*, 30: 33 (1952).

CHAPTER III

The Elements in a Positive View:
The Entrepreneur and His Organization

1. Economists familiar with the ideas of John R. Commons as expressed in his later works, and especially in his *Economics of Collective Action* (1950), will note some parallelism of thought with parts of what follows. I regret to have to admit that I was not familiar with this line of thought in any useful way until the present book was nearly completed. At that time my attention was called to group organizations, "going concerns," and the like by my friends Professor Benjamin M. Selekman and his wife, who had reviewed Commons' last book in the *Harvard Business Review* for November, 1951 (vol. 29, pp. 112–128).

2. See p. 10 above.

3. M. P. Follett, *Dynamic Administration* (1941).

4. Here there may seem at first blush to be an inconsistency or at least a confusion of thought as to where in business units the entrepreneurial function is located, just who is "the entrepreneur." More specifically, it can well be asked, "If there is an ultimate authority, why should he not be identified as bearer of the function and appropriate bearer of the title? Why not take the possessor of this ultimate authority as *the* entrepreneur for purposes other than the current analysis?"

The answer is at least twofold. The traditional identification in economic literature of a single-person entrepreneur with the entrepreneurial function is untrue to the facts, at any rate in modern business life; and second, the possessor of final authority in a given action-situation is not necessarily the only person participating cooperatively and with some authority in that action.

An analogy with governmental conditions may serve quickly to elucidate the relationship. There is no doubt that the President carries the final responsibility for decisions in the executive branch of the federal government administration; but the executive function is also clearly dispersed among many officers in the administration. And one may properly consider the relations of "the President and his organization" as a means of understanding better the manifestations of the executive function in the federal government.

5. The degree to which the top executives are "policy-clinching" would depend much upon the constitution of that executive or its relations to a board of directors.

6. I made an effort to suggest some important lines of literary evolution in an essay entitled, "Conspectus for A History of Economic and Business Literature," which appeared in the *Journal of Economic History*, 17: 333–388 (1957). This essay was reprinted under a slightly different title as Brochure No. 12 of the Kress Library, Harvard University Graduate School of Business Administration.

7. See in particular the essay, "The Role Structure of Entrepreneurial Personality," by L. H. Jenks in *Change and the Entrepreneur* (1949), pp. 108–152. No effort will be made here to reproduce the elaboration of a sociological schema especially pertinent to entrepreneurship that Professor Jenks presents there. No one at the Center has added significantly to the system devised in 1948 by him.

8. R. R. Wohl, "An Historical Context for Entrepreneurship," *Explorations*, 1 (No. 2): 12 (1949).

9. My attention has recently been called to an article by Professor Robert K. Merton entitled "The Role-Set: Problems in Sociological Theory," which appeared in the *British Journal of Sociology*, 8: 106–

120 (June, 1957). Professor Merton draws the very useful distinction between "role-set" and "status-set" anent the occupier of any social status; e.g., teacher, doctor, etc. In relation to the entrepreneur, the distinction would be this: the entrepreneur as such is, as it were, the focus of several interests, those of stockholders, staff, customers, employees, in the sense that each such group expects something individual and distinctive as far as its interests are concerned. On the other hand, the individuals carrying the entrepreneurial roles, or occupying that status, are simultaneously in their own persons occupying other statuses, as, for example, fathers, church members, perhaps members of school committees or political parties.

In the ensuing analysis, the concept of role-set will appear most appropriate and important, although I am inclined myself to feel that the term "role-set" is hardly strong enough to carry the complex of entrepreneurial relationships that I am disposed to think significant. The term "role-galaxy" might be more suitable. As to status-set, however, one will observe its utility when the discussion touches upon the relation of the entrepreneurial actors to their families, to their professional associations, etc. Both the terms—and the concepts—are worth keeping in mind.

10. Bendix, *Work and Authority in Industry.*

11. Wilson, *History of Unilever,* vol. II, *passim.*

12. T. R. Navin, *The Whitin Machine Works* (1950), *passim.*

13. The partnership agreement will be rewritten on the death of a partner, but the new group may be a mere reorganization of the earlier one.

14. K. E. Boulding, *The Organizational Revolution* (1953); W. Z. Ripley, *Main Street to Wall Street* (1927); Gordon, *Business Leadership in the Large Corporations;* J. Burnham, *Management Revolution* (1941); O. Knauth, *Managerial Enterprise* (1948).

15. See below, pp. 238 ff.

16. *General Motors Builds Its First Fifty Million Cars* (1954).

17. See below, Chap. IV, *passim.*

18. O. W. Nestor, "History of Personnel Administration, 1890–1910" (1954).

19. Here I refer again to the recent article by Professor Merton (see above, n. 9) in which he elaborates the notion of role-set." Obviously, the several "interests" expect different actions of the entrepreneur, and they are in some measure willing to exert sanctions to get their respective ways. The entrepreneur is the bearer of a role viewed divergently by the several parties in his organization.

As Mr. Frank W. Abrams, erstwhile of the Standard Oil Company of New Jersey, once wrote, "The job of professional management, as I see it, is to conduct the affairs of the enterprise in its charge in such a way as to maintain an equitable and workable balance among the claims of the various directly interested groups. Business firms are man-made instruments of society. They can be made to achieve their greatest social usefulness—and thus their future can be best assured —when management succeeds in finding a harmonious balance among the claims of the various interested groups: the stockholders, employees, customers, and the public at large." F. W. Abrams, "Management's Responsibilities in a Complex World," *Harvard Business Review,* 29: 29–30 (1951).

20. R. G. Layer, *Earnings of Cotton Mill Operatives, 1825–1914* (1955).

21. The movement of prices, especially after the mid-1890's, adds confusion.

22. See above, p. 53.

23. See above, p. 10 f.

24. Regarding Mr. Abrams, see below, pp. 201 ff.

25. C. C. Abbott, "Broad View of Administration," University of Virginia *Alumni News,* October, 1956.

26. Quoted by T. C. Cochran, "The Organization Man in Historical Perspective," *Pennsylvania History,* 25: 18 (1958).

27. Berle, p. 70.

28. *Ibid.,* pp. 51–52.

29. T. C. Cochran, "The Organization Man . . . ," p. 22.

30. *Ibid.,* p. 18.

CHAPTER IV

The Elements in a Positive View: The Entrepreneurial Stream

1. See below, p. 107.

2. The nature of the interrelations of producing institutions, advertising organizations, marketing units, and the consuming public is exhibited by H. R. Tosdal in his new study, *Selling in Our Economy: An Economic and Social Analysis of Selling and Advertising* (1957).

3. A. A. Young, "Increasing Returns and Economic Progress," *Economic Journal,* 38: 539 (1928).

4. See above, Chapter III, n. 5.

5. A representative case of intellectual immaturity is provided by Roderick H. Smith's *Science of Business* (New York, 1885). After two preliminary chapters entitled "The Direction of Motion" and "The Rhythm of Motion" he presents a sequence of specific chapters as follows:

"Part Second; I. General Business, II. Iron, III. Railroad Building and Consumption of Rails, IV. Immigration, V. Stocks, VI. Exchange,

VII. Foreign Trade, VIII. Grain, IX. The Balancing of Prices or Equilibration, X. Summary and Conclusion."
6. E. C. Kirkland, *Dream and Thought in the Business Community, 1800–1900* (1956), p. 13.
7. T. C. Cochran, *Railroad Leaders, 1845–1890* (1953), p. 82.
8. I have in mind the varied activities of seeking tariff protection, promoting banks and railroads, etc.
9. L. Benson, *Merchants, Farmers, & Railroads* (1955), pp. 208–209.

CHAPTER V

The Elements in a Positive View: The Social Conditioning of Entrepreneurship

1. C. S. Belshaw, "The Cultural Milieu of the Entrepreneur," *Explorations*, 7: 151 (1954–55).
2. S. L. Thrupp, "Entrepreneurial Theory and the Middle Ages," *Explorations*, 2: 161 (1949–50).
3. B. Bailyn, "The *Apologia* of Robert Keayne," *William and Mary Quarterly*, 3d ser., 7: 568–571 (1950).
4. A. Gerschenkron, quoted by H. Rosovsky, *Explorations*, 6: 208 (1953–54).
5. J. S. Duesenberry, "Some Aspects of the Theory of Economic Development," *Explorations*, 3: 73 (1950–51).
6. J. C. Riemersma, "The Role of Religion in Economic Development," *Explorations*, 2: 302 (1949–50).
7. H. Bridges, *Iron Millionaire* (1952), *passim*.
8. See the unpublished dissertation (1950) by C. A. Foster, "Honoring Commerce and Industry in 18th Century France."
9. H. Rosovsky, "The Serf Entrepreneur in Russia," *Explorations*, 6: 207–253 (1953–54).
10. S. Rottenberg, "Entrepreneurship and Economic Progress in Jamaica," *Inter-American Economic Affairs*, 7: 74–99 (1953–54).
11. Lane, pp. 45–53.
12. Perhaps a classification comparable to that of Danhof's might be devised, this one on degrees of boldness!
13. I do not mean to posit a "spirit of enterprise" or its equivalent. Entrepreneurship calls for the display of varied qualities of mental ability and conditioned valuations. All that I mean to imply above is that the threshold of entry is not a straight horizontality. To some men the role of entrepreneurship is more congenial than to others.
14. E. F. Heckscher, *An Economic History of Sweden* (1954), p. 98.

15. Danhof, *passim.*
16. Duesenberry, pp. 72, 73. Based upon Talcott Parson's "Economic Motivation," contained in his *Essays in Sociological Theory and Its Applications* (1949).
17. Riemersma, p. 302.
18. T. de Scitovszky, "On the Decline of Competition," *Social Change,* 3: 31 (1941).
19. Sawyer, "Strains . . ."; Landes, "Business . . ."; W. N. Parker, "Entrepreneurial Opportunities and Response in the German Economy," *Explorations,* 7: 26–36 (1954–55). A new, improved analysis of the situation, giving some of the influences of past experiences upon present-day conditions, is contained in Landes' article in *World Politics,* 9: 329–349, entitled "Observations on France: Economy, Society, and Polity."
20. de Scitovszky, p. 32.
21. Parker, p. 32.
22. See also *L'Artisan de la fortune, ou les moyens de s'avancer dans le monde* (1691); but on the whole, I have found less attention to the theme in Continental literature.
23. R. R. Wohl, "The 'Rags to Riches Story'" in *Class, Status and Power* (1953), pp. 388–395.
24. *Change and the Entrepreneur* (1949), pp. 23–24.
25. It also seems true that the young man who took the older woman to acquire the attached privileges of printing also took the opportunity later to annex a young woman as a second wife — who, in turn, acquired a younger husband. Whether this system could be defended on grounds other than the control of industry may well be doubted.
26. H. G. J. Aitken, *The Welland Canal Company* (1954), *passim.*
27. J. B. Hedges, *The Browns of Providence Plantations* (1952).
28. R. K. Lamb, "The Development of Entrepreneurship in Fall River, Massachusetts, 1813–1859" (1935).
29. S. D. Clark, *The Social Development of Canada* (1942).
30. On the frontier entrepreneur see pp. 161 ff. below.
31. For the ensuing data on innovations and on cooperation, I am indebted to Professor Clarence H. Danhof, whose findings I had hoped sometime since to have published as agent of the Committee on Research in Economic History.
32. A. H. Cole, "Agricultural Crazes," *American Economic Review,* 16: 622–639 (1926).
33. See below, pp. 143 ff.
34. Benson, p. 228.
35. See below, pp. 171 ff.
36. See below, pp. 175 ff.
37. See below, pp. 193 ff.

38. The engineer as entrepreneur is a subject that has engaged the attention of Professor John B. Rae of the Massachusetts Institute of Technology. See his article, "The Engineer as Business Man in American Industry," *Explorations*, 7: 94–104 (1954–55).

39. G. B. Baldwin, "The Invention of the Modern Safety Razor," *Explorations*, 4: 73–102 (1951–52).

40. T. Veblen, *The Engineers and the Price System* (1921).

In this section I am concerned only with the movement of entrepreneurs, not handicraftsmen or workmen.

42. O. Handlin and M. F. Handlin, "Ethnic Factors in Social Mobility," *Explorations*, 9: 1–7 (1956–57).

43. See for example, G. Ranis, "The Community-centered Entrepreneur in Japanese Development," *Explorations*, 8: 80–98 (1955–56); K. I. Choi, "Tokugawa Feudalism and the Emergence of the New Leaders of Early Modern Japan," *Explorations*, 9: 72–90 (1956–57); and J. Pelzel, "The Small Industrialist in Japan," *Explorations*, 7: 79–93 (1955–56).

44. H. B. Lamb, "The Indian Business Communities and the Evolution of an Industrial Class," *Pacific Affairs*, 28: 101–116 (1955).

45. See above, Chap. II. *passim*.

46. A. H. Cole, "An Approach . . . ," *Journal of Economic History*, 6: 10–11 (1946).

47. A. H. Cole, "A New Set of Stages," *Explorations*, 8: 99–107 (1955–56).

48. Professor F. C. Lane tells me of the day-long buzzing among merchants that appears to have gone on on the Rialto; and Dr. Redlich reminds me of the importance that commercial exchanges and coffee-houses seem to have played in commercial life in various mercantile centers, not excluding the American seaboard cities.

49. W. R. Maclaurin, *Invention & Innovation in the Radio Industry* (1949), p. xv.

50. S. Diamond, *The Reputation of the American Businessman* (1955).

51. See above, pp. 58 f.

52. See above, p. 81.

PART TWO

Entrepreneurial Realities

1. Those familiar with German material would also recall the work of Wiedenfeld and Eulenburg.

2. F. L. Redlich, "European Aristocracy and Economic Development," *Explorations*, 6: 78–91 (1953–54).

3. Foster, "Honoring Commerce and Industry . . . ." I should in all honesty add that Dr. Redlich, on reading this section of my manuscript, has expressed a disagreement with my interpretation of Dr. Foster's materials. I hope that before long the latter will publish his own summary — or better, an extension of his thesis.

4. See, however, Redlich's very recent essay entitled "Der fürstliche Unternehmer: eine typische Erschunung des 16. Jahrhunderts," which appeared in *Tradition*, 3: 17–34, 98–112 (1958).

5. See H. J. Habakkuk, "Economic Functions of English Landowners in the Seventeenth and Eighteenth Centuries"; H. Kellenbenz, "German Aristocratic Entrepreneurship: Economic Activities of the Holstein Nobility in the Sixteenth and Seventeenth Centuries"; R. Konetzke, "Entrepreneurial Activities of Spanish and Portuguese Noblemen in Medieval Times." These articles all appeared in *Explorations*, 6: 92–120 (1953–54).

6. Foster, p. 308.

7. Professor D. S. Landes wrote about the French businessman in 1949. Professor Sawyer presented a broader view somewhat later.

8. J. E. Sawyer, "The Entrepreneur and the Social Order: France and the United States," in *Men in Business* (1952), p. 9.

9. See their essays in larger or narrower frames: D. S. Landes, "French Entrepreneurship and Industrial Growth in the Nineteenth Century," *Journal of Economic History*, 9: 45–61 (1949); J. E. Sawyer, "Strains . . . ," and D. S. Landes, "Business . . . ," in *Modern France: Problems of the Third and Fourth Republics* (1951), pp. 293–312 and 334–353, respectively; and J. E. Sawyer, "The Entrepreneur . . . ," pp. 7–22.

10. Sawyer, "Strains . . . ," p. 299.

11. Landes, "Business . . . ," p. 336.

12. Sawyer, "Strains . . . ," p. 303, and Landes, "Business . . . ," pp. 341–343, 348–349.

13. Parker, "Entrepreneurial Opportunities"; H. B. Lamb, "Business Organization and Leadership in India Today"; H. B. Lamb, "Development of Modern Business Communities in India"; Choi, "Tokugawa Feudalism . . ."; Rottenberg, "Entrepreneurship and Economic Progress . . ."

14. See above, p. 105 f.

15. Danhof, "Economic Values in Cultural Perspective."

16. Rosovsky, "The Serf Entrepreneur in Russia."

17. Easterbrook, "The Climate of Enterprise."

18. Of course, this latter case could be interpreted as the entrepreneurial units providing their own security and not really being deterred by the existing uncertainties.

19. Hedges, *The Browns* . . .

20. Here I draw on the unpublished Ph.D. dissertation (Cornell, 1950) of Miss I. D. Neu, entitled "A Business Biography of Erastus Corning."

21. Professor C. L. Marquette of the University of Mississippi investigated the life of Washburn for his doctoral dissertation at Wisconsin. He presented it in 1940 under the title, "The Business Activities of C. C. Washburn."

22. Some years ago Professor Frederick Merk of Harvard inspired a series of doctoral dissertations on the lumbering industry as it progressed across the country. They are not well known and are worth citing here for the data that they contain on entrepreneurship in pioneer areas, particularly, of course, in connection with lumbering companies: R. G. Wood, *History of Lumbering in Maine, 1820–61* (1935); A. M. Larson, *History of the White-pine Industry in Minnesota* (1949); E. S. Meany, Jr., "History of the Lumber Industry in the Pacific Northwest to 1917" (1935).

23. R. R. Wohl, "Three Generations of Business Enterprise in a Mid-western City," *Journal of Economic History,* 16: 514–528 (1956).

24. R. K. Lamb, "The Development of Entrepreneurship . . .";
"Entrepreneurship in the Community," *Explorations,* 2: 114–27 (1949–50); "The Entrepreneur and the Community," *Men in Business* (1952), pp. 91–119.

25. See above, p. 124.

26. See above, p. 45.

27. Butters and Lintner, p. 14.

28. I have taken the ensuing data mainly from R. R. Wohl's unpublished Ph.D. thesis entitled, "Henry Noble Day, the Development of an Entrepreneurial Role." He contributed a preliminary sketch to *Men in Business* (1952) entitled, "Henry Noble Day, A Study in Good Works, 1808–1890," pp. 153–192.

29. Wohl, "Henry Noble Day, A Study . . . ," p. 158.

30. Day sampled teaching and the law before turning to the ministry.

31. Wohl, "Henry Noble Day, A Study . . . ," p. 167.

32. *Ibid.,* pp. 172–173.

33. A. H. Cole, *The American Wool Manufacture* (1926), I, 91–93.

34. J. T. Lincoln, "Material for a History of American Textile Machinery," *Journal of Economic and Business History,* 4: 263 (1931–32).

35. F. L. Redlich, "The Leaders of the German Steam-Engine Industry during the First Hundred Years," *Journal of Economic History,* 4: 121–148 (1944).

36. See above, p. 44.

37. The ensuing sketch is based upon W. C. Scoville's *Revolution in Glassmaking* (1948).

38. Cf. O. Knauth, *Business Practices, Trade Position, and Competition* (1956).

39. J. A. Schumpeter, *History of Economic Analysis* (1954), p. 897.

40. *Ibid.*, p. 895.

41. H. C. Passer, *The Electrical Manufacturers, 1875–1900* (1953), and "E. H. Goff: An Entrepreneur Who Failed," *Explorations*, 1: 17–25, No. 5 (1949).

42. Bruchey, pp. 370–73. The fact that the author had studied under Professor Frederic C. Lane, author of *Andrea Barbarigo*, and dedicated his book to the latter, makes the comparison doubly "nice." Both are excellent studies.

43. Bailyn, *The New England Merchants* . . . , pp. 88–90.

44. R. Davis, "Merchant Shipping in the Economy of the Late Seventeenth Century," *Economic History Review*, 2nd ser., 9: 67 (1956).

45. G. M. Butel-Dumont, *Histoire et commerce des colonies angloises* (1755), pp. 263–264.

46. Letter of Professor J. B. Hedges to the author, April 15, 1957.

47. K. W. Porter, *The Jacksons and the Lees* (1937), I, 99.

48. Bailyn, "The *Apologia* . . . ," also *The New England Merchants* . . . , *passim*.

49. *Ibid.*

50. Cochran, *Railroad Leaders*, p. 9.

51. *Ibid.*, p. 34.

52. *Ibid.*, p. 82.

53. *Ibid.*, p. 56.

54. See Sawyer, "Entrepreneurial Error . . . ," p. 200.

55. Wilson, *History of Unilever*, I, 165–175, 237–239.

56. W. R. Maclaurin, *Invention & Innovation in the Radio Industry* (1949).

57. W. Miller, "The Business Elite in Business Bureaucracies," *Men in Business*, pp. 286–305.

58. Abrams, pp. 29–34.

59. *Ibid.*, p. 32.

60. *Ibid.*, pp. 29–30.

61. Heckscher, Chap. III, *passim*.

62. P. W. Bamford, "Entrepreneurship in Seventeenth and Eighteenth Century France," *Explorations*, 9: 204–213 (1956–57); R. M. Westebbe, "State Entrepreneurship," *Explorations*, 8: 205–232 (1955–56). In connection with the entrepreneur and the state I should call attention to what, in a way of speaking, was an identification of entre-

preneurship and the state — the ruler acting as entrepreneur. See essay by Dr. Redlich noted in n. 4, above.

63. See above, pp. 171 ff.

64. The books sponsored by the Committee include: O. Handlin and M. F. Handlin, *Commonwealth: A Study of the Role of Government in the American Economy, Massachusetts, 1774–1861* (1947); L. Hartz, *Economic Policy and Democratic Thought: Pennsylvania, 1776–1860* (1948); M. S. Heath, *Constructive Liberalism: The Role of the State in Economic Development in Georgia to 1860* (1954); J. N. Primm, *Economic Policy in the Development of a Western State: Missouri, 1820–1860* (1954). An able survey of this series is contained in the *Business History Review*, 29: 81–96 (1955). The author is R. A. Lively.

Among Professor Goodrich's essays may be cited: "Public Spirit and American Improvements," *Proceedings of the American Philosophical Society*, 92: 305–309 (1948); "National Planning of Internal Improvements," *Political Science Quarterly*, 63: 16–44 (1948); "The Virginia System of Mixed Enterprise. A Study of State Planning of Internal Improvements," *Political Science Quarterly*, 64: 355–387 (1949); "Local Planning of Internal Improvements," *Political Science Quarterly*, 66: 411–445 (1951); "The Revulsion Against Internal Improvements," *Journal of Economic History*, 10: 145–169 (1950); and (with H. H. Segal) "Baltimore's Aid to Railroads. A Study in the Municipal Planning of Internal Improvements," *Journal of Economic History*, 13: 2–35 (1953).

65. The ensuing sketch is based upon H. G. J. Aitken's *The Welland Canal.* . . .

66. See above, p. 124.

67. See above, p. 45.

68. Aitken, *The Welland Canal* . . . , p. 31.

69. D. R. Fusfeld, "Heterogony of Entrepreneurial Goals," *Explorations*, 9: 8–18 (1956–57).

70. S. Diamond, "From Organization to Society: Virginia in the Seventeenth Century," *American Journal of Sociology*, 63: 457–475 (1957–58).

71. Charles W. Moulton, *The Library of Literary Criticism* (1901), I.

72. Aitken, *The Welland Canal* . . . , p. 12.

73. R. G. Wellington, *The Political and Sectional Influence of the Public Lands, 1828–1842* (1914), *passim*, especially Chap. 3.

74. Aitken, *The Welland Canal* . . . , pp. 116–118.

75. S. J. Stein, *The Brazilian Cotton Manufacture* (1957).

76. H. G. Aubrey, "Investment Decisions in Underdeveloped Countries," *Capital Formation and Economic Growth* (1955), p. 424.

77. United Nations Economic and Social Council, Economic Commission for Latin America, *Economic Development of Latin America and Its Principal Problems* (1950).

PART THREE

Postlude: Process of Entrepreneurial Change

1. As a partial result of the disregard of the duration of the spans of life of business units, we know more about the life expectancy of cows, probably of insects, than we do of corporations.

2. Marshall, p. 379.

3. K. F. Helleiner, "The Vital Revolution Reconsidered," *Canadian Journal of Economics and Political Science*, 23: 9 (1957).

4. A. H. Cole, "Conspectus . . ."

5. H. Heaton, "An Economic Historian's View of Enterprise" (1956); E. F. Gay, "The Rhythm of History," *Harvard Graduates' Magazine*, 32: 1–16 (1923–24).

6. W. N. Parker, "Coal and Steel Output Movements in Western Europe, 1880–1956," *Explorations*, 9: 229 n. (1956–57).

7. Heckscher, p. 4.

8. See my comment above, p. 39 f.

9. See especially Chaps. III, IV.

10. D. C. McClelland *et al.*, *The Achievement Motive* (1953); D. C. McClelland, "The Psychology of Mental Content Reconsidered," *Psychological Review*, 62: 297–303 (1955); D. C. McClelland, "Some Social Consequences of Achievement Motivation," *Nebraska Symposium on Motivation*, III (1955); *Studies in Motivation* (1955). Unfortunately, I became familiar with this literature too late to make proper use of it.

11. P. F. Drucker, *The Practice of Management* (1954), p. 175.

12. See above, p. 82.

13. I. G. Wyllie, *The Self-made Man in America* (1954).

14. Much of the "case" material used for instruction in schools of business is based on the assumption of such internal stresses.

15. See F. L. Redlich, *History of American Business Leaders* (1940), I, 22–30.

16. J. A. Schumpeter, "The Creative Response in Economic History," *Journal of Economic History*, 7: 149–159 (1947).

17. E. Dahmen, *Svensk industriell företagarverksamhet* (1950), I, 414.

INDEX

INDEX

Dobb, Maurice, 181
Dolge, Alfred, 69
Donaldson, James, 107
Donham, Wallace B., 242
Drucker, Peter F., 73, 234
Dudley, Massachusetts, 172
Duesenberry, James S., 100, 104
Dun & Bradstreet, 90, 102, 244
Du Pont family, 57, 58
Durfee family, 163
Dutch, 20, 100, 120, 157. *See also* Holland

Eagle Works, 201
East India Company, 101, 105, 191, 206
Easterbrook, W. Thomas, 21, 99, 102, 138, 158, 159
Economic Development: Theory, History, Policy, 40, 41
Edison, Thomas A., 181–84
Egells, F. A. J., 174
Eliot, Charles W., 10
Emerson, Ralph W., 94
England and Englishmen, 6, 9, 17, 22, 54, 56, 57, 60, 66, 80, 87, 92, 102–105, 107, 114, 116, 119–21, 128, 131, 142, 145, 146, 148, 151, 152, 157, 161, 174, 191, 206, 208, 210–11, 217–18, 220, 235, 238, 242. *See also* Britain and British
Erie Canal, 213–15
Essay in the Theory of Profits and Income Distribution, 36
Esso Standard Company, 202
Europe, 20, 65, 105, 113, 114, 116, 119, 120, 141, 142, 144, 145, 147, 155, 159, 160, 189, 197, 210, 211, 229, 242
Explorations in Entrepreneurial History, 32, 138–40, 207

Fall River, Massachusetts, 110, 163
Fall River Iron Works, 163
Far East, 189, 191
Faulkner, William, 23
Federal Reserve System, 127
Federal Trade Commission, 23
Flanders, 119

Follett, Mary Parker, 51
Forbes, John Murray, 60, 117, 194–97, 241
Forbes family, 191
Ford, Henry, 44, 176
Ford, Henry, II, 18
Ford family, 57
Ford Foundation, 204
Forstmann & Huffmann Company, 120
Fortune, 125
Foster, Charles A., 140–42, 145, 147
France, 21, 42, 57, 60, 87, 101, 106, 108, 120, 121, 128, 131, 141, 142, 145, 146, 149, 150, 160, 207–209, 220, 223, 235, 238
Frankfurt-am-Main, 101
Frederick the Great, 114
French Canada, 159, 160
Freund, Georg Christian, 174
Fur Trade in Canada, 159
Fusfeld, Daniel R., 215

Garelin, 153, 156
Gary, Elbert H., 66
Gay, Edwin F., 89, 98, 99, 229, 242
General Electric Company, 16, 239
General Motors Corporation, 18, 63, 204
George, Henry, 126
Georgia, 192
Germans and Germany, 17, 20, 22, 42, 57, 60, 69, 101, 106, 119, 120, 128, 131, 137, 142, 144, 151, 174, 220, 223, 235, 242
Gerschenkron, Alexander, 21, 99, 101
Gillette, King C., 118
Girdler, Tom, 127
Goff, E. H., 184–86
Goodrich, Carter, 213
Gordon, Robert A., 16, 138
Gould, Jay, 61, 110, 183, 236
Grachev, 153, 156
Gras, N. S. B., 62
Great Britain, 47. *See also* England
Greeks, 120
Gustavus Adolphus, 206
Gustavus Vasa, 141

281

INDEX

Habakkuk, H. J., 32, 142
Hamburg, 189
Hamilton, Alexander, 10, 148, 206, 220
Handlin, Oscar, 120
Hannibal & St. Joseph Railroad, 194
Harkort, Friedrich, 174
Harper, William R., 10
Hartford, Connecticut, 189
Harvard Business Review, 89, 203
Harvard Business School, 20, 242
Harvard University, 10, 19, 38, 41, 53, 89, 137, 140, 171, 207
Haugwitz, Count Karl Otto, 144
Heaton, Herbert, 229
Heckscher, Eli F., 206
Hedges, James B., 162, 190
Helleiner, Karl F., 144, 229
Heralds' College, 104, 148
"Heterogony of Entrepreneurial Goals," 215
History of Economic Analysis, 181
Hitler, 59
Holland, 105, 206, 210, 211, 235
Holstein, 142
Hong Kong, 191
"Honoring Commerce and Industry in Eighteenth-Century France," 140
Hope Iron Furnace, 162
Hoppe, Theodor, 174
Houqua, 194
Houston, E. J., 185, 186
Hudson, Ohio, 165, 166, 168
Hudson's Bay Company, 161
Hughes, Howard, 118
Hungary, 144
Hunt's Merchants' Magazine, 86
Huron tribe, 160
Hutchinson family, 189

Illinois Central Railroad, 198
India, 119, 121, 151
Indonesia, 5
Industrial Management, 87
Industrial Relations Counselors, 204
Industrial Revolution, 87, 102, 116
Innis, Harold A., 3, 159
Iran, 121

Iron Age, 86, 124
Iroquois tribe, 160
Italy and Italians, 44, 57, 103, 119–21, 142, 144, 235
Ivanovo, 153, 154, 156

Jacobi, Gottlob Julius, 174
Jamaica, 102, 151
Japan, 42, 121, 151
Jefferson, Thomas, 217
Jenks, Leland H., 20, 53, 72, 99
Jersey City, New Jersey, 201
Jesus College, Cambridge, 47
Jewett City, Connecticut, 172
Jews, 105, 120
Journal of Commerce, 86

Kansas City, 109, 163
Keayne, Robert, 100, 125, 192
Keirstead, Burton S., 36–38
Kellenbenz, Hermann, 142
Knauth, Oswald, 16, 94
Koch, Paul, 101
Korea, 58
Krueger, Ivar, 118, 129

Lake Erie, 214, 216
Lake Ontario, 214, 216
Lamb, Robert K., 110, 163
Landes, David S., 57, 105, 106, 138, 149, 150
Lane, Frederic C., 16, 141, 207
Latin America, 17, 109, 131, 221. *See also* South America
Layer, Robert G., 70
Leahy, Emmet J., 242
Lebanese merchants, 102
Lenihan, Richard, 243
Lever, William (Lord Leverhulme), 47, 199
Lever Soap Company, 80
Libbey, Edward D., 176–80
Libbey Glass Company, 177–80
Liege, 210
Lintner, John, 20, 164
Lloyd, Henry Demarest, 126
London, 57, 63, 151, 184, 189, 192
Louis XI, 146

INDEX

West Virginia, 178
Western Electric Company, 70
Westebbe, Richard M., 207, 211, 212
Western Reserve University, 165, 168
Westinghouse, George, 175, 182
Weyerhaeuser Company, 20
What's on the Worker's Mind, 70
Wheeling, West Virginia, 177
Whistler, George W., 118
Whitin Machine Works, 58
Whitney, Eli, 125
Whitney, John Hay, 118
Wilkinson, David, 174
Willem I, 211, 212
Williams, Whiting, 70

Willits, Joseph H., 242
Wilson, Charles, 47, 57, 138, 151, 199
Wohl, R. Richard, 53, 72, 138, 165–67, 235
Wöhlert, Johann F. L., 174
Work and Authority, 55
World War I, 70, 222
World War II, 48, 49, 102, 222, 223, 242
Wyllie, Irvin G., 235

Yale University, 45, 165, 167
Yates, John B., 216, 218–20
Yorkshire, 172
Young, Allyn A., 84

71
75
26
77
79
8)
83
85
88